Y0-ASW-099

HELP FROM ABOVE

Air Force Close Air Support
of the Army

1946–1973

John Schlight

AIR FORCE HISTORY AND
MUSEUMS PROGRAM
Washington, D. C.
2003

For sale by the Superintendent of Documents, U.S. Government Printing Office
Internet: bookstore.gpo.gov   Phone: toll free (866) 512-1800;   DC area (202) 512-1800
Fax: (202) 512-2250 Mail: Stop SSOP, Washington, DC 20402-0001

ISBN 0-16-051552-1

Library of Congress Cataloging-in-Publication Data

Schlight, John.
 Help from above : Air Force close air support of the Army 1946-1973 / John Schlight.
     p. cm.
Includes bibliographical references and index.
 1. Close air support--History--20th century. 2. United States. Air Force--History--20th century. 3. United States. Army--Aviation--History--20th century. I. Title.

 UG703.S35 2003
 358.4'142--dc22
                                            2003020365

Foreword

The issue of close air support by the United States Air Force in support of, primarily, the United States Army has been fractious for years. Air commanders have clashed continually with ground leaders over the proper use of aircraft in the support of ground operations. This is perhaps not surprising given the very different outlooks of the two services on what constitutes proper air support. Often this has turned into a competition between the two services for resources to execute and control close air support operations.

Although such differences extend well back to the initial use of the airplane as a military weapon, in this book the author looks at the period 1946-1973, a period in which technological advances in the form of jet aircraft, weapons, communications, and other electronic equipment played significant roles. Doctrine, too, evolved and this very important subject is discussed in detail.

Close air support remains a critical mission today and the lessons of yesterday should not be ignored. This book makes a notable contribution in seeing that it is not ignored.

Contents

Foreword iii

Photographs vii

Introduction xi

1   **The Birth of Close Air Support** 1
    World War I 2
    Between the Wars 19
    World War II 32

2   **Close Air Support Enfeebled 1945–1950** 53
    On the Road to Independence 54
    Independence 72
    Reduction of Tactical Air Command 83
    Congress and Close Air Support 95
    Further Attempts to Improve Air-Ground Operations 98

3   **Close Air Support in Korea** 113
    The War in Outline 114
    The Close Air Support System in Korea 141
        The Demand Side: The Air-Ground Operations System 142
        The Supply Side: The Tactical Air Control System 145
        The Joint Operations Center 145
        Tactical Air Control Parties 149
        Mosquitoes 151
        Aircraft Issues 153
    The Bottom Line: Command and Control 159

4   **Close Air Support Under the New Look** 179
    The Services, The New Look, and Close Air Support 182
    Further Attempts to Create Joint Air-Ground Doctrine 201
    The Close Air Support Challenge from Organic Army
        Aviation 221

5   **Close Air Support and Flexible Response: 1960–1965** 233
    Early Stirrings of a Close Air Support Revival, 1961–1963 236
    The Army Proposes Its Own Airmobile Force: The Howze
        Board 242

      The Air Force Defends the Existing System: The Disosway
         Board 251
      A Joint Examination of Close Air Support 257
      Field Testing the Opposing Close Air Support Concepts 279

6   The Vietnam Era: 1965–1973 . . . .**299**
      Air Force Close Air Support Validated in Vietnam 301
      Armed Helicopters Also Legitimized 335
      Toward a Specialized Close Air Support Plane 352

7   Conclusions **365**

Notes **385**

Glossary **415**

Bibliography **419**

Index **447**

Figures

1. St. Mihiel, September 12–16, 1918 16
2. Curtiss A–12 Shrike 25
3. Details of Target Selection. 30
4. Approximate Location of Targets. 31
5. Cover of Aviation in Support of Ground Forces 34
6. Air-Ground Operations, August 1946 59
7. Far East Command, June–August 1950 116
8. Korea 119
9. FEAF Sorties, June 26, 1950–July 27, 1953 134
10. General Almond's Proposed Organization for Close Air
     Support 170
11. Joint Air-Ground Operations, Immediate Air Request System,
     September 1, 1957 214
12. Joint Air-Ground Operations, Preplanned Air Request System,
     September 1, 1957 215
13. Air Force General Purpose Forces, FY 1961–1965 239
14. Organization of the 11th Air Assault Division, 1963–1964 291
15. Joint Air-Ground Operations System 307
16. Major Battles and Significant Localities, Vietnam 321

Contents

17. 1st Cavalry Division (Airmobile) Organization 340
18. 1st Aviation Brigade Organization, August 1, 1968 344

Photographs

An F–111F releasing high drag bombs over a range. xvi

Gen. John J. Pershing addressing Air Service personnel at
 Tours, France on July, 29, 1918 (top); Maj. Gen. Hugh A.
 Drum (right); Gen. William Mitchell in cockpit at Selfridge
 Field, Michigan during Daytona races in 1922 (bottom). 4

British De Haviland DH–4 observation plane (top left); British
 Handley-Page bomber (top right); Italian Caproni A–12 bomber
 (center); French Brequet bomber (bottom left); French Spad 13E
 fighters in formation (bottom right). 8

Lt. Benjamin D. Foulois in the first aircraft owned by the U.S. Army,
 a Wright type B, at Fort Sam Houston, Texas. 13

German Junkers all metal monoplane (top); German Halberstadt
 (center); British Sopwith Camel (bottom). 17

A presentation ceremony on April 16, 1920, at Kelly Field, Texas
 (top); Air Corps machine shops at Barksdale Field, Louisiana
 (bottom). 23

Silhouettes of a Curtiss A–3 (left); Curtiss XA–8 (top). 26

A Curtiss Y1A–18 (top); A Douglas A–20 (bottom). 27

Lt. Henry H. Arnold in Wright B aircraft at College Park, Maryland
 in 1911 (bottom); Gen. George C. Marshall, Chief of Staff in
 1939 (right). 33

A Consolidated F–7A reconnaissance aircraft. 36

Boeing F–9 reconnaissance aircraft (top); Lockheed F–5 reconnaissance
 aircraft (center); North American F–6 reconnaissance aircraft
 (far right). 37

Curtiss C–46 cargo and troop carrying transport (top left); Douglas
 C–47s on line (top right); Douglas C–54 over Mt. Whitney,
 California (center); Douglas C–54 interior (bottom left);
 Fairchild XC–82 (bottom right). 39

Help from Above

Gen. Dwight D. Eisenhower congratulates Lt. Gen. Carl A. Spaatz on being awarded the Legion of Merit on September 16, 1943 (left); Lt. Gen. Elwood R. Quesada (right). 56

Langley Field, Virginia (top); March Field, Riverside, California (bottom). 63

A Douglas A–26C at Lawson AFB, Georgia, February 26, 1947. 64

View of the Capitol building from a Lockheed P–80 Shooting Star. 65

A 20-mm cannon installed in a Lockheed P–80 Shooting Star. 68

A Northrop P–61 Night Fighter. 69

Lt. Gen. Ira C. Eaker 76

Col. William W. Momyer 80

Gen. Carl A. Spaatz 85

Maj. Gen. Richard E. Nugent (left); Maj. Gen. Robert M. Lee (right). 89

Lt. Gen. Glenn O. Barcus 100

Construction at Wright-Patterson Field, Dayton, Ohio in 1941. 102

Lt. Gen. George E. Stratemeyer 115

An air reconnaissance photo. 121

Lt. Gen. Otto P. Weyland (left) and Lt. Gen. Earle E. Partridge (right) 125

A Boeing B–29 after a mission over North Korea. 127

Enemy fuel truck hit by F–51 east of Kumchon (top); F–80 attacks on North Korean tanks. Photo taken by gun camera (bottom). 128

Brig. Gen. James Ferguson 147

A Stimson L–5, over Korea. 152

A North American T–6. 153

Napalm bombs being assembled (top); napalm being dropped from a Lockheed P–80, at Eglin Field, Florida (bottom). 156

Contents

A Soviet MIG–15 Fagot. 157

A North American XF–86. 158

An F–100 Sabre 45 (top); A Martin B–57A Night Intruder
(bottom). 183

An illustration of a Douglas B–66A. 185

A drawing of an F–101A showing a portion of the cockpit interior. 188

A McDonnell F–101A. 189

A Cessna XL–19B, the world's first turbine-powered light aircraft. 193

Gen. Hoyt S. Vandenberg 198

Maj. Gen. Curtis E. LeMay 235

Brig. Gen. Gabriel P. Disosway 253

A German Fieseler Fi–156 (top); A German Junkers Ju–87
(bottom). 268

A British Westland Lysander in France (top); A French Mureaux
115–R.2 (bottom). 269

Col. Gilbert L. Meyers 282

An F–111F refueling from a KC–135E Stratotanker. 289

Secretary of the Air Force Eugene M. Zuckert 295

Maj. Gen. Ernest Moore 305

A B–52 bomber. 309

The F–4E Phantom II. 312

Several F–4D Phantom IIs taxi on a runway with their drogue
chutes extended. 313

An A–7K Corsair II flying with an A–7D Corsair II (top) and an
A–37 Dragonfly (bottom). 314

An OV–10 Bronco. 319

A Fairchild C–123 transport. 322

Help from Above

A Marine with an M–16 rifle. 329

An XM–198 155-mm howitzer. 330

A drawing of a Lockheed C–130. 333

A Soviet 7.62-mm AK–47 assault rifle. 347

A Soviet-made ZU–23 23-mm antiaircraft gun. 348

A Soviet-made M–1939 37-mm antiaircraft gun. 349

An AH–56A Cheyenne attack helicopter, Fort Polk, Louisiana. 355

An A–10 Thunderbolt II during an exercise (top) and an A–10
    Thunderbolt II firing a GAU–8/A 30-mm cannon (bottom). 361

A UH–1H Iroquois during a training flight. .377

Crewman mans an M–60 machine gun on an Iroquois helicopter. 382

Introduction

> Close Air Support—air action against hostile targets which are in close proximity to friendly forces and which require detailed integration of each air mission with the fire and movement of those forces.
> — JCS Pub 1, 1964

It is important for nations such as the United States, whose military force is disbursed among separate air, land, and sea services, to devise ways to temper any institutional lack of unity. Past compensatory measures, however, have at best only eased, rather than dispelled, service resistance to further unification. This resistance has sprung in part from each service's interpretation of its mission, of the best equipment and procedures for achieving that mission, and often of a strong sense of service pride. While these elements are healthy, and often essential, in an effective fighting force, enhancing both the devotion and effectiveness of the individual fighting man, they also frequently intensify differences that clash when the interests of the services overlap.

Attempts to secure unity have taken both organizational and doctrinal forms. Organizationally, such measures have ranged from the creation of formal joint organizations with service representatives to coordinate the services' efforts, to less formal, lower level programs of interservice exchanges, training, and indoctrination. On the doctrinal level, attempts to forge interservice cooperation extended from the strict notion of operational control of assets by one service to such more amorphous formulations as *integration* or *coordination*. Because of their vagueness, these latter concepts prompted a variety of interpretations.

Among the flashpoints are the missions of the U.S. Army and the U.S. Air Force and the question of close air support. For example, the Army has traditionally viewed close air support more as a ground-support fire akin to artillery rather than as part of an air campaign in which it forms a triad with interdiction and air supremacy missions. Likewise, within the Air Force, the close air support mission has usually been viewed more as it relates to these other tactical air missions than as one of several ground support weapons. Only on rare occasions has the Army included the Air Force's interpretation, and the Air Force the Army's, in their analyses of close air support.

Help from Above

The practice of the Air Force to regard close air support as but one element within a larger package called tactical air support challenges the researcher. Even though close air support is but one of several types of tactical air support, this latter phrase is frequently used in documents and speech to indicate close air support. The task of deciding when tactical air support is so employed, as opposed to when it carries its full generic meaning, falls to the author. Sometimes the context surrounding the phrase suggests its narrower meaning. On other occasions it is not possible to distinguish close air support from tactical air support. It has been the author's practice in this volume to interpret tactical air support as meaning close air support only when the context clearly dictates such an identification. When such a distinction has not been possible, the author has used the term tactical air power on the assumption that what is true of the generic term is also valid, *a fortiori*, for all of its species.

Despite minor variations in formulation, the general elements of close air support have remained constant over the decades. Both the Army and the Air Force have defined close air support as air attacks against enemy ground targets that are close enough to friendly ground troops to require detailed integration between the strike planes and the friendly ground units. The two unchanging elements in this formulation are (1) proximity of the opposing ground forces, and (2) the need to coordinate air and ground operations.

Consensus has been less noticeable, however, in attempts to implement these two generalizations. As to the first, namely, the proximity of the ground forces, efforts to agree on detailed close air support measures have often led to controversy between soldiers and airmen. For example, while both sides see close air support as attacks against enemy troops in contact, unanimity has usually ended when it came to when, where, and how these attacks should be mounted. The issue of when to use planes rather than other forms of available ground fire has at times become embroiled in the larger question of the relationship between artillery and aircraft. It has also carried with it overtones of interservice rivalry where each service believes its solution in a given instance to be preferable.

Controversy over timing in the employment of aircraft for close air support has been part of a larger disagreement between the two services over the role of tactical air power. While the Army and Air Force were in accord on the general nature of close air support, on the definition of aerial interdiction as air strikes outside the battle zone that need not be coordinated with the ground forces, and on the view that air superiority meant preventing enemy air power from interfering with ground operations, their views diverged when it came to the details of these tactical missions and assigning relative values to them. The priorities accorded to tactical air missions were colored by the overall goal of each service. For example, the Air Force has always been and remains convinced that, as a general rule, strikes carried out closer to the ultimate source

Introduction

of an enemy's power were more effective than those made against enemy forces that had already been dispersed to the field. This meant, in the case of the air superiority mission that the most productive strikes were those mounted against all forms of enemy air power wherever they were found, whether on the ground or in the air, or whether distant from or directly over the friendly ground forces. This view was not shared by the Army, which wanted aircraft to serve only as umbrellas over the ground troops, shielding them from enemy air attack. The same philosophy and controversy prevailed in the question of close air support. The Air Force held as a fundamental belief that air attacks behind the front lines were more productive, less costly in aircraft and pilots, and ultimately advanced the objective of the ground campaign more than did strikes against troops in contact. The genesis and attempts to settle this disagreement provide one of the themes of this book.

The size of the close air support zone has also occasionally become a source of dispute as steady advances in military technology have gradually expanded the range of artillery and with it the battle zone. Most differences of opinion, however, centered on the means of conducting close air support. In this regard, controversy has accompanied such issues as the best type of aircraft for close air support (high- or low-performance planes, fixed-wing or rotary vehicles, single-purpose or multipurpose aircraft, or planes stressing survivability or responsiveness), the most effective types and combinations of ordnance, whether those controlling the planes during actual strikes should be airborne or located on the ground, and how best to operate at night and during periods of foul weather.

The second element in the definition of close air support upon which the Army and Air Force have agreed, namely, the need for integration between the ground and the air, has also had a less than harmonious history when it came to formulating specific measures to bring about this integration. The word "integration" was amorphous enough to lend itself to antithetical interpretations, each reflecting the doctrine of its parent service. The desire of both the Army and the Air Force to maintain majority control over the close air support mission resulted in a constant tug of war over many of the specific subordinate issues relating to the mission. Since the Air Force traditionally viewed close air support as but one of several elements that go to make up an air campaign, it insisted on maintaining the same control over the assets needed for that mission as it did over resources for its other tactical missions. It continued throughout the period to assert its prerogative to design and develop close air support planes and ordnance and to plan how their missions would be conducted. The Army, on the other hand, regarding close air support as an integral supportive element of the land battle, increasingly sought to have greater involvement in both the development and employment of close air support resources. The tension between these two aspirations was constant throughout the period.

Help from Above

This issue of control expressed itself in other areas of *integration*. Attempts by both services to settle on a set of institutions and techniques for executing close air support missions frequently foundered on the perception by one or the other service that it was surrendering too much control. Here, too, the Army's insistence that the ground commander control the planes that were supporting him flowed from the interpretation of close air support as an element of the ground battle. The Air Force's determination that control not pass out of its hands was also consistent with its view that air power formed a continuum across the entire spectrum of operations and that no one element, such as close air support, should be broken away. In the face of these unyielding positions, the best that could be accomplished was a series of ad hoc manuals proposing close air support mechanisms—manuals that were accorded only temporary acceptance. Agreement on a permanent, jointly approved set of procedures continued to elude the authors of the doctrine. This lack of a joint doctrine for air-ground operations in turn complicated joint training and maneuvers, which depended for their success on a meeting of the minds.

In addition to these issues over the meaning of close air support, several other recurring themes have infused the history of close air support in the three decades following World War II. These themes have, in turn, influenced the outcome of the controversies over close air support. One such topic was the twofold struggle within the Air Force to decide, on the one hand, the relationship of tactical to strategic air power and, on the other hand, the proper niche for the close air support mission within the varieties of tactical air power. These questions matured during the period of cold war controversy between the United States and the U.S.S.R.—a controversy that strongly affected the development of close air support thinking and resources. National security policy during most of the period saw the U.S.S.R. as the principal potential enemy and nuclear deterrence of Soviet adventurism as the main strategy to contain the threat. In their struggle to preserve a close air support capability in the face of this strategic inundation, some airmen came to abandon the belief that the means available to deter nuclear war could also prevent lesser conflicts. Efforts of these men to create a conventional deterrent by, in part, improving the Air Force's close air support capabilities, permeate the age.

A second theme that generated many of the close air support disagreements during the period was the rejection by an influential segment of Air Force leaders of any implication that aircraft were merely *support* weapons. Suggestions, chiefly from the Army, that airplanes be resubordinated to the ground forces were anathema to that generation of airmen who had devoted their careers to demonstrating that the airplane could perform missions separate from the ground forces, and to realizing that idea by creating an Air Force divorced from the Army. At one point Air Force doctrine even banned the use of the word *support*, and there were frequent attempts to find alternate formu-

Introduction

lations. Lying behind virtually every Army/Air Force disagreement over close air support was this basic difference of perception as to the nature of the air vehicle.

Despite their aversion to being considered solely a support organization, advocates of tactical aviation believed that the Air Force possessed both the required close air support resources and the desire to use them on behalf of the Army. A major theme of the period was the Air Force's efforts to demonstrate this in the face of the Army's skepticism and efforts to acquire its own close air support capability. A large proportion of soldiers, on the other hand, convinced that the Air Force was less than cooperative, sought to obtain its own organic resources for self-support. The competition between the two to demonstrate which form of close air support was more effective and efficient constitutes another major subject of this volume.

An F–111F releasing high drag bombs over a range.

1 | The Birth of Close Air Support

> We should not dissipate our effort on ground attack aviation. If the development of aviation as a whole proceeds as dictated by its efficiency for reaching a decision in war, the ground attack aviation will be used only in peacetime maneuvers.
>
> — Memo, Air Corps Tactical School, 1936
>
> Maximum air support for land operations can only be achieved by fighting for and obtaining a high measure of air superiority in the theater of operations.
>
> — Arthur Coningham, 1943

Many of the close air support issues over which the U.S. Army and the U.S. Air Force contended after World War II were foreshadowed before the war and solidified by it. Many of these issues were first encountered during World War I.[1] The most basic question was that of command and control: Was it more effective to have a central air commander or a local ground one in charge of the aircraft that were assisting the ground forces? From this question flowed such subsidiary concerns as who should decide when, where, how and why to conduct air missions, which aircraft and armament should be used, and which targets should be hit. Since military aviation was still in its infancy during World War I, and the Air Service was part of the Army, this issue was only beginning to surface. Air doctrine, the contextual guidelines for employing aircraft, was also first enunciated during the Great War, although in halting terms. In addition, technological issues, such as the relative effectiveness of multipurpose and single-purpose planes, arose during the wartime period. Embryonic efforts

Help from Above

were made during the conflict to coordinate the activities of air and ground units, inaugurating what would turn out to be a long history of problems with communications between the two. The onset of a sense of difference between air and ground personnel during the war presaged the later movement of the air units to become independent from their ground cowarriors. The conflict also featured the first experiments with the close air support tactics of strafing and bombing enemy troops and equipment. The issue of joint training between air and ground forces, which would increase in prominence in the future, was virtually nonexistent in World War I.

Close air support issues of command and control, doctrine, technology and tactics proceeded at an uneven rate after World War I. Officers in the Air Service and Air Corps, although still members of the Army, sought to gain expanded control over ground-support aircraft. Air doctrine was often contradictory, simultaneously picturing military aviation's primary role as supporting ground forces and as attacking the enemy's homeland. Until 1935 attack aviation received considerable attention. Several attempts were made to develop a plane solely for close air support (attack). Tactics for close air support were refined at, and also confined to, the Air Corps Tactical School. The professional gap between air and ground officers continued to widen between the wars. As many Air Corps officers after 1935 began to identify independence with strategic bombing, interest in attack aviation lessened. The outbreak of hostilities in Europe in 1939 signaled a return of attention to tactical close air support in the United States.

Many of the close air support issues that previously had been only partially developed matured during World War II. The first close air support field manual was issued during the war, addressing questions of command and control, tactics, communications, and an elementary Tactical Air Control System. This manual set the stage for vigorous postwar debate and revisions. Other major wartime developments, such as the use of fighter-bombers and intensive joint training, filled in some of the prewar gaps in the close air support picture. Of all the close air support developments that emerged from the war, however, airmen looked upon the autonomy that they achieved from ground control as the most beneficial influence on the close air support mission.

World War I

At the time the U.S. Army took delivery of its first airplane from the Wright brothers in 1909, the military organizations of the Western world were already firmly wedded to offensive strategies. The campaigns of Frederick the Great and Napoleon, as filtered through the partially misinterpreted writings of the nineteenth-century Prussian theorist Karl von Clausewitz, had had their

The Birth of Close Air Support

impact on the doctrines of military planners in Germany, France, Italy, Great Britain, and the United States.[2]

A key tenet of these offensive strategies was the conviction that the enemy's army was the most important objective in warfare. Clausewitz's recognition of the importance, under certain circumstances, of less obvious targets, such as an enemy's capital, his leader, his command center, or the glue that held his alliance together,[3] went unheeded in the nineteenth-century rush to realize the Prussian writer's vision of the essence of war as total violence. Concrete examples during that century of successful military campaigns against targets other than armies, such as Gen. William T. Sherman's successful assault on the will of the people in the southern United States, were seen, when considered at all, as deviations from the true path of Napoleonic totality.

Enemy armies, in contemporary thinking, were to be assailed by other armies, spearheaded by the infantry. Artillery and cavalry were instruments designed to support the infantry. While artillery barrages prepared the way, cavalry gathered intelligence and undertook peripheral attacks on the flanks and rear of the opposing army. These priorities were enshrined in the U.S. Army whose *Field Service Regulations* in 1914 stated unequivocally that "the infantry is the principal and most important arm," while the artillery and cavalry provide support.[4]

The new aerial weapon entered this military climate of opinion on a par with artillery and cavalry, as an adjunct to ground operations and to the infantry. Its main function, according to the chief of the Signal Corps, to which aviation belonged in 1913, was observation and the collection of information.[5] While other military branches served offensive purposes, the offensive value of aviation had yet to be demonstrated.[6] The desire to escape this early defensive view of aviation was to form one of several justifications used by later air forces to attach secondary importance to ground support missions.[7]

America experienced its first significant air combat during its brief, but relatively intense, involvement in World War I. Following a year of preparation, a disappointing record of aircraft production at home, and several minor initial combat experiences, Gen. John J. Pershing's American Expeditionary Force (AEF) launched its contribution to the allied war against the Central Powers in April 1918. During the ensuing seven months, until the November armistice, American forces spearheaded two campaigns: a four-day engagement in mid-September to reduce a German salient around the northeastern French town of St. Mihiel; and a campaign farther north, begun later that month and lasting until war's end, to blunt a German offensive through the Ardennes and then to push back the armies of the Central Powers.

During World War I, the chief of the Air Service in Europe was a non-rated Army officer and a member of the Army-controlled AEF staff, which decided the general direction of the air war. The ground officers who planned the AEF's organizational structure retained control of their air resources at the

Help from Above

Gen. John J. Pershing addressing Air Service personnel at Tours, France on July 29, 1918 (top); Maj. Gen. Hugh A. Drum (right); Gen. William Mitchell in cockpit at Selfridge Field, Michigan during Daytona races in 1922 (bottom).

The Birth of Close Air Support

field army level.[8] Air units were parceled out to divisional and subordinate headquarters only for specific operations. Ironically, the Army would later abandon this system of centralized control and decentralized execution, while the Air Force would fight to maintain that system.

Mission orders were issued by either the AEF's Information (G–2) or Operations (G–3) section of the General Staff or, in the case of artillery adjustment flights, by the artillery commander. The Air Service was left to flesh them out.[9] Although ground officers at times delegated some initiative to the air commanders, such as during the September campaign around St. Mihiel when the First Army's chief of staff, Col. Hugh Drum, placed 1,500 pursuit and bombing planes in the hands of Col. William "Billy" Mitchell, ultimate decisions normally remained with the soldiers. Mitchell complained loudly about unknowledgeable nonflyers making decisions about air missions.[10]

Airmen in the field, too, frequently expressed dissatisfaction with the negative effects these command arrangements were having on their ability to prosecute the war. The most recurring criticism was that nonflyers, being unfamiliar with the strengths and limitations of airplanes and aerial equipment, often ordered missions that were beyond the capability of their aircraft.[11] "I know of instances," recorded one pilot, "where Groups were given missions of such magnitude that weeks would have been involved in their execution."[12] The chief radio officer of the Air Service expressed frustration with the arrangement that made ground radio receiver operators responsible to a ground artillery officer rather than to the Air Service. "The receiving operator," he reported, "must be familiarized with every detail of the airplane observer's duties and difficulties" so that he could develop loyalty to the observer whom he is serving.[13] There were repeated recommendations that engineers, armament officers, radio operators, and motor transport men be taken out of the Corps of Engineers, the Ordnance Department, the Signal Corps, and the Motor Transport Corps, respectively, and placed directly under Air Service control to eliminate the division of authority, which the flyers contended, was slowing down critical projects.[14]

These complaints might be dismissed as part of a universal antipathy field forces frequently display toward a perceived lack of sensitivity to the requirements of combat on the part of behind-the-lines superiors, except that this command and control dissatisfaction apparently went deeper. During the Chateau-Thierry campaign in July 1918, for example, Mitchell seriously disagreed with the ground corps commanders over control of the observation squadrons.[15] The situation became grave enough to warrant Pershing's personal intervention (on Mitchell's behalf) and mention of the incident in the postwar final report by the chief of the Air Service.[16]

American air doctrine was borrowed largely from the European allies. By 1917, French and British aviation experience in the war was instrumental in forming American perceptions of how aircraft should be used. The French were particularly influential in supplying the Americans, not only with planes, but with doctrinal literature for using them.[17]

By 1917, Mitchell, then in Europe, was beginning to go beyond the allied doctrine by making somewhat of a distinction between tactical and strategic aeronautical functions. The former, which the Europeans had been pursuing for three years, involved observation, control of artillery fire, and protection of observation planes from enemy aircraft by pursuit planes. The strategic function, which he admitted, had received very limited application, required groups of airplanes organized separately from those directly attached to Army units.[18]

Yet the writings of Mitchell and other Americans remained more as think pieces than as official statements of doctrine. The air weapon was too new and changes too rapid to provide the luxury of organized debate over the implications of what was happening. A few airmen rose above day-to-day concerns and produced thoughtful tracts on how the air weapon should be used, but none found its way into official doctrine. Aircraft missions remained principally those of observation, adjustment of artillery fire, and protection of observation planes from enemy aircraft—all tied directly to ground action and determined by the needs of the infantry.

One doctrinal element that appears with regularity in mission reports and manuals is that of the moral, as opposed to the physical, effect of aerial attacks on the enemy. Analogous to, and possibly inspired by, the contemporary French emphasis on the superiority in warfare of moral over physical force, American airmen repeatedly stressed the moral effectiveness of their weapon. One principle promulgated by the Air Service, for example, stated that:

> The moral damage [airplanes] do with their bombs and machine guns is to the material damage as about twenty to one, but success in battle comes from the destruction of the enemy's morale, and not from the enemy's annihilation.[19]

The purpose of attacks on ground targets was not only physical destruction but, more importantly, to sow confusion along the enemy's front lines, disperse his infantry, distract his machine gun fire, demoralize traffic, and delay the approach of reinforcements.[20] Postflight reports from strafing runs regularly mentioned the unquantifiable, but nonetheless real, sense of fear that the flyers believed their attacks instilled in the enemy. One summation described a successful battle as one in which only a limited portion of the enemy's army is destroyed "while holding over the remainder the threat of impending destruction."[21] Belief among airmen in the deterrent power and moral effectiveness of their air weapon was real, and would blossom during the succeeding two decades as the basis of a doctrine of strategic bombardment.

When America declared war in April 1917 military planners set ambitious goals for aircraft production. Since even semiaccurate plans for the number of

The Birth of Close Air Support

aircraft needed to support ground forces must be based on the types of missions to be flown and the requirements of the ground forces themselves, American estimates, not based on prior experience with ground support, fluctuated wildly. In August 1917 alone, for example, the goals for the production of DH–4 observation planes changed from 7,000 to 5,000, then to 15,000, and then down to 6,000. By February of the following year the number had decreased to 4,500.[22] Yet the first American-built DH–4s did not arrive in France in appreciable numbers until May 1918, and the first American unit did not use them in combat until August, three months before the Armistice. Aside from JN–4 training planes, American attempts to build pursuit and bombing planes faltered and U.S. flyers had to rely on French and British aircraft for these missions.

During the early years of the war, before America's entry, both sides initially had employed separate types of planes for separate missions, the Allies using Spads and Nieuports for pursuit, Brequets for day bombing, DH–4s and Salmsons for observation, and Handley Pages and Capronis for night bombing. Inevitably, as flyers experimented with new possibilities and pushed against the frontiers of their equipment, they added new missions to the original ones. DH–4s were soon found to be capable of tactical bombing in addition to observation, while pursuit planes, designed for combat against enemy aircraft, added strafing ground troops and carrying small bombs to their operations. All the nations except Germany were content to divert pursuit, observation, and bombardment planes from their normal missions to attack functions.

Despite this growing tendency toward multipurpose planes, however, the tradeoffs that accompanied these attempts quickly became apparent. As summed up by one American air commander:

> The war has shown that there is no universal or multiple purpose plane which can be used for pursuit, reconnaissance, and bombing work. Each particular work calls for a different type of plane, specializing either in speed, maneuverability, climbing ability, carrying capacity, or long distance range. In order to embody one of these characteristics in a plane, others must be sacrificed.[23]

Thus began a long-running controversy between proponents of multipurpose aircraft and those who believed that, since each additional mission detracted from an aircraft's ability to perform its principal role, there should be a different type of airplane for each function. This difference of opinion would become a recurring theme throughout the history of close air support.

The ancillary role of aircraft gave rise to many of the issues that would continue to confront later practitioners of close air support. The most urgent requirement for two or more military branches acting in unison is an ability to

Help from Above

British De Havilland DH–4 observation plane (top left); British Handley-Page bomber (top right); Italian Caproni A–12 bomber (center); French Spad 13E fighters in formation (right); French Breguet bomber (bottom).

The Birth of Close Air Support

communicate clearly and rapidly with each other. The underdeveloped ability to do so limited the effectiveness of close air support in World War I. For coordination, each squadron sent an Air Service Liaison Officer to the headquarters of the army and division it was supporting. As a link between the ground and the air, this officer's job was to keep the squadron informed of tactical plans and to advise the ground commander of the best way to use his aerial resources. This required an experienced observer who could inject an aerial perspective into planning. The liaison officer worked closely with the operations and information officers to keep abreast of the ground situation and of future plans. From the signal officer he learned the system and codes being employed for receiving radio and dropped messages from aircraft. Officers in the Artillery Brigade kept him informed of the location of artillery units and which ones needed aerial observation for their fire control. He passed this information, along with any changes in the ground situation, by telephone or radio to the squadrons. He also acted as an informal inspector general, visiting artillery battalion and infantry brigade command posts to determine whether the airplanes were providing good service and whether they were receiving adequate cooperation from the ground.[24] As slow and cumbersome as were the activities of this prototype air liaison officer, it was widely agreed that he was extremely useful, and that the assignment of liaison officers should be made permanent.[25]

The absence of efficient radio communications between the ground and the air was a serious impediment to close cooperation between Air Service and infantry units. In order to contact the infantry or artillery, pilots and observers used wireless telegraphy, dropped messages or, on occasion, dispatched carrier pigeons. Ground troops, unable to reach aircraft by radio, signaled their location or intentions with Bengal flares, Very pistols, cloth panels, mirrors, projectors and, when all else failed, by waving coats or other available garments. Artillery spotting, infantry liaison, and observation planes carried French "Y" Type wireless radios, which they used to report in code the accuracy of artillery rounds and the location of friendly and enemy lines. Many pilots complained of time wasted in preflight checks of this radio equipment and of its unwieldiness in the cockpit. Planes on photo reconnaissance or protection missions carried no wireless equipment.[26]

Since, in the eyes of the flyers, ground radio operators often did not know how to use their equipment,[27] wireless communication proved relatively unreliable and airmen more often resorted to dropping written messages. Predetermined drop areas were clearly marked and manned by watchers with a telephone and a motorcycle messenger. Where drops proved impractical, the pilot landed at the nearest field and delivered his missive to the closest message center.[28]

On at least one occasion, flyers dropped messages to inform their own troops that they were operating. Exasperated by what he perceived as the infantry's failure to appreciate the Air Service's contribution to the fighting at St. Mihiel, Mitchell ordered leaflets released over American soldiers informing

Help from Above

them of the ways in which aircraft were supporting them. Addressed "From the American Scrappers in the Air to the American Scrappers on the Ground," the leaflet contained a sentence that would echo down through future decades as the airman's statement of the often unobservable but real benefits of air power: "Do not think we are not on the job when you cannot see us—most of our planes work so far in front that they cannot be seen from the lines."[29]

Even less effective and more unwieldy than dropped messages were projectors and other types of signal lights to which aircraft observers occasionally resorted. With projectors the flyer was unable to indicate which unit he wished to contact, while cartridges for Very pistols sometimes added to the weight of the airplane and on occasion were accidentally discharged inside the plane. Misfires, delayed discharges, and failures of rockets to explode added greatly to the observers' difficulties.[30] In some cases a klaxon horn or peculiarly timed burst of machine gun fire was used to alert a ground crew to the imminent dropping of a message.[31] Most curious of all was the sight of an observer hefting a wicker basket of carrier pigeons into his DH–4 before taking off on a reconnaissance mission.[32]

To contact an airplane, the infantry had to employ equally primitive measures, the most common of which was to display white cloth panels on the ground indicating the location of the front line. Intricate rules and codes were devised for panel signaling. The panels were to be kept clean and placed in positions not observable by the enemy. They were to be constantly moved about so as to be more easily detected by aircrews. By rearranging panels into predetermined configurations, the infantry troops could ask the aircraft questions concerning the location of the unit's command post, its advanced elements, what the observer saw to the left or right, or could inform the plane of its present status.[33]

Where the use of panels proved impractical, doughboys could speak to the planes with colored fireworks and rockets requesting barrage fire or indicating that their objective had been reached, their intention to advance, or that friendly artillery fire was hitting them.[34]

The rudimentary nature of these communications necessarily limited the quality of air support that the Air Service could render. The absence of two-way radios ruled out rapid reaction to fluid situations, with the result that most missions were planned well in advance. Although planes not assigned specific missions on a given day were often kept on alert for 15-minute takeoffs, even these missions had to be briefed before they were airborne.[35] The chances of changing plans in midair were slim. While these *immediates* were of some value when the ground situation was stabilized in the trenches, they were less effective during the relatively rapid movements of the St. Mihiel and Argonne campaigns.

Another consideration—the need for order in planning—probably influenced the airmen's preference for preplanned missions. It was more efficient,

The Birth of Close Air Support

although not necessarily more effective, when coordinating the activities of a large number of units, to plan individual missions within the larger context of other requirements. Yet the future controversy over planned versus immediate missions was foreshadowed in the dissatisfaction some flyers felt with missions designed too far in advance. "To call for such missions by schedule from the day before," protested one Corps Observation Group commander, "is a useless sacrifice of officers; when called for, even when the troops are not advancing, as it has been, is simply to invite the squadron C.O. [commanding officer] refusal under any pretext he happens to think of at the time."[36]

There arose during the war a divergence of attitudes between ground and air fighters that would remain a persistent factor in the later development of doctrine and organization. This intraservice rivalry had several parents. Some airmen saw its origin in the large presence of erstwhile civilians within the ground military ranks, entrepreneurs who often brought with them "the selfish competition of business and commercial affairs, the desire to build up one service…at the cost of another."[37] As noted by one air training chief:

> Competition is the mainspring of civil activity: cooperation and united effort are the mainsprings of military effort. What in civil life would be a laudable effort toward self-advancement may become in military life a menace to a service.[38]

Contributing to the diverging outlooks was the newness of the Air Service and its unproven record before September 1918. At first General Pershing gave every appearance of knowing and caring little about aviation. Although his attitude changed as the Air Service proved itself, doubts remained among many top-level ground officers of the AEF about the position of aviation.[39]

Most, however, interpreted the flyers' sense of individualism and lack of discipline as an inherent consequence of the nature of flying. Unlike the ground soldiers, airmen were volunteers who saw little practical application for the Army's traditional training methods. An airplane could not "be made the subject of order and direction in the same manner as can the handling of a rifle or the management of a pack." The feeling on the part of an airman that, unlike the foot soldier, he ultimately was alone in the air and was the sole judge of what he had to do, led to impatience with Army discipline, which appeared irrelevant at best, and at worst, detrimental to his operations.[40]

This attitude of separateness and, at times, superiority toward ground troops was reinforced by outward, more conspicuous manifestations of their differences, such as flying insignia worn by the airmen,[41] and reinforced by the soldiers' purported ignorance of the functions and capabilities of the Air Service. One flyer called this the heaviest of tactical handicaps.[42] Some resentment also was engendered in airmen by the fact that mission orders were issued by ground representatives of G–2 "who are not familiar with the Air Service and are not qualified to prescribe them."[43] In Mitchell's view, the General Staff was trying to run the Air Service "with as much knowledge of it as a hog has about skating."[44]

The most frequent criticism against the airmen was their lack of discipline. Ground troops were not the only complainers. The rated commander of an air training center reported that training had been hampered by gross disrespect shown superior officers by students, including throwing mud while drilling.[45] Although the Air Service's final report at the end of hostilities exonerated the flyers, concluding that their behavior was no more blameworthy than that of other AEF officers, the causes that gave rise to this sense of difference would continue to exert a strong influence on future doctrine and policy.[46]

The best substitute for combat experience is training and maneuvers. Although the Air Service developed an effective program to train the large influx of civilians in the art of flying, shortage of time permitted only sporadic joint training between airmen and soldiers. For four months before being thrown into heavy combat, the flyers were sent to Toul, a quiet sector where they were gradually introduced to combat flying. Some joint exercises with different infantry units were held there to acquaint the soldiers with aircraft operations and to hone the airmen's skill at working with ground troops. The 90th Aero Squadron conducted a school for 200 infantry officers and noncommissioned officers (NCOs) at a time, teaching them to identify flying aircraft, how to show their position to airplanes overhead, how to send messages to aircraft, and, in general, the importance of close liaison between the infantry and airplanes. In return, the squadron sent observers to the Infantry Division, Brigade, Regiment, and Battalion's command posts to instruct them in the air mission and to find out what the airmen could do for them.[47] Individual squadrons were encouraged to use their spare time and personnel to conduct joint training behind the lines.[48]

Judging from the outpouring of protests from flyers about the unpreparedness of ground troops to operate with them, this ad hoc training was ineffective. Some squadrons reported that they were already overworked and undermanned and could not divert resources from their missions to conduct joint maneuvers. Such training, they contended, should have been performed before arriving at the front. On numerous occasions, lack of instruction was blamed for the infantry's refusal to display its panels for a circling aircraft, which it could not distinguish from an enemy plane.[49] Many flying hours and tactical opportunities of artillery-spotting planes were wasted because radio operators at the artillery reception stations were poorly trained. The Chief of the Air Service, Gen. Benjamin D. Foulois, observed that artillery, infantry, and cavalry officers all needed training in how to give ground signals to airplanes.[50] Lack of familiarity with aircraft resulted in American artillery shooting down several planes of the 1st Aero Squadron, and some Air Service liai-

The Birth of Close Air Support

son officers were met with blunt refusals by ground commanders to cooperate in joint training.[51] Ironically, the virtually unanimous clamor of airmen to consider closer training and working relationships between the air and the ground was in part responsible for the postwar organization that decentralized the Air Service by dividing its resources among the Corps areas in the United States—a decentralization that ran counter to the direction in which the budding air doctrine was moving.

Several tactics that signaled the tentative beginnings of close air support were introduced during the war. One was the practice of strafing and bombing ground troops and supplies. Two factors encouraged the spread of ground attacks. First, the frustration both sides experienced as the war settled down into a defensive, trench-centered struggle. The warriors' natural aggressiveness found outlets in new forms of offensive equipment and tactics in an effort to restore mobility to the battlefield. On the ground, the British introduction of the tank in 1916 was a response to this frustration. In the air, the offensive spirit was signified by an increasing number of direct aerial attacks against ground forces. A second factor, a technological one, contributed to the success of these attacks. The invention of deflector plates on propellers, which allowed aircraft-mounted machine guns to fire through whirling propellers, stepped up the intensity not only of air-to-air combat but of air-to-ground missions as well.

European air forces pioneered strafing and bombing tactics several years before Americans took to the field, with the Germans and British leading the way. As early as 1916, during the Battle of the Somme, British observation air-

Lt. Benjamin D. Foulois in the first aircraft owned by the U.S. Army, a Wright type B, at Fort Sam Houston, Texas.

Help from Above

craft, after completing their reconnaissance missions, strafed targets of opportunity along the German trench line. In July of that year, during a raid near the Flanders coast, the Germans diverted a bomber squadron to attack and strafe ground units. For months, however, these remained isolated missions with neither dedicated aircraft nor preplanned targets.[52]

Alone among the belligerents, the Germans organized attack squadrons (called battalions) and introduced a plane configured specifically for the ground support mission. Buoyed by the effectiveness of their 1917 aerial attacks, they converted some escort squadrons, originally designed to protect reconnaissance planes, into ground support units to strike at all points of resistance to the infantry's advance. That same year they developed the all-metal Junkers-Fokker CL–1 attack plane, protected by one-fifth-inch armor, armed with two fixed guns firing to the front, one to the rear, and carrying about 200 pounds of bombs and high-explosive grenades. This plane was soon superseded by the Hannoveraner and Halberstadt CL planes, which were lighter and unarmored, and depended on speed and maneuverability, rather than armor, to escape the effects of ground fire.[53]

By March 1918, approximately one-third of the 1,000 airplanes the Germans had concentrated on a 50-kilometer front near Amiens were attack planes. Organized into flights of from six to nine aircraft each, and united into squadrons of three or four flights, these attack airplanes used strafing and bombing to assist the German infantry during its offensives and to prevent reinforcements from reaching the battlefield.[54] By the end of the war the German Air Force had 38 attack squadrons with 228 aircraft dedicated to this close air support mission.[55]

The Allies did not go as far as the Germans. Although the British began designing special attack planes, none appeared at the front before the end of the war. They did, however, divert their Sopwith Camels and Bristols from pursuit and observation duties for attacks on troops. The French considered attacks on ground troops as emergency measures and never organized a specialized branch for that work. They used Spads, Nieuports, Moranes, and Brequets as weapons of opportunity. The Americans, who had no American-made planes during the war, had their pursuit Nieuports, Spads, and Camels double as attack planes.[56]

Pilots of the two American squadrons that flew with the Royal Air Force (RAF) early in 1918, before the United States had its own squadrons ready for combat, absorbed much from the experience with strafing and bombing. Although ground strafing was not new, it greatly intensified during a German offensive in Picardy during March and April of that year. Periodic British supremacy in the air freed their pursuit planes for ground attacks. Both British and American pursuit and observation pilots experimented with strafing tactics. For a week they tried sending out flights of six planes every half hour. Splitting up when they reached the lines, each plane attacked targets of oppor-

The Birth of Close Air Support

tunity. It was quickly realized that ground attacks were more effective when they were continuous. Consequently, they then switched to sending two-plane flights every 15 minutes. During this period, the Americans gained experience for the day they would be conducting their own missions.[57]

While working under RAF control, the American squadrons also learned to cooperate with allied tanks. During an offensive in August 1918 against the Germans around Montdidier, pursuit planes of both nations flew low over the British tanks, hitting antiaircraft guns and machine gun nests that stood in the path of their advance. In this action the British tanks scored a major victory, completely surprising and capturing a German headquarters. Although none of the official mission descriptions for these early American sorties included strafing and close-in bombing, this form of air support became widespread, and operational orders during the last few months of the war increasingly called for such aerial attacks.

Such was the case with the American squadrons in their two campaigns of the war late in 1918, namely, those of St. Mihiel and Meuse-Argonne. In the former, American ground units were assigned the task of reducing a German salient around the town of St. Mihiel in northeastern France (**Figure 1**). Throughout the day of September 12, American pursuit planes of the 12th Aero Squadron, along with French pursuit planes, rained machine gun fire down on the German troops, guns, and transports that were retreating north-eastward along the road between Vignuelles and St. Benôit. The enemy columns were thrown into confusion by allied air attacks that sealed off their escape routes. This enabled American troops, who encircled the enemy behind Vignuelles the following day, to capture 15,000 immobilized prisoners, 440 guns, and large stores of materiel. For two more days the planes continued to strafe fleeing troops along the St. Benôit-Chambley and the Chambley-Mars-la-Tour roads. By the time the American units embarked on the subsequent Meuse-Argonne operation, strafing and bombing attacks against enemy units had become so effective that, according to intelligence reports, the mere sight of allied planes was causing confusion in the enemy's ranks. In his final report on the war, the Chief of the Air Service noted that "the attack by aircraft upon ground troops, using machine guns and small bombs, showed very clearly that this has a most demoralizing effect."[58]

During the campaign the following month, the American squadron was originally charged, among other things, with protecting 500 French tanks from hostile aircraft. Unable to contact the tanks directly, the planes turned their attention to targets of opportunity, but the precedent had been set for greater cooperation between planes and tanks in future years.[59]

Pilots returning from missions debated the relative advantages and disadvantages of strafing and bombing. Some saw reconnaissance missions as more productive than attacking enemy troops.[60] Others believed that strafing missions were not important enough to risk the lives of highly trained

Help from Above

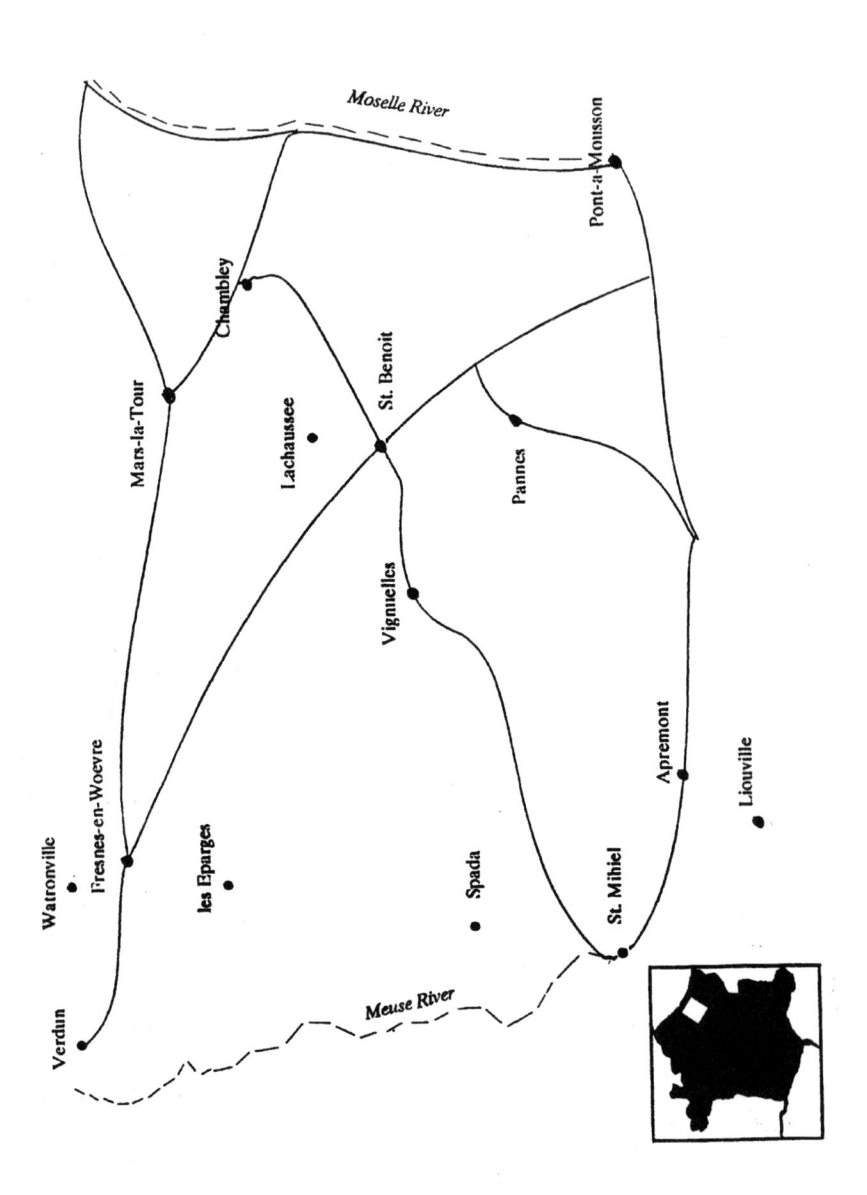

FIGURE 1
St. Mihiel, September 12–16, 1918

The Birth of Close Air Support

German Junkers all metal monoplane (top); German Halberstadt (center); British Sopwith Camel (bottom).

observers.[61] Most, however, viewed this opportunistic mission as beneficial, and strafing became almost a daily feature for pursuit planes.

Through trial and error, flyers gradually devised tactics for striking ground targets. Pilots of observation planes, whose fixed, forward-shooting guns required the plane to dive in order to strafe, were advised to fly straight and level and let the observer fire his two guns, which were mounted in the rear on a movable tourelle.[62] During the later stages of the Meuse-Argonne offensive, American observation planes performed the twin functions of the absent cavalry. In addition to locating the enemy for the ground troops, their strafing pointed out the enemy's positions, including his hidden machine gun nests, to the American soldiers below.[63]

Pursuit planes were instructed to cross the front lines at 1,000 meters, drop their bombs at about 500 or 600 meters, and then strafe with machine guns at about 250 meters.[64] This latter altitude was deemed to be the best compromise between achieving accuracy and avoiding ground fire, which was the greatest threat. One estimate placed the casualties from ground fire at 75 percent. Some pilots felt that it was safer to strafe at an altitude below 200 meters, where the plane quickly passed out of range of ground fire and more rapidly changed its angle of sight.[65]

Mission directives did not distinguish between attacks on troops that were in contact with friendly forces (later called close air support) and strikes against ground targets out of artillery range of the front lines (interdiction). The closest they came to this differentiation was a distinction in the flight orders between trench strafing and troop strafing.[66] The former approximated later close air support, while the latter was roughly equivalent to interdiction. Until World War II, close air support and interdiction would be lumped together in the term *attack aviation*. Despite this lack of distinction, the idea of using aircraft to affect directly the outcome of the ground battle was born.

Two wartime developments, seemingly insignificant at the time, were to grow into challenges to the Army's conception of close air support. First were the initial stirrings of the idea among airmen of separating the Air Service from the rest of the Army. These ideas were inspired by the example of the British, who accomplished such a separation in 1918, and by mounting evidence that the air weapon had potentialities far beyond its direct service to ground troops. Although many of the flyers who addressed the issue, including General Foulois, opposed autonomy, the seeds of independence had been sown, an independence that when finally achieved would vastly complicate the ability of air and ground forces to work together.

The other event with implications for the future was the arrival of the personnel to man three U.S. Marine squadrons in Calais at the end of July 1918. Unable to acquire their own planes, they flew DeHavillands on bombing missions for the RAF.[67] Although they were not supporting ground troops, the expansion within a decade of this newborn Marine aviation into a close air sup-

The Birth of Close Air Support

port organization was to present a strong alternative to the direction that Army close air support would take.

The U.S. Army Air Service emerged from World War I with the rudiments of a close air support concept, system, and organization, as well as early indications of future close air support problems. Moreover, despite limited combat experience, its pilots had assimilated tactics for strafing and bombing ground troops and for protecting friendly tanks. The doctrinal distinction between strategic and tactical operations also began to appear, although the term *attack aviation* still did not distinguish between close air support and interdiction. Finally, some elements of a future system for requesting close air support strikes, for controlling them, and for coordinating them with ground commanders surfaced. The lesson of applying technological advances to warfare were clearly learned.

Yet many air-ground problems that arose during the war were bequeathed to future generations of airmen. Mitchell's arguments with his superiors over who should control the aircraft foreshadowed later major debates over the command and control of close air support planes, and disagreements during the war concerning which was more effective, a multipurpose plane or one tailored to a specific mission, became sharper after the war. Also, the air-ground communication difficulties experienced by both airmen and soldiers would be passed on to succeeding generations, and the inability of planes to strike the enemy at night would present a continuing challenge to future airmen. The relative merits of preplanned missions over immediate strikes would continue to be debated, and the lack of effective air-ground training would continually plague the Air Service and its successors. The diverging attitudes between airmen and soldiers, which originated in World War I, would intensify with time to become a major tacit ingredient in future air-ground deliberations.

Between the Wars

Concentration by historians and others on the evolution and eventual primacy of strategic bombing concepts within the Army Air Service in the two decades between the wars has obscured the fervid debates that took place among advocates of tactical and ground support aviation. Tactical doctrine, command and control, technology, and tactics initially made considerable progress both at the service schools and in the field, at least until the establishment of the Army's semiautonomous General Headquarters (GHQ) Air Force in 1935 reversed many of these gains. Tactical aviation throughout the period took two forms: pursuit and attack. The former was dedicated largely to gaining control of the air, which all agreed held first place in the priority of missions. Within attack aviation, still no distinction was made between interdiction and close air support.

Help from Above

Air Service thinking in the immediate postwar period was strongly shaped by the separatist ideas and polemics of Billy Mitchell. Possibly in reaction to the counterproductive effects of his tendentious methods, air power advocates became more subtle and, some would say, more subversive, following his court martial in 1925 and resignation early the following year.

For the next decade Air Corps (the name change occurred in July 1926) doctrine moved simultaneously along two seemingly contradictory paths. On the one hand, many of the writings and teachings at the Air Corps Tactical School, the seedbed of doctrine, repeated the Army General Staff's adage that the mission of air units "is to aid the ground forces to gain decisive success." This, in War Department thinking, was to be accomplished principally by attack aviation normally controlled by the ground commander. Even bombardment aircraft were to support ground forces.[68]

At the same time, a powerful competing train of thought stressed, with increasing repetition, that air power was an instrument not directly of the ground forces but of national policy. This placed air power on an equal footing with ground power. Its purpose was to destroy not the enemy's army but his will to resist, and the best means for doing this was to attack the interior of his country.[69]

So impressed had the AEF been with the results of ground attacks, particularly during the St. Mihiel and Meuse-Argonne campaigns, that General Foulois, in his final report on the war, strongly urged the establishment of attack units and approved an immediate postwar manual for their employment.[70] These instructions, written by Mitchell who had become an enthusiastic supporter of the offensive potentialities of attack planes, provide the first clear doctrinal statement for attack aviation.

Attack aviation became synonymous with the direct support of the ground forces. Its primary mission included what would later become the separate missions of close air support and interdiction. Initially, attack aviation was organized, equipped, and trained primarily to destroy light material objectives and concentrations of troops before, during, and after ground battles. Secondarily, attack planes were to strike aircraft on the ground, airbase facilities, light vessels, personnel in coast defense operations, antiaircraft defenses, hostile lines of communication, supply and manufacturing establishments, light bridges, and transportation equipment. Its principal weapons were chemicals, light bombs, and machine guns.

For the first time, the United States had attack squadrons, with eighteen planes apiece, and groups, each with three squadrons. Officers at the Air Corps Tactical School developed missions, tactics, and techniques for attack planes. When the ground troops were on the offensive, these planes were to roam overhead and in front of the infantry to strike the enemy's forward infantry lines and harass his forward artillery. In addition, they were to break up his movement of reinforcements to the battlefield and interdict his lines of communi-

The Birth of Close Air Support

cation. Some aircraft would be kept on alert when friendly forces were on the defensive. At such times, the planes' targets became the enemy's second and third assault waves. If the enemy were using tanks, the attack squadrons were to separate the tanks from their infantry support by attacking the latter with bombs and strafing them with cannon fire. A major contribution of attack planes was in strengthening the confidence and morale of friendly forces.

This doctrine recognized the need to build planes with sufficient protection against ground fire and with adequate radio communication with the ground, and of the importance of intensive training, especially of flight leaders, in close formation and flight-following procedures.

As a secondary mission, attack squadrons were to act in conjunction with bombing squadrons. The doctrine stressed the importance of concentrated, continuous, uninterrupted engagement at the decisive time and place. In a departure from wartime practice, attack planes were not to be assigned other missions, but were to be dedicated solely to the air-ground task. This codified the lesson supposedly learned during the war about the superiority of single-purpose aircraft and inaugurated a search for an effective attack plane. The ideal attack plane was originally envisioned as a single seater, armored plane with two fields of fire—one forward and one below.[71]

So new was the idea of attack aviation that the flying veterans who were called upon to capture in writing their wartime ideas found it difficult to incorporate attack aviation into doctrine. By the early 1920s, they had conceptually divided the Air Service into two distinct categories: the air service and the air force. The former was made up of observation planes operating as auxiliaries of the infantry. The air force, on the other hand, which many considered the *true arm*, consisted of attack, bombardment, and pursuit planes. Since the air service performed in a more support-overled role and the air force a more direct combat role, and since bombardment, pursuit, and attack aircraft had accounted for three-fourths of all planes on the western front at the end of the war, it was this latter category that was emphasized.

The missions of observation, bombardment, and pursuit aircraft were quite distinct from each other. Observation craft were closely tied to ground forces. Bombardment and pursuit planes had little to do directly with the ground, while attack aircraft had to coordinate with both pursuit planes, which defended them from enemy aircraft, and the ground forces they were supporting. As a result, attack aviation became the focal point of an intense controversy between those who stressed the ground support function of aircraft and their more independence-minded fellow airmen. Most early theorists in the Air Service considered that, since the bond between attack and pursuit planes was stronger than that between attack planes and ground forces, both pursuit and attack aircraft should be directed by an air, rather than a ground, commander.[72] In this way the role of close air support aircraft was bound up with the question of command and control at an early stage.

Help from Above

These visions of centralized control under air commanders were not realized until the mid-1930s, and then only partially. Immediately after the Great War, Air Service units were parceled out to the four continental Army Corps areas as well as to the Philippine, Hawaiian, and Panama Canal Departments. By 1926, the number of Army Corps areas whose commanders controlled the planes of the Air Service had increased to nine, the three overseas departments remaining unchanged.[73]

Attack aviation, as a distinct organization, came into being in September 1921 with the conversion of the First Surveillance Group and its four squadrons into the 3rd Attack Group at Kelly Field, Texas. Three years later, two of the squadrons were inactivated, and the remaining two decreased in size. Under the overall five-year Air Corps expansion program announced in 1926, the attack group gained new life. In 1927 it moved to Fort Crockett in Galveston, Texas, and two years later its two squadrons were reactivated. By 1933 the group had joined with a pursuit group at Barksdale Field, Shreveport, Louisiana, to form an attack wing that operated 52 attack, 50 pursuit, 6 observation, and 2 cargo planes. In 1935 a second Attack Group, the 17th, was formed at March Field, California. Yet the low priority attached to attack aviation on the eve of World War II is suggested by the distribution of Air Corps squadrons on September 1, 1939:[74]

Bombardment	15
Pursuit	15
Observation	10
Reconnaissance	8
Attack	7

The mission of attack squadrons had undergone subtle changes by 1939. In the 1920s and early 1930s their principal targets were ground units such as troop columns, troop concentrations, corps and army reserves, and concentrations of artillery.[75] There was general agreement that the use of attack aviation was not warranted "within the range of artillery, or within the area eight miles in the rear of the enemy front lines."[76] This stipulation was inspired not by any animus toward cooperating with ground troops, but by the difficulty, at the time, of providing effective support so close to friendly troops. During the 1920s and into the early 1930s, studies and exercises of attack operations at the Air Corps Tactical School shared equal time in the curriculum with those of pursuit aviation. Emphasis on bombardment and observation tactics lagged behind.

By 1938, when the B–17 was harnessed to a national policy of hemispheric defense, the attack mission began to shift. First priority was now given to supporting the bombers by destroying aircraft on the ground, attacking light vessels in coastal defense operations, and neutralizing antiaircraft defenses.

The Birth of Close Air Support

A presentation ceremony on April 16, 1920, at Kelly Field, Texas (top); Air Corps machine shops at Barksdale Field, Louisiana (bottom).

Support of ground forces before, during, and after the battle, which had been the first priority for attack planes in 1921, now fell to last.[77]

Air attack tactics and targets were hotly debated. Student texts included lessons on attacking mechanized and motorized columns, troops on the march, airfields, and antiaircraft installations.[78] Information on air tactics was gleaned from all available sources, both theoretical and actual. In 1928, for example, for use as a text at the school, the Chief of the Air Corps received a detailed briefing from the Marine Corps Commandant on the Marines' air experience in Nicaragua. From this interchange the Air Corps reinforced, and in some cases refined, its views on types of aircraft, the best altitudes and formations to fly, the effectiveness of aerial and ground weapons, the importance of surprise, and the relative merits of preplanned targets versus those of opportunity.[79]

Attempts during this period to develop attack aircraft were frustrated by the limitations of technology and continued controversy between, on the one hand, planners who wanted to get the most out of their economically limited

23

Help from Above

number of airplanes, and, on the other hand, theorists who argued constantly against using pursuit, bombardment, or observation planes for attack. Suggestions to use pursuit planes in the attack role were countered with the argument that adding bombs, bomb racks, four forward guns, and their associated equipment, would add 525 pounds to the plane, decreasing its critical speed in the face of hostile pursuit aircraft. Observation planes as substitutes were ruled out as incapable of carrying attack equipment in addition to their observation instruments. Bombardment planes lacked the necessary speed and maneuverability to serve as attack vehicles.[80]

It was still the unanimous judgment from the field that a dedicated attack plane was needed. This view was reinforced after the creation of the GHQ Air Force in 1935, when attack aviation assumed two, seemingly incompatible, missions: support of the growing bomber force and ground support missions. Most believed that no one plane could perform both missions effectively. Support of bombers by destroying antiaircraft installations and enemy aircraft on the ground, called for a plane with great range. To acquire this long range, however, other characteristics essential for effective ground support had to be sacrificed.[81]

Attack aircraft that were developed and flown operationally during most of these two decades were designed to counter ground fire and antiaircraft artillery by their speed and maneuverability rather than by heavy armor, which would reduce the aircraft's speed.[82] For the first decade after the war, the Air Service's attack planes were originally designed for other purposes—DH–4s that survived the conflict, the XBIA, the Douglas O–2, and the Curtiss A–3. This latter plane was merely a Curtiss O–1 observation plane that was fitted with four immovable guns in the wings.

As the requirements for attack missions became increasingly sophisticated, these observation/bombardment planes proved inadequate. The A–3s, for example, which had become the standard attack planes in 1928, were neither fast enough to evade ground fire nor heavy enough to carry enough bombs for the attack mission.[83]

Beginning in 1931, the Air Corps experienced a brief flirtation with planes designed solely for the attack mission. In that year it introduced the Curtiss A–8 which, despite many drawbacks, was the first of a series of planes with built-in capabilities to perform the attack function. In 1933 the aero group converted to the Curtiss A–12 Shrike (**Figure 2**), a single-engine, two-seater monoplane with four wing-mounted .30-caliber fixed machine guns and two flexible .30-caliber guns in the rear seat. With a full load of four externally carried 100-lb. demolition bombs, it could reach a speed of 186 mph.

Between 1935 and 1938 attack units acquired greater speed, range, and bombload capacity with the single-engine Northrop A–17 attack plane.[84] This aircraft, which cost $26,483 (less its engine), carried a crew of two and 654

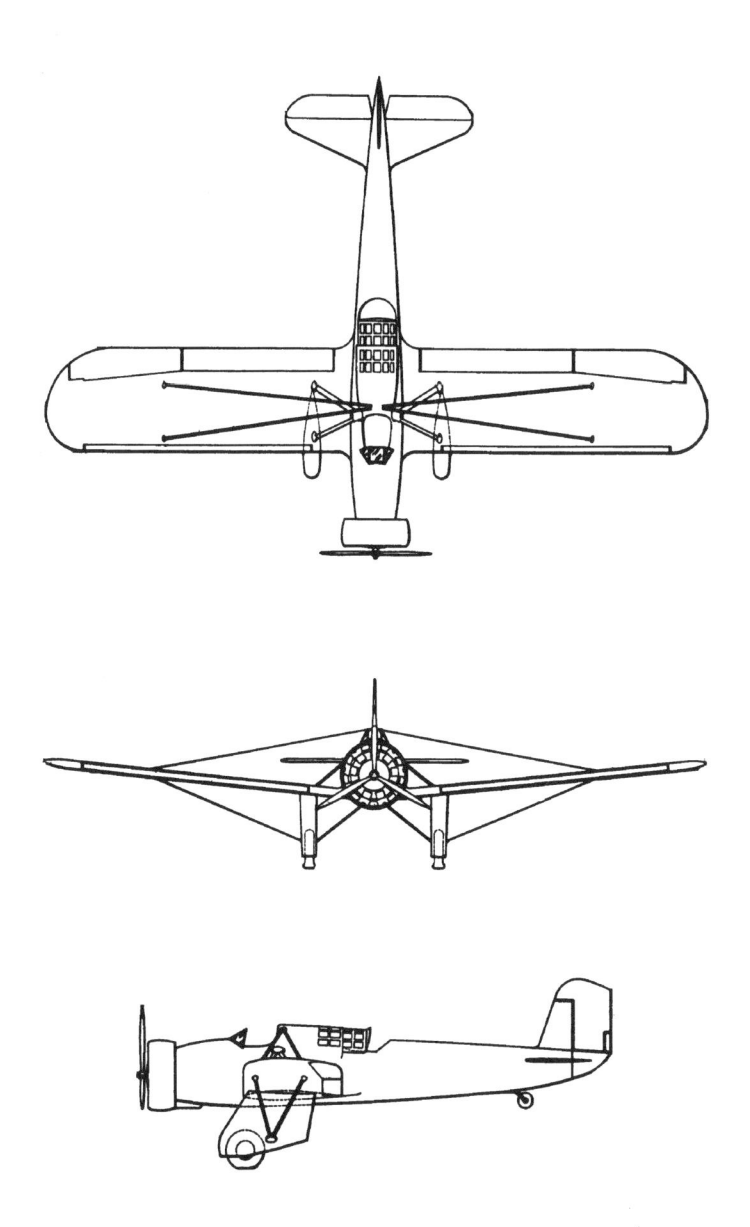

FIGURE 2
A–12 Shrike

Help from Above

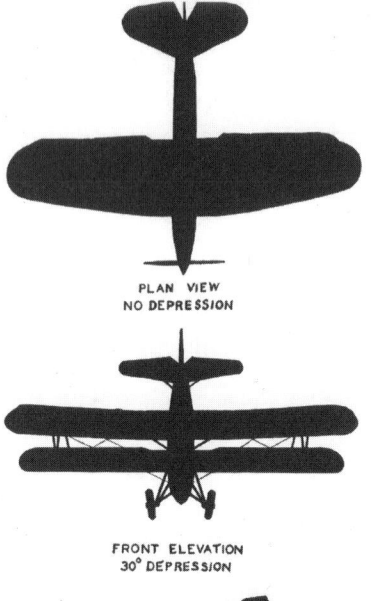

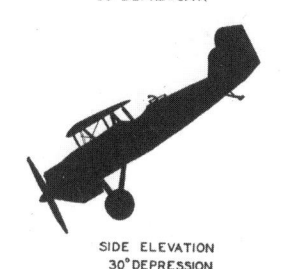

PLAN VIEW
NO DEPRESSION

FRONT ELEVATION
30° DEPRESSION

SIDE ELEVATION
30° DEPRESSION

Silhouettes of a Curtiss A–3 (left); a Curtiss XA–8 (top).

pounds of bombs, had an operating speed of 180 mph, and an operating range of 1160 miles with an overload of fuel. While the A–17 was effective in the ground support role, the shift of GHQ Air Force priorities for attack aviation away from ground support and toward counter-air force missions, led to the 1938 introduction of a two-engine attack plane, the A–18. It was believed that the A–18 would be more useful in defending bombers by destroying enemy aircraft on the ground, by striking base facilities, and by neutralizing antiaircraft defenses. This shift to a two-engine attack plane was also encouraged by reports from the Spanish Civil War recounting the disasters encountered by insufficiently armored attack planes. Close air support operations in the Spanish Civil War also convinced airmen of the superiority of tactical bombing over strafing.

The employment of the A–18 as the standard attack plane signaled the beginning of the end of the Air Corps' short flirtation with aircraft designed solely for the close air support function. The termination of the experiment took place shortly thereafter in 1940 when attack groups were redesignated as

The Birth of Close Air Support

"light bombardment" units.[85] Subsequently, during World War II, multipurpose fighter-bombers became the choice for close air support aircraft.

Consistent with its new emphasis on light bombers rather than single-purpose attack planes, the Air Corps by 1939 was switching over to twin-engined A–20s, the main attack plane with which it entered the war. Suggestions, however, to develop dive bombers came to naught. Since dive-bomber technology was not sufficiently advanced, the Air Corps rejected the idea of generating new aircraft specifically for close support.

On a par with the frustrations attack enthusiasts experienced from the Army's insistence on decentralization and the Air Corps' drift toward strategic

A Curtiss Y1A–18 (top); a Douglas A–20 (bottom).

Help from Above

bombing were the unsuccessful efforts between 1921 and 1939 to acquire reliable aircraft radios. Efficient and reliable two-way radio contact between the ground and the air was essential for a Tactical Air Control System, the heart of any close air support operation. Yet field tests during the first half of the 1920s with the SCR–130 series of radios were disappointing. Serious attempts by the Signal Corps to develop voice communication were thwarted by its lack of success in grounding airborne radios in wooden planes, by wave absorption in metal planes, and by engine and aircraft noise in the open cockpits of both types of aircraft. The use of trailing wire antennas further complicated these early experiments. Antennas interfered with formation flying, frequently snapped off during tight maneuvers, and often were caught on trees and other ground objects during low passes.

Until the early 1930s pilots and ground personnel continued to rely on proven World War I methods to contact each other: dropping messages, setting out panels, flares, rockets, smoke, or whatever other imaginative means of contact they could devise.[86] In 1927, for example, during the sole substantial combat use between the wars of aircraft for ground support, the Marines in Nicaragua became aware that one of their battalions was under siege by the Sandino rebels only after a Marine pilot, flying without radios, landed by chance near the action, heard of the siege from natives, and flew back to his airfield to alert reinforcements.[87] During the refueling experiment in the Los Angeles area two years later, the crew of the Question Mark airplane received information from the ground either by notes attached to the end of the refueling hose, or by reading messages scrawled on a huge blackboard attached to a plane that flew alongside.[88]

Even as more efficient aircraft radios were coming into use in the early 1930s, funding constraints created long delays in getting the equipment installed in the planes. Pilots continued to rely on a combination of radio and visual signals to direct operations. As late as 1933, during an exercise at Fort Knox, Kentucky, each squadron of 22 aircraft possessed only six two-way radios and five receivers. Air Corps pilots had difficulty the following year, when called upon to fly the airmail, in achieving radio contact with the incompatible equipment of civilian airways.[89]

Another staple of successful close air support, joint training between air and ground forces, failed to make progress in the United States before World War II. Although the Air Service and Air Corps held annual maneuvers and air demonstrations, these seldom came closer in practicing ground support than interdicting enemy movements toward the front or enemy supplies behind the lines. Even those exercises at the Air Corps Tactical School that were designed for close ground support pitted aircraft in prearranged strikes against dummy targets representing soldiers, horses, carts, or communication centers (**Figures 3 and 4**).[90] These sterile exercises lacked the realism that would have been achieved against live ground troops capable of evasion, camouflage, and

The Birth of Close Air Support

defending themselves with antiaircraft weapons and small arms. No Tactical Air Control System emerged from these maneuvers. Despite the Army's insistence on giving first priority to ground support, the Air Corps often used these exercises as opportunities to bring their scattered air resources together to practice operating with each other rather than with the infantry.[91]

By the mid-1930s, the slow pace of technological progress in attack aviation, the growing resentment among flyers toward the General Staff's insistence on tying aircraft closely to ground forces, and the fervent belief that the airplane's future lay in offensive operations away from the immediate battlefield, combined to accelerate the shift of Air Corps priorities away from attack and pursuit aviation and toward strategic bombardment. This change of direction is reflected in a recommendation from the Tactical School's Tactics and Strategy Department, made in the midst of the debate over whether attack aviation should support bombers rather than ground forces:

> Until we accomplish the provisions of an adequate M-day Air Force we should not dissipate our effort on ground attack aviation. If the development of aviation as a whole proceeds as dictated by its efficiency for reaching a decision in war, the ground attack aviation will be used only in peacetime maneuvers.

The memo went on to suggest that merging attack and bombardment aviation could assuage the ground arm's suspicion of the emphasis on strategic bombardment, "particularly if 'support' could be disconnected from the idea of directly maiming personnel."[92]

While the U.S. Army Air Corps continued to move in the direction of strategic air power, the newly revived German Air Force was traveling in the opposite direction. During the first several years after its rebirth in 1934 the *Luftwaffe*, like Britain's RAF, had been enamored of long-range bombers. The realization, however, that its position as a land power surrounded by potential enemies required, unlike the United States and Great Britain, an air force to support its army from the opening day of a war, led to a shift of emphasis toward tactical air resources. This change toward close air support was further encouraged by the presence in the *Luftwaffe* of many officers who had been ground soldiers in World War I and by the success of the gull-winged Ju–87 Stuka bombers in supporting Nationalist ground forces in Spain.[93]

As a result, the Germans took the lead in creating an air-ground system. Although the *Luftwaffe* was an independent service, the Iberian experience impressed on its leaders the need to share a common objective with the ground forces and to concentrate its effort on supporting the army. Like its American and British counterparts, the German Air Force had yet to distinguish between close air support and battlefield interdiction, as each was nec-

Help from Above

DETAILS OF TARGET CONSTRUCTION

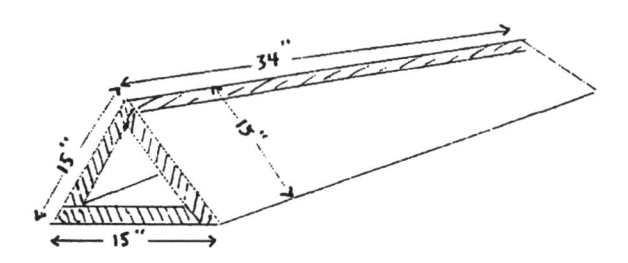

[Diagram of triangular prism target with dimensions: 34" length, 15" width, 15" height]

1. STANDING FIGURE: Two targets placed end to end, and in upright position. Total height 5 - 8"

2. KNEELING FIGURE: One target placed on end. Total height 2' - 10"

3. PRONE FIGURE: Two targets placed end to end and flat on the ground. Height 13"

NOTE: (1) Some of the targets are not made exactly according to specifications, usually exceeding the dimensions given above.

(2) Standing and prone figures expose considerable more surface than would the body of a man.

(3) The surface of a kneeling figure is approximately one-half that of a standing or prone figure.

(4) Targets representing animals were hastily improvised and were much too small.

FIGURE 3
Details of Target Construction

APPROXIMATE LOCATION OF TARGETS

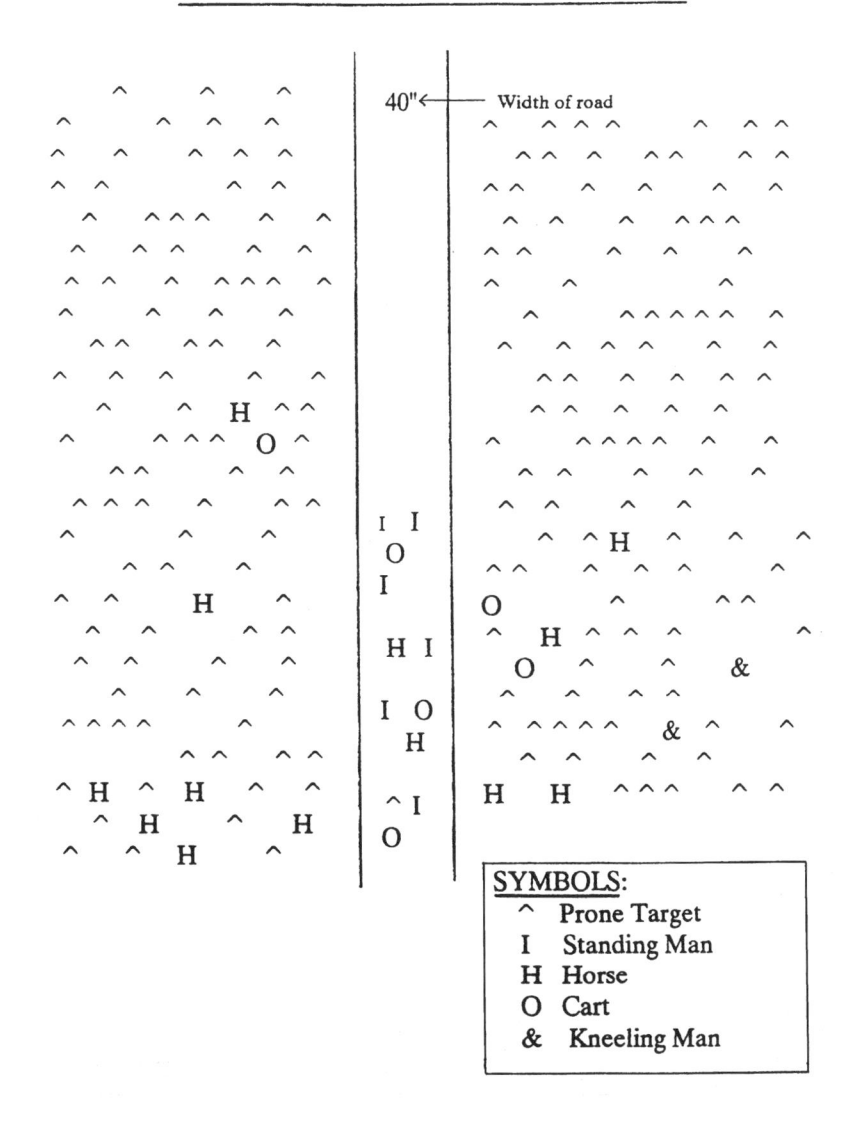

SYMBOLS:
- ^ Prone Target
- I Standing Man
- H Horse
- O Cart
- & Kneeling Man

FIGURE 4
Approximate Location of Targets

Help from Above

essary at different times in the course of battle. By 1939 the *Luftwaffe* had several close air support squadrons, divisions, and corps, that had trained extensively with the ground forces. In addition to fighters, these units contained reconnaissance and transport planes.

Air divisions and corps were assigned to ground units for particular operations and air and ground commanders, whose headquarters were collocated, planned jointly. Most missions were planned the day before, but the air commander could divert sorties during emergencies. The German Air Force assigned officers and NCOs to army corps and divisions (Air Signal Liaison Teams) to report back the ground commander's situation and intentions. In addition, Ground Attack Teams, assigned to each level down to regiments, directed close air support strikes. By the time war engulfed Europe, this German close air support system set the standard for its time.[94]

World War II

The decline of attack aviation in the United States leveled off in 1939 with the opening of hostilities in Europe and the start of American mobilization. The arrival of Gens. Henry "Hap" Arnold as Air Chief and George C. Marshall as the Army Chief ushered in a more cooperative and compromising period in air-ground relations. Marshall, unlike his predecessors at the helm of the Army, accepted offensive bombing as a major mission of the air forces. He continued to insist, however, that all aircraft, regardless of mission, be tied to the ground forces and be commanded by a ground officer. Arnold, on the other hand, while remaining a bomber advocate, acknowledged the military and political advantages of providing attack (now called tactical) aircraft.

The need for aerial attack support for the ground forces was reinforced by force structure decisions made on the eve of the war in reorganizing the War Department. Among these changes was the decision to forgo investment in very heavy artillery and even to limit the amount of heavy artillery for the ground forces. It was decided that the money saved by not developing and shipping these weapons be used by the Army Air Forces (so named since March 1941) to enhance its ability to substitute close air support for the missing artillery.

The new conciliatory attitude between Generals Arnold and Marshall became evident in April 1942, when a major step was taken to rectify the lack of a "joint" doctrine for close air support.[95] German successes with tactical air support in Poland and France in 1939 and 1940, a host of weaknesses in American air-ground support procedures uncovered during maneuvers in the United States during 1940 and 1941, and some early experiences in the Pacific war, combined to convince the Army Air Forces to improve guidelines for close air support.

The Birth of Close Air Support

Lt. Henry H. Arnold in Wright B aircraft at College Park, Maryland in 1911 (bottom); Gen. George C. Marshall, Chief of Staff in 1939 (right).

The resultant Field Manual (F.M.) 31–35, titled *Aviation in Support of Ground Forces* (**Figure 5**) was clearly a compromise. For the first time it separated close air support from the other tactical functions of interdiction and air superiority by omitting the latter two. It also distinguished between command and control by centralizing control in an air support commander[96] who, however, served as a staff member to an army, theater, or task-force ground commander. The ground commander was responsible for determining the mission, the method of air support, the units to receive support, and the area of operations, and also made the final decision on the priorities assigned to targets. The air commander decided the method of attack and the equipment to be used and issued orders to his air units, laying out priorities, attack times, bomb loading, and flight routes. The air commander was also in charge of air support control and Air Support Parties, which consisted of airmen attached to lower ground headquarters.[97]

Field Manual 31–35 also fleshed out some of the details that make close air support work, and it outlined a method for ground units to request air support. Air and ground alerts were also discussed. A small group of airmen, the air support control, located at ground-force headquarters, directed aircraft operations and advised the ground commander of the capabilities of the air

Help from Above

FIELD MANUAL 31-35
Aviation in Support of Ground Forces
April 9, 1942

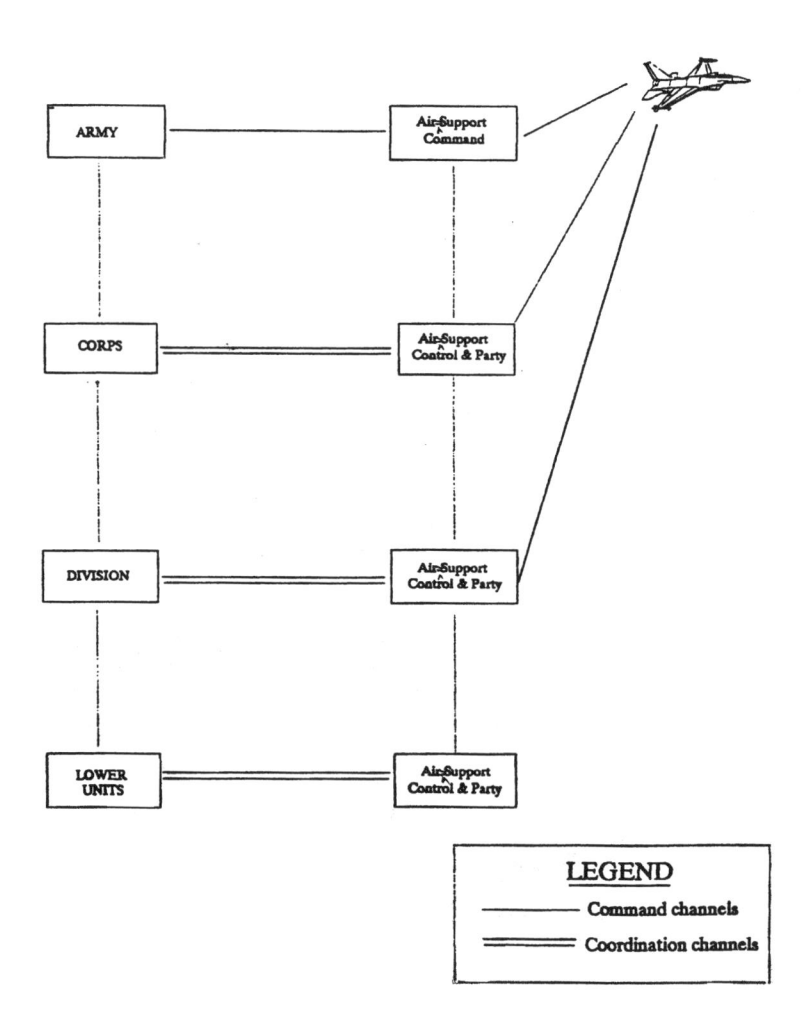

FIGURE 5
Cover of Aviation in Support of Ground Forces

The Birth of Close Air Support

resources. The air support control had airmen, Air Support Parties, posted with subordinate ground units in the field to relay requests for air support. Even when, on rare occasions, an air unit was assigned to a specific ground unit, the air commander retained control of the operational details. Assignment to a ground unit did not imply subordination of the aviation force to the supported ground unit. Only observation aircraft remained organic parts of ground units.[98]

Air targets included any defensive forces in the path of the friendly army, particularly mechanized and armored units, hostile ground elements moving toward the operational area, antitank forces, and hostile aircraft when no other friendly aircraft were available to confront them. Air Support Command aircraft were also to clear and maintain landing zones for parachute and airborne troops.[99] Although the manual excluded air superiority and interdiction from its discussion of tactical air support, it did include both reconnaissance and air transport operations in that category. Three years earlier the War Department, in establishing functional groupings for military aviation, had defined combat, reconnaissance, and air transport as ground support roles.[100]

The continued unreliability of radio communications between air and ground was reflected in the manual's provisions for siting radios and identifying targets. No radio sets for air-ground communications were to be located at levels below divisions. Ground signals, familiar since World War I, were still recommended, and arrows pointing to the target, vehicles in prearranged formations, tracers or smoke, signal lamps and lights, and pyrotechnics were all suggested. Pointing to the future, the manual also made provision for observation craft to "lead in" combat planes.[101]

Since World War I the Army had considered observation aircraft as an essential component of air support. Until 1935, however, these planes were used exclusively for visual surveillance. In that year the GHQ Air Force developed the first aircraft for long-range reconnaissance missions. In February 1940 the Air Corps activated the 1st Photographic Squadron. A year later, encouraged by reports from Europe of the effectiveness of photoreconnaissance and a growing realization that observation squadrons were being trained "under directives and concepts based on the last war," Army ground troops were trained to rely on aerial photographs rather than existing maps.[102]

With the new emphasis on photoreconnaissance, the familiar debate arose as to whether to develop a plane specifically for the reconnaissance mission or to equip on-the-shelf aircraft with cameras and other reconnaissance equipment. Several experiments demonstrated that a unique reconnaissance plane would be impractical. Reports from Europe indicating excellent results from modifying fighter or pursuit planes for photography pushed the Army Air Forces (AAF) in that direction, and initially, photographic equipment was installed in some P–40s. During fall maneuvers in 1941, similar equipment was placed in P–38s (at first called F–1s) with satisfactory results, and early the following year, some P–39s and A–20s joined the growing list of planes modified

Help from Above

A Consolidated F–7A reconnaissance aircraft

for reconnaissance. The coming war was to see P–47s and P–51s (F–6s) pressed into service for tactical reconnaissance and later model P–38s (F–5s), B–17s (F–9s), and B–24s (F–7s) performing strategic reconnaissance roles.[103]

Field Manual 31–35 made observation squadrons and groups organic to theater, army, corps, and armored or cavalry divisions, with these air units having three missions: reconnaissance, liaison, and artillery spotting. It was envisioned that visual and photographic reconnaissance missions would be flown both day and night. Liaison flights would obtain or transmit special information information or orders, and artillery missions would locate targets and observe artillery fire as "elevated observation posts" rather than as vehicles for adjusting artillery.[104]

The other relatively new ingredient in the Army's conception of air support was air transport. Although the Air Corps had been using an assortment of planes, including bombers, since the 1920s to move its own scarce supplies from base to base, the idea of using them to support ground forces grew and was tested during exercises in the late 1930s. The concept of combat airlift was given added urgency by successful German airborne operations against Norway in 1940 and in Crete the following year. As a result, the Air Corps placed its combat airlift resources in a Troop Carrier Command, separate from its more routine Air Transport Command.[105]

Troop carrier planes, according to F.M. 31–35, would be used to deliver parachute and airborne troops as well as to move emergency supplies to the combat theater. The air support commander, with one exception, retained control of the air units. When parachute troops were carried, control of individual aircraft could be relinquished to jumpmasters on the final approach to their objectives. Emergency supplies could be delivered either by parachute, by gliders, or by landing airplanes. Included in the air-transport concept were those of air evacuation and target towing.[106]

The Birth of Close Air Support

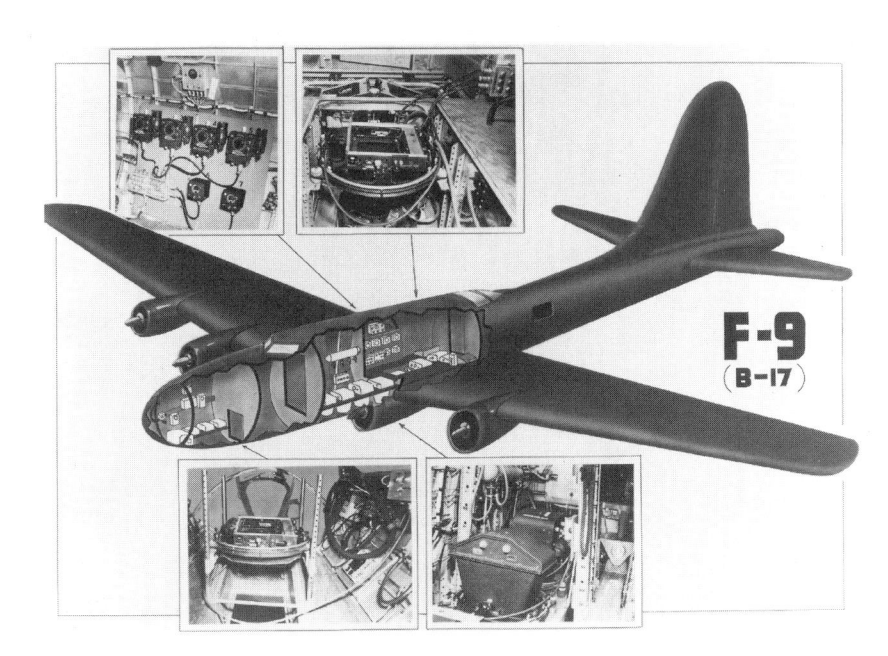

Boeing F–9 reconnaissance aircraft (top); Lockheed F–5 reconnaissance aircraft (center); North American F–6 reconnaissance aircraft (right).

Help from Above

At the very time of the issuance of F.M. 31–35, the AAF was clarifying the combat role of its troops carrier units and making critical decisions on the best aircraft for Army support. It had been decided that, in a theater of war, troop carrier units would carry paratroops, regular airborne groups, and infantry across the front lines into enemy territory and from sector to sector along the front lines. The airplanes would then supply the landed forces until ground transportation could take over. Transport aircraft was also expected to supply armored columns after they broke through enemy lines and to rush emergency material to hard-pressed ground forces. In all of these scenarios, the air units would evacuate the wounded.[107]

For the remainder of 1942 the various air and ground commands concerned with troop carrier operations sought the best aircraft for the purpose. Three models were considered: the C–47, C–46, and C–54. It was concluded that the C–47 met more of the requirements than did the others and that it should become the mainstay of the troop carrier effort, at least until it could be replaced by the then experimental but promising C–82 Packet. Throughout the following year, however, production of this converted DC–3 by the Douglas Aircraft Company was given a priority well behind that of the B–17. Finally, in January 1944, due to an urgent demand for transports for the invasion of Normandy, the production schedule was accelerated, and during the next six months over 28 of the planes flowed from production lines.[108]

The carefully crafted compromise achieved in F.M. 31–35 was weakened within a year of its publication, during its first combat test in North Africa. The performance of the XII Air Support Command (ASC) in supporting the American Fifth Army after its November landing was dismal. Although the Fifth Army had serious internal problems that contributed to this failure, these were accompanied by deficiencies in the XII ASC as well—green, untrained pilots; inferior, untested equipment; poor logistics; ineffective command arrangements; the diversion of large numbers of close air support aircraft to the Middle East, Russia, and the Western Desert; foul weather that turned airfields to mud; poor communications; and an inefficient use of aircraft.

Any one of these factors, taken in isolation, could have explained the poor showing. In a review of the campaign in the following year by both air and ground analysts, predispositions seemed to influence judgments more than did objective analyses of these debilitating factors. The ground forces attributed the failure of the aircraft to protect them from the *Luftwaffe* to a lack of interest on the part of the airmen who, they believed, were more concerned with strategic bombing than with supporting ground troops. These suspicions were holdovers from the previous fall when the AAF reneged on an agreement to provide aerial support for joint air-ground exercises. Although General Arnold and Gen. Lesley J. McNair, the commander of the Army Ground Forces, agreed at the time that worldwide demands for American aircraft were largely to blame, ground officers' perceptions of the airmen's indifference per-

38

The Birth of Close Air Support

Curtiss C–46 cargo and troop carrying transport (top left);
Douglas C–47s on line (top right); Douglas C–54 over Mt. Whitney,
California (center); Douglas C–54 interior (bottom left);
Fairchild XC–82 (bottom right).

39

Help from Above

sisted.[109] These suspicions were understandable. For the AAF, the campaign in North Africa was an unwelcome diversion of resources from the nascent strategic bomber buildup by the Eighth Air Force in England. Airmen, on the other hand, convinced that air superiority and interdiction missions were often necessary preludes to close air support missions, attributed the poor results of the campaign to the command and control structure that hobbled their performance.[110] In their view, the excessive demands, by the ground forces, for their airplanes to act as umbrellas over the ground troops had too often prevented them from carrying out the other tactical missions they considered more fruitful.[111]

Regardless of which view correctly reflected the battlefield realities, it was this latter position that prevailed in the combined counsels at Casablanca in January 1943. With the strong support of Field Marshal Bernard L. Montgomery and Air Vice Marshal Sir Arthur Coningham, the command and control arrangements of F.M. 31–35 were modified in favor of the British command organization and doctrine that had succeeded against Rommel west of Cairo since 1940.

The British, like the Germans, had come to a belated appreciation of the importance of tactical aircraft for supporting their ground forces. Until the outbreak of war the RAF, independent since World War I, had hewed closely to the strategic warfare theories of Giulio Douhet (1869–1930). The need for tactical air resources came about through a recognition of the importance of air defense. The British fiasco in trying to defend their ground expeditionary force in France from the air early in 1940 led to the creation in December of an Army Cooperation Command to develop doctrine and procedures for close air support. Many of the air-ground procedures employed by Coningham's Desert Air Force and Montgomery's Eighth Army in Africa evolved from ideas generated by this command.[112] A key principle for close air support was enunciated in September 1941 when Churchill informed the British army forces, then battling Rommel, that they must not expect "as a matter of course" to be protected against aerial attack. "Above all," continued the order

> the idea of keeping standing patrols of aircraft over our moving columns should be abandoned. It is unsound to distribute aircraft in this way and no air superiority will stand any large application of such a mischievous practice.[113]

The Casablanca conferees adapted two salient features of this British system to allied use: tactical aircraft were centralized in the hands of air commanders, who were elevated to a level equal to that of ground leaders; and air resources were, from then on, to be employed first to wrest control of the air from the *Luftwaffe*, then to stanch the flow of materiel and personnel to the battlefield. Only after these two operations had succeeded, would the planes be

The Birth of Close Air Support

used in direct support on the battlefield. These priorities were implied by Coningham:

> The attainment of this object [maximum air support for land operations] can only be achieved by fighting for and obtaining a high measure of air supremacy in the theatre [SIC] of operations. As a result of success in this air fighting our land forces will be enabled to operate virtually unhindered by enemy air attack and our Air Forces be given increased freedom to assist in the actual battle area....[114]

These implied priorities were seen by airmen as priorities in time, not necessarily indications of relative importance. They regarded tactical air power as an indivisible trinity whose effectiveness was achieved through a step-by-step application in three phases. Close air support was not less important than air superiority or interdiction—but its effectiveness was in direct proportion to the degree that these other two preconditions had been met.

This new program was inaugurated in February 1943 with the consolidation of all British and American tactical planes into the Northwest African Tactical Air Force (NATAF), commanded by Coningham. Although the time span for its application narrowed as close air support assumed third priority, the quality of support increased. Within days of NATAF's creation, for example, Coningham sent some concentrated air units, which now included the XII ASC, to extricate American ground forces from attacks by Rommel's tanks at the Kasserine Pass.[115]

In the final push toward Bizerte and Tunis between March and May 1943 Coningham's strategic plan unfolded in almost textbook fashion. The first two months were devoted to emasculating the *Luftwaffe* and destroying Axis shipping, supplies, and depots. During the final weeks, Allied planes, facing little hostile air activity, turned to close air support.[116]

The North African campaign became a laboratory for close air support. In addition to the Allied changes in command and control procedures, the campaign revealed the inadequacy of light and medium bombers in the close air support role. German antiaircraft artillery forced the A–20s, B–25s, and B–26s to altitudes from which they could not support the ground troops.[117] In addition, the bombers' strong point, their longer range, was better suited to the Pacific theater than to operations in North Africa, as was foreseen in the coming European campaign. As an alternative, airmen turned again to British precedent, equipping fighter planes with bomb racks to attack targets on the front line, and P–38s and P–40s increasingly performed the close air support mission. The large demand elsewhere for the still growing force of fighter planes slowed the evolution of tactics and techniques for these new weapons—an evolution that would accelerate during the fighting in Europe. The two-

41

Help from Above

decade-long search for a dedicated attack plane was abandoned, however, and two more decades would pass before the search resumed.

Not all of F.M. 31–35 was discarded in North Africa. Air and ground units used and improved the system of Air Support Parties and air support controls to request air strikes. Communications, however, continued to hamper the effort. Fighter-bombers, whose introduction solved so many other problems, were unable to carry the heavy radios necessary for effective air-to-ground communication. Pilots often still had to resort to many of the older, more primitive methods of contact. During operations preceding the battle at Kasserine Pass in February, for example, the orders for an American regiment to fall back were delivered by messages dropped from two P–39s. Yet the conclusion remains valid that "… in Africa the AAF mastered in a short time and at small cost the basic principles of the difficult science of air-ground cooperation which it was to apply decisively in the overthrow of Fortress Europe."[118]

General Arnold and the Air Staff were quick to enshrine the lessons from North Africa in an official pronouncement. In what was record time for the composition and publication of a doctrinal statement, the War Department approved and disseminated, within two months of the fall of Tunis, a new manual (F.M. 100–20) for the use of air power.[119] Although General Marshall approved and signed the document, it was not coordinated with the Army Ground Forces. Significantly, the word *support* appeared nowhere in the publication.

The new regulation explicitly affirmed the equality of air and land power. In an operational theater, the ground commander and the air commander were to report separately to the theater commander, not one to the other. Air commanders, from then on, were to join with ground commanders in devising the logic for military operations.

Field Manual 100–20 made more specific the three-phased priorities for tactical air operations at which Coningham had hinted, namely, air superiority, isolation of the battlefield, and close air support. In an attempt to discredit and bury the implied priorities of F.M. 31–35, the new manual stated that destruction of the enemy's airplanes, both on land and in the air, "is much more effective than any attempt to furnish an umbrella of fighter aviation over our own troops."[120]

The choice of the three-phase nomenclature in the document led to confusion and, according to the airmen, misrepresentation of their view of close air support. This third phase—attack on enemy ground forces—was not the lowest form of tactical air activity. On the contrary, it was the highest form, the culmination and end toward which the gaining of air superiority and interdiction led. Further, the three phases were not exclusive, and when necessary, all three could be performed simultaneously.

In addition to the ground commander's loss of command over tactical aircraft, Army Ground Forces also questioned the narrow interpretation of close air support in the document. Although, as a third priority, tactical air strikes

The Birth of Close Air Support

were to be flown against objectives in the battle area, strikes against troops-in-contact were discouraged. Missions against an enemy locked in combat with friendly forces, noted the document, were difficult to control, most expensive, and least effective. Besides, there was always the possibility of striking your own troops. "Only at critical times," stated the manual, "are contact zone missions profitable."[121]

Despite the fact that this proscription of air strikes within the range of friendly artillery was merely a repetition of the doctrine that had been taught at the Air Corps Tactical School, it has been pointed to by ground historians as further evidence of the aviators' intransigence and unwillingness to cooperate. "No more concise and challenging criticism," wrote one, "was ever written about close air support."[122] Given the state of the art at the time, however, this caveat in the manual appears to be more a reasonable statement of fact than of philosophy. By the summer of 1943, neither aircraft, communications systems, nor tactics had been honed to the point where aircraft could confidently strike very close to friendly lines without incident. The numerous instances in North Africa and later of airplanes bombing and strafing their own troops, of which the ground forces rightly complained, justified this cautious appraisal by the authors of F.M. 100–20. The fact that this prudent statement of reality was quietly laid to rest after the invasion of Normandy, when improved technology and tactics permitted closer cooperation, further portrays this statement as one of discretion rather than of doctrine.

The general provisions of F.M. 100–20 left ample room for improving techniques of close air support. During the 38-day Sicilian campaign in September 1943 the XII ASC and II Corps experimented with mobile air control parties that used very high frequency- (VHF) radio-equipped jeeps to direct fighter bombers to their targets. In addition, radar mounted on landing craft off the assault beaches warned night fighters of approaching German planes, thereby reducing losses. Small liaison planes were used to advantage in directing artillery fire. American forces also set up communications between air headquarters, ground headquarters, and their agencies located with ground units, which the new command structure introduced.[123]

Further experiments with air-ground techniques were performed during the subsequent Italian campaign. In order to provide closer coordination, the Fifth Army and the XII ASC located their forward command posts within a few hundred yards of each other and the method for requesting air strikes was streamlined. Requests were funneled upward to Fifth Army headquarters, which evaluated them and then asked the ASC to execute only those missions that contributed directly to the ground objective. This dampened the tendency of corps and division commanders to dissipate the air effort by asking for unnecessary air support. The air support commander, on the other hand, relieved of having to deal directly with commands below army headquarters, was able to improve the response times of his aircraft.[124]

Help from Above

Other modifications contributed to more effective close air support in Italy, where a new air section (G–3 Air) was established at army headquarters. Army ground liaison officers, sent out to ground units from this new section, took over the responsibility for requesting immediate sorties from the Air Support Parties. Ground liaison officers were also posted at each of the air units, including the reconnaissance outfits, where they assisted in briefing pilots on the ground situation.

Eighty percent of the ground-support missions were preplanned, that is, were decided upon at a joint air-ground conference the evening before. The air commander held back two to four squadrons each day for immediate missions that might arise in response to unforeseen emergencies. He also could divert aircraft already in flight to immediate missions.[125]

The mobile air control parties, which had been introduced in Sicily, were strengthened in northern Italy by the addition of airborne controllers in L–5 liaison planes who led fighters to ground targets, using either radio or visual signals. Although the AAF experienced difficulty installing radio sets in these light observation planes, the experiment held promise for the future.[126]

While top commanders at the theater and army levels, and their superiors in Washington, were pleased with the accommodations worked out in Italy between the Fifth Army and the XII ASC, subordinate ground commanders did not always share this enthusiasm. Response times for immediate air strikes were still running about 90 minutes, due in part to the cumbersome method for requesting air assistance. Further, as a result of the new three-phase system for tactical operations, only about 20 percent of the air missions were flown as close air support. The other 80 percent were in response to requests by higher air headquarters.[127]

The greatest remaining problem in air-ground cooperation, in the view of the ground forces, was the inadequacy of the intelligence it was receiving from air reconnaissance units. Ground commanders attributed this to the higher priority accorded to photography more useful to the AAF, such as air targets and bomb damage assessment, than to ground objectives. This resulted, in their eyes, from a preponderant use of aircraft, such as the P–51, which provided its pilots with excellent oblique vision, but was deficient in obtaining what the army needed most, vertical photographs of the terrain below. The army also complained that the priority for developing photographs in the labs gave preference to pictures of use to the air campaign, thereby delaying the distribution of time-sensitive intelligence to the field.[128]

Frequent and sometimes disastrous instances of American ground and air forces firing on each other because of misidentification in North Africa, Sicily, and early in the Italian campaign, highlighted the critical deficiencies in radio communication between air and ground. In 1943 the AAF installed in its aircraft VHF radios that proved incompatible with the Army's surface equipment.

The Birth of Close Air Support

Many Army officers saw this as a deliberate attempt of airmen to retain control of the aircraft. They also believed that the Army's adoption of VHF equipment would result in fewer accidental firings of air and ground forces on each other, in shorter response times to requests for air support, and in increased ground control of the aircraft.

Successful stateside Army experiments with VHF equipment, however, did not lead to its acceptance. The Army Ground Forces pointed to the stipulations of F.M. 31–35 that placed the responsibility for communications on the air forces. It also maintained that only airmen on the ground were qualified to talk to airmen in the air. Since such an exchange of personnel did not exist at the time, VHF radios were not needed. As a substitute, the Army Ground Forces increased its emphasis in training on aircraft identification and the use of visual signals.[129]

Developments in the air-ground system hammered out in Italy were transferred to England in planning for the upcoming campaign on the continent. The AAF's role in the invasion and subsequent push to the German heartland followed the three-phase program of F.M. 100–20. For three months before the landings on June 6, 1944, Allied air forces wrested control of the air over France by destroying *Luftwaffe* units on the ground and in the air, forcing the German Air Force to retreat to the safety and defense of its homeland. During and immediately after the landings, in the second phase, air power concentrated on isolating the battlefield by interdicting enemy traffic headed for the front lines. Ground support primarily took the form of parachute drops and reconnaissance. Only after the breakout in July and the subsequent push across France and Germany did Allied tactical air units turn their full attention to the third phase—close air support of the advancing armies.

The Ninth Air Force, which had been created in England late in 1943 to support the continental campaign, while concentrating on air supremacy and interdiction during the first two phases, simultaneously prepared for its eventual close air support roles.[130] While the Ninth's fighters were helping to destroy German aircraft and their support facilities across the English Channel, members of the command underwent intensive training in England. In addition to practicing the tactics and techniques of close air support, flyers engaged in joint exercises with the U.S. First Army, which it would be supporting on the continent. In simulated invasion exercises, air and ground commanders practiced the exacting close air support procedures that they would soon be called upon to employ. These preparations in England were strongly influenced by the Italian experience, since many of the air and ground leaders who had worked out the close air support system on the Italian peninsula brought with them their experiences when they were transferred to England. The Ninth Air Force developed an extensive exchange program with airmen in Italy, thus increasing the transfer of knowledge and techniques. Even during the actual invasion and its subsequent interdiction campaign, close air support was not totally ignored.

Help from Above

On the day of the landing 6 of the 18 fighter groups that accompanied the ground forces provided close air support.

When movement inland from the beaches began, the AAF inaugurated the third phase. Lt. Gen. Elwood R. Quesada's IX Tactical Air Command (TAC), successor to the IX ASC,[131] set up its headquarters adjacent to that of Gen. Omar N. Bradley, the First Army commander. Air staff officers and army ground officers (G–2 Air and G–3 Air) operated under the same roof in a combined operations center. As in Italy, requests from army units for air combat and reconnaissance assistance were consolidated and screened by the Army and agreed to in nightly conferences with airmen. Ground liaison officers were assigned to air units to familiarize flyers with ground plans, and ground-to-air communications were improved by posting airmen (forward controllers), equipped with VHF radios, to ground units.[132]

These arrangements quickly proved themselves when the hedgerows of the Normandy countryside immobilized the medium and light tanks of the newly landed allied forces. Attack planes and artillery succeeded against the more potent German tanks and dug-in enemy positions.

The breakout of allied forces from St. Lo on July 25, 1944, according to Army analysts, "marked the beginning of the most effectively sustained close air support in history." In the space of less than three hours, 2,450 heavy-, medium-, and fighter-bombers blasted a gap in the enemy's defenses. As Americans poured through the disorganized German lines, experienced airmen, equipped with VHF radios, directed fighter-bombers from the lead tank of each armored column. Through instantaneous communication with the planes, they received warnings of obstacles in their path and directed P–47s against ground targets. This tactic of close armored column cover proved to be one of the more innovative close air support measures developed during the war.[133]

The new command and control arrangements for close air support again proved their effectiveness in the subsequent campaign in western France. Throughout August and early September 1944 tactical air power worked so well with Gen. George S. Patton's Third Army in its historic "end run through France" that the American ground commander entrusted his entire right flank along the Loire River to Gen. Otto P. Weyland's XIX TAC. Continuous reconnaissance and fighter-bomber attacks on massed German troops provided Patton the needed mobility and flexibility to capture a German force of 20,000 early in September.[134]

During the period of static warfare that preceded the Germans' December counterattack, while the TACs were concentrating on interdiction and moving their resources closer to the front, the ground forces continued to request close air support for a variety of operations. Fighter-bombers operated increasingly closer to American lines. In a 12-day assault on Aachen, American aircraft carried on a sustained attack on the entrenched enemy. At

The Birth of Close Air Support

river crossings, tactical planes assured the expansion of bridgeheads by striking moving enemy troops and protecting the flanks and front of attacking allied forces.[135]

When the Germans counterattacked through the Ardennes in December 1944 the IX TAC devoted all of its resources to supporting American ground forces within the Bulge, while two other American TACs and one British Tactical Air Force harassed the enemy at the base of the salient and on its northern and southern fringes. The main air effort was directed against German tanks, which led the infantry in the counterattack.[136] The challenge of navigating aircraft over snow-covered ground and distinguishing friendly from enemy snow-covered tanks was met by an unorthodox use of radar. The SCR–584, designed originally as an early-warning radar, was linked to a Norden bombsight and pressed into service for ground control and identification. Ground operators were able to identify tanks for airborne pilots.[137] This conversion of radar from defensive to offensive use represented one of the more significant technological contributions to the growing corpus of close air support practices.[138] When the 101st Division was besieged at Bastogne, IX TAC fighter-bombers struck close-in targets that ground artillery was unable to hit. By the end of December the U.S. First and Third Armies, strongly supported by fighter-bombers of the IX and XIX TACs, were driving the Germans from the salient.

A continuing problem throughout the war was the ineffectiveness of night operations. Prewar experiments in strafing surface targets at night showed promise when the targets were illuminated by searchlights, and fighter-searchlight teams had been successfully tested in Hawaii in 1940. Flares, however, proved disappointing, as they burned out too quickly, they drifted, and the difference in their light intensity made it hard for the pilots to locate targets.[139] Moreover, throughout World War II, night operations suffered from pilots, navigators, and bombardiers who lacked experience in night missions. There was no effective system of pathfinding and no adequate planes or equipment. As the *Luftwaffe* waned, however, so did the need for defensive night operations. The several squadrons of P–61 night fighters in the theater were then used as intruders, shooting down enemy planes returning to their bases rather than supporting ground forces.[140]

Nighttime close air support and interdiction, in General Quesada's experience, was nonexistent. The IX TAC resorted to several gimmicks to compensate. Before sunset, for example, planes would seed roadsides with the largest available bombs equipped with delayed fuses. The bombs would go off after dark, giving the impression of a night attack. But these were only palliatives and, as noted in the postwar history of the Ninth Air Force, "the inadequacy of the night force was sharply felt, as always."[141]

The AAF's combat support of ground forces in the Pacific took a somewhat different path from that in Europe. Most close air support in the Central

Help from Above

and South Pacific was performed by naval air units, while the AAF was predominant in the Southwest Pacific. General George C. Kenney, in Gen. Douglas MacArthur's command, eschewed dividing his Fifth Air Force into ASCs. In his view, the concept of an ASC, dedicated solely to ground support, did not fit the situation in the Pacific. This decision not to create a counterpart to the European TACs represented an even greater centralization of air power and was made possible by the early absence in the Pacific of competition from a strategic bombing campaign.

The lack of competition for resources from a strategic air campaign, at least at the outset, permitted Kenney to hold a broader interpretation of air flexibility than that practiced in Europe. Much to the disappointment of the ground forces in the European theater, flexibility took place mostly within the functional area of each class of aircraft. Centrally controlled heavy bombers were moved about and concentrated principally for strategic bombing missions, mediums and lights for attacks on airfields and communications, and fighter-bombers for operations in areas on and around the battlefield. The absence of this limitation on flexibility in the Pacific allowed Kenney greater centralization of his aircraft. "Whenever the necessity arises," he told Arnold, "all or an appropriate part of the striking power of the Air Force is assigned to the tasks of supporting the ground forces."[142]

Without ASCs to work with specific ground units, there was no need in the Pacific for adjacent air-ground headquarters, as were already being used in North Africa. Instead, ground liaison officers, assigned by the ground forces to the A–2 and A–3 sections of the Air Staff, represented the ground forces in general, rather than particular ground units.[143]

There developed in the Pacific a distinction, unknown in Europe, between direct air support and close air support. The former included air strikes against combatant targets such as troop concentrations and bivouac areas far enough from the front lines that coordination with the ground forces was not necessary. In Europe these types of missions were included in the general category of interdiction. Close air support, in the Pacific as well as in Europe, referred to air attacks designed to help friendly ground troops in taking or holding ground.[144]

In most other aspects, however, Kenney's organization followed the stipulations of F.M. 31–35 (**Figure 5**) more closely than did his tactical European counterparts. Air and ground units exchanged personnel for close coordination. Air support control and Air Support Parties were assigned to ground units, while ground liaison officers worked closely at air headquarters.[145] Specially trained officers were assigned to the A–3 section of his staff. In addition to going into the field, these officers worked to draw up air support doctrine for the Southwest Pacific.[146]

Close air support reached its highest point in the Pacific in amphibious landings and the island fighting that followed. As a result, it was used offen-

The Birth of Close Air Support

sively more often than was the case in Europe. In the early campaigns of Guadalcanal and New Guinea, AAF support of the III Marine Division was foiled by poor communications, by the climate, and the terrain. Jungle foliage also presented problems. Pilots had difficulty finding the lines that troops attempted to demarcate by using smoke, and ground commanders, fearful of casualties to their own troops, were therefore reluctant to request air assistance. Attempts of air liaison parties to use radio-equipped jeeps were frustrated by the climate, the terrain, and a shortage of radio operators.[147]

It was during these early campaigns in the Pacific, however, that fighter-bombers were first used to attack surface targets with bombs, thereby introducing a close air support practice that would be one of the most innovative in both the Pacific and European theaters.[148]

Air operations improved during the next campaign in Bougainville. Air liaison parties posted early to the III Marine Division, indoctrinated ground troops in the use of air support, and ground commanders gradually increased their willingness to request air support. Air-to-ground radio communications vastly improved and planes struck closer to friendly troops than at any time during the Pacific war.[149]

It was in the tortuous march across New Guinea that the Fifth Air Force learned how to render effective aid to the ground forces, aid that it would later provide in the Philippines, as its P–38s, P–39s, P–40s, and P–47s hit hard at ground targets. On short missions, P–38s and P–47s were able to carry larger bombloads than the A–20s, loads comparable to those of the B–25s. Target marking improved by using gridded oblique photographs, artillery and mortar smoke shells, lead-in aircraft, and verbal descriptions by air-ground radio.

Although air support communications improved, they were still not to the point where planners could dispense with the need to request strikes the day before they were to be used. This was not as critical in the Pacific as it was in Europe, however, since only on rare occasions were planes needed to bomb within a few hundred yards of the front lines. In general, air support against Japanese troops in open terrain was usually devastating. When the enemy took refuge in caves, however, air support was "merely another weapon, albeit a useful one."[150]

The larger distances between islands made close air support in the Central Pacific different from that employed in the South and Southwest Pacific. Whereas land-based planes were effective in assaulting undefended beaches in the south that were in close proximity to one another, carrier planes were needed against the more heavily defended landing areas in the northern islands. The preponderance of air support in the Central Pacific was required during the assaults on the islands. Given the small size of most of the eastern islands, comparatively little support was needed after the troops were established ashore.

Control of air support aircraft was as centrally controlled by the Navy in the Central Pacific as it was by the Army farther south. During amphibious

Help from Above

landings, a commander of support aircraft (CSA) aboard the task-force flagship controlled the air support. Air liaison parties (ALPs) went ashore with the landing force to relay requests for air support to the CSA and to keep him informed of the position of front line troops, the results of close air support missions, and the location of promising targets. Seldom did ALPs control air strikes. Airborne air coordinators flew over the island to report and, on occasion, lead fighters to their targets. Navy centralization of air support was as rigid as that practiced by the Army.[151]

It was not until Iwo Jima in March 1945 that some control of support aircraft was turned over to a land-based commander. Even then, however, this represented a compromise between the Navy system of centralized control and the Marine commanders' desire to have the ALP control the air.[152]

Marine principles for close air support were developed between October 1944 and January 1945 as Marine aircraft trained on Bougainville for the assault on the Philippines. Due to logistical problems, Marine aircraft missed out on the drive across the Central Pacific, and therefore had adequate time to prepare for a new mission. Their doctrine aimed at eradicating two weak spots in the complex Army and Navy control systems—long reaction times and the reluctance to schedule attacks too close to friendly troops for fear of hitting them. These two weaknesses were related. It was the desire to avoid short rounds that led to the relatively complex control system, which in turn lengthened the time it took planes to respond. Both limitations had made the ground force commanders hesitant to call for aerial assistance.

Marine doctrine stressed that Marine airmen were soldiers first, flyers second, and that airplanes represented but one of a number of ancillary weapons the ground commander could use to support his infantry. Therefore, close air support "should be immediately available [to the ground commander] and should be carried out with deliberation and accuracy and in coordination with other assigned units."[153]

The three months of training by the Marines with the Army's 37th and Americal Divisions paid handsome dividends and again showed the critical importance of joint training. Ground units gradually gained confidence in the ability of aircraft to support them. When the two Marine air groups began to operate on Luzon in January, they were folded into the existing control system, joining with AAF fighter-bombers under control of the 308th Bombardment Group. Within several weeks Marine ALPs were directing both Army and AAF planes onto targets as the U.S. forces captured Manila and then the rest of Luzon. In all, Marine air flew about 15 percent of Fifth Air Force's ground support sorties.[154]

The Marine system of close air support in the Pacific was more a confirmation than a repudiation of the centralized control arrangements of the Army and Navy. First, the use of ground parties to direct attacks was not entirely new. Army Air Force ALPs had earlier directed Army planes onto tar-

The Birth of Close Air Support

gets in the Admiralty Islands and, when appropriate, in several other campaigns during the march across the islands to the Philippines. Second, much of the success must be credited to the three months of joint training, a luxury denied to AAF flyers. Third, unlike the AAF planes, which had to juggle air superiority, interdiction, and close air support missions, the Marine aviators concentrated on close air support, with expected satisfactory results. Finally, the Marine system, as executed, fell short of Marine doctrine. Although flights were often directed from the front lines, the Marine planes were still controlled by Fifth Air Force, which assigned them their missions on the basis of requests through normal channels.[155]

* * *

Following tentative beginnings in World War I, the major close air support issues underwent two decades of uneven advancement. Monetary limitations between the world wars slowed down technological progress in some close air support areas, and the authors of doctrine, still undecided as to how military aircraft could best be used, vacillated between treating them as support or independent weapons. As a result, the decision as to who should control them remained unanswered and controversial. Joint training proved largely unaffordable. Initial advances made by attack aviation during the period were slowed after 1935 by the growing interest in bombardment, air defense, aircraft, and missions. Only the outbreak of war in Europe four years later revived the fortunes of the close air support mission.

The practice of using tactical aircraft in close coordination with ground troops matured in World War II. Many elements coalesced during the war to bring about this maturity: new methods of commanding and controlling aircraft; improved planes, weapons, and communications; a superabundance of resources and a highly developed logistical system to deliver them; rigorous joint training both before and after the invasion of the European continent; an unprecedented spirit of cooperation between air and ground commanders in both theaters; innovative battlefield tactics; and weakened German and Japanese resistance in the air.

This maturation of the close air support mission in World War II, however, introduced a set of issues that would remain controversial between the Army and the Air Force for several decades. Behind virtually every future disagreement over the mission lay a different explanation of exactly what happened during World War II and how the air action was to be interpreted. Predispositions colored postwar judgments. The AAF, which earlier had temporarily postponed its prewar march toward independence, attributed the effectiveness of close air support primarily to the freedom tactical air commanders enjoyed to command and control their own airplanes.[156] This was a logical position for airmen whose independence from the ground forces was virtually assured.

Help from Above

Airmen credited progress in other close air support areas to this autonomy that they achieved during the war. The rapid mobility and critical flexibility without which close air support would have been less successful was viewed as a by-product of the new command arrangements. The unparalleled spirit of cooperation between air and ground combat commanders was nurtured, in the flyers' view, by the added responsibility and trust accorded them. The ability to exercise individual judgment was seen as responsible for such technological innovations as the evolution of fighter-bombers and their employment as the main close air support aircraft, the transition of radar and radio from defensive weapons to offensive ones for controlling fighter-bomber missions, and the development of air-ground communications. The evolution of imaginative close support tactics and techniques, particularly the use of armored column cover and armed reconnaissance, was fostered by the freedom given airmen to control their own resources.

One of the more significant developments for close air support was the gradual abandonment of the proscription on strikes anywhere within the range of artillery. The gradual narrowing of the ban, which by war's end excluded fighter-bomber attacks only from those targets that could effectively be hit by artillery, was also attributed by airmen to the flexibility granted to air commanders. Equally important for the future history of close air support was the embryonic development of a set of priorities for the use of tactical aircraft. While the relative importance of air supremacy, interdiction, and close air support missions was not completely decided upon, the groundwork was set not only for the establishment of a set of priorities but for a spirited controversy over them as well.

The top echelons of Army command agreed with the general assessment of close air support as successful, even though they did not necessarily attribute this success solely to the Air Forces' small taste of independence. Generals Marshall, Bradley, and Dwight D. Eisenhower supported full independence for the air forces upon a promise of continued support of the ground forces. Many commanders below their level, whose wartime experience with air support had been less than satisfactory, however, continued to hold reservations about the degree to which a separate service would provide such support. The reconfiguration of the world and the adjustment of national policies and strategies in the immediate postwar period seemed to justify this skepticism.

While most of the factors that brought about a flowering of close air support in World War II would be enshrined in future doctrine and practice, two elements unique to the war were to prove more frangible, with important negative consequences during the immediate postwar period. These elements were the national wartime policy and strategy and the remarkable cooperation forged in battle between leaders of the ground and air components of the military services. The rapid disappearance of both was to jeopardize many of the gains achieved during the war.

2 | Close Air Support Enfeebled 1945–1950

> If the Air Force continues its present relatively negative tactical air policies for a period of four to six years, the Army will have compiled a dossier of facts which will completely justify its requisitioning a budget for its own air force.
>
> — USAF Tactical Review Board, 1949

In the last year of World War II, the United States spent $42 billion to train, equip, and support its ground, air, and sea forces of over 12 million. In order to take advantage of what a later generation would call a *peace dividend*, and determined to avoid inflation and to balance the budget, Pres. Harry S. Truman for half a decade after the war clung to a policy of funding the military with money left over after other national needs were met. As a consequence, authorizations for the Army and Navy during the first postwar year plummeted by two-thirds, to less than $14 billion, an annual ceiling that remained in effect until the Korean War.

Of all the elements that conspired to reduce the AAF's impressive World War II close air support capabilities to a token force in the short space of five years, these budgetary restrictions were the most fundamental, forcing draconian choices upon all the military services and, in the process, heightening interservice competition. The Army envisioned a ground force of 10 divisions, the Navy a fleet of 600 combat ships, and the AAF a structure of 70 combat groups plus 42 separate squadrons.[1]

Aggravating this fiscal stringency were the demands engendered by demobilization and reorganization, and the absence of a clear and specific national security policy against which to weigh these expenditures. The future Soviet threat was slow to materialize and, with a clouded view of the future, only the past remained as a guide to developing policy and force structures.

Help from Above

The U.S. Army was the slowest to accept the revolutionary nature of atomic weaponry. The U.S. Navy, somewhat quicker to realize the altered nature of warfare, attempted to carve for itself a share in the nuclear future. Only the AAF, young and brash, and convinced of its essential, and even decisive, role in defeating the Axis powers, claimed to have a clear picture of the future, a future dominated by nuclear power and with little need for ground and sea forces. The AAF's unwavering adherence to a nuclear future, however, owed much to the past. Its view of the future was, in part, intertwined with its long-standing quest for separation from the Army.

Lacking a road map for what lay ahead, the services relied heavily upon the doctrines that had proved successful in the recently concluded conflict. The AAF's doctrine of strategic bombardment, developed in the late 1930s and, at least in its eyes, justified during the war, proved more compatible with the way things actually turned out, thus giving the airmen a dominant position in the military hierarchy. Having won its independence, the new Air Force became increasingly convinced of the centrality of strategic bombing, not only to its own future, but to its hegemony among the services as well. The emphasis on the strategic, however, gave the appearance, if not the reality, to many in the ground forces of an almost supercilious disdain on the part of the Air Force toward any form of warfare short of total. This perception had direct and adverse effects on the development of close air support within the Air Force.

On The Road to Independence

The AAF's view as to where the close air support mission should fit within the hierarchy of air power missions was reflected in its initial plan for postwar reorganization. Close behind independence as a goal, AAF planners wanted an air force that emphasized strategic air power and a force-in-being based on the traditional principles of centralization, flexibility, and indivisibility which, they were convinced, had accounted for their success in the war. The postwar air force, they argued, should be organized to reflect these principles and should harness them to serve primarily a strategic striking force. As early as 1943, when planning for the postwar period got under way, many airmen saw the wartime practice of dividing air assets between strategic and tactical organizations as a violation of the principle of indivisibility that viewed air power, unlike ground power, as a seamless and indivisible continuum across the entire spectrum of air warfare. To fragment this unified air power into specific entities, such as strategic or tactical, would violate that principle and deprive air power of its strongest characteristic, namely, unity. They also viewed such separation into *penny packets* as weakening the flexibility air commanders needed to be able to concentrate all their resources at decisive points.

Close Air Support Enfeebled

Consequently there was early support among many planners for the concept of placing all future air combat forces in one single strategically oriented combat command that would give the commander full freedom to exercise these principles. A single combat command, they argued, had been tested and proven effective in the Pacific, under General Kenney, and in Europe before the Normandy invasion. In both instances, the air commanders had been able to shift their aircraft, both strategic and tactical, as the battlefield situation changed, often diverting heavy bombers to support ground troops and fighter and medium bombers to assist strategic campaigns. It also seemed to some that, with the anticipated paucity of funds, it made fiscal sense to use individual aircraft in as many different roles as possible.

The combat command idea, however, ran the risk of alienating the Army whose support, in the face of the Navy's opposition, was crucial in the coming campaign for Air Force independence. At the same time, the AAF's support was important for the Army, which was leading the drive for unification of the armed services. General Eisenhower, who became the Army's Chief of Staff in November 1945, and his other top wartime ground commanders, strongly supported a separate Air Force. Eisenhower's experiences in World War II, coupled with assurances by AAF leaders that, when independent, they would preserve tactical air power to support the Army, made him a key voice in the Air Forces' drive for independence.[2]

Despite Eisenhower's opinion, there remained substantial sentiment within the Army's ground forces for retaining control of the tactical air resources, and particularly the close air support function. These were field-grade and company-grade officers who had commanded regiments, battalions, and even companies during the war, and whose experiences with air support had been either nonexistent or infelicitous. Responsible only for their own relatively limited objectives and not involved in planning the overall scheme of operations, they often evaluated air support as inadequate. Memories remained vivid among them of instances where airplanes had missed their targets with disastrous results, such as the misdropping of parachutists the night before D-Day and the death of General McNair and hundreds of ground troops around St. Lo from errant firing by American planes. Later these officers, having risen to positions of command, were to form the cadre within the Army that would push to acquire its own air support capability.[3]

The idea of the Army keeping control of its own air support was fueled by a drumbeat of frequently contentious statements by airmen depicting future warfare as atomic. Even the normally cautious and diplomatic General Arnold on one occasion called for the elimination of "all arms, branches, services, weapons, equipment, or ideas whose retention might be indicated only by tradition or sheer inertia."[4] Other members of the AAF were also of the opinion that the new Air Force would be better off if it left the tactical forces with the Army and concentrated on its strategic mission. In that way the Army would

55

Help from Above

Gen. Dwight D. Eisenhower congratulates Lt. Gen. Carl A. Spaatz on being awarded the Legion of Merit on September 16, 1943 (left); Lt. Gen. Elwood R. Quesada (right).

bear the financial burden of researching, producing, testing, and maintaining tactical aircraft, thereby freeing the Air Force to spend its money on strategic forces.[5]

Rather than risk alienating so powerful a supporter of autonomy as Eisenhower, Gen. Carl A. Spaatz, acting Chief of the AAF, gathered around himself in the Pentagon a high-level group of airmen to persuade both Congress and the Army that the present AAF, including its tactical air resources, should be transferred intact to the new Air Force. Included in this group was General Quesada, a preeminent wartime tactical air commander, whose high credibility with the Army leaders helped to dampen their appetite for retaining tactical air resources. Army fears were further allayed in January 1946 when Spaatz, abandoning the idea of a single combat command, ordered the activation of three separate, functional commands: the Strategic Air Command (SAC), the Air Defense Command (ADC), and the Tactical Air Command (TAC). Two months later these new commands became a reality.[6]

Throughout these high-level debates and decisions, the term *close air support* rarely arose. Airmen spoke more generically of *tactical* air power, in which they lumped together the missions of air superiority, interdiction, and direct support of ground forces on the battlefield. Their conception in 1946–1947 of close support was a broad one, embracing airlift and reconnaissance in addition to combat support. Even though the AAF, and air power, was now divided into three commands, they attempted to preserve, as much as possible, the principle of indivisibility within each command. Within the TAC this took the form of treating the command's three combat functions as in-

Close Air Support Enfeebled

separable parts of a unified whole. Wherever possible, as in the past, the same aircraft would serve all three functions.

The Army, on the other hand, used the term *tactical* almost exclusively as a synonym for close air support, that is, as another form of fire support like artillery that the ground commander could direct against an enemy who was in direct contact with his forces. This semantical difference was part of a more fundamental disagreement between the services over the words *support* and *coordination*, a disagreement that cut to the very purpose of military aircraft and one that would never be fully settled.

Even before the question of postwar organization was resolved, the AAF began to confront some of the close air support issues that would plague it in future years. In 1944 it directed its AAF Board to undertake a comprehensive review of the past, present, and future of tactical air power.[7] This initiative, called the "Tactical Air Force Development Program," proceeded in haphazard fashion until April 1946 when its projects were more clearly organized and defined.[8] Several of these projects related directly to close air support and, together with the activation of the TAC a month earlier, signaled to the Army that the AAF was sincere in its desire to support the ground forces.

While one of the program's goals was to evaluate the progress in aircraft design "from the standpoint of ground cooperation," it was less than objective in setting the ground rules. The guidance for the project counseled:

> Evidence must be produced to show that the present high speed, experimental aircraft can accomplish the ground cooperation mission, otherwise the question of a specially designed airplane for cooperation with the ground forces in Phase III [close air support] operations will have to be considered. This is undesirable....[9]

This allergic reaction to developing a close air support fighter plane had several origins. Fiscal constraints was one. In the existing economic climate it made sense to build aircraft that could perform several missions, at least in the case of close air support, which had traditionally enjoyed the lowest priority for tactical air power. In the words of the program planners, "any airplane designed for Phase III missions would be of limited use for Phase I [air superiority] and II [interdiction], which are of primary importance."[10]

The experiences of World War II were also used to support this position. During 1944 in Europe, according to the guidance, 36 percent of Ninth Air Force's fighter-bomber sorties were in close support of the ground forces. While this number might seem substantial, it was high only because the Allies enjoyed complete superiority in the air. Had the German Air Force been at equal strength with the Allies, far fewer close air support missions likely would have been flown. Furthermore, only 20 percent of the medium- and light-bomber sorties supported the battlefield directly, and only 8 percent of the Eighth Air Force missions were of the close air support variety.[11]

Nevertheless, the stated purpose of the program was to remedy World War II deficiencies "from the standpoint of fulfilling total obligations of a full-fledged member of the air-ground operations team." Among these deficiencies were the inability to operate efficiently at night and during poor weather, the lack of a means of delineating front lines, and the experimental nature of much of the electronic equipment used in the war.

An early product of the board was a revision of the wartime air-ground manuals F.M. 100–20 and F.M. 31–35, to incorporate lessons of the war. The result, published in August 1946, was a new F.M. 31–35, this time titled *Air-Ground Operations*. Like its predecessors, the new manual concentrated heavily on the command and control aspects of close air support, as indicated by its chapter titles: Organization and Command, Planning, Air-Ground Operations System, Tactical Air Control System, and Communications. These command and control principles differed little from those of F.M. 100–20. The manual, ignoring the wartime experiences in the Pacific, closely mirrored the organization that had been created in the European theater. This was not surprising since the manual relied heavily on two European-oriented wartime air-ground training circulars (#17 and #30), and was consciously patterned after the Ninth Air Force, the wartime parent organization of TAC's first commander, General Quesada.

The revised manual reflected the dilemma faced by the AAF in attempting to satisfy two seemingly contradictory pressures. On the one hand, the planners in their work had to preserve the principle of independence and retain the airmen's control of air resources. On the other hand, pulling in the opposite direction, was the realization, coming out of World War II, that future wars would be joint ventures requiring unified action between all the services. Nowhere did these conflicting tendencies come into sharper focus than in the case of close air support.

Field Manual 31–35, in setting up procedures for close air support, tried to accommodate these competing demands by providing for two parallel structures, on the ground side an Air Ground Operations System for requesting air strikes, and on the air side a Tactical Air Control System for supplying them (**Figure 6**). Both systems were joined only at the top, at the field army and the tactical air force level, in a Joint Operations Center where both air and ground intelligence and operations officers worked together to coordinate air support to ground units. No joint planning or operations existed below this level, at either corps, divisions, regiments, or battalions.

Requests for air strikes worked their way up the Air Ground Operations System from the ground commander through the division and the corps to the Joint Operations Center. Even though airmen (air liaison officers) were often

Close Air Support Enfeebled

Field Manual 31-35
AIR-GROUND OPERATIONS
Aug 1946
(used in Korea)

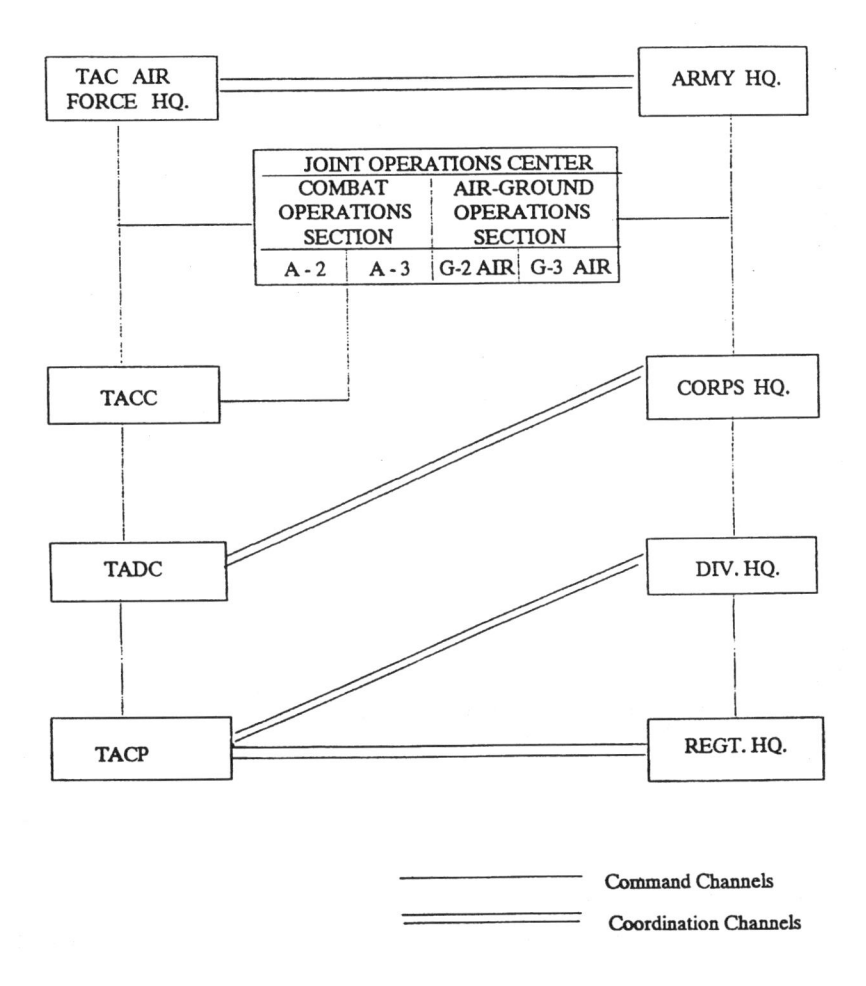

```
TAC AIR                                              ARMY HQ.
FORCE HQ.
              JOINT OPERATIONS CENTER
              COMBAT      |  AIR-GROUND
              OPERATIONS  |  OPERATIONS
              SECTION     |  SECTION
              A-2  |  A-3 | G-2 AIR | G-3 AIR

TACC                                                 CORPS HQ.

TADC                                                 DIV. HQ.

TACP                                                 REGT. HQ.
```

——————— Command Channels
═══════ Coordination Channels

FIGURE 6
Air-Ground Operations, August 1946

59

Help from Above

present at each of these intermediate ground levels, they were not allowed to request air strikes. The most they could do was advise the soldiers as to the suitability of targets and how the Tactical Air Control System worked.[12]

Once officers at the Joint Operations Center approved a request, strike orders were dispatched down the Tactical Air Control System through, in descending order, a Tactical Air Control Center, which controlled and tracked all air units, and a Tactical Air Direction Center, which directed aircraft within a restricted area, to Tactical Air Control Parties. These parties consisted of a forward air controller and his assistants to provide on-the-spot ground direction of strikes onto the target.

When the ground troops were on the offensive, the forward air controller could operate from a tank or an armored car from which he guided the aircraft in protecting a tank column or clearing obstacles in the path of advancing ground units.[13]

The nerve center controlling all the elements of the Tactical Air Control System was the Tactical Air Control Group. This group, composed of both aircraft control and aircraft warning squadrons, provided the communication facilities and information that allowed the various segments of the system to operate.[14]

The field manual appeared, on the surface, to relax the rigid three-phased priorities for tactical missions that the earlier manual prescribed. Now the decision as to how to apportion the effort between air superiority, interdiction, and close air support missions was left to the air commander. This seemed to favor the ground forces who had chafed under the earlier regulations that relegated close air support to last place. The change was more apparent than real, however. Air commanders were enjoined in the manual to base their priorities on the long-term effectiveness of the missions to the overall force, rather than on the "immediate local success gained by a portion of that force."[15] Since all agreed that air superiority had to precede other tactical missions, this left interdiction, whose effects were of longer duration to a larger force than were those of close air support, as the more desirable. The manual, in more subtle fashion, retained the priorities of the earlier document.

The emphasis on command and control in F.M. 31–35 shortchanged other important close air support measures. By emphasizing the past, it did not consider the implications of future technological and doctrinal changes. There was no acknowledgement, for example, that past practices would require adjustments because of jet aircraft, which were just coming into the inventory. It had little to say about the tactics and techniques of aerial strikes. The airborne forward air controller, who had begun to come into his own during the war, was dismissed with the one-sentence suggestion that "it may be desirable at times that additional forward air controllers operate airborne as tactical air controllers."[16] Night operations were similarly ignored, as was the question of target selection. No mention was made of joint training.

Close Air Support Enfeebled

Even though the War Department and the Army Ground Forces (AGF) approved the new close air support manual, some ground officers felt it did not faithfully reflect the system that had operated so well during the war and did not accord sufficiently with Army doctrine on command and control. In their eyes, there was less, rather than more, jointness than before, and the revised system would prove less beneficial to the infantry, which was the main customer for close air support.

This undercurrent of discontent was later expressed most clearly by Lt. Gen. Mark W. Clark who, while praising the air support he received during the war, continued to insist that the absence of joint organizations for close air support below the theater level, "constitutes a fundamental defect in command relationships." He deplored what he called "command by mutual cooperation," which in his view:

> reserves to the supporting arm the authority to determine whether or not a supporting task should be executed. The theory of divided command in the face of the enemy is foreign to the basic concept of warfare wherein the responsible commander exercises undisputed directive authority over all elements essential to the accomplishment of his missions.[17]

These views were muted at the time by signals from General Eisenhower to his commanders that the two services would work together toward unification and that any Army criticism of the Air Force was to be kept in-house and within the confines of the services. When Gen. Jacob L. Devers, the commander of the AGF, for instance, was quoted in the *Washington Post* as being critical of the Air Force for "gold-plating" its aircraft and its airfields, the Army chief mildly rebuked him, reminding him that proper channels existed for such comments and that "only damage to the Army can result from public criticism by Army personnel of any sister service."[18] Nevertheless, expressions such as Devers's mirrored an underlying dissatisfaction among combat soldiers with airmen who, in their opinion, had lost contact with the ground as they sought to build aircraft that could fly faster and higher. This disquiet continued to fester just below the surface, the source of a later movement among midlevel Army officers to create for the Army its own close air support capability.

Fundamental command and control differences between the Army and the AAF continued to exist and the need remained to expand close air support doctrine beyond the reactionary prescriptions of F.M. 31–35. Other more pressing issues took precedence, however, and it was only on the eve of the Korean War, by then too late to affect the war, that a serious attempt was made to write a joint directive for close air support.

Part of the problem that hindered the creation of joint doctrine was the disproportionate nature of the doctrine-making organizations within the Army,

Help from Above

on the one hand, and the AAF, on the other hand. While the Army centralized its doctrine-making responsibility in the AGF, the air forces, and later the Air Force, lacked a central official locus for writing and disseminating doctrine. This responsibility was shared by the commands, air forces headquarters, the AAF Board (at first), and the Air University. Whereas the AGF could distribute its doctrine throughout the Army with assurance of acceptance, Air Force authors of doctrine could only request adherence. Internal disagreements within the Air Force over many doctrinal issues prevented it from presenting a united front to the Army. An even greater obstacle was presented by the Navy, whose basic close air support doctrine was diametrically opposed to that of the Army and its air forces.

Even before publication of the revised F.M. 31–35, General Quesada, the wartime commander of the IX TAC, set his new TAC to cooperating with the other services. On May 27, 1946, he moved his command from Tampa, Florida, to the former Air Transport Command base at Langley Field, Virginia, close to the headquarters of the AGF, which was scheduled to occupy nearby Fortress Monroe in October, and to the headquarters of the Atlantic Fleet at Norfolk. In addition to being charged with the creation and dissemination of Army doctrine, the AGF was responsible for joint operations and training in the United States and for supervising the widespread system of Army service schools.

On paper, this move replicated the system of coequal adjacent headquarters that had proved so successful in Europe during the war. In reality, TAC, lacking sufficient units, schools for training, and control over doctrine, became a junior partner of the AGF.[19] Further, the AGF occupied the same command level as the AAF itself, of which the new TAC was a subordinate unit. Although Quesada was personally unaffected by being outranked by his Army counterpart, General Devers, this difference in rank and authority, combined with the relatively anemic nature of TAC, sent a further signal to some in the Army that the AAF was less than serious about cooperating with the Army on close air support matters.

Demobilization and postwar fiscal parsimony depleted the AGF as much as the air forces. By the first anniversary of V-J Day, Army ground contingents had shrunk from a peak of 89 divisions to 10. One armored, one airborne, and one cavalry division, were stationed stateside, while the remaining seven divisions were posted to occupation duty in Europe and the Pacific.

The new TAC had three numbered Air Forces, the Third, the Ninth, and the Twelfth. The Third Air Force, at Greenville, South Carolina, had ten squadrons of troop carrier aircraft (C–46s, C–47s, and C–82s) organized into four groups. The Ninth and Twelfth Air Forces, called tactical air forces, had functions similar to those the IX TAC had performed in Europe during the war. The Ninth Air Force, in El Paso, Texas, contained a light-bomber group of

Close Air Support Enfeebled

A–26s, a fighter group of P–51s, and a reconnaissance group, also with P–51s. The Twelfth Air Force, at March Field in California, initially had only one group of four squadrons of the P–80s, America's first jet fighter.[20]

Although impressive in theory, few of these units were combat ready and their total size was inadequate to carry out TAC's multifarious missions, such as participating in joint operations with ground and sea forces, cooperating with the ADC in defending the nation, operate independently in offensive operations, training units to maintain tactical forces in all parts of the world, and cooperating with the AGF in training airborne troops.[21] In addition, TAC was saddled with numerous secondary public relations enterprises that detracted from its ability to concentrate on the purely tactical portion of its mission. It had commitments to the Air Reserve and the Air National Guard, and was called upon to ferry aircraft, tow targets, provide aerial demonstrations for Reserve Officer's Training Corps (ROTC) units and Air Scouts, and even

Langley Field, Virginia (top); March Field, Riverside, California (bottom).

63

Help from Above

establish weather stations in Alaska. Also, the command had a major and time-consuming responsibility to train its fliers.

Critical for the niche close air support occupied in this melange of missions was the combat philosophy of General Quesada. As a leading developer and practitioner of tactical air operations in the European war, he held strong convictions as to how tactical aircraft could best be used in ground battles. While he agreed that strategic bombing was important, he felt, with equal conviction, that the untapped potential of tactical air power could be liberated only if it were organized as a distinct force, untethered to strategic operations. In his experience, tactical air power's greatest contribution to a ground campaign lay in its indirect, rather than its direct, assistance to the ground forces.

First in priority among these indirect contributions was gaining control of the air. He was unopposed on this score, even by Army ground officers. Close behind, in his estimation, was tactical air power's potential, through concentrated campaigns of interdiction, to "prevent opposing armies from coming into contact." In this regard he considered the experience of World War II, where tactical air power had not prevented such clashes, as only a starting point for further tactical development. If tactical air power realized its potential by keeping warring armies apart, there would be little or no need for
close air support. To him, close air support should ideally occupy a relatively small niche in the continuum of tactical air operations.[22]

As commander of TAC, Quesada found himself cast once again in the familiar role he had played during, and in the Pentagon since, the war—as a bridge, or more accurately, as it turned out, a buffer, between senior air and ground leaders with diverging doctrines. He was determined to prove the

A Douglas A–26C at Lawson AFB, Georgia, February 26, 1947.

Close Air Support Enfeebled

AAF's sincerity and its ability to support the Army, not with words, but by actual aerial demonstrations of tactical air power, including close air support. His goal became creating and publicizing, through air demonstrations, such an effective air support structure that both the Army and the public would be convinced that tactical air power truly belonged with the AAF.[23]

During the first three months of his tenure as TAC commander, Quesada's eagerness to satisfy all requests from the ground forces for air demonstrations cut so seriously into unit and individual training programs that, in July 1946, he declared that TAC was "in a horrible state," and called a halt to demonstrations. As a result of what he referred to as the "futility of scrambling like hell from day to day and trying to keep everybody happy and meeting needs as they arose," he organized an Air Indoctrination Course to present to all the Army ground schools controlled by the AGF.[24] The course was to serve the two-fold function of making young Army officers of all branches aware of the complexity and effectiveness of close air support, while at the same time providing his own pilots additional training in air-ground operations.

While the course contained segments on troop carrier and reconnaissance operations, the bulk of the material dealt with close air support. The first part described the two legs of the air-ground system: the Air Ground Operations System (Army) and the Tactical Air Control System (AAF). Woven into the course was the AAF's doctrine that the success of the system depended on

View of the Capitol building from a Lockheed P–80 Shooting Star.

65

Help from Above

cooperation between the air and ground elements rather than subordination of the air to the ground commander.

The course depicted the Air Ground Operations System as a means for each commander to exchange such current battle information as the location of forward elements and bomb lines, requests for and reports on air missions, and plans for impending operations. It then examined the Joint Operations Center, that level at which true jointness was supposed to take place. Again it pointed out that here the air commander controlled the means of translating ground force air requirements into "cooperation" missions. Lectures on the Tactical Air Control System explained each of its components (the Tactical Air Control Group, the Tactical Air Control Center, the Tactical Air Direction Center, the Tactical Air Control Parties, and air liaison officers), again stressing that this part of the system operated in coordination with, not in subordination to, the Air Ground Operations System.[25]

During the second phase of the course, attendees did some joint planning and were introduced to the close air support equipment that was to be used. The course concluded with an aerial demonstration of fighter-bombers on immediate-call missions destroying heavily fortified positions that were holding up a ground attack, and light-bombers strafing ahead of a friendly ground attack. The course placed special emphasis on planning and controlling strike missions rather than upon their execution. Designers of the program clearly stated their purpose as "to correctly present the Tactical Air Doctrine as it exists today."[26]

Ninth Air Force, which had moved from Texas to North Carolina and replaced the Third Air Force the preceding fall, presented the Air Indoctrination Course twice in 1947. Between February and May, 2,300 students at Army and AAF schools were flown by TAC to Fort Bragg. At nearby Lawson Army Field each group received five days of instruction and demonstrations.[27] The course was repeated at Bragg for 2,000 students in October under the name Combine.

These attempts to convince the ground forces of the coequal status of air and ground forces in close air support operations met with only partial success. After the May exercise, TAC reported to AAF headquarters that, despite the excellent understanding and cooperation of General Devers and his staff, "some senior ground commanders failed to digest the import of the Air Indoctrination Course." Some ground commanders, it noted, were still planning joint exercises, including the air portions of the exercises, unilaterally without consulting the air commander.[28] A later letter from Fort Monroe to the Army staff characterized the Air Indoctrination Course, and its spin-off Combine, as "strictly Air Force shows" intended to sell Air Force concepts as expressed in F.M. 31–35, which it maintained, were "inadequate and obsolete." It bemoaned the fact that Army students were getting only one side of the story.[29]

In addition to demobilizing after the war, recruiting and training its own personnel and units, performing air power demonstrations, and conducting the Air Indoctrination Course, TAC simultaneously tested equipment, tactics, and

Close Air Support Enfeebled

techniques as part of the Tactical Air Force Development Program. While operational doctrine for close air support, and the rather feeble attempts at joint exercises based on it, reflected wartime experiences, rapid technological changes introduced new issues between the Army and the Air Force. Items of close air support equipment and techniques that came under review in the Development Program included the new P–80 Shooting Star jet, the use of night fighters, the role of the light-bomber in ground support, instrument bombing equipment, gun bomb sights, and the development of new radars to control fighter aircraft.

America's first turbojet airplane, the P–80,[30] was produced by Lockheed in 145 days in late 1943. Shortages of parts and engines, however, kept the plane out of the war. By the time TAC was activated in early 1946, the AAF possessed 300 of these Shooting Stars. In February 1946 the AAF Board, as part of the Tactical Air Force Development Program, ordered extensive combat testing to determine the aircraft's effectiveness in all phases of TAC's mission. Twenty thousand flying hours, over 2,000 bombs, and 158,000 rounds of .50-caliber ammunition were consumed in putting the plane through its paces in strafing, dive-bombing, intercepting other planes, escorting bombers, aerial combat, night and instrument flying, and formation flying.[31]

A report the following year from TAC's First Fighter Group and the Air Proving Ground concluded, in general, that the P–80A would not fulfill the close air support requirements of the Air Force, principally because its limited range permitted its use only on short missions. Other problems with the P–80A as a vehicle for close air support were encountered: only two of its four guns could be fired simultaneously without damaging the plane's nose, and both the rate of fire and the effective range of the guns proved unsatisfactory against ground targets. Low-altitude bombing was ruled impractical due to excessive fuel consumption. The study recommended that the P–80A serve as an interim aircraft until other advanced fighters were procured.[32]

The prewar controversy over whether to build aircraft for single or multiple missions continued into the jet age. Many Army commentators, in summing up their wartime experiences, saw a need for airplanes designed and built specially for close air support. The advent of jets exacerbated the problem. Implied in his earlier criticism of AAF aircraft procurement policies was General Devers's opinion that aircraft loaded down with equipment for many diverse types of missions could perform none of them satisfactorily. Some Army leaders came to believe that jet aircraft, with their limited range, minimum time over the target, and excessive speed, which caused the pilot to miss many targets that were visible from slower, propeller-driven aircraft, were not adaptable to the close air support mission. These objections were variations on the theme, which had taken on the dimensions of a cult among many ground officers, that the airmen's ever widening quest for faster and higher planes with which to fly "into the wild blue yonder" was separating them both physically and psychologically from the ground and the needs of those who had to fight on it.[33]

Help from Above

Although the numerous role and mission agreements of the period clearly assigned to each service the responsibility for developing its own equipment, some influential Army leaders gradually came to feel that, as the customers for close air support aircraft, not only should some aircraft be designed solely for the close air support mission, but also that they should have some input into the design of these aircraft. Fiscal stringency, combined with the AAF conception of the role of tactical fighters, made this an impossibility at the time. These ideas lay below the surface for the time being, as top Army leaders, particularly General Eisenhower, maintained a solid front with the AAF in opposing the Navy's attempt to scuttle the movement toward integration of the armed services and independence for the Air Force.

In addition to evaluating the new jet aircraft as a vehicle for tactical air operations, including close air support, the TAC was also involved in a development program to do something about one of the major wartime weaknesses, the inability of tactical aircraft to reconnoiter and attack at night and in poor weather.[34] During the latter part of the war, and most dramatically during the Battle of the Bulge, the enemy carefully planned his operations to synchronize with periods of bad weather when Allied tactical air operations were limited. Throughout the conflict, he resupplied himself at night with impunity. There was clearly a need for better aircraft and equipment for blind-bombing, navigation, night photography, as well as for electronic equipment.[35]

In the nighttime role, the P–61 had proved unsatisfactory during the war and two new jets, the F–89 and F–94 were still being developed. Difficulties

A 20-mm cannon installed in a Lockheed F–80 Shooting Star.

A Northrop P–61 Night Fighter.

with them assured that they would not be ready until 1950. Also, these jets were designed as interceptors, not as ground support fighter-bombers. An interim propeller-driven plane was needed to replace the P–61. Consequently, the nighttime close air support mission was assigned to TAC's 47th Bombardment Group, which still had its A–26s from the war.

In its final report, the First Fighter Group concluded that visual bombing at night should be attempted only as a last resort. If visual bombing missions were flown, the best technique was for one pathfinder plane to illuminate the target with flares at 2,000 feet, a second to drop a marker bomb on the target, and the rest of the bombers to aim at the marker.

Existing airborne radars were not refined enough to pinpoint targets, although they were excellent for navigation. Short-range Radar and Navigation (SHORAN) equipment was effective for locating targets, but only within 200 miles of a SHORAN station.

Night strafing was entirely different from daytime strafing, because targets were harder to identify in darkness and there was a tendency for pilots to fire longer bursts. Also, since the range of vision was shorter at night, pilots

Help from Above

often pressed their attacks too closely. To compensate for this it was recommended that the copilot and bombardier-navigator keep their eyes on the instruments during strafing runs so they did not fly too close to the ground. Firing rockets proved to be hazardous, since they temporarily blinded the pilot on his attack run.[36]

The report revealed the need for a better bombsight and improved marker munitions, flares, gunsights, extended SHORAN coverage, radar, and night training. In short, "inability to operate effectively at night was one of the outstanding weaknesses of the Air Forces during World War II and very little has been done since then [1951] to overcome this deficiency."[37]

The close cooperation and understanding between Devers and Quesada was matched by the top Army and AAF leaders in Washington. Between the end of the war and early 1947, as the drive for integration of the armed services and independence of the Air Force accelerated, top Army ground leaders, including Lt. Gen. Joseph L. Collins, Generals Bradley, Devers, and Eisenhower repeatedly expressed to Congress their faith in the AAF's sincerity, and their belief that an independent Air Force would support the Army's ground forces.[38] Both Army ground and air forces leaders wished to institutionalize the unified commands that had proved so successful during World War II. In addition to their experiences with air power in the war, such developments since then as the Air Staff's verbal promises of future support, Quesada's aggressive cooperation with the AGF, and the ubiquitous sensitivity of air officers to the Army's concerns, eased these higher level soldiers' anxieties. Equally important, the Army strongly wanted the backing of its air forces in the battle for unification that the War Department was spearheading and the Navy Department was attempting to head off.

The Navy's opposition to unification of the services was fueled by its institutional fear that it would be submerged in any unified defense organization. Naval officers were concerned that unification would see them outnumbered two to one by the Army and Air Force in policy and budgetary matters; that they would not have a substantial role in the future of atomic warfare; and that an independent Air Force would take over their Marine and naval aviation, a large portion of which was devoted to close air support.

Paradoxically, their arguments aimed at gaining naval participation in the nuclear future were contradictory. On the one hand, they set out to cast doubt on the military significance of atomic weapons. Naval analysts pointed to a purported American limited potential for producing such weapons, the possibility that the United States would turn over its nuclear arsenal to the United Nations, the moral dubiety, expense, and public negative reaction to using atomic weapons, and to the fact that the Air Force could not successfully deliver such weapons.

At the same time that the Navy was attempting to minimize the military effectiveness of atomic weapons, it gave every appearance, at least to the

Close Air Support Enfeebled

AAF, of trying to carve out for itself a role in the very nuclear mission it was denigrating. The most dramatic symbol of this contradiction was the laying of the keel in July 1947, just as the hearings on unification were completed and the National Defense Act of 1947 was signed, of a supercarrier, the 65,000-ton CAV–58, designed to launch nuclear-armed strike aircraft. This action, coming as it did hard on the heels of the Navy's publication several months earlier of an official mission statement classifying enemy industrial infrastructures and transportation networks as naval targets, was interpreted by the Air Force as a move by the Navy to obtain a strategic atomic mission.[39]

Although the Navy failed to claim a share of the nuclear mission at that time, it was more successful in its insistence on retaining its Marine and naval aviation. Despite the AAF's repeated assurances that it did not envision incorporating the naval air forces into the new autonomous Air Force, the Navy argued its position strenuously during the unification hearings. In order to emphasize the importance of retaining its own aviation it had to argue, or at least felt it had to argue, against the record of the AAF in supporting ground forces. Even though Navy witnesses couched their testimony in terms of tactical air support, rather than close air support, the prominence in the hearings of Marine aviators, whose sole expertise was in close air support, indicated that, for the most part, close air support was what they were debating.

Such debates had been going on in Congress since war's end. In 1945 the Navy argued that the AAF's emphasis on atomic warfare would weaken its support for the Army. Some witnesses suggested that the Army's failure to integrate its tactical air power into its ground forces had led to the present move for autonomy. Others slighted the record of the AAF during the war. One Marine general flatly denied that the AAF had provided any close air support to the Army throughout the war.[40] The Navy's distrust of an independent Air Force was evident in the testimony of its officers, who used close air support as one of its arguments against unification during the hearings in the spring of 1947.[41]

The National Security Act, as signed by President Truman on July 26, 1947, represented a series of compromises between service positions and doctrine. The act failed to establish a unified armed service, but instead, designated three separate, cabinet-level secretaries for the Army, Navy, and a new Air Force, under a relatively weak Secretary of Defense. The Navy retained its own aviation as well as that of the Marine Corps, leaving the conflict between the new Air Force and the Navy unresolved. The absence in the act of specific, workable functions for the armed services prompted the president on the same day to issue an Executive Order spelling out these functions in more detail.[42]

Both documents finessed the issue of close air support by submerging it in general statements about air support. The Executive Order, designed to specify service roles and mission in more detail than did the act, enumerated the Air Force's missions as those of strategic bombing, air supremacy, airlift and

Help from Above

air transport, supporting land forces and strategic reconnaissance. It did not distinguish between interdiction and close air support, combining both under "supporting land forces."[43] It was assumed that further differentiation of this function would be worked out between the Army and the Air Force. By declining to make an unequivocal statement on the issue, these guidelines permitted continued debate between the two services over priorities within tactical air power.

Perhaps of even greater consequence for the future of the close air support controversy than the disagreement over priorities was the assignment to the Army in both documents of "such aviation and water transport as may be organic therein." This was intended to limit Army aviation to those liaison aircraft that had remained under the control of AGF since 1942. It was also the sense of the act that Army aviation would be limited to transport aircraft. The inclusion of the word "organic," however, left open the future possibility, and eventuality, that as the Army mission changed so would its interpretation of what it viewed as organic.[44]

As a substitute for failing to create a truly unified armed service, the National Security Act and its complementary Executive Order were sprinkled with exhortations concerning joint planning and operations. This presented some difficulties for the new Air Force. Despite the exertions of Quesada and Devers to bring the Army and Air Force closer together, there was lingering suspicion elsewhere in the new service that an excess of jointness would detract from the Air Force's primary mission of strategic preparation and would nudge it back toward the ancillary status from which it had just emerged.

Independence

The Air Force was born on September 18, 1947, with the clearly stated mission of defending the United States against air attack and being prepared to wage strategic atomic air warfare, but with little specific guidance concerning its operational relationship with the Army and Navy. The National Security Act did not assign functions, roles, and missions to the services, and President Truman's attempt to do so with his Executive Order left many questions unanswered. The order was too general to help the Joint Chiefs settle the innumerable nagging issues surrounding roles and missions.

A first attempt to revise the Executive Order and clarify service roles and missions was undertaken by the new Secretary of Defense, James Forrestal, in March 1948. Emerging from a series of meetings between him and the Joint Chiefs at Key West that month was a directive, signed by the president, listing the functions of the armed forces and the Joint Chiefs of Staff. Despite its attempt to define service roles, it came no closer than the earlier documents to settling the question of close air support vis-à-vis interdiction. It repeated the earlier assignment to the Army of "such aviation...as may be organic" to it, and now included close air support of land operations as a "collateral" (secondary) function of the Marine Corps.[45]

Although the Key West directive gave the Air Force a primary mission of furnishing close combat and logistical support to the Army, it defined this support as airlift, support, and resupply of airborne operations, aerial photography, tactical reconnaissance, and interdiction of enemy land power and communications. Nowhere did it clearly assign to the Air Force the close air support mission that the Air Force defined as "the attack by aircraft on hostile ground or naval targets which are so close to friendly forces as to require detailed integration of each air mission with the fire and movement of those forces."[46]

In language that probably seemed clear enough at the time, the Key West agreement appeared to give each service the exclusive right to research and develop the weapons it needed to carry out its primary mission. The only exception was the caveat that each service "coordinate with the others in matters of joint concern."[47] Within a year, however, divergent interpretations of this authorization would result in divisive quarrels between the Air Force and Navy, and to a lesser degree between the Air Force and the Army, over the right of one service to have a say in the weapon procurement decisions of another.

Continuing unease with the inexactitude of roles and missions led to a second conference between the secretary and the chiefs at Newport, Rhode Island, in August 1948. While no further decisions concerning close air support of the Army emerged, these deliberations addressed the distinction between the primary and collateral missions that appeared in the Key West directive. By acknowledging that each service had exclusive responsibility for planning and programming resources for its primary missions, it warned that the collateral functions "shall not be used as the basis for establishing additional force requirements."[48] This seemed to rule out Army participation in the research, design, and production of Air Force aircraft that provided close air support to the Army's ground combat forces. This became an escalating issue between the two services.

The stipulation in the National Security Act and subsequent documents granting the Army "such aviation...as may be organic to it," was the official charter for the Army's subsequent creation of its own aviation branch, which eventually expanded to include a capability for close air support. It breathed new life into Army aviation, which had been organized under the artillery in 1942. In that year the Army was authorized two Piper Cub light planes for each artillery battalion and each higher artillery headquarters, to be operated, however, solely as individual planes, not as units, and only for artillery spotting. Three years later the War Department approved the expansion of the

Help from Above

Army's organic aircraft by assigning them, in addition to artillery units and headquarters, to tank battalions, reconnaissance battalions, armored divisions, infantry regiments, engineer battalions, cavalry groups, and signal battalions. By war's end the AGF had 1,700 aircraft, according to one estimate, 3,000 according to another. By 1947, the absence of funds and high-level interest, combined with the uncertain future of Army aviation in the face of an independent Air Force, had reduced the inventory of planes to about 200.[49]

Imbedded among the many agreements between the Army and Air Force when the latter became independent was the stipulation making the Air Force responsible for organizing, equipping, and operating liaison aircraft for the army.[50] Supervision within the Army of their organic aircraft fell to General Devers and the AGF. The interest of some Army officers in aircraft was quickened by, among other things, their continuing desire to increase the Army's mobility. The airplane promised to fill that need.

During the war General Devers, an armor officer, had become impatient with the number of artillery shells that were wasted because fixed-wing spotter planes were unable to pinpoint enemy targets over the horizon.[51] In 1947, and increasingly during 1948, his desire to supplement the Army's fixed-wing liaison planes with helicopters grew. Initially his interest in helicopters was motivated by the need for a vehicle to observe artillery fire without having to fly over enemy lines. After visiting Coast Guard helicopter rescue operations on Long Island and Marine experiments with Piaseckis in Philadelphia, he became convinced of the potential of the helicopter.

The AAF had used a few helicopters in Europe during World War II, principally for rescue and medical evacuation. In 1947 the helicopter was still experimental, capable of a top speed of only 70 knots and not sufficiently stable to serve as a gun platform. In the following year, as helicopters were improving in speed and stability, Devers convinced General Spaatz, with whom he had worked in Europe during the war, of the potentialities of rotary-winged aircraft. The Air Force procured some and sent them to Fort Wolters, Texas, where Air Force pilots trained light-plane operators as helicopter pilots.[52]

As the military budget tightened, however, the Air Force cut back on many research and development projects, helicopters among them. The Air Force's chief of research and development, Maj. Gen. Curtis E. LeMay, informed the Army, "it was found necessary to eliminate many projects...intended primarily for ground forces use."[53] A later Air Force reply to Maj. Gen. James M. Gavin's request for additional helicopters was, according to Gavin, to the effect that the helicopter was aerodynamically unsound.[54] These statements by the Air Force were motivated, in the view of young Army aviators, not by fiscal limitations but rather by the Air Force's indifference to the needs of the ground forces.

Devers and others in these early days saw helicopters primarily as vehicles for artillery spotting. "I wasn't thinking much about anything else," he

Close Air Support Enfeebled

later recalled, "but I said that eventually they could take the place of a truck." Ground leaders responsible for Army aviation were beginning to develop ideas about the possibility of using this new machine to carry soldiers, supplies, and ammunition quickly to the battlefield. "In this way," said Devers, "we could put the infantry in the air."[55]

Ironically, as these ideas were germinating within the AGF, General Eisenhower, the Army Chief of Staff, was assuring the Secretary of Defense that "basically, the Army does not belong in the air—it belongs on the ground."[56] Thus, before Korea, visions of an Army-controlled air support capability were confined to a small group of lower level soldiers virtually in opposition to official Army policy.

However, these ideas remained inchoate for the time being. The exhortation in the National Security Act that the services plan and operate jointly, which served as a substitute for true unification, acted as a spur to the ongoing efforts of TAC and the AGF (which was renamed the Army Field Forces in March, 1948) to train and instruct their people in air-ground cooperation. During the first year of Air Force independence, the two organizations made some progress, in part through a series of exercises and demonstrations, in honing and familiarizing their personnel with the instruments of air-ground cooperation. In March, for example, they repeated the Combine indoctrination course of the previous year. In the same month, Twelfth Air Force jet fighter-bombers, reconnaissance planes, and tactical control units practiced with the Army Mountain Winter Warfare School at Camp Hale, Colorado, in exercise Timberline. This operation reinforced TAC's opinion that jet aircraft did a better job than artillery of supporting ground units in the mountains and yielded valuable lessons in using jet aircraft for ground support. A notable example of the jet's effectiveness was provided in Timberline when 20 F–80s dropped 40 100-lb. practice bombs on a 20 x 30 foot target, scoring 37 direct hits. The fact that the target was 10,000 feet above sea level and surrounded by 14,000-foot peaks, showed that the new jet aircraft had been measurably improved in the past two years and could successfully perform ground support operations at high altitude and in precipitous terrain.[57]

In a May 1948 exercise, called Mesquite, Twelfth Air Force units trained with the Army in providing column cover for attacking ground forces. On four occasions during 1948, TAC performed smaller demonstrations of air-ground doctrine in infantry battalion defense and infantry-artillery attack exercises.[58]

Throughout 1948 TAC and the Army Field Forces moved beyond static displays to joint field exercises to test the close air support provisions of F.M. 31–35. Although these were not true maneuvers, they represented a realistic improvement on the demonstrations of the previous year. In addition to testing troop carrier operations, such as air drops and resupply, these exercises provided some correctives and fine-tuning to many of the detailed procedures of

Help from Above

Lt. Gen. Ira C. Eaker

the air-ground operations system, the Tactical Air Control System, and photoreconnaissance methods.

The command and control provisions, to which the Army objected during the war and with which it was becoming increasingly uncomfortable since the publication of the manual, remained unchanged. The ground forces continued to be nettled by those provisions that kept joint planning and operational control of aircraft at the higher tactical air force-field army level. Most of the problems uncovered in these exercises were caused, in the Army's view, by the absence of joint planning and the lack of direct control of aircraft by corps, division, regimental, and battalion commanders.

Transcending the technological and organizational changes that had been made in the area of close air support, and to some degree influencing them, was the Air Force's unyielding fidelity to the command and control principle of coequality of surface and air forces and its hesitancy to join with the other services in any operation that suggested turning over control of air power to them. This presented some difficulties for the Air Force. Tactical Air Command limited its joint participation to exercises and maneuvers that provided useful training for its personnel and that conformed to its ideas on command and control. For example, although General Quesada usually sought to cooperate actively with the Navy in joint amphibious exercises, he was reluctant to take part that year in a Navy-designed amphibious joint training exercise on Vieques, an island east of Puerto Rico. Tactical Air Command's objections to the exercise were two-fold. Besides judging the proposed operation as unrealistic, it also opposed the Navy's plan to control the air resources. "Such a philosophy was not acceptable," noted TAC's special projects officer, "in that the Air Force never accepted the Navy's thesis of the command and control of amphibious operations." The Air Force interpreted this proposal as an "encroachment into the command of an airborne operation."[59] By resisting the

Close Air Support Enfeebled

Navy's plan, the Air Force did two things. On the one hand, it reinforced its adherence to the idea of coequality of air and surface forces. At the same time, however, it added to the growing perception within the Navy, and increasingly within the Army, of the Air Force's intransigence and nonreceptivity to joint exercises.

The Air Force's record of cooperation with the Army during 1948 was better than that with the Navy. During an exercise in May, called Assembly, a joint task force composed of the 82d Airborne Division and both troop carrier and fighter planes from the Ninth Air Force, recaptured Camp Campbell, Kentucky, from guerrilla bands who had seized the post. Responsibility for planning and operating the Tactical Air Control System fell to the Air Force's only Tactical Control Group, the 502d, which installed a Tactical Air Control Center at Smyrna, Tennessee, a Tactical Air Direction Center at Franklin, Kentucky, and assigned two Tactical Air Control Parties to the Army division. Twenty-four Ninth Air Force F–51s provided close air support for the 30,000 friendly troops and air cover for the troop carriers, while nine F–6s flew reconnaissance missions. Eight F–47s supported the aggressors.

Overall, both Army and Air Force observers were satisfied with the performance of the troop carriers, although the Army pointed out some shortcomings in the adequacy of the C–82 Packets for air drops. As to fighter air support, assessors found it difficult to evaluate the adequacy of air-ground doctrine since the Air Task Force was supporting only one division, whereas in actual combat it would have to support several. As a result, there was more air support than was needed, raising expectations for the future beyond what could be expected in actual combat and resulting at times in sending fighters against inappropriate targets. Another element of unreality was introduced by the short distances between the air bases and the division, distances that would be much larger in actual combat.

Air Control Parties—those airmen assigned to the ground units to direct the air strikes—had difficulty keeping up with the infantry, and their radios were not up to the task. It was recommended that four, instead of two, such parties be assigned to each division. This recommendation was adopted in the following exercises.

One of the most critical elements in close air support is the speed with which fighters respond to immediate calls for assistance. During Assembly these reaction times were often too long to make the aircraft effective. Given the many elements that made up the request system, there were several potential points along the request chain that caused delays. Requests that originated at the battalion level frequently took longer to reach the division than it did for them to transit the rest of the system, that is, from the division to the Joint Operations Center for approval, then to the fighter units that were alerted, flew to the target area, and contacted the forward air controller. In an attempt to speed up the process the Army recommended two correctives. The first suggestion, which was strictly an internal Army communication problem, was to stop using the already overburdened command channels and start using the artillery request channels for immediate strike requests. During combat operations the command channels were in constant use to transmit all orders and directives affecting the employment of units. Adding air strike requests, in the Air Force's view, would overburden these radios. On the other hand, the artillery request net, which was already being used to request artillery firing, was relatively unburdened and could efficiently handle air requests.

Unlike this first recommendation, which the Army could adopt by itself, the second suggestion fed the command and control controversy. This was a proposal to create Fire Support Coordination Centers (FSCCs) at regimental, division, corps, and army levels. A team of representatives of each fire support agency, such as artillery, air support, heavy mortars, tanks, and so on, would be located at these centers to determine the most appropriate type of fire support for a given battlefield situation.[60] Although the Air Force viewed this proposal as potentially weakening the doctrine of centralization of command and control at the higher levels, FSCCs were tested in later exercises.

The largest divergence of views between the Army and the Air Force to emerge from Assembly centered on doctrinal positions both sides held going into it. The Army, as in earlier exercises, attributed the most serious close air support deficiencies to inadequate joint planning before the maneuver began, and the lack of proper (i.e. Army) control of aircraft during its progress. Joint planning and operations had taken place, as called for in F.M. 31–35, at the Joint Operations Center located at the tactical air force-field army level. The Army's recommended remedy was to set up Joint Operations Centers at corps and even division levels to avoid what it characterized as an "unsound tendency" to centralize heavily at the upper command levels. In a statement reminiscent of those of many ground commanders before, throughout, and since World War II, the Army's report asserted that joint operations centers must be decentralized and "charged with planning for and directing the employment of aircraft allocated to their particular units." The report deemed this decentralization "imperative," and recommended that the air liaison officer at each division be given the authority to use aircraft working with the division as the division commander desired without having to clear target and mission changes with the upper level joint operations center. In a bold statement reflecting discontent with F.M. 31–35, the report declared that employment of air by the division "must be decided at the division level."[61]

Both of these recommendations flew in the face of the Air Force's close air support doctrine, which saw a threat to its principles of mobility, flexibility, and the concentration of force in such decentralization. Although the second Army suggestion was not acted upon at the time, together they indicated that the ground forces had not abandoned hope of regaining more control of air

Close Air Support Enfeebled

resources. They also represented a further step in the Army's gradually increasing dissatisfaction with the close air support manual.

While these Army comments addressed some specifics of the air-ground system, and did not constitute a repudiation of F.M. 31–35, they did signal a growing dissatisfaction on the part of the Army with that document, which it had helped to write. A report submitted by a Marine observer at the conclusion of exercise Assembly, however, went much farther than did the Army. By maintaining that control of the aircraft should have been given to the ground force commander who was responsible for the action, the Marine report showed the unbridgeable doctrinal gap that existed between the Navy and the Air Force/Army on the question of close air support. Two earlier attempts to revise F.M. 31–35 by creating a joint air-ground manual had been aborted by the unwillingness of the two sides to abandon their basic doctrinal tenets, principally on this command and control issue. A third attempt, being staffed at service headquarters at the time of exercise Assembly, was about to meet a similar fate in the face of the Air Force's refusal to abandon the principle of coequality as expressed in F.M. 31–35.

Tactical Air Command's hard-hitting response to the doctrinal implications of the Marine's critique, written by its Director of Plans and Requirements, Col. William W. Momyer, reflected the Air Force's philosophy of close air support then and since. The Air Force, wrote Momyer, had consistently held that air and ground forces are coequal and that air power is neither subordinate nor subservient to a surface force. This had been adequately proven in World War II and enshrined in F.M. 100–20 and F.M. 31–35. All Marine air, on the other hand, was assigned to ground units and, consequently, seldom concerned itself with the overall objective of a surface campaign. By restricting itself to close air support, which the author equated with front line artillery, Marine/Navy air lacked responsibility for gaining control of the air, isolating the battlefield, or carrying out interdiction, measures which the Air Force viewed as "determining criteria" in assisting ground forces in a surface campaign. Had this Navy doctrine, as practiced in the Pacific, been adopted by Allied air forces in Europe, asserted Momyer, "the German Air Force would have been the victor," since it would have gone unopposed by Allied air power. Conversely, the adoption of this Navy doctrine of close air support by the German military establishment during the war was instrumental in its destruction.[62]

This Navy doctrine of close air support, although not overtly expressed in the critique, underlay the Marine observer's critique on specific close air support measures taken during the exercise. For example, the report criticized the paucity of Tactical Air Control Parties and the fact that a Tactical Air Control Center was not located adjacent to the Army field command headquarters.

To the first objection, Momyer pointed out that the land forces in exercise Assembly were opposed, not by a hostile army, but spasmodically by guerrillas. Consequently, not all components of an air-ground system were needed.

79

Help from Above

Col. William W. Momyer

In an interesting observation, the future commander of the Air Force in Vietnam opined that "the utilization of Air Power against isolated guerrilla activities is a useless waste of manpower and equipment with a small resultant damage inflicted on the hostile force."[63]

In reply to the second objection, he noted that it was the Tactical Air Force, not the Tactical Air Control Center, that was adjacent to the field army in Army/Air Force close air support doctrine. He reiterated the function of the Tactical Air Control Center as an Air Force agency through which the air commander disseminated and controlled his air operations once he had received his instructions from the Joint Operations Center. The Army had no direct connection with the Tactical Air Control Center, which is strictly an Air Force operation. Once again, the basis for this arrangement was the Air Force's compulsion to avoid subordination to the ground forces.

The TAC report got to the heart of the matter when it noted that

> There can be no argument that a ground commander with all the means assigned to him...can secure any type of support more rapidly than if required to go through other channels of communication.... The utilization of air power in (the close air support) role is most eagerly sought by ground commanders, regardless of whether air superiority and the other aspects of a military campaign were achieved, providing it assists that commander in the dilemma that presently confronts him.[64]

Yet the Air Force's answer to this apparent dilemma was to defend its holistic interpretation of close air support, namely, that since in and of itself close air support normally results in the elimination of an immediate danger rather contributing to the larger objectives of a campaign, it must be applied only when it is clearly connected to and does not detract from that final objective.

The largest demonstration of air-ground capabilities during 1948 took place in October and November. Combine III brought together units from the TAC's Ninth and Twelfth Air Forces, the Third Army, the Air Marine Fleet Atlantic, the Naval Air Fleet Atlantic, SAC, and the Air Proving Ground Command. As with the previous courses, Combine III served the dual purpose of instructing students of the Army's service schools as well as providing training for the participating units in joint planning, staff procedures, and operations.[65]

A simulation employed in the course, which was held at the Air Proving Ground at Eglin Air Force Base (AFB), Florida, touched on all the elements of air-ground cooperation. A hypothetical amphibious and airborne invasion and the capture of an enemy capital was illustrated with skits and air power demonstrations. The students were introduced to the planning and operations of an air superiority campaign, an interdiction campaign, and close air support of a friendly force. The 60-day campaign was compressed into a three-day scenario of skits, static displays, and aerial demonstrations. The observers first viewed simulated planning conferences on Joint Chiefs of Staff, Army, Navy, Air Force, and Task Force-Combine III levels, a display of tactical aircraft and their ammunition, ordnance, and guided missiles, and a demonstration of loading cargo aircraft. Next, they observed skits depicting close air support techniques at a battalion command post, a Tactical Air Control Center, a Tactical Air Direction Center, and a Joint Operations Center. They also examined equipment used to control aircraft, including the MPQ–2 SHORAN. Air power demonstrations, including close air support missions of the Infantry, Artillery, Tank, and Air Team, rounded out the program.[66]

The fruits of two years of technological development in electronic control and communications equipment were also on display for the attendees. The Tactical Control Group, which was responsible for operating the Tactical Air Control Center and for providing its radar and communication apparatus, introduced the students to a microwave early-warning radar, an improved version of the radar that Quesada had shoddily rigged in Europe during the war to control his fighters. This new version had a range of 220 miles. Other long- and medium-range radars and height finders, both portable and permanent, ranging in weight from 5,000 to 23,000 pounds, and requiring anywhere from 2 to 15 operators, were also demonstrated.

Communications equipment used in the Combine III exercise also illustrated the technological advances that had been made since the war. Among the items exhibited was an air transportable kit containing all the components required for setting up a Tactical Air Control Center—telephone equipment, plotting tables, and other items needed to receive information on aircraft move-

Help from Above

ments from outlying observation posts or radars and to filter this information for controlling fighter planes. Additional communications equipment included VHF direction finders that could be mounted in vans or small transportable shelters, VHF air-ground transmitters and receivers, high-frequency (HF) air-to-ground and point-to-point transmitters-receivers, and new frequency-modulation (FM) transmitters and receivers.[67]

Despite the great amount of energy and time that went into the preparation and presentation of the exercise, and the encouraging reports at its conclusion, Combine III was still only a static simulation that lacked important characteristics of a joint exercise such as uncertainty and joint participation. Equally ominous for the future, it was an exhibition of potentiality rather than of readiness, since the constrictive 1948 military budget left the Air Force with but one Tactical Control Group, stationed in North Carolina. Significantly, none existed in either Europe nor the Far East.

The Navy was not the only service to challenge the Air Force's jealously guarded prerogative of maintaining control of air assets in joint operations. Increasingly anxious over close air support, early in 1948 the Army requested modification of the earlier agreement that made the Air Force responsible for organizing, equipping, and operating liaison squadrons for the Army.[68] The Army proposed that it organize its own flight detachments of liaison planes, using its own resources. It argued that it was not satisfied with the performance of the Air Force's liaison squadrons and that, since liaison planes were not an integral part of air power, they should be placed under the Army. In addition, the Army requested that the liaison planes be assigned in units, not as individual planes.

Tactical Air Command viewed this proposal as "the camel's nose under the tent," fearing that if this step were approved, the Army would next ask for its own transport aircraft. "Once troop carrier was lost," it predicted, "it was conceivable that reconnaissance, fighter, and bomber aircraft would follow."[69] Implications for close air support of the request were obvious. Tactical Air Command argued against the proposal on two fronts. On the one hand, it stoutly maintained that liaison aircraft were an integral part of air power and, as such, could not be separated from the main body without having the entire corpus of air power unravel. If the Air Force accepted the premise that liaison airplanes could be broken off from the main body and given to the Army, then it would, to be consistent, have to agree to a similar detachment of other aircraft, including fighter-bombers and light bombers employed in close air support. "[The Army's] position is indefensible," responded TAC, "and will only provide a future basis for the Army to seek transport aircraft as organic to an Airborne Division and fighter-bombers and reconnaissance aircraft as organic to infantry units."[70] This line of reasoning also explains why the Air Force did not give up the close air support mission, even though it did not place it high on its list of priorities.

The other argument was that the Army's proposal represented a quantum leap to a total of 3,926 L–16 and L–17 liaison planes. The plan to organize these planes into units was seen as a breach of earlier agreements. Also, "the magnitude of the force alone will necessitate the Army creating an organization designed in accordance with the Air Force concept for the employment of Air Power."[71]

Following a year of discussion and coordination of positions as to what constituted the Army's organic aircraft, the two services in May 1949 agreed to define two types of Army organic aircraft, while at the same time limiting their size and missions. Army fixed-wing planes were not to weigh more than 2,500 pounds, while Army helicopters were to remain below 4,000 pounds. These planes and helicopters were to be used by the Army only for aerial surveillance and route reconnaissance, control of march columns, camouflage inspection, courier service, emergency aerial evacuation, limited aerial resupply, and limited front line photography.[72] Seemingly innocuous at the time, this agreement in hindsight did, indeed, nudge the Army camel's nose forward in its quest for an organic close air support capability.

Reduction of the Tactical Air Command

Combine III was the last joint exercise performed in the 1940s by TAC as a major Air Force command. Upon his installation as the new Air Force's first full-term Chief of Staff in April 1948, Lt. Gen. Hoyt S. Vandenberg undertook a reorganization of the service that still was only partially divorced from the Army. Despite his own tactical background and experience in World War II as commander of the Ninth Air Force in Europe, Vandenberg, like Spaatz and Arnold before him, was not comfortable with the existing division of the Air Force's resources into "strategic" and "tactical" forces.[73] Although it proved politically impossible at the time, due to Army and congressional opposition, to fully implement the earlier combat command concept, Vandenberg took a step in that direction. On the first of December 1948, the Tactical Air and Air Defense Commands (ADCs), lost their major command status and were redefined as administrative units within a newly created Continental Air Command (CONAC), headquartered at Mitchel Field on Long Island under Lt. Gen. George E. Stratemeyer. Although the reorganization was pictured as primarily a response to a presidential order to strengthen the civilian components of the armed forces (the Air Reserve and the Air National Guard), it clearly reflected the growing preeminence of the Strategic Air Command, which was greatly strengthened by the changes. It was also a move to create Air Force command areas to match those of the Army. Tactical Air Command's two numbered air forces, the Ninth and Twelfth, and ADC's four air forces, became six regional air forces under CONAC, corresponding to and working closely with the six existing Army command areas in the United States.[74]

Help from Above

The reduction of TAC mirrored the continuing division within the Air Force over the nature of air power in the environment of the late 1940s. Most of the top command of the Air Force supported the primary role of the strategic forces, the new command organization, and the official relationship between nuclear and conventional conflict. The advent of the atomic bomb and the intransigence of the USSR, highlighted most recently by their blockade of Berlin in 1948, had convinced most of them, including such tactical airmen as Vandenberg, that a protracted war of local campaigns like World War II was no longer likely. According to this majority view, the potency of atomic weapons, which had yet to be adapted to the battlefield, was such that any future war, regardless of how it started, would quickly escalate into global conflict aimed at the enemy's economy and heartland rather than at his armies, and would end fairly quickly. According to this scenario, ground forces, no longer needed to fight enemy armies, would only have the missions of mopping up after the atomic devastation and of keeping the peace, neither of which tasks required a tactical air organization in being or a close air support capability. This view was a direct descendent of the earlier immediate postwar idea of a single combat command in the Air Force. The creation of CONAC was seen as a step in this direction by increasing centralization and flexibility. As in World War II, strategic aircraft could perform tactical and defensive functions and tactical aircraft could perform strategic missions. According to Air Force proponents of this philosophy, "It is not sound in the face of limitations imposed by economic and other similar considerations, to design and organize separate forces tagged and earmarked for specific functions to the exclusion of others."[75]

Proponents of the Air Force's tactical functions, on the other hand, were unconvinced that conventional wars were a thing of the past, and were unwilling to concede that there would not be wars other than nuclear ones.[76] They continued to believe in the need for a tactical air arm in being and ready to go, an air arm that included in its mission close air support of the ground forces. Both Quesada and the recently retired Spaatz were "very, very distressed" by TAC's abridgement, which they saw as an abrogation of their earlier promises to support the Army. To Quesada the downgrading of TAC, which was motivated by a parochial desire to prevent domination by the Army, was "a sad day for the Air Force." To him the move was a repudiation of the philosophy he had been pursuing since the war. Throughout his tenure as TAC commander, he had taken the approach that the best way to keep the Army from dominating the tactical air forces was to satisfy the Army's need for air support so completely that it forestalled any desire on its part either to create its own air force or to reach its tentacles so deeply into the Air Force's operation as to control it. He rejected the notion that the close working relationship between him and Devers was leading to Army domination as "completely false."[77] Unable to convince the Air Force of the soundness of his

Close Air Support Enfeebled

approach, Quesada was reassigned from TAC in November 1948, one week before the command was downgraded, as a special assistant to the Chief of Staff, General Vandenberg, for matters pertaining to the reserve components. His deputy, Maj. Gen. Robert M. Lee, was tapped to head the greatly reduced TAC. Although still in existence, the command became an operational headquarters of about 150 people for planning and conducting joint exercises with the Army and the Navy.

The reduction of TAC reduction was seen by most airmen as a glass being half-full, while the proponents of a tactical air force in being interpreted it as a glass half-empty. In the eyes of the former, the Air Force had not done away with its tactical and close air support capability, but rather, moved it closer to the ideal of indivisibility of air power. In theory, the reorganization fit neatly into the Air Force's doctrine of centralization. Tactical and defense air resources were consolidated at a higher level, where they could be massed and centrally controlled for either air defense or tactical air operations. The continuation of separate commands for air defense and for tactical operations with surface forces was deemed as a "relatively inflexible and 'stylized' employment of available forces," which was not "in consonance with the principle of economy of force."[78] Tactical air control adherents, on the other hand, who were working day in and day out with the Army, emphasized the losses and inefficiencies introduced by the move. To them the scattering of its assets among local commands appeared as a decentralization and distribution of its

Gen. Carl A. Spaatz

Help from Above

resources into those very *penny packets* against which Field Marshal Montgomery had railed during World War II and the Air Force had opposed since then.

In the 1948 reorganization TAC lost control over its own units and had to request them from CONAC whenever they needed them for joint exercises. Besides the complications and inefficiencies introduced by the new requirement for additional coordination, the TAC was stripped of its institutional memory, the opportunity to train its own people, and the ability to improve its close air support procedures through lessons learned in the joint exercises. At the completion of each exercise, the air units returned to their own commands, leaving TAC without the benefit of lessons derived from the experience.

Even though the reduced TAC charter emphasized cooperation with the Army in joint land operations and with the Navy in amphibious exercises, and even though General Lee was as dedicated to interservice cooperation as his predecessor, the reorganization had deleterious effects on relations with the Army. Army doubts about Air Force sincerity, which until then had remained muted and largely within the Army, now began to surface at high levels.

Tactical Air Command's contraction reinforced the view of many Army commanders that the Air Force would readily sacrifice its tactical resources on the altar of strategic bombing which, indeed, was claiming an increasing share of the Air Force's attention. While not denying the primacy of the strategic force, many Army leaders saw in the reorganization further evidence that, as budgets shrank, tactical aviation would bear the brunt of any reductions. The economy was assuredly a factor in the decision to reorganize. In the summer of 1948 President Truman imposed a budget ceiling of $14.4 billion on the services for the coming fiscal year of 1950, and refused to raise it, forcing all the services to tighten their belts. The Air Force chose not to spread the cuts across the board, but to reorganize its nonstrategic elements so as to preserve the strategic force intact for its primary mission. In defense of its decision, the Air Force noted that "the monetary limitations of the…budget reveal unmistakably that the weapons and resources of the USAF [United States Air Force] will not be quantitatively adequate to support both [an Air Defense and Tactical Air Command]."[79]

The Army was concerned with more than this particular instance. Looking to the future, it feared that in any future reductions imposed on the Air Force, units dedicated to supporting the Army would be the first to go. Typical of this concern were the sentiments expressed in an Army Field Forces's study that examined the Air Force's own predictions of its posture if forced to reduce from 70 to 58 groups. All 12 groups that would be lost were tactical air groups, while strategic bomber and reconnaissance groups remained untouched. The report prophesied that whenever the USAF was

Close Air Support Enfeebled

required to reduce its forces, the cut would be made in those types of aircraft that support the ground forces.[80]

Within months of the reorganization General Devers bluntly voiced the Army Field Force's disappointment in a letter to General Vandenberg:

> Until the reorganization of the USAF, Ninth and Twelfth Air Forces were basically charged with tactical air force missions, operating under Tactical Air Command. As near as I can determine, USAF reorganization has not charged any numbered air force or lower headquarters with tactical air force functions and missions. I do not know what plans you may have to keep alive the complex machinery of close support and to allow this specialized activity to progress. My own experience tells me that unless an operating agency is charged with the responsibility for planning, experiment, development, and operations, when the operational need arises last minute improvisation with resulting ineffectiveness will result. I am therefore quite concerned over the absence of Tactical Air Force organization.[81]

Reaction to Devers's well-reasoned complaint was swift, bringing to the forefront once again the question of close support. Continental Air Command, which had already been planning to create an agency within TAC for closer coordination with the ground forces, activated it in July as the Tactical Air Force (Provisional). The new organization, which formed an operational headquarters for conducting joint exercises, was empowered to deal directly with the other services on joint matters. In an attempt to avoid a loss of institutional memory, the new agency was ordered to "maintain sufficient assigned personnel adept in the current concepts and knowledge of the employment of tactical air."[82]

The Tactical Air Force (Provisional), however, proved to be more of a Band-Aid than a curative. While it refined the machinery used by the Air Force for planning and operating with the other services, it did not address Devers's concerns about experiment and development. Decisions concerning aircraft procurement and testing remained with CONAC where, in the eyes of the Army, those dealing with close air support were certain to be subordinated to those of air defense. Above all, TAC did not regain its own units, making subsequent joint air-ground exercises and maneuvers largely unproductive from the aspect of training.

Devers's views bore fruit in the Pentagon, as well. In May 1949, the top leaders of both services met there to discuss the issues. Representing the Army were General Bradley, the Chief of Staff, General Devers, and a dozen other Army generals. Generals Vandenberg, Quesada, Lee, and Lt. Gen. Lauris Norstad spoke for the Air Force. High-level examination of Army and Air

Help from Above

Force differences was also undoubtedly encouraged by impending congressional hearings on the Navy's objection to the B–36 bomber and on the status of service unification.

The disappearance of TAC as a major command was a watershed in the history of close air support by the Air Force between World War II and the Korean Conflict. It threatened the healthy spirit of interservice cooperation that had developed between Quesada and Devers. It confirmed the suspicions of many Army officers about the fragility of the promises of support made by their air counterparts. Largely as a result of this new situation, both the Army and the Air Force doubled their efforts to seek accommodation between their conflicting positions. Between the time of the reorganization and the outbreak of hostilities in Korea in mid-1950, serious and important discussions about close support took place in the Pentagon, in Congress, and at Langley/Fort Monroe between the impoverished TAC and the Army Field Forces. Several attempts during this period by TAC and the Army Field Forces to write a joint manual for close air support failed, in the Air Force view, because of the Army position on command and control of aircraft in close air support operations. At these joint discussions representatives of TAC felt that the experiences of air-ground operations in Europe during World War II were being ignored. They were determined that those hard-won lessons would prevail in future air-ground operations.[83]

In response to criticisms such as those of Devers and the press regarding the reduction of TAC, the Air Force established in June 1949 a Board of Review for Tactical Operations to examine the entire question of support for the Army. Chaired by General Quesada, it was made up of wartime tactical air commanders, including Maj. Gen. Richard E. Nugent and General Weyland who, along with Quesada, had commanded Ninth Air Force's three TACs in Europe during World War II.[84] Between June and October the board, in six sessions ranging from half a day to three days, examined the Air Force's current doctrine, tactics, procedures, and equipment for supporting the Army, and the Army's view of them.

Quesada set the tone for the board by stating at the outset that it was not to be a "whitewash" of current Air Force practices in the tactical arena, but was to look seriously at the shortcomings of tactical air support.[85] To substantiate this, he invited General Collins, the Army's Vice Chief of Staff, who within a month was to ascend to the top Army job, Lt. Gen. Albert C. Wedemeyer of the Army staff, and Maj. Gen. Robert C. Macon, who represented Devers and the Army Field Forces, to present the Army's position to the board. Members also heard from General Lee of TAC and Lt. Gen. Ennis C. Whitehead, the new CONAC commander.

The Army representatives, as was to be expected, confined their remarks almost solely to that which was of most immediate concern to them, namely, close air support. They displayed less interest in air superiority and interdiction, which in their view, affected them only indirectly. Behind their comments

Close Air Support Enfeebled

Maj. Gen. Richard E. Nugent (left); Maj. Gen. Robert M. Lee (right).

was the Army's desire that the Air Force provide both an organization and aircraft specifically designed to provide close air support as a primary function. It was also obvious from their remarks that the Army no longer considered F.M. 31–35, which encompassed the Air Force's concept of close air support, acceptable. They unequivocally disagreed with three key aspects of close air support as it was then being pursued: command and control, the Air Force's priorities, and the types of aircraft the Air Force was using for close air support, hinting at their dissatisfaction at being excluded from decision making concerning the nature and development of these planes.

While expressing satisfaction with the idea of a Tactical Air Force (Provisional), which was just being formed, they proposed going even further by setting up a Joint Tactical Air Support Center at Fort Bragg to develop joint doctrine, tactics, and techniques; to test and evaluate specialized equipment, and conduct joint training. Although it was not spelled out in the discussion, the board interpreted the proposed joint center as an amalgam of the newly formed Tactical Air Force (Provisional) and V Corps, under the Army Chief of Staff. This was seen by the Air Force board members as an attempt by the Army to increase its control over close air support missions and was unacceptable to them.[86]

Other command and control suggestions by the Army officers seemed, on the surface, surprisingly minor. They wanted an Army liaison officer assigned

Help from Above

to the Air Proving Ground and a USAF air liaison officer to work with the Army Board. These proposals reflected the Army position that, as users of tactical aircraft, they should be kept abreast of, and even have some input into, the development of these aircraft. Finally, they proposed an inclusion in any revised air-ground manual of the statement "Tactical Air Support of Ground Forces is the application of tactical air power in the furtherance of a ground campaign *as required by the ground force commander to achieve his mission.*"[87]

Army desires to modify the Air Force's existing priorities for tactical air operations, which they believed still placed close air support last, emerged in the soldiers' request to have the current joint manuals rewritten. Specifically, they pointed to that most annoying burr under their saddles, the statement in F.M. 100–20 that "missions against units in the zone of contact are most difficult to control, are most expensive, and are in general least effective." From the ground forces' perspective, this was not necessarily true and should be reworded.[88]

While acknowledging that it was the Air Force's prerogative to develop and select aircraft for tactical air missions, the Army officers expressed concern at the Air Force's complete acceptance of jet fighters and its abandonment of reciprocating-engined fighter-bombers for close air support.[89] Virtually nothing about jet aircraft appealed to them. Jets were limited in performing the close air support role by their vulnerability to ground fire, limited range, large takeoff requirements, inadequate armament, high fuel consumption, and short endurance over the battlefield. The Army preferred a modified version of the P–47 of World War II.

They also made a strong plea for the development of light-bombers, with an effective combat radius of up to 1,000 miles, to occupy an intermediate position between fighters and medium-bombers. Medium-bombers, whose combat radius was between 1,000 and 2,500 miles, in their view tilted the tactical air effort too far in the direction of interdiction.

General Collins and company also disliked the term "penetration fighter" that recently replaced fighter-bomber in the lexicon of military definitions. As with medium-bombers, the new term suggested to Army ears the idea of operations away from the battlefield to the exclusion of close air support. The board agreed and proposed reinstating the earlier term.[90]

It was clear throughout the Army officers' testimony that they were unhappy with the emasculation of TAC and were concerned about the implications it had for joint training. They pointed out, for example, that the 2d Division at Fort Lewis, the Armored Division at Camp Hood, and the three divisions in the eastern United States could not test and maintain the techniques of close air support unless tactical air units constantly worked and trained with them. Such intimate working relationships, they noted, "would dispel current fears of lack of cooperation and inability [of the Air Force] to support."[91]

In presenting TAC's position before the Board, General Lee reaffirmed the Air Force's broader view of tactical air operations and, in the process, illus-

Close Air Support Enfeebled

trated the gulf that continued to exist between the Army and the Air Force on the question of close air support. While the Army talked only of close air support and within the framework of a ground campaign, the Air Force placed close air support within the larger, holistic context of tactical air operations, and placed tactical air operations within the even larger backdrop of an overall air campaign. There were, Lee noted, three inseparable aspects of tactical air operations: support of the strategic air offensive, support of a limited surface campaign, and support of a major surface campaign. Tactical air operations supported the strategic air offensive by attacking, concurrently with the strategic forces, enemy targets, such as his air and ground forces, communication centers, transportation facilities, rolling stock, bridges, and viaducts, which sustained his infrastructure but were not assigned to the strategic forces. The same tactical forces supported limited surface campaigns by removing obstacles to friendly ground forces that were attempting to seize advanced base areas for the strategic forces. If called upon to support a major surface campaign "in the magnitude of the last war," tactical air operations would accelerate the advance of the ground forces by maintaining air superiority over the operational area, by preventing the enemy from moving troops and supplies into the battle zone, and by destroying enemy forces that were engaged with friendly units or posed a threat to their advance.[92]

Gaining air superiority and keeping enemy forces from arriving at the battlefield were tactical responsibilities in all three of these aspects. Close air support, however, was pursued only in the third aspect, namely the support of a major surface campaign, and then only if interdiction had failed to prevent a clash of arms. The purpose of future major surface campaigns, in TAC's view, would be not to defeat an enemy nation, but to assist the strategic air offensive in doing so. As a result, if the air superiority and interdiction campaigns succeed, "close air support actions will be of relatively limited significance." Therefore, "close air support activities must of necessity be placed in a lesser category of importance when viewing the total requirement necessary to be accomplished by tactical air operations."[93]

The TAC briefers suggested that World War II had given the Army a distorted picture of close air support. According to them, the reason the AAF had been able to provide such a relatively large amount of support to the ground forces in the later stages of the war was because tactical air had by then achieved total supremacy in the air and had already carried out an effective isolation campaign. By concentrating only on the final, close air support aspect, the Army had obtained too narrow a vision of the broad nature of tactical air operations.

Corollary to this depiction of tactical air power as an indivisible entity was disagreement with the Army's contention that a ground force commander should direct the air effort and should determine the targets and the time, duration, and methods of air attacks. The Army's suggestion that the Air Force dedicate a specific amount of close air support to each battalion and regiment was

Help from Above

tantamount, in Lee's view, to repudiating the lessons of World War II. Control and direction of tactical air operations, regardless of the specific task to be performed, was an Air Force responsibility that could not be delegated to ground forces regardless of the magnitude of the operation.[94]

Tactical Air Command's response to the Army's discontent with jets also flowed from this unified conception of tactical air operations. Aircraft must be designed and configured, it believed, primarily to wage the battle for control of the air. Secondarily, they must be able to perform interdiction operations. If aircraft were properly designed with characteristics for these first two functions, they would automatically possess the minimum acceptable attributes for close air support. While granting that such aircraft would not be as effective as would ones designed specifically for close air support, TAC maintained that aircraft should not be designed by stressing characteristics totally suitable to the "least significant of the three functions that must be performed."[95]

The Langley officials buttressed these doctrinal arguments for jets with the results of a series of tests conducted by the Air Proving Ground Command at the Las Vegas gunnery range. They had tested Air Force jets (F–80s, F–84s, and F–86s) against Air Force and Navy prop planes (F–47s, F–51s, F–82s, AM–1s, and AD–2s) in every category of tactical air operations. In aerial gunnery, the jets outperformed the reciprocal planes 13.4 to 3.5 in percentage of hits on targets. For close air support, the jets' advantage in ground gunnery was 56.75 to 50.5 percent. Ninety-seven percent of skip bombs fired by jets hit their target, compared to 94 percent for the propeller driven aircraft. In dive-bombing tests, the average circular error for jets was 82 feet, compared to a 132 feet for the others.

The advantages enjoyed by jets in these tests were attributed in the main to the absence of propeller or engine torque, which reduced accuracies in conventional aircraft, and to the use of dive brakes, which permitted the jets to slow down quickly while still enjoying the advantages of higher speed at other times. The briefers concluded that jet planes were already superior to conventional aircraft in tactical operations, and that they would improve as new equipment such as gunsights became available. Propeller-driven aircraft could not survive, they predicted, nor satisfactorily accomplish the ground support role in modern warfare. It remained TAC's position that the Air Force should continue to develop jet fighters for ground support and not consider developing conventional-powered fighters.[96]

General Lee also noted at the meeting that several amphibious exercises with the Army and Navy during the past three years had failed to produce appreciable progress in developing joint doctrines and procedures. The Air Force frequently was excluded from the planning of these exercises or invited late. Control of the aircraft also remained a major matter of dispute and although agreements were reached on the command structure for each exercise, a permanent solution to this problem remained elusive. The principal unresolved issue was between the Navy and Air Force over this question of control. As in World War II, the Navy insisted on its amphibious doctrine, which provided for naval control of all operations, including air, prior to an amphibious landing. With the establishment of an Expeditionary Force commander ashore, control of aircraft was transferred to the ground commander. The Air Force had yet to write its own doctrine on the matter of command and control, but TAC strongly opposed yielding control to the Navy for any portion of a joint undertaking. Since these exercises involved support of Army units after the initial landings, this issue had important implications for the command and control aspects of close air support.[97] Tactical Air Command wanted the issue resolved through a joint decision.

During a September 1949 meeting of the Board's Air Force members, Quesada characterized the existing TAC as impotent and, undoubtedly still smarting over the rejection of his approach. He also predicted that if the Air Force did not meet the Army's needs within five years, the Army would be in a position to justify its own air force.[98]

In its final report, the Board reaffirmed the contradictory principles that air and surface forces must be fully integrated and coordinated, that the air commander must have centralized control of his aircraft in order to concentrate them, and that the air commander, after consulting with surface commanders, must allocate his resources between air superiority, interdiction, and close air support missions. The proportion of aircraft the air commander devotes to each mission would depend upon the particular situation.[99]

The Board further observed that, just as the Air Force had a strategic striking force in being, so it should have a tactical air component in being, as opposed to its present reliance on borrowed units, reserves, and mobilization. This tactical air component should be self-contained, inherently capable of planning, administration, operations, and logistics. Until it recreated a TAC with subordinate Tactical Air Forces, the Air Force would remain open to justifiable criticism from the Army.[100]

In its conclusion the Board rejected the Army's idea of creating a Joint Tactical Air Support Center as duplicative of what the Air Force's Air Proving Ground Command was already doing at Eglin AFB. It considered it inappropriate for the Army to evaluate air tactics and techniques. Nor should the Army, it said, be involved in assessing Air Force equipment for close air support.[101]

The Board agreed to assign Army Intelligence and Operations officers to Air Force headquarters in Washington and to the TAC. It also concurred with the idea that an Army liaison officer be assigned to the Air Proving Ground, believing that such an assignment would prove beneficial to both services. While differing with the Army's contention that jet aircraft were unsuitable for close air support, the board did recommend that air-defense fighters and long-range strategic escort fighters be modified to perform close air support and other tactical fighter missions. It saw no need for light-bombers, opting again

Help from Above

for larger fighter aircraft with heavier payloads and longer range. Members sided with the Army that the term "penetration" fighter should be changed back to fighter-bomber. They also recommended that the question of planning for joint exercises, which had so upset TAC, be resolved at Air Force Headquarters level with the Army and Navy.[102]

In short, the Board reaffirmed the Air Force's view of close air support as a secondary mission that should be prepared for and performed within the context of the other missions of supporting the strategic forces, gaining superiority in the air, and interdicting the battlefield. It disagreed, however, with the Air Force view that a tactical air force in being was unnecessary.

In a separate memo addressed to the Secretary of the Air Force, Stuart Symington, shortly after the Board disbanded, Quesada expressed his opinion that, although the Air Force had not disregarded the importance of tactical air power and close air support of the Army, it had constantly put its worst foot forward. He attributed the surface forces' perception of the Air Force's inability or lack of desire to participate in joint operations "to our consistent ability to present our contribution in the most unfavorable manner."[103]

The division of tactical air into tactical and air defense commands was a cardinal error, giving the impression of lack of cooperation. This fragmentation of tactical forces along offensive and defensive lines did not exist within the strategic forces, and there was no reason for it to be pursued with tactical resources. The idea of *operational control*, whereby units were meted out to the TAC only for the duration of an operation, had long since been proven unsatisfactory. The Air Force has also hurt itself in the eyes of the surface forces, Quesada wrote, by redesignating fighter groups as penetration groups. The 20 fighter groups in the Air Force's 48 groups appear on paper as:

Penetration groups	8
Ground support groups	1
Interceptor groups	6
All-weather groups	5

By characterizing them this way, he said, the Air Force has sold itself short and raised the distrust of the surface commanders. Since penetration fighters also performed close air support functions, why not call them fighter-bombers? Then the mix would look more realistic and appealing to the Army:

Fighter-bomber groups	9
Interceptor groups	6
All-weather groups	5

The final, and most important, irritant to the ground forces was, in Quesada's opinion, the strong tendency of the Air Force to shy away from joint

Close Air Support Enfeebled

operations because they feared domination by the other services. He had experienced little or no tendency on the part of the surface forces to dominate the Air Force. On the contrary, surface commanders fully accepted the principle of coequality and of the essentiality of air power to surface operations. He urged the secretary to eliminate the distinction between offensive and defensive tactical air power by creating a Continental Tactical Air Command as well as TACs in Europe, Alaska, and the Far East. He also suggested that the Air Force assume an aggressive attitude toward joint operations, not only seeking opportunities to participate in them, but going so far as to create them.[104]

Congress and Close Air Support

While the Army and the Air Force were attempting to draw closer on the specifics of close air support during 1949, the close air support issue arose and was projected into a larger background in the Capitol. In August, the House Armed Services Committee investigated a Navy claim that the Air Force's procurement of the B–36 intercontinental bomber was riddled with fraud and abuse. Although these claims were quickly dismissed, the hearings did raise larger questions of national security and the status of military unification.

The Navy's brief against the B–36 was motivated in part by its deep distress over the cancellation in April of the supercarrier by the new Secretary of Defense, Louis Johnson, without Navy concurrence. Johnson, an ardent supporter of the president's military austerity program, invoked the Newport stipulation that a service should not use a collateral function to justify new weapons. The cancellation was a serious blow to the Navy's ambition to acquire a nuclear mission, and left SAC as the preeminent American nuclear strike force. In reaction, its spokesmen questioned not only the Air Force's investment in the B–36 bomber, but the entire Air Force nuclear strategy.

Congress expanded its inquiry from the question of the effectiveness of the B–36 as a satisfactory weapon to a full-scale examination of the roles and missions of the Air Force and Navy, with particular attention to Navy and Marine aviation. In the process, it touched upon two issues central to the question of close air support. The first issue was whether one service should have a voice in the development of weapons by another service. The termination of the supercarrier seemed to contravene the portion of the Key West agreement that the Navy interpreted as authorizing each service to develop its own weapons. However, in making that argument the Navy was caught on the horns of a dilemma. If it argued that it had the right to develop the supercarrier without interference from the other services, it would then have no case to oppose the Air Force's development of the B–36. On the other hand, if it argued that it had the right to oppose the B–36, it lost any claim it might have had to complain about the cancellation of the supercarrier, *United States*.

Help from Above

In their testimony, Adms. Louis E. Denfeld and Arthur W. Radford attempted to straddle the dilemma by claiming for each service the right to develop its own weapons for its primary mission through the prototype stage, "otherwise some weapons of great value will remain undeveloped." When it came to procurement of weapons, however, no one service should be allowed to proceed unilaterally, lest "weapons of doubtful value" be reproduced, with "consequent waste in manpower and funds."[105]

This same issue, of course, was one that existed between the Army and the Air Force, both of which were dancing around the question of how much influence the Army should have in decisions affecting the type of close air support aircraft the Air Force should procure. Although on the west side of the Potomac River at the Pentagon during the summer of 1949 the Army was quite firm in expressing its desire for more influence, its statements to Congress were more moderate. General Collins for the Army and General Vandenberg for the Air Force both spoke with one voice in the hearings by agreeing with the Navy position except when the weapons being developed were so costly that their unilateral development would adversely affect the mission of the other services.[106] In a letter to the committee, the Army Secretary Gordon Gray seconded this position, noting that the high cost of developing the supercarrier would be detrimental to the overall defense effort.[107] By taking this position, the Army could support the Air Force in opposing the development of a supercarrier, which was certainly costly enough to decrease the other two services' portion of the budget, while preserving for itself the ability to intervene in the Air Force's research and development of close air support aircraft programs, which were hardly of a magnitude to affect the budget of the other services.

Congress supported the Army/Air Force position, concluding that in cases where the expenditure of tremendous sums and effort by one service in developing its weapons seriously interfered with the creation of minimum balanced forces, the Joint Chiefs and the other services should participate in the decision to proceed with the development of that weapon.[108]

The second issue that the Navy raised before Congress was the assertion that, by concentrating on strategic bombing, the Air Force neglected tactical aviation and the development of adequate fighter aircraft and fighter aircraft techniques. This was a claim with which many in the Army, and some in the Air Force, concurred, although it had yet to surface as an official Army position. In his testimony, Admiral Radford did not argue in terms of the relative number of strategic and tactical planes in the inventory. Since the number of strategic groups outnumbered those that could be used primarily for tactical missions by only 18 to 11, an argument on that basis would have weakened his position. Instead, he contended that the Air Force had earmarked only six percent of its research and development funds for tactical and fighter aircraft. In his view, this purported lack of adequate fighters might have grave consequences for future security, and it could well be disastrous to spend scarce budget dollars on bombers "dedicated to an unsound theory of war."[109]

Army and Air Force rebuttals on this issue were devastating. Army Secretary Gray expressed complete confidence that the Air Force would support his service in both training and in developing joint doctrine. Alluding to the discussions that were taking place in the Pentagon, he expressed satisfaction that currently planned Air Force programs would adequately support the Army. To maintain the Army's bargaining position with the Air Force over types of close air support planes, he did note that "present development trends in types of aircraft designed to support ground forces may require some modification."[110] General Collins, while testifying that he would like to see more air groups for close air support, stated that the Air Force was definitely cooperating. He pointed out that, although Congress was still debating the size of the future Air Force, if the Air Force were authorized 48 groups, 23 of these could be used for ground support. If the Air Force were to grow to 58 groups, 38 of them would support the ground forces.[111] Air Force Secretary Symington told Congress that "upon mobilization, more than 80 percent of the Air Force would consist of groups primarily equipped for purposes other than strategic bombardment." General Vandenberg was more specific, asserting that SAC had 942 aircraft, of which 132 were tankers, 96 reconnaissance planes, 150 fighters, and 24 transports. The remaining tactical groups and squadrons of the Air Force operated 2,304 aircraft. Thus SAC accounted for only 29 percent of the combat and combat-support aircraft of the regular Air Force.[112]

As with the question of the supercarrier, Congress projected the issue into the overarching context of attaining balanced forces. It concluded that, although there would never be enough money for all the strategic and tactical aircraft that were desirable, it was up to the Joint Chiefs to decide the basic strategic concept and to establish properly balanced forces to carry it out.[113]

Close air support resurfaced in testimony when the congressional hearings resumed in October. Marine Brig. Gen. Vernon E. Megee, Associate Director of Marine Aviation, sought to depict the inadequacies of the Air Force's close air support resources, doctrine, and command and control arrangements. He took the AAF to task for having ignored ground support before and during the initial campaigns of World War II, preferring instead to concentrate on independent air operations. He asserted that tactical aviation, not strategic bombing, was the decisive factor in both the Atlantic and Pacific during the war, and praised the ability of Marine close air support aircraft to strike targets within 100 yards of friendly troops. This reference to distance from friendly troops illustrated a basic difference between Marine and Air Force close air support. Unlike Army operations, Marine amphibious landings were made without concurrent artillery support. Consequently, close air support planes had to serve as artillery by striking as close to the friendly lines as possible. The Air Force and Army split the responsibility of fire support

Help from Above

between artillery and aircraft, and defined close air support as strikes close enough to friendly lines as to require close coordination with the ground units. This attempt to measure the success of close air support in terms of proximity to friendly lines was seen by the Air Force as an attempt to divert attention away from the real nature of close air support.

In pitting the Marine system of close air support against that practiced by the Air Force, Megee emphasized that the Air Force's "traditional doctrinal insistence of coequal command…deprives the Army commander of operational control of his supporting element," forcing decisions in case of disagreements to be made at the highest command level, thereby introducing delay and inefficiency into combat operations.[114]

Addressing the question as to whether the Air Force had weakened its tactical air capability by stressing strategic bombardment, he maintained that the Air Force did not have enough tactical air units to support the Army. His own experience had shown that one ground division required four groups of supporting aircraft. According to him, the Air Force lacked the 16 groups that would be needed to support the Army's planned peacetime force of four divisions.

Megee's testimony brought into stark relief the gulf between Marine and Air Force conceptions of close air support. To the Marines, whose operations were carried out on shallow fronts, normally unsupported by artillery, and not directly involved in gaining air superiority or performing interdiction, tactical operations were synonymous with close air support. In its rebuttal, the Air Force pointed out that this identification of tactical air with close air support was too narrow a definition of tactical aviation. If that was all that tactical aviation meant, then the Air Force could possibly be considered deficient. Yet such a view overlooked the inherent flexibility and indivisibility of air power that permitted an air commander to apply all aircraft, including bombers, to whatever air task, as well as close air support, was required at a given moment. Viewed from this perspective, the Air Force's tactical air assets were fully capable of supporting the Army in a protracted surface campaign.[115]

The Air Force rejected Megee's call for four groups per division as unrealistic in the face of present budget restrictions and unnecessary in light of the Air Force's ability to use all its air power for any given purpose. It defended its close coordination and cooperation with the Army, which had resulted in joint training exercises and sincere attempts to develop joint directives for them.[116]

Further Attempts to Improve Air-Ground Operations

Although the Army representatives had emphasized the high level of cooperation between the Army and Air Force in both joint training and the development of joint doctrine, progress in the field in both areas was slow and hardly reflected their testimony before Congress. In the spring of 1949 the two

Close Air Support Enfeebled

services participated in an exercise, Tarheel, in the area around Fort Bragg, North Carolina. This was the first training exercise since the demotion of TAC the previous December, and the Air Force was uncertain as to whether it could provide aircraft. By the time the Air Force decided to participate, it was too late to plan for a joint task force. A separate air task force was created to support the ground task force, making Tarheel essentially a ground exercise with air participation, rather than a joint exercise. The Joint Operations Center, which had been the bone of contention in the earlier Assembly exercise, was located adjacent to the headquarters of the two task forces, thereby avoiding a showdown over who should control the aircraft.

Whereas the earlier exercise emphasized troop carrier operations, Tarheel stressed air-ground measures. F–84Bs, RF–80s, F–47s and F–51s supported a ground thrust of the 82d Airborne Division and three tank battalions against an aggressor force that landed west of Fort Bragg. The aggressors were supported by F–51s. Between May 11 and 18, 1949, this air-supported ground force enveloped the enemy, forcing him to surrender.

While the Army was effusive in its praise of the air support, several close air support weaknesses surfaced. This was the first large field test of the ability of jet aircraft to perform the close air support mission. The Tactical Air Control Center, the Tactical Air Direction Center, and the Tactical Air Control Parties had little difficulty controlling the jet planes. The air task force commander, Maj. Gen. Glenn O. Barcus, believed the jets, both F–84s and RF–80s, had proven they were not too fast to support ground troops.

Yet this view was not universally shared. The jets were "severely handicapped" by high fuel consumption, which prevented them from remaining in the target area long enough to find targets of opportunity. The need for so much fuel overworked the petroleum, oil, and lubricants (POL) support people and their equipment. In addition, the jets' extremely wide radius of turn made it very difficult for their pilots to pinpoint targets. The F–84 was only marginally suited to the close air support role. [117]

Difficulties with forward air controllers experienced in the earlier exercise continued throughout Tarheel. One squadron called them totally inadequate. In many cases pilots were unable to contact them due to poor radio equipment. When they were contacted, they rarely gave the pilots targets to strike. For the most part, the forward air controllers were unable to work with more than one flight of planes at a time. Most of these problems were attributed to the fact that TAC, since its absorption into CONAC and loss of its own units, was suffering from a lack of continuity. Continental Air Command's need to borrow units for individual exercises had weakened its training program.

One command and control difference did arise during the maneuver. The Army division experimented by setting up a central organization, called a Fire Support Coordination Center (FSCC), to coordinate artillery and air support strikes. The Air Force's senior Tactical Air Control Party was located at this

Help from Above

Lt. Gen. Glenn O. Barcus

center, from which it delegated final control of air strikes to the three other parties at the battalions. The Army was delighted with the results and sought to incorporate the FSCC into Army doctrine. The Air Force was more cautious and held out for further testing. A joint training directive that appeared the following year included a description of the FSCC, but with the inclusion of an air liaison officer rather than a Tactical Air Control Party.

The Air Force, however, did not rely solely on exercises with the Army to decide the suitability of jet aircraft for ground support missions. Even though the National Military Establishment (the predecessor of the Department of Defense) had approved the total conversion of the Air Force to jets, various commands continued extensive testing to determine the strengths and weaknesses of the existing aircraft.

In the spring of 1949, aircraft manufacturers, the Air Materiel Command, and the Air Proving Ground Command ran exhaustive trials of the three currently operational jets—the F–80C Shooting Star, the F–84E Thunderjet, and the F–86A Sabre. Since the aircraft were being evaluated for their effectiveness across the entire spectrum of tactical air operations, including air superiority, interdiction, and close air support, the planes were rated according to both their air-to-air and air-to-ground capabilities. The evalua-

Close Air Support Enfeebled

tors, sensitive to the Army's claims that jets were less suitable for close air support, addressed such Army concerns as the jets' vulnerability to enemy fire, their short range and low endurance, their gunnery and bombing accuracy, their purported excessive airfield requirements, and the logistical requirements of jets for fuel, maintenance, and supply.

Vulnerability tests predicted the damage that both jet engines and jet airframes could be expected to sustain in battle. The results of the engine tests ran counter to the common perception that one or two bullet holes in a jet engine would cause a disastrous fire or explosion. In a wind tunnel, evaluators fired .50-caliber machine guns into the engine of a jet clocked at 350 mph. They concluded that the jet, in this case an F–80, could take two or three rounds through the combustion chamber and 10 to 15 scattered rounds through the tail cone and tailpipe, and still return to base with only local damage to the engine's structure.[118]

Tests performed at the USAF Propulsion Laboratory at Wright-Patterson Air Force Base revealed some potential vulnerabilities of jet engines in the face of enemy fire. The plane would probably disintegrate if a bullet struck the compression wheel or turbine wheel. For this to occur, however, the bullet would have to be fired directly up the tail pipe—an unlikely occurrence on ground attack missions. A severed fuel line also would cause a serious fire and eventual explosion. Although this was also true for conventional aircraft, the fire would occur more quickly in jets and therefore the loss rate for jets might be higher than that for propeller planes. Numerous safety precautions were being built into later models of jets to minimize this risk. The jet's oil system, which is the most vulnerable part of any aircraft engine, was less vulnerable than that of conventional planes because it used less oil and the system was more compact.[119]

Experiments at both Lockheed, the builder of the F–80, and at Wright-Patterson showed that the jet's airframe, too, was less vulnerable to enemy fire than was commonly perceived. The .20-mm ammunition fired into the wing caused, at the most, a relatively harmless crater two inches in diameter. Peeling of the skin after battle damage was shown to be not a serious factor. Concern that a wing would explode from a sudden change of internal pressure caused by the entry of a bullet proved groundless. Tests showed further that a head-on hit in the leading edge of the wing at high speeds had very little effect on the aircraft.[120]

Aside from these tests, TAC maintained that, for several reasons, jets were less vulnerable to light antiaircraft fire than were conventional planes. Since they operated at greater speeds, and had a greater ability to roll and zoom, jets presented a more fleeting target. In addition, the jet's relatively silent approach to a target gave it the advantage of surprise that helped to protect it from defensive fire.[121]

The jet's range and endurance were still lower than those of conventional planes, but they were catching up. The F–80, without extra fuel in tip tanks and

Help from Above

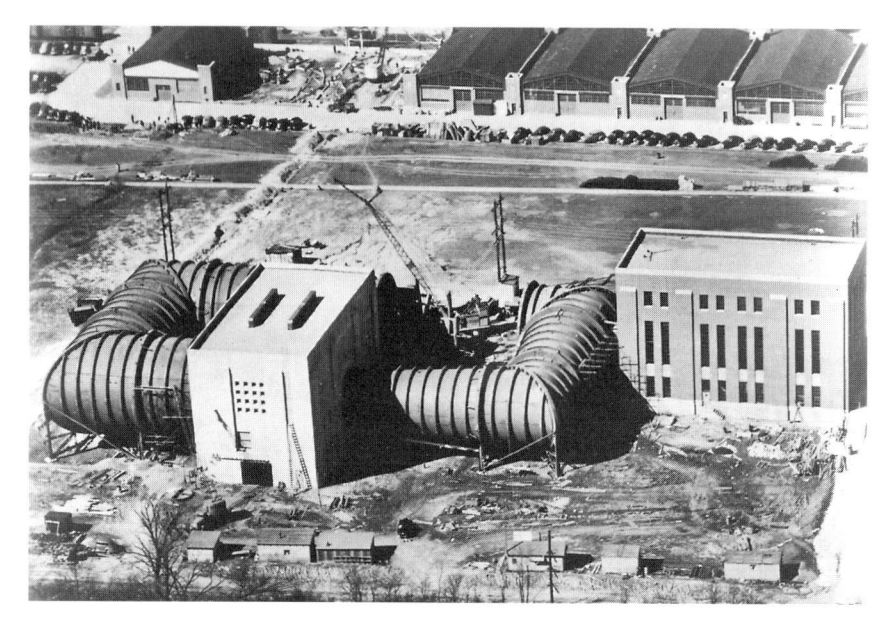

Construction at Wright-Patterson Field, Dayton, Ohio in 1941.

with a full bomb load, had a radius of action[122] of only 150 miles, about half that of a P–47 with an equivalent load. Although this distance would normally be enough for close air support missions, its loiter time over the battle area was unacceptably short. The problem here was the jet's voracious appetite for fuel at low altitudes, the very altitudes at which they must fly on close air support missions. Tactical Air Command's only answer to this problem was to oppose the use of jets on air-alert, or immediate missions, which required longer loiter times to identify targets. While TAC considered such immediate missions wasteful and historically was reluctant to perform them, the Army favored them over preplanned missions since they provided more flexibility and quicker responses to the ground commander. It was this difference of opinion that formed one of the Army's main complaints about jet aircraft.

Even the problems of range and endurance, in the eyes of the Air Force, were being solved in newer jet models. The F–84E, which had just entered the inventory in the Spring of 1949, had a combat radius of 650 miles when carrying two 500-lb. bombs, and of 800 miles when armed with eight rockets. It could loiter in a target area 300 miles from home base for two hours.[123]

These encouraging advances in extending the range of jet fighters, however, were counterbalanced by the inability of the Tactical Air Control System to keep pace with aircraft technology. Although in early 1949 the ground control and navigational systems were adequate for the short-range fighters, which had to takeoff, fly directly to the target, accomplish the mission, and return

Close Air Support Enfeebled

directly to home base, there was some apprehension over the future ability to provide the new fighters of very high speeds and longer range with adequate control and navigational guidance. In short, improvements in aircraft performance were outstripping improvements in aircraft control.[124]

Results of a recent fighter gunnery meet, which pitted jets against conventional planes, convinced TAC that the jets were superior in gunnery and bombing accuracy. The jet's predominance was particularly noticeable in strafing operations, a key element of close air support, and was attributed to the absence of torque and vibration, better visibility, and the better handling qualities of the jets. Jets also had the advantage of nose-mounted guns that fired straight ahead, rather the wing-mounted weapons of most World War II planes that forced the pilot to cope with the problems of converging fire.[125]

Another Army concern was that jet aircraft would require longer and more permanent airfields, particularly those located at high altitudes and in areas of extreme heat. The experience of jet fighter pilots to date, however, was that under wartime conditions similar to those in France and Germany in World War II, 6,500-foot airfields with pierced-steel plank (PSP) surfaces were adequate for jet operations. Although concrete, hard-surface runways were preferable, the job could be done from planked airfields. The only negative effect of the PSP was the minor one of extending the takeoff roll somewhat, due to the tendency of the planks to pile-up in front of the wheels. Yet recent increases in jet engine thrust and such improvements as water injection and afterburner removed the need for unusually long runways for jets.

The problem of launching jets from high-altitude fields or in high temperatures was overcome by attaching temporary jet pods [jet assisted takeoff (JATO)] to the wings of the planes to increase their takeoff thrust. Tactical Air Command believed that JATO was a temporary expedient and that it would not be needed in the future as added thrust was built into later jet engines.

Most of these conclusions were based on actual laboratory or field tests, since the Air Force had, in early 1949, no actual experience with the logistic problems posed by an all-jet force either in combat or in field exercises. Exercises with the Army up to that time had been carried out under strictly controlled conditions that did not allow for the unexpected logistical complications that traditionally arose in combat. The best the Air Force (as well as the Army) could do at this point was rely on the knowledge and predictions of its most experienced logistic personnel.

The most important logistical question was that of fuel. The Air Force acknowledged that jet aircraft required four times the amount of fuel that conventional planes needed in World War II. Logisticians predicted, however, that the increased efficiency of jet aircraft would result in fewer sorties with a consequent reduction in fuel requirements. At the same time studies suggested that, since jet planes were less complicated and required fewer spare parts than reciprocating aircraft, both maintenance and supply should be easier.[126]

Help from Above

In its overall evaluation of the three jets, the Air Force concluded that none of the three completely fulfilled all the requirements for a tactical fighter. As for their predicted effectiveness for close air support, only the F–84E was deemed adequate. The Shooting Star proved incapable of carrying the mixed load of bombs, rockets, and napalm tanks that close air support missions needed, since these loads had to be suspended from the wing tips. When carrying the needed armament, the planes could not simultaneously carry wingtip fuel tanks, thereby reducing their radius of action below an effective range, in some cases as low as 90 miles. Although the F–86A Sabre's speed and maneuverability made it an excellent air-to-air fighter, its combat radius when fully loaded was, on the average, even less than that of the F–80 and it was poorly designed to carry air-to-ground armament. Only the F–84E Thunderjet possessed the requisite combat radius and was able to carry a large air-to-surface armament load. The Thunderjet was configured to carry either a mixed or alternate loading of air-to-surface armament, and its estimated combat radius of between 560 and 900 miles, depending on its armament load, was more than twice that of the two other aircraft.[127]

While judging the Thunderjet an adequate, although admittedly interim, close air support airplane, evaluators felt that much of the doubt about jets that existed in both Army and Air Force circles was engendered not by the jets themselves but by a past lack of proper ordnance, of correct armament installation, and of weaknesses in the Tactical Air Control System.[128]

In addition to testing the ability of jet aircraft to perform close air support missions, in 1949, the Air Force sought to convince the Army of the jet's effectiveness by providing orientation rides for members of the Army Field Forces and Army Headquarters. At first these indoctrination flights were made in two-seater F–80s, developed two years earlier. Later, an F–84E was modified with a second seat for the same purpose. These orientation flights and demonstrations were having the effect of dampening some Army doubts about the effectiveness of jet aircraft as close air support vehicles. After a demonstration for the Army the following spring, in which conventional aircraft were measured against jets, General Clark, who had replaced Devers as Chief of the Army Field Forces the preceding October, told General Lee:[129]

> I want to let you know how deeply I appreciate the trouble you and your command went to in making it possible for me to see first hand a demonstration of air support and a comparison between the conventional type airplane and the jet in their ability to support ground troops.
>
> You know, I have had some misgivings as to the suitability of your fighter-bomber jet which you are using in close-support

Close Air Support Enfeebled

mission[s]. Your demonstration this morning completely dispelled that question from my mind.[130]

On the eve of the Korean War, two joint exercises again uncovered weak spots in the USAF's close air support system. The first exercise was an Army, Navy, and Air Force joint amphibious and ground attack on Vieques Island, east of Puerto Rico, appropriately named Portrex. Below the surface of the generally laudatory postmortems of this operation lay strong indications that the Air Force was ill prepared for close air support operations.

The scenario called for dropping airborne troops near the island's beach, followed shortly by an amphibious Marine landing on the beach. An initial mistake was made in deciding to cover the landing with naval, rather than air, gunfire to protect the adjacent airborne troops. The Air Force's Tactical Air Control Party did not train with the airborne force to which it was assigned before the operation got underway. Further, the party did not jump with the troopers, but traveled to Vieques by ship. Not only was this unrealistic, but the party lost valuable time in joining up with the ground force and in agreeing on techniques that should have been developed and rehearsed beforehand.[131]

A number of shortcomings surfaced during the ground battle that followed the landing. Although close air support planes were called in from orbit points near the battle area, it still took them an unacceptably long 25 minutes to respond to requests. This was due to lack of training, the overloading of the tactical air direction communications net, and poor target designation and identification. The failure of the ground forces to mark front lines and targets with either panels, arrows, or smoke shells often made it necessary for the control parties to rebrief the pilots, adding to the reaction time.[132] This again emphasized the critical importance of joint training and the consequences of its omission.

Both the Marines and the Air Force had control parties with their respective ground forces. Whereas the Marine parties had trained with their units for three weeks before the exercise, the Air Force controllers did not join their Army ground units until two days after the landing.[133]

As was becoming habitual in such exercises, the afloat task force commander, a Navy captain, in his final report, concluded that the operation would have been even more successful had "the power of decision as to the employment of particular squadrons or flights [been] decentralized to the headquarters of the unit being supported." This was an obvious allusion to the fact that during the exercise Marine aircraft, having to seek approval to strike from fewer intermediate staff levels than did Air Force planes, responded more quickly. The Army generals who participated in Portrex were of two minds. The Army commander on the scene proposed that a flight of close air support aircraft be assigned to each assault battalion. His superior, however, the Army's Joint Task Force commander ashore, countered that such a recom-

Help from Above

mendation would require too many aircraft and that the priorities for aircraft decided at the division and higher level took precedence over "piecemeal" assignment to lower echelons. He also argued that such fragmentation of air assets would destroy the flexibility of higher headquarters to mass their aircraft against key targets.[134] The two sides in the debate seem to have been influenced more by the operational level they occupied than by the service they represented.

Communications during the exercise were plagued by the familiar problem of overloaded frequencies. Tactical control frequencies were continually jammed with calls. Radio call signs were unnecessarily long and cumbersome. The radar used to control the fighters, the AN/CPS–5, could not track individual jet planes. More sophisticated radar equipment was needed.[135]

The TAC's loss of units the year before produced some logistical weaknesses during Portrex. Just as the exercise was about to begin, the F–84Es of one of the two fighter-bomber groups were grounded for bearing problems, forcing the remaining group to serve double duty. Both the bearing problem and the below normal in-commission rate experienced by the second group were due to the division of logistical responsibilities, in the absence of a TAC deputy for materiel, between two numbered Air Forces. This resulted in poor planning for parts and lengthy supply lines—deficiencies that would not have occurred had the pre-December 1948 TAC been in existence.

Close air support operations were further delayed by the late arrival of its nerve center, the 502d Tactical Air Control Group. Equipment needed to operate the Tactical Air Control Center, the Tactical Air Direction Center, the radar station, and the control parties was loaded haphazardly on eight different ships. Not having been combat loaded, the equipment needed first was unloaded last. Men and equipment were not mated, in some cases, until near the end of the exercise, and radar sets, which had not been waterproofed, shorted out, requiring many man-hours for repair. These breakdowns were blamed on the absence of a single TAC logistics agency.[136]

Further, in order for the Tactical Air Control System to work properly, at least two Tactical Air Direction Centers with interlocking communications were needed. During Portrex, one Tactical Air Direction Center was placed on the main island at Ramey AFB as a small control center. The other was sited on Vieques but, being alone, could not function properly as a control center.[137]

Although the second exercise, called Swarmer, stressed troop carrier and strategic airlift operations, considerable effort was expended in gaining air supremacy, interdicting an aggressor force, and providing close air support for a counterattacking friendly ground force. This was a very large exercise between April 28 and May 3, 1950, in the Fort Bragg area and involved 26,000 ground troops, 4,000 trucks, 2,000 trailers, 350 tanks, 70 heavy guns, and 3,344 air sorties flown by airlift, fighter-bomber, fighter-interceptor, light-

Close Air Support Enfeebled

bomber, and reconnaissance aircraft. The importance of the Air Force's role in the exercise is indicated by the assignment of its Deputy for Operations, General Norstad, as the maneuver commander.

Army observers expressed general satisfaction with the air support they received, but the Air Force was more critical. The results showed that many of the weaknesses noticed in the earlier exercises and predicted in earlier studies continued to plague the close air support phase of the test. As suggested by earlier evaluations, lapses in the Tactical Air Control System were more detrimental to the exercise than weaknesses of jet aircraft.

Familiar problems persisted with forward air controllers. Their lack of training showed up, as they often gave incoming fighter pilots only map coordinates for targets rather than talking them onto targets. This was attributed to TAC not possessing its own units, requiring them to use untrained officers as forward air controllers. For security reasons, forward air controllers who dropped with the paratroops were not given ground authentication. This caused serious delays in their ability to control incoming fighters—a delay of 10 hours in one case. The forward air controllers were also handicapped by their AN\TRC–7 radios, whose weak signals were frequently blocked by aggressor aircraft that gained operational control of friendly aircraft and turned them against their own ground troops.

This same lack of training showed up in the poor performance of personnel in the Tactical Air Control Center. In the postmortem on the exercise, the center was criticized for not controlling the fighter-bombers tightly enough. Too often the center cleared immediate flights into the battle area without specific missions. Once inside the zone, these flights interfered with preplanned missions, creating congestion around the airhead. The need for training also showed up in the inaccurate or incomplete logs kept by the controllers, in their poor coordination with the Joint Operations Center, and in their absence of radio discipline. Part of the congestion problem was caused when the controllers were forced to direct sorties using only two VHF radio channels. Reconnaissance flights, in particular, were almost forced off the airwaves.[138]

Six months later, looking back with hindsight from a perspective atop Korean hilltops, the 502d commander characterized Swarmer and Portrex as lacking realism. "People know how to drive down paved roads," he noted, "park on old runways and set up equipment that hasn't been moved actually since they loaded it." Yet none of this prepared them for trucks turning over on narrow roads, people having to climb mountains and build camps, and equipment being loaded and unloaded several times and jostled on ships and ground transport. Never in prewar training, said the commander, had the Group been employed as a unit. In Swarmer, two of the three Tactical Air Direction Centers were diverted, one to control airlift planes and the other as a control center for the enemy forces. Again, as in Portrex, only one radar was available for directing friendly aircraft to their targets and that, lacking interlocking communications, was unable to provide coverage in the required depth.[139]

While the front line troops praised the air support, Air Force observers realized that the continued excessive number of available support sorties, which had also characterized earlier exercises, was unrealistic and could redound to a criticism of the Air Force when, in an actual combat, fewer sorties were available.

Coordination and teamwork between the air and ground forces needed improvement. Despite earlier predictions, the radius of action of the F–84Es, with a full ground-attack combat load, proved to be only 300 miles. This left them only 10 minutes over the target. While this was usually adequate for preplanned missions where the targets were known beforehand, it was unacceptable for immediate flights which, seeking out unplanned targets, needed at least 30 minutes in the combat area. Although the jets, armed with 5-inch rockets, were effective against tanks during daylight and good weather conditions, they were unable to perform at night and when the weather was bad.

Congestion resulting from the small number of radio channels reduced the number of targets struck, in one estimate, by 50 percent. Tactical Air Command's earlier observation that improvements in jet aircraft had outpaced the system for controlling them was borne out. The World War II type ground radars that were still being used lacked the range to control friendly aircraft.

The Army portion of the close air support system experienced difficulties as well. The signal company that operated the air-ground liaison communication system performed poorly. Poor radios, antiquated ciphering devices, and insufficient and inexperienced operators degraded the system for requesting air strikes. One Army observer classified the efforts of the Army's Air Ground Operations System as "futile in view of completely inadequate communications."[140]

Tactical air control advocates were acutely aware of the weaknesses of the Air Force's close air support system and attributed many of its problems to the demotion of TAC. The maneuver commander for the exercise, General Norstad, upon reviewing the evidence, recommended to the Chief of Staff that TAC be given its own units, which would provide continuity and training in the weak areas. This recommendation in effect called for restoring TAC to its former command status.[141] Within six weeks after the exercise, before this and other recommendations could be acted upon, the North Koreans invaded South Korea and the USAF went to war with a close air support system still displaying the shortcomings exhibited in these exercises.

In addition to participating in joint exercises, TAC also had the responsibility for planning, and in some ways its efforts in this area during 1949 and early 1950 exceeded those in the arena of joint exercises. While Air Force headquarters and the Air University concentrated on developing strategic

Close Air Support Enfeebled

bombing doctrine, the small TAC contingent continued its attempts to obtain the Army Field Forces' concurrence with a joint tactical doctrine. Although command and control differences frustrated these attempts, the two organizations agreed to separate publication of a common directive for close air support procedures.

This final product, a *Joint Training Directive for Air-Ground Operations*, was published simultaneously by TAC and the Army Field Forces in September 1950, three months after the Korean War began. In general, it made only minor modifications to the close air support procedures contained in the earlier F.M. 31–35.

Air Force headquarters approved use of the directive for TAC in its training and instruction. The Air Force's hopes of elevating the directive to a uniform air-ground Defense Department doctrine, however, were dashed by objections from both the strategic-minded Evaluations Division of the Air Staff and the Air University.[142]

Seeking to redress what it perceived as a tilt too far in the direction of considering tactical air solely as support of ground campaigns, and ominously, for close air support, an air staff study in December stated that tactical air power could take action against enemy forces independently of friendly ground forces. It went so far as to question whether air forces should cooperate equally with ground forces.[143]

The fragmentation of doctrinal responsibility prevented the training directive from being issued as a department-wide statement of joint doctrine. While foreswearing any right to comment on the specific air-ground procedures contained in the directive, the Air University commander, citing his responsibility for doctrine on command and employment of air forces, deemed the document unacceptable on philosophical grounds. He disputed the first two paragraphs of the 195-page document that, in his view, set the doctrinal tone for all that followed. Specifically, he challenged the implication in those paragraphs that theaters of operation were always predominantly theaters of surface action, and its corollary that the general mission of tactical air forces was always that of supporting a surface battle to defeat surface forces. He further objected to the impression given in the document that gaining air superiority was nothing more than general support for a ground campaign, rather than a key element of an air campaign independent of surface activity.[144] Once again the issue of command and control posed a barrier to the issuance of a Department of Defense approved joint doctrine. Although never published as such, the Joint Training Directive became the operative doctrine for close air support during the Korean War.

The fortunes of close air support between 1945 and 1950 bear a similarity, in microcosm, to those of attack aviation between the two world wars—initial progress, followed by retrenchment. Just as the Air Service/Air Corps, during the first decade after the Great War, set out to improve attack aviation, there also was substantial acceptance by AAF leaders, immediately after World War II, of the idea of cooperating with the Army's surface forces. This was due partly to the successful performance of tactical air power, and particularly of its close air support component, during the conflict. The contribution of wartime close air support impressed those ground force commanders, especially General Eisenhower, whose support was essential in the upcoming debate over an independent Air Force. The AAF left no stone unturned in its campaign to strengthen support for its independence, and one important element of this campaign was the promise to the Army that Air Force tactical forces would continue to support it.

In addition, until 1947, the euphoria of victory was still in the air, and the future Cold War had yet to assume a definitive shape. The initial postwar reorganization of the AAF, by rejecting the idea of a combat command, institutionalized the distinction between strategic and tactical air power. This decision was based on the assumption that future wars would not differ substantially from the recently completed one that tactical air power, including close air support missions, had helped to win. Close air support advocates benefitted from this initial organization, which included a TAC working closely with its Army counterpart. Wartime cooperation between air and ground commanders carried over into these early postwar years. The collocation of the new TAC and the AGF headquarters in coastal Virginia represented a measure toward cooperation. An attempt to capture in writing the close air support lessons of the war, resulted in the issuance of the new F.M. 31–35 in 1946. Yet the sincerity, ingenuity, and hard work that went into trying to forge cooperation was insufficient to overcome the intractable underlying service differences over the nature of future warfare and the place that close air support would occupy in it.

These differences over air-ground cooperation were forced onto the front burner by the Air Force reorganization of 1948. Analogous to the demise of attack aviation in the 1930s, the advent of General Vandenberg accelerated an Air Force's emphasis on strategic bombing that was already underway and resulted in a cutback of close air support assets. Looking back on this period many years later, the leading figures of TAC, at the time, remembered it as one in which Air Force doctrine was alive and vigorous, but in which the availability of equipment, the tactical control system, and the number of people assigned to the numbered tactical air forces had all shrunk to a dangerous level. While internal Air Force doctrine was making some progress, joint doctrine for close air support stagnated. The demotion of the TAC made joint exercises with the Army unproductive. The Tactical Air Control System, which was the heart of close air support missions, was stagnating from a lack of continuity and of trained personnel. Furthermore, although the Army was reluctantly coming to accept jet aircraft as vehicles for close air support, it was insisting on a larger input for itself into the design of close air support planes,

Close Air Support Enfeebled

more air-ground training, air controllers better trained in air-ground tactics, and, above all, operational control of aircraft assigned to support its ground troops.[145]

Just how low the level of close air support resources, doctrine, and training, had fallen by the middle of 1950 was soon demonstrated after the North Korean attack on South Korea.

3 | Close Air Support in Korea

> The only assurance a ground commander can have that any supporting arm will be employed effectively, or at all, is by having operational control over that supporting arm.
> — Maj. Gen. Edward M. Almond, U.S. Army, 1951
>
> It is illegal to assign to any unit a weapon whose effective range far transcends the limits of the area for which the unit is responsible...The airplane should be no exception to this sound principle. It is equally unwise to restrict the potentialities of a weapon deliberately. The fallacy of the concept of the airplane as nothing more than a flying artillery was amply demonstrated in World War II.
>
> — Barcus Report, Dec 1950

The steady deterioration in both significance of and resources for close air support during the closing years of the 1940s was dramatically halted and temporarily reversed by the North Korean invasion of South Korea in June 1950, and the subsequent three years of peninsular warfare. The surprise Communist assault threw into relief, more starkly than could any other event, how unprepared were American air and ground forces to cooperate with each other on the battlefield. The outbreak of this conventional limited conflict should have put the lie to the idea that the weapons designed to deter nuclear war were adequate to prevent conventional conflict. Instead, the Korean struggle was seen by most influential decision makers as merely a diversionary first phase of a European conflict that could well become nuclear.

Help from Above

Previous emphasis on a nuclear future weakened America's arsenal of conventional planes, guns, and ammunition, and left its military personnel, both air and ground, without the experience they needed to respond quickly and effectively to the conventional invasion. The initial weeks of the war were particularly illustrative of the substandard condition of air-ground cooperation. The American military force structure both at home and in the Far East, geared to the air defense of the territory taken in World War II, was ill-equipped for offensive ground action. Aircraft and pilots were better prepared to defend Japan against a Soviet nuclear air attack than to support a ground war against invading North Koreans. Many of the basic requirements for successful air-ground cooperation and effective close air support were not in place at the beginning of hostilities. The paucity of communications and good intelligence was sorely felt. The absence of a network of airfields in South Korea severely limited close air support missions. The Air Force had no organization in place in the Far East for the centralized direction of multiservice American air strikes.

This lack of readiness was a result of the earlier inability of the Army and Air Force to agree on a joint doctrine for air-ground cooperation and, consequently, to improve cooperation through serious joint exercises. The Joint Training Directive of 1950, which improved somewhat on the earlier air-ground cooperation manuals, but failed to provide a joint doctrine for close air support, was not approved by both services until after the initial North Korean thrust was stopped and the perimeter established around Pusan.

Many of the close air support issues, which during peacetime had either become dormant or whose solution seemed to lack immediacy, once again assumed increased urgency. Differences of opinion sharpened over such questions as to what was the best close air support plane, who should control it, which tactics and techniques were most effective, how were communications between air and ground to be handled, which targets and armament were most productive, and who should determine them. Yet of all these and other close air support questions that were given new life in the Korean War, the most potent was also the oldest—the issue of command and control. Once again, as earlier, the positions of the antagonists in this controversy were colored by the conflicting interpretations of the nature of conventional warfare and the place that aircraft should occupy in it.

The War in Outline

Of the several potential flash points between communist and noncommunist forces around the globe in 1950, the former chose a showdown in June the Far East that contained the largest concentration of American overseas military forces. Four of the U.S. Army's five overseas divisions were in Japan, another was in Europe, and the five remaining divisions were at home. Eight of the Air Force's 48 wings, comprising about 1,172 aircraft, 350 of them combat planes, were also in the Far East—five in Japan and one each on Okinawa, Guam, and the Philippines. While 37 percent of the Navy's fleet was in the Pacific, only one-fifth of that was in Far Eastern waters.

At the beginning of June 1950, the forces in the Far East were part of General of the Army Douglas MacArthur's Far East Command (FEC). From his GHQ in Tokyo, MacArthur, who served as the Supreme Commander Allied Powers (SCAP) in Japan, sat as Far East Commander with three subordinate component commands to assist him, one for each of the participating services: the Naval Forces, Far East (NAVFE), commanded by Vice Adm. C. Turner Joy; the Far East Air Forces (FEAF), under the command of General Stratemeyer; and U.S. Army Forces, Far East (USAFFE), which MacArthur himself commanded. Two weeks after the war began, on July 8, MacArthur assumed the additional title of Commander in Chief, United Nations Command (CINCUNC). (These command arrangements are depicted at **Figure 7**.)

By making himself the de facto Commander in Chief of the Army Forces, Far East (CINCAFFE), MacArthur was able to use CINCAFFE's Army officers to staff his FEC headquarters. He defended his failure to create a truly separate Army component command on the grounds that to do so would duplicate his functions as Commander in Chief FEC (CINCFE) and create an unneeded bureaucratic layer between himself and the subordinate Army commands.[1]

The practical result of this peculiar arrangement, however, was that the FEC was a de facto Army command, peopled almost entirely with Army personnel, rather than a joint command with proportionate representation from the interested services.[2] This had the effect of elevating each of the subordinate Army commands (the Eighth Army, the Ryukus Command, and the Marianas-Bonin Command) to the level of FEAF and NAVFE. More critically, it assured

Lt. Gen. George E. Stratemeyer

Help from Above

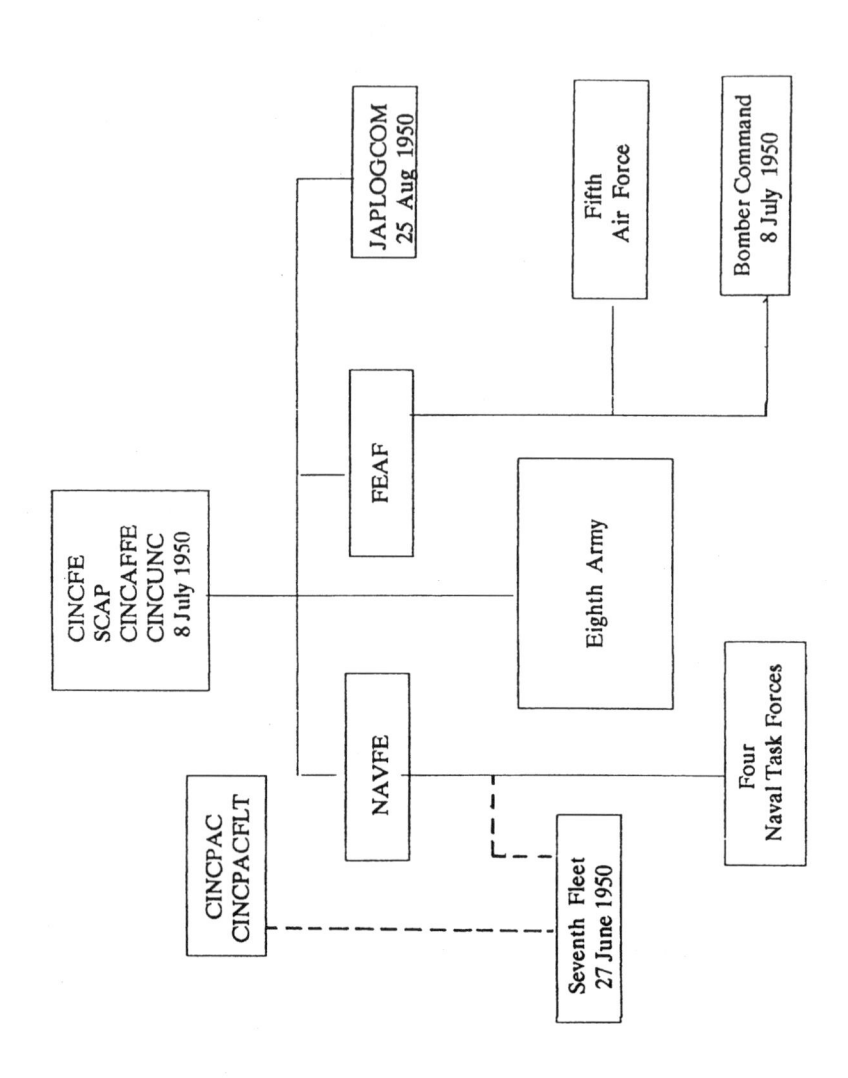

FIGURE 7
Far East Command, June–August 1950

that strategy, planning, and operations for the campaign in Korea were filtered through the prism of Army doctrine. This arrangement fractured the unity of command for air operations in several respects. Early in the war its poor knowledge of how to use air power led CINCFE to interfere "shamefully" in selecting targets and deciding which aircraft to use, both prerogatives that properly belonged to FEAF and the Fifth Air Force. Later, in preparing for the Inchon invasion, CINCFE again split control of the tactical air forces by giving the invading force, X Corps, its own (Marine) air component, thereby depriving the responsible command, Fifth Air Force, of control over theater naval assets and even many land-based aircraft.[3] Both the Navy and the Air Force objected to this melding of the Army and Far East commands, which virtually guaranteed that prewar Army and Air Force differences over the role of tactical air power, and particularly of close air support, would carry over into the new conflict.

Since 1949 Korea was outside MacArthur's command. When the 40,000 American troops withdrew from the peninsula in that year, there remained only a small 500-man advisory group, assigned to the U.S. Ambassador, to help train the Republic of Korea Army (ROKA), largely an internal constabulary force.

The mission of American ground forces in the Far East, before war erupted, was to support the occupation of the former enemy territories and to defend them against external attack. Consequently, the four army divisions in Japan, which were only at 70 percent of their authorized strength, contained large numbers of noncombat personnel. Their training had been essentially in defensive measures. They had not cross-trained with the Air Force in air-ground operations, since the need for such expertise was not foreseen.

Air Force units in the Far East were also there for defensive purposes. The sole mission of the eight Air Force wings and their supporting units in FEAF was to defend the captured islands.[4] Three of the five wings in Japan, which constituted the Fifth Air Force, were equipped with F–80C jet interceptors, with a sprinkling of F–82 propeller-driven twin mustangs for all-weather work. Closest to Korea, 130 miles from Pusan, was the 8th Fighter-Bomber Wing at Itazuke Air Base, on the southern island of Kyushu. The 49th Fighter Bomber Wing at Misawa Air Base, on the northern tip of Honshu and over 700 miles from Korea, was on alert against any air threat from the north. In between and close to Tokyo, at Yokota Air Base, was the 35th Fighter Interceptor Wing. The two remaining wings were a light-bomber wing of B–26s, the 3d, at Johnson Air Base near Tokyo, and the 374th Troop Carrier Wing at nearby Tachikawa Air Base. Rounding out FEAF's eight wings was a fighter-interceptor wing of F–80Cs on Okinawa, a fighter-bomber wing of F–80Cs in the Philippines, and a medium-bomber wing of B–29s on Guam.

As with the ground forces, defensive strategies, training, and equipment had permeated FEAF. Large, permanent ground radars, of limited utility in a fast-moving ground war, scanned the skies over Japan around the clock for

Help from Above

signs of enemy attack. Air-defense control centers were equipped primarily to direct aircraft against opposing planes rather than enemy ground forces. The aircraft were configured and armed, and the pilots trained, primarily for air-to-air combat. No joint training with ground forces had taken place in the Far East.

When six of the North Korean Peoples Army's (NKPA) eight infantry divisions, supported by Russian T–34 tanks, stabbed southward across the 38th Parallel on the morning of June 25, only three of South Korea's eight divisions were stationed around or north of Seoul to meet them (**Figure 8**). The others were in the southern part of the peninsula. Four of the NKPA divisions and two regiments headed down two corridors toward the South Korean capital, there to press down the main road system in the south. A fifth division pushed down the center of the peninsula, while a sixth moved southward down the east coast.

Seoul fell on June 28 as the South Korean retreat continued. Three days later the first American troops—an advanced party of the 24th Infantry Division—flew from Japan into Pusan, in the southeastern corner of South Korea. From there it moved quickly to a position north of Osan, 20 miles south of Seoul, in an attempt to slow down the advancing enemy along the main road system. Within two weeks the remainder of the division had arrived and taken up positions around Taejon. The 25th Infantry Division moved to Korea between July 11 and 15, followed by the 1st Cavalry Division between July 19 and 23. These three divisions formed the Eighth U.S. Army, Korea, whose forward headquarters were established 60 miles north of Pusan, at Taegu.

While the ground troops were deploying and fighting a rear guard action in South Korea, the Air Force experienced an equally sudden and wrenching alteration of its mission. In addition to continuing to defend Japan and the islands, it now was called upon to fight on the continent. Much of the debate over the Air Force's conviction that one type of airplane possessed enough flexibility to perform multiple tactical roles centered on how effectively the Air Force made the transition during these early days of the fighting in Korea.

To meet the emergency, the Air Force moved 18 of its 28 Far East squadrons closer to Korea, while simultaneously supporting the retreating Korean and American ground forces. The day after the invasion, the medium-bomber wing[5] of B–29s on Guam began a 1,200-mile move to Okinawa. The next day the fighter group from the northern Japanese base at Misawa started operating in Korea, while at the same time, moving its personnel and equipment southward to the Kyushu bases at Ashiya and Itazuke. That same day, July 27, the B–26s were also moved closer to the action, from Yokota to Ashiya. Between July 4 and 9 two additional B–29 wings were transferred to the Far East and began operations on the thirteenth of the month. At the same time, FEAF directed the Twentieth and Thirteen Air Forces on Okinawa and in

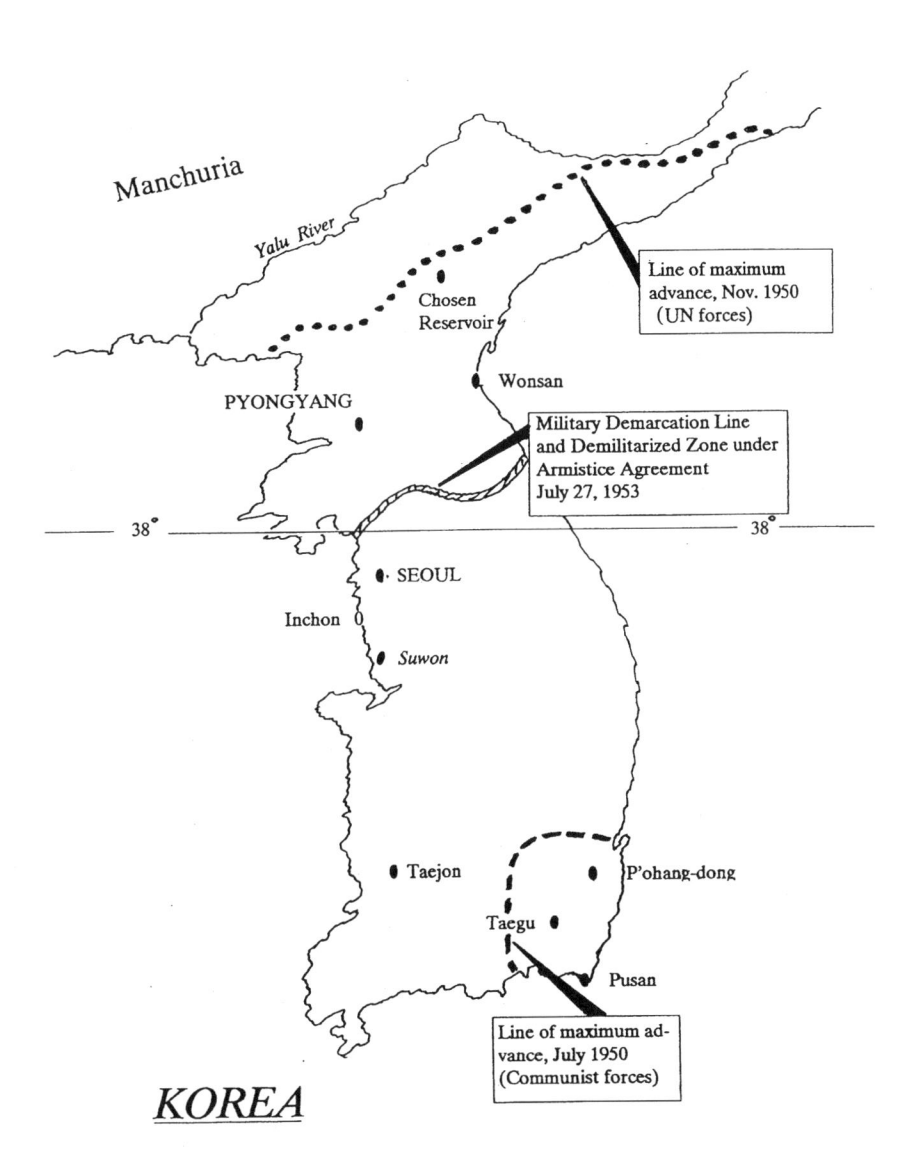

FIGURE 8
Korea

Help from Above

the Philippines to deliver all but 75 each their F–80s to Japan to reinforce the fighter units there.

For the first month of operations, which saw the steady advance of the North Koreans on all three fronts, FEAF attempted to compensate for the relative weakness in heavy artillery of the U.S and Korean ground troops with air power. Sixty-two percent (3,251) of FEAF's 5,232 sorties supported the South Korean and American ground forces. A mere 13 percent (689) tried to interdict units and equipment and destroy bridges behind enemy lines. The remaining flights contended with the weak North Korean Air Force, assisted in the evacuation of noncombatants, and flew reconnaissance missions.

At first, most of the close air support flights were performed by F–80Cs and a smaller number by B–26s, all from Japan. World War II F–51s, too, flew close air support missions after their arrival near the end of July. Even the newly arrived B–29s, at FEC's urging, joined in with some close air support missions. On July 14, for example, 10 of FEAF's 232 close air support sorties were flown by medium-bombers that attacked bridges and highway and railroad junctures in the battle area. For the following three days, B–29s flew, respectively, 10 of 267, 8 of 319, and 8 of 267 close support missions.

The results of these missions were disappointing, and Lt. Gen. Emmett O'Donnell, the commander of the FEAF Bomber Command that had been established on July 8, strongly opposed FEC's insistence on using the medium-bombers for close air support. Given the altitudes from which the bombers were forced to operate, he argued, the crews required more preflight time for target identification briefing than the FEC had been giving them. O'Donnell's point was brought home on the seventeenth when three B–29s, engaged in close support flights, accidentally bombed the wrong target, killing 22 Korean civilians. Still enamored of the medium-bombers in the close support role, MacArthur relented only to the point of instructing his operations people to allow 48 hours advance notice in all cases where B–29s were to be used for close air support.[6]

The fighter- and medium-bombers had other problems to contend with in providing close support. Inadequacies of communication and target information, adverse flying conditions, a lack of airfields in Korea, and the long distance from the battlefield to the Fifth Air Force bases in Japan, sharply curtailed this close air support during the early weeks of the war.[7] Probably the most serious of these impediments was the lack of communications and combat intelligence, since the ground forces lacked the ground communication the intelligence units needed to request air strikes. There was only one such unit in the Army, the 20th Signal Company, and it was in the states. The absence of this unit during the first four months of the war prevented the Army from establishing separate air communication nets for their G–2 and G–3 Air officers, for their clear-voice reconnaissance system, and for their ground liaison officers. All of these units were forced to use general command channels to

An air reconnaissance photo.

communicate, thereby overloading them and slowing down the operation of the air-ground system. The seriousness of this situation was illustrated on July 7 when Lt. Gen. William F. Dean, at the time commanding the ground forces in Korea, had to place a personal telephone call to General Stratemeyer in Japan, naming four targets for FEAF to attack.[8]

Photographic intelligence also suffered at the outset from the absence of an Army photo-reproduction team at the Joint Operations Center (JOC) and of Army photo-interpretation teams at the JOC as well as at corps and division headquarters. The absence of a photo-reproduction team wasted valuable time by having to develop photoreconnaissance prints at Itazuke in Japan and fly them back to the JOC. The lack of photo-interpretation teams at the JOC and at corps and division headquarters caused many profitable air targets to be missed completely or located too late to be useful.

The Air Force's sole Tactical Air Control Group, essential for providing communication and radar equipment for directing air strikes, was also stateside. As a result, pilots at first confined their close air support attacks almost entirely to the targets of opportunity they spotted while flying over the battlefield. In the absence of communications for a proper request net, various expedients were employed. Divisions had to request strikes by word of mouth, usually by sending a courier to an air unit. On one occasion, Lt. Col. Dean E. Hess, the commander of the first F–51 squadron in Korea, was awakened in his tent at three in the morning by couriers from the Advisory Group "sticking their heads in the tent and requesting an air strike over a city at a certain time and then they disappeared in the night." At times, even the ground force commanders personally made requests to the flyers. "We've had General Walker directing out there for two or three days at a time," and "we have had General

Help from Above

Kean in our own combat operations stating where they would like the air strikes made."[9]

The Air Force began to remedy this situation with the dispatch of the first two Tactical Air Control Parties (TACPs) to the theater on the last day of June, and by using T–6 training planes, called Mosquitoes, as airborne forward air controllers to direct fighters to their targets.

This lack of contact with the ground assured that most of these initial missions, although directly supporting the ground forces, were not particularly close air support missions, even though most reports called them that. Many were what would later come to be called battlefield air interdiction missions— that is, missions on the battlefield close enough to the front line to receive some direction by either a ground or airborne controller.[10] These missions struck, for the most part, tanks, roads, bridges, and clusters of enemy soldiers in the battle zone. As ground-to-ground and ground-to-air communications improved throughout July, these missions came more and more to resemble true close air support.

The short range of the F–80s, which were over 300 miles from the battlefield when the war started, left them only 10 or 15 minutes over the front lines, barely sufficient time to identify and attack targets when they were not controlled from the ground. On July 23, 145 F–51 Mustangs arrived in Japan aboard the carrier *Boxer*. Six of the F–80 squadrons were converted to these World War II fighters, and by early August were operating from fields at Pohangdong and Taegu in Korea and at Itazuke and Ashiya in Japan.

On July 5 Fifth Air Force set up a rudimentary JOC at 24th Division Headquarters at Taejon, but found no Army personnel to man the request side of the center, the Air Ground Operations System. As a stopgap measure, until the Army could supply personnel, the JOC borrowed some airmen and equipment from Air Force TACPs that by then had increased to six in the country.[11]

During these first chaotic weeks, the Army's and the Air Force's concepts were in harmony as to how tactical aircraft should be used to support the ground forces. The Air Force agreed to use its combat planes primarily to supplement firepower of the ground forces, at least until reinforcements arrived and the situation stabilized. Stratemeyer even ordered the three B–29 wings to assign close support as their first priority. The Army ground commanders were effusive in their praise of FEAF's tactical air support. To them this meant close air support, since it was all they could see. At the end of the first month of operations, General Dean told Stratemeyer that the Air Force had blunted the initial North Korean thrust and it was doubtful if he could have withstood the onslaught without this continuing air effort.[12] General Kean, the 25th Division commander, General MacArthur, and Maj. Gen. Walton H. Walker were equally impressed with the effectiveness of Fifth Air Force's close support.[13]

Close Air Support in Korea

Near the end of July, when it appeared likely to the Air Force that the United Nations' (UN) forces[14] would hold, the first fissure appeared in Army/Air Force unanimity on close air support. The split came about when Army officers on the FEC staff, unfamiliar with the employment of air power, wanted to continue using the B–29 medium-bombers almost exclusively for close air support. In conferences with General MacArthur and his chief of staff, Generals Almond and Stratemeyer emphasized the difficulties inherent in using the B–29s for close air support. He pointed out that bomber missions required extensive advanced planning to allow for thorough crew briefings and for placing proper armament on the aircraft. The length of time it took to prepare a B–29 for a mission made it impractical, he said, to change targets and missions on short notice. The B–29 program was being hampered by frequent mission changes at the eleventh hour.[15]

Behind these complaints lay the Air Force's conviction of the most effective ways to use tactical aircraft, which in this war included medium-bombers. By the end of the first month of fighting, sufficient forces had been rushed to the theater, or were on the way, to justify in Air Force eyes, a shift of priorities away from close air support and toward an interdiction program to isolate the battlefield. The Army, still being pushed back toward the southeastern corner of the peninsula, wanted to continue concentrating aerial firepower on the battlefield.

These conceptual differences were raised to the highest level during a visit to the theater by General Vandenberg in mid-July. In discussing the matter with MacArthur, the Air Force chief underscored his conviction that tactical air strikes against widely dispersed and well-entrenched enemy units on the battlefield would pay a much lower dividend in the long run than would an interdiction campaign against troops, supplies, and key transportation and communication lines leading to the battle area. While MacArthur agreed in principle with Vandenberg's view, he stressed that the extraordinary situation being faced by the ground forces required that the preponderance of FEAF's effort continue to be used for close air support, regardless of its relative value compared to other roles.[16]

This disagreement came to a head over the question of how to use the medium-bombers. As it became apparent that the UN forces were not going to be evicted from the peninsula, the fissure widened between the Army-dominated Target Selection Group at GHQ and the Air Force's FEAF Target Section. The Target Selection Group in Tokyo was an ad hoc committee composed of an Army colonel from GHQ's intelligence section, who had been an information and education specialist and military attaché; an Army lieutenant colonel from GHQ's operations section; a military policeman, who had been an intelligence staff officer with Ninth Army during World War II; and a naval commander, who had been a carrier gunnery officer. The recommendations of these part-time targeters went directly to Gen. Edward M. Almond, who normally strongly supported them.[17]

Help from Above

Frequent and often heated differences between the two targeting organizations made it necessary at times to buck target-priority problems up to MacArthur for his personal decision. Stratemeyer found this situation intolerable and pleaded for an overall agreement on the role of tactical planes.[18]

On July 20, MacArthur approved a recommendation by Stratemeyer to establish a Joint Target Selection Board comprising general officers from both Army and Air Force. Appointed to the Board were the FEC's Vice Commander and Intelligence Officer, Gens. Doyle D. Hickey and Charles A. Willoughby respectively, and General Weyland, who two days earlier had arrived from the Air Staff as FEAF chief of operations.

Weyland lost little time in pushing for the recognition of the Air Force's tripartite tactical air doctrine among the Army officers in the FEC. On July 23, he sent a memo to the FEC's chief of operations, noting that the targets the FEC had been coming up with were wrong, being too numerous and too small to be identified by B–29 bombardiers. The poor results to date of using medium-bombers as close air support vehicles, and particularly the accidental bombing on the seventeenth, showed that the aircraft were being misused. He recommended that targeting be turned over to FEAF, which would plan a proper interdiction program to isolate the battlefield.[19]

This memo energized MacArthur's volatile chief of staff, General Almond, a man, according to the Army's official history, both feared and obeyed throughout the FEC.[20] Before the war, Almond attended the Air Corps Tactical School with the result, according to Maj. Gen. Earle E. Partridge who befriended him at the school, that Almond believed "he knew more about employing aircraft than anyone in the world." Partridge, among others, characterized the Chief of Staff as a "very difficult guy to work with…who flew off at the slightest provocation…and got purple in the face."[21] Of all the Army generals in Korea, Almond took the greatest detailed interest in air support and proved to be the most critical of the Air Force's system.

The day after Weyland submitted his memo, Almond called the members of the newly created Joint Target Selection Board into his office and strongly criticized Weyland's views. MacArthur, he said, had not approved an interdiction program along the lines suggested by Weyland, the medium-bombers must continue to provide close air support in the immediate battle area, and FEAF was being uncooperative and causing trouble.

Almond tried to end the session by asking Weyland if he understood the directives Almond had given him. Weyland, unintimidated, responded that he did not, since MacArthur had clearly and unequivocally approved the interdiction program in a personal discussion with Stratemeyer. He went on to point out that he had worked closely and effectively with General Patton during World War II, but that the cooperative attitude he had enjoyed then was missing in the FEC, where policy was being dictated from above without due regard for the tactical air aspects of the problem. The Board had been established, he concluded, for the express purpose of exchanging viewpoints and working out mutually satisfactory selection of targets, and he intended to continue to express his views.

The board members continued to voice their divergent viewpoints after Almond's departure. The Army officers stressed the critical nature of the ground situation, where three U.S. divisions were facing nine enemy divisions. They argued the Air Force did not hit targets when directed, and that only a small percentage of FEAF's planes were flying close air support missions. They complained that Fifth Air Force did not have enough planes to do the necessary close support job by itself.

Weyland responded that the situation had been critical since the beginning of the war, and, therefore, critical had become normal. It was time to back off from day-to-day operational problems and take a longer view from the standpoint of the ultimate outcome of the struggle. The old GHQ Target Section Group had specified far too many targets in the battle area and many of these were unidentifiable. There were many technical difficulties in having the medium-bombers operate in the same area with Fifth Air Force's fighter-bombers and light-bombers. Almond's claim that the Air Force was not operating as directed was untrue. Far East Air Forces' aircraft had followed directives every day since June 25. The relatively low percentage of B–29s operating in the battle area was due to bad weather, not bad attitude. Since these bombers operated at higher altitudes than the fighters and light-bombers, the low clouds and poor visibility which characterized the period had a greater

Lt. Gen. Otto P. Weyland (left) and Lt. Gen. Earle E. Partridge (right).

Help from Above

adverse effect on the B–29s than on the other aircraft. Fifth Air Force, he concluded, far from lacking enough planes, had, according to its commander, General Partridge, more fighter-bombers than there were profitable targets in the battle area.

As a result of these discussions, the Board proposed, and MacArthur subsequently approved, a plan to use two of the medium-bomber wings in a systematic interdiction program to isolate the battlefield, retaining the third wing for close air support.[22] Although on this occasion both sides modified their desires—for more close air support by the Army, and for more interdiction by the Air Force—it was clear that the basic underlying doctrines remained undisturbed.

The first phase of the war, the UN retreat, came to an end early in August as the North Korean drive, slowed by interdiction attacks against their overextended lines of communication, ground to halt. By August 4, the UN forces had established a 100 x 50-mile defensive perimeter around the southeastern port of Pusan.

Defense of this perimeter against frequent major enemy attacks, which constituted the second phase of the war, lasted from August 4th until September 18. Fifth Air Force planes, providing close air support to the Eighth Army, were joined by two Marine squadrons flying carrier-based propeller-driven Corsairs and by Navy planes also flying from carriers. The Marine pilots flew principally in support of the provisional 1st Marine Brigade that was temporarily attached to the Eighth Army.

General Headquarters now agreed that the situation had become stabilized enough to divert some planes to interdiction missions. On August 4, it authorized B–29 interdiction attacks south of the 38th Parallel, and two weeks later, on the twenty-fifth, it approved the diversion of a larger number of Fifth Air Force fighters to interdiction measures north of the parallel. Whereas in July, 61 percent of all FEAF's sorties flew close air support missions, many of them by B–29s, this figure dropped to 48 percent in August. Conversely, the percentage of interdiction sorties rose in August to 20 percent from 14 percent the preceding month.[23] Although close air support sorties continued to outnumber those devoted to interdiction, the real story is told in the composition of these sorties. Almost one-fifth of the interdiction sorties that ravaged communication and transportation lines and supplies in the north after August 4, were performed by B–29s, whose armament loads far outweighed those of the fighter- and light-bombers flying close air support missions in the south.

This tilt toward interdiction widened further the gap between FEAF, which wanted to limit the volume of what it considered relatively unproductive close air support missions, and the ground forces who argued for all the fire support they could obtain. Even so, the move toward more interdiction was interrupted on several occasions by enemy attempts to pierce the perimeter. During a fierce four-day battle early in August, for example, close air support

Close Air Support in Korea

strikes helped the 24th Division throw back a determined enemy drive that succeeded in crossing the Naktong river, the western boundary of the perimeter. On August 31, the NKPA opened a concerted series of attacks all along the perimeter, and by September 6 had reached within eight miles of Taegu. General Walker's ability to shift his forces along interior lines within the perimeter, assisted by a growing preponderance of ground forces and devastating close air support and interdiction strikes, brought the threat to an end by the twelfth of the month.[24]

Since the Marine squadrons involved in defending the perimeter were designed and trained to provide flying artillery support for landing ground forces, they were organized to emphasize their subordination to the infantry. Each Marine division owned its own wing of Marine aircraft, complete with ground control intercept and tactical air control squadrons. Each Marine infantry battalion had its own air observers, the equivalent of the TACPs in the Army/Air Force system.

While supporting the Eighth Army in the southwestern end of the Pusan perimeter, the Marine squadrons were in some ways operating in an alien environment. The basic directive for control of aircraft when Marine, Navy, and FEAF planes were assigned missions in Korea, gave "coordination control" to General Stratemeyer.[25] Being self-contained for close air support, many of the Marine support units duplicated those of Fifth Air Force and adjustments were made. When the Marine squadrons were supporting their own Marine infantry, they were excused from reporting to the JOC and were allowed to use their own air control system. They dedicated 45 missions per day to close air support of Marine ground units.

Between August 7 and 14, Eighth Army elements on the extreme left wing of the perimeter, called Task Force Kean and composed of two Army regiments and the one provisional Marine brigade, tried unsuccessfully to coun-

A Boeing B–29 after a mission over North Korea.

Help from Above

Enemy fuel truck hit by F–51 east of Kumchon (top); F–80 attacks on North Korean tanks. Photo taken by gun camera (bottom).

Close Air Support in Korea

terattack and push the North Korean 6th Division westward. Following initial successes in the mountaintop fighting, the UN forces ended the one-week campaign where they had begun.[26] Marine air saw action for the first time, with two carrier-based squadrons supporting principally the Marine infantry on a narrow, 10-mile segment of the front. At the same time the eight squadrons of FEAF's fighter bombers were supporting, not only the Army and ROKA units on that flank, but along the entire 150-mile length of the perimeter.

The Eighth Army's first experience in Korea with Marine close air support came during this counterattack and showed how pervasive was the desire among many Army officers for tighter control of Air Force close air support aircraft. On the very day that the unsuccessful counteroffensive ended, August 14, a United Press correspondent published a syndicated article that, while not alluding to the ultimate failure of the campaign, described how at one point the Army had become bogged down while the Marines had driven back the North Koreans using a deadly new battle tactic—close air support. This "new" tactic, wrote the author, that had taken the Marines eight years to develop and constituted the most destructive weapon the enemy had faced since the war began, featured Marine propeller-driven planes, which were superior to the Air Force's jets, directed from control jeeps below, striking enemy units only 50 yards ahead of Marine troops. This, claimed the author, was at last a scientific approach to the coordination of air and ground forces.[27]

Pressured by the Air Staff to look into these claims of superiority of Marine tactical air over FEAF's close air support, Stratemeyer solicited the reaction of, among others, General Walker, who commanded the operation. After acknowledging certain inaccuracies in the article—the claimed 50 yards, for example, was more like 300—and reiterating his earlier praise for the support he had received from Fifth Air Force, the Eighth Army commander continued: "I must say that I, in common with a vast majority of officers in the Army, feel strongly that the Marine system of close air support has much to commend it."

The features of the Marine system that appealed to Walker were that Marine aviation was designed, equipped, and trained for the sole purpose of close air support, and that, by training constantly with ground units, the Marines had perfected air-ground communication and coordination. He particularly appreciated the fact that the Marines had Tactical Air Support Parties at every level down to and including the infantry battalion, and that they were able to keep their Corsairs over the battlefield at all times. "In short," wrote Walker to a disappointed Stratemeyer, "...I feel strongly that the Army would be well advised to emulate the Marine Corps and have its own tactical support aviation."

Stratemeyer saw in this reply a reflection of what he termed an "undercover campaign" spearheaded by the commander of the Army Field Forces, Gen. Mark W. Clark, to secure tactical aviation as part of the Army.[28] In

Help from Above

response, the FEAF commander pointed out that, far from becoming bogged down, the two army regiments in Task Force Kean had been three to five miles ahead of the Marines and had to wait for them to catch up. He disputed the "newness" of the close air support tactic by pointing out that, not only had the Air Force employed essentially the same system of close air support in World War II, but FEAF had been supporting the ground forces successfully in Korea daily for 51 days.[29]

The Marines, continued Stratemeyer, were indeed able to keep aircraft overhead continuously because they were guarding 3,000 men across a very narrow front, "frequently measured in yards," while FEAF close support aircraft were defending 150 miles of battlefront. Fifth Air Force was doing this so effectively, in the FEAF commander's judgment, that the ground forces or airborne controllers were often unable to produce targets as rapidly as the fighter-bombers were destroying them.[30] Were the Marine system of dedicated aircraft and continuous coverage over the battlefield extended from their narrow front to the entire perimeter, it would prove economically and militarily impossible. If extended to a proposed Army of 100 division, the Marine system would require 7,500 aircraft just for that one mission. Even General Walker, realizing the impracticality of this, modified his underlying desire for the Army to adopt the Marine system by noting that "even if our economy were many times as strong as it actually is, we could not support such a program."[31] The Air Force preferred to keep its close air support aircraft on alert, from which they could be directed to any segment of the perimeter that needed immediate assistance.

As for TACPs, Stratemeyer pointed out that the Air Force had at the time 20 TACPs, plus Mosquito airborne controllers, operating with the ground forces along the entire perimeter. Since there were four divisions there, this amounted to five TACPs per division as opposed to the normal Marine complement of one control party per regiment, or three per division. Furthermore, the FEAF commander saw it as an established fact that propeller-driven aircraft could operate only as long as they were unopposed by modern enemy jets. The F–80, in his opinion, could do everything the slower and more vulnerable F–51 could do and could do it better.

Walker's reaction suggested that the desire of some within the Army to acquire its own tactical aviation was reaching to higher levels. It had not yet risen to the top, however.[32] General Joseph L. Collins, the Army Chief of Staff, had indicated in several conversations with Stratemeyer that he was satisfied with FEAF's efforts and cooperation and, like General Eisenhower before him, opposed the idea of the Army possessing its own tactical air capability.[33] As subsequent developments will show, this probably represented, not so much an abandonment of the Army's desire to control close air support, as a tactical retrenchment that, while acknowledging the current political and economic unreality of the Army possessing its own tactical air force, continued to chip

Close Air Support in Korea

away at the existing air-ground system. The subsequent measures taken in this indirect approach would include proposals for dedicating tactical aircraft to specific ground units, developing aircraft solely for the close air support mission, extending operational control of tactical air downward to corps commanders, increasing the number of TACPs (which gave the Army a larger measure of control of strikes), and Army participation in the development of close air support aircraft.

During the six weeks of defending the Pusan perimeter, Fifth Air Force planes flew over 10,000 close air support sorties with an additional 6,000 devoted to interdiction strikes.[34] Medium-bombers from the FEAF Bomber Command joined in the latter. On September 1 the two Marine squadrons were withdrawn from the lines to prepare for the coming landing at Inchon.

MacArthur's staff in Tokyo continued to press for, and FEAF's Bomber Command continued to resist, using B–29s for close support operations around the perimeter. Stratemeyer was caught in the middle. The medium-bombers did fly one such mission on August 16 against North Korean forces that crossed the Naktong River, creating a powerful salient on its east side. Ninety-eight B–29s dropped 1,000 tons of high-explosive bombs on a three-by-seven-mile rectangle where an estimated four enemy divisions and several armored regiments were believed to have concentrated opposite the 1st Cavalry Division. Since Eighth Army forces did not enter the area after the bombing, however, no one was able to prove any military advantage to the operation.

A second close air support carpet-bombing mission had been planned for three days later. Once again the Air Force view of the most effective use of its aircraft came into conflict with the Army staff in Tokyo where General Almond, despite opposition to the second mission from Generals Stratemeyer, Partridge, Walker, and O'Donnell, insisted that the second mission be performed as planned. Stratemeyer brought his objections directly to MacArthur.

The medium-bombers, he informed the FEC commander, would create a "serious hazard" to our own front line troops. Further, the area selected for the air attack provided cover to the enemy ground forces, which would greatly reduce the effectiveness of the carpet-bombing. Citing Walker's evaluation, he noted that the use of the B–29s might be advantageous if the ground troops were prepared to follow-up with a breakthrough, since the main advantage of carpet-bombing was psychological shock and disruption. Fighter-bombers and light-bombers, however, were better suited for such a limited attack, which was designed only to reduce the salient and drive the enemy across the Naktong River. Further, when B–29s were operating in an area, it was necessary to curtail fighter-bomber and light-bomber operations. It would be better to use Navy carrier planes rather than B–29s to supplement FEAF's tactical strikes, since these would not interfere as greatly with the operation. In addition, the B–29s had been targeted for interdiction strikes up north to help isolate the

Help from Above

area around Seoul to prepare for the September 15 invasion at Inchon. Diversion of the bombers from this mission to close air support around the southern perimeter would jeopardize these critical northern plans. Finally, the supply of 500-lb. bombs used by FEAF's Bomber Command was critical and should be used only to prepare for Inchon. MacArthur, convinced by Stratemeyer's arguments, called off the proposed mission, undoubtedly adding to Almond's perception of the Air Force as uncooperative.[35]

Navy carrier planes were also active in close air support around the perimeter, leading to a major command and control flap with the Air Force. The July 8 directive on command and control gave to FEAF operational control of all Navy and Marine aircraft performing FEAF missions. Such was the case with the close air support operations around the perimeter. This meant that Navy planes coming off the carriers had to check in first to the JOC, which then directed them to either a TACP or an airborne Mosquito plane to control their strikes. In prewar training exercises, the Navy had been reluctant to relinquish control of their planes to Air Force control, and this reluctance turned to strong dissatisfaction in Korea. Navy pilots and their commanders complained at length about the inefficiency of the system. In many cases where both Air Force and Navy strike planes were over the same target, the controllers gave preference to Air Force jets which, flying from Japan, had a very short time over the target and had to expend their armament quickly to return home. As a result, the Navy planes were frequently made to wait until their loiter time ran out. In addition, Navy pilots complained about poor communications that often resulted in their being unable to contact ground controllers and being forced to jettison their cargoes unproductively before returning to ship.

The third phase of the war began on September 15, 1950, with the landing of UN forces behind enemy lines near Seoul at Inchon and the breakout of the Eighth Army from their Pusan confinement three days later. The Inchon landing force, which included the 1st Marine Division, was supported by Marine and Navy planes. Far East Air Force's prior interdiction campaign and earlier destruction of the small North Korean Air Force played a major role in keeping the landing area virtually free from enemy air and ground forces. To the south, however, FEAF's close air support was critical to the fortunes of the Eighth Army.

On September 18, preparing the way for the northward surge of the UN ground forces, 49 B–29s, diverted from the interdiction campaign, struck the point of the breakthrough near Waegwan, while Fifth Air Force planes flew 286 additional close support sorties. The following day this number jumped to 361, with Mustangs dropping napalm and strafing enemy positions within 50 yards of the front lines. The reinforced UN forces, now made up of the newly formed I Corps and led by a wedge of close air support aircraft, broke out of the Pusan confinement near Waegwan and pursued a demoralized disintegrating NKPA northward. The Eighth Army moved 170 miles in 11 days and linked up with the X Corps near Suwon on September 29.

In September close air support sorties outnumbered interdiction sorties by only 39 percent to 25 percent, and by October, as the allies pushed the enemy past the 38th Parallel and into North Korea, the interdiction effort surpassed that devoted to close air support by a margin of 28 percent to 19 percent (**Figure 9**).[36] The need for intensive ground support decreased between the end of September through most of November. Air Force commanders viewed these developments as justification of their insistence on flexibility, which allowed them to shift missions along with the changing vicissitudes of the war.

A further conflict between Army and Air Force positions on control of support aircraft took place as the northward moving Eighth Army entered the X Corps zone in the Inchon/Seoul area. General Almond, a leading opponent of the "cooperation type support" that was agreed upon by the Army and the Air Force, was given command of the X Corps Inchon invasion force, which was made up of the 1st Marine Division, the 7th Infantry Division, and a regiment of Korean Marines. In accord with Navy doctrine for amphibious operations, air cover for the landing was supplied by naval carrier aircraft. On September 21, after the troops were safely ashore, and during the march to nearby Seoul, Almond took command of all units (including land-based Marine air units) in the Seoul Objective Area. When the Seoul Objective Area was disestablished on October 3, the land-based Marine air was supposed to revert to FEAF's operational control.[37]

Anticipating the disestablishment of the objective area and the return of control of aircraft to FEAF, on September 25 General Partridge sought to move a fighter-bomber wing to Suwon airfield, inside the objective area just south of Seoul. His purpose was to advance his units to forward bases as rapidly as they were secured by friendly ground forces, thereby placing him in a position to render the most effective close air support to the Eighth Army. This move was preparatory to FEAF's assumption of operational control of all land-based missions. Almond, however, was reluctant to relinquish control of his Marine planes, even though he, as MacArthur's chief of staff, had earlier signed the directive granting FEAF "operational control of naval land-based air when not in execution of naval missions."[38]

Three days later, Almond approved the deployment of Partridge's wing to Suwon, but only on the condition that "all tactical aircraft operating in this area will be under the control of the X Corps Tactical Air Command," that is, himself. Partridge, already suspicious of Almond's views from his earlier encounters with him, was furious. In his view, to consent to have his unit controlled by X Corps simply because the newly recovered airfield lay within the Objective Area, would lessen his control over his own unit and weaken his ability to provide close air support to Walker. Also, to yield to Almond now would

Help from Above

Month	Close Support	Inter-diction	Counter Air	Recon naissance	TOTAL COMBAT	TOTAL COMBAT SUPPORT
Total	92,603	221,162	86,818	60,971	461,554	249,332
July 50	3,942	2,256	546	336	7,080	1,419
August	6,774	3,912	317	659	11,662	3,924
September	6,250	3,528	126	676	10,580	5,259
October	3,340	4,551	117	565	8,573	8,061
November	3,652	4,210	916	664	9,442	8,674
December	3,336	6,462	760	748	11,306	6,878
January 51	2,671	7,794	876	1,322	12,663	7,711
February	3,002	6,178	536	1,332	11,048	7,662
March	5,405	7,371	1,159	2,259	16,194	7,592
April	2,598	8,655	1,576	1,847	14,676	7,935
May	2,824	8,224	1,748	1,602	14,398	9,091
June	2,030	7,037	1,599	1,658	12,324	9,071
July	1,084	5,939	1,011	1,469	9 503	6,411
August	818	6,565	1,148	1,673	10,204	7,252
September	862	8,686	1,561	2,947	14,056	5,255
October	1,000	9,753	1,981	3,219	15,953	5,934
November	1,136	8,735	1,118	2,689	13,678	5,488
December	302	8,347	2,291	2,701	13,641	5,687
January 52	394	6,805	2,451	2,303	11,953	6,628
February	162	6,268	2,624	1,636	10,690	6,282
March	1,081	6,437	3,427	1,675	12,620	7,033
April	711	6,288	3,870	1,759	12,628	5,913
May	1,031	8,126	5,151	2,428	16,736	7,218
June	1,910	5,603	2,883	2,169	12,565	7,071
July	2,082	4,104	2,673	1,396	10,255	6,379
August	1,854	4,978	2,923	1,723	11,478	6,859
September	1,822	5,120	3,649	1,655	12,246	6,685
October	3,009	6,357	4,321	1,942	15,629	7,342
November	2,416	5,330	2,614	1,630	11,990	5,756
December	1,713	5,650	3,557	1,554	12,474	6,721
January 53	1,218	5,714	3,579	1,593	12,104	6,786
February	1,545	4,858	2,936	1,235	10,574	6,009
March	1,187	4,264	3,741	1,660	10,852	7,189
April	2,617	5,310	4,955	2,022	14,904	8,190
May	3,887	4,706	4,831	1,654	15,078	8,186
June	7,078	3,450	4,210	1,465	16,203	7,705
July	5,860	3,591	3,037	1,106	13,594	6,076

Source: Operations Statistics Division, DCS/Comptroller, USAF, Table 21.

FIGURE 9
FEAF Sorties, June 26, 1950–July 27, 1953

Close Air Support in Korea

create greater control problems later, when the Objective Area was disestablished, over the Marine air resources that had just settled in at Kimpo. Partridge wired Stratemeyer that Almond's precondition was unacceptable. The wing would not be moved to Suwon unless it was clearly understood by all concerned that command and control of the units remained with him.[39] Stratemeyer appealed to MacArthur, arguing that all Fifth Air Force units established in the X Corps area must remain centralized under Fifth Air Force to carry out their overall missions. Since the Inchon operation had passed well beyond the amphibious phase, he noted, "control of all land-based aircraft, including Marines remaining at Kimpo, must pass to the Commanding General, FEAF," as set forth in the policy letter of July 8.[40] The issue over who should control the Fifth Air Force units within the Objective Area was overtaken by events when collateral combat damage by the invading 7th Infantry Division so chewed up the airfield at Suwon that Partridge was unable to move his aircraft there until after the Objective Area was disestablished. The other part of the issue, namely control of the land-based Marine planes at Kimpo, remained an open sore and clearly indicated future trouble over the issue of control when the X Corps repeated its amphibious operation at Wonsan.

MacArthur agreed, and on October 1 placed the elements of the 1st Marine Air Wing at Kimpo under FEAF's control, but with the understanding that Almond would resume control when he embarked on his forthcoming second amphibious invasion against Wonsan on the east coast.[41] Although Almond's appetite for direct control of close air support aircraft was temporarily curbed, his favorable impression of Marine close air support was to influence his future opinions and, through him, those of the Army's chief of staff.

Close air support of the Eighth Army continued to occupy the majority of Fifth Air Force's planes until the end of September. In October, as Walker's forces continued their northward push, the number of interdiction sorties outpaced those devoted to ground support. With a prohibition against bombing north of the Yalu River boundary with Manchuria, however, and as the distance between the front lines and the Yalu River shrunk, the number of profitable interdiction targets decreased. Yet from October 1950 until the final month of combat, June 1953, with a few memorable exceptions, Air Force close air support sorties were overshadowed by interdiction and armed reconnaissance flights, sometimes by a ratio as high as twenty-five to one.[42]

As preparations for the Wonsan landing proceeded, a tug of war developed over control of the Marine airplanes at Kimpo. Although MacArthur had given control of them to Partridge until they were needed for the Wonsan operation, a disagreement ensued between Almond and FEAF over when and how these Marine resources would proceed to Wonsan. The operational plan called for the Marine units to revert to Almond's control, process out through the port of Inchon, sail around the peninsula, and land at Wonsan.[43] Far East Air Forces objected to this plan, maintaining that the Marine air units should remain under Fifth Air Force's control for supporting the Eighth Army until the last minute, and then be flown across the peninsula to Wonsan. To follow the operational plan would be to immobilize these units for two weeks before Wonsan at a critical time in Walker's offensive. Further, at the time of the discussion ROKA forces were approaching Wonsan, and it was apparent they would capture it within days. It appeared unrealistic to FEAF to withdraw Marine close air support from Walker for even a limited period of time.[44] Weyland's oral briefing of this view convinced the Navy and Marine commanders, and the Marine planes were retained at Kimpo until the field at Wonsan was secure and operational.

Almond's measures regarding close air support were the boldest attempt of any Army commander in Korea (or Washington) to act on an increasingly widespread conviction within the Army, "contrary to all written documents," that ground commanders should have control of all types of firepower that support their forces. Most other commanders either straddled or ignored the issue. MacArthur, for example, responding to a claim in *Time* magazine that he was behind the Army's fight to take tactical aviation away from the Air Force, told Stratemeyer that nothing could be farther from the truth.[45]

As he had at Inchon, however, Almond attempted to retain control of his own close air support resources, still the 1st Marine Air Wing. Although the landing at Wonsan was an administrative rather than a combat landing, requiring no close air support, Almond and the FEC treated it as a combat operation by applying the command and control procedures of a true amphibious landing. For example, control of close air support planes remained in the hands of the ground commander, Almond, until the amphibious landing area was discontinued. Weyland and Partridge objected to this delineation, seeing it as a fiction perpetrated so as to exclude FEAF from the northeastern part of Korea.

The suspicions of the Air Force commanders seemed justified when, after the forces of X Corps were ashore, Almond proved reluctant to give up his "own" air force. While planning for the landing, Weyland earlier had dissuaded MacArthur from making the Marine Air Wing a separate air command and giving it to X Corps. He pointed out to the UN commander that such an arrangement contravened both the official roles and missions agreement for U.S. forces, in which the Air Force was to support the Army (X Corps contained both a U.S. Army and a ROKA division), as well as MacArthur's own directive of July 8 giving operational control of all land-based close air support aircraft to FEAF when they were used for FEAF missions.[46]

As soon as he was ashore, Almond claimed that the poor communications made it impractical for him, on the east coast, to rely on the JOC across the mountainous peninsula at Seoul. Due to geography, poor communications, and personal antipathy, X Corps on the east coast was not placed under the western Eighth Army, but rather remained a separate task force. The self-imposed isolation of X Corps from Eighth Army and from Fifth Air Force's

JOC continued even after it established teletype communications with Eighth Army and radio communications with GHQ in Tokyo at the end of October.[47]

A tug of war ensued between Almond and FEAF over the question of X Corps sending, as called for by F.M. 31–35, G–2 Air and G–3 Air officers to handle close air support requests at the JOC. In a meeting with Partridge on November 3, Almond maintained that it would be a waste to send these officers, since the poor state of communications would prevent them from operating effectively. Instead, he would send a liaison officer. Partridge reminded the X Corps commander that communications for the Tactical Air Control System were the responsibility of the Army.[48] He was convinced that this was more of a doctrinal than a communications issue.

At the meeting Almond also renewed an earlier request for additional TACPs from Fifth Air Force for his forces. In a difference of opinion with FEAF, Almond considered TACPs superior to airborne controllers, probably because he had more control over the earthbound Air Force parties that were collocated with his ground forces. The Mosquito controllers, on the other hand, returned to their air bases after each mission. Also, it was undeniable that TACPs had much more intimate contact with the ground forces they were supporting, and consequently were more familiar with the details of ground operations. Although Partridge promised to provide four more TACPs when he could get them, he clearly felt that Almond had exceeded his share of the control parties.[49]

The situation was resolved by compromise. X Corps did not send G–2 Air or G–3 Air officers to the JOC, thereby signaling that it could perform its mission without close air support from the Air Force. Partridge offered Almond whatever Fifth Air Force air support he would need but, as a practical matter, none was needed or requested. All but one of the major urban objectives of the northward drive were on the coast, within range of naval gunfire. The Marine air units proved to be more than sufficient to provide air support further inland. Enemy resistance was light as X Corps drove toward the Yalu. Still Almond's stance posed a doctrinal problem to the Air Force, particularly in light of the fact that Almond was in constant contact by letter with General Clark at the Army Field Forces and with the Army Chief of Staff, General Collins.[50]

The doctrinal controversy was ratcheted up a notch when, on November 16, Almond asked Stratemeyer for 34 more TACPs. To Stratemeyer this request made "about as much sense as if…I had told him to have ten nicely upholstered sedans, painted Air Force blue, to meet me at the airfield at Yong-po Dong when I landed." On a visit two days later, Partridge told Almond that he did not at the moment have enough qualified pilots to satisfy his request and, further, that he could not supply the parties until X Corps sent the JOC the communications and personnel it was supposed to. Almond replied that he knew that, but had made the request to get it on the record. The record was one he was keeping of the Air Force's "unwillingness" to cooperate.[51]

Help from Above

Almond's readiness to herald the superiority of Marine close air support over that of the Air Force was a source of puzzlement to FEAF's commanders, since Almond had never, throughout his operations in Korea, experienced Air Force support.[52] Those Army commanders who had been supported by FEAF, on the other hand, were effusive in their praise of Fifth Air Force's support. During the summer retreat of June and July, General Walker had admitted that if it had not been for the Fifth Air Force, his army would not have been able to stay in Korea. In July, before his capture by the North Koreans, General Dean, commander of the 24th Division, avowed that without Fifth Air Force's close air support it was doubtful that his thinly spread troops could have could have withstood the onslaught by a vastly superior enemy.[53] During the defense of the Pusan perimeter in August and early September, General Kean, the 25th Division commander, credited Fifth Air Force with saving his division "as they have many times before."[54] General Hobart R. Gay, whose 1st Cavalry Division captured the North Korean capital of Pyongyang on October 19, told Partridge that it could not have been done without Fifth Air Force's "magnificent" close air support. When it appeared that victory was within grasp early in November, Walker again praised the Air Force in Korea for its support of the Eighth Army.[55] This discrepancy between the views of those Army commanders who had operated with Air Force close air support and Almond, who had not, convinced the FEAF air leaders that the X Corps commander's opinions emanated from a preconceived doctrinal position rather from the combat experience in Korea.

The fourth phase of the Korean War began on November 26, 1950, when the Chinese Communist Army, which had been infiltrating from Manchuria, launched a full-scale offensive against the UN forces in both the western and central sectors of the front. Air power was not able to prevent the Chinese counterattack because, since October, the bomb line was on the Yalu River in many places, and aircraft were prohibited from bombing across the river. There was little room for interdiction.

A month after the Chinese offensive opened, Lt. Gen. Matthew B. Ridgway replaced General Walker, who was killed in an automobile accident. To many the Chinese intervention introduced a whole new war whose opening phase was a repetition of the action during the previous June and July when the UN forces had to trade space for time. Between late November 1950, and the middle of January 1951, all available aircraft were assigned to close air support missions in relief of the retreating Eighth Army. As in the earlier campaign, all-out close air support prevented the retreat from becoming a complete disaster. In the east, Marine close air support, assisted by 438 FEAF support sorties, extricated Marine ground units from a trap at the Chosen Reservoir, as X Corps retreated to Hungnam and, on Christmas Eve, embarked there for Pusan, where it was finally consolidated with the Eighth Army. This move raised great hopes among the airmen that with X Corps now a part of the

Eighth Army, many of the close air support command and control problems that existed when the corps was separate would be resolved.[56]

In the west, FEAF close air support of the retreating Eighth Army inflicted devastating casualties on the advancing Chinese forces. Characteristic of the effectiveness of the more than 4,000 close air support sorties flown by Fifth Air Force in support of the Eighth Army during the last week in November and in December were those flown on November 30 to extricate some 8,000 motorized troops of the 2d Infantry Division near Kunuri, north of Pyongyang. The division was serving as a rear guard blocking force while the Eighth Army's other divisions moved south. Their road was blocked by Chinese troops firing down on them as they tried to pass through a narrow defile. The Air Force captain in charge of the TACP contacted a Mosquito control plane whose pilot within four minutes had four fighter-bombers destroying the enemy with napalm and strafing runs within yards of the Americans. "Never before," related the assistant division commander, "have I had metallic links from machine gun fire drop on my head, nor have I seen napalm splash on the road. The support was that close." It was not only close but effective. Although the division lost all of its artillery in the action, the Division commander, Maj. Gen. J.B. Keiser, credited Fifth Air Force with preventing disastrous casualties to the division.[57]

Along with their ground forces, the Chinese communists introduced MIG–15s into the war. The United States deployed an F–86 wing from the states to counter them, thereby releasing the F–51s, F–80s, and the newly introduced F–84s, to concentrate on close air support. As the distance between the Yalu and the front lines increased, air interdiction attacks on North Korean road and railroad networks gradually came to outnumber support strikes and became increasingly effective. The combination gradually brought the Communist drive to a halt south of Seoul.

As the front lines stabilized around the original 38th Parallel, and armistice talks got underway in July 1951, the need, in the eyes of airmen, for continuous close air support decreased. For the next two years, until the last two months of the war, June and July 1953, FEAF's main attention was focused on attacking enemy logistics (**Figure 9**). Ground commanders, however, continued to request close air support, even though it was much less effective against an enemy who was anchored in dugouts and underground shelters.

The earlier dramatic success of close air support missions against the enemy, when the front line was moving up and down the peninsula, had conditioned the ground commanders to expect similar success in the new static phase of the war. Such hopes were not realized, as close air support missions experienced greater difficulties in rooting out an entrenched enemy. In Weyland's view, close air support now reached the point of diminishing return. Each increase in the number of close air support sorties meant a reduction in

Help from Above

the number of more remunerative interdiction sorties, and the overall gain on the front was not worth the additional effort put into close air support. He saw close air support in such static situations as an expensive substitute for artillery fire. Close air support in such situations pays off only after interdiction has immobilized the enemy by cutting off his logistics. Only then can close air support be decisive in massed coordination with ground action.[58]

The Army's view of close air support, so laudatory earlier when aircraft were saving the ground forces from destruction, turned critical during this period of static warfare. Most of the Army's battlefield-derived criticism of the Air Force's close air support in Korea, as distinguished from its doctrinal disagreements, dated from these last two years. One would expect ideally that doctrinal positions would flow from experience in battle and that the two positions would coincide. In Korea, however, it is possible to distinguish between those Army criticisms of close air support that were derived from ground combat in the theater and those that stemmed from prewar doctrine and perceptions, which the flow of battle did little to change.

Despite their reservations about the effectiveness of close air support, FEAF and Fifth Air Force provided more than adequate close air support when elements of the Eighth Army were actively engaged with the enemy. Even when there were no contact battles a rather high-level of air support sorties were flown to keep the Tactical Air Control System in being and proficient.[59]

By the end of May 1952, the enemy had succeeded, despite the interdiction program, in moving large quantities of equipment, supplies, and personnel up to the front line. To forestall a new enemy ground offensive, a majority of fighter-bombers again shifted their missions back to close air support. Between June and the end of the year, close air support missions were flown for the Eighth Army whenever the limited ground action required. In September, for example, a daily average of 292 close air support missions were flown in support of UN ground forces. Fifth Air Force claimed destruction of 450 gun positions, 802 bunkers, and an unspecified number of enemy casualties.[60]

A final close air support surge took place at the very end of the war. In June and July 1953 the Communist ground forces, in a last-minute attempt to improve their positions before the armistice was signed, opened up an offensive against the South Korean sector of the Eighth Army's line. All available airpower, more than half of it devoted to close air support, was diverted to this sector. During the two months FEAF aircraft flew 11,000 close air support sorties and 7,000 interdiction flights, as the enemy offensive was contained.[61]

The effectiveness of FEAF's combat aircraft in all these phases of the war confirmed, in the minds of Air Force leaders, the soundness of their World War II-derived doctrine for employing tactical air power. The key to success, which in their view was proven in Korea, was FEAF's ability to orchestrate its fleet of fighter-bombers, light-bombers, and medium-bombers,

Close Air Support in Korea

moving them about almost effortlessly between air combat, close air support, interdiction, and strategic bombing missions. While laudatory in its praise of the Marine close air support of Marine infantry units, and admitting that at times the Marine system of close air support displayed some advantages over the more complex Army/Air Force system, Air Force leaders became even more convinced than before that, for operating across an entire theater for which the Air Force was responsible, their system was not only superior but necessary. They were quick to contrast Marine tactical air, which was organized and controlled to support relatively small-scale assault operations involving shallow penetration on a narrow front with the Air Force's system, which was designed to support operations on wide fronts involving either deep penetrations or retreats.[62]

Air Force leaders did not hesitate to remind their Army counterparts at every opportunity that it was two air factors that made possible the kind of ground action that had taken place. One factor was the defeat of the enemy's air force, both at the outset of the war and later after the introduction of Russian jets. These airmen were concerned lest the ground forces become so accustomed to operating free from enemy air attacks, that they would overlook the efforts of FEAF that made it possible. The second air factor that, to Air Force eyes, greatly eased the soldiers' burden was air power's unseen, and therefore often unappreciated, role in preventing enormous quantities of enemy men and materiel from reaching the front line. To the airmen, these efforts were as important, if not more so, than direct close air support in determining the outcome of the battles.

Top Army commanders, such as MacArthur and Walker, whose responsibilities extended to the entire theater, tended to agree that all facets of air power were important. But even they were impressed with the local results of Marine air support. Lower-level commanders who were the beneficiaries of FEAF's close air support were also laudatory concerning the support they received. Yet, as in most wars, prewar doctrine, as well as the postwar status and organization of each service, played a major role in judgments relating to tactical air support. The air-ground system in Korea was cumbersome enough, and posed enough problems, to instill a desire for a better system of support in the minds of many Army commanders.

The Close Air Support System in Korea

Any system as complex as that derived from World War II, and applied in Korea, to coordinate air strikes with ground movement can be only as effective as its weakest link. As stipulated in F.M. 31–35, to be fully effective the close air support system required intimate and uninterrupted cooperation on many levels between those requesting air strikes, those evaluating the requests,

Help from Above

those transmitting the requests to operating units, and those responsible for ordering and performing the air missions.

The Army (demand) side of this structure, the air-ground operations system, was responsible for determining and requesting the air support it needed. It was the task of the Air Force (supply) side, the Tactical Air Control System, to furnish whatever support was validated. For a number of reasons, both technical and political, the system as it unfolded in Korea contained several weak links.

The Demand Side: The Air-Ground Operations System

Even before the onset of hostilities in Korea, many Army officers, particularly at the Army Field Forces, had become disenchanted with the command and control provisions of F.M. 31–35. Nevertheless, this manual, along with the Joint Training Directive, remained the bible for both the Air Force and the Army throughout the war. This document clearly spelled out the responsibilities of both the ground and air forces.

On the ground side, it prescribed specific obligations for army, corps, and division commanders. Experienced ground officers, who were familiar with the principles of air power, as well as with the characteristics, armament, capabilities, limitations, tactics and techniques of aviation, were to be assigned at each of these levels. The most important echelon on the demand side of the system was at the field army level (in Korea, the Eighth Army) where direct coordination and planning took place with its corresponding Air Force, the Fifth. Ground commanders at subordinate levels were prohibited from dealing directly with their Air Force counterparts on the supply side.

In theory, the Eighth Army was responsible for placing G–2 Air (Intelligence) and G–3 Air (Operations) officers at a JOC and ground liaison teams at tactical air force fighter and reconnaissance units, for organizing a photo-interpretation center, and for using its own signal company to install and maintain communications for the Army's air-ground operations system.

The smooth functioning of the entire demand side of the system depended primarily on the G–2 Air and G–3 Air officers at this army level in the Air-Ground Operations Section of the JOC. The former, as head of the intelligence staff, supervised the Army's photo-interpretation center, controlled the Army's ground liaison officers who were stationed at Air Force reconnaissance units, and supervised those activities of the Army's signal company that related to reconnaissance. The G–3 Air at the army level was the linchpin between requests for air support coming up from lower levels and those passed on to the Air Force. His job was to coordinate these lower-level requests with the army plan of operations, to approve or reject them, to place them in priority, and to pass them on to the Air Force's Combat Operations Section (also at the JOC) for final joint decision and action.[63]

These arrangements were repeated at the subordinate corps and division levels. The corps level was also supposed to contain G–2 Air and G–3 Air branches, communication facilities of the signal company, and ground liaison officers. The officers at this level received requests for air support from subordinate units, integrated them with the corps plan of operations, and passed them up to the army level for processing and presentation to the tactical air force. As at the higher army level, the corps G–2 Air was responsible for processing all lower-level requests for visual and photoreconnaissance missions and submitting them to the army level G–2 Air.

The division's G–3 Air staff funneled air support requests up from subordinate units to the corps G–3. Unlike the higher levels, there was no G–2 Air at division headquarters. Intelligence and reconnaissance duties, normally performed by a G–2 Air, were handled there by the chief photo interpreter. None of these components of the air-ground system existed below the division. Teams to handle these duties could, however, be attached to subordinate levels in emergencies.[64] One of the Army's major complaints with the system was that the planning and execution of air support was handled at too high a level, namely the Army/Air Force level, stripping commanders of lower-level units, who were closer to the enemy, of many important decision-making powers over matters concerning their own support.

For a number of reasons these arrangements developed slowly and often in haphazard fashion during the first critical six months of the war. The Eighth Army, in full retreat down the peninsula, could spare few personnel for the system. One reason they had almost no soldiers to spare for the air-ground operations system was their (as well as the Air Force's) unpreparedness. The prewar defensive orientation of the ground troops, coupled with the sorry state of joint training before hostilities began, found the Army without officers who were trained and ready for detailed coordination with the Air Force. By August 9, for example, 46 days after the war started, there were still only nine Army personnel distributed throughout the entire air-ground system.[65] This prompted Stratemeyer four days later to inform MacArthur that Eighth Army's failure to provide G–2 Air and G–3 Air officers, a photo-interpretation center, ground liaison officers, and a signal company was preventing it from getting as much air support as was available. The FEC apparently thought this matter was not too important. In a reply nearly three weeks later it told Stratemeyer that it was aware of the deficiencies and was taking steps to correct them.[66]

In the absence of Army G–2 Air and G–3 Air officers from the Eighth Army during the first weeks of hostilities, the Air Force picked up the slack as best it could. By the second week of August the Air Force had flown six TACPs to Korea and had diverted some of these airmen to set up a rudimentary JOC until ground officers were in place.

There was only one Signal Company, Air-Ground Liaison, in the entire U.S. Army (the 20th), but it was in the United States and did not arrive in

Help from Above

Korea until September 1950. Not until December was the company able to furnish a satisfactory air-request communications net between divisions, corps, and the JOC. It was this interim lack of communications with which to request air strikes that required General Dean to call Tokyo to obtain them.[67] Without an air-request net during the first week, requests for air strikes followed the circuitous route of being sent first to the Korean Military Advisory Group, which forwarded them to the FEC headquarters in Tokyo. Far East Command, in turn, sent them to FEAF which relayed them to Fifth Air Force at Itazuke, Japan. It took, on the average, four hours for these requests to travel from a field commander to Fifth Air Force.[68]

In order to provide some ground communications until an Army system was organized, a provisional Air Force Tactical Control Group, the 6132d, devised a makeshift air-request net connecting divisions to the JOC by scrounging and giving each Army division an SCR–399 HF radio and some airmen to operate it.[69] It was not until December that the 20th Signal Company organized an SCR–399 radio net between the JOC and the army's air liaison officers at airfields in Korea. Even after the signal company arrived and set up an air-request net, the system was not fully effective. The G–3 nets it organized were chronically short of personnel, and it did not set up a G–2 intelligence net until well into 1951, after the immediate emergencies had passed.

X Corps, which remained separate from the Eighth Army during the first six months of the war, did not even go this far, resisting Fifth Air Force's urgings to send representatives to the JOC. General Almond's stated reason for not establishing an air-ground operations system, namely lack of communications, was valid. The communications lapse, however, was an Army omission.

Virtually all of the difficulties the Air Force had with X Corps over close air support stemmed from Almond's refusal to furnish communications and G–2 Air and G–3 Air officers to the JOC. When General Partridge visited the corps in late November 1950, he discovered that neither Almond nor his staff was familiar with F.M. 31–35. Without ground communications for requesting air strikes, ground officers in the Corps were using TACPs and Mosquito aircraft to contact the Marine Tactical Air Control Center directly, thereby bypassing the JOC, which was responsible for overall control of air strikes. Partridge detected a "sly attitude" among officers in the X Corps headquarters who, in his judgment, "thought they were getting away with something."[70]

Also, X Corps in the critical month of December 1950 had difficulty obtaining intelligence photos of the battlefield. This was traced in large part to the failure of the corps to provide a G–2 Air with concomitant photo interpreters, ground liaison officers, and reproduction facilities. Again the problem was ameliorated in makeshift fashion when the Air Force and Marines filled the void. General Almond's repeated calls for more TACPs, one for each battalion, were resisted by Fifth Air Force, partly on the grounds that the assignment of such a large number of parties would bankrupt its resources, and part-

Close Air Support in Korea

ly on the observation that these parties would be useless until the corps provided the communications the parties needed to do their job.[71]

The abundance of available sorties, both from Navy and Air Force aircraft, papered over many of the weaknesses of this shoddily built air-ground operations system during the critical opening months of the war. Yet it remained the judgment of the Air Force that the Army, throughout the war, did not place enough emphasis on the air-ground operations system to allow it to exploit as fully as it could the assistance the Air Force was ready and eager to provide. Some Army commanders in the field, on the other hand, unaware of the underlying reasons for frequent long reaction times or poor targeting, tended to blame the *supply* side of the system, which they could see before their eyes, rather than the weaknesses of the *demand* side that were largely invisible to them. Such judgments perpetuated the spreading cult among future-oriented Army officers that the Air Force was not interested in supporting the Army and that the Army would have to look to itself for support in the future.

The Supply Side: The Tactical Air Control System

Just as requests for air support worked their way up the Army's demand side of the system from the fighting man to the army's centralized Air-Ground Operations Section in the JOC, the Air Force's organization to supply that support moved down for implementation from its counterpart Combat Operations Section in the JOC through a series of control centers to the fighting man. After decisions were made jointly in the JOC, they proceeded through a series of Air Force agencies—a Tactical Air Control Center (TACC), Tactical Air Direction Centers (TADC) and, finally, to the Air Force controllers on the front line in TACPs.

The Joint Operations Center

On July 5, within two weeks of the North Korean invasion, Fifth Air Force flew 10 officers and 35 airmen to Taejon to set up a Joint Operations Center at 24th Division Headquarters. Since no Army personnel were available, they organized what was in effect the Air Force's portion of a JOC, a Combat Operations Center. Nine days later, anticipating the fall of Taejon to the North Koreans, this center moved back to Taegu where it became part of the Eighth Army/Fifth Air Force joint headquarters. The collocation of the JOC with its TACC and Fifth Air Force Headquarters established command and control in one location. Despite several moves in the next 10 months, these three elements were never separated during the remainder of the war.[72]

By the time of the move to Taegu, sufficient heavy communications equipment was beginning to arrive and the outlines of a full-scale JOC began to emerge. The only items still absent were radar and direction-finding facilities.

Help from Above

Two experts, Col. James Ferguson (later Brig. Gen.) and Col. Gil Meyers, were imported from the Tactical Air Command to improve the system. As late as a month later, however, the Army's Air-Ground Operations Section of the JOC was still short 15 officers and enough clerks to staff the work of the section, and still lacked a photo-interpretation center to process reconnaissance materials.

The creation of a JOC that mirrored the stipulations of F.M. 31–35 was accompanied by birth pangs and misunderstandings. On August 4, for example, Partridge complained to Walker not only of his failure to provide the necessary communications that would allow him to support the Eighth Army fully, but also of the exclusion of the Air Force from the planning of ground force troop movements. Precipitous retreats by the 24th and 25th Divisions, without Air Force knowledge, had left several uninformed TACPs stranded and at the mercy of the enemy. Partridge suggested that the Army's G–3 Air, currently assigned to the JOC, be given the complete confidence of Eighth Army planning personnel so that he could perform his function of coordinating Army and Air Force plans and operations.[73]

There was also some initial controversy over the location and control of the JOC. Since Eighth Army's participation had so far been minimal, and Fifth Air Force was in fact controlling the agency, Partridge had been treating it as an Air Force outfit. Walker objected. In a meeting on August 13 the two commanders had a "very crisp, but pleasant" difference of opinion over the use and location of the JOC. Despite Stratemeyer's assertion, at the time, that F.M. 31–35 clearly stated that the JOC was an Air Force function,[74] such was not the case. The intent was that it be a true joint agency with neither service in charge. This issue appears to have been one more of cosmetics than of substance. It was not raised again overtly, and Fifth Air Force continued to assume responsibility for its operation. This, perhaps, in part accounts for the reluctance in some quarters, such as X Corps and the Navy, to participate in its operations.

The JOC had no trouble controlling land-based Marine fighters after the Inchon landing, once they were released from their amphibious landing duties. Control of the Navy's carrier planes was another matter. For the first six months of the war, Navy planes, which were also performing close air support, were controlled separately by Seventh Fleet. Seldom did Fifth Air Force and Seventh Fleet know what the other was doing, with the result that the JOC was unable to incorporate the Navy's daily close air support flights into the big picture. Until direct communications between the two controlling agencies were established in February 1951 the requests for Navy close air support missions had to be relayed from the JOC to the naval task force through naval headquarters in Japan.

The February establishment of direct communications between the two controlling agencies did not mean centralized control, however. It was not until the final month of the war, in July 1953, that the Navy fully accepted JOC control by setting up a Navy Liaison Section there, comparable to that of the Army's Air-Ground Operations Section. By then it was not needed.

Brig. Gen. James Ferguson

The JOC's vehicle to order and control close air support air strikes was the Air Force's TACC. This was the nerve center through which the Fifth Air Force commander controlled and monitored his air activities. The senior air officer in the JOC passed his mission requirements down to the TACC, which in turn, relayed them to the airfields where the strike aircraft were stationed. Direct local control of close air support strikes was performed at still lower levels by TADCs and TACPs. The TACC's main responsibility was to consolidate all the information available about the immediate air situation and display it for easy use by controllers, operators, and the decision makers in the JOC.

Until enough TADCs were established in Korea, the TACC also directed aircraft on close air support strikes. This was not its normal function, and it relinquished it as soon as TADCs became operational. Some TADCs were located at corps headquarters. The air-traffic controllers at the TADCs had the massive job of identifying all aircraft flying within their area, distinguishing between friend and foe, preventing saturation in the operating area, and passing close air support aircraft of the Air Force, Navy, Marines, South Korea, Australia, Greece, and South Africa on to TACPs for final direction of their strikes.

General Quesada's pioneering use of radar during World War II to direct close air support strikes was the focus of much development after the war. Considerable energy had been devoted to acquiring new equipment, and Korea was the first war to attempt its systematic use.

Help from Above

According to F.M. 31–35, a Tactical Air Control Group was supposed to provide and maintain the radar equipment and personnel for the TACC and the TADCs. This equipment was particularly critical for air support operations at night and during bad weather. When the war began, the Air Force's sole Tactical Air Control Group, the 502d, was stationed at Pope AFB, in North Carolina. Although its four Aircraft Control and Warning Squadrons encountered some difficulties with both equipment and coordination with ground forces during prewar training exercises, it had learned a great deal about controlling air strikes. Unfortunately, this expertise was not applied during the early, critical months of the war, because the 502d did not reach Korea until October 1950. In the meantime, a temporary group without proper equipment or trained personnel did its best to help FEAF fighters support the Army.

Problems encountered by the 502d Tactical Air Control Group in its move to Korea present, in microcosm, a picture of the unpreparedness of many defensive-oriented Air Force units at the beginning of the war. Just prior to departure from the United States, the group was stripped of a large number of the vehicles it needed to establish radar sites on hilltops and to keep up with the fast-moving front. The group's commander, who arrived in Korea during the first week of September, believed that, had he been able to get radars on the hills above the Naktong River during the defense of the Pusan perimeter, he could have kept the North Koreans out of the 10-mile assembly area west of the river they were using to mount attacks against the defending Eighth Army.

Rough handling by stevedores damaged much of the sensitive radar equipment when it was shipped across the Pacific. It took an average of eight days, rather than the normal 12 hours, to repair and make it operational after its arrival in Korea. In addition, as a result of poor combat loading, equipment components, personnel, and vehicles were shipped separately, requiring additional time to mate them in the theater of operations.

More critical early deficiencies experienced by the group, however, were caused by the unrealistic nature of the prewar joint training exercises with the Army. Peacetime, eight-hour schedules did not prepare the operators for the rigors of round-the-clock operations. Having trained in the United States, where they had to "fake so many things due to lack of real estate," the technicians and mechanics were ill-equipped to climb mountains to install the radar equipment. The group had never been tactically employed or used as a group during the prewar maneuvers. According to its commander, the group was hampered by "a lot of people who had not the pioneer spirit whatsoever."[75]

Nevertheless, by October one of the group's squadrons was operating the TACC and the other three had established TADCs at Kimpo, Taegu, and Taejon. As the Eighth Army moved north of the 38th Parallel in November, the 502d set up a direction center at Sinanju and was directing strikes by B–26s in support of the advancing ground troops.[76]

Close Air Support in Korea

In January 1951, the group experimented with a new type of control agency, the Tactical Air Direction Post (TADP). Three of these "Tadpoles," as they were called, were set up close behind the front lines, one with each of the three American Corps[77] that then made up the Eighth Army, and moved with the front as it advanced or fell back. They proved highly successful in controlling fighters and light- and medium-bombers in close air strikes. Pilots found the MPQ–2 radars, which guided them to their targets and plotted their bomb release points, good for operations at night and during periods of bad weather.

In late April the Army G–3 Air in the JOC sent FEAF a glowing detailed report of radar-controlled night bombing along the front lines of all three corps during March and April. In I Corps, prisoners of war had reported heavy casualties and enormous destruction of supplies. In one case an enemy unit was reduced from regimental size to battalion strength just before they attacked. In another instance, MPQ–2 radar bombing reduced three enemy regiments to a battalion, forestalling their offensive. An enemy attack that had penetrated the American lines was stopped cold by two radar controlled B–26s, which dropped their loads less than 1,000 yards from the friendly positions. Intelligence reports from IX and X Corps were equally enthusiastic.[78]

Ironically, the very success of these night radar-directed missions revived one aspect of the doctrinal issue of close air support. Upon reading these reports, Stratemeyer was struck by the contrast between the Army's euphoric tone in this instance and the deluge of complaints over close air support he had received from them the preceding summer. Since Stratemeyer had used about one-third of his B–29s for these MPQ–2-controlled close air support missions during March and April, he suspected that the Army's praise was a prelude to a renewed attempt by GHQ, similar to the one that he had successfully diverted the previous summer, to use all the B–29s for close air support "regardless of the tactical requirement." To the FEAF commander it was a matter of preserving his prerogative to select targets for his aircraft.[79]

Early in 1952 the MPQ–2 radars were replaced with improved MSQ–1s, and from June 1952 until the end of the war, B–29s and B–26s at night supplemented daytime fighters in providing 24-hour close air attacks against the enemy's limited-objective offensives.[80] Stratemeyer's concern over a massive diversion of the medium-bombers from interdiction to close air support did not materialize.

Tactical Air Control Parties

In Korea, a Tactical Air Control Party (TACP) was a team of airmen, led by an experienced fighter pilot, called a forward air controller (FAC), who was assisted by one or two enlisted radio operators and an enlisted radio mechanic, assigned to a battalion or regiment to direct close air support strikes in its unit's vicinity. In addition to his controller duties, the FAC also served as an

Help from Above

agent of the Air Force, explaining the capabilities and limitations of air power to the soldiers in his assigned unit.[81]

At first, FACs were selected from the fighter squadrons operating in Korea for temporary duty of several weeks with ground units. Later, they were Mosquito pilots assigned temporarily from within the Tactical Control Group. The loss of experienced combat fighter pilots to serve in TACPs caused a hardship to fighter squadrons, and throughout the war some argued that this problem could be alleviated by using nonrated officers as FACs.[82] Although General Almond experimented with this expedient in X Corps, air commanders believed that only rated Air Force officers were fully conversant with Air Force equipment, tactics, thinking, and terminology, and therefore only they could be effective in the job. Near the end of the war the Army and Air Force agreed to modify the TACP system by having the Army assign equipment and enlisted men for the parties, while the Air Force continued to supply pilots as FACs.

The first group of control parties encountered enormous difficulties. Lack of information on Army plans left several parties stranded after their ground units had moved out. In some cases, the Army field troops were unable to pass on their location because they did not know it themselves.[83] By early July, three TACP members had been killed, leading to a ban (lifted in October) against assigning TACPs below the regimental level.

An even greater problem for these initial control parties was the inadequate World War II equipment with which they had to work. Their radio-equipped jeeps were unprotected from the weather or from enemy fire.[84] They had no shock mountings, with the result that the fragile radio equipment was damaged on the primitive Korean roads and mountain passes. Also, the antiquated TRC–1 radios in the jeeps broke down with regularity. Even when they were operating properly, they lacked a remote capability. This meant the FAC was tied to his jeep and could not sally into more advantageous front line positions from which to direct incoming strikes.[85] This factor, more than any other, led to the expedient of placing FACs in light planes, which gave them more mobility and greater perception of the battlefield.

Equipment for the ground-control parties improved as the war progressed. By the latter part of the conflict they were using new M–39 jeeps, each carrying an aircraft-type generator, a weatherized and shock-mounted removable radio-equipment container, an ARC–3 VHF radio set with 16 channels, an ARC–27 UHF radio set, and an ARC–7 radio set with a 100-foot remote-control cable that allowed the FAC to operate from dug-in positions distant from his radios with added personal safety during enemy artillery and air attacks.[86]

The initial two TACPs, which were hastily summoned at the beginning of hostilities, had grown by the final year of the war, on to an average of between 48 and 60 control parties operating with the Eighth Army. As a general rule,

Close Air Support in Korea

each U.S. division had between four and six parties. The Air Force, considering that the conditions in Korea weakened the ability of TACPs to operate as effectively as airborne tactical air coordinators, judged that six was the maximum number a division could gainfully employ. Some division commanders, however, insisted that they could use 10 or more.[87] General Almond in X Corps was particularly avaricious. In late 1950 he had 37 TACPs (some Army) with his three divisions, while the five divisions of General Walker's Eighth Army in the west had 20 parties.

At first, each South Korean division received only one TACP. The Air Force was well aware that this was inadequate. In the early stages of the war, however, the South Korean army was poorly disciplined and frequently fled in wild disorder at the approach of the enemy, leaving the TACP behind in hostile territory where no one spoke English. Even the later doubling of the number of TACPs, as the South Korean army improved, did not provide fully effective control of air strikes. An attempt in 1952 to train South Korean Air Force personnel as FACs resulted in only three indigenous TACPs, all assigned to the I ROKA Corps. Language difficulties, and the preference of the South Korean airmen to remain with their own units, resulted in only moderate success for this program.[88]

Mosquitoes

Field Manual 31–35 had little to say about airborne FACs, other than to note, in passing, that "it may be desirable at times that additional forward air controllers operate airborne as tactical air coordinators."[89] However, the initial difficulties of the ground FACs with communications and equipment led to one of the more effective air experiments in the conflict—the development of airborne Tactical Air Coordinators, popularly called Mosquitoes.

These airborne control flights began with the 24th Division at Taejon on July 5th using an L–5 Stinson Sentinel as a reconnaissance plane with the call sign "Angelo." The L–5 was too light and its generator too weak to support the sustained operation of their VHF radios. Within days, an experiment with the heavier T–6s proved successful, as it was more durable and survivable than the L–5. The T–6 had a single 600-horsepower radial engine with a cruise speed of about 140 knots. There was no system to these early flights. The pilots, with an Army observer in the back seat, armed with only a map and a radio, would fly behind enemy lines and reconnoiter the roads. If they discovered a target, such as tanks, they would transmit through various radio channels until some fighters answered. They then gave the fighters the targets.

On July 14, the airborne controller operation fell back to Taegu with the 24th Division, the JOC and Fifth Air Force Advance Headquarters. By then the decimated TACPs were prohibited from operating below the regimental level, and the airborne Mosquitoes, took their place. The organization still had

Help from Above

A Stimson L–5, over Korea.

only two airplanes and four pilots and was not part of any formal Air Force unit.[90]

The Mosquito operation spread rapidly. On August 1, the T–6 operation formally became the 6147th Tactical Control Squadron, and by the following month, it had 27 planes and 55 pilots. The planes kept moving their home base to keep up with the battle line. In October, they moved from Taegu to Seoul, and by the beginning of November, the squadron's 34 T–6s were stationed at Pyongyang. By April of the following year, the Mosquito organization had split into two squadrons of 25 planes each, and joined with a third, a TACP squadron, to form the 6147th Tactical Control Group. Having airborne Mosquito and ground FAC officers in the same group allowed experienced airborne controllers from the T–6 squadrons to serve temporary stints as FACs.[91]

Until the breakout from the Pusan perimeter on September 16, the Mosquitoes operated almost exclusively in close air support of the Eighth Army. Up until that time they had directed successful strikes against 183 tanks, 119 trucks, and 778 other vehicles. During the enemy's retreat to the Yalu River, the Mosquitoes added other missions to those of close air support and visual reconnaissance. The T–6s often directed air strikes ahead of the retreating enemy, scattered safe conduct leaflets, helped rescue downed airmen, directed B–26s at night, and adjusted artillery.[92] Throughout their existence, in addition to whatever other missions they performed, the Mosquito pilots acted as the eyes of the JOC, flying visual reconnaissance missions and contributing to the corpus of intelligence the center needed to make its decisions.

Close Air Support in Korea

Once the war settled down to a stalemate around the 38th Parallel early in 1951, each side reinforced its lines, making it increasingly dangerous for the slow and unarmed T–6s to fly far beyond enemy lines in search of targets. By summer the Mosquitoes were prohibited from flying more than two miles beyond the front. Attempts to replace the T–6s with F–51s or L–19s were not successful. Instead, tactical air coordinators modified their methods to provide as much safety as possible. For example, they stopped talking fighters to their targets and marked targets with rockets, instead.[93]

Despite their superb record during the war, most aviation observers believed, inaccurately as it turned out, that airborne observers in slow, unarmed planes would be too vulnerable to play a substantial role in controlling close air support fighters in future wars.

Aircraft Issues

Before the war in Korea, two of the more divisive close air support issues separating the Army and the Air Force concerned the relative effectiveness of propeller-driven and jet-powered aircraft, and the question as to whether the Air Force should develop a single-mission aircraft to support the

A North American T–6.

Help from Above

ground forces, or whether its general-purpose tactical aircraft could do the job. The war went a long way toward resolving this first issue. By end of the conflict it was generally accepted by most, including the Marines who had adopted them, that jet planes were superior and represented the future of close air support.

This result was far from apparent at first. The F–80 Shooting Stars with which the Air Force entered the war were initially criticized by ground troops for their inability remain "on station" for long periods of time. The long distances from their Japanese bases, coupled with their high rate of fuel consumption, did in fact limit their time over the target compared with the F–51 Mustangs, the other close air support fighter that was introduced soon after the war began. The F–80s had been converted from air-defense fighter-interceptors to close air support fighter-bombers by equipping them with retractable rocket-launching posts and six .50-caliber machine guns. Shackles on the wing tips allowed them to carry either bombs or external fuel tanks, but not both simultaneously.[94] This forced a tradeoff between distance and firepower.

Much of the early criticism of the F–80 stemmed from the ground troops' desire for aircraft constantly overhead to bolster their morale and lower that of the enemy. The Shooting Stars also came in for criticism, at first, for their inability to carry napalm, a deficiency that was later corrected with the addition of pylon bomb racks.

In June 1950, two possible remedies existed for the short-range problem—either base the planes in Korea or extend their range. Until airfields in Korea were improved to handle the jets, the second solution was attempted, unofficially. One group fitted its external fuel tanks with extra center sections, which increased the capacity of each tank from 165 to 255 gallons and added 30 minutes to the loiter time of each sortie. The consequent decrease in aircraft maneuverability and the frequent breakage of wing-tip shackles due to increased weight, however, made this expedient a temporary one, until the first Shooting Stars were stationed in Korea, at Taegu, at the end of September.[95]

On July 22, 1950, 145 F–51 Mustangs arrived from the United States. This was widely interpreted at the time as an admission that jets were unsuitable for the close air support role. Actually, FEAF had requested an additional 150 F–80s, only to find that the Air Force possessed only one-third of that number. Since the Air Force had over 1,500 World War II Mustangs, it convinced FEAF to convert six of its jet squadrons to its more numerous F–51s. The absence of North Korean jet air opposition made this solution acceptable to FEAF. The real reason for turning to Mustangs, namely the absence of jets in the inventory, could not be stated for national security reasons.[96]

Approximately one-sixth of the F–80 sorties, and one-fourth of the F–51 flights during the war were in close air support,[97] at times not more than 25 or 30 feet in front of friendly forces. Each type of aircraft had its own advantages

Close Air Support in Korea

and disadvantages, but on balance the jet, which was constantly improving, had the edge. The slower and older Mustang could operate from unprepared airstrips and had more range than the F–80. The F–80, on the other hand, was faster and better fulfilled the Air Force's requirement for an air-to-air fighter. In many ways the two planes complemented each other. Initially, the Mustangs were assigned missions with bombs and napalm, while the Shooting Stars attacked with rockets and machine guns. When midwing pylon racks were added later, the jets also began carrying napalm and bombs.

Ammunition loads for the two planes were approximately equal: 1,800 rounds for the F–80, 2,000 for the F–51. The F–80s' M–3 machine guns, however, fired twice as rapidly as the Mustangs' M–2s, and their parallel firing was far more effective against ground targets than the converging fire from the Mustang's guns. Two other features gave the jet an advantage. The absence of torque from the jet's engine allowed prolonged bursts from longer distances without the pilot having to compensate for changes in speed and altitude, and the virtually noiseless attack approach permitted the jet to achieve complete surprise.[98]

Other factors, each perhaps minor in itself but significant when taken in aggregate, favored the F–80. The loud noise and vibrations took a toll on pilots of the conventional aircraft, contributing materially to the buildup of combat fatigue. Because of its speed, the F–80, was less vulnerable to ground fire than the Mustang, resulting not only in fewer losses, but also in less mental strain on jet pilots. The vulnerability of the F–51 to ground fire was a major concern, due to its propeller's exposure to cable traps, to the vulnerability of the coolant and oil sections of the aircraft's engine, and to the shallow rate of climb away from the target, exposing it to enemy fire for a much longer period than was the case with the jet.[99] By the end of December 1950, for example, 115 Mustangs had been lost to ground fire, compared to 50 F–80s.

The Shooting Star proved to be a very rugged combat aircraft. In one instance, for example, an F–80 struck the ground in a pass on a target, bounced into the air, and flew back to base. In another, an F–80 ran out of fuel on a combat mission and bellied into a field. The aircraft was later jacked up, the gear extended, the plane refueled, and then flown back to base where relatively minor repairs were required to return it to combat status.[100]

The jet had better equipment. The F–51s' four-button SCR–522 radios were inferior to the jet's ARC–3 radios. The F–80 could fly above bad weather, whereas the F–51 normally had to fly through weather on instruments. Maintenance was easier for the jets, which had fewer parts, than for the conventional planes. This was also accounted for by the fact that the F–80s were newer. Moreover, it was more difficult to perform adequate armament maintenance on the F–51 than on the F–80.[101]

One of the prewar *a priori* objections to using jets for close air support was the contention that their speed would cause pilots to miss many ground

Help from Above

Napalm bombs being assembled (top); napalm being dropped from a Lockheed P–80, at Eglin Field, Florida (bottom).

156

targets that they would have observed from the cockpits of slower, reciprocating-engine fighters. Experience in Korea laid this concern to rest. Fifth Air Force's Director of Combat Operations, who had flown over 200 combat missions in P–40s and P–47s during World War II and close to 80 F–80 missions in Korea, was emphatic in his praise of the superiority of the jets. "I can see as much at 300 miles an hour," he said, "as I could see before when I was going 170 to 180 miles." This was due, he explained, to the ability of the jet pilots to adjust to the pace and to concentrate on looking for certain targets while blotting out other distractions. He compared it with the gradual increases over time in the speed of automobiles. Modern drivers at 70 or 80 mph could see road signs and pedestrians as well as could motorists when the top speed for cars was 34 mph.[102] Pilots of F–84s made similar observations.[103]

Jet superiority over conventional planes for close air support was further illustrated with the introduction of F–84E Thunderjets in December 1950.[104] Within seven months the number of Thunderjets assigned to committed units in Korea surpassed the number of Shooting Stars, and by war's end two years later outnumbered them 215 to 5.[105] The Thunderjets flew, not only the greatest number of close support missions, but also the largest percentage of their missions was in support of the ground battle.

The second Army/Air Force issue, namely whether the Air Force might develop a plane solely for close air support, was not settled by the war. From a strictly technological perspective, it should have been resolved in favor of all-purpose aircraft. The technological performance and flexibility of FEAF's fighter-bombers, particularly the jets, provided little support for those who favored developing a close support airplane. With minor and rapid modifications, the F–80 had been shifted from a vehicle for air defense to a plane that performed all three tactical missions with equal ease. Likewise, the F–84, which until its appearance in Korea was used principally as a fighter escort for

A Soviet MIG–15 Fagot.

Help from Above

A North American XF–86.

bombers, proved to be an even more effective close air support plane, while still able to carry out interdiction and counter-air missions. Even the F–86, the FEAF's premier weapon against enemy MIGs, was used for ground support and interdiction on occasion with satisfying results.

Some problems were encountered in the initial transition of these planes from their prewar to their wartime missions, but no major difficulties originated with the aircraft themselves. The biggest problem in the transition stemmed from the absence of prewar joint training with the ground forces. "We have not," noted one of the earliest Thunderjet pilots in Korea, "had sufficient work with the ground forces to understand their problem or to pin-point small targets in rough terrain." Within the 30 days before it was assigned to Korea in December 1950, for example, the 27th Fighter Escort Wing had escorted SAC bombers across the North Atlantic twice, made various trips to the Caribbean, and escorted bombers on training missions "anywhere, in any weather, at any time." It was the pilots' contention that tactical fighter units in the United States should not be limited to one type of mission but should be prepared for any mission that might be assigned them.[106]

Most of the other problems that slowed down the transition centered around periodic shortages of spare parts and support equipment—such as

Close Air Support in Korea

rockets and napalm tanks, radar gun sights, servicing trucks, and fuel- and bomb-handling equipment—and personnel, such as armament and electronics specialists. Even within these limitations, the F–84 jets at Taegu, for example, were able to maintain an in-commission rate of 80 percent of their aircraft, compared to about half that for the propeller-driven twin Mustang F–82s, which they replaced.[107]

The absence of technological evidence to support the superiority of a single-purpose close air support aircraft meant that the basis for continued disagreement on the issue would be economic and political. The Air Force would continue to maintain that single-purpose aircraft were uneconomical and disruptive of its doctrine of the flexibility of air power. Behind the avowed reasons for Air Force opposition to developing a close air support plane was the realization that the existence of such aircraft would make it easier for the Army to take control of aircraft whose sole mission was to support it. The Army, on the other hand, while openly pointing to supposed tactical and technological deficiencies in multipurpose fighter planes in Korea, was basically interested in gaining more command and control of the planes supporting it. Thus, although on the technological level, the Korean War showed that multipurpose aircraft could do the job effectively, this had little bearing on the controversy which continued unabated after the war.

The Bottom Line: Command and Control

The Air Force's air combat support of the Army in Korea underwent closer scrutiny than most facets of air operations. Teams from both services scoured the theater attempting to learn whether the provisions of F.M. 31–35 and the Joint Training Directive had proved effective, or whether they should be modified or abandoned in favor of the different arrangements. Interviews, discussions, briefings, and conferences were held at all levels with representatives of all the services, and testimony was elicited from enemy prisoners of war.

The first of these investigative teams, in point of time, was a party sent out late in the fall of 1950 by the Army Field Forces, headed by Brig. Gen. Gerald J. Higgins, the Director of the Army's Air Support Center at Fort Bragg, North Carolina. The team's purpose was to investigate alleged deficiencies in Air Force support, the purported superiority of the Marine system of close air support, whether jet or conventional planes were better for close air support, and the soundness of the existing doctrine.

Interviews with the commanders of Fifth Air Force and Eighth Army, all corps commanders, all but one division commander, many regimental and battalion commanders, naval and Marine officers, and visits to airfields, combat operations centers, and the JOC, left the group with such a wide variety of conflicting impressions that they were unable to generalize. They found instances

Help from Above

where a battalion commander disagreed with the remarks of his regimental commander, and members of their staffs held views different from their division commanders. The viewpoint of one corps commander regarding air support was diametrically opposed to that of another corps commander. Air Force personnel disagreed among themselves, as did Navy and Marine personnel. The team concluded that, quite often, a smaller unit commander was unaware of special situations in the larger context that directly influenced the availability of close support aircraft and that practically all of the personal adverse remarks about air support could be attributed to lack of information, or even misinformation, on the subject.[108] Surprisingly, it did not suggest that prewar opinions on the issues of air-ground cooperation might have been important factors in the observations of their interviewees.

The investigators isolated five factors unique to the Korean Conflict that profoundly effected close air support. First, the UN ground forces enjoyed air superiority and almost total freedom from effective flak or antiaircraft artillery practically from the beginning, making it rarely necessary to divert planes from close air support to air combat or flak suppression. The report warned against taking this situation for granted in future combat. Second, the narrowness of the Korean peninsula allowed carrier-borne aircraft to overfly the entire area from either side. Third, the extremely mountainous terrain, lack of adequate roads, and the type of farming presented most unusual problems, particularly in regard to communications. The fourth factor to be taken into account when judging the effectiveness of close air support was the flat, wide, hard-bottomed rivers, easily forded in most cases, and the hundreds of railroad tunnels that served as bomb shelters for trains, convoys, and massed troops. Finally, those judging close air support must take into account that up to the time of the report the Army had been unable to mass its artillery on lucrative targets, since its divisional artillery was too spread out (at times across 15-mile fronts) and it had no corps or army artillery. Therefore, fighter-bombers were frequently called upon to counteract enemy actions that normally would have been handled by organic or attached artillery. This was a major factor in evaluating their effectiveness.

The Higgins Report concluded that, within the context of these factors, the air-ground system was sound and that air support was effective. It found major deficiencies in only two areas—the lack of proper communication facilities, and the lack of training in the techniques for requesting, processing, and applying close air support. Most of these deficiencies existed on the Army's side of the support system. It even modified these conclusions by noting that these defects had been corrected to a degree by improvisation and battle experience.

Of equal importance is what the investigators concluded about the relative effectiveness of Marine and Air Force close air support. In sum, they concluded that the Marine air system in Korea was initially superior to the

Close Air Support in Korea

Army/Air Force system, but it would be dangerous to impose such a system on the Air Force and the Army. The report arrived at this conclusion as it did the others—by placing the issue in its larger context. General Higgins recognized that Marine forces were organized for amphibious operations that required them to stay in continuous action for relatively short periods of time. In order to perform these quick, short strike campaigns, the Marines dedicated an entire Marine Air Wing of 216 planes to each Marine division. This was true in large part because, unlike with a normal Army operation, the aircraft had to compensate for the absence of Marine ground artillery. At the height of operations in World War II, the Army Air Forces supported each division of the 12th Army Group with only 35 planes. To the 216 planes the Marines were providing each division in Korea must be added the Navy planes that flew top cover and general air support during amphibious landings. To replicate this force of planes for the six Army divisions in Korea, General Higgins estimated it would take 1,296 aircraft for close air support alone, and about 2,600 for total aircraft support. The cost of such support, according to the report, would be beyond the nation's economic industrial capacity.[109]

No report so at variance with Army doctrine on close air support could long survive, and the Higgins Report was virtually ignored by the Army in favor of a more doctrinally correct study produced by the X Corps commander, General Almond, late in December and sent to FEC headquarters and the Army's chief of staff. The Almond Report began by rejecting General Higgins's joint perspective. In a sweeping initial assumption, it excluded from consideration any "Air Force or budgetary policies, priorities, or missions."[110] By confining itself solely to determining the Army's requirement for tactical air support, the report from its outset assured that its conclusions would be driven by Army, rather than joint, doctrine.

Given that localized perspective, which ignored the larger context of the overall war, General Almond concluded that the close air support provided by the 1st Marine Air Wing was superior in every respect: First, Marine aircraft were designed, he said, solely for close air support, whereas Air Force planes were designed primarily to fight other planes in the air. It would be unreasonable to expect, according to Almond, that such aircraft could be used as efficiently in close air support as aircraft designed solely for that mission. Planes used for close air support must be dedicated to that mission, while air defense, air superiority, and interdiction should be performed by other aircraft tailored to those missions. He recommended, therefore, that close air support aircraft should be designed for that primary function, and that the Army should take part in both determining the characteristics for such a plane and in shouldering the financial burden for developing it.

Second, Marine planes had tactical air support as their primary and usually only mission, whereas in Air Force doctrine of close air support enjoyed a priority no higher than third. Any military unit performs its primary mission more efficiently than lower priority missions. Therefore, the primary mission for Air Force tactical units should be close air support.

A third advantage of Marine close air support noted by Almond, was the extensive air-ground training the Marines had undergone before the war, with the result that Marine pilots were totally familiar with the tactics, problems, and techniques of the ground units they were supporting. He remarked that the Army long before learned that combined training by tank, artillery, and infantry units proved to be the key to success on the battlefield. This applied equally to air-ground training, which unfortunately, had not taken place between the Army and the Air Force. The general opted for joint air-ground training at all echelons, using the same units each time to form permanent teams.

Almond considered one of the major advantages of the Marine system to be the inclusion of a Tactical Air Control Party as an organic part of each Marine battalion and higher unit. The Air Force policy, as he saw it, of providing one TACP for each division was less effective. According to him, a TACP cannot effectively control air strikes, report battle results, and advise the ground commanders on air operations unless its members are located at the front line along with artillery and tank representatives with whom they coordinate directly. The Air Force's TACPs were located at too distant a level to function properly. In short, the overextended frontages of modern warfare dictate the presence of one TACP at each infantry battalion and each higher unit, with infantry company observers stationed at each infantry battalion. Such an increase in the number of Air Force TACPs was one that Almond had fought vigorously for throughout his tour in Korea.

The fifth Marine measure that Almond deemed superior was at the heart of the matter and, in his estimation, flowed from the other objections. This was the fundamental question of the command and control of air resources. According to him, the advantage of the Marine system was that the senior ground commander, not the senior air commander, had operational control of the supporting aircraft. He was not talking about the senior Marine ground officer having control, for throughout his time in Korea, he contended constantly with the Marine commander, Gen. Oliver P. Smith, over such control. He was here opting for control by the senior army or corps commander. Falling back upon the argument from unity of command, Almond argued that since the ground commander was responsible for what happens on the land, he must have authority to order, not ask for, the air support he needs. "The only assurance a ground commander can have that any supporting arm will be employed effectively, or at all," he concluded, "is by having operational control over that supporting arm."[111] Consequently, field army or separate corps commanders should have operational control over supporting tactical air units. This proposal, of course, struck directly at the Air Force's doctrine of command and con-

Close Air Support in Korea

trol and threatened to turn the clock back to the pre-1943 days when such an arrangement had been tried and proven unworkable in the sands of North Africa.

The X Corps Commander next pointed to the specific dedication of Marine close air support planes to Marine units down to the infantry battalion. In his judgment, at least one tactical air squadron of 24 Air Force planes, but preferably an entire group of three squadrons, should be dedicated to each ground division. Since his previous point gave operational control of the planes to the senior ground officer, this proposal for the dedication of planes meant in effect assignment of the planes to each division. Assignment of a group of planes would permit each division to control, not only its own strike aircraft, but also photo-reconnaissance planes and laboratory facilities, Mosquito aircraft for airborne FACs, and helicopters for command and rescue missions. To Almond, this extensive decentralization of command and control would correct the excessive subordination of the close air support mission to other tactical air missions, which in his view, had caused the virtual disappearance of close air support prior to the Korean War.

General Almond also found the Marine's simplified and localized communications system far superior to the complex arrangements for coordination required of the Army/Air Force system. In Korea, he bridled at the need for him to communicate with the usually inaccessible JOC, which was 100 to 200 miles away over rugged mountains, when he had a complete and efficient Marine system of communications within his own command. The time delay in relaying operational messages, according to him, frequently precluded effective close air support by Fifth Air Force at the desired time and place. Partridge recognized this difficulty in communications and authorized X Corps to submit its requests for emergency air support directly to the Marine 1st Air Wing.[112] As a result, Almond deemed virtually all requests for air support as emergencies[113] and practically never called upon Fifth Air Force close air support assets during the fall and winter of 1950, raising in the mind of more than one observer the question of how he could possibly compare Fifth Air Force's close air support with that provided by the Marine's 1st Air Wing.

Analyzed from the perspective set down by General Almond at the beginning of the study, namely, from the view of Army rather than joint doctrine, these recommendations appeared logical and would undoubtedly have met Army requirements for close air support. Nevertheless, from the more inclusive perspective of joint operations, which considers warfare throughout the entire theater of operations, these recommendations appear as limited iterations of prewar Army doctrine, unaffected by the experiences of Korea.

The attempts by General Almond at the end of 1950 to support his conclusions with testimony from the Korean fighting were questioned by the Air

Help from Above

Force, most notably by General Weyland. Both he and General Partridge failed to see how Almond's analysis of Marine and FEAF close air support could have stemmed from actual experience in Korea, since X Corps received virtually all of its air support from Navy and Marine aircraft and practically none from the Air Force.[114] Weyland also pointed out that, contrary to Almond's belief, close air support was not given a fixed priority within the missions of tactical air power, but rather was assigned relative importance according to the situation in consultation with ground force representatives. There was certainly ample evidence of this so far in the war, where close air support had occupied top priority during the first three months and, at the time of study, was once again coming into prominence in slowing down the intervening Chinese armies.

General Weyland could only agree that tactical air units had insufficient training in air-ground operations. One major reason for this, he suggested, was Eighth Army's reluctance to participate in joint maneuvers before the outbreak of war. Additionally, he disputed Almond's contention that the Air Force was restricted to supplying only four TACPs to each ground division. He pointed to the air-ground doctrine as approved in the Joint Training Directive, which did not specify any ratio of TACPs to ground units, but rather made their allocation contingent upon the tactical situation.

As with the question of command and control of air assets, the recommendation that a specific number of aircraft be assigned to a field army or corps was one that had been made many times and rejected just as often, not only by the USAF, but by other air forces around the world. The argument for the indivisibility of air power, and against separating air power into penny-packets, went back at least as far as to Field Marshal Montgomery in World War II and was based on the assumption, which Almond totally rejected at the outset of his study, that close air support is but one portion of a larger air campaign that must be considered whenever questions arise concerning any one aspect of tactical air power.

The strongest evidence that General Almond's position on close air support was inspired as much by Army planners in the Pentagon as by his Korean experience comes from the remarkable similarity, both in content and in style, between the X Corps commander's study of November 1950 and a memorandum that General Collins, the Army Chief of Staff, had sent to General Vandenberg one month earlier. In this seminal document on the close air support of ground operations, the Army chief set down clearly and succinctly the Army's complaints with the support it was receiving from the Air Force and its recommendations for improvement. The chief's missive constitutes, in fact, a check list of Army/Air Force disagreements over the issue. Almond's study of the following month follows it closely.

At the outset, Collins reaffirmed his earlier position that, despite the suggestions of "many observers," he had no interest in taking over the Tactical Air

Close Air Support in Korea

Force or in creating an Army Air Force. As had his predecessor, General Eisenhower, the chief remained convinced that any attempt on the part of the Army to assume responsibility for close air support would result in duplication of effort and excessive cost.[115]

However, continued Collins, he was not satisfied with the close air support that the Air Force was furnishing the Army. Further, it would not improve until the Air Force adopted a system of close air support that took into account the Army's views and the Army's requirements for training and combat support.

What these Army requirements were quickly became apparent. Basic to all of them was the familiar appeal for increased command and control of fighter and reconnaissance aircraft by ground commanders. In a formula virtually identical to that prescribed a month later by Almond, the chief called for the assignment of one fighter group to each Army division and one reconnaissance group to each field army "at the earliest possible date." Not only should these air units be assigned, but Army tactical commanders, down to include the corps level, should be given operational control of them. Collins saw a precedent that could be used as a model for such operational control in another activity in which the Army and Air Force had to share units, namely, air defense. Three months earlier, he and Vandenberg completed an agreement that gave Air Force commanders of air defense units in the United States operational control over Army antiaircraft artillery units when they were working with Air Force squadrons on air defense missions. In such cases, the Air Force commander exercised his control by announcing the basic principles of engagement for both the ground and aviation defense units.[116] Collins envisioned a similar arrangement, in reverse, whereby tactical ground commanders could be given the same type of operational control over the tactical air units that were providing reconnaissance and "fire support" to ground units. With the approval of the Army group commander, these close air support aircraft could be released for other roles when not required for ground missions.[117]

The next step, according to General Collins, in correcting existing deficiencies in Air Force support was to procure an aircraft that was designed primarily for close air support. By this he meant an aircraft with a maximum ability to locate and attack promptly, under all conditions of weather and visibility, all targets close to the supported ground unit; an aircraft with reasonable operational endurance; and an aircraft that could operate from advanced strips in combat zones. Further, the Army should participate in determining the general requirements for such a close support plane and should be consulted in its development, and in its testing and evaluation. On this score, the Army chief had to be careful not to step over the boundary set by earlier agreements that made each service responsible for developing its own equipment. Collins claimed that the Army had no vested interest in the detailed characteristics of Air Force equipment, but rather was seeking participation only in determining the broad military qualities of the close support plane. His rationale for expect-

Help from Above

ing such participation was the fact that, since close air support was so closely integrated with ground combat operations, the determination of operational capabilities and of certain military characteristics was considered to be a joint function of the Air Force and the Army.[118]

Finally, Collins addressed the questions of TACPs, communications, and joint training. Although this memo made no recommendation concerning specific numbers of TACPs, the implication is clear that the Army wanted a reexamination of personnel and equipment requirements with an eye toward increasing them. General Almond's later study filled in the details. Collins's call for the Air Force to "provide adequate and suitable communications equipment" is baffling since up to that time a major obstacle to a smooth functioning air-ground operating system in Korea had been the Army's inability to provide communications equipment and personnel for the air request net. Perhaps this was not yet clear to the Army staff when this memo was produced in November.

Concurrent with the Higgins and first Almond reports were the conclusions of an Air Force team, headed by General Barcus and Dr. Robert Stearns, concerning close air support in Korea.[119] Since the starting point and underlying assumptions of this evaluation were different from those of the Higgins and Almond studies, it did not directly address some of the Army's dissatisfactions. In the course of the investigation, however, many of the underlying factors behind the Army's positions were examined.

The Air Force report agreed with the Army that the absence of joint training in air-ground procedures in the Far East before the war was responsible for a disorganized close air support system during the initial weeks of conflict. It attributed this training weakness to the nature of the Army's occupation mission and the state of training of the ground forces.

Investigators recognized the limitations placed on TACPs by the relatively poor regard in which the assignment was held, by inferior equipment, by short tours, by the many poorly trained radio personnel, and by the FAC's inability to direct strikes in those zones beyond their vision but inside the bomb line. They recommended several measures to improve the TACP system. In order to acquire better controllers, their tours should be lengthened to at least six months and controllers should be chosen from the pick of the Air Force—"definitely not the unwanted or the misfit." The aura of the position should be heightened by giving serious consideration to such an assignment as a prerequisite for promotion and for assignment to the command of a combat unit participating in a joint operation. As to the number of TACPs per Army unit, this should be left flexible and dependent on the need for close air support and not, as the Army wanted, fixed at a standard number. This recommendation was probably inspired by General Almond's demand for more and more TACPs that he was using, in the absence of a proper air-ground operations system in X Corps, to request air strikes.

Close Air Support in Korea

Poor equipment, particularly communications equipment, with which the TACPs had to work came in for indictment. The group recommended that the ground controllers be given proper radios to communicate with a POMP and artillery forward observers and with direction centers associated with its lead element, as well as with liaison and combat planes. Also, the equipment should be sturdy enough to be used in remote locations and well protected from shocks, rain, snow, and dirt. The radio equipment should be mounted in vehicles similar to those used by the supported outfit so that they could go anywhere the supported unit went.

While the T–6 Mosquitoes came in for praise for supplementing the TACPs, as well as for performing such other tasks as covering tank columns, performing front line reconnaissance, and providing a channel for strike requests, the analysts warned that they could not be relied on in a nonpermissive environment where they would face the hazards of enemy aircraft and automatic weapons. They should be used as long as the environment permitted, but should never be permitted to replace TACPs in unit organization.[120]

The fiasco surrounding the deployment of the 502d Tactical Control Group, which made it unavailable at the very time when it was most needed, led the group to recommend that in the future similar groups be shipped by echelon, rather than as a unit, so that portions of the equipment could be employed without having to await full deployment. In order to do so, it recommended that these groups be reorganized in such a way as to allow in future for such contingencies as the immediate airlift of equipment for two small-scale TADCs, one TACC, and connecting communications. The remaining equipment should follow by the most expeditious means, including airlift if available.[121]

Many of the defects that fueled the Army's dissatisfaction with close air support, according to Barcus's analysts, stemmed from the Eighth Army's failure to fully staff the air-ground operations system. The resulting loss of effectiveness prevented the Army from taking full advantage of Fifth Air Force's assets. Far from being the result of indifference, low priority, or an Air Force animus toward close air support, the barriers to full and total close air support were a result of the Army's failure to staff its system, either because of lack of personnel, as with the Eighth Army, or because of failure to understand the communication and personnel requirements of F.M. 31–35, as was the case with X Corps.

So by early 1951, by which time the most important close air support operations had already taken place and the services had begun serious examination of what had occurred, both the Army and the Air Force still retained their prewar incompatible assumptions about the nature of and requirements for close air support. In July, General Almond produced a second major statement detailing X Corps's position on close air support in Korea, which he forwarded to the Army's Chief of Staff for Plans.[122] For 27 days, from May 10

Help from Above

through June 5, the X Corps, now a part of the Eighth Army, faced Chinese forces in the central part of the peninsula. During the first week of operations, the corps readied itself for a Chinese counterattack against its positions. The next seven days were spent in successfully parrying the enemy's thrust. In the final two weeks the corps went on the offensive and drove the Chinese back well beyond the positions they had originally occupied.

Sixty percent of the 25 close air support strikes during this campaign were flown by land-based Marine F4Us and carrier-based Marine and Navy F4Us, ADs, F9Fs, and F7Fs. Far East Air Forces F–80s, F–84s, F–51s, and B–26s, based in both Korea and Japan, provided the remaining 40 percent. The X Corps commander considered the Air Force support inadequate, due principally to the average time of 67 minutes that elapsed between request and delivery of air strikes.[123] He attributed this long response time to two factors: the complicated system for requesting strikes and the long distances between airfields and the front.

As regards response time, General Almond maintained that the average 6.5 minutes it took for requests to travel from the originating battalion to the JOC could be cut by more than half by allowing battalion commanders to request strikes directly from their local TADCs. This, of course, was what he had done earlier, much to the annoyance of the Air Force, when his corps was operating in eastern Korea separate from the Eighth Army. This arrangement eliminated the time consumed by regimental, division, corps, and Army G–3 Air officers in evaluating battalion requests. These intermediate echelons, in Almond's plan, would simply monitor the requests, stopping any they disapproved. Such a system was being used to advantage in calling in artillery fire and it seemed to Almond to be a practical method for requesting air support. Although nothing came of the suggestion at the time, a similar measure would be adopted a dozen years later in Vietnam.

Just as time was wasted in the request part of the system, so was it on the supply side, according to Almond. The average land-based plane was stationed 160 miles from the front, from where it took propeller-driven planes 48 minutes, and jets 25 minutes, to reach the action. This left the jets between 10 and 20 minutes of operating time over the target and the others between 60 and 100 minutes. The value of bases close to the front line was illustrated by the base at Pyongtaek (K–6), 80 miles from the front, which was being used by the Mosquitoes. Being so close to the battle line allowed the T–6s to remain over the front for more than three hours. Unfortunately, the only other nearby base, at Hoengsong (K–46), which was 40 miles distant and handled Marine F4Us, was unsurfaced, resulting in an unacceptable degree of damage to the aircraft propellers, plexiglass noses, and leading edges.[124]

The study recognized communications difficulties as one of the major problems of air support in the campaign. For ground communications, Army units used a telephone system to connect battalions to the JOC; a radio net

Close Air Support in Korea

made up of SCR–399s along with Air Force SCR–193 to connect corps headquarters with ROKA divisions; and a Teletype system from divisions to X Corps and from X Corps to the Eighth Army and the JOC. The telephone system experienced many difficulties, mainly from mountain ranges that interfered with the VHF relays and from a 250 percent overload on telephone switchboards. The radio net, on the other hand, was very dependable and effective. The Teletype system was too time-consuming. Frequently, Teletype operators were not available, and it required a phone call to tell a station to answer the Teletype.[125]

Almond's report concluded with the by now familiar plea that close air support squadrons be placed under the operational control of the field army commander, who would further allocate them to his corps commanders. To illustrate his proposal, he laid out a detailed description and organizational chart (**Figure 10**). Corps commanders, operating through Army Corps Air Officers, should be empowered to plan and supervise fighter-bomber strikes, air reconnaissance missions, column cover sorties, and the employment of TACPs. These Corps Air Officers should command all Air Force units supporting the corps, advise corps commanders on air matters, determine whether planes could fly based on mechanical or weather conditions, recommend procurement of air units, supervise detailed plans and annexes to operations orders, and prepare and supervise training programs for the air units under their command. In short, Army Corps Air Officers should replace Air Force commanders. The only things they should have to request from the Air Force would be night strikes, medium- and heavy-bomber missions, deep air reconnaissance and aerial photography missions, air transport and air rescue sorties. Citing the principle of unity of command, General Almond proposed ending the system of dual command. A responsible ground commander, he noted, must be able to direct, not request, air support.[126] Given the prevailing attitude within the Pentagon, this proposal went nowhere. It is useful, however, as an example of one of the more specific delineations of the Army's eternal quest for control of the close air support function.

The change of guard early in 1951 in the top military levels of the FEC ushered in no changes in the theater or service attitudes regarding close air support. Nor should changes have been expected. The attitudes in Korea were mere reflections of service doctrine that could be altered only at home through interservice agreement. General Ridgway, who replaced General Walker after the latter's accidental death just before Christmas of 1950, harbored as reserved an attitude toward Air Force close air support as had his predecessor, and he carried these views with him to Tokyo when he replaced MacArthur the following April. His replacement that same month at the helm of the Eighth Army, Lt. Gen. James A. Van Fleet, and Lt. Gen. Frank F. Everest, who took over Fifth Air Force in June, viewed close air support essentially has had their predecessors.

Help from Above

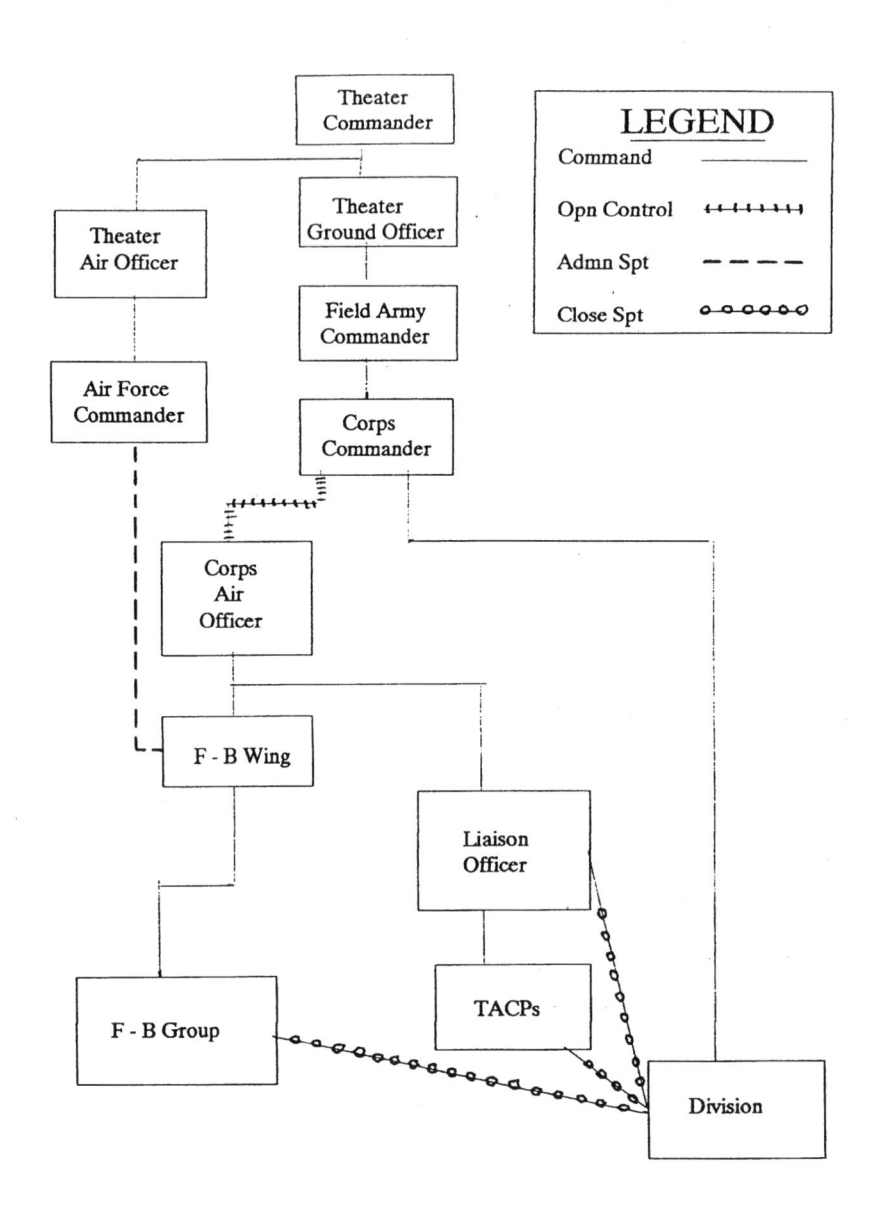

FIGURE 10
General Almond's Proposed Organization for Close Air Support

Close Air Support in Korea

General Collins's campaign to gain for the Army operational control over Air Force close support aircraft, which had begun late in 1950 with his letter to Vandenberg, picked up momentum in 1951. This was reflected in Korea in December when Van Fleet admitted to Everest during a visit that "Mark Clark has finally convinced Joe [Collins] that he is right, and Joe is ready to move." Clark had been pushing for such operational control for several years and Fifth Air Force interpreted Van Fleet's visit as the "first shot to be fired in the long anticipated argument." Noting that he was receiving pressure from both above and from his corps and division commanders, Van Fleet was probing to see how much, if any, support he could expect from Everest for a proposal assigning a squadron of fighter-bombers to each of his corps and stationing these squadrons as near the front as possible. According to the Eighth Army commander, such an arrangement would put an end to the squabbling that was going on between his corps and division commanders, who were in constant competition with each other for the air support that was allotted to Eighth Army. By giving each corps commander a specified amount of air support upon which he could depend, each corps commander could then apportion it according to his own plan and requirements, and Van Fleet and Everest would then only have to monitor its use.[127]

Everest's reply was twofold. First, even if he believed in splitting up his resources in such a manner, which he did not, he did not have the authority to set aside the established principles of air power. "The battleground for this inter-service argument," he reminded Van Fleet, "is in Washington, not Korea." Second, he firmly believed that the adoption of Van Fleet's proposal would destroy the existing flexibility to shift aircraft from one unit to another as the battlefield situation demanded and would result in fewer available daily sorties than Eighth Army currently enjoyed.

Despite Everest's unenthusiastic response, the Eighth Army commander made a formal written proposal on close air support to Ridgway several days later. By way of prologue, he stated that the time had come, in light of the Korean experience, to reexamine the existing arrangements for command and control in joint operations and to make whatever changes seemed indicated to render the joint effort more efficient. Van Fleet claimed to be expressing his own opinion, as well as that of all the ground commanders from company to corps level, in stating that close air support in Korea had not lived up to expectations.[128]

Specifically, seven correctable weaknesses dogged close air support in Korea. First, according to General Van Fleet, an inadequate number of close air support sorties was available. Second, the airfields from which close air support planes flew were not located near enough to the front lines, nor where they situated laterally across the peninsula, so as to reduce travel time to the target areas. Third, centralized control of all aircraft in the JOC added unnecessary delays between the time strikes were requested and the time they arrived.

Help from Above

Fourth, much time was wasted in placing aircraft on their targets after they reached the target area. This, in the view of Van Fleet, was due to the inexperience of the pilots and the insufficiency of ground control facilities. Fifth, there were not enough TACPs with the ground forces. This forced the ground units to rely excessively on the Mosquito airborne controllers, who may not be available in a war in which control of the air had not been won. Sixth, these TACPs were handicapped by their initial inexperience and their short tours of duty. Finally, Van Fleet stated that close air support suffered from the absence of a special aircraft and armament developed specifically for that mission.[129]

The remedy for most of these ills was the by now familiar one of assigning aircraft to corps commanders for close air support. Van Fleet used the analogy of the Army's contemporary organization in which combat units such as infantry divisions or field artillery battalions were attached to the basic combat organization, the corps, to assist the corps in accomplishing its mission. Close air support aircraft should be attached in a similar way.[130]

Given these factors, Van Fleet proposed assigning three of FEAF's Marine squadrons in Korea to the Eighth Army, which in turn, would delegate control over them to the three corps commanders in the theater. Not only would these aircraft perform close air support, but would also be used to attack "close interdiction targets" (20 to 40 miles beyond the front lines) that were directly affecting the battle. Army officers, specially trained by the Air Force, would control these air strikes. Air Force FACs would be replaced as much as possible by air observers and forward observers of the field artillery.

Requests for close air support would not go to a JOC, but instead would be processed at each corps headquarters and filled from aircraft under the operational control of each corps. The army headquarters would keep enough control over these close support aircraft so that in case of bad weather or a particular tactical situation, flights could be shifted from one corps to another. Unused sorties would be made available to Fifth Air Force.

Viewed from the ground perspective, this proposal would produce nothing but benefits to the air support program. It would provide more close air support sorties without subtracting from the interdiction or counter air effort. Closer airfields would reduce travel time to the targets. The overburdened communications traffic to and from the JOC would be reduced. Once they arrived in the target area, aircraft would deliver their ordnance more rapidly. The Mosquitoes would be eliminated, and control of air strikes would be given to trained army personnel permanently assigned to subordinate units within an infantry division.[131]

Although based on the Collins approach to the question, Van Fleet's revolutionary proposal carried the chief's philosophy further by applying it to specifics. Fifth Air Force's response was predictable, conservative, and suggestive of the position the Air Force would continue to embrace after the war was over.

Close Air Support in Korea

In response to General Van Fleet's call for a reevaluation of the air-ground practices in light of the Korean experience, the Fifth Air Force noted that these practices had been developed laboriously over a long period of time by staffs of expertly qualified officers, and that the air-ground experience in Korea was atypical and would probably not be repeated in future conflicts. Furthermore, it disputed evidence from Korea to the contrary.

As to the complaint that close air support had been inadequate and not lived up to expectations, the Army, argued Fifth Air Force, was being too inexact in its use of the phrase "close air support." By definition, close air support referred only to "air attacks against hostile surface targets which are so close to friendly forces as to require detailed integration of each air mission with the fire and movement of these forces." The geographical area encompassed by this definition was that which was within the range of ground weapons, principally artillery. The only time true close air support (as the Air Force understood it) would be required would be when these other ground weapons could not do the job. Army unit commanders below division levels in Korea preferred to use artillery, which was cheaper, more sustained, more accurate, and more controllable than air support and was available day and night in fair weather and foul. Except in special cases such as tank attacks, they preferred to see the air support used in areas beyond the range of concentrated artillery. The Air Force had supplied more than enough sorties for this type of close air support where it was necessary and practical. Where it had run into occasional shortfalls was in filling requests from division and corps commanders who called for air strikes against targets of opportunity, largely to gain advantage in competition with other division and corps commanders. Even in these cases, where the requests were merely expedient rather than necessary and practical, the Air Force had complied in a great many instances.

Fifth Air Force denied that airfields were not located laterally across the peninsula, pointing to the string of airfields from Suwon and Seoul (K–13 and K–16) in the west, through Hoengsong (K–46) in the center, to Kangnun (K–18) near the east coast. By December 1951 these four fields were home to fighter-bombers used for close air support. There were good reasons why airfields were not located closer to the front lines. The logistics and transportation to support such fields had to be shared with the Army. To the degree that logistical assets were used to construct forward airfields, they were unavailable to ground units. On occasion, the Army had been able to support airfields in forward locations, such as at Suwon and at Seoul when the U.S. I Corps first retook those cities. In general, however, the frequent shifting of the front lines in Korea had not justified the establishment of forward air bases until the lines settled down and became permanent.

Most ground commanders had become convinced that the requirement for them to request aircraft from the JOC imposed unnecessary administrative delays in getting the aircraft to the target. Van Fleet proposed taking the con-

Help from Above

trol of close air support aircraft away from the JOC at Army level and placing it at the FSCCs, which controlled artillery and other firepower at corps and division levels. The Air Force estimated that the only time saved by doing this would be the minuscule amount of time it took the JOC to contact either an airborne fighter-bomber or an airfield. It considered the time-saving argument to be largely a cover for the more deep-seated doctrinal disagreement over control of close air support planes.

The Army preferred using TACPs over using airborne Mosquitoes to control air strikes because they retained more control over the ground FACs than they did over the flying tactical air coordinators. Fifth Air Force also preferred ground controllers over airborne ones, but for different reasons. To provide visual airborne coverage over the entire front in Korea would require a prohibitive number of pilots and would detract from the Air Force's ability to man fighter-bombers and other close support aircraft.

To Van Fleet's complaint that the TACPs lacked familiarity with army procedures, Fifth replied that the TACP's job was to provide the experience and perspective of a combat pilot and not necessarily a great deal of knowledge about the Army. It was the job of the G–3 Air, which was the TACP's counterpart in the air-ground system, to supply the perspective of an Army officer. The two were supposed to work together.

Fifth Air Force wisely refrained from making extended comments on Van Fleet's analogy between tactical air units and Army ground units other than to note that there was no conceivable task for air capabilities at these levels that could not be accomplished effectively under the present arrangement. The question of command and control transcended the theater level and was so central to Army/Air Force relations that its determination could only be made in Washington.

The Air Force saw in the Van Fleet proposal to place three Marine squadrons under the operational control of his Eighth Army as an attempt to install the Marine system of close air support into Fifth Air Force. Such an arrangement would raise many questions. Where would the Koreans, who now were being supported by FEAF through the JOC, get their air support? Who would set the priorities between Army and Air Force aircraft missions? If squadrons were operating from forward bases, or airheads, who would set the priorities for airlift? Who would build airfields for loaded cargo aircraft? Who would fly cover for Marine aircraft? Would Fifth Air Force have the option of refusing to attack heavily defended targets requested by corps commanders when the Air Force did not consider that the value of the target warranted the effort? When corps aircraft could not fly, would Air Force planes be expected to fly their missions without preparation or training? Most of these questions were asking, in effect, who would assume the many "peripheral" functions then being performed by the JOC but which would go wanting with its demise. For example, whoever commanded the air effort in a specified zone also had the responsibility for reconnaissance to develop intelligence for target study and for damage assessment. The Van Fleet idea made no provision for such responsibilities.

On the recommendation that the Army take over the responsibility of providing TACPs, the two sides agreed. Army personnel for the TACPs would undergo special training by the Air Force. Already existing air observers and forward observers of the field artillery would be used as much as possible, and signal equipment would be borrowed from the Air Force and the Marines. The Air Force's willingness to entertain this change was probably motivated by its desire to stanch the flow of qualified fighter pilots into ground observer activities.

In conclusion, Fifth Air Force disagreed with the purported advantages of the proposal. To General Van Fleet's assertion that his arrangement would provide more close air support sorties without reducing Fifth Air Force's air effort, General Everest's command replied that the sorties given to the Army would be expended primarily against targets of opportunity in the front lines rather than in necessary close air support, and that the arrangement would result in a 15 to 20 percent reduction in Fifth Air Force's fighter-bomber effort. To the Eighth Army commander's assertion that travel time would be reduced to a minimum if the planes flew from fields within the corps areas, Fifth Air Force estimated that the maximum round-trip time saving would be 25 minutes, which would be more than offset by the additional aircraft turnaround time and their maintenance periods at unimproved forward fields.

The Van Fleet proposal was not adopted. In fact, in his conversation with Everest the Eighth Army commander pictured it as a recommendation for use only if the offensive battles resumed in Korea, which they did not. Nevertheless, the specificity of the proposal, its appearance at this particular time, and its continuity with the earlier ideas of Generals Collins and Almond, point to the direction in which the close air support controversy developed after the guns in Korea were silenced.

Three years of war on the Korean peninsula ended in a stalemate, as neither service was able to work its will on the other. Military and psychological initiatives by both factions resulted in a situation not substantively different from that which existed at the beginning of hostilities. Convictions held in July 1953 differed hardly at all from those of June 1950. In many ways, it was as if no war had taken place at all. Frequent discussions during the three years had convinced neither service to accept the other's position. The large volume of military activity and battlefield successes and failures had not swayed the antagonists' opinions. While one side remained convinced of the soundness of its prewar preference for centralized planning and control, the other adhered with equal resolve to its faith in the critical importance of disbursing power. The parties to this standoff were, of course, the United States's Air Force and Army. The deadlocked issue remained that of command and control of close air support.

Help from Above

There were changes on the margins. Aircraft and armament improved, as did the tactics of air support, and the importance of having airfields close to the action was reinforced. Some communication difficulties were overcome, both by the acquisition of better equipment and by agreements on how it was to be used, while the experiment with airborne FACs, although forced on the Air Force by the ruggedness of the terrain, was nonetheless a positive step in the direction begun by the occasional use of airborne controllers in World War II. Also, the installation of ground radar made successful close air support missions possible at night and during periods of foul weather.

On many occasions, air strikes compensated for a deficiency of ground firepower in defeating Chinese human-wave assaults, and air and ground commanders gained valuable experience in integrating artillery and air strikes. A major agreement between the two services called for the Army to provide the equipment and personnel for the TACPs, while the Air Force would continue to provide the FACs, who were still to be rated fighter pilots.

Once the opening shock of the invasion passed, the Tactical Air Control System, after some early jury-rigging, did well in controlling jet aircraft on close air support missions and in concentrating air power on threatened areas. Unfortunately, late and sporadic participation in the JOC by the other services made it, by default, appear to be too much of an Air Force, rather than a joint, instrument for coordinating and controlling air strikes. The animus that this impression built up toward the center during the conflict would figure prominently in postwar modifications of the air-ground system.

The major legacy of the Korean War for close air support was the reinstatement of the Tactical Air Command shortly after hostilities began. Within two months of the North Korean invasion, in August 1950, the command regained administrative and logistical control of its own units from the Continental Air Command. On December 1, TAC was restored to the level of a major air command, a status it would retain for four decades. The war had loosened purse strings, leading to a large buildup of ground forces, a new emphasis on tactical air power to support them, and the restoration of TAC to provide the support. The rebirth of TAC interrupted the trend toward organizing the operational units of the Air Force into a centralized, nonspecific combat command—a trend that would not be resumed until after the disappearance of the USSR more than 40 years later.

Beneath these positive aspects, however, lay the still unanswered question of who should control close air support assets. Although the picture was a blurred one, and the Army was not able to prove definitively from its Korean experience that the Air Force/Army air-ground system had failed and should be replaced, its prewar dedication to the concept of air power as an alternate form of battlefield firepower that it should control, continued to dominate its postwar plans and concepts. Its adherence to this concept was reinforced in Korea by the performance of Marine aircraft. Generalizing from the impressive close air support provided by these planes in a limited situation and believing that such a performance could be duplicated on a larger scale, many Army leaders carried into the postwar period a renewed desire for their own close air support resources. In this sense, the war changed little. Desirous before the war of a return to the pre-1943 status of close air support aircraft as an integral part of a combined arms team, the Army emerged from the war even more determined to achieve such control. The Air Force, on the other hand, could not accept the Army's perception of close air support as simply more firepower on a par with artillery or missiles or tanks. Unlike aircraft, these surface firepower weapons were geographically limited by terrain. Aircraft, on the other hand, possessed a unique capability to move to a geographic location on or behind the battlefield and to attack where none of these other weapons could. In Air Force eyes, this mobility, constituted the aircraft's greatest advantage and the very reason for its existence. Corps and division commanders, however, had no need for this mobility. To give them control of the aircraft would be to prevent the planes from being used to their fullest capability.

These differences would be exacerbated in the postwar decade by the Army's quest for a mission in the face of expanding doctrinal and budgetary emphasis on strategic deterrence and war fighting capability.

4 | Close Air Support Under the New Look

Usually close air support actions contribute less to the furtherance of surface actions than do the gaining and maintaining of air superiority and the interdiction of the enemy's lines of communication.

— AFM 1-3, April 1, 1954

The Army holds that interdiction of the battle area and close air support are integral parts of land warfare and that air forces engaged in such combat missions are not engaged in air warfare, but in land warfare, and are therefore subject to the general direction of the supported (Army) commander.

— Maj. Gen. Paul Adams, USA 1955

The high performance airplanes are flying away from us: they have left the battlefield.

— Gen. Maxwell D. Taylor, USA 1956

The encouragement that tactical airmen derived from the revival of interest in close air support and tactical air power during the Korean War was short-lived after the war ended and the steady rise of the USSR (Union of Soviet Socialist Republics) brought increased emphasis on American nuclear military power. More and more, the Korean Conflict came to be seen as an aberration that would never be repeated, and the prevailing opinion was that American troops would never again be sent to fight a conventional ground war, especially in Asia. Consequently, even TAC, whose rebirth during the Korean War at

Help from Above

first seemed promising for the future of tactical air power, had to adapt its mission to the reality of strategic nuclear preeminence.

The Air Force close air support program, during the post-Korea 1950s, moved simultaneously on several levels. The Air Force was comfortable in its role as the principal agent for America's deterrence and containment of the USSR, and tactical resources and functions often became handmaidens to the strategic mission. Seeing the question of close air support as a corollary to the larger issue, most influential Air Force leaders began to assert that strategic nuclear forces could deter both total war and limited conflicts. Tactical airmen struggled to keep the close air support mission alive, while most strategic airmen would just as soon have seen the Army take over its own air support. The subtle nuances of debate between these two approaches within the Air Force stemmed from the first level of analysis of the close air support issue during the 1950s.

The intensity of discussion within the Air Force over close air support of the Army was matched by the debate that the issue engendered within the Army. Here, two schools of thought existed, although the dividing line between them was not always well defined. The first group, mostly more senior leaders, wanted more control of close air support aircraft, but stopped short of proposing that the Army assume responsibility for the close air support mission. Taking a more cautious and gradualist approach in dealing with the Air Force on the question of close air support, despite their commitment to reducing reliance on the Air Force, these officers worked largely within existing channels and agreements.

Throughout the 1950s the Army continued to struggle, as it had since the end of the World War II, to define its mission within the nuclear world and the new national security policy of containment and deterrence. Its attempts to join in the nuclear mission, in particular in the field of surface-to-surface missiles, affected its perception of the Air Force's support role. Even though two of the chiefs during the decade, General Ridgway and Gen. Maxwell D. Taylor, had commanded in Korea and shared a general disappointment with the close air support they received from the Air Force in that conflict, they remained reluctant to fight for total Army control of the close air support mission.

Such could not be said for the second group, made up of a growing number of lower ranking Army officers. In a movement reminiscent of the "young Turk" revisionists that espoused Brig. Gen. William "Billy" Mitchell's ideas of autonomy in the 1920s and 1930s, these younger Army aviators, initially in the face of considerable official displeasure, developed both the doctrine (air mobility) and equipment (armed helicopters and fixed-wing planes) they hoped would provide the Army with an organic close air support capability.

While Air Force leaders were dealing with this first group of more moderate top Army officers on interim agreements, such as the size and mission of army aviation and joint training and doctrine, these lower ranking army aviators

Close Air Support Under the New Look

were starting to demonstrate that Army units having their own armed helicopters and fixed-wing planes could provide the Army with its own close air support. By the decade's end, the armed helicopter was rapidly gaining acceptance in the Army and all that remained was to test it in the field, decide where it would best fit within the Army organizational structure, and await the arrival of a defense secretary sympathetic to its incorporation into the Army's force structure.

For the most part, during the second half of the 1950s, Army and Air Force decision makers approached close air support issues with an open mind. In Korea the two agreed on some air-ground procedures, and both stood to gain from a settlement of their remaining differences. The persistent contention over air support of ground forces had sprung from the positive desire on each side to perform its mission as effectively as possible. Disagreements, although at times quite vicious, were a natural by-product.

The common starting point for both services in the decade was the shift of national security policy, in 1950, from the earlier reliance on diplomatic and economic methods to a more militant response to Soviet expansionism. Perhaps even more important for relations between the Army and the Air Force than the North Korean invasion in June, 1950, was Pres. Harry S. Truman's signing, two months earlier, of a National Security Council (NSC) Paper (NSC 68) officially sanctioning the policies of containment and deterrence of communism. Whereas the Korean War in many ways forced the Army and Air Force into closer cooperation on the battlefield, NSC 68 was a step in the opposite direction. Produced in reaction to the USSR's explosion of an atomic weapon and the communist takeover in China, both in August 1949, the new policy introduced a world that was to shape America's national strategy and the defense budgets to support it, as well as diplomatic, political, and economic moves, for the next four decades.[1]

The new policy called for abandoning the arbitrary budget limitations for defense that had remained at an annual $13.5 billion since the end of World War II. It recommended an increase in annual funding of up to 20 percent of the gross national product for "substantially increased general air, ground and sea strength, atomic capabilities, and air and civilian defenses to deter war" and, should war occur, to win it.[2] The subsequent three years of warfare on the peninsula largely deferred action on the new policy. No sooner had the armistice been signed in July 1953, however, than a new president, Dwight D. Eisenhower, set to work to modify the containment and deterrence policy.

Korea turned Eisenhower against limited wars. The conflict convinced him that a series of such limited wars would bankrupt the American economy, and that America should never participate in a war whose goal was less than total victory. Above all, he believed that his veiled threat to use atomic weapons against North Korea was instrumental in bringing about the armistice. As a result, his New Look policy, unveiled in October 1953 with the signing of NSC 162/2, was based on the premise that the American nuclear

Help from Above

deterrent was less costly than a conventional one, and that the presence of an American nuclear arsenal would serve to deter, not only a nuclear war, but wars at all levels of conflict as well. This latter idea was based on the assumption that the strategic nuclear deterrent would keep the USSR from initiating a limited war for fear that it may grow into a general war it could not win. Most importantly, the new policy ushered in a period of emphasis on tactical nuclear weapons. This new policy of strategic nuclear deterrence further complicated the already thorny issues of close air support.

The military implications of this security policy became clearer three months later with the announcement in January 1954 of the military strategy of Massive Retaliation. This strategy ruled out the previous strategy of conventional defense of local areas, claiming that this failed approach gave the initiative to the communists. In its place, the United States would seize the initiative by placing itself in a position to be able to retaliate instantly with nuclear weapons "at times and places of our own choosing."

The New Look policy and Massive Retaliation in many ways represented the culmination of the Air Force's long campaign for recognition of its supremacy among the military services. Together they promised a rosy future for the service in the areas of both budgets and prestige. For the Army, on the other hand, the turn away from limited wars and toward reliance on nuclear weapons, which for the most part were delivered by air, foreshadowed a further reduction in the size and importance of the ground force that had just begun a revival, thanks to the Korean War, from the low point following World War II. Once again, as it had before Korea, the Army was forced to search for a mission. It was within the context of these mission developments that the story of the Air Force's close air support of the Army unfolded between 1955 and 1960.

The Services, The New Look, and Close Air Support

Less than two months after Secretary of State John Foster Dulles's announcement of Massive Retaliation, General Weyland arrived from FEAF to replace Gen. John K. Cannon at the helm of TAC. In on the ground floor of the new strategic and nuclear-oriented national military strategy, Weyland found himself in a position analogous to that which General Quesada had occupied in the previous decade. It became Weyland's task to preserve whatever tactical force and mission in the Air Force that he could in the face of the preponderant Massive Retaliation, as represented by SAC. To save what he could, he shifted the brunt of tactical operations away from their traditional joint-operations missions and toward becoming primarily a complementary element of the Air Force's massive retaliatory force. Airmen from TAC took on the protective coloration of Massive Retaliation by tilting toward nuclear weapons and

Close Air Support Under the New Look

**An F–100 Sabre 45 (top);
A Martin B–57A
Night Intruder (right).**

strategic retaliation and away from (although not completely) conventional warfare and close air support capabilities. This middle ground was illustrated by the Composite Air Strike Force (CASF), which combined the nuclear power of national policy with the mobility and flexibility needed to support ground forces anywhere in the world. Although supporters of tactical air power were not overly enthused with this choice, it represented to them a better option than its alternative, absorption by SAC and the disappearance of any capability to support ground operations.

Starting in 1953, the development of tactical air power became keyed to the use of nuclear weapons as atomic thinking dominated fighter design. Although some conventional air wings to support the Army continued to exist during these years, after 1954 these wings were seen only as subordinate to the primary strike force. In that year, as soon as they were nuclear equipped, TAC's light-bombers (B–26s and B–57s) and fighter-bombers (F–84s, F–86s, and F–100s) began their atomic delivery training. The command's concept of operations for 1955–1956 barely mentioned a conventional capability. Although the Air Staff's policy required that tactical aircraft, even though designed primarily as atomic carriers, retain a supplementary conventional bomb capability,[3]

183

Help from Above

this capacity was usually overshadowed by nuclear priorities in doctrine, training, and armament and munition procurement.

A conventional capability, including that for close air support, however, never completely disappeared.[4] Despite TAC's nuclear-dominated concept of operations, there remained within the command a healthy controversy as to where the balance should lie between conventional and nuclear readiness. In 1954, for example, two F–86 wings received intensive atomic training and were sent to Europe, but for the rest of TAC's forces qualification in atomic delivery was secondary. The following year, TAC compromised on the issue by requiring its best qualified pilots to be trained for atomic delivery and the remaining aircrews for conventional operations. Each fighter-bomber squadron was to keep five aircrews available for best-qualified duties. By the time of the joint nuclear exercise Sage Brush in the fall of 1955, atomic delivery had become the primary mission for most fighter-bomber units, with only "familiarization," rather than proficiency, with conventional weapons required of aircrews.[5]

The TAC continued to emphasize the ability of its aircraft to deliver both nuclear and nonnuclear weapons, despite the conclusion from Sage Brush, the first major joint exercise, that nuclear delivery should receive primary consideration and the fear that assignment of a dual role would dilute the capabilities in both fields. Although the command attempted to train its aircrews in both roles at the gunnery range at Wendover, Utah, severe shortages of 20-mm ammunition and of guns resulted in a *de facto* preponderance of nuclear-delivery training.[6]

One practical problem that complicated attempts to use the aircraft in dual delivery roles was the many hours required to physically reconfigure the planes from one type of operation to the other. A large part of the difficulty arose from the need for different pylons for conventional and nuclear weapons. Throughout 1956 the Air Force's Research and Development Command was unable to come up with a universal pylon that could serve both types of munitions. Sticking to its policy, TAC did not accept the compromise suggested by its field commanders that specific squadrons concentrate on one or the other type of delivery.[7] The emphasis on nuclear delivery became even more pronounced in 1956 when TAC introduced two more nuclear-delivery aircraft, the B–66 light-bomber and the F–100D. The latter was to become the backbone of TAC's offensive force.

By 1958 some field commanders felt that the requirement for fighter crews to be only familiar with, rather than proficient in, the tactics and techniques of conventional weaponry had severely diluted the command's ability to do a satisfactory job with conventional weapons, either in close air support, interdiction, or air-to-air combat. This sentiment was reinforced that same year when TAC sent composite air task forces to both Lebanon and Taiwan. Although no fighting ensued, American policy precluded the use of tactical nuclear weapons in the event conflict had erupted. In the view of one of these task force commanders, "U.S. forces would have been overwhelmed in conventional fighting," meaning that TAC's fighters could not support a ground

Close Air Support Under the New Look

An illustration of a Douglas B–66A.

force in a conventional, limited war. The commander of the other air task force was horrified to discover that his F–100 aircrews, all of whom had received familiarization training with conventional weapons, were not qualified to deliver high-explosives. As a result of these experiences, many in the TAC became convinced of the need to increase conventional training, even at the expense of nuclear training.

These warnings went unheeded at the time. Maj. Gen. Thomas D. White noted truthfully but unhelpfully that it would take years to build high-explosive weapons and forces.[8] Rather than build up TAC, the Air Force further reduced the command in late 1958 and early 1959, terminating, among other things, the Air Force's program for developing conventional bombs and limiting nonnuclear training to two F–104 squadrons. As a result of halting the research and production of conventional weapons in 1958, conventional weapons did not keep up with the improved delivery systems. The weapons stockpile came to be made up of munitions that had been manufactured before production had ended, many of which could not be delivered successfully at jet speeds. In order to maintain even the semblance of a nonnuclear tactical air support capability, TAC was forced to rely on the Navy's conventional weapon development program.[9] General Weyland, just before his retirement the following year, warned again that preoccupation with strategic bombing and missiles would "leave us unprepared to fight limited war."[10]

Help from Above

A malaise in the area of air-ground cooperation in the 1950s is also suggested by the uneven attendance record at the Air-Ground Operations School (AGOS), the one joint school dedicated to training officers of both services to cooperate on the battlefield. The school, which TAC had been running since 1951 at Southern Pines, North Carolina, to immerse Air Force and Army officers in the doctrine, tactics, and mechanics of air-ground operations, was having trouble filling its quota of Army officers throughout the 1950s.

Instruction at the school was based on the 1950 version of the Joint Training Directive. Both the faculty and student body consisted of Army and Air Force officers with an Air Force commandant and deputies from the Army and Air Force. The Marine Corps and the British RAF had permanent faculty representatives to broaden the area of issues considered by the students. By the end of 1953, 10,500 students in grades lieutenant colonel through lieutenant general had graduated from one or more of the three courses that made up the curriculum: the Indoctrination Course, the Specialist Course, and the Forward Air Controller Course. A five-day Indoctrination Course dealt with the broad subject of air-ground cooperation, and a following, longer, ten-day Specialist Course, held at Pope AFB, covered the details of the tactical air control system, the JOC, and the air-ground operations center. Special emphasis was placed on the roles of the G–2 Air and G–3 Air, ground liaison officers, air liaison officers (ALOs), the integration required in planning and executing joint operations, target selection and marking, and the process of requesting air support by line units. In the Forward Air Controllers Course, Air Force officers became acquainted with the details of the tactical air control system, the air-ground operations system, and the JOC. They also studied ground force weapons, the relations between controllers and ground commanders, the control of aircraft on close air strikes on front line targets, target marking, FAC equipment, and how the ground forces were organized.[11]

Included among the alumni were 150 civilians with equivalent rank and 75 Allied officers. During the decade after the Korean War, however, Army interest and enrollment in the school shrank to less than half the quotas assigned to it and many of the unfilled slots went to Air Force officers. It was also discovered that only a small percentage of Army officers assigned to G–2 Air and G–3 Air positions had attended the school.

For the vast number of officers who could not attend AGOS, TAC instituted the Joint Air-Ground Instruction Team (JAGIT), which traveled to various locales to introduce personnel to the fundamentals of joint operations. While less thorough than AGOS, these instruction teams were deemed of some value in building bridges between air and ground forces. Unfortunately, the inability of the two services to agree on doctrine, which the school taught, prompted an observer in 1954 to note that what began as a "monument to interservice cooperation has come to more nearly resemble a gravestone."[12] Overall, this poor performance in air-ground instruction

Close Air Support Under the New Look

added to the impression of general lack of interest in cooperation existing within both services.

The close air support picture in the 1950s was not a totally bleak one, however. The majority of TAC's supersonic F–100s, for example, were designated as fighter-bombers with close air support as one of their missions. The first of these planes, the A and C models, that became operational in the fall of 1955, were designed as day fighters and air superiority vehicles. The Air Force, however, bought only 679 of them.[13] Almost twice as many (1,274) of the F–100s, on the other hand, were D models that entered operational service in September 1956 with the primary mission as fighter-bombers. As such, these planes served as TAC's primary close air support planes. The almost two-to-one ratio in the number of D models over A and C models reflected the Air Force's determination to preserve some air-ground capability. It was true that the close air support mission had to share the assets with the interdiction mission, and that nuclear deliveries, which favored interdiction over close air support, predominated. It was also true that the F–100Ds, like the Cs, experienced difficulty in delivering conventional weapons. For example, in 1957 the F–100Ds had problems dropping napalm fire bombs, leading the TAC historian to state that "in theory, if not in practice, TAC retained a napalm potential."[14] Nevertheless, the close air support mission remained alive and a factor in aircraft procurement.

Even some of the Air Force's 805 F–101 Voodoos, originally designed to escort B–36 bombers, were put into service as fighter-bombers. When SAC changed its mind in September 1954 and announced that it had lost interest in the Voodoo as an interceptor, TAC requested that the plane, which had been successfully tested that month, be reconfigured as a fighter-bomber. Equipped with four 20-mm cannons, missiles and rockets, 77 A models served with tactical fighter wings from 1957 to 1965. While most Voodoos were B model interceptors and photoreconnaissance aircraft, a small number of C models also were equipped with 20-mm cannons and nuclear bombing stations for the fighter-bomber role in close air support.[15]

The C model of the F–104 Starfighter interceptor was also a fighter-bomber, equipped with a 20-mm cannon and able to carry two missiles and 2,000 pounds of bombs. While this first jet plane to exceed the speed of Mach 2 was soon passed over by the services and became a stalwart of arms sales abroad, a number of the fighter-bomber models served with tactical fighter wings until the mid-1960s.[16]

That the Air Force intended to maintain a close air support capability was also reflected in its development in the late 1950s of a supersonic jet whose primary role was as a tactical fighter-bomber. The F–105 was designed to carry an armament load one and a half times the weight of that carried by B–17 bombers in World War II. In addition to a fixed 20-mm cannon on its nose, the Thunderchief could carry up to 8,000 pounds of nuclear weapons in

Help from Above

A drawing of an F–101A showing a portion of the cockpit interior.

its bomb bay and 4,000 pounds of external ordnance for close air support, including cluster bombs and over 1,000 rounds of ammunition. As the probability of its delivering nuclear weapons decreased, the bomb bay was modified to accommodate either fuel tanks or additional conventional weaponry.[17]

This close air support capability was increased in mid-1959, when the chief of staff directed that five of TAC's stateside fighter wings, and one each of the tactical wings in Europe and the Pacific, qualify aircrews in high-explosive delivery within one year. This inaugurated a program aimed at making all tactical aircrews dual qualified.[18] Newer first-line fighter-bombers, the F–104s, F–105s, and F–100Ds, were modified during the next two years to carry an even greater assortment of nonnuclear weapons than before. This development greatly accelerated after Defense Secretary Robert S. McNamara's announcement in May 1961 that nonnuclear war forces would be strengthened.

At every opportunity Weyland attempted to clarify the new role of tactical aircraft, stressing that the Air Force continued to have a responsibility to support the Army in air-ground operations, and that the introduction of nuclear weapons had in no way changed the fundamental principles of tactical aviation.[19] A major theme of his tactical air philosophy in the 1950s, and one that justified continued support of the ground forces, was that while SAC was the chief deterrent to the outbreak of a major war by the communists, it was relatively ineffective in deterring or fighting "wars of less than major proportions."[20] "It is obvious to me," he told Congress in 1956, "that we must have adequate tactical air forces in being that are capable of serving as a deterrent to the brush-fire type of war just as SAC is the main deterrent to a global war." In his view, the strategic nuclear deterrent had not prevented the outbreak of

Close Air Support Under the New Look

the limited military conflicts in Korea, at Dien Bien Phu in Indochina, or in Malaya. Needless to say, on this point the Army agreed. Throughout the decade Weyland continued to pound home the idea that the tactical air forces needed genuine support rather than lip service.[21]

Yet Weyland and other proponents of tactical air support found themselves constantly called upon to perform a balancing act between the still dynamic Douhetian claims being made for air power by most in the Air Force and their (the tactical air supporters') relatively small role in preserving conventional forces to support the Army. Most flyers remained convinced that air forces were the dominant factor in war and rejected the traditional tenet that the object of war was to defeat the enemy land forces in battle. Air power had introduced a third dimension to warfare, according to this theory, making it possible to hurdle the barrier of enemy ground forces to strike directly at the sources of the enemy's power. Since land forces did not have to be destroyed to win the decision, it was no longer appropriate that air forces be placed in support of ground forces.[22] There were increasing calls to examine whether or not the historic roles of the military forces should be reevaluated and reversed.[23]

Despite TAC's view that it possessed a reasonable close air support capability in the 1950s, the Army continued to express its dissatisfaction with the Air Force because the latter bought only multipurpose tactical aircraft. Army leaders, impressed with the light close air support planes of World War II and Korea, kept pressure on the Air Force to develop a dedicated, light, subsonic, close air support plane that could operate from forward fields and could be controlled by ground commanders at lower levels.

This control at lower levels, of course, was precisely what the Air Force wished to avoid. Throughout the 1950s for doctrinal, economic, and tactical reasons, the Air Force adhered to its policy of flexibility by developing its new "Century" series as long-range multipurpose tactical planes, capable of per-

A McDonnell F–101A.

forming close air support and interdiction missions as fighter-bombers, and air superiority and air defense roles as day fighters. Although several of the new models were designated primarily as fighter-bombers, all fighter aircraft were expected to support each other's mission under certain combat conditions. Fighter-bombers, for example, whose primary mission was to attack enemy airfields, troops, and equipment on the ground, on occasion flew combat air patrol or intercept missions. Conversely, day fighters were to be ready, when called upon, to depart from their primary patrol and intercept missions to attack ground targets.[24]

To the Air Force, the policy of developing multipurpose aircraft reflected both doctrinal, economic, and tactical realities. By not limiting individual types of aircraft to specific missions, this practice accorded with the Air Force's conception of air space and air power as indivisible. This approach was also the result of the relatively limited budgets the Air Force had for procuring tactical aircraft, budgets that, throughout the 1950s, were about half those of SAC. Purchasing aircraft that could carry out several functions appeared to be a wiser investment than buying planes that served only one purpose. Finally, Air Force leaders were sincere in their conviction that light, subsonic close air support planes could not survive the air defenses of the modern nuclear battlefield.

Most Army officers, of course, disagreed. For one thing, many Army leaders believed that the Air Force's low esteem for close air support would ensure that the vast weight of effort of these supersonic, multipurpose planes would be devoted to missions other than those supporting the ground forces. In addition, many ground commanders were convinced that military equipment designed to perform multiple roles could perform none of them satisfactorily. Finally, the Air Force's emphasis on nuclear weaponry suggested a further de-emphasis of the ground support mission. The fact that the Air Force continued to proclaim that "the capability to fight 'iron bomb' (conventional) wars will be maintained at the highest possible level," did little to allay Army discontent.[25]

The willingness of the Air Force to maintain what it considered a reasonable degree of close air support capability among its resources did not impress the Army, whose leaders continued to complain that they were not consulted in the development of these planes, that they had virtually no input into the arming of and targeting for these aircraft, and, of course, that they lacked ultimate control of their operations. The most frequently heard plaint was that the Air Force's preoccupation with heavy-bombers and supersonic tactical planes had diverted its attention from close air support. In mid-decade the Army chief of staff, General Taylor, for example, informed his commanders that "the high performance Air Force planes are flying away from us: they have left the battlefield."[26]

In the face of the technological evidence, however, it is hard to avoid the conclusion that the Army's stated dissatisfaction with the purported inadequa-

Close Air Support Under the New Look

cies of jets and nuclear weapons for close air support masked a much more fundamental resentment. During the 1950s the Army was fighting for its very existence while the Air Force enjoyed overwhelming political and economic support. If the Army were to remain a viable military force in the nuclear age, its leaders would have to carve out for it a mission that would ensure for it a place in the sun and in the annual defense budget. The outlines of this new mission began to take shape in the mid-1950s, during General Taylor's tenure as chief of staff.

Taylor's predecessor, General Ridgway, who served as Army chief of staff between 1953 and 1955, had strongly disagreed with President Eisenhower's New Look policy and its concomitant strategy of Massive Retaliation. He rightly perceived that the logical consequence of such strong reliance on nuclear forces for deterrence or retaliation would seriously diminish the role of ground forces. His concern was reinforced by a pervasive, although not necessarily universal, conviction within the Air Force that land warfare, whose object was to defeat an enemy's land forces in battle, was a thing of the past. The emerging Air Force basic doctrine, first published in 1954, was quite clear in assigning to air forces the dominant role in warfare and in maintaining that it was no longer necessary to defeat an enemy's ground force in order to destroy his strength.[27] This doctrine led frequently to statements that the Army found contentious, such as that of one speaker early in 1955 at the Air War College, who suggested that "it may now be possible to reverse the (traditional) order and place the armies in support of air forces."[28]

Major among the Army's many concerns with the New Look policy was the fear that the Air Force, in its embrace of Massive Retaliation, would abandon close air support altogether and turn away from whatever progress had been made in interservice cooperation in Korea. Specifically, the Army looked with growing apprehension at what it perceived as the Air Force's procurement of strategic bombers and fighters to the detriment of tactical support planes. It did not share the Air Force's confidence that jet fighters, even those with primary missions of air fighting or interdiction, could perform the close air support mission satisfactorily.

The Army's response to the close air support issue was far from monolithic. It took two approaches to challenging the Air Force's stewardship of the close air support function. The first challenge was more moderate and operated within the framework of traditional interservice negotiations. It took the form of a reinvigorated campaign from the top down to modify the existing command and control arrangements by acquiring a larger degree of control over both the development and operations of Air Force planes for the Army. This challenge, up front and aboveboard, formed the agenda of many interservice conferences and studies during the decade. The Army members of this school, who for the most part represented the upper echelons of command where compromise with the Air Force was the order of the day, continued to

Help from Above

deny any ambition to create a close air support capability within the Army.

The second challenge, which sought more substantive changes to the traditional methods of tactical air support, was more covert and therefore more the subject of Air Force suspicion. Its champions, mostly officers of lower rank, embarked on a grassroots effort to develop the Army's organic aviation, particularly helicopters, with the goal of taking over portions of, not only the close air support mission, but also of the airlift and reconnaissance functions from the Air Force.

The moderates operated through normal channels. Their complaints with Air Force close air support were summed up in an article which the Secretary of the Army distributed in May 1955 to every Army unit. The article, titled "Army Aviation," had appeared in the journal *Air Facts*, a magazine for pilots.[29] Although the article was a pitch to sell light aircraft to the Army, its thrust was a litany of Air Force deficiencies in the area of close air support. The Air Force's close air support in Korea, according to the author, had been either nonexistent or too late to be of value. "Day after day" one of three things would happen to requests from beleaguered ground troops for air support. Either it would be decided that the target was not worth the risk of a $500,000 plane, or that other simultaneous requests for air support were more urgent, or

> An hour or so after the request was made there might come a jet steaming along at five hundred miles per hour at ten thousand feet flown by essentially an acrobatic and instrument pilot, now having to fly by pilotage, studying his map and looking at the ground trying to figure out just beyond what cross road they were talking about. Even though the ground unit might have had him in sight, they were not permitted, even with suitable code identification, to talk him down to the target. As a result, the unit, having received no close air support or at best much too late, had to take its losses and extricate itself as best it could.

Despite statistical evidence to the contrary, the writer repeated this widespread parody of Air Force close air support in Korea calling such support "sporadic, tardy, and extremely limited in quantity."[30]

The article, distributed throughout the Army for "information" purposes, stated clearly what many soldiers believed, but hesitated to say openly. It declared that the first priority accorded to air superiority by tactical air power "for long periods" prevented aircraft from supporting ground forces. It directly attacked Air Force tactical doctrine by maintaining that "many times" the United States had been pushed back on the battlefield even when it had air superiority, and that "air superiority has only a negative value to ground forces."[31]

Close Air Support Under the New Look

A Cessna XL–19B, the world's first turbine-powered light aircraft.

The author, who was trying to sell low-and-slow airplanes to the Army, attributed much of the Air Force's purported weakness in providing close air support to its "reverence for speed." For the Air Force, he maintained, speed is as much a weapon as fire power. Yet the man on the ground, pinned down under heavy fire, wanted fire power, not speed. He dismissed the Air Force's concern about the vulnerability of slow planes in the battle area with the assertion that the Army knew from its experience with the Cessna L–19s in Korea that light planes could survive.[32]

Finally, the author ridiculed the command and control system for close air support by contrasting the ground commander's ability to control his tanks and artillery with his lack of control over his close air support. "He's got to have his close air support," concluded the article, "not only along with him like his tanks and trucks and artillery, but subject wholly to his command."[33]

The relevance of this document resides less in what it said, which reflected basically the Army's position on close air support, than in the fact that the Army headquarters used it as a vehicle to disseminate its views throughout the organization, thereby preserving the option of denying the official nature of those items challenged by the Air Force.

Army officers repeated these basic ideas in conversations with the Air Force in July 1955. Although these meetings dealt primarily with resolving potential disagreements arising from the Army's development of its own organic aviation, the basic Army philosophy of close air support shines

Help from Above

through the discussions. Among its objectives, the Army included equal partnership in developing the characteristics of aircraft used in joint operations. The chief Army representative, Brig. Gen. Hamilton H. Howze, also insisted that the Army have "general direction" over aircraft of other services supporting Army forces in the land battle. To support this position he pointed to the statement contained in a JCS paper of the previous March (1692/9) to the effect that:

> The Army holds that interdiction of the battle area and close air support are integral parts of land warfare and that air forces engaged in such combat missions are not engaged in air warfare, but in land warfare, and are therefore subject to the general direction of the supported (Army) commander including such directions as designation of targets or objectives, timing, duration of the supporting action and other instructions necessary for coordination and for gaining the greatest advantage.
>
> The Army's position on tactical air support is the same as for any other type of support; that is, to be effective, supporting forces must operate under the direction of the supported commander.[34]

While the weight of Army opinion on close air support reflected this view, there was some disagreement with it within the service. One Army artillery officer questioned, in an article, the Army's assumption that the Air Force's position violated the principle of unity of command. Pointing to the fact that the Army itself did not give its own local infantry commanders control of the noninfantry artillery that was supporting them, he asked why tactical air should be controlled by local ground commanders when the artillery was not. Paradoxically, he continued, it was the very principles of war of mass, economy of force, and unity of command that kept the Army from giving control of supporting ground weapons to those who most directly used them—the squad, company, battalion, regimental, or division commanders. This same principle should continue to be applied to air support. The Army's disgruntlement with the Air Force putting air superiority first also came in for criticism in this analysis. The Air Force was fully justified in this priority by another principle of war set forth in Army doctrine, namely, that of security. This principle meant security for ground forces as well as for aircraft. "Our own close support activities cannot possibly be effective," he wrote, "if the enemy is in a position to challenge us seriously in the air." The author of the article found it inconsistent for the Army to readily accept, in the name of unity of command, the Navy's doctrine of command and control of its air support for amphibious

Close Air Support Under the New Look

landings while rejecting the Air Force's identical doctrine for air-ground operations.[35]

Rightly pointing out that it was largely circumstances that dictated whether interdiction or close air support occupied the second priority for tactical air, the writer reminded his fellow soldiers that almost all the targets that could be seen from the ground (or from low-flying aircraft) could be hit more effectively, more accurately, more quickly, and more repeatedly by ground weapons than from the air. Airplanes can contribute more directly to the land victory by "beating up on the rear areas, lines of communications, supply depots and command posts, than they can spraying a vaguely defined front line with machine guns, bombs and napalm."[36]

Even the Army's cherished argument that it needed a cheaper, more maneuverable, and more effective close air support plane than the Air Force's jets came in for rebuttal. The author envisioned, during the battle for air supremacy, large numbers of these limited aircraft and expensive pilots sitting idly by as attractive targets for enemy attack. If the air battle were lost, these planes would be unable to operate. Even if the air battle were won, modern antiaircraft weapons would make their use extremely hazardous. In addition, a resort to low-and-slow conventional aircraft for close air support would eliminate the psychological bonus over enemy ground forces enjoyed by jets. In conclusion, the author found the Air Force doctrine of command and control of close air support aircraft sound in terms of the principles of war and comparable accepted doctrine of naval air support for ground forces.[37]

Needless to say, this was a lonely view within the Army. Nevertheless, the moderates still did not go so far as to favor the Army replacing the Air Force with its own close air support resources. Rather, they preferred that the Army obtain operational control of supporting aircraft, which would still belong to either the Air Force, the Navy, or the Marines. Although by 1955 some young Turks were beginning to push for Army possession of its own close air support resources, the more moderate top leadership continued to speak in conservative terms.

One such moderate was Brig. Gen. John E. Dahlquist, the commander of the Continental Army Command (CONARC). He disagreed with some of his subordinates, notably Brig. Gen. Carl I. Hutton, the commandant of the newly organized Army Aviation School, who believed that the Army should own its own close air support resources. Dahlquist thought the Army should possess only aircraft that "may in the future replace trucks." Close air support and other tactical support aircraft "should be under our operational control but...belong to either the Air Force or the Navy." He objected to Army plans to test light aircraft in the close air support role. His objections were more economic than doctrinal. Given the tight budgets, the Army would have to sacrifice in other areas in order to assume the burden of close air support, and Dahlquist could find no candidates for reduction.[38]

Help from Above

By 1955, General Ridgway's outspoken criticism of President Eisenhower's New Look policy led to his retirement after only one two-year tour as the Army's chief of staff. He was succeeded by General Taylor, another member of the "airborne club" and critic of the Air Force's close air support record. Unlike his predecessor, however, Taylor came to the job not only dissatisfied with the Air Force's cooperation, but with a proposed remedy. During his subsequent two tours as chief of staff he would devote his diplomatic skill and persuasive writing ability to an attempt at convincing the decision makers that Massive Retaliation was a flawed strategy that could not deter, much less prepare the United States to win wars less intense than all-out nuclear conflict. In this he agreed with Weyland who had been attempting to preserve tactical air resources for this very reason. Both leaders agreed that, in addition to nuclear war, resources were also needed to prevent, and win if necessary, conventional, limited, and insurgent types of warfare. Unfortunately, traditional and deep-seated service differences on the most fundamental level prevented this agreement in theory among these leaders from being translated into comfortable cooperation at the top military level. Although Taylor's doctrine of Flexible Response made little headway outside the Army during Eisenhower's tenure, it would be enshrined as national strategy by his successor, Pres. John F. Kennedy.

Taylor's push for a more flexible capability coincided with his conviction that, since it became independent in 1947, the Air Force had reneged on its promise to support the Army. The Air Force, in his view, was using the Army's need for Air Force close air support as a lever to blackmail the Army into accepting its views on close air support procedures, on control of the airspace over the battlefield, development of support aircraft, on limitations on Army aircraft, on the ranges of Army missiles used in close support, and on the radius of Army activities ahead of the battle line.[39]

Taylor was particularly exercised by what he saw as the Air Force's two-pronged shirking of its responsibility to the Army in ground combat. On the one hand, he said, its emphasis on high-performance aircraft designed primarily for air-to-air combat ill prepared the Air Force to discharge its obligation. While not providing enough of its own resources, the Air Force, on the other hand, was preventing the Army from doing so by restricting the size and weight of Army planes. "The Army must be freed from this tutelage," wrote Taylor, "and receive all the organic means habitually necessary for prompt and sustained combat on the ground."[40] Despite the emphasis by Taylor and the highest Army levels on the development of organic aircraft for the Army, limited budgets kept progress modest in the 1950s.

The gray area between Air Force and Army aspirations in the area of close air support that allowed Taylor's campaign to make some headway resided in the roles and missions assigned to each service. From the very beginning of its independence, the Air Force had repeatedly been given, and

Close Air Support Under the New Look

the Army prohibited from exercising, the close air support mission. President Truman's executive order that accompanied the National Security Act in 1947 listed "air support of ground forces" as a specific function of the new Air Force. This Air Force responsibility was further defined in the Key West functions paper the following year as "close combat...air support to the Army."[41]

An agreement between Generals Bradley and Vandenberg in 1949 specified the types of aircraft the Army would have and what they would be used for. Army aircraft were restricted to aerial surveillance, route reconnaissance, control of march columns, camouflage inspection, courier service, emergency evacuation, wire laying, limited serial resupply, and some front line aerial photography. Close air support or any form of aerial combat was not among the functions.[42] This restriction was reaffirmed two years later by the Army and Air Force secretaries, Frank Pace, Jr. and Thomas K. Finletter, who agreed that Army aircraft would not "duplicate the functions of the Air Force in providing the Army, by fixed-wing and rotary-type aircraft, close combat support." Army planes were specifically limited to aerial observation, control of Army forces, command, liaison and courier missions, wire laying, and transport of Army supplies and small units within the combat zone. A second agreement by the two secretaries in 1952 repeated the prohibition against using Army planes to duplicate the Air Force's mission of providing close air support.[43] In November 1956, Secretary of Defense Charles E. Wilson issued a memorandum that limited Army planes to performing the four functions of liaison and communications; observation, fire adjustment and topographic survey; limited airlift of personnel and materiel; and aeromedical evacuation. It specifically prohibited the Army from using its aircraft to perform close combat air support, interdiction, or strategic airlift, and reiterated that the close air support mission belonged to the Air Force.[44] Some Army leaders interpreted this memorandum as a serious blow to their aspirations of taking over some of the Air Force's tactical air support functions.

Throughout the 1950s questions persisted over Army and Air Force roles and missions. In a further effort at explanation, Secretary Wilson issued another directive in March 1957.[45] His intent was to make more explicit the boundary between the functions of Army and Air Force aircraft and to ensure that the Army did not duplicate any of the Air Force's missions. Specific weight limitations were placed on Army aircraft, which once again were prohibited from performing strategic and tactical airlift, tactical reconnaissance, interdiction, and close air support. Army aircraft were limited to the same functions as in the memorandum of the previous November.

Despite its attempt at elucidation, the directive left room for further debate. It admonished the Air Force "at all times to meet the reasonable (support) requirements specified by the U.S. Army," and said that it "shall devote an appreciable portion of its resources to such support."[46] The use of the subjective adjectives "reasonable" and "appreciable" defeated the purpose of the

Help from Above

Gen. Hoyt S. Vandenberg

directive. What appeared as reasonable and appreciable within the context of Army doctrine and tradition was viewed as excessive by the Air Force.

The Army considered these pronouncements by the secretary as defeats and set about to study the issue of tactical air support in greater detail. Late in 1959, the new Army chief of staff, General Taylor's successor, Gen. Lyman L. Lemnitzer, directed his operations staff, the DCSOPS or deputy chief of staff for operations, to develop a contingency plan for the Army to take over those missions of tactical air support it deemed necessary so that the Army could efficiently perform its primary role. The resultant plan was based largely on the "Tactical Air Support Feasibility Study" developed by the Aviation Division within DCSOPS, headed then by Brig. Gen. Clifton F. von Kann.[47]

In analyzing the Army's future requirements for close air support during the 1965–1970 period, the study began by calling for the removal of arbitrary restrictions placed on the Army's ability to accomplish its mission by the Secretary of Defense's 1956 memorandum and 1957 directive. It also called for modification of the currently assigned roles and missions to allow the Army to develop "organic systems" it deemed necessary for land operations.[48]

The Army study reviewed all the functions of tactical air support, including air superiority, tactical air reconnaissance, intratheater tactical and administrative airlift, interdiction, and close air support. Faulting the Air Force's earlier and continuing preoccupation with long-range nuclear strike operations and air defense, and its present emphasis on missile and space activities, the study concluded that the Air Force would not be able, during the 1965–1970 period, to provide tactical air support to the Army in the combat zone. This conclusion was based on its assessment that Air Force aircraft were generally not suited to the mission, that the Air Force was neither organized for nor inclined to be sufficiently responsive to Army requirements, and that many of these functions that were currently being performed by manned aircraft would be performed better in the future by other means.

Close Air Support Under the New Look

The two-part report, issued late in 1959, made much of what it pictured as the Air Force's failure to meet the "reasonable" and "appreciable" criteria of the secretary's memoranda. The Air Force fell only slightly short, it maintained, of meeting the quantitative Army requirements for close air support of one tactical fighter wing for each of the Army's 14 divisions—the Air Force had 13. It was the quality of the support that the Army found seriously deficient. It objected strenuously to the Air Force's practice of diverting aircraft theoretically programmed for Army support "for its own purposes." It hit hard the Air Force's emphasis on procuring aircraft for its own missions and disregarding the development of planes for close air support. Since World War II, it claimed, multimission aircraft, with characteristics that indicated they were designed for air defense, offensive counter air and interdiction missions, had overshadowed the requirement for close air support to which scant attention had been paid.

To support this contention, it noted that none of the planes currently in the Air Force inventory, or those planned for the future, met the criteria the Army proposed for close air support aircraft: penetrability, attack speeds on the order of .6 or .7 Mach, a capability of slow speed and great agility, and the ability to operate from relatively unimproved areas. The F–86F Sabre had the required attack speed capability, but could not fly slowly enough, nor was it sufficiently agile. Also, it needed a minimum of 4,000 feet of runway. The F–100 had the same drawbacks as the Sabre—lack of low-speed and agility coupled with lengthy runway requirements. The F–105 was also inadequate because it was extremely heavy, it lacked a low-speed capability, and its runway requirements were "completely unacceptable." Although the F–106, which came into the inventory that year (1959), could operate from level area runways as short as 2,500 feet, it carried no guns or bombs, only air-to-air rockets. It had no air-to-ground capability.[49]

As to the future, the study concluded that the Air Force had no plans to procure a single-purpose close air support plane, although several were available. The Navy, on the other hand, had reversed the trend toward speedier aircraft by developing new subsonic planes, like the AD–4, AF–2, and AD–6 for the close air support role. The Air Force even opposed use by non-U.S. NATO forces of an excellent lightweight strike fighter, the G–91. According to Army calculations, only three-tenths of one percent of the Air Force's 1961 research budget for fiscal year 1961 was to be spent for TAC. While only 1.7 percent was to go to airlift, the remaining 98 percent belonged to SAC and air defense. The only Air Force aircraft under development was the B–70 bomber.[50]

To illustrate the Air Force's unresponsiveness to the Army's "reasonable" requirements, the study cited many instances where the Army believed that the Air Force was diverting aircraft that had been programmed for Army support for its own purposes. Instances spread across the entire field of tactical air support, including airlift, reconnaissance, interdiction, and close air support. For the latter function, the study cited a case (May 1959) in which Gen.

Help from Above

Laurence S. Kuter, the Air Force commander in the Pacific, informed Gen. George H. Decker, the UN and Eighth Army commander in Korea, that he would not, unless ordered by higher authority, send a sophisticated and expensive aircraft such as the F–100 to deliver a conventional weapon in view of the small return on the investment. In the United States, CONARC was reporting that the quantity of Air Force support for small-unit exercises was 60 percent, and only 25 percent for large-scale exercises, and that the Air Force's inflexibility in stateside exercises had repeatedly required that the most minor issues go to the CONARC-TAC level for resolution.[51]

Differing philosophies regarding command and control of close air support aircraft compounded the problem. It was the Army's consistent view that it was the theater commander's prerogative to allocate forces to accomplish his mission. He determined which missions each service would perform, set the priorities for the effort, and established policy. The Army and Air Force component commanders planned jointly to determine what was needed for each mission and then the Army commander placed a requirement for support from the Air Force. The Air Force, the Army felt, was then responsible for providing the requested support. The Air Force, on the other hand, considered the theater air commander as the agent of the theater commander for employing all air forces. It was up to him to decide which planes would be used in which roles and to determine the timing, tactics, techniques, and weapons. The inability of the services to agree on a compromise position resulted in many problems over the years. As the Army saw it, Air Force units refused to participate in exercises in which Air Force-delivered atomic weapons were allocated to Army forces and delivered in close air support operations under the control of Army commanders. In fact, TAC had advised that all Air Force support would be withdrawn during those phases of exercises where the air commander did not have final air control authority.[52]

A key question discussed in the 1959 study, and one that formed the basis for many of the contending issues, was that of control of the airspace over the combat zone, whose depth the study set at 300 miles into enemy territory. As the Army saw it, up until then the Air Force clearly had the responsibility for controlling aircraft over the combat zone since they were the primary users of the air and had the principal antiair and close air support weapons. Conditions had changed, however, and the airspace once occupied almost exclusively by Air Force planes had now to be shared with Army artillery, surface-to-surface and surface-to-air missiles, observation aircraft, transport aircraft, drones, and conventional supporting fires, most operated by the Army. Paradoxically, the Army, which had resisted the emphasis on atomic weapons, was now using its own possession of such long- and short-range nuclear missiles as the Davy Crockett, Honest John, Little John, Corporal, Sergeant, and LaCrosse, as arguments against continued Air Force control of the air. Consistency in argument, however, has never been a strong suit in military planning, nor has its absence

Close Air Support Under the New Look

often interfered with arriving at doctrinal conclusions. To the Army, aircraft had become a secondary resource for the ground commander's mission in the combat zone. Since the bulk of the resources that would operate in the airspace over the combat zone of the future would come from the Army, the Army commander should have control of all these weapons.[53]

The study concluded that the Army should assume all tactical air responsibilities with the exception of part of the interdiction mission. This included taking over complete control of the airspace, tactical air reconnaissance, interdiction in nuclear warfare, intratheater airlift, and, above all, close air support. In nuclear war, aircraft would participate only as a supplementary means of close air support; in nonnuclear war, as a primary means.[54]

The plan called for each Army division to have a direct support battalion of 36 aircraft. These planes must have short takeoff and landing capabilities and be capable of carrying a maximum armament and munitions load of 3,000–5,000 pounds. They should be able to cruise at 200–300 knots, be able to loiter on station for three hours, and be able to fly under instruments and at night. Finally, they would be single-place machines.[55]

This plan did not specifically call for the Army to possess its own tactical air resources, but rather implied that the Army should assume responsibility by taking over control of the functions then being performed by the tactical aircraft of the other services. Concurrently with his plan, General von Kann, in a public statement, dismissed the notion that the Army wanted to take over TAC. "We are perfectly happy to have the Air Force do it [the TAC mission]," he wrote, "but we insist it must be done."[56] His words were echoed at the end of 1960 by the Army's new chief of staff, General George H. Decker. In the course of discussions with the Air Force chief, General White, Decker stated:

> I think as long as the Air Force has the [Tactical air support] mission and can do it they ought to do it. We don't want to take it over, but there is that kind of pressure, as you probably know. I want you to know that is not my position.[57]

The pressure he was talking about was that exercised from below by the less moderate Army officers whose experiments with Army aviation, by 1960, constituted a substantial challenge to the Air Force's hegemony in the close air support arena.

Further Attempts to Create Joint Air-Ground Doctrine

Despite these deep-seated doctrinal differences at the higher levels, Air Force leaders at the operational levels in the United States, the Far East (FEAF),[58] and Europe (USAFE)[59] continued to work with the Army in con-

Help from Above

ducting joint exercises throughout the 1950s. It was their hope that these exercises would aid in the development of a joint doctrine for air-ground operations. Tactical air supporters had a natural ally in the Army in opposing the dismantling of forces for limited wars. Unfortunately, two conditions prevented the tactical proponents from solidifying this natural alliance. On the one hand, in order to prevent TAC's total absorption by SAC, Weyland emphasized his command's ability to provide an independent tactical nuclear deterrent and war-fighting capability. In so doing, he, too, played down, more than he liked perhaps, its air-ground mission. On the other hand, enduring interservice differences proved stronger than the common desire to preserve conventional war capabilities, and prevented both sides from taking advantage of the opportunity to improve upon the advances in cooperation that had been achieved in Korea. In short, the doctrinal differences over command and control, aircraft development, weapon and target selection, and the host of minor differences that had come between the two services before the advent of nuclear weapons, carried over into the new atomic era, making more difficult the creation of firm joint agreements.

The obstacles to reaching agreement were most pronounced in joint training and joint doctrine. The two were closely related, and both languished until near the end of the decade. Most of the joint training disagreements that arose during the period resulted from an absence of a joint doctrine to provide clear guidelines for command and control of operations. In 1951 and 1952, for example, Army and Air Force differences over command and control of tactical aircraft and weapons in Korea were matched by similar disputes in exercises at home. A joint exercise at Fort Bragg, North Carolina, in August 1951, called Southern Pine, in which TAC's Ninth Air Force field tested, among other things, its ability to support ground forces, was seriously delayed during the planning phase by disagreements over how the opposing forces would be controlled. As a result, the planners had to make revision after revision right up until the exercise began. The main bone of contention was the Air Force's refusal to give the maneuver director, an Army general, complete control of all forces during the exercise.[60] The Army insisted on controlling air-delivered weapons at the lower corps level, while TAC, adhering to the Joint Training Directive (JTD), insisted that they be controlled by the JOC at the higher Army/Air Force level. To the Air Force, this dispute was merely the tip of the iceberg. Airmen saw the Army's insistence on decentralizing control of atomic weapons as merely a prelude to a concerted effort to decentralize control of all tactical air support. Although temporary agreement was reached, valid only for that maneuver, the subject of joint doctrine was referred to the Joint Tactical Air Support Board.[61] Instead of simplifying the process of creating joint doctrine, the interjection of this board added one more player to the already overcrowded field of participants and, in effect, created another arena for the airing of Army/Air Force differences.

Close Air Support Under the New Look

Similar disruptions accompanied exercise Long Horn, where simulated nuclear weapons were used on a small scale, during March and April the following year. After a simulated aggressor force landed at Corpus Christi and extended its sway over a portion of eastern Texas, including San Antonio, two divisions of the Army's IV Corps, supported by tactical air power, drove the invaders back into the Gulf of Mexico. Little progress was made during this exercise in settling the question that had disrupted the previous maneuver, namely that of operational control of fighter-bombers and weapons. The Army chief of staff, Gen. Lawton J. Collins, reflecting the criticisms he was hearing from Korea, particularly from General Almond, after a staff visit to the exercise, noted that "the present system of close support...is too slow and unwieldy." Even evidence the Air Force presented, showing that the problem was exacerbated by the Army's burdensome request system and that the support received by specific units was always coordinated with higher echelon Army commanders, did not convince the general that the corps commander should not have direct control of air support and air-delivered weapons.[62]

Army complaints with the Air Force throughout these maneuvers were not limited to what the Air Force called close air support, but often extended to other facets of Air Force support. The Army included in its definition of air support such other support functions as airlift, reconnaissance, airborne operations, aeromedical evacuation, operation of aerial port squadrons, and even interdiction. In both the Southern Pine and Long Horn exercises, for example, a time-consuming disagreement took place over who should perform aeromedical evacuation.[63] During joint exercises in New York State in 1953, the Army's chief of operations, Lt. Gen. Anthony C. McAuliffe, complained to General Vandenberg that the Air Force failed to provide proper aerial port facilities and pathfinder teams for the airborne troops.[64] General Cannon, who was still commanding TAC at the time, pointed out in reply that the blame should be shared by the Army for failure to make the proper requests or provide the Air Force with sufficient information. Cannon's staff, however, was less diplomatic. It saw the complaint as part of a calculated plan "to build a case against the Air Force for use later in Army efforts to usurp Air Force responsibilities." It was this continuing suspicion on the Army's part that the Air Force was purposely slighting support of the ground forces, matched on the other side by a hovering belief by many Air Force officers that the Army was attempting to develop its own air support, that colored relations between the two on the issue of close air support.

Resolution of this distrust lay in hammering out a mutually acceptable joint doctrine for air-ground operations. The delay in achieving unanimity, however, came as much from internal disagreement within the Air Force as from differences between the Army and the Air Force. Both the Army and TAC had agreed in September 1950 to implement the JTD. The Army Field Forces headquarters at Fort Monroe had the authority to enforce the directive and to

Help from Above

make it official doctrine for use in all Army schools. On the Air Force side, however, there was no clear-cut channel for creating doctrine. Although doctrinal responsibility was split between the Air Staff, the Air University, and the major commands, the Air Staff had charged the Air University with being the focus for its development. While major commands, such as TAC, might have inputs, these were to be filtered through the Air University. Tactical Air Command supported the JTD as a practical manual of instruction for operating with the Army, while the Air University rejected it on the theoretical grounds that it pictured theater operations as basically surface action, relegating tactical air units to the support of surface forces against other surface forces. This, maintained the Air University's analysts, contravened accepted Air Force doctrine and should not be preserved in any training directive.[65] In their eyes, the only valid statement of doctrine on the subject of air-ground cooperation then in existence was the F.M. 31–35 of 1946.

In an attempt to alleviate the unhealthy condition caused by reliance on two different sets of concepts, TAC asked Air Force headquarters to approve the JTD as an interim replacement for F.M. 31–35 until a permanent manual could be produced.[66] In true Solomonic fashion, Air Force headquarters authorized TAC to use the JTD "as an amplification of F.M. 31–35" in its instruction in air-ground training.[67] While this satisfied neither side to the controversy, it did reiterate that the directive, as originally conceived, was an interim document, thereby spurring TAC and the neighboring Army Field Forces to try again to find common ground.

Early in 1951, representatives of the two organizations once more set about to revise the JTD and arrive at a mutually acceptable doctrine for air-ground operations. In a series of meetings throughout June, it became obvious to the five delegates from each command that they were approaching the revision from opposite points of view. The Army members, whose basic doctrine was set forth in manuals elsewhere, viewed the directive as simply an operational and procedural guide rather than as a staff manual containing doctrine. By 1951, the Air Force had yet to publish its basic doctrinal manual. Consequently, the Air Force representatives wanted to include tactical air doctrine in the directive. Since intelligent use could not be made of procedures and techniques unless they were based on doctrine, a procedural manual without a doctrinal foundation would serve no purpose. Because the doctrinal matters that TAC insisted upon could not be resolved at the TAC/Army Field Forces level, the committee was stalemated. As a result, each agency set about to write its own manual.[68]

Attempts to buck the problem up to the Joint Tactical Air Support Board, which in September 1953 was assigned the task of establishing joint doctrine and procedures for air-ground operations, also foundered on service intransigence. Tactical Air Command objected to the idea of a joint board devising a joint doctrine without Air Force consultation. It believed that it had already

Close Air Support Under the New Look

made substantial progress in formulating joint doctrine for air-ground operations as evidenced by the imperfect, but still basically useful F.M. 100–20, F.M. 31–35, and the JTD itself; that the Joint Chiefs were usurping the command's prerogative to formulate doctrine; that TAC and the Army Field Forces were on the brink of agreement on a revised manual; and that a joint board, whose predecessors had traditionally intensified, rather than dampened, interservice differences, would offset all that had been achieved.[69] Its specific objections to the joint board's early draft of a manual went to the heart of the close air support controversy. Tactical Air Command representatives could not accept the proposed degree of Army participation in planning for air operations in the theater, the recommended greater degree of ground commander influence over air strike priorities, and an attempt in the proposal to organize unified commands below the theater level. The tactical air proponents saw the latter as an attempt to tell the Air Force how it should be organized.[70] As it turned out the Army, Navy, and Marine Corps, fed up with Air Force intransigence over the control question, withdrew from the project in mid-1954 and continued to prepare their own manuals. The intervention of the Joint Chiefs had set the process back. It would be two years before TAC and the Army Field Forces (renamed the Continental Army Command on February 1, 1955) resumed attempts to settle the issues.

Similar doctrinal disagreements between air and land forces were transported across the Atlantic in 1953 when American, British, and Canadian contingents of NATO gathered to formulate an air-ground doctrine for their forces in defending the European continent. Convening in England that August, air, ground, and naval representatives from the three nations to the ABC Conference, as it was named, mirrored the positions of the American contingents back home. While the TAC delegates and the Canadian and British members substantially agreed over the question of control of tactical aircraft, the U.S. Army and Navy raised the same objections they had put forth at home. Unable to settle any of the main issues, the conference skirted them by producing a document, the *ABC Manual for Tactical Operations*, which simply listed the positions of both sides without evaluating or adopting any of them.[71] The main dispute, as usual, revolved around the relative roles of air and ground commanders. The Army and Navy insisted that tactical air be described as a supporting element of ground operations, while the Air Force clung to its belief that tactical air was an independent force that operated "in coordination with" surface units. What might sound like semantic quibbling to the uninitiated went to the heart of the matter for those involved. Acceptance of the concept of tactical air as "support," according to the airmen, would place tactical air at "the whim of an Army commander who could use it as an extension of his artillery because of his lack of appreciation of air power." Despite general concurrence with the document on the part of the British, the Canadians, and the USAF, the U.S. Army failed to endorse it, and TAC was not displeased to see it pass into oblivion.[72]

Help from Above

Meanwhile, it was hoped that joint exercises at home, which traditionally had been the hallmark of collaboration between TAC and the Army Field Forces, would provide opportunities for joint agreement. The relationships between field exercises and doctrine were reciprocal. Maneuvers suffered in the absence of an agreed-upon joint doctrine, while joint doctrine was forged in the experience of maneuvers. The maneuvers of the mid- and late 1950s were important since both the air and ground forces were moving rapidly into the age of tactical nuclear weapons. Field testing was needed to answer a myriad of questions concerning atomic weapon sizes, height of air bursts, delivery tactics, types of aircraft, times of delivery, the effectiveness of the Air Force's Mark 7 nuclear weapons against enemy nuclear weapons and airfields, the effects of radiation exposure on the ground troops, whether a mission could be accomplished with conventional high-explosive weapons, and so forth. Unfortunately the exercises in the middle of the decade seemed to sharpen rather than minimize the differences between the two services.

The first major joint exercise to test the effects of nuclear weapons on the battlefield was set for late 1955 in Louisiana. Sage Brush, as it was called, again nearly aborted over doctrinal differences. To anyone but TAC and its Army counterpart, CONARC, these doctrinal controversies assumed the air of a theoretical academic debate. To those two agencies, which represented the working-level point of contact between the services, the differences, however, were a practical, not academic, matter. The outcome of these exercises and debates could contribute to their success in developing joint doctrine, procedures, tactics, and techniques.

Since TAC had agreed to take part in the exercise before General Weyland took over its helm in April 1954, the new commander restrained his lack of enthusiasm for the command's participation as too disruptive to his organization and went along with the decision. He was named maneuver director. After a bit of minor wrangling, it was agreed that this position was equivalent to that of theater commander with all its responsibilities and privileges. Principal among these prerogatives was the maneuver director's right to decide joint doctrine and procedures for an exercise when TAC and OCAFF (Office of the Chief of Army Field Forces) could not agree beforehand.

Weyland's main challenge as maneuver director of Sage Brush was to accomplish the exercise successfully without forsaking the Air Force's doctrine on close air support and in the absence of an agreed-upon joint doctrine. After many years of divided responsibility and authorship, the Air Force finally, by 1954, possessed a series of basic doctrinal manuals, several of which contained elements of close air support doctrine. While these manuals presented no revolutionary ideas, essentially reiterating the service's traditional philosophy of air power, they toned down some of the more contentious language that had characterized previous manuals. They abandoned, for example, the earlier statements of priorities for tactical air operations that suggested

Close Air Support Under the New Look

close air support missions occupied a largely inferior third place behind counter air and interdiction. "The priority in which these functions will be accomplished," stated the new doctrine, "cannot be prescribed by arbitrary methods." Rather, the priorities keep changing with the degree of success and should be determined by the overall effects of air operations.[73] It is in no way imperative to complete one of these tasks before performing another. On the contrary, all are of a continuing nature and are often executed simultaneously.[74] Despite this seeming like an assignment of equality to all tactical air tasks, the time-honored axiom that close air support missions were less effective remained alive:

> The results of air effort in the immediate battle area are often the ones most apparent to surface forces, but usually these close air support actions contribute less to the furtherance of surface actions than do the gaining and maintaining of air superiority and the interdiction of the enemy's lines of communication leading to the combat zone.[75]

The new manuals also outlined a change in the level at which the Army and Air Force would coordinate close air support missions. Recognizing the expanded battlefield area technology was introducing, the new doctrine called for, in addition to the familiar tactical air force/field army cooperation, a second tactical air command/army group level of collaboration to plan and conduct close air support.[76] In effect, this represented an increase in centralization and flew in the face of the Army move to decentralize the control of tactical aircraft down to at least the corps level.

Reflecting the experience of Korea, where the Army had objected to the organization of the JOC by the Air Force and its attachment to Fifth Air Force, the new manual clearly depicted the JOC as an Air Force facility established at the tactical air force/field army level. The manual described it as the combat operations room of the tactical air force, which contained representatives from the surface forces for requesting and coordinating purposes.[77] This very description rendered the title "joint" meaningless, and this agency was soon to change its shape.

Yet for the most part, the new consolidated Air Force doctrine for close air support reiterated the earlier principles. Once again avoiding any suggestion that air power was merely a support for ground action, it stressed the idea that assistance and support were two-way streets. Surface forces, by appropriate maneuver and tactics, could support air forces by creating situations favorable to the air weapon. In air interdiction campaigns, for example, the ground forces could support the efforts of aircraft to slow down or stop the movement of enemy resources to the battlefront by engaging with the enemy, thereby causing him to expend his resources. Air and ground forces were to function as a team, each supporting the activities of the other.[78] Therefore, "air elements are not placed under the command of other component commanders." Instead, "each component operates under its own command structure and each component supports the other." Close air support is most effective when it assists friendly forces in breaking through enemy lines and breaching hostile positions, in advancing with armored columns, in preventing major enemy offensives or counteroffensives, and in striking targets in the immediate battle area that the organic weapons of the ground forces cannot hit.[79]

This was the air doctrine that General Weyland was challenged to preserve in Exercise Sage Brush. Since the exercise's scenario called for a large amount of close air support by both the aggressor and friendly sides, the question of control of nuclear weapons became paramount. As early as the fall of 1954, Weyland and his staff became aware of the doctrinal differences between the Army and Air Force over the question of using nuclear weapons for close air support. On several earlier occasions the Air Force had withdrawn from nuclear portions of joint exercises because, in its view, the Army employed its own doctrine, rather than accepting a joint one. Specifically, Weyland objected to the unilateral Army doctrine that allotted air-delivered nuclear weapons to the Army and empowered ground commanders to decide whether to use conventional or nuclear weapons in a given situation and to select the type of nuclear weapon.[80] The controversy over command and control that raged throughout the years around conventional close air support operations was now being transferred to the nuclear arena.

The Army interpreted the shift to nuclear warfare as substantial enough to call for new rules. General Weyland, on the other hand, in a series of letters to the Army Field Forces commander, General Dahlquist, emphasized that the basic roles and missions documents, such as the Key West Agreement and the 1951 Joint Action Armed Forces (JAAF) papers of the Joint Chiefs, remained valid and that the advent of atomic weapons in no way abrogated the principles of close air support contained in those charters. Furthermore, he noted, the JTD of 1950, which had been successfully battle-tested in Korea, contained adequate joint guidance for Sage Brush. Those documents made close air support a primary function of the Air Force and assigned to it the responsibility for developing doctrines, procedures, tactics, and techniques employed by the Air Force.[81]

Subsequent meetings between staffs of TAC and the CONARC to prepare for the upcoming Sage Brush exercise failed to resolve the impasse. Army representatives at the conferences remained loyal to Army doctrine that insisted on ground control of certain Air Force-delivered nuclear weapons, and they noted that the Army probably would not participate in the exercise unless Army doctrine was followed. Weyland strongly objected to this attempt to reduce the Air Force to "merely a delivery agent" for applying nuclear weapons to targets chosen by ground commanders. When his recommended compromise, whereby ground commanders would control ground-delivered weapons and air commanders, in coordination with ground commanders,

Close Air Support Under the New Look

would control air-delivered weapons in close air support operations, was rejected, Weyland gave up and submitted the entire matter to the Air Force and Army chiefs of staff for resolution.[82]

At the end of June 1955, the chiefs of staff replied to Weyland's request for clarification of the doctrine for Sage Brush. The chiefs made it clear that the rules they were presenting were valid only for this exercise and would have no bearing on future agreements.[83] Weyland's position as maneuver director was confirmed, and he was advised to allocate weapons to commanders below the theater level and to decentralize the authority to fire weapons at targets of opportunity. The Army was to control its own nuclear artillery, but was told to coordinate its firing through the JOC to avoid hitting aircraft operating in the impact area. The Army commander was also instructed to route his requests, including the desired yield, time of delivery, height of burst, and ground zero, for close air support nuclear strikes through the JOC. These procedures for the control of atomic weapons were flexible enough to allow the exercise to proceed. Nevertheless, the need to seek advice from Washington pointed up once again the critical need for agreement on joint doctrine.

Of even greater importance for the future of the close air support issue than the question of control of nuclear weapons was the Army's request to test its experimental Sky Cavalry concept in Exercise Sage Brush. The Sky Cavalry, formed in June 1955 and incorporated into the 82d Airborne Divisional Reconnaissance Troop, was a reconnaissance patrol group of helicopters and light fixed-wing aircraft equipped with television and long-range cameras to give the ground commander an immediate view of enemy territory. The Air Force had been keeping a close eye on the Army's burgeoning inventory of helicopters and organic light fixed-wing aircraft. Although it was attempting to slow down this process by circumscribing the weight and missions of these planes, the Air Force was convinced that the growth of Army aviation was a prelude to Army assumption of further Air Force missions, progressing from airlift to reconnaissance to close air support.

As maneuver director, General Weyland decided against permitting the Sky Cavalry experiment on the grounds that this proposed use of Army aircraft forward of the battle area should be interpreted as airborne operations and therefore violated earlier agreements between the Army and Air Force. When the Army, claiming that its organic aviation was an integral part of its force structure rather than airborne support, appealed to the Army secretary, the decision was reversed by Air Force Secretary Donald A. Quarles. While Quarles agreed with Weyland's position and principles (unstipulated), circumstances led him to advise the maneuver director to "permit the Army to take advantage of the opportunity afforded by Sage Brush to carry out their Sky Cavalry tests." As with all decisions from the Pentagon surrounding this exercise, this one also was advertised as being "without prejudice to the joint doctrine involved."[84] In short, the matter of joint doctrine, particularly for close air support, had become too hot for any responsible agency to propose anything other than *ad hoc* and temporary solutions.

The exercise took place between November 15 and December 4, 1955, in the environs of Camp Polk, Louisiana, with both conventional and nuclear weapons use simulated in numerous close air support operations. Although both sides proclaimed Sage Brush useful, the Army evaluation once again highlighted that service's dissatisfaction with the close air support it was receiving from the Air Force. The commander of the aggressor forces, Maj. Gen. Paul Adams, stated in his final report on the exercise that the Army had an increased need for close air fire support "of the tank and bunker busting variety," but that "even when weather and available aircraft made close fire support possible, the Army's requirements could not be completely met due to the Air Force's preference for using atomic weapons and arming their planes accordingly."[85]

Some in the Army deemed the Sky Cavalry test a success and recommended that a battalion of Sky Cavalry units be provided at each corps under direct Army command because "The present relationship of mutual cooperation between the Army and the Air Force units leaves much to be desired."[86] This recommendation was not acted upon because the final Army afteraction report, written by nonaviator evaluators, deemed the Sky Cavalry trials as inconclusive.[87]

The maneuver also highlighted the woeful inadequacies of the 1950 JTD. Even before the exercise, in January 1955, General Ridgway, the Army chief of staff, rejected the JTD as not adequately expressing the Army's views on doctrine for ground operations.[88] Since joint exercises and training schools were relying on the directive for guidance, it was now more imperative than ever to revise it and settle, not only the basic issue of command and control, but also many of the antiquated procedures of the directive that had been made obsolete by new technology. A main element of the old directive that needed updating was the concept of the JOC. The nuclear weapons and rapid communications of modern warfare were placing a premium on dispersal and flexibility. The JOC had proved too immobile and inflexible to be able to react quickly enough to the new demands. No one was more aware of the need for revision than General Weyland, who noted in his final Sage Brush report that:

> although they [the joint doctrine and procedures] were found to be workable in Sage Brush, they do not completely satisfy needed requirements in this field. It is considered mandatory, therefore, that joint doctrine on air-ground operations employing both conventional and nuclear weapons which would be applicable not only to U.S. air and ground forces but also for U.S. forces working with allied forces, be firmed up and approved at the earliest possible date.[89]

Close Air Support Under the New Look

Acting upon this urgency, early in 1956, Weyland obtained the agreement of CONARC's new commander, Gen. Willard G. Wyman, to convene a working group from the two commands to revise the JTD. At first, the meetings showed promise. Army representatives did not object to TAC's new concept for tactical air operations, which involved moving the tactical air force's partnership upward from the field army (where it had been placed in both F.M. 31–35 and in the JTD) to the army group, creating an Air Operations Center (AOC) at the Tactical Air Force headquarters to control air operations, and splitting the old JOC in two: an Air Force installation called an Air Support Operations Center (ASOC), and an Army installation, the Tactical Support Center (TSC). The Army raised few objections since TAC could make most these changes unilaterally with only the coordination of the Army.

As soon as the conferees reached the sensitive issue of the availability and allocation of aircraft for close air support, however, the meetings deadlocked. The Army members held that a specific number of close air support sorties should be made available to the Army group commander for a specific length of time, sorties that he could then suballocate to his field armies as they needed them. The airmen replied that the Army would receive more reliable close air support if the sorties were made available to ASOC based on priorities set by the Army. Fundamentally, the Air Force representatives saw in the Army proposal a further attempt to gain operational control over Air Force aircraft, and an inference that the ground commander was as capable of directing close air support planes as was the air commander—the worst kind of heresy to TAC.[90]

Following a summer of discontent, disagreement, and inability to narrow the doctrinal gap, both sides agreed, in September 1956, to commit their positions to writing. These statements show the contending views in stark relief. Each agency's definition of close air support, which were not too far apart, stressed the elements important to that organization. Tactical Air Command defined close air support operations as those assisting (not supporting) surface forces in the immediate battle area, which it defined as the area, not to exceed 25 miles, between the friendly surface forces and the bomb line. There could hardly be any serious doctrinal objection to this definition. Continental Army Command members proposed a different, but not necessarily contradictory, definition. To them, close air support included visual, photographic, and electronic reconnaissance by tactical support planes as well as the destruction of enemy forces as required by the ground force commander to support (not assist) his mission. Nothing in either of these concepts was so diametrically opposite that compromise could not be reached.

In an attempt to circumvent the close air support definitional barrier, Army representatives at one point suggested replacing the term close air support with "air fire support" or "offensive air support." This, they contended, would make a clear distinction between air-delivered fire support and recon-

Help from Above

naissance support. The Air Force members were suspicious of this proposed change and opted for continued use of close air support. Navy and Marine observers agreed with the Air Force, and the Army eventually dropped its suggestion.[91]

The two agencies defined a combat zone essentially the same way, as being the area extending from the rear boundary of the field army through the area of contact out to the maximum range of organic or attached supporting weapons. The Air Force specified a limit of 25 miles out from the area of enemy contact. The Army did not seem to object.

Doctrinal sparks flew, however, over two elements of control, namely, who should control the airspace above the battlefield and who should control nuclear weapons. The resolution of both items was essential to any agreement on close air support. The question of airspace control also went to the heart of air-ground disagreements and was merely a more recent formulation of the reasoning behind the schism that had separated air from ground forces in the first place. In the Air Force's *horizontal* interpretation, the airspace above the battlefield was connected not with the ground below but with the rest of the airspace surrounding it. Unlike the terrain below, the airspace could not be divided into sections with different rules and capabilities for each section. In short, it was a continuum without seams. The rules governing the application of air power were identical throughout the continuum. In that portion of airspace that happened to have friendly military forces engaged below it, it was necessary to integrate and coordinate with that military activity in order to be more effective. That airspace, however, remained an integral part of the air, not ground, scheme and "it is necessary that the Air Force have the responsibility for airspace control."[92]

Nothing could be farther from traditional military ground thinking. As opposed to the Air Force, the Army's view of airspace was *vertical*. The space above the battlefield was an integral part of battle zone and was to follow the rules of ground warfare. Control of this airspace was analogous, in the Army view, to the control the Army exerted in the space under the battlefield, such as against tunnels, which it would later meet in Vietnam. The space above the battlefield was a medium to be used by weapons that supported ground operations, whether they be artillery, missiles, or air strikes. Consequently, according to CONARC "the field army commander exercises control of the air-space over the combat zone and regulates the movement of all aircraft in this area."[93]

Differences also existed on the question of control of nuclear weapons used in close air support. It remained the Air Force's position that the power to make the ultimate determination of which air weapons system to use against enemy targets in the battle zone rested with the air commander. He was to coordinate with the ground commander who designated the target, the effects desired, and the time of delivery. The Continental Army Command wanted the ground commander to have "authoritative direction" over air-delivered nuclear

Close Air Support Under the New Look

weapons. This meant that the ground commander, far from simply coordinating with the air commander, could determine unilaterally the time on target and the characteristics of the air weapons to be used.[94]

Attempts to compromise on some of these points were showing promise when, in November 1956, the Army's backbone and resistance were stiffened by a memorandum from the Secretary of Defense, Charles Wilson, with the somewhat misleading title of "Clarification of Roles and Missions to Improve the Effectiveness of Operations of the Department of Defense." This memo only partially succeeded in its purpose of settling doctrinal differences between the services, and the Army and the Air Force interpreted some paragraphs entirely differently. Particularly disruptive to the ongoing close air support discussions between TAC and CONARC was the assignment of responsibility for surface-to-air missiles for point defense to the Army and for area defense to the Air Force.[95] Army conferees interpreted this as supporting their position that they controlled the space over the battlefield. The Air Force made no such interpretation, and the battle over airspace control continued.

Finally, Generals Weyland and Wyman made enough progress in a personal meeting in March 1957 to allow the process to resume. Although they did not resolve the major question of responsibility for the airspace over the combat zone, their meeting produced a compromise that allowed the committee to continue its work. To TAC's original statement that the tactical air control system "provides the tactical air force commander with the organization and equipment necessary to direct and control air operations," they agreed to add the modification "...and coordinate air operations with other services."[96] Such face-saving measures settled no major issues, but allowed the group to complete the manual.

By the following July, the two commanders were able to sign a *Joint Air-Ground Operations (JAGOS) Manual* (**Figures 11 and 12**), which was published on September 1, 1957.[97] Both TAC and CONARC agreed not to coordinate the manual through their respective departments, for this would have entailed long delays and possibly disapproval. That neither side was completely satisfied with the product is clear from the commanders' avowal in its preface that the purpose of the directive was to establish "jointly acceptable operational procedures through mutual compromise, where necessary, of divergent doctrinal positions."[98] The manual made no pretense to being a definitive statement of doctrine. Instead, like its predecessors, it was a guide to procedures to be followed in joint training exercises, leaving doctrinal differences intact.

Indicative of the fact that the new manual lacked the aura of joint doctrine was its separate designation by the Air Force as TACM 55-3 and by the Army as CONARC TT 110-100-1. In many ways, the *JAGOS* represented a move away from the jointness that had characterized its predecessor, the JTD of 1950. Since the publication of the earlier document seven years before, on

Help from Above

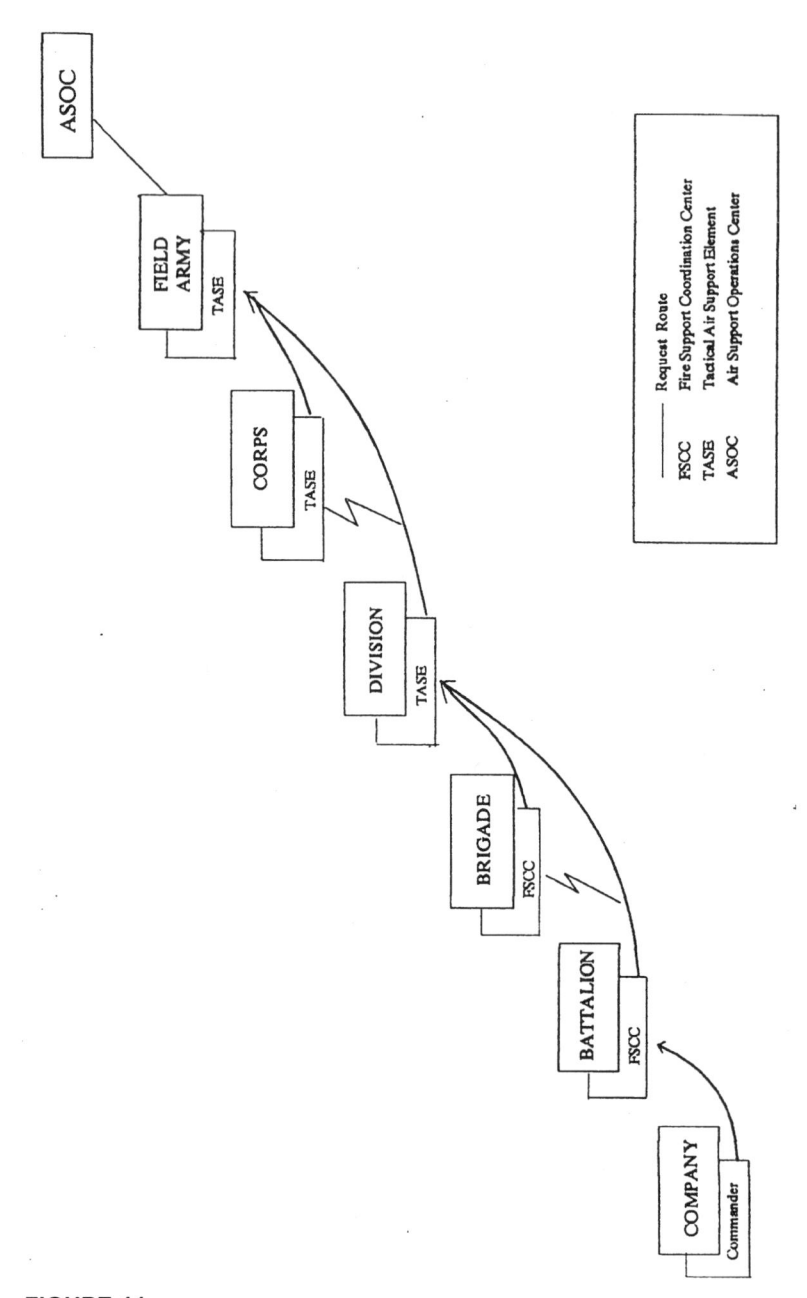

FIGURE 11
Joint Air-Ground Operations
Immediate Air Request System, Sept. 1, 1957

Close Air Support Under the New Look

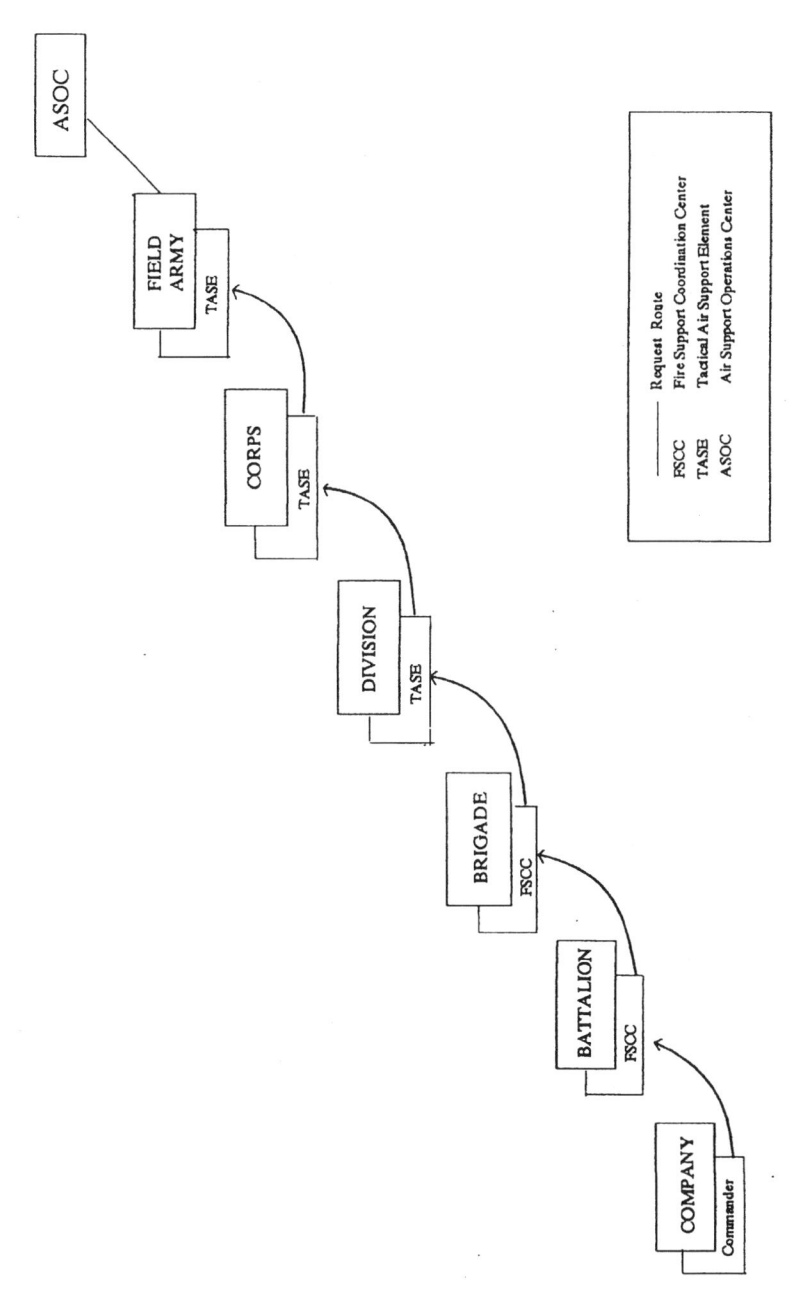

FIGURE 12
Joint Air-Ground Operations
Preplanned Air Request System, Sept. 1, 1957

Help from Above

the eve of the Korean War, both services had experienced major transformations in doctrine, tactics, and equipment. These changes were reflected strongly in the manual that, in many ways, depicted an arbitrary coexistence of two service positions with little more than a thinly veiled attempt to coordinate them. Recognition of the important differences between the Army and Air Force positions over command and control and use of the close air support forces was noticeable only by its absence.

Key to the rest of the document was the agreed-upon definition of close air support. So great remained the differences over control and procedures that the common denominator of agreement resulted in a definition that, although acceptable to both sides, left room for interpretative debate. The manual defined close air support as:

> ...the application of air fire power within the combat zone at the request of the field army commander against enemy targets capable of interfering with current combat operations of friendly forces. Air fire power delivered on targets in the vicinity of friendly forces must be integrated with the fire and movement of surface forces to insure troop safety and maximum efficiency in expenditure of effort. Normally, close air support should not be requested for targets which are within the means and capabilities of organic ground weapons unless the added fire power delivered by aircraft will produce decisive results.[99]

This final sentence reaffirmed earlier agreements that the Air Force's close air support, unlike that of the Marines, who relied less than did the Army on field artillery, was directed for the most part at that part of the battlefield and against those targets that Army artillery or other ground weapons could not cover. By expanding the perimeter of the battlefield to 100 miles in front of the line of contact with the enemy, the manual extended close air support strikes into territory that formerly had been considered the region for interdiction. The gradual extension of the battlefield, occasioned by technological advances in artillery and other ground weapons, was slowly forcing a division and more specific delineation of the concept of close air support. The newly acquired outer regions, which contained enemy forces not in close proximity to friendly forces but whose disruption would have an immediate effect on the operations or scheme of maneuver of those friendly forces, fell in a gray geographical as well as conceptual area between traditional interdiction and traditional close air support. It would not be long before air attacks in these border areas would be graced with the title *battlefield air interdiction* to distinguish them from close air support missions that struck closer to friendly forces and from interdiction strikes that did not require coordination with the ground. This

Close Air Support Under the New Look

refinement of the concept would come later. For the time being, all such attacks were called close air support.

The most important organizational change from its predecessors brought about by the *JAGOS Manual* was the disappearance of the JOC, the subject of earlier debate. The Army had two objections to the JOC. First, since the JOC had become part of the Air Force's Air Control Center and moved with it, it often happened that the representatives of the field army commander were operating at considerable distances from army headquarters, leading to delays, confusion, and misunderstanding. The Army felt that the supporting force commander (air) should physically "come to" the supported force commander (ground). The Army objected in the second instance to what it perceived as too much discretionary authority given to the tactical air commander to approve missions.[100]

Largely in recognition of these objections, and of the expanded size of the modern battlefield brought about by the introduction of nuclear weapons, more rapid communication, and faster aircraft, the *JAGOS Manual* moved the Tactical Air Force up from cooperating with the Army at the field army level to operating with it at the higher army group level, where its new AOC received Army requirements and allocated planes to meet them. Back down at the field army level, the two former parts of the now-disbanded JOC were separated into a TSC for the Army and an ASOC for the Air Force. Each field army headquarters was to have an ASOC to control and coordinate the aircraft that were supporting the field army. This ASOC was supposed to be highly mobile and to move each time the field army moved, thereby answering one of the Army's criticisms with the old JOC. The ASOC would now move with the Army's TSC instead of army personnel having to move, as formerly, with the JOC.[101]

This divorce of these two agencies was critical. Although the manual envisioned the two operating "in the same general location" and maintaining "adjacent sites,"[102] an examination of their functions clearly indicated that both services were showing signs of decreasing interest in a joint approach to the close air support question. This was due mainly to the inability of their representatives to resolve the tough command and control questions in the conferences that fashioned the manual. It also reflected the Army's growing emphasis on mobility in the nuclear age and the growing expectation among some of its members that their increasing number of organic light fixed-wing aircraft and helicopters would someday take over a portion of the Air Force's tactical air support mission.

The clearest example of the Army's success in legitimizing its control over a portion of its own rapidly growing air arm is seen in the composition and functions the *JAGOS Manual* allotted to its TSC. Located within a field army's command headquarters, and headed by that army's operations officer (G–3), this agency's job was to coordinate all tactical support available to the field army commander, including artillery, missiles, organic air, and tactical air. The distinction between organic (Army) and tactical (non-Army) air support is consistent throughout the manual, which gives the Army's TSC "*control* of organic tactical support and *coordination* of non-organic tactical support." The organic tactical support referred to here is not yet close air support—the manual directs the Army to continue to refer its requirements for close air support to the Air Force.[103] However, the surprising acquiescence by the Air Force to providing the Army with a mechanism whereby it could plan and control the flights of its own aircraft and helicopters in an air space the Air Force claimed as solely its own, was a major step toward the not too distant future when the capabilities of these light aircraft and helicopters would expand when the addition of armament made them capable of close air support.

It is probable that the Air Force underestimated the determination and ability of the Army to build its own close air support capability. In 1957 it appeared willing to compromise on this apparently secondary issue in order to achieve its objectives, such as the centralized control and decentralized execution of the command system in the area of operations elsewhere in the agreement. In addition, the Air Force maintained control of air-delivered atomic weapons with the tactical air force commander allocating them to ASOC for close air support of the field army.[104] The army commander, through his TSC, was to specify the target, the desired results, and the time over target, and could also recommend the height of the burst and the desired yield. The air commander in ASOC, however, could change any of these specifications or recommendations.

Except for a bewildering array of name changes, the Air Force's portion of the system, the Tactical Air Control and Operations System, remained essentially unaltered. Control of aircraft was still centralized in the hands of the air commander at the AOC located at Army group level, assisted at the next lower level, the field army, by ASOC sited near the ground TSC. As the central operational facility for final control of the aircraft, ASOC in turn, was supported by a number of communications and radar agencies to keep track of the aircraft, guide them to their targets, and warn of enemy aircraft.[105]

One change in the manual that emanated from the Korean War made the Army assume responsibility from the Air Force for supplying the jeep, the radios, the driver, the radio operator, and the mechanic for the Air Control Teams, the former TACPs. The team leader, the FAC, however, still had to be an experienced Air Force fighter pilot.[106]

The inability of TAC to create close air support doctrine for the entire Air Force was once again illustrated by the negative overseas reaction to the *JAGOS Manual*, and many of the provisions of the *JAGOS Manual*, were incompatible with the NATO practices and procedures that governed the operations of the European air force.[107]

Close Air Support Under the New Look

By the 1950s, USAFE, had become the dominant air force in Western Europe, and its commander, General Everest, wore several hats. As the air component commander of the unified U.S. European Command (EUCOM), he was responsible for joint military planning and training with U.S. Army troops based in Europe, while as the USAFE commander, he had housekeeping responsibilities in Europe as well as supervision of the foreign military assistance programs. Although USAFE was not formally a part of the NATO military structure, most of its numbered Air Force units were integrated into NATO's air arm, the 4th Allied Tactical Air Force, for maneuver purposes. In time of war, these units would come under the direct operational control of NATO. As a result, the close air support doctrine and methods practiced by USAFE units were guided not as much by agreements made back home between TAC and CONARC as by the exigencies of joint and combined operations in the European scenario.

General Everest's first disagreement with the new manual was that the compromises made in the document were compromises between positions held by TAC and CONARC and did not recognize the close air support issues that existed between the various nations of Europe, as well as between EUCOM and USAFE. While in general these issues were the same as those being discussed at home, their specific manifestations differed in the European context. A 1954 SHAPE (Supreme Headquarters Allied Powers Europe) manual for tactical operations, for example, was criticized by EUCOM and Seventh Army headquarters for its emphasis on the Air Force's doctrine of centralized air power. Seventh Army also complained about the absence of any reference in the document to the Army's organic aviation. On the other hand, USAFE's main tactical air force, the Twelfth, objected to the manual's suggestion that a part of the available air capability might be allocated to an Army corps, which was contrary to Air Force policy.[108] In USAFE's view, the new JAGOS manual did little to settle these and other specific close air support matters existing in Europe.

Moreover, the section of the *JAGOS Manual* on communications was deemed to be so general as to be useless. The requirements for Europe were not the same as those elsewhere, and the existing communications directives provided specific guidance for use in that area.[109]

The manual's definition of close air support was also unusable in Europe. Whereas it delineated the combat zone for close air support as extending 100 miles forward and 100 miles to the rear of the line of contact, NATO defined the combat zone as extending to the international boundary, that is, to the Iron Curtain. According to the NATO commander (the Supreme Allied Commander, Europe [SACEUR]), the international boundary was also the bomb line.[110]

The concept of a TSC that figured so prominently in the manual, was controversial with the U.S. Army in Europe, which did not support the idea.

Help from Above

Also, the manual prescribed certain Army functions in close air support with which General Everest did not agree.

Air leaders in Europe also found the manual's description of ASOC inconsistent with what they were doing, since their ASOC exercised far less control than called for in the manual. In Europe, it had no control or even communication with, the tactical wings. All it could do was divert flights. There the ASOC merely received a tentative allocation of sorties and monitored their operations. The intricate communication agencies, such as Control and Reporting Centers and Control and Reporting Posts that the manual described, were superfluous in Europe, where direct high-frequency communication between the ASOC and the on-site control parties (ALOs and FACs) was fully adequate.[111]

Nor did the manual's treatment of the control of atomic weapons fit the European arrangements. In NATO, nuclear weapons were controlled and allotted, not at the ASOC level, but by SACEUR, and not to specific organizations but to various types of operations, such as interdiction, counter-air, support of regional commanders, and so forth.[112]

One of USAFE's principal objections to the *JAGOS Manual* spoke to the sensitive doctrinal question of control of airspace. The European air command deemed as fallacious the manual's reference to the "undeniable right of all services to operate in the airspace over the combat zone." This statement, according to USAFE, failed to recognize airspace as a distinct combat zone. Further, since each service did not have an undeniable right to operate in land or sea combat zones, why were they given the right to operate in the air combat zone? The integrity of control in each combat zone, as delineated in the Key West and subsequent agreements, must be maintained. Acceptance of this principle, in USAFE's judgment, could pose far-reaching problems in the Central European Area if the Army insisted on it, since it would give the field army commander the power to regulate the use of air space.[113]

Given the incompatibility between the stateside compromise and actual conditions in the field, General Everest concluded that, "we do not plan any further action on the manual in this area."[114] Ironically, the *JAGOS Manual*, which was patterned after the close air support practices of World War II in Europe, was rejected on the very continent that had originally inspired it. This was a further indication of a quickened pace of change resulting, not only from advances in nuclear and aircraft technology, but also from America's burgeoning role in the world. In the Far East, on the other hand, whose World War II experiences with close air support had been rejected in postwar close air support doctrine, the revised air-ground manual was to form the basis for close air support operations in Vietnam.

Close Air Support Under the New Look

The Close Air Support Challenge from Organic Army Aviation

Side by side with the Army's official position in the late 1950s, which denied any ambition to take over close air support, ran the halting beginnings of an effort to extend the activities of its own organic planes and helicopters from peripheral to combat missions, from support to close air support operations. Not everyone in the Army looked with favor on this development. Some Army agencies opposed it as a diversion of scarce resources. Other soldiers were reluctant to engage in the momentous conflict with the Air Force that such a program would foster. A third group was suspicious of the move that appeared to be leading to the creation of a separate aviation branch within the Army. Yet despite such opposition, supporters of the movement, who represented a younger, more eager group of Army officers uninhibited by the responsibility that their superiors bore of living peacefully with the Air Force, made significant progress before the decade was over.

In several ways this movement resembled the earlier crusade within the Army in the 1920s and 1930s that led to a separate Air Force. In both cases the leaders were relatively junior officers. Many of their methods were furtive and many of their ideas ran counter to existing agreements and regulations. In both cases, their goal was not initially universally accepted by the service's top leaders.

Yet in one essential aspect these later Army officers differed significantly from their predecessors. The goal of Mitchell and company had been to enter new territory by creating roles, missions, doctrine, and tactics for a completely new military vehicle that possessed potentialities that, in their view, were being stifled by conservative thinking. Far from trying to restore to the Army a lost potential, they had sought to replace the traditional thinking and practices of ground warfare with a new set of principles derived from the nature of the aerial vehicle. To them, the old concepts that confined warfare to terrain and saw the enemy's army as the target had to be replaced with an expanded vision made possible by the advent of the airplane. This attempt at revolutionary overthrow was bound to fail, leaving the airpower apostles the choice between capitulation or separation.

The revisionists of the 1950s, on the other hand, were basically reactionary. Their experiments to arm light aircraft and helicopters, far from being a bid to create something new, aimed at rejuvenating within the Army some of the mobility that had been sacrificed with the disappearance of the cavalry just before World War II. Their attempt to harness aviation to ground power was in part motivated by the need to redress this existing imbalance between firepower and mobility. Throughout the history of ground warfare, the preeminence of one or the other of these two critical factors had swung back and forth, pendulum-like. The initial mobility that the medieval knight exercised gradually disappeared with the introduction, along with innovative tactics, of

Help from Above

weapons of greater firepower, including the longbow and gunpowder. After the Civil War, the United States accelerated the practice of substituting firepower for manpower. Advances in automatic weaponry and field artillery in the second half of the nineteenth century, coupled with a lack of progress in making the foot soldier more mobile, increased the preponderance of firepower over mobility, leading to a trench-warfare stalemate in World War I. Reaction to the lack of mobility during World War I led to a swing of the pendulum back in the direction of greater mobility. While firepower remained essentially unchanged between the wars, tanks, trucks, airplanes, and airborne divisions were integrated into armies, giving mobility the upper hand. Mobility's hegemony ended, however, at the conclusion of the World War II when firepower, in the form of atomic weapons, once again gained the ascendancy.[115]

The Korean Conflict did little to weaken firepower's dominance. After the war the Army had two alternatives: it could work on improving mobility along the surface, or it could explore the potentiality of aerial vehicles. It pursued both. Despite imaginative attempts to speed up surface forces, including organizational experiments such as mobile task forces, however, the capabilities of ground vehicles remained inherently limited and predetermined by the location and routes of highways, railroad tracks, or waterways.[116]

It was within this milieu that the young Army revisionists began experimenting after Korea with the second alternative, the aerial vehicle. The purported unresponsiveness of the Air Force's close air support resources led these officers to focus on their own aerial vehicles—the light, fixed-wing planes and helicopters that constituted Army aviation.

Army aviation improved little during Korea for several reasons. Even though budgets eased during the Korean War, aviation occupied an inferior niche within the Army and did not share in the improvements enjoyed by major Army branches. Part of this was the result of traditional ground force thinking, while part derived from the limitations the Department of Defense placed on Army aviation. These restrictions were enforced by a president and defense secretary who were determined to honor earlier roles and mission agreements that stipulated that the Army was to fight on the ground, the Navy on the sea, and the Air Force in the air. The administration was dedicated with equal vigor to rooting out duplication of effort.

Taken together, these agreements, which since 1947, sought to define the nature and mission of what that year's National Security Act meant by the Army's "organic" aircraft, actually represented a small step forward for Army aviation. The 1949 agreement, which was formalized in JAAFAR (Joint Army and Air Force Adjustment Regulations) 5-10-1 and in both Army and Air Force regulations that year, limited fixed-wing aircraft to 2,500 pounds and helicopters to 4,000 pounds.[117] Because technological advances rendered these weight ceilings anachronistic, the Air Force acceded, in 1951, to having them removed and to defining organic aircraft by function rather than by

Close Air Support Under the New Look

weight. Both service secretaries agreed to define Army organic aircraft as utility fixed-wing aircraft and helicopters of unlimited size that the Army considered integral and essential for it to perform its combat and logistical function within the combat zone (between 50–70 miles deep). A key stipulation, however, prohibited these aircraft from duplicating the Air Force's close air support, interdiction, reconnaissance, and troop carrier functions.[118] This was a major advance for Army aviation. By removing the weight restrictions in 1951, it permitted the Army to gain experience with larger and larger aircraft and helicopters. Despite the existing injunction against duplicating Air Force's missions, the Army's growing familiarity with procuring, maintaining, and operating large aircraft would eventually provide another example of the principle that function follows form, as Army planes replaced some Air Force functions in all of the four *prohibited* areas.

As Army planes and helicopters grew in size, a new agreement the following year, 1952, reinstated a weight limit on fixed-wing aircraft (5,000 pounds empty), but not on helicopters. This weight limit, however, could be waived by the Secretary of Defense should technological advances dictate, thereby rendering it virtually unenforceable. The combat zone was increased to "fifty to one hundred miles in depth," and the ban on duplicating Air Force functions remained. The Air Force, preoccupied with providing nuclear capabilities for its tactical forces, acquiesced in this expanding role for Army aircraft, although it was aware of the potentiality for duplication. Shortly after the 1952 agreement, the Air Force issued a policy statement to the effect that it would not actively oppose the Army's attempt to increase its own air support aviation, though it continued to emphasize the phrase in the new agreement that denied any intention to "modify, alter or rescind" any of the missions, including close air support, assigned to the Air Force at Key West. This agreement, and the Air Force's reaction to it, represented another step forward for Army aviation by encouraging the Army to budget for more aircraft.[119]

Following Korea, the pace of Army aviation development accelerated. In 1953, the Army began to train some of its own helicopter pilots, the first step in its drive, completed three years later, to take over from the Air Force the responsibility for training all of its own fixed-wing and rotary-wing pilots. Army aviation gained additional clout in 1953 with the establishment of an Army Aviation Branch within Maj. Gen. James M. Gavin's G–3 (Operations) division of the Army staff in Washington. Later in the year, the division also organized a Doctrine and Combat Developments branch, headed by an ardent advocate of Army aviation, Col. John J. Tolson. The influence of Army aviators in the Pentagon, if not everywhere in the field, was growing.

The forging of a mission for the rapidly growing aerial force advanced further in June 1955 with a policy statement from General Ridgway, still chief of staff, to all his commanders. Appealing for new thinking in the area of air mobility while reaffirming the Army's position that it must be ready to fight and defeat local aggression as well as general war, Ridgway noted that the Army's ability to move its forces to any point in the world had not kept pace with the increasing weight of its equipment. He envisioned an even greater need in the future for all types of airlift: helicopters, convertiplanes, light utility planes, and the Air Force's troop carrier aircraft. This was in many respects the official opening gun of the Army's crusade toward air mobility. Although Ridgway's statement was confined to airlift, with no explicit mention of other tactical air missions, it concluded with the ominous (for the Air Force) statement that "After assuring the achievement of the air mobility capability, consideration then will be given to the achievement of the maximum feasible capability for sustained combat."[120] Within a decade this general exhortation would have become a reality.

The uncoordinated growth of Army aviation came to an end in November 1955 with the issuance of a complete plan for the long-term development of Army aviation. The blueprint called for the creation of an Aviation Division in the G–3 section of the Army staff; the establishment of an aviation center at Camp Rucker, Alabama, along with an aviation test board; the assumption by the Army from the Air Force of depot maintenance and supply; the strengthening of procurement control from the Air Force; and the formation of an aviation branch within the Army. The chief of staff approved most of the plan early the next year, and the Army assumed from the Air Force responsibility for depot storage and maintenance of its growing aviation fleet. Following a bruising battle with the Air Force, the Army in 1956 took over all of its own pilot training. For this purpose, the Air Force turned over Wolters AFB to the Army in July and Gary AFB in December.

That same year the Army announced that its aviation school, until then a small operation designed to support artillery at Fort Sill, Oklahoma, would move to an old tank repair base at Camp Rucker, Alabama. Brigadier General Hutton was assigned commander of the new post, which was completed the following February and designated a permanent station—Fort Rucker—in October. At the same time an Army Aviation Board, responsible for testing Army aircraft, was organized at Rucker. The institutional organs of Army aviation were slowly falling into place.

Early in 1955 the Army took a major, but hardly noticed, step in gaining control over its aircraft development and production contracts. Until then the Air Force, as the procurement agent for the Army, channeled all development and procurement money to the contractor and supervised all Army aviation contracts. The Army was becoming increasingly dissatisfied with the time-consuming delays in clearing contract changes and engineering modifications this system entailed. In 1955, the Army centralized its research and development organization to make it ready if and when the Army needed it for its own procurement and development. Many top Army leaders felt it was inevitable that Army aviation, given its growing importance, would reach that point with-

Close Air Support Under the New Look

in several years. They saw the reorganization of their research and development practices as the first step in preparing the Army to administer its own aeronautical program.[121]

Accompanying this slow advance in acquiring resources for Army aviation was a gradual expansion of the meaning of the term *air mobility*. While the term was widely used, there was little unanimity in the early and mid-1950s as to what it meant or how it should be accomplished. Early in the decade the Army emphasized the helicopter as a mode of transporting soldiers and equipment to the battlefield. An Army plan to place a cargo helicopter company at each division and one at each corps ran into opposition from the Air Force, which was still responsible for procuring the helicopters. When the Army chief of transportation ordered 3,000 helicopters, the Air Force saw this as a challenge to its airlift mission, which included air assault.

Although this initial emphasis on helicopters as airlift vehicles did not challenge the close air support role of the Air Force, the next logical steps in the development of Army aviation did. Some soldiers were beginning to point to the value of helicopters in the reconnaissance role, suggesting experiments with rocket-armed rotary-wing aircraft, equipped with reconnaissance gear, for direct fire.[122] By early 1954, when he had become the Army's operations chief, General Gavin was proposing the establishment of units that combined armored cavalry with light armed helicopters or aircraft for tactical mobility.[123] The creation within his office that year of a general officer position to supervise and coordinate the Army's aviation program, and his appointment of Brigadier General Howze to the position,[124] greatly strengthened the Army's push for its own autonomous air force. The evolution of Army aviation, both helicopters and fixed-wing planes, was inching toward arming these vehicles and, by the Air Force's definition, employing them in a close air support role in combat.

As defined by one commander of the Army Aviation Center, air mobility went beyond its traditional meaning of mobility of personnel, equipment, and supply to include mobility of firepower, a "new aspect we have been bordering on for some time." By mobility of firepower, he envisioned organic Army vehicles flying to a predetermined target, "delivering its fire mission," and returning home—in short, close air support. Although at the time of this statement Army aviation was still experimenting with planes and helicopters for reconnaissance, the commander foresaw that, "in time, air mobile units will also do this final, but crucial job"—fighting.[125]

When the objectives of Army aviation were finally agreed upon and written down in 1959, armed combat enjoyed a prominent place in the concept of operations. Armed aircraft were to provide both offensive and defensive fire where the ground forces were engaged with an enemy and augment the aircraft of other services against enemy personnel and materiel in point, area, and air-to-air targets.[126]

Help from Above

While most Air Force theorists viewed armed attack helicopters, developed in this period, as a close air support vehicle whose attacks against close-in enemy ground forces required coordination with the friendly troops, many in the Army did not even consider them as fire-support systems, much less close air support systems. Rather, many Army officers argued that they were maneuver units, so closely integrated into ground maneuver units that they were more closely related to the tank than to the airplane.[127]

Despite this later rationalization, it was clear that the original organicists of the late 1950s, who developed armed helicopters, hoped to supplement, and possibly even supplant, Air Force close air support capabilities with Army rotary-wing aircraft, and perhaps even with fixed-wing planes. Among the most outspoken and daring in this regard was the commandant of the Army Aviation School and commander of the Army Aviation Center at Fort Rucker, Brigadier General Hutton. To him, interdiction and close air support, while very distant cousins, faced in opposite directions. Interdiction was a by-product of the tactical air effort, while close air support was of value as a firepower element only to the extent it was coordinated with the ground battle. For this reason, for him interdiction clearly was a function of the Air Force, which had the equipment to perform it, while close air support, as an integral part of the ground battle, should be an Army function. It must be totally responsive to the will of the commander. He firmly believed that the function agreements and statements should be revised to confirm the Air Force's dominance in the interdiction role and the Army's dominance in the close air support role.[128]

Hutton was a strong advocate of expanding the mission of helicopters by the Army from simply transporting soldiers to battle to using them as air fighting vehicles. He envisioned many types of air fighting helicopters for different air tactical roles. A division, in his view, could contain a group of light, high-speed helicopters for reconnaissance, another as a fast striking force, and yet another as a heavy fighting unit. Although none of these aircraft existed in the mid-1950s, the pace of technological advances made such visions attainable in the future.[129]

Disappointed by the poor showing of the Sky Cavalry unit in the Sage Brush exercise, but inspired by the ideas General Gavin expressed in his *Harpers* article and taking advantage of his position as commander at Fort Rucker, Hutton set in motion in June 1956 a special project to design and test weapons systems for helicopters. Although earlier jury-rigged incidents of soldiers firing from helicopters had been executed by the French in Algeria and the Americans in Korea, these earlier efforts involved men firing handheld weapons. The experiments at Rucker aimed at devising built-in firing systems.

This attempt to arm helicopters represented a qualitative as well as quantitative change in the use of rotary-wing aircraft. Although General Hutton and others initially saw the helicopter as a means of increasing the mobility of the foot soldier, they had now extended their view to regard the helicopter also as a means of suppressing ground fire during air mobile assaults. With this step the revisionists crossed the line from airlift to close air support.

The Rucker experiments began without official sanction. Fearing a turndown, Hutton initially did not ask the approval of his superiors at CONARC. The members of his group, who devoted their time after duty hours and on weekends to the project, at first had little to work with—a few helicopters, several guns and rockets salvaged from an earlier unsuccessful attempt to arm light fixed-wing airplanes, and no gun sights. Scrounging trips to Air Force and Navy depots produced bomb sights, machine guns, and pieces of scrap. As described by the Director of Army Aviation: "By trial and error methods and with a commendable application of the soldierly principles of initiative, imagination, and moonlight requisitioning, this group demonstrated the practicability of using the helicopter as a weapons platform."[130]

The unofficial nature of the experiment with armed helicopters changed in July 1956 when the new CONARC commander, General Wyman, requested from all his commanders new concepts on mobility and flexibility.[131] Hutton took advantage of the request to inform Wyman of his idea of placing ground soldiers in aerial vehicles and of experimenting with existing helicopters as fighting aerial vehicles. Wyman was more inclined to encourage Army aviation than had been his predecessor, General Dahlquist. He not only approved what Hutton was doing but requested a broad, overall plan for army aviation.[132]

Assured of official support, Hutton pushed ahead with the completion at Rucker of a new Sky Cavalry unit which, in order to avoid semantic confusion with the earlier Sky Cavalry experiment, was renamed an aerial combat reconnaissance (ACR) company. Still with no formal research and development assistance and no design or evaluation personnel, the group opened its own machine shop and fabricated and tested any armament idea suggested by members of the unit. The road to success was paved with some bizarre failures. In one case when a helicopter pilot fired his 2.75-inch rockets, the rockets took many of the firing tubes with them. The designers had not allowed for expansion of the rockets, with the result that the tightly packed rockets could not fire free. On another occasion, a short circuit caused all fifteen 2-inch rockets to fire simultaneously, starving the helicopter engine of oxygen and causing it to crash. Some helicopters were damaged when they were overloaded with weapons and ammunition, and the 2-inch rocket gasses caused severe corrosion to the flanks of the helicopters.[133] Gradually these and other bugs were ironed out and the ACR unit demonstrated the feasibility of using the helicopter as a weapons platform.

The ACR unit was designed to perform all the classic missions of the cavalry, such as reconnaissance, security of open flanks, seizure of critical areas, pursuit, and exploitation. Its OH–13, UH–19, H–25, and CH–21 helicopters were armed with machine guns and rockets.[134] The Aviation School

Help from Above

took on the task of winning over opponents of the air mobile idea, both inside and outside the Army, by staging impressive demonstrations. Throughout 1957 and 1958, in addition to performing for its own students at the Aviation School, the unit gave glimpses of the emerging air mobile tactics at Forts Knox, Benning, and Bliss, at the Redstone Arsenal, and at conferences of the Army Aviation-Industry and the Joint Civilian Operations.[135] In addition to firing the various helicopter-mounted weapons at these presentations, a platoon-size formation of seven armed reconnaissance helicopters, a utility helicopter, and two light cargo helicopters illustrated the versatility of the rotary-wing vehicles in a firepower display.[136] These irregular experiments paid off when this helicopter unit was officially sanctioned by the Army in March 1958:[137]

> The early work of the ACR company at Fort Rucker inspired other Army commands to experiment with air mobility and helicopters. Army planners were so impressed with the company's tactical demonstrations that in 1959 CONARC directed the Army's Armor School at Fort Knox to organize an armed helicopter mobile task force, the Aerial Reconnaissance and Security Troop (ARST), patterned after the experimental ACR company at Rucker and designed to perform and augment the traditional missions of armored cavalry. Early the following year the unit moved to Fort Stewart, Georgia, for training and testing.[138]

Army developments of fixed-wing aircraft during the period appeared on the surface to pose more of a challenge to the reconnaissance and airlift missions of the Air Force than to its close air support function. By 1960, the Army had developed a twin-engine, turboprop airplane, the OV–1 Mohawk, as a tactical observation aircraft and planned to have 250 of them by 1965. Since the plane weighed almost 10,000 pounds, it had to receive the first waiver of weight limitations from the Secretary of Defense. This was also the first quantum leap in the size of Army fixed-wing planes from the earlier light, single-engine planes (Otters, Beavers, Bird Dogs, Chickasaws, Ravens, and Seminoles) that the Army had been flying. The Army's development of the Mohawk, and its simultaneous acquisition of the 32-passenger Caribou, inspired General White to observe that "these planes are probably as big as our bombers were eighteen or twenty years ago." Size was not the only objection the Air Force had to these planes, particularly the Mohawk. The OV–1, although described and tested as a reconnaissance vehicle to supplement ground surveillance, was potentially a gun platform, a fact that impressed suspicious Air Force planners with the possibility of another challenge, in addition to the armed helicopters, to its close air support mission. That these suspicions were not unfounded became clear two years later when, at the end of a

Close Air Support Under the New Look

period of intensive testing of both helicopters and aircraft, the Army recommended providing each of its divisions with 24 armed Mohawks and 36 Huey helicopters armed with 2.75-inch rockets.[139]

Air Force leaders were fully aware of what was going on. Despite their uneasiness at what they clearly perceived as potential incursions into their close air support mission, several factors combined to somewhat dampen their reaction. First, the question of close air support occupied a minor niche in the New Look environment, as the attention of Air Force leaders remained focused on the nuclear aspects of their mission. There even remained an element within the service that favored letting the Army take over its own close air support.

Second, until the end of the 1950s, the Army itself was having a hard time defining what its force structure should be for a nuclear ground war. One observer compared the Army's attempts to devise an aviation plan in this fluid environment to "tailoring a suit to fit a man whose height and waistband measurements are going to change any minute."[140] The Army reorganized its divisions in 1957, which resulted in further alterations in aviation planning. Such constant changes provided the Air Force with nothing more than a moving target, making it difficult to oppose.

Third, by 1960, the firepower part of the helicopter equation had yet to surface as a major mission for rotary-wing aircraft. Helicopters were still envisioned primarily as means of transportation and logistics. Field tests of rotary-wing aircraft as an integral part of an air mobile division were still three years in the future.

Fourth, it remained a firm conviction among most Air Force officers that low-and-slow aircraft were a phenomenon of the past and that the Army would learn the hard way that light fixed-wing aircraft and helicopters could not survive in an area where the enemy's aerial and ground countermeasures were under electronic control.

Fifth was an appreciation at the highest levels of the necessity of accommodating other services at least as long as there was no serious doctrinal compromise. The case of the OV–1 Mohawk was a good example of this and of the different reactions within different Air Force levels. The Tactical Air Command took the position that if approval were given to arm the Mohawk, it would be only a matter of time until the Army was flying high-performance combat aircraft. This would necessarily happen because high performance in an aircraft was necessary for it to survive. The Air Force had already learned this through experience, and the Army would also learn it with the result that, before long, the Army would be flying the same kind of high performance planes as the Air Force was flying. However, TAC was not represented on the air staff that negotiated with the Army. In TAC's view, the air staff was not as aggressive as it could have been in demonstrating to the Army why it made more sense to apply its resources to other systems.[141] The reaction of the Air Force chief of staff, General White, for example, to an Army briefing on army

Help from Above

aviation in late 1960 reflected the ambivalence of his position. While agreeing with the Army concept and stating that he could not quarrel with the Sky Cavalry idea, he openly questioned how this would develop in the future as Army fixed-wing planes got larger and larger and Army helicopters increased their firepower. "How do we get along?" he asked. "Because the air does clash at a certain point."[142]

Finally, despite advances in Army helicopter armament, Air Force leaders continued to rely on the fact that every roles and mission statement and agreement since 1947 had reaffirmed the Air Force's primacy in close air support and prohibited the Army from intruding on this mission. They had no reason to believe that this attitude would change. In this they were naive, possibly underestimating the depth and persistence of the Army's ongoing campaign to alter these agreements. General Gavin, for example, made no secret of his opposition to Secretary Wilson's 1956 directive on roles and missions, which the general said would "unquestionably prevent" the Army from fulfilling its mission.[143] Virtually all those officers involved in Army aviation took Gavin's lead, as opposition to the existing arrangements became the order of the day.

The Air Force's doctrinal objection to the Army's drive for air mobility was clear in 1960 on the eve of the Army's successful test of the concept and its introduction into Vietnam. The Air Force viewed the growth of Army organic aviation, which ranged from heavy fixed-wing transports to light helicopters and had grown from 3,633 planes in 1954 to about 6,000 by 1960, as leading not only to a duplication of functions for which the Air Force was responsible but also to capabilities inferior to those currently possessed by the Air Force.

As the Air Force saw it, air mobility affected not only its close air support mission but its counter-air, interdiction, tactical reconnaissance, and airborne assault functions as well. Far from acting simply as attached support units, the Army wanted to integrate the aerial vehicle into its very force structure for every mission. The Army aviation program sought to integrate Army maneuver units in the air with maneuver units on the ground; to integrate Army air firepower with ground firepower; to integrate Army air surveillance with ground surveillance; and to integrate Army air supply with ground supply. This integration would take place by placing the control and execution of air mobile operations in the hands of the ground commander. The Air Force opposed this view of aerial responsibilities, which it termed "environmental," as an unwarranted departure from the time-tested assignment of responsibilities by function. The "environment" of the ground soldier, which the Air Force imputed to the Army, was one that included the atmosphere above the combat zone. "The adoption of the Army's concept," noted an Air Force study, "could well lead to the uneconomic and ineffective proliferation of aviation resources for employment within narrow and arbitrary geographic boundaries."[144]

Close Air Support Under the New Look

* * *

By the end of the 1950s, as the Kennedy administration was about to take office, opposition was strong to the New Look strategy of Massive Retaliation, and cries were loud for a more inclusive strategy that would more directly deter wars smaller than total nuclear conflict. Within the context of this controversy over strategy, the issue of close air support loomed large. The Army and the Air Force, however, had largely papered over, rather than faced squarely, their differences about close air support. Foremost among these differences continued to be, as it had been from the beginning, the question of command and control. Minor accommodations in the air-ground agreement of 1957 failed to dent the Air Force's bedrock doctrinal conviction that aircraft, to be most effective and efficient, had to be controlled from one central source, which could mass them and dispatch them to strike wherever they were needed. Approaching the issue from an entirely different perspective, namely that of the requirements of the ground commander, the Army consistently pressed for more control over the aircraft that supported them. Rebuffed at every turn, some Army officers turned to aviation assets they already possessed. Unable to achieve control over already existing Air Force close air support resources, they would convert those aircraft into air support assets. At first, experiments with these aircraft were held under the mantle of air mobility, which on the surface, suggested that they would be confined to transporting troops into battle. But early Army tests with arming both helicopters and light fixed-wing planes, coupled with statements by some responsible Army leaders, convinced many Air Force commanders that the air transportability of these vehicles was merely an opening wedge employed by the Army to attain it own close air support capability. By decade's end the revisionist Army aviators had come a long way toward convincing many skeptics within the Army that armed helicopters and Army-owned fixed-wing aircraft could perform what the Air Force viewed as the close air support role. What remained was to devise an organization within the Army that could make best use of these new aerial vehicles.

Still, the official Army position remained that of the more moderate leaders who, while agreeing that the Air Force should retain the close air support mission, wanted to hold the Air Force to its responsibility, yet wanted a greater input into decisions concerning the development and control of the aircraft the Air Force assigned to the mission. These decisions included the design and procurement of a plane specifically for close air support; the assignment of specific numbers of sorties to ground commanders; and the need for ground commanders to determine targets, strike times, armament, and so on. In 1960, the Air Force still believed that, while a specific close air support plane might

Help from Above

represent a minimum increase in effectiveness, this was more than offset by the inefficiency that resulted from depriving such an aircraft of the ability to defend itself against enemy aircraft or to attack enemy resources outside the battle area. At the same time, it continued to resist Army pressure to delegate to ground commanders the right to make those tactical decisions it deemed the sole prerogative of air commanders who were most conversant with the capabilities of their aircraft.

5 | Close Air Support and Flexible Response: 1960–1965

> This (the Air Force's tactical air support system)...is not responsive to many of the day-to-day legitimate requirements of the Army for close support.... This can only be achieved if the pilots are part of and under the command of the ground elements.
>
> — Howze Board Final Report, 1962

> In our opinion, the Army (Howze) Board fails to consider the interaction of air and ground forces in terms of joint operations.... Further increases in Army mobility can be most effectively achieved by the aviation organic to the Air Force performing the missions of air superiority, interdiction, close support, reconnaissance, and intra-theater airlift.
>
> — Disosway Board Final Report, 1962

The early years of the 1960s were critical in determining the future of the Air Force's close air support mission. The Army's challenge to the Air Force's hegemony in that role, which had been gaining force during the closing years of the preceding decade, came to a head during these years. Antithetical ideas that had been festering below the surface were brought into the open for evaluation. The catalyst for the controversy was the desire to take advantage of rapidly improving technology to improve the mobility of American ground forces. The Air Force believed that this was best done by improving its already existing tactical air support capabilities and harnessing them to existing Army divisions. The Army, on the other hand, saw increased mobility coming from the creation of a new type of division with its own

Help from Above

organic aircraft. The close air support mission figured prominently in this airmobile controversy.

The controversy was propelled to the forefront by the ascension to the presidency of John F. Kennedy in 1961 and his espousal of the new deterrent policy of Flexible Response. Long before becoming president, Kennedy had voiced doubts about the Massive Retaliation strategy and championed the cause of larger American ground forces. As early as 1954, even as Secretary of State John Foster Dulles was announcing the new nuclear strategy, then Senator Kennedy warned in Senate speeches that the emphasis on nuclear retaliation, with its concomitant disregard of conventional forces, was encouraging the communists to expand in areas where they believed the United States would not make a nuclear response and could not make a conventional one. Four years later, in a Senate speech, Kennedy opined that the commitment to Massive Retaliation was creating a Maginot mentality dependent "upon a strategy which may collapse or may never be used, but which meanwhile prevents the consideration of any alternative." In 1959, Senator Kennedy mirrored Army Major General Taylor's contention, which Taylor published that same year in *The Uncertain Trumpet*, that Massive Retaliation had endangered America's national security. "We have been driving ourselves into a corner," the senator said, "where the only choice is all or nothing at all, world devastation or submission."[1]

Kennedy carried these views into the White House, where they were reflected in some of the people he chose as his military advisors. In April 1961 he appointed Taylor, who two years earlier had retired as Army Chief of Staff and in whom he had a great deal of personal confidence, as his adviser on military affairs until he could return him to the Army as Chairman of the Joint Chiefs, which he did the following year. The president's instrument for making the new Taylor-inspired policy of Flexible Response work was his new Secretary of Defense, Robert S. McNamara. Kennedy assigned the Defense Department team the task of implementing the concept of Flexible Response, that is, of a military strategy, and modifying the military force structure so that it would respond successfully to threats across the spectrum of warfare from local infiltration to nuclear attacks. He charged his defense secretary with fashioning a strategy for a world in which nuclear war was no longer thinkable and with developing a military force structure capable of responding to military threats in a controlled manner, graduated to meet a variety of levels of aggression.[2] While firmly embracing this view, the secretary's main contribution to the administration was to bring rational order to the Pentagon's weapons-acquisition process, which he viewed as out of control.

On the other hand, his selection of Major General LeMay as Air Force Chief of Staff in June 1961 signaled his intention that the new conventional capability would be added to rather than supplant the nuclear deterrent forces in the nation's arsenal. The arrival of LeMay, a lifelong strategic bomber advo-

Close Air Support and Flexible Response

Gen. Curtis E. LeMay

cate and the architect of SAC, at the top Air Force post just as the president was seeking to modify the national policy upon which SAC's preeminence rested, guaranteed future disagreements with parts of the new policy. LeMay, in turn, installed many of his own strategic-minded protégés in key positions within the Air Force. For example, in October 1961 he appointed as head of TAC (a command he had tried to eliminate in the late 1950s), Gen. Walter C. Sweeney, Jr., who had worked for LeMay and whose background in strategic bombers went back to B–29s.

McNamara challenged the services' existing strategies and force structures to decide which arms the nation needed for each level of potential military response and to provide them as economically as possible. To determine the goals and the instruments needed to reach them, he relied heavily upon systems analysis, which placed a premium on quantification and gave less weight to experience and intuition. In so doing he met with considerable resistance from the professional military, who believed that their background and seasoning was being accorded insufficient recognition in the development of strategy.

McNamara directed his searing scrutiny at all levels of the military strategy and force structure. At the level of strategic nuclear deterrence, he slowly weaned the Pentagon's strategy away from the *counterforce* principle of primary retaliation against military targets and toward a nuclear stance that emphasized, in the event of war, *countervalue* strikes against USSR urban and

Help from Above

industrial complexes. He believed that this form of deterrence did not require a vast number of weapons. As a result, he blocked further development of the B–70 manned bomber, the successor bomber to the B–52, and opposed the deployment, but not the development, of an antiballistic missile (ABM) system. On the other hand, he favored offensive nuclear weapons such as the Polaris and Minuteman long-range ballistic missiles.

At the level of more conventional warfare, whether total or limited, the secretary became involved in virtually every aspect of procurement, opposing nuclear surface ships, supporting the massive C–5A transport plane and the M–16 rifle, and unsuccessfully promoting a fast development logistics (FDL) ship. One of his more noted, and unsuccessful, initiatives in the area of close air support was to develop a common fighter-bomber, the F–111, that could be used by both the Air Force and the Navy as a replacement for the Air Force's principal future close air support planes, the F–105s and F–4s. Although early in the planning the secretary hoped that the plane could be used for ground support, he subsequently dropped this expectation in the face of unanimous opposition. His encouragement of the Army's concept of flexible response and airmobility, however, had important consequences for the future of close air support.

It was McNamara's steps to make the Army more mobile, however, that had the most enduring repercussions on the Air Force's mission of providing close air support, and it was within this context that close air support developments unfolded between 1960 and 1965.

Early Stirrings of a Close Air Support Revival, 1961–1963

In response to the Kennedy administration's move away from sole reliance on a nuclear rejoinder to threats from the USSR, the Air Force, during the first two years of the new presidency, took some initial steps to improve its tactical, nonnuclear capabilities. The process was slowed by the need to maintain a strong strategic force, by the lingering influence of nearly a decade of nuclear strategic emphasis, and by conflicting philosophies, vested interests, and industrial lag times. As late as the summer of 1962 General Sweeney was still exhorting the Air Staff to accelerate the conversion of his fighter-bombers so that they could deliver conventional as well as nuclear weapons: "If we are going to fight large scale non-nuclear conflicts we must radically raise our force structure because we aren't even in the ball park now."[3]

Despite these obstacles, some close air support improvements were realized in weapons and munitions, joint and unit training, cooperation between soldiers and airmen, and preparation for limited warfare overseas. In 1961, the Air Force's Systems Command proposed 43 new kinds of conventional munitions, many for use on close air support missions. These included pod-mount-

Close Air Support and Flexible Response

ed 20-mm guns for fighter-bombers, a white-phosphorous bomblet, improved firebombs, blunt-nosed railway mines, smoke-trailing ammunition to increase the accuracy of ground strafing, and rockets and rocket launchers for use against small-point targets and for marking targets.

Advances were also made in the employment of flares. Night close air support had been neglected during the era of the New Look. Emphasis on an all-nuclear Air Force had made TAC's nuclear daytime role primary, while night attack training was neglected. The Cuban Missile Crisis in the fall of 1962 revived interest in the night close air support role. Planning for a Cuban contingency revealed a lack of night-attack capability among tactical fighter aircraft. The biggest problem was the outdated and totally inadequate flares (the MK–6s) then in use for illuminating targets. These flares, designed 12 years earlier, could produce only an inadequate one million candlepower of light for three minutes, and they could be dropped only from aircraft flying slower than 250 knots. Due to their age, they frequently malfunctioned. This was clearly prejet equipment. On October 24, 1962, the day after President Kennedy publicly announced a quarantine of Cuba, the Air Force inaugurated a crash program to obtain better aerial flares. Tests showed that MK–24 flares, which provided three million candlepower of light, could be used for close air support. The Army released MK–24s to the Air Force but dispensers were not immediately available. By modifying the launchers it had on hand (LAU–10s), by the spring of 1963, TAC successfully tested the flares on F–100s in strafing, skip-bombing, and rocket attacks. This "Night Owl" operation was further tested under operational conditions in Swift Strike III that summer, and it was decided to equip all jets with the flare system while working to improve the flares' burn time to four minutes and brilliance to four million candlepower.[4]

In February 1963 TAC, in a program called Full Scope, evaluated the effectiveness of its conventional close air support weapons against individual, as opposed to area, targets at Eglin AFB, Florida. Individual targets were more characteristic of tactical missions, while area targets were usually the goal of strategic warfare. The tests revealed that air-launched rockets could penetrate most targets, that the 20-mm guns were effective, that modified railroad mines dropped from aircraft destroyed their targets, and that cluster bombs (in this case the CBU–2A) showed great promise as antipersonnel weapons in close air support. On the negative side, the napalm used in the tests burned too rapidly despite attempts to adjust the mixture, 750-lb. bombs were too large to be effective against small-point targets, and the 2.75-inch rockets were more effective against area targets than against individual ones. Full Scope produced important recommendations that would improve the Air Force's tactical air support capability. Suggestions to improve fuze mechanisms and napalm mixes, to require a 50-foot altitude for delivering munitions, test a 40-mm cannon on jets, and devise a method of retarding the fall of the 750-lb. bombs, were among those that illustrated the renewed importance that the Air Force was attaching to close air support of the Army in the early 1960s.

Thus, even before the acceleration of interest in tactical air support, particularly in close air support, in 1963, Tactical Air Command was well on its way to completing a comprehensive evaluation of its close air support capabilities and weaknesses. TAC pronounced Full Scope, which concentrated on the effects of conventional air weapons and on producing a photographic record of the Air Force's tactical air ability, a success and viewed it as a blueprint for increased emphasis on tactical air support.[5]

Between 1961 and early 1963, the Air Force's slowly reviving interest in close air support and other tactical missions was also reflected, in addition to its improvement in weapons and munitions, in a resurgence in its most important peacetime function, namely, training. The pendulum was swinging in the direction of stressing close air support in joint training exercises with the Army and, to a lesser degree, in individual and unit training within the Air Force. In the 18 months between the beginning of 1962 and the middle of 1963, the Strike Command[6] hosted 32 joint exercises. It had a similar number scheduled for the following year.

Despite this nod in the direction of nonnuclear tactical air capabilities, the primary emphasis in training Air Force commanders, supervisors, aircrews, and weapons load teams, during the early 1960s, continued to be placed on the nuclear capability. Aircrew proficiency in the two main close air support aircraft, the F–100 and F–105 (**Figure 13**), was still weighted in favor of nuclear proficiency. While F–100 crew members, for example, had to qualify every six months in three types of nuclear weapons delivery, be familiar with two other types, attend a refresher course, and be recertified as proficient in nuclear weapons delivery, they had to qualify only annually in nonnuclear delivery and simply be familiar with, not proficient in, delivering nonnuclear weapons. The same basic imbalance existed for F–105 aircrews.[7]

This primacy of nuclear weapons had, up to this time, made it more difficult for aircrews to improve their expertise with non-nuclear weapons. For example, techniques for delivering *free fall* nuclear weapons, as opposed to *retarded* ones, were extremely complex and required a considerable amount of training time—time taken from training in nonnuclear delivery. Yet these priorities were slowly shifting. New techniques in the early 1960s for delivering retarded nuclear weapons were gradually reducing the required training time. In addition, procedures for delivering retarded nuclear weapons were almost identical to those used in close air support with napalm, cluster bomb unit (CBU) bomblets, and skip bombing. At the beginning of 1963 the Pacific Air Forces (PACAF) reduced nuclear weapons delivery training and increased nonnuclear training by 40 percent. In mid-1963 TAC's new training manuals for F–100s and F–105s allotted 21 percent and 27 percent, respectively, of the

Close Air Support and Flexible Response

	FY61	FY62	FY63	FY64
Tactical aircraft	1826	2338	2071	2045
Fighter bomber wings	16	23	21	21
Tactical bomber wings	2	2	1	1
Reconnaissance squadrons	14	18	14	14
Interceptor squadrons (overseas)	12	12	11	11
Active Forces				
Tac Fighters				
F-84F	-	300	222	129
F-86	-	75	-	-
F-100	910	860	757	660
F-101	75	66	66	66
F-104	72	129	54	54
F-105	122	265	419	516
F-4C	-	-	-	93
Total	1179	1695	1518	1518
Total wings	16	23	21	21
Intercept Aircraft				
F-89	12	12	-	-
F-102	287	275	269	243
Total	299	287	269	243
Total squadrons	12	12	12	11
Tactical Bombers				
B-57	48	48	48	48
B-66	48	-	-	-
Total	96	48	48	48
Tactical Reconnaissance				
RF-84	-	72	-	-
RF-101	144	128	128	128
RF-4C	-	-	-	18
RF-66	108	108	108	90
Total	252	308	236	236
Total Squadrons	14	18	14	14
TOTAL ACTIVE AIRCRAFT:	1826	2338	2071	2045

SOURCE: Draft memo, SOD to the President, 3 Dec 1962, subj: Recommended FY 1964-1968 General Purpose Forces, OSAF file 1297-62 reprinted in George F. Lemmer, Strengthening USAF General Purpose Forces, 1961-1964. (USAF Historical Division Liaison Office, 1966), p. 82.

Figure 13
Air Force General Purpose Forces, FY 1961–1965

Help from Above

semiannual training time to nonnuclear weapons delivery against 16 percent and 11 percent, respectively, for nuclear weapons.[8]

Another factor that reduced training time for aircrews in nonnuclear and close air support functions was the requirement for overseas commands to maintain aircraft on quick-reaction alert. Both in Europe and in the Pacific each tactical squadron had to keep from four to six planes on alert 24 hours a day. In the Pacific, where these planes were kept at forward-deployed bases, this meant that six to eight planes were away from their home base at any one time, making them unavailable for close air support training. This alert, together with the lack of an all-weather capability on the F–100, was imposing a great strain on manpower and resources and severely limiting nonnuclear training effectiveness.

The obstacles that aircrews encountered in obtaining adequate nonnuclear training also existed for ground crews. They received very little training in loading live conventional weapons and were hindered by the many different types of pylons needed to carry the various weapons. The F–100 had 16 different pylon configurations for attaching nuclear and nonnuclear weapons and fuel tanks. The development of a universal pylon, which as yet eluded researchers, would greatly enhance close air support efficiency.

A proliferation of conventional air weapons in the early 1960s compounded the close air support training and maintenance problem. As new weapons came into the inventory, old ones were not retired, although attempts were made to alleviate this logistics problem. The overseas commands and TAC, for example, consolidated munitions skills into a single squadron for each tactical wing, and PACAF established a weapons-loading evaluation team to increase nonnuclear efficiency by standardizing loading techniques.

Close air support training was also constrained both in Europe and at home by a shortage of weapons ranges close to tactical bases. Poor weather and the small size of ranges available in Europe forced aircrews stationed in England and continental Europe to deploy twice each year to Libya to qualify in weapons delivery at Wheelus AFB. At home, TAC had eight weapons ranges to support eleven tactical wings and three combat crew training schools. Things were better in the Pacific where established weapons ranges were available within a few miles of each base. In addition, the Air Force made good use of Army weapons ranges in Korea and on Okinawa for demonstrations and joint exercises.

For its part, the Army matched Air Force measures to improve the training and indoctrination of Army soldiers in air-ground operations. In a 1961 annex to the *JAGOS Manual*, CONARC required all soldiers to be introduced to air-ground operations, moving progressively from basic to advanced unit training and instruction by units of the combat arms. Individually, ground soldiers were supposed to become familiar with procedures for marking friendly positions, with passive air defense measures, what to do as part of an Air

Close Air Support and Flexible Response

Control Team, how to process requests for tactical air support, and the proper use of communications and staff procedures.[9]

Cooperation between TAC and CONARC had widened in the same period to include contacts between the personnel of Army divisions and Air Force wings, the mutual exchange of FACs, ground liaison officers, and air liaison officers; the establishment of a close air support briefing team to make presentations to Army combat units; the inclusion of additional close air support sorties in the combat crew training program; and the initiation of a close air support competition program between tactical fighter wings.

An informal agreement between TAC and CONARC, in October 1962, to increase personal contact between soldiers and airmen at divisions and wings[10] showed some increase in cross-training by early the following year. In April, 45 Army commanders and staff officers of the 1st Armored Division at Fort Hood visited Cannon AFB in New Mexico for air-ground orientation. Twenty Air Force officers returned the visit to Fort Hood later in the month. The commanding officer and major unit commanders of the 82d Airborne Division were taken on orientation flights to acquaint them with the capabilities and limitations of high-performance close air support aircraft. In the Pacific, a cross-training program called Exercise Teamwork matched airmen of the Fifth Air Force with ground officers of the Eighth Army.

In September 1963, General Sweeney reported that TAC had permanently assigned air liaison officers to the Army's XVIII Airborne and III Corps, and one liaison officer and two FACs to each of the Army's eight continental divisions. In addition, the command had attached TACPs to every Army level of command during each large scale joint exercise. Each 12-aircraft TAC fighter squadron was required to have at least 10 fighter pilots fully qualified as FACs, with four of these jump-qualified. Both the Ninth and Twelfth, TAC's two combat air forces, had a hard-core of trained personnel to man the elements of the Tactical Air Control System: the Air Force Command Post, the TACC, and Direct Air Support Centers.[11]

A similar renewed interest in close air support was in evidence overseas. In Europe, during the summer of 1963, the Air Force activated a Tactical Control Squadron and an ASOC, and initiated a program to work with the Seventh Army in simulated close air support missions and each month Air Force fighter-bombers flew 360 sorties to support the Seventh Army. Tactical fighter units were aligned with specific Army divisions to improve coordination, joint training, indoctrination, and close air support. The same type of projects were pursued in the Pacific. In January 1963 the PACAF command performed a series of joint exercises near the demilitarized zone in Korea in which close air support with live ordnance was provided to American and Korean army forces. F–86s, B–57s, and F–100s delivered napalm, general-purpose bombs, 2.75-inch rockets, and 20-mm and .50-caliber ammunition. Each tactical aircrew participated in at least one such close air support exercise each year. In addition, 79 of the command's tactical aircrews served four-month tours as FACs in Vietnam. Twenty-one other crews were assigned short Vietnam tours as air liaison officers. In a newly established PACAF Weapons School, eight academic hours were devoted directly to close air support, and many other hours were spent on related procedures such as nonnuclear munitions and delivery techniques. Pacific Air Forces personnel were also exchanging one-week orientation tours with their soldier counterparts in the U.S. Army of the Pacific (USARPAC). While Air Force officers were assigned to front line Army combat units, Army officers visited tactical air bases and at times received orientation flights.[12]

Despite all of the factors militating against a strong close air support capability in the Air Force by the service's strategic orientation, its tactical doctrine, which continued to devalue close air support, and its basically nontactical force structure, which could not change overnight, the period between 1961 and 1963 was one of considerable movement preparatory to an accelerated revival of close air support after 1963.

The Army Proposes Its Own Airmobile Force: The Howze Board

While airmen were gradually adapting to Flexible Response and beginning to adjust their thinking and resources toward greater cooperation with the Army, Army aviators continued to develop both the doctrine and resources of airmobility. On April 19, 1962, Secretary McNamara signed and sent two memos, one personal and one official, to Secretary of the Army, Elvis J. Stahr, Jr., expressing his dissatisfaction Army attempts to incorporate aircraft into its ground units. Both memos noted that greater mobility and potential monetary savings could be realized by substituting air for ground transportation in many areas. The memos exhorted the Army to take a bold new look at its mobility in land warfare and to explore the feasibility of breaking with traditional means of mobility, by looking closely at what would be required for aviation to achieve "quantum increases in mobility." While the tenor of both messages seemed to equate mobility with transportation, the reference in the memos to "aerial artillery" and to aircraft serving as "weapons platforms" opened the way for a broader interpretation of mobility to include weapons, as well as of personnel, which in this case, would encompass the close air support role.[13]

These memos provided implicit support for the ongoing airmobility experiments. Nevertheless, while they lauded the doctrinal concepts that had emerged from the earlier Army studies on the air mobility division, airmobile reconnaissance regiments, and aerial artillery units, they decried the fact that these concepts had not been put into effect. These memos appear, therefore, to have been vehicles to apply pressure from above to implement the ideas of the revisionist aviators, and references to aerial artillery and weapons platforms

Close Air Support and Flexible Response

suggested that close air support should be among the roles investigated. They also encouraged the Army secretary set up a "managing group of selected individuals" to reexamine its aviation requirements, and the personal memo named nine of the Army's leading uniformed and civilian organicists to head up the review committee.[14]

A student of the bureaucratic decision making process in the Pentagon has examined the background of these memos and concluded that they were written for McNamara's signature by an Army colonel on the secretary's staff, working together with a sympathetic civilian in the systems analysis shop. In addition, to bypass the Army hierarchy, which was not yet fully comfortable with the idea of airmobility, these authors included the suggestion (order) that the final report of the board be sent directly to the Secretary of the Army and the Secretary of Defense without staff review. The authors clearly wanted to avoid giving the uniformed Army staff, sections of which were opposed to the idea, an opportunity to water down the recommendations. Opposition to airmobility within the Army stemmed basically from those who saw in the growth of Army aviation a threat to the funding of other weapons systems. Although the opponents included some artillery and airborne officers, the main resistance came from armor officers who believed that, within a fiscally constrained Army, room would have to made for any new airmobile units by their displacing existing armor divisions.[15]

Army leaders found themselves in an ambivalent position regarding Army aviation. While they did not wholeheartedly endorse the growing movement for increased organic aircraft in the Army, and privately resented efforts of the civilian leadership to make radical changes in the Army without its concurrence, neither did they strongly oppose or attempt to control it. A number of interesting reasons for this vacillation have been suggested. For one, decisions in the joint atmosphere of the Pentagon were customarily arrived at through bargaining and compromise with, rather than annihilation of, opponents. This attitude fostered a relatively tolerant approach toward the Army aviators. Also, by the early 1960s aviation had become entrenched within the Army to the point where reversing the development would have been extremely difficult, if not impossible. Furthermore, some types of Army aviation, such as the small liaison planes, were useful to the top brass who enjoyed the luxury of using them. Moreover, the movement for a new Army air force had no organized center, and its presence was felt within many Army agencies, making it difficult to isolate. Also, most of the supporters of the movement maintained a low profile and were hard to identify, while the attention of the top Army leaders was usually focused elsewhere, especially in debates with the Air Force over missiles. Another factor in the revisionists' survival within the Army was their tenacity and the fervor of their crusade. Finally, even though the top leadership was aware of the disadvantages of too wide a spread of the airmobile concept, at the same time it recognized the value of Army aviation that could be used as a blue chip in bargaining with the Air Force.[16] Yet there remained within the staff some powerful forces opposing airmobility, and the proaviation authors of the memos hoped to skirt them, thereby avoiding time delays and alterations these forces would introduce. One of the leading revisionists, officially, commenting on the steps that led up to the critical memos, noted that:

> There was a nucleus of Army aviation oriented officers both in the office of the Secretary of Defense staff and Army Staff who recognized the possibility of capitalizing on Mr. McNamara's [sympathetic] attitude to sweep aside ultraconservative resistance within the Army itself. Finally there was an opportunity to present to the Secretary of Defense for his signature directives that would cause the Army to appoint an evaluation by individuals known for their farsightedness and to submit recommendations directly to the Secretary of Defense in order to avoid intermediate filtering.[17]

While, on the one hand, this same participant depicted the results of these bureaucratic tactics as fortunate, on the other hand, he indicated his awareness that it was unprofessional. "For the record, it should be noted," he continued, "that General Howze [who was to be the principal beneficiary of the move] knew nothing of this background maneuvering and would have sternly protested had he been aware."[18]

The result of these memos was the creation of the Army Tactical Mobility Requirements Board, better known as the Howze Board after its chairman and chief author, Lt. Gen. Hamilton H. Howze, Commander, XVIII Airborne Corps. The Board, which met during the four summer months of 1962, had an executive committee of 15 officers and five high-ranking civilians, and was supervised and supported by CONARC, and was headquartered at Fort Bragg, North Carolina. In setting guidelines for the Howze Board, the Army staff took advantage of the opportunity provided by the memos to institutionalize its own ideas. The Army, for example, had been chafing for years under the weight and performance limitations the Defense Department placed on its airplanes. In a clear attempt to skirt these limits, the staff instructed the Board not to be restricted in its deliberations by current limitations on characteristics of organic Army aircraft.[19] Its charter called for it to undertake a comprehensive study of the Army's aviation requirements during the period 1963–1975.

Composed as it was of a majority of Army officers who were already convinced of the superiority of airmobility over the existing Army divisional organization, the Howze Board did not set out to perform an objective evaluation of the effectiveness of airmobility. Rather, it examined various types of force structures and organizations to determine which would be the most effective for the airmobile concept. To avoid time consuming debate with

Close Air Support and Flexible Response

those who might challenge Army aviation, and in order to meet the secretary's stringent deadline of four months, the executive committee closed its meetings to any whom it deemed untrustworthy. Since Air Force planes were needed, an Air Force representative was invited to be present at the Board's field tests. None was asked to attend the meetings of the executive committee, however, because there was too much discussion of "what was wrong with the Army–Air Force interface."[20]

The creation of the Howze Board and its subsequent deliberations added to the growing conviction within TAC that the Army's interest in the airlift area was just a first step in its campaign to make inroads into the entire spectrum of tactical air support, including close air support, reconnaissance, and communications and control functions. While the Howze Board was convening, General Sweeney proposed to General LeMay that as the Air Force Chief of Staff he ought to negotiate with the Army to turn over all of its fixed-wing aircraft to the Air Force rather than see the Army duplicate Air Force research, development, and training. Since Sweeney realized that TAC did not have the resources to support the Army as fully as the Army wanted, he also recommended that the Air Force accelerate its program to acquire the needed weapons and control systems.[21]

Throughout the summer of 1962, over 100 Army officers, enlisted men, and civilians, not counting divisional troops engaged in field exercises, attached to the Howze Board bent to the task of comparing the existing Army division, the Reorganization Objective Army Division (ROAD) that contained fewer than 100 planes and helicopters, with a proposed air assault division, which would have over 400 flying vehicles. The analysis tested the viability of the Army's mobility concept at all levels of conflict from full-scale conventional war through limited wars to counterinsurgency. Convinced that the airmobile concept was superior to the existing arrangement, they set about determining what structural changes should be made to create the most efficient and effective type of airmobile unit.

Development and field testing took place simultaneously. It would have been better to perform these functions sequentially, but time (four months) did not permit that. Tasks were assigned initially to a group of seven working subcommittees, each headed by an Army brigadier or major general. These committees dealt with target acquisition, tactical mobility, firepower, logistics, operations research, policy, and field tests. In response to over 300 letters sent to aircraft industries, the Board received valuable suggestions for using aircraft and helicopters to improve, among other things, its firepower. A group of experts was asked to review prospects for technological advances during the next decade. The findings of all the committees were analyzed by operations research organizations.[22]

One subcommittee oversaw war-gaming, which sought to provide a quantified measure of the superior effectiveness of an airmobile organization over

Help from Above

its surface transported counterpart. This portion of the Howze Board's activities, however, was the weakest. The shortness of time required the war-gamers to take a number of shortcuts that led to overgeneralized conclusions. Lacking time, the analysts were often able to conduct only one-of-a-kind examinations, preventing them from establishing a broad base. Since the experiments in airmobile organization and weapons were new, and in most cases without historical precedent, much of the work was, of necessity, subjective. Some board members visited Southeast Asia to explore the applicability of their airmobile ideas to the growing insurgency in Vietnam. Simultaneously, Fort Bragg's Special Warfare Center undertook an analysis of the board's concepts and requirements for special warfare.[23]

All of the airmobile ideas generated by these conceptual committees were subjected to field tests at Forts Bragg, Benning, and Stewart, and in the mountains of western Virginia. Three battle groups of the 82d Airborne Division joined with 150 Army planes and 16 Air Force C–130s to conduct over 40 tests of three general types. One type of test evaluated the firepower and other aspects of airmobile organizations. These included live-fire exercises and three major week-long maneuvers.[24] A second tested the new organization's efficiency in counterinsurgency operations. Finally, side tests were conducted of new equipment and techniques, including armed helicopters and fixed-wing aircraft.[25] Reluctant to seek the assistance of wary Air Force officers, Army aviators sought advice from the Navy on how to load and drop bombs from their Mohawk fixed-wing airplanes.[26]

Air Force suspicions of the Army's intent did not lessen the amount of support the Air Force provided to the Board's field tests, even though it believed the Howze Board's findings would have a serious impact on vital Air Force missions. This support was provided by an Air Force mission headed by Brig. Gen. Tarleton H. Watkins, the operations chief of the Ninth Air Force. After six weeks of Army briefings and studies, Watkins was more convinced than ever that the Army was intent on assuming a greater close air support role and in acquiring some transport aircraft even heavier than the twin-engine C–7 Caribou. He reported his belief that the Army went so far as to attempt to extend its influence to air-to-air combat under certain circumstances. As a result of his observations, he concluded that the Army intended to use its aircraft to fly column cover, which was a close air support function, whenever its aircraft were operating in the objective area. What he saw and heard persuaded him that the Army would intensify its campaign to place all aircraft under its jurisdiction during all ground-oriented operations.[27] The head of operations at TAC interpreted the findings of the Howze Board as an extension of the ideas General Taylor expressed in *The Uncertain Trumpet*. In his view, the Army would reduce the Air Force support role to air superiority, and in any joint operations, the Army would have full command and control over operations in the battle area.[28]

Close Air Support and Flexible Response

There was plenty in the Howze Board's final report, submitted in August 1962, to justify such concern. By declaring that "air-delivered firepower by the several services must be complementary," the Board was attempting to elevate the close air support function of Army aircraft to the same level as that of the Air Force. It attempted to further institutionalize the close air support role of Army aircraft, which it called "airmobile firepower," by noting that it must be closely integrated into both conventional and airmobile unit structures. Finally, it pushed for the creation of air fighting units, which it called air cavalry combat brigades, whose purpose was to assume the Air Force's close air support mission of fire suppression during helicopter landings.[29]

In outlining its tactical concepts, the Howze Board provided examples where attack helicopters could supplant Air Force aircraft in providing close air support, and even in engaging in air-to-air combat. Airmobile forces would be able to hold sectors of the front, according to the Board, through the ability of its attack helicopters, armed with 7.65-mm and 20-mm machine guns, to apply airborne firepower in very heavy quantities, with surprise, on targets of opportunity. These attack helicopters could even be used to attack other helicopters.[30]

Anticipating objections to the airmobile idea, principally from the Air Force, to the effect that helicopters and slow fixed-wing aircraft were too vulnerable on the modern battlefield, the report claimed that overall tests and other evidence showed that Army aircraft were "less vulnerable than most previous estimates indicated." Army flyers, it stated, had reduced aircraft vulnerability by adopting a series of measures, such as varying their flight patterns, having flank and overwatching aerial firepower accompany the troop-carrying helicopters, coordinating with ground firepower, intensive air battle drill, flying at very low altitude, taking evasive action, and relying on surprise.[31]

In its final report the Howze Board recommended that the Army undertake a modernization program to improve by eleven standard ROAD divisions, five air assault divisions, three air cavalry combat brigades, and five air transport brigades. It also recommended approval for a 1968 force of 10,922 aircraft for combat and 3,300 more for training. These aircraft, both helicopters and fixed-wing planes, would perform missions across the entire spectrum of tactical support—airlift, reconnaissance, close air support, air assault, interdiction, and even air-to-air combat.

The air assault division, with 429 helicopters and 30 fixed-wing airplanes, would increase the Army's tactical mobility. Eighty-seven of the helicopters would be attack helicopters armed with antitank or antipersonnel weapons and heavy quantities of ammunition. Twenty-four of the fixed-wing Mohawks would be similarly armed for close air support. Each division would contain all of the elements of striking power it needed to sustain itself, and its organic fire support (close air support) would permit the execution of completely integrated airmobile task force missions. Not only were helicopters

Help from Above

envisioned as replacing a portion of the Air Force's close air support, but they were also seen as supplanting much of the ROAD division's artillery support. In concept, the new air mobility division would substitute an aerial rocket battalion of 36 attack helicopters, each with 96 rockets, for the 155-mm and 8-inch howitzers of the ROAD division.[32]

The Board also recommended the creation of air cavalry combat brigades, air fighting units that could destroy the enemy by aerial maneuver, surprise, and a heavy application of firepower delivered by 144 attack helicopters. Its purported mission duplicated much of what Air Force fighter-bombers had been doing during and since World War II. These attack helicopters were seen by the Howze Board members as assisting ground units in defense of river lines and other obstacles, in opposing enemy armored and mechanized forces, in blocking an enemy breakthrough, and in seizing terrain features such as bridges or defiles in advance of friendly ground forces.[33]

Much of the Board's recommendations existed, as yet, only on paper, and much research and development would be needed to make them a reality. Therefore the Howze Board recommended funding an entire family of close air support weapons for Army aircraft: tank-killing weapons, air-delivered antitank mines and antipersonnel bomblets, variable delayed antipersonnel mines, helicopter-delivered napalm bombs, and antiradar missiles. It also advocated a new generation of helicopters and fixed-wing aircraft, many fashioned specifically for close air support. The most ambitious of these suggestions was an improved version of the existing HU–1B armed helicopter that could operate with troop-carrying helicopters to protect them from attack during flight and provide fire (close air) support in the course of ground operations.[34]

Even more suspect in Air Force eyes were the Board's follow-on, long-range plans for the 1970s. Relying heavily on the data it had accumulated from the civilian technological forecasts and from industry, the Howze Board made an H. G. Wellesian leap into the future, visualizing the air assault divisions as developing logically into air mobility divisions and the air combat cavalry brigades becoming "armor brigades" between 1969 and 1975.[35]

These envisioned air mobility divisions of the 1970s would contain 12,000 men, 450 light ground vehicles, and 1,250 aircraft. Each armor brigade would be made up of 4,000 men, 125 light ground vehicles, and 450 aircraft for rapid strike and *fire brigade* (close air support) action. Improved armored and mechanized divisions, in which the helicopter would be substituted for personnel carriers wherever possible, would round out the ground force of the next decade.[36] By the middle of the next decade, the Army would have created its own air force consisting of 29,100 aircraft.

The current tactical concepts behind the airmobile idea, as outlined in the Board's long-range plans, assumed that many Air Force close air support missions would henceforth be performed by Army helicopters and fixed-wing aircraft. In its view, airmobility would allow tactical envelopment of the enemy

Close Air Support and Flexible Response

up to 300 miles. Within this distance army aircraft would be able to make their presence felt "with maximum shock effect." Front lines and "forward edges of the battle area" (FEBAs) would disappear in the battlefield of the future. The battle would be everywhere, and victory would go to the side that could move the fastest to bring killing firepower to bear. The difference between victory and defeat would be determined by airmobile assault forces relying for close air support on air-mounted artillery and air cavalry.[37]

Among the weapons seen as performing these close air support firepower missions was a follow-on to the existing HU-1 helicopter, a weapons helicopter called a Surveillance Attack aircraft (SA). These armed helicopters would accompany troop-carrying helicopters into battle, protecting them from attack during flight and attacking ground threats to the column. They would also provide suppressive fire and close air support after the troops had landed. For this mission they would be armed with all the weapons needed for close air support—antipersonnel and antimateriel area weapons, antitank missiles, machine guns, bombs, and rockets. The close air support function of these airmobile units would be additionally enhanced by vertical-takeoff-and-landing (VTOL) aircraft as surveillance attack vehicles and as artillery weapons systems. In the latter role their primary mission would be indirect fire support with direct fire from the air as their secondary mission.[38]

This vision even included using Army aircraft in air defense and interdiction roles. "Attacking enemy high and low performance aircraft," declared the Final Report, "must first be destroyed by a combination of Air Defense missiles, organic Army aircraft, and the over-all USAF battle for air supremacy."

Members of the Howze Board were well aware that their prescription for the Army to assume many close air support functions would be met by strong resistance from the Air Force, to whom these functions had been delegated by law. They attempted to face the issue in their final report by making a theoretical distinction between two types of close air support. After acknowledging a continuing Air Force role in air superiority, interdiction, deep reconnaissance, and close air support, the authors went on to write that the existing method of close air support, in which the JOC allocated missions, was effective for massing air power on a single target system, but was not responsive to the day-to-day requirements of the Army for close air support. While agreeing that Air Force planes could escort helicopter borne forces and perform the close-in reconnaissance needed for airmobile operations, many of these missions, to be effective, required the most intimate coordination with ground combat elements (infantry, tanks, and armor) and this coordination could be achieved only if the pilots were part of, and under command of, the ground elements, lived with them, and operated their aircraft from fields close to the headquarters they serve.

The Board embellished the familiar theme: that command and control of aircraft by the ground commander was essential for effective close air support. "It is impossible," its report read, "for a commander to brief an unknown pilot,

Help from Above

whom he has never met, by radio or telephone as well as he can a familiar face in a tent before a map. It is also unrealistic," it continued, "to expect a stranger to understand the interrelation of artillery and missile fire, tank and infantry maneuver, air reconnaissance, and air-delivered fire if he has not seen the plan of operation about to be placed in effect and does not have detailed knowledge of the situation and terrain. It is not a question of courage or will. The Army pilot, who may be inferior in both of these qualities, would still be infinitely more useful because he lives and works in an Army environment, and the chain of command that governs his action is direct and unequivocal."[39] This latter statement was a plaint against the complex system of communications that Army ground commanders had to employ when requesting close air support from the Air Force.

This plea for ground control of close air support aircraft and helicopters was buttressed by the testimony of Army officers interviewed during the Howze Board's visit to Southeast Asia during the first week in July 1962. Even though that summer the American military services represented a relatively small advisory force to the South Vietnamese army and air force, the Army's experience with the helicopters and fixed-wing Caribous of its three aviation companies, the Marines employment of 24 helicopters in its task unit, and the Air Force's eight months of operations by the composite fixed-wing aircraft that made up its Farm Gate organization in South Vietnam, provided a basis for evaluating the Army's airmobile proposals.

In interviews designed to determine the feasibility of the airmobile idea, particularly in a conventional war against the Chinese, most Army officers serving in South Vietnam approved of the proposed airmobile organizations. Marine and Air Force interviewees, on the other hand, were cool to the idea of arming helicopters on the grounds that the helicopter would not provide an efficient weapons platform and would not survive in a truly hostile environment.[40] Army officers felt differently. With certain modifications, they embraced the idea of mixing air mobility and standard divisions, and believed such a combination would be successful in Southeast Asia.

One major modification to the existing system that most Army officers espoused was to decentralize the control of Army aviation. They told Board members that the existing air traffic control procedures under the JOC concept were too restrictive. For the airmobile concept to work, in their view, all elements must be entirely and directly responsive to the needs of the commander charged with accomplishing the mission. This could only succeed if Army planes were released from the "restrictive processes of a highly centralized agency." In arguing further for ground control of close support aircraft, other officers in the theater repeated the familiar view that aerial weapons had to be responsive to the ground commander, and that only if he had control of aircraft could he coordinate aerial weapons fire with that of other fire-support elements and with the maneuver of the supported force.[41]

Close Air Support and Flexible Response

While some of these arguments favoring ground control of aircraft made sense, others seemed to stretch the point. Some Army officers in Vietnam, for example, were of the opinion that, since it was so difficult to distinguish between friend and foe in the jungles of Vietnam, armed aircraft had to be used with discrimination "and under the direct control of the ground commander."[42] The implication that centralized control of aircraft resulted in indiscriminate operations was insupportable.

In its Final Report, the Howze Board recommended that the Army adopt its airmobile concept and begin to transform some of its divisions into airmobile units. It called for the conversion of only a portion of the Army's force structure to the new airmobile configuration, with the remaining divisions continuing to be surface-transported but improved with additional aircraft. Illustrative of its lack of a joint perspective, the Board recommended that the new units be evaluated through a continuing program of field tests, but under the general supervision of the Army's test command, the Combat Developments Command, rather than under the Joint Strike Command. This failure to integrate Army aviation with the existing tactical air assets of the Air Force, both within the report and in the recommendation for subsequent field testing, stood in the way of peaceful integration of the two aerial forces for close air support.

The Air Force Defends the Existing System: The Disosway Board

The Air Force adopted two simultaneous and pervasive responses to the Howze Board's airmobility idea and to the close air support segment of that doctrine. Its first position was that it fully agreed that the Army needed more mobility and that the Air Force should help the Army achieve it. Even while the Howze Board was still in session, TAC fully supported this position, although well aware that acceptance of the Board's findings by the Secretary of Defense could have a serious impact on vital Air Force missions. After the Board submitted its report, General Sweeney emphatically stated that the Air Force should show a sincere desire to meet Army requirements, not merely deride the Army's concepts as infeasible. General LeMay charged all commanders, particularly the TAC commander, to support field tests, war games, engineering tests, and analytical studies relating to the concept of airmobility.[43]

While agreeing that the Army had to become more mobile through the air, the Air Force's second position, dealing with how to accomplish this, challenged the Howze Board's prescription of relying principally on Army aviation. The Air Force maintained, and set out to prove, that the means for augmenting the Army's mobility already existed or would soon be available within Air Force resources. For the next several years TAC and other Air Force commands acted to prevent the expansion of Army aviation into the fields of airlift, reconnais-

Help from Above

sance, and close air support by improving the Air Force's ability to provide these services to the Army. These measures included convening a board to examine the Howze conclusions, establishing a Tactical Air Warfare Center to support tests of Air Force tactical support resources, reexamining doctrine in an effort to update the joint air-ground manual, improving the tactical air control system, performing unilateral and joint tests of the Air Force's tactical conventional war-fighting potential, and developing a close working relationship with the Joint Strike Command to demonstrate that it could fill the bill.

The earliest Air Force reaction to the Howze panel was to create a parallel board to examine the same questions. In August 1962, a month before the Howze Board submitted its findings to the Secretary of Defense, General LeMay ordered the formation, by TAC, of a panel to analyze and comment on the imminent Army report.[44] Leadership of the committee, called the USAF Tactical Air Support Requirements Board, fell to General Sweeney's vice commander, Lt. Gen. Gabriel P. Disosway, who contributed his name to the unofficial title of the panel. Disosway was assisted by 10 officers, both generals and colonels, from the affected areas of the Air Force—the Operations, Plans, and Operational Requirements directorates of the Air Staff in the Pentagon, the Military Air Transport Service, the Logistics and Systems commands, and the operations chiefs from both the European and Pacific commands.[45]

The Disosway Board divided into working groups paralleling those of the Army board. Written sections of the Army's report were made available by the Air Force liaison officer assigned to the Army board at Fort Bragg. The final 36-page report of the Board, submitted in mid-September, followed the format of the Howze product, commenting on each item in turn.

The Disosway comments on specific issues disclosed three underlying themes: that all military forces in a theater, including tactical air power, belonged to the unified or theater commander and could not be planned for unilaterally by any one service; that while agreeing to the need for more airmobility, the Air Force strongly opposed the use of Army aviation for missions that duplicate what the Air Force could do and already was doing; and that the Air Force was fully equipped and willing to provide all the support, including close air support, that the Army wanted.

The Disosway Board was critical of the Howze panel's methodology. Since it considered the field tests to be the most important element in Howze's examination, the Air Force board saved its harshest censure for them. While agreeing that these tests were of some value in disclosing problem areas in equipment and tactics, Disosway pointed out the Howze Board's lack of time prevented it from applying what was learned in one test to the design of the follow-on experiment. The Air Force also found a weakness in the lack of statistical analysis of the test results. Without such statistical analysis, the conclusions were based on the judgments of the evaluators, which they deemed as subjective and not conclusive.

Close Air Support and Flexible Response

Brig. Gen. Gabriel P. Disosway

The Board's strongest criticism of Howze's methods, which trailed over into a substantive issue, was that the Army analysts had examined airmobility strictly *in vacuo*, looking solely at Army resources without considering the interaction of air and ground forces in terms of joint operations. The Disosway group regretted that no appraisal was made of Air Force equipment, tactics, and techniques as an alternate approach to increasing the Army's mobility.[46] For example, the Army did not factor into its planning the Air Force F–84s, F–100s, F–105s, B–57s, or B–66s, all of which contributed to close air support of the Army. The Air Force had over 2,000 tactical fighters and bombers in its active force, and another 532 in its reserves, that could support the Army's mission.[47] Throughout the report, claims for the need for Army aviation were made without acknowledging the fact that in most cases the Air Force already possessed such capabilities.

The Air Force report responded to the many Howze Board arguments for decentralizing control of Air Force planes by placing them under ground commanders during combat situations. Repeated emphasis on the superior authority of the unified commander over his component service commanders was the committee's rejoinder to the Army's recommendation to increase the responsiveness of air units by locating them with and under the command of ground force commanders. On the contrary, noted the Air Force reply, economy of force and responsiveness are improved when air units in a unified command

253

Help from Above

are controlled by the air-component commander according to priorities set by the unified commander. This principle had a long history dating back to World War II, where it was discovered in the crucible of conflict, and in Korea where it was applied with some success. It had received the praise of General Eisenhower who, after the North African campaign, wrote that "the new administrative and operational organization successfully solved one of the basic problems of modern warfare—how to apply air power most effectively to support land operations."[48] The greatest advantage of this newly organized centralized air power, in the view of the commander of the European Theater of Operations (ETO), was that:

> aircraft of different combat formations could be fused in a single mission as the need arose, and as a result the local commander had for direct support the combined weight of the strategic and tactical forces when he most needed it.[49]

The Disosway Board also rejected the argument for Army control of Air Force planes built on the contention that low-and-slow aircraft based close to the front were more responsive than high-performance jets flying from bases far behind the action. Modern jets, which could cover 100–200 miles in a matter of minutes, removed the prior limitations on basing areas and permitted short response times to almost any target requested by the Army in close support. To station low-and-slow Army planes close to the front, on the other hand, would create logistical and supply problems incommensurate with their value. The Air Force report did not fail to take advantage of the opportunity to mention, again, that the Air Force was constantly being criticized for taking so long to respond to calls for close air support, although it traditionally took longer to process and evaluate a request through the Army request net than it did to fly the mission.[50]

Finally, in the controversy over command and control, Disosway's panel rejected the Army's notion that an airman had to live with a soldier in order to understand his problems. Coordination and daily contact between the Tactical Air Force Commander and the field Army commander was sufficient for mutual understanding, without requiring a flight commander and tank commander to be colocated. This arrangement worked well in World War II and in Korea, where FACs in leading tanks were in contact with the fighter-bombers covering the tanks' movements. This system paid off handsomely during General Patton's plunge to the Rhine, illustrating that mutual respect for the needs and capabilities of the other can exist without one force being placed under the command of the other.[51]

On the question of the vulnerability of Army aircraft to enemy defenses, the Disosway group stated that it could find little substantive evidence to support the Army's claim that "Army aircraft [were] less vulnerable than pre-

Close Air Support and Flexible Response

vious estimates indicated." On the contrary, based on the wartime experiences of its members, the Air Force board believed that, if the Army used its aircraft as it proposed, it would sustain unacceptable losses to enemy ground fire from rifles, automatic weapons, rockets, and antiaircraft guns. Citing a vulnerability analysis that it had conducted, the board concluded that the Army's AO–1 Mohawk was four times as vulnerable to ground fire than was the Air Force's principal close air support plane, the F–105, or the promising F–4 then undergoing tests. It found that the F–4 would have a 50 percent chance of completing a mission in an area where the Mohawk would have only a 5 percent probability. As to helicopters, the board found questionable, to say the least, the Army's assertion that the achievement of air superiority and the elimination of ground defenses would prevent helicopters from suffering unacceptable losses. The problem was that it was simply an assertion that required more exhaustive and authoritative examination before it could be considered a conclusion.[52]

Turning to the 16-division (11 ROAD, 5 airmobile) force structure Howze proposed, Disosway recommended postponing any decision until joint tests and joint war games either validated or rejected such a radical reorganization. He was unhappy with the fact that this recommended reorganization had been determined unilaterally by the Army without being placed in the context of existing Air Force close air support, airlift, and reconnaissance capabilities. If no restrictions were placed on it, noted the report, each military service could superficially justify a requirement to be entirely self-contained and self-sufficient, just as each unified commander could justify having all the forces he needed permanently under his command. The prohibitive cost in dollars, manpower, facilities, and equipment, however, rendered such arrangements patently impossible. The Air Force rejected, therefore, any proposition such as the present one that would establish another air force in the Army that duplicated Air Force capabilities.[53] It equally rejected the Howze recommendation that the Army test its new concept unilaterally, but rather recommended that any testing that took place be done under the aegis of the unified Strike Command, which would test both the Army's idea that it could provide for its own tactical air support and the Air Force concept that it was fully capable of supporting the Army.

The Disosway report hammered away at the theme that the Air Force with its existing tactical aircraft and experience could already do, and in many cases do better, what the Army was promising to accomplish with its airmobile forces. At a demonstration at Fort Bragg on July 24, for instance, Army Mohawks, although primarily reconnaissance planes, performed attack missions normally executed by Air Force fighter-bombers. Had the F–4 Phantom, expected in the inventory within a year, been used in the same mission, it would have delivered, with equal accuracy, six times the firepower at two-and-a-half times the speed. In addition, the Phantom in a combat situation would be able to live and fight in gaining air superiority, while the Mohawk "would

Help from Above

suffer the same fate as the Stuka," which disappeared from combat in World War II after Allied fighter-bombers dominated the skies over Europe.[54]

Disosway and his companions rejected the distinction the Army group tried to make between two types of close air support, namely, "close-in" for Army aviation and "other" for Air Force planes. Based on what they observed Army planes doing in the field tests, and the fact that they carried the same munitions as Air Force planes, including 1,000-lb. bombs, 2.75-inch rockets, and 20-mm guns, it appeared that Army aircraft of the proposed airmobile units would be performing close air support missions identical to those that Air Force planes were already executing. This conclusion was reinforced by Air Force board members who visited South Vietnam and saw Army helicopters and Mohawks performing close air support, airlift, and reconnaissance missions.

By way of a final conclusion, the Disosway panel recommended that the creation of a new Army force structure, the procurement of new equipment, and the functional reassignments needed for the force structure the Howze Board proposed, be held in abeyance until further field tests and war games determined which was the better way to improve the Army's mobility—by using already improved Air Force tactical resources or by creating the airmobile system. These future evaluations should be conducted by the Joint Strike Command, which should base its evaluations on the needs of unified commanders in the field, not on those of individual service commanders. The Air Force believed this approach would avoid a repetition of what the Air Force considered to be a major drawback of Howze's effort, namely, analyzing Army mobility from a unilateral service perspective rather than from a unified viewpoint. Further, the future tests of Army mobility should pit the Air Force's concept of tactical air support against the Army's notion of airmobility to determine which was more effective and economical. Finally, the Disosway Board recommended that the Army discontinue acquisition of the Mohawk and Caribou aircraft that presented the clearest challenge to Air Force close air support and airlift functions.

Both the Howze and Disosway reports came to Secretary McNamara in September 1962, the former directly from the Army secretary without intermediate scrubbing by the uniformed Army staff, the latter from Disosway through LeMay and the Air Force staff. McNamara's initial reaction was far from encouraging for Army aviators, as the Army study failed to convince him of the economic viability of the airmobile concept. In reporting on the Board's findings to Congress the following February, he voiced reservations about some of the Board's recommendations.[55] In a memo that same month to both service secretaries he noted that the Army recommendations would entail new aircraft and associated expenses that would amount to $1 billion a year. He had no intention of duplicating close air support and other resources that already existed within the Air Force and could do the job. He acknowledged that the Air Force was showing a new interest and was developing new methods and proce-

Close Air Support and Flexible Response

dures for making its close air support more responsive. Specifically, he alluded to a recent competition at Nellis AFB, which showed a "realism in dealing with the discovery and attack of ground targets heretofore not demonstrated."[56]

Given the radical nature of the Army's recommendations and their close relation to the Air Force mission, McNamara accepted Disosway's recommendation and, in his February memo, requested (ordered) the services to undertake two follow-up measures. First, he instructed the Army and Air Force to examine jointly the contemporary status of close air support and recommend improvements. As he saw it, there were still major problems of communications, target location and identification, delivery accuracy, and responsiveness.[57] Secondly, he urged the Joint Chiefs of Staff to direct General Adams's Strike Command, which had been activated late in 1961, to test both the Army and Air Force concepts as they had been stated by the Howze and Disosway conclaves.[58]

A Joint Examination of Close Air Support

Reaction to the first of Secretary McNamara's two instructions, namely to analyze close air support, was forthcoming at all levels. During the first months of 1963 the Defense Department embarked on a close support study, the Strike Command undertook a review of Air Force air control procedures, and TAC and the Army's Combat Development Command once again tried to produce a unified doctrine for air-ground operations.

In the Pentagon, the Army and Air Force headquarters staffs tried to winnow down, and come to some agreement over, what they saw as the kernels of their disagreements over close air support, battlefield mobility, and control of airspace. In a substantial exchange of ideas, early in 1963, the vice chiefs of both services attempted to close the gap and settle the outstanding issues. The task proved too daunting. Each side remained wedded to a central philosophy that proved incompatible with the other side's. While the central positions and the specific issues that flowed from them dealt only with all the elements of tactical air support, close air support occupied a cardinal position in the discussions. Despite the obvious sincerity of both sides in the search for an acceptable middle ground, an examination of both the central positions and the specific disagreements indicates that both sides approached the issue from diametrically opposed directions. The Army, in its stated central position, did not see the issue as one of roles and missions. The Air Force saw it as principally that.

In stating his service's central position on organic aircraft, the Army's Vice Chief of Staff, General Barksdale Hamlett, denied that the Army harbored a desire to take over any Air Force mission, or any portion of one that the Air Force could perform to the Army's satisfaction. He stated repeatedly that the

Help from Above

Army wanted to leave the existing roles and missions arrangements intact. McNamara, however prodded the Army to improve its mobility by incorporating state-of-the-art technology, principally aircraft, into its inventory. Therefore, the Army would increase its mobility by transporting its troops to the battlefield in Army helicopters, and these helicopters would be protected by the kind of organic fire-support that had always been an integral part of maneuver units in all armies—machine guns, mortars, antitank weapons, and so forth. With existing technology, this translated into using armed helicopters to provide this fire-support. In the Army's view, to arm helicopters or other Army aircraft amounted to no more than simply elevating the gun platform of ordinary ground weapons, making Army aircraft a competitor, not with the fighter-bomber, but with the artillery, the 1/4-ton truck, or the armored carrier. The use of fire-support from aerial platforms came under the same doctrine and precepts as did the use of any other type of organic fire-support, not under a doctrine that would compete with the Air Force close air support mission. Hamlett saw no fragmentation of close air support. There is no "division of the close air support function into two parts," he wrote, because the function performed by the Army is not, in fact, a part of the same basic mission that the Air Force performs.

In the same vein, the Army would replace the traditional light vehicles and trucks, which in the past provided logistic support, with appropriate aircraft. To Hamlett, the Army's operation of such vehicles no more constituted an invasion of Air Force roles and missions than did the arming of trucks with machine guns or the movement of mortars in armored personnel carriers. Since the need for immediate and continuous support to ground forces was the concern of the ground commander's alone, the Army had to have the dominant voice in supplying it. The Air Force could provide it only if the Air Force units involved were permanently attached to the parent Army unit so that they could live and train as well as operate with that unit 24 hours a day.[59]

The basic and unchanging conviction behind all these expositions of the Army position was that there was nothing unique about aircraft that required them to be judged or employed in any way other than as a weapon of war generically similar to those martial instruments that armies had employed since the advent of warfare. The Army's arguments were totally consistent with this fundamental interpretation. Substituting aerial fire-support for ground fire-support, helilift for truck transportation, and Army aerial reconnaissance for ground surveillance was simply a matter of raising these traditional activities a bit above the ground. There was nothing generically different about them.

To the Air Force, of course, this limited perception of the nature of aircraft struck at the very reason for having an air force separate from an army. In the airman's view, the airplane had revolutionized warfare by introducing a whole new category of principles. To emasculate the aerial weapon by confin-

Close Air Support and Flexible Response

ing it within the strait jacket of traditional military thinking would be to suppress air power's potential and prevent it from functioning to best advantage. The imperative that aircraft be employed according to criteria different, not only in degree, but also in kind from those of ground forces had largely been recognized and codified in numerous agreements and statements on roles and missions since World War II.[60] Therefore, the Air Force's position, unlike that of the Army, was anchored in the existing agreements on roles and missions that it considered fundamental and unchangeable.

In outlining his service's central position, the Air Force's Vice Chief of Staff, Maj. Gen. William F. McKee, emphasized these past agreements on roles and missions. He noted that each service had been given a specifically defined area of responsibility. According to the agreed upon roles and missions, there was only one authority responsible for directing combat operations and that was the unified commander. There were no longer any unilateral combat services. The services contribute their resources to unified commanders who decided how to use their forces. The strategies and tactics for applying these forces had to be established in the context of joint operations. They must be used where they would be most effective from a theater standpoint, not from the point of view of an individual service. The Air Force would direct all its available air effort to targets and situations that were most important, not in the eyes of the local ground or air commanders, but in the eyes of the man carrying the responsibility for both, the unified theater commander.

The Air Force's controversy with the Army sprang in part from its opinion that the Army was developing concepts for land battle in a vacuum, without taking into account the concept of the unified command and with no acknowledgement that the Air Force already had close air support resources in being to support it. Since the Air Force was convinced, and was currently in the process of illustrating in field tests, that it possessed the resources, experience, and will to provide exactly what the Army said it wanted, it could never agree to any proposition that would create an Air Force in the Army, nor to any proposed duplication of Air Force capabilities. The increased mobility the Howze Board wanted for the Army could be attained with existing Army and Air Force resources. A selective combination of strategic airlift, Air Force troop carrier airlift, and Army helicopters supported by Air Force and reconnaissance planes could do the job. It would be irrational to duplicate unnecessarily a capability that already existed. As regarded the close air support function, the Air Force saw no valid reason to develop a duplicative capability to strike close air support targets, particularly when the Army proposed to use the same types of munitions, tactics, and techniques, but to deliver them by an aircraft whose survivability was questionable. New requirements could be satisfied as they arose more readily by the Air Force than by the Army.

While McKee recognized that the Army could fruitfully replace some of its surface vehicles with helicopters for observation, artillery spotting, and

Help from Above

courier missions, he believed that any increased capability to deliver aerial firepower from aerial platforms must be achieved by the Air Force. In an ideal world without restrictions, each military service could probably justify having resources that would make it fully self-contained and self-sufficient. In the real world, however, the prohibitive cost in dollars, manpower, facilities, and equipment would make that impossible, regardless of how convincing the arguments and rationale of the service chiefs.[61] This Air Force contention that it was fully willing and able to support the Army, and that the Army's attempts to develop its own aerial support resources were both economically and doctrinally unsound, formed the background for all close air support discussions in the period immediately preceding the major deployments to Vietnam.

The response to Secretary McNamara's exhortation for a joint examination of close air support got underway within three months of his February memorandum. In May, a board convened at Fort Meade, Maryland, to act on the secretary's directive. Although called a joint board, the committee actually consisted of two groups, an Army Close Air Support Board, headed by three Army generals from Fort Meade, CONARC, and Fort Ord, and an Air Force Close Air Support Board, chaired by the major general who commanded the Twelfth Air Force.

The Close Air Support Board examined the essential elements of close air support—air-ground command relationships, close air support aircraft, tactics and techniques, training and indoctrination programs, and resources for close air support—and submitted its final report in August 1963. The results were mixed. While the conferees reached some agreement in the areas of tactics and techniques, training and indoctrination, and resources, they differed on two other major issues: command relationships and the type of aircraft to be employed.

For purposes of its study, the joint board modified the definition of close air support by increasing the area where this function could be performed. Whereas the official joint definition then in effect identified a close air support area as the region between the FEBA and the bomb line,[62] the Board extended this zone to include targets out beyond the bomb line that were of immediate concern to the ground commander. This change recognized the fact that the longer ranges of modern weapons and the increased mobility of modern forces made the ground commander more vulnerable than previously to forces outside the bomb line. Specifically, the Board mentioned two types of targets in this new, extended area that now became targets for close air support strikes—combat troop units capable of attacking within six hours and which were located within four or fewer hours march distance from the front line, and artillery units that could fire on our forces. This new definition represented a subtle shift toward the direction that the Air Force had always espoused. By agreeing to change the basis for defining close air support from a geographical (how close-in to the front line the strikes were) to an operational (targets of "immediate

Close Air Support and Flexible Response

interest" to the ground commander) one, the Army was coming close to the age-old Air Force contention that close-in close air support was less effective than that performed farther out beyond the battlefield. This consensus, to move the center of gravity for close air support missions out beyond the bomb line and abutting the region of interdiction, was another step toward creating a new category of close air support called "battlefield air interdiction."[63]

The first area where the two parts of the Board were at loggerheads was over the perennial question of command relationships relative to close air support aircraft. The continued inability of the services and Joint Chiefs to agree on a formal joint doctrine for close air support permitted both the Army and Air Force members to reiterate and refine their familiar service positions regarding air-ground command relationships. The Army proposed, once again, that operational control of close air support airplanes be given to field army commanders. The Air Force, it maintained, had not lived up to its responsibility to meet the "reasonable requirements" of the Army and to devote an "appreciable portion of its resources" to such support.[64] The Air Force's interpretation of *cooperation* in close air support did not satisfy the Army's view that combat power was best applied by giving the commander at each level the resources, and the authority he needed to accomplish his mission.

Army board members also stressed two failures of the current system: the Air Force's close air support was neither habitual nor sufficiently responsive. Even though the amount of close air support needed at the field army and corps levels varied with changes in the ground battle, it was never zero. These levels of Army organization always have a bona fide continuing need for some close air support. Yet the existing system, which employed the same planes for air-to-air fighting, for interdiction, and for close air support, did not assure that a consistent amount of close air support planes would be available. The current system also provided the least responsive support. The need for air and ground commanders to *cooperate* in getting close air support missions violated the principle of unity of command. In addition, the existing arrangement kept the ground commander guessing as to whether he would receive the sorties previously promised to him or whether the planes would have been unilaterally diverted by the air commander who controlled them. As long as this one element of his combined arms package remained questionable, the ground commander could never field a truly integrated team of combat and combat support elements.

The Army board members again, therefore, recommended that the Air Force replace the existing practice of assigning a specific number of sorties to close air support with a program of placing particular air divisions under the operational control of field army or independent corps commanders. While the method of assigning aircraft by sorties rather than by units allowed the air commander to mass all his forces rapidly and gave him the flexibility to adjust, they argued, it deprived the ground commander of the assurance of receiving a given amount of close air support. At the same time, it increased the response

Help from Above

time when the proper ordnance was not immediately available. Finally, the Army remained convinced that the assignment by unit rather than sorties would create a feeling of mutual interest and responsibility between the air and ground units that would contribute to the success of ground missions. Conversely, while the proposed assignment of support by units rather than by sorties would deprive the Air Force of some flexibility, this would be greatly outweighed by the advantages to the overall mission and to the ground commander, who could then plan his operations in advance with reasonable assurance that he would have the support, and who could integrate and tailor his air and ground fire-support resources and maneuver elements to achieve the best results.[65]

Board members from the Air Force disagreed with almost every one of these points, arguing for retention of the existing command and control arrangements. They pointed out, once again, that the system proposed by the Army had been tried in World War II with almost catastrophic results. They deemed it essential for an air commander to retain the authority to mass any or all of his aerial resources to satisfy the immediate demands of air operations, be they for air superiority, interdiction, close air support, or a combination of the three. Tying an air unit down to a particular field army, they wrote, would deprive it of the ability to support another field army that might be more hard-pressed, or to perform the other aerial roles when these were judged more important. To illustrate the superiority of the existing command arrangements, the Air Force panelists used the example of a field army front of 100 miles, where the inherent capability of the forthcoming F–4 Phantom fighter-bomber allowed it to range over the area in support of at least three field armies. This would be impossible if the fighters were tied down under the control of one field army.

Furthermore, a particular field army commander, to whom the Army proposed giving operational control, was not, in the opinion of the Air Force, in a position to weigh and judge his own immediate close air support requirements against the entire requirement for air support. Finally, in its rebuttal of the Army position regarding command and control, the Air Force asserted that better responsiveness would be achieved by improving tactics, techniques, training, and indoctrination rather than by changing the command structure. Since tactics and techniques could be improved only in the field by operating organizations, the Board recommended a Joint Air Support Center be established for that purpose. The Air Force board also pointed to the impressive increase in training underway within the Air Force and to the fact that TAC in the past few years had gone far to change the state-of-mind of Air Force personnel. It was on improvements in these areas, rather than on changes in command relationships, that the Army should rely for increases in responsiveness.

Finally, the Air Force rejected the Army's contention that it was the Air Force's system of centralized control that caused the flow of close air support to the Army to be inconsistent. This problem, it maintained, resulted from either poor planning or unexpected battle reversals, neither of which would necessarily disappear under the Army's proposed system. In conclusion, the Air Force's participants on the Close Air Support Board recommended no changes to the existing command relations, but suggested that both services continue to improve their procedures for requesting and supplying close air support missions and that they emphasize cross-training of service personnel.[66]

The second area where the two boards failed to adjust their differences was over the question of whether high- or low-performance aircraft could better perform the close air support mission. As it had argued in the case of command and control, the Army wanted a plane that would be most responsive to its requests for support. As in the case of command relationships, the Army anchored its arguments for a specific aircraft on its need for responsiveness. Responsiveness, in its view, was determined by an airplane's all-weather capability; its vulnerability to ground fire; its basing requirements; its combat radius, payload, and loiter time; and whether it was dedicated solely to the close air support mission or was a multipurpose aircraft.

As to the requirement that the ideal close air support plane be able to operate effectively at night and in poor weather, the Army contingent on the board concluded that for the time period being considered (1965–1970), it was unlikely that any plane could provide more than limited close air support at night and under low ceilings and reduced visibility. The problem was not in navigating but in developing equipment that could locate, identify, and attack targets during these periods. Even if such equipment were developed, ran the argument, it would be so heavy and bulky as to make the aircraft ineligible for the close air support role on other grounds.

Aircraft vulnerability was a major element of responsiveness. The Army board members viewed vulnerability to surface-to-air weapons as primarily a function of speed and altitude, and secondarily of maneuverability, distance from the weapons, and exposure time. Although it accepted the dictum that a higher speed and lower altitude improved chances for survival against surface-to-air weapons, it argued fervently against the oft-stated Air Force contention that supersonic speed was necessary to survive in a sophisticated air defense environment. Relying principally on a RAND study,[67] it maintained that a ground battery could offset the supersonic speed of an attack aircraft by changing its firing pattern. Unless a plane were flying above Mach 3 and below 300 feet, the ground battery could launch enough missiles to achieve a high probability of hitting any tactical aircraft that flew through its engagement envelope. Survivability depended more upon a clear assessment of the threat and adoption of countermeasures than it did on supersonic speed.[68]

On the other hand, the Army board considered a maneuvering speed of 300 knots or less as an essential qualification for a close air support plane. This ability to fly at slower speed was needed not only to permit the pilot to identi-

Help from Above

fy his target, but also to make his attacks on the target more precise by reducing the turning radius of the aircraft and the G-force pressure on the flyer.

The Army panelists considered basing requirements as another major factor that determined responsiveness. To be as responsive as the ground commander wished, close air support planes should be stationed as close to the front line as possible. How close they could be to the action depended on their logistic needs. To meet the criteria, the planes should not need elaborate and vulnerable fixed facilities, they must be able to operate from short, semiprepared landing strips, and they must be reliable and relatively easily maintained under these conditions. After surveying airfields around the world, the board concluded that enough bases were available only if the close air support planes operated from semiprepared runways of 3,000 feet or less. Air Force close air support jet fighters needed at least 5,000 feet. Reducing the required runway length from 5,000 to 3,000 feet would almost double the number of available bases worldwide. Even more striking was the estimate that planes that could use semiprepared landing strips would be able to use eight times as many airfields as those that needed permanent-surface runways.

A review of the potential theaters of operations around the globe led the Army officers to set the criteria of a 200–300 nautical mile combat radius, an ordnance load of 4,000 pounds, and a loiter time of one hour as the minimum requirements for a close air support plane. In addition, the ideal close air support plane should have a ferry range of 2,500 nautical miles, a speed between Mach .3 and .9, and a short-takeoff-and-landing (STOL) ability from sod or semiprepared strips. The plane should be able to attack approximately 25 percent of its targets at night. In poor weather it should be capable of taking off and landing in minimum visibility and of hitting targets under ceilings of 1,000 feet with three miles visibility. About 15 percent of close air support sorties would have to strike their targets within 15 minutes of the time they were called, and about 20 percent of the total close air support effort must be able to respond within 30 minutes or less. Finally, some portion of tactical air must be responsive to the ground battle in all active combat situations.

The strongest statements of the Board's Army contingent, however, were reserved for its arguments against using multipurpose planes for close air support. In the first place, the design of any plane that performs more than one function must necessarily represent a compromise between the competing demands of the various functions. The design of the Air Force's multipurpose jet fighters, moreover, which flew air superiority, interdiction, and close air support sorties, was weighted toward supersonic speed essential for air combat, but not for close air support. Therefore, degradation of the close air support role was likely. Second, the close air support function could be further degraded, as crews were trained to perform primarily in the air superiority role. While multipurpose fighters increased the air commander's flexibility, this flexibility was often attained by sacrificing the of quantity and availability of

Close Air Support and Flexible Response

aircraft for close air support. Finally, multipurpose, supersonic aircraft were extremely heavy, complex, and expensive. They required large bases with long, hard-surfaced runways, which reduced their ability to respond to ground needs. They were three to four times more expensive to procure and maintain than were smaller, lighter planes of less but adequate performance. The F–4C Phantom, which the Air Force adapted from the Navy and which would be its main tactical fighter in the late 1960s, cost $2.8 million each, and required about $460,000 a year to maintain. Smaller attack planes, like the Navy's A4D–5 cost $800,000 to buy and $260,000 a year to operate.

None of the Air Force's fighter planes then in the inventory or planned for future development satisfied the Army as a close air support aircraft. The Air Force's fighter-bombers (F–100s, F–105s, F–4Cs, and F–111s) all needed elaborate and vulnerable fixed bases with long runways. The F–100 could not carry enough munitions and had too short a combat radius and insufficient loiter time. The European Fiat G–91, which was being proposed as a close air support plane for the North Atlantic Treaty Organization (NATO), along with the F–5A, also failed the payload, combat radius, and loiter time tests. The Navy's A6A attack plane was ruled out because it too needed permanent bases, while its A4E lacked the payload, combat radius, and loiter time and needed too long a runway. In the Army's view, major modifications would be needed to existing light attack planes or newly developed ones to make them suitable for close air support.

On the other hand, a visual light attack (VAL) plane the Navy was proposing, seemed to fit most of the Army's criteria for maintenance, logistic support, responsiveness, and the ability to fly off semiprepared 3,000-foot runways. The Navy had decided in the spring of 1963 that its carrier attack planes, which had been developed for nuclear strikes under the New Look concept, were inadequate for nonnuclear limited wars. Bypassing the Joint Chiefs, the Navy received Secretary McNamara's blessing to develop a subsonic plane with a long loiter time and a capacity to carry a large bomb load.[69] This type of plane appealed to the Army members of the Close Air Support Board.

The Air Force basically accepted the Army's list of characteristics desirable in a close air support plane. It did not agree, however, with the priorities the Army placed on them.

While the Army quite understandably stressed responsiveness, the Air Force, with equal logic, emphasized the need for aircraft survivability. In a direct contradiction of the Army's dismissal of supersonic speed as the principal requirement for survivability, the Air Force concluded that high-performance characteristics and the ability to defend itself were the key to attaining an acceptable attrition rate. In 1963 high performance meant that an aircraft could carry and deliver munitions at a speed of Mach .9 and still have enough additional speed to cope with enemy fighters and surface-to-air missile (SAM) sites. Other characteristics that contributed to an aircraft's high performance

Help from Above

included reliable navigation, radar and fire control equipment, munitions carrying, and STOL ability.

Unless attrition[70] were reduced to an acceptable level or eliminated entirely, the Air Force would be unable to furnish the requested close air support sorties. Studies showed that in the past a one percent attrition rate, such as that experienced in World War II, would reduce the size of the D-Day force by 50 percent within 100 days. A 10 percent attrition rate would reduce the force to 25 percent within two weeks, and to 12 percent within three weeks. There were two ways around this problem: either reduce attrition, or accept attrition and replace losses with new production. While the latter practice had saved the U.S. in the past, the escalation of costs, the advent of more modern technology, and the unfavorable distribution of materials had made massive replacement a less dependable solution. It was more reliable, argued the Board, to reduce the attrition rate as much as possible. This was done by diminishing the effectiveness of their causes. For the most part, future attrition was pictured as a result of attacks on friendly air bases, air-to-air engagements, and hits by enemy SAMs. Assaults on friendly air bases could be reduced by locating them farther from, rather than nearer to, the battle zone. With the speed of modern jets, proximity to the front line was not a necessity, but could even be a disadvantage. High-performance aircraft were necessary for successful air-to-air engagements and to survive against all types of enemy air defense. Only high-performance aircraft possessed the speed, missile delivery effectiveness, and radar warning devices and electronic countermeasures needed for survival.[71]

The Air Force members of the Board then analyzed the effects of an aircraft's speed on its vulnerability and concluded that speed was the most valuable single characteristic needed for survival against sophisticated enemy air defenses. They maintained that higher speed improved survivability by making it more difficult for the ground defense weapons to detect and lead a plane, by decreasing the number of rounds that could be fired at the aircraft while it was within firing range, and by increasing the effectiveness of anti-SAM and air-to-air weapons. This latter advantage of high-performance over low-performance aircraft, according to the conferees, was inspired by the fact that the current antiradiation standoff weapon missile, the Shrike, could not outdistance the enemy's SA–2 and SA–3 missiles when delivered subsonically, but had a longer range than those two ground-launched missiles when launched at supersonic speed, thus making supersonic aircraft speed critical to survivability.

In defending the effectiveness of high-performance close air support planes, and opposing the use of low-and-slow aircraft over the battlefield, the Air Force personnel on the board thought the Army was contradicting itself. Elsewhere the Army was arguing that it could gain "control of the land" with effective antiaircraft defenses. At the same time it wanted a low-performance close air support plane that could loiter for an hour in the vicinity of an enemy that would also doubtless possess the same effective air defenses.

Close Air Support and Flexible Response

To the Air Force, the question of the survivability of low-performance close air support planes had already been settled in World War II, which was replete with examples of special-purpose aircraft that could not live in the battlefield environment. Despite the glamorization in Army literature of the wartime feats of American light-plane pilots, artillery spotters seldom ventured deeply behind enemy lines and survived largely because of the enemy troops' fear of Allied counterbattery artillery fire. Initial British attempts in 1939 to use low-performance Westland Lysanders to support the Army in France proved disastrous. They were phased out within two years and the RAF turned to fighters for close air support. At the beginning of the war both the French and Germans tried to use slow STOL airplanes (Mureaux-115s and Henschel Hs 126s) for close air support and reconnaissance, only to withdraw them entirely from service in mid-1941, by which time they were proving to be hopeless against high-speed fighters. British and French pilots were unanimous in their conviction that slow, unarmed planes had no place near the front in modern warfare. The Germans had to withdraw the famed slow-flying Ju–87 Stuka from combat on the western front as early as 1940 due to its vulnerability to antiaircraft fire and Allied fighters. Also, their excellent, little low-performance plane, the Fieseler (Fi–156) Storch (Stork), suffered such heavy losses on liaison missions in front areas that the German high command turned down requests to use them for artillery spotting. Finally, the Air Force believed that the logistical difficulties the *Luftwaffe* experienced in supporting a great number of low-performance planes at many scattered locations on the Russian front suggested that the U.S. Army would face the same problems if it tried to maintain a large fleet of small planes.[72]

Attrition also figured into the question of cost-effectiveness. The Army pictured it as more cost-effective to buy cheaper, low-performance aircraft rather than expensive, high-performance models. The Air Force replied that cost-per-kill, rather than the original purchase price, was a better measure of the cost-effectiveness of various aircraft. By including corollary expenditures, such as those incurred for bases, passive and active defense, and so on, in the total system's cost, the difference in cost between low-performance and high-performance planes became relatively small, suggesting that the expected advantage of a *cheaper* aircraft could be spurious. Additionally, it was more cost-effective to cut the attrition rate by buying more survivable aircraft in the first place than it was by buying cheaper planes. The sophistication of high-performance aircraft would cut attrition and in the process reduce the cost-per-kill.[73]

Following this long disquisition on the essentiality of survivability for close air support aircraft, the Board considered the other criteria that the Army had set forth. The location of air bases in relation to the front line should be determined, it said, not solely on the basis of how rapidly its planes could respond to immediate requests for close air support, but also out of considera-

Help from Above

A German Fieseler Fi–156 (top); A German Junkers Ju–87 (bottom).

tion for the fields' vulnerability to enemy attacks and for their logistical requirements. They should be located far enough behind the front line to be safe from enemy artillery (30–50 nautical miles), and even farther back depending on the fluidity of the battle line. Given the speed of modern jets, aircraft based as far as 200 miles behind the lines would still be highly responsive to the Army's needs. As to logistical support, the report noted that the farther forward the bases were, the more complicated it became to support them. The Board also observed that no high-performance aircraft was projected for the 1965–1970 period that could take off vertically or from short unimproved runways. All the aircraft under consideration would require a 4,000–5,000-foot hard-surface runway.

Close Air Support and Flexible Response

A British Westland Lysander in France (top); A French Mureaux 115–R.2 (bottom).

The Air Force conferees agreed that close air support planes should be able to operate at night and in poor weather. They should be able to navigate to the target, to identify the target, and to deliver munitions accurately. While noting that the current state of the art provided excellent navigation, it did not permit the planes to acquire their targets and strike them with pinpoint accuracy. Improvements were being made, however, and planes were now able to spot their targets in ceilings below 1,000 feet and in three-mile visibility.

Although the state of the art could not provide all of the required characteristics in one close air support airplane, the Board came up with a set of feasible (closest possible to required) characteristics against which to measure the existing and planned close air support planes. These traits included the ability to takeoff and land on a 5,000-foot runway, a 200-nautical-mile radius of action, a one-hour loiter time, a Mach .9 cruise speed at sea level, a ferry range of 25 miles without refueling, and a 10,000-lb. munitions payload.

Help from Above

The members then applied these criteria to all the existing and projected close air support aircraft. The Navy's A4D single-engine attack plane had a low loiter time and small payload, no night or all-weather navigation or delivery system, a limited ferry range and speed, and poor takeoff capabilities. The VAL plane, which the Navy had proposed and the Army elements on the Board had recommended as the close air support plane of the future, was judged to have a limited speed and payload and lacked a night and all-weather capability. General LeMay strongly opposed this plane. Before the Senate Armed Services committee he condemned the fact that the plane's proponents had bypassed the Joint Chiefs and testified that Air Force F–101s, F–105s, and F–4s could do a better job than the VAL.[74]

Another Navy plane, the A6A all-weather and night attack aircraft, could carry a large load of munitions and remain in the target area for over an hour, but it needed too much runway for takeoff, could not be refueled in the air, had limited speed, and was without guns or gun pods with which to defend itself. The F–5A Freedom Fighter, which was being developed for sale to foreign air forces, could carry all the Air Force's munitions and was supersonic at sea level, but was poor on takeoff, had no all-weather navigation or delivery system, and neither guns nor an air-refueling ability. The F–100D could carry a wide variety of munitions and 1,200 rounds of ammunition for its four 20-mm cannons. It had also showed that it could be maintained at very austere locations. Yet it needed too long a runway to land, it lacked an all-weather delivery system, and both its payload and ferry range were limited. The F–105D, which at the time was the Air Force's primary close air support plane while awaiting delivery of the F–4C, also required a long runway, had too short a loiter time, and could not deliver its munitions at night or in bad weather. The F–4C, which was expected off the production line later in 1963, would carry Sparrow missiles for self-defense and would be able to deliver its munitions in all weather conditions against well-defined radar targets. Its loiter time in the target area, however, was short and it had trouble hitting pinpoint targets at night and in bad weather. Only the F–111A, which was expected to enter the inventory in 1968, would be able to fly at supersonic speed at sea level and loiter in the target area for almost three hours. It was expected to meet or exceed all the criteria for a close air support aircraft.

This review of close air support planes illustrated the importance that both services attached to developing a high-performance, vertical or short takeoff and landing tactical fighter-bomber that could navigate and detect and strike pinpoint targets at night and in foul weather. The Board did not take sides as to whether these characteristics should be added to already programmed multipurpose fighters or whether they should be incorporated into a specialized close air support aircraft. This would depend upon future research. If these close air support capabilities could be added to existing

Close Air Support and Flexible Response

planes without detracting from their ability to perform air superiority and interdiction missions, this should probably be done. If this proved impossible, consideration should then be given to tailoring part of the fleet for close air support alone.

This latter suggestion represented a significant softening of the Air Force's heretofore stubborn opposition to using single-mission airplanes for close air support. Since the introduction of the fighter-bomber in World War II, the Air Force had clung tenaciously to the view that to employ an airplane that could perform only one of the three tactical air combat missions was unacceptable, both doctrinally and operationally. This suggestion in 1963, while attempting to preserve the doctrine of unity of air power, was one of the first steps that, within a decade, would result in the introduction into the Air Force's inventory of the first exclusively close air support plane, the A–10, since before the World War II.

The Air Force board's choice for an eventual close air support plane settled, predictably, on the F–111A as measuring up best to all the requirements. Until that swing-wing two-seater became available in 1968, however, the F–4C Phantom II, which was less effective than the F–111, but more capable than the other aircraft considered, should be used in the close air support role.[75] The Phantom, a Navy carrier-launched fighter attack aircraft that, at the urging of Secretary McNamara, was being modified with Sparrow and Bullpup missiles, napalm, conventional and nuclear bombs, and cannons, to allow it to perform all of the Air Force's tactical air missions, had been accepted by the Air Force three months earlier, in May 1963. In November it would enter operational service with a training wing, and the following January the first operational tactical fighter wing would begin receiving its Phantoms.

Despite the inability of the Army and Air Force conferees to compromise their differences over command relationships, or to agree on a suitable aircraft for close air support, they did much better in softening their disagreements in three other areas, namely on questions of tactics and techniques, training and indoctrination, and the resources (other than aircraft) for close air support.

Regarding the first of these issues, they agreed that some of the tactics and techniques then in use should be modified. The existing procedures were still those that TAC and CONARC had developed in 1957 and published separately in the *JAGOS Manual*.[76] Unfortunately, at the time they were promulgated, these procedures had not received the imprimatur of the Joint Chiefs, so they remained valid only for testing, and were not official expressions of the doctrines of the two services. Subsequent attempts to frame a joint doctrine for close air support had foundered on the shoals of service doctrinal purity and obtuseness. The most recent joint proposal for a mutually acceptable set of close air support procedures emerged in a draft manual issued by the Strike Command in April 1963, and both the Army and Air Force reviewers on the board evaluated these modifications to the 1957 system.[77]

Help from Above

A major factor that intervened between the publication of the 1957 manual and its reexamination six years later, was the pervasive effect of the new defense policy of Flexible Response and the increasing attention being paid during these years to the insurgency in Southeast Asia. The introduction into Vietnam late in 1961 of Army Special Forces and an Air Force unit equipped with propeller-driven planes to support them, the threat to Laos the following year, and the increasingly successful guerrilla attacks by the Viet Cong government's forces in South Vietnam, led the Board to examine the applicability of its current close air support procedures, not only to general nuclear and full-scale nonnuclear wars, but also to the seemingly more urgent categories of counterinsurgency and limited wars. While the Board found that the existing measures were generally adequate for the full-scale conflicts for which these procedures had been originally designed, they had to be modified for the smaller types of war the Board believed would typify future international relations.

The principal weakness of the tactics and techniques contained in the JAGOS system was that the procedures for getting strike aircraft to their targets for immediate, as opposed to preplanned, strikes often introduced unacceptable delays in the planes' response times. This was due to several flawed links in the air request chain: it took too long for the Army to process requests for immediate assistance; the Air Force units that controlled the aircraft in the field were not mobile enough to move rapidly with the changing battlefield environment; the Army lacked reliable communications equipment, especially for the air-request net; and there were problems with many of the practices within headquarters that often delayed responses.

The first, and in many ways the main, problem was with the procedures in use for operating the air request net. As prescribed in the *JAGOS Manual*, after a ground commander, at whatever level, asked by radio for emergency air strikes in a critical battlefield situation, the request had to work its way sequentially from the originator up through a chain of command all the way to the field army headquarters before it was passed over to the Air Force. At each of the intervening stops, which could number as many as five, the request was analyzed in light of other potential methods of supporting the request, and either rejected or accepted and passed on to the next level. While this procedure had the advantage of providing each of the intermediate headquarters the chance to decide if it could provide better fire-support from its own organic resources than from air support before passing the request on, this advantage was far overshadowed by the time-consuming delays it created in getting the job done. This sequential procedure of the existing system did not allow for concurrent planning either at each succeeding Army echelon or by the participating Air Force units. Each headquarters had to wait until coordination was completed at all its subordinate levels before it could begin its own coordination.

The change to this method proposed by the Strike Command's draft manual would allow requests for immediate air strikes to go from the requestor at the battalion level simultaneously up the Army channel and across to the Air Force's Direct Air Support Center that had the authority to scramble the planes. As the request moved up the Army channels to the top it was not stopped for coordination at each headquarters, but rather each echelon monitored the request as it went by and indicated its concurrence by remaining silent. Army commanders still kept control of the request authority by being able to cancel any request for air at any level and substitute other fire-support that they deemed more appropriate. Besides preserving the ground commanders' jealously guarded command prerogatives, this new procedure would have the advantage over the sequential one of alerting the Air Force beforehand to forthcoming requirements that might exceed its existing allocations and giving it time to request additional sorties to answer the call.[78]

Although this new procedure would not change the response times of planes on air alert (under both systems it took from 13–22 minutes for the planes to hit their targets), it was estimated that it would reduce the response time from ground alert by about one quarter. Based on past experience, the board judged that under the existing arrangements it took fighter-bombers on ground alert between 47–53 minutes to respond to immediate requests. It was estimated that the proposed changes would reduce this time to between 38–43 minutes, a sizable and critical reduction in situations where every minute counted.[79] A second weakness in the existing arrangements, as viewed by the Army, was the relative immobility of Air Force units within the system. One of the continuing complaints the Army voiced was with what it interpreted as reluctance on the part of the Air Force to provide as many front line air liaison officers (ALOs) and FACs as the Army believed it needed. The assignment of Air Force controllers and their tactical air control parties to the lower operational levels, the battalions and brigades, was important because it increased mobility by allowing these parties to move with the battle action. The Air Force had been somewhat hampered in assigning ALOs and FACs by its own requirement that these positions be filled only with qualified pilots.

The Strike Command's proposed system, which the Board seconded, called for making the Air Force responsible for providing both the personnel and equipment needed to support the TACPs at both the battalion and brigade levels. These changes would almost triple the number of assigned Air Force officers. To ameliorate the pilot shortage problem, the plan recommended that 106 pilot spaces could be saved by eliminating the ALO at the battalion level and by dispensing with the requirement that the battalion FAC be a qualified pilot.

To compensate for the loss of battalion ALOs, the Board suggested that NCOs fill the radio operator positions in the TACPs and in addition be trained

Help from Above

to perform most of the FAC's functions. They could then assume some of the FAC duties by acting as assistant FACs.

A third factor in the current air-ground operating system that increased response time stemmed from the Army's past inability to provide reliable communications. Both the air request and the air response segments of the system depended heavily upon rapid, clear, and dependable radio contacts. Not only did the various ground headquarters rely on dependable communication links for requesting air strikes, but air-to-ground and ground-to-air radio transmissions were critical if the planes were to find and hit their targets. The biggest problem in the past had been the incompatibility of Army and Air Force communications equipment. To change this, the Board proposed that, for the first time, the Air Force furnish the ground vehicle and radio equipment, along with a driver, mechanic, and radio operator for the tactical air control parties. It specified in great detail the types and numbers of radio equipment that the parties in battalions and brigades should have.[80]

A fourth cluster of weak links resided in a host of less dramatic but ultimately critical institutional practices within the various headquarters for requesting and dispatching air strikes. Any system as complex as that for coordinating and controlling close air support strikes would of necessity contain a large number of small working parts, each of which must operate effectively for the whole process to function at full capacity. The effectiveness of even the best system for requesting air strikes, such as, for example, the one proposed by the Strike Command and supported by the Close Air Support Board, would be impaired by defects in such day-to-day routines within headquarters as processing requests, using standard terminology, assigning priorities to targets, and marking targets. Although often overlooked, these seemingly minor procedures at operational headquarters could often determine the success or failure of close air support in the field.

The absence of standard terminology, for example, was a significant hindrance to commanders who must understand the concepts of employment of a variety of fire-support systems. Even though the Joint Chiefs were continually issuing definitions that were supposed to be standard,[81] service publications often diluted them by using different terms and meanings. One instance was the various interpretations of such phrases as bomb line, interdiction, and armed reconnaissance. Some publications had been substituting the phrase fire-support coordination line for bomb line, while others retained the original term. The Joint Chiefs distinguished two types of bomb lines: a tactical bomb line, beyond which the ground commander determined that properly coordinated bombing would not endanger his troops, and a forward bomb line, prescribed by the troop commander, beyond which he considered it unnecessary to coordinate with his own forces. The FAC normally controlled strikes in the area short of the tactical bomb line. Yet the absence of a need to coordinate strikes beyond the forward bomb line gave the mistaken impression that the Army was

Close Air Support and Flexible Response

not concerned with Air Force strikes against deep targets within the combat zone. This led to confusion on the operating level over the terms interdiction and armed reconnaissance. Theoretically, from the Army's point of view, an attack on any major target had to be coordinated, regardless of its location, if the target had any effect on present or future Army operations. Yet it was recognized that in certain situations the Air Force should have free rein to strike targets of opportunity within the combat zone without prior coordination. Armed reconnaissance, a term devised for these situations, was also defined in myriad ways. The original fuzziness of terms led each separate, operational headquarters to add, amplify, and clarify the basic definition to further, as they put it, "local understanding of the term." The net result was confusion and the recommendation to eliminate all variations in definitions concerned with close air support. The Joint Chiefs of Staff (JCS) definitions should be used and any local clarifications be appended to the basic definition.[82]

The Board also recommended that other practices at headquarters affecting close air support be sharpened. Improvements needed included better communications, improved administrative techniques, more people, and greater command interest. Target marking also came in for review, since the speed of modern close air support airplanes rendered many methods of marking targets obsolete. While no set of standard techniques could apply to all situations, the Board made some general observations. Strike pilots received their information on the friendly situation from Army ground liaison officers (GLOs) whose intelligence originated at the field army level. Since this information was often stale and inaccurate, it was recommended that GLOs be assigned from an echelon much closer to the requesting unit. Also, the time-honored arrangement of ground troops marking their position by panels, while it could no longer be done continuously without informing the enemy, was still effective if coded displays were used for short periods of time.[83]

The escalation of interest in close air support within both the Army and the Air Force in the two years since the advent of the Flexible Response doctrine was acknowledged by the board members. The Strike Command, TAC, and CONARC, as well as overseas commands, had increased the emphasis they placed on close air support in their individual, unit, and cross-service training programs. Many proposals, some of which had already been field tested, were being advanced to improve response times and traffic control in the battlefield. The Air Force System Command had inventoried its hardware and capability for providing close air support and was preparing a shopping list of new equipment to enhance its support of the Army. As beneficial as these measures were, they lacked the necessary permanence as long as they were not backed up by a joint doctrine for close air support. What was needed, in the Board's view, was a permanent bilateral Army/Air Force Air Support Center to develop and test close air support doctrine, tactics, procedures, and airborne and ground equipment. The presence in the center of both Army and Air Force members would replace the present imperfect system of coordination with full and enthusiastic bilateral participation. Further, a permanent joint Air Support Center would save the time and continuity currently being sacrificed in organizing, disbanding, and reconstituting the plethora of special boards and study groups that had been examining close air support issues. Such boards, including the present one, rarely had the needed time to investigate problems thoroughly. Particularly unrewarding were the attempts to tie together the recommendations of so many boards and studies. A single permanent agency would solve these problems. In addition, the center would also provide a focal point where industry and the military could work together to improve weaponry and munitions that were lagging behind improvements in aircraft.

Substantial agreement was also reached by the board members on the problems surrounding close air support training and indoctrination. After analyzing all types of training for close air support—individual, unit, and joint—the board judged that despite recent improvements, insufficient attention was still being paid by the Air Force to nonnuclear training, particularly for close air support. This situation was caused by the excessive amount of training time Air Force pilots needed to become proficient in delivering existing types of air-delivered nuclear weapons, the round-the-clock assignment of aircraft to nuclear alert at overseas bases, training problems created for weapon load crews by the vast number (over 200) possible loading combinations, the paucity of weapons delivery ranges for practice, and the absence of a joint training directive that would provide uniform guidance to all commands, including those overseas.

These deficiencies could be corrected by eliminating all free-fall nuclear weapons from the Air Force's stockpile and replacing them with retarded nuclear weapons. The latter were available, could provide varied yields and burst height options, and reduce the training time for delivery by one-third, thereby making available more time for nonnuclear training. Additionally, the list of Quick Reaction Alert targets could be pared down to include only those that would have to be destroyed one or two hours after hostilities began. This would release a large number of planes and crews for close air support training. The Board urged accelerated attempts to develop a universal aircraft pylon that could be used for all ordnance and fuel tanks, thereby cutting down considerably on the training needed by loading crews.

To alleviate the shortage of firing ranges for aircrew training, the Board recommended that the Army's artillery ranges be made available for tactical air units. It also strongly advised the publication of a joint Army/Air Force directive for air-ground operations that would reflect the doctrines of both services and provide a firm foundation for standardize training.

Air-ground training at both Air Force and Army schools needed to be expanded. For example, the curriculum at the Air Force's AGOS should include courses for enlisted men of both services who were expected to act as

Close Air Support and Flexible Response

members of G2 and G3 Air parties, Army Control Teams and TACPs, and within ASOCs and Direct Air Support Centers (DASCs). The number of mandatory offerings in air-ground instruction should be increased throughout the entire professional military education system. The Board discovered that the Army was sending only 45 percent of its allocation of 226 officers to attend the Air Force's AGOS. The Air Force picked up the slack by sending 439 officers against an allocation of 412 slots. Placing mandatory quotas on Army units to send students to the school would train more ground officers in the doctrine, tactics, techniques, and procedures used by both the Air Force and the Army in combined combat operations.

In its most controversial suggestion, the Close Air Support Board urged that company-level combat arms leaders, artillery forward observers, and army aircraft pilots be trained to serve as backup FACs. The Board took the position that the existing requirement that a FAC be a rated pilot was causing too many combat-ready aircrews to be diverted from the cockpit. In its view, the FAC did not have to be a rated pilot. The British, for example, trained Army officers to perform as FACs. American Army officers could also be trained in the procedures and techniques of guiding strike aircraft to close air support targets. This training could take place with little or no difficulty by using the existing Air Force ALOs and FACs who were already assigned to Army units to train unit personnel in the capabilities and limitations of close air support planes, in the air-ground radio communications procedures and equipment, and in how the air-ground system operates. The Air Force ALOs and FACs could also take their Army students on orientation flights in close air support aircraft to familiarize them with how a target appears to a strike pilot.[84] This recommendation had ramifications far outside the area of personnel and effectiveness of the air-ground system. To many airmen it also appeared to be one in a series of steps whereby the Army hoped to increase its control over Air Force strike planes by inserting its own people further into the operations of the air-ground system.

The final area that the Board examined, and on which both the Army and Air Force panelists concurred, was the status of resources, both existing and planned, for close air support. The examiners found them totally inadequate for effective close air support operations in the 1965–1970 time period. Serious acceptance and implementation of the Board's recommendations, however, would at least bring about significant improvements.

Inadequate resources in the current air base arrangements were highlighted. Overseas, aircraft were heavily concentrated on air bases, making them vulnerable to enemy air and ground attacks. In addition, these bases were far behind the potential front lines, reducing the effectiveness of their close air support planes. Also, the permanence of their equipment and facilities reduced their mobility. The inability of air base construction to keep up with the rapidly moving ground forces had been one of the major weaknesses of close air support in Korea. Close air support aircraft would be used more effectively if the fighter units operated from austere forward bases with their major maintenance performed at rear maintenance facilities. The F–4C, which would be the Air Force's main close air support plane during the last half of the 1960s, could operate from such forward dispersed airfields. It was capable of taking off from a 5,000-foot runway with sufficient munitions for close air support sorties. The desired mobility could be realized by adopting a system that the Marines developed for building forward air bases rapidly. Called the "Short Airfield for Tactical Support," (SATS), it consisted of an entire airfield complex packaged for delivery by air. Eighty percent of its 1,500-ton weight was taken up by aluminum matting for a runway 5,000 feet long and 72 feet wide, and for 214,000 square feet of taxiways. The package included runway lights, approach lights, a ground-controlled approach (GCA) system for guiding planes into the field, tactical air navigation (TACAN) radios for in-flight navigation and reporting, a control tower, and 24 vans for support equipment and local maintenance. It took 72 hours to install one of these prepackaged airstrips, but only 12 hours to establish one on a taxiway or other hard surface.[85]

Better communications resources were needed across the board. In addition to detailed recommendations for improving communications equipment of both the Army and Air Force, the Board urged field testing and adoption of the Air Force Air Request Net system, which TAC and the Strike Command had proposed. To replace the existing Army immediate-request system with one in which the Air Force used its own communications net to request immediate strikes directly from the DASC, the Air Force would need additional communications personnel and equipment. To accommodate this, the Board recommended reorganizing the TACPs at the brigade and battalion levels. The former would include two vehicle-mounted ultrahigh-frequency (UHF) radios, one manpack radio for use when the FAC was away from his vehicle, one VHF radio to communicate with Army ground forces, and one radio for remote contact with Army or Air Force aircraft. Communications equipment at the battalion level would be the same except for one, rather than two, UHF radios.[86]

The Close Air Support Board also saw great potential in using electronic equipment to identify and control close air support planes, especially in bad weather and reduced visibility. First, it noted that the use of light-weight ground surveillance and height-finding radars would appreciably increase mobility. Close air support strikes could be conducted in poor weather if the planes were directed by electronic devices that were light enough to be manpacked to most forward positions. Following their missions, close air support planes could be recovered at their home bases in poor weather by using a single-package navigation device that included a precision GCA radar, an electronic surveillance control instrument, and a TACAN unit. The Board urged continued improvement of this equipment.[87]

Close Air Support and Flexible Response

Despite the advances that had taken place in the past two years in developing and testing nonnuclear munitions, much remained to be done before the close air support capability could be called adequate. The Air Force had to improve its ability to deliver general-purpose iron bombs, and improve the quality of napalm, its target-marking procedures, its incendiary and fire bomblet delivery, and its effectiveness in using standoff missiles. The Board suggested that the Air Force investigate the Navy's Snakeye retarded bomb and Walleye TV-guided missile, as well as some of its antimateriel cluster bombs, for possible use on close air support missions. It also recommended that the Army and Air Force prepare a joint publication containing munitions effectiveness values for use in selecting munitions for specific targets.[88]

The deliberations and conclusions of the Close Air Support Board provided a midyear report on the status of the major elements of close air support, as well as a catalog of items to be evaluated in the unilateral and joint field tests mandated by the secretary and performed during the succeeding two years.

Field Testing the Opposing Close Air Support Concepts

In his February memo, Secretary McNamara instructed the Army and the Air Force to field-test their opposing concepts of tactical air support—the more radical airmobility idea of the Howze Board, and the existing air-ground operations system that entailed Air Force support of the existing ROAD divisions. For this purpose, in April 1963 the Strike Command issued a Test and Evaluation Plan[89] for examining the relative operational and logistical merits, as well as the overall cost-effectiveness of both plans.

Even before the recommendations of the Close Air Support Board were fully digested, however, a joint test in the summer of 1963, called Swift Strike III, evaluated some of its proposed changes. These modifications were made in large part to address the Army's complaints with close air support, specifically with the still-too-long response times to Army requests for immediate close air support sorties, with the difficulty Air Force control units in the field had in keeping up with a moving battlefield, and with the poor status of communications that hampered the effectiveness of the air request net in the past.

The exercise took place during the last week of July and the first two weeks of August 1963, in the maneuver areas of North and South Carolina. The Strike Command performed the overall evaluation of the exercise, which featured the full range of tactical air support operations—airlift, counter-air, air defense, reconnaissance, interdiction, and close air support.

Some important modifications to the way the Air Force supported the Army with close air support missions emerged from Swift Strike III. An experimental method of requesting support was tried in an attempt to reduce response times. Instead of having the requests work their way up through each interven-

Help from Above

ing command level between requestor and supplier, they were transmitted by an ALO at the originating headquarters directly to the Air Force's DASC at the closest corps headquarters. Army officers at each of the intermediate headquarters monitored the requests, acknowledged them and, if they concurred, remained silent.[90] Even though this was a limited experiment and additional, larger-scale testing of the new method would be needed, this represented an initial step toward a major improvement of the tactical air control system.

Other major changes to the air-ground system were hinted at in Swift Strike III. The Joint Task Force commander was given the authority to establish priorities between air and ground power to be used in various phases of the operation. This authority included making allocations between preplanned and immediate sorties. Preplanned sorties were scheduled first, normally the night before they were needed. Those left over after all preplanned mission needs were satisfied were made available to a DASC to satisfy immediate requests.[91]

The appearance of the new control center, DASC, as a replacement for the ASOC, which was prescribed in the 1957 air-ground manual, was an important concession to the Army's desire for more control and decentralization of close air support missions. Unlike the former ASOC, which was more of a coordinating and monitoring unit for close air support flights, the new DASC had the authority, in the absence of Army objections, to allocate and scramble aircraft for immediate missions. In addition, the DASC was located at the corps level, whereas the old ASOC was at the higher army level. Control had moved one step closer to the battlefield.

Also in line with the earlier proposals, the Air Force in Swift Strike III experimented with providing almost all the ground support for their new air request net, including ALOs, radio operators, radios, drivers, and wheeled vehicles. The only exception was that the Army provided tracked vehicles or radio-equipped tanks in specific cases where these might be needed. Previously, the Army had supplied all radios, vehicles, and operating personnel for the Air Force TACPs. The Army remained responsible for maintaining the vehicles of the TACPs serving with Army units.[92]

Communications remained a weak spot of the tactical air control system. Despite valiant attempts to improve radio equipment, the commanders of the joint task forces and field elements that participated in Swift Strike III deplored the supporting communications. For example, when DASC tried to use a new UHF radio, the ARC–27, to control the fighters, it could not maintain continuous connection with the aircraft. It turned out that the new equipment was not powerful enough to meet the range requirements of the control center. Moreover, the communications equipment used by the Air Force ALOs stationed with an airborne division was too large to be dropped from the air. Normally the equipment was air-landed and moved into place, an operation that in Swift Strike III took four days to complete. While waiting for their

Close Air Support and Flexible Response

radios and telephones, the members of the TACP had to rely on portable UHF equipment and an airborne DASC to operate the air request net. "We hear about exotic equipment," wrote one of the task-force commanders:

> but none of it ever seems to be available to operators in a contingency. Our field telephones with the hand-magneto appear to be little different from those used in World War I. I can think of no piece of equipment that would offer a bigger improvement to the field command and control system than a modernized telephone system.[93]

Not all of the communication ills were attributable to poor equipment. As noted by many of the exercise's reviewers, communications operators and maintenance personnel were poorly trained. This led, in the experience of the deputy controller of the exercise, to some "surprising things." For example, at one time a DASC was controlling 58 flights that were awaiting targets. Some never made it. One flight leader was directed to orbit for 15 minutes directly in the center of a Hawk antiaircraft battalion. The general estimated that about 75 percent of the missions in the air request net were handled professionally.[94]

Overall, the new Air Force air request net was rated by both air and ground officers as sound and responsive to the needs of close air support. The commander of one of the task forces in the exercise, Gen. William C. Westmoreland, remarked on the improvement that had taken place in the responsiveness of tactical aircraft. He would soon become better acquainted with that responsiveness.

Following Swift Strike III, at the beginning of November 1963, the Air Force activated, under TAC, a Tactical Air Warfare Center (TAWC) at Eglin AFB in Florida to manage its participation in the field tests of the Howze and Air Force concepts. The staff of the TAWC commander, Maj. Gen. Gilbert L. Meyers, included officers from TAC, SAC, the Military Air Transport Service, the Air Force Systems Command, and other agencies with a professional stake in the outcome of airmobility.

The TAWC was charged with exploring every possible means of using tactical air power to increase the mobility of joint forces. It was to analyze the Air Force's ability to "provide all or most of the air support functions that are required by the Army with its already existing systems," and to make good on the Air Force promise "to provide all Army air requirements other than the very light courier, liaison, and observation functions."[95]

Specifically, the TAWC was charged with two important missions relating to the field tests. First, it was assigned the task of adapting, analyzing, and testing the effectiveness of traditional tactical air missions in light of the current rapid technological progress. Second, the charter highlighted, although in

Help from Above

Col. Gilbert L. Meyers

very general terms, those issues of controversy between the Army and the Air Force in the areas of close air support, airlift, and reconnaissance. In the case of close air support, this included questions of response time, the desire of the Army for uninterrupted availability of aircraft overhead, the question of command and control of tactical aircraft, and the willingness of the Air Force to accede to modified requirements. This latter included the matter of the Army's participation in the design and construction of close air support aircraft. All of these issues had been festering for years and had been raised anew, most recently by the Close Air Support Board. Now the TAWC joined the search for solutions.

The initial activities of the TAWC were designed to take advantage of the developments that were already underway in conventional warfare and to improve unilaterally the Air Force's equipment, materiel, and procedures for supporting ground forces so that it would be in good shape for the subsequent Strike Command joint evaluations. This led to some modifications of the tactical air control system.

One element of the tactical air control system upon which there was some disagreement within the Air Force was the question as to whether FACs had to be Air Force fighter pilots or whether nonrated, or even Army, officers could perform the job just as well. General Sweeney was concerned over repeated suggestions, both from inside and outside the Air Force, that trained, rated FACs be replaced with nonrated personnel. Both the Strike Command and the Close Air Support Board were recommending that this exchange be made at the battalion level. The latter had even recommended, again that year, that Army officers serve as backups for Air Force FACs.[96]

In opposing the idea of nonrated FACs, the TAC commander exhorted the Air Force's overseas tactical air commanders to impress on the other tacti-

Close Air Support and Flexible Response

cal commanders the full scope of responsibilities of the FAC. According to him, those who advocated using personnel other than tactical fighter pilots were of the mistaken notion that all the FAC did was direct strike planes to their targets. In addition to this, Sweeney reminded the others, these officers had to advise Army commanders and their staffs on air tactics and capabilities, and indoctrinate ground troops on tactical air power so that they could take full advantage of it. Obviously, neither nonrated Air Force officers nor Army officers could perform these functions adequately. Moreover, it was imperative that the Air Force commander have direct representation in the ground battle area. Sweeney also noted that, since the Air Force was responsible for close air support, it was self-evident that air commanders had to have complete control of all elements and all personnel, including FACs, associated with the system.[97] His argument prevailed and assignments as FACs continued to be reserved for fighter pilots. This decision, while consistent with Air Force doctrine, within a few years placed an added strain on the relatively thin ranks of available fighter pilots in Vietnam.

The original Strike Command's test and evaluation plan in 1963 had called for field-tests, engineering tests, analytical studies, and war-gaming of the Army's and Air Force's competing mobility proposals. Budgetary limitations, however, canceled all but the field-tests, two of which were retained. Gold Fire I, scheduled for October and November, 1964, was to test the Air Force's concepts by teaming appropriate Air Force units with an Army brigade. Gold Fire II, slated for the following year, was to take place in two phases: a test of the Army's airmobile 11th Air Assault Division, and a division-size test of the Air Force concept, both against the same division-size aggressor force.[98]

During the spring and summer of 1964, the Air Force conducted a graduated, three-phased series of exercises at Eglin AFB to prepare for the Gold Fire I tests. Called Indian River I, II, and III, these operations trained Army and Air Force units for Gold Fire I, while allowing the Air Force to refine its mobility concepts through test data before the coming competition with the Army.

Indian River I took place in June, Indian River II in late July and early August, and the final, culminating, test, Indian River III, between August 24 and September 22, 1964. Indian River III employed 6,400 Army troops in a full infantry brigade of the 1st Infantry Division from Fort Riley, Kansas, an artillery and aviation battalion, a headquarters support command, and assorted platoons and companies. The Air Force contributed 2,600 personnel and 93 planes distributed between an assault airlift headquarters, a test wing, an Air Control and Warning Squadron, and a Tactical Fighter Squadron. More than half of these 93 planes (51) were F–100, F–105, and F–4C fighter-bombers, which performed close air support missions. Twenty-six C–130s and CH–3C helicopters were used for assault airlift, and 15 jet planes for reconnaissance.[99]

Help from Above

The command structure for Indian River III directly reflected the Air Force doctrine that a single joint force commander must integrate the combat power entrusted to him, and that no single service could fulfill all of its own combat requirements. The Tactical Air Control System used for close air support and reconnaissance, which came with minor modification from the TAC manual,[100] permitted the Air Force commander to exercise centralized control of his forces while allowing for decentralized execution of tactical air operations. One minor modification substituted a Direct Air Support Team (DAST) at the division level for a DASC, which would normally function at the (absent) corps level. This experimentation with a DAST at the division level was part of the Air Force's constant search for an answer to the Army's perennial complaint that the Tactical Air Control System was not mobile enough to keep up with a rapidly advancing ground force. When the division's command post was moved near the end of the exercise, the van-mounted DAST, together with its communications equipment, moved along with it without breaking contact with its subordinate tactical air control parties or its parental TACC.[101]

The use of an airborne DAST in the exercise increased the Air Force's ability to move its units about in changing combat situations. Tactical air control parties at brigade and battalion headquarters handled immediate requests for close air strikes, employing the new method of forwarding them directly to the DAST while intermediate headquarters monitored them and either disapproved or remained silent. The FAC members of these parties were still qualified fighter pilots who controlled the strikes from their positions on the ground with air-ground radios. A Control and Reporting Center (CRC) provided radar surveillance and control of the airspace over the area of operations. This radar was complemented by a light-weight, portable radar (the UPS–1) to cover the lower altitudes that the CRC could not reach. All of these familiar elements of the system were vehicles for implementing the Air Force doctrine that the air commander must maintain centralized control of his air assets, although their control was decentralized for operations.

The Air Force made a major effort in Indian River III to shorten response times. Observers recorded times at nine critical points in the train of events leading from the time of the initial request until the first ordnance fell. These critical points were when the Army made the request, the DAST approved and sent the scramble order to the fighter unit, the crew was briefed, the aircraft was scrambled, the plane climbed to altitude, the pilot was vectored to the target area by a CRC, the pilot contacted the FAC and received target information from him, the pilot acquired the target, and the pilot released his ordnance. Through practice and the telescoping of several administrative procedures, the planes significantly reduced the average response time to immediate requests from 70 minutes in Indian River II to 55 minutes in Indian River III. While at first glance 55 minutes seems excessive, this was

Close Air Support and Flexible Response

an average between the shortest (5 minutes) and the longest (75 minutes) reaction times. The effectiveness of the close air support response was illustrated, not by these raw numbers, but rather by whether the planes struck when the ground commanders needed them. Response times were not equally critical in all cases because, in some instances, the ground commander did not want the strikes too soon. Also, second waves of strike planes necessarily held back, thereby raising the averages. In order to allow for these variations, ground commanders in the exercise included in each request a time after which the strikes would be of no value—a "not later than" (NLT) time. The average NLT time in Indian River III was 71 minutes. A remarkable 86 percent of the aircraft flew their close air support missions under that requirement.[102]

In preparation for the upcoming Gold Fire test, the Indian River exercises also concentrated on measuring and improving the ability of fighter-bombers to be diverted in flight from one target to another. The Air Force proved, at least to its own satisfaction, that the heavyweight, multiple-stores carriages on the F–4C and the F–105 permitted these planes to carry sufficient variety of ordnance to allow them to shift back and forth between air-to-air, interdiction, and close air support missions without increasing their response time. Adapters on the nine stations under the newly acquired F–4C, which was first used in Indian River, permitted it to carry virtually every type of ordnance in the inventory.

The exercise also addressed the issue of the need for close air support planes to be based on fields close to the front line. Indian River confirmed the airmen's earlier opinion that tactical fighters were flexible enough to operate around the clock from either permanent rear-echelon bases or from austere forward operating bases closer to the battlefield. During the exercise aircraft were flown from both types of bases. Those that operated from bases 150 nautical miles behind the front, after entering the battle zone, loitered 20 miles behind the front line for 50 minutes before striking targets 45 miles beyond the front line, and then remained in the target area for 15 minutes. Distance from their bases did not degrade their performance. Even greater flexibility and responsiveness would be realized, concluded the evaluators, if the planes were refueled in the air. Nevertheless, recognizing that there would be times when these high-performance planes would have to fly close air support missions from forward operating bases, the exercise directors also experimented with using austere airfields. Despite some advantages, the Air Force concluded that such bases were more vulnerable and required greater logistic support than permanent fields. During Indian River, the fighters stationed at rearward bases, thanks to the permanent maintenance facilities that produced a superior in-commission rate, completed 99.15 percent of their scheduled close air support missions. Such operational readiness and effectiveness would not be possible at austere forward bases, which

Help from Above

the survey concluded, should be used only where permanent facilities did not exist.[103]

Results from Indian River III also confirmed an earlier study at the Air Proving Ground Command that showed that there was no significant decrease in the ability of a pilot to detect targets from aircraft flying between 350–550 knots and that of pilots flying at slower speeds.

During Indian River III fighters flew 27 close air support "Night Owl" sorties during the hours of darkness, delivering napalm, air-to-ground rockets, and 20-mm ammunition. The planes carried their own flares and used the buddy system to illuminate targets. One aircraft dispensed the flares while the remaining planes of the flight made their attacks. Flares dispensed at 1,500 feet lit up approximately one and a half miles of the battlefield, enough for the planes to achieve the same accuracy as during daylight hours. Aside from the need to improve flares and target orientation techniques by the FACs, both aircrews and Army observers judged the night operations to be effective.[104] Exercise directors were also satisfied that the planes could operate during poor weather. Fifty-two close air support sorties were flown successfully in weather conditions ranging from heavy precipitation at takeoff to marginal visibility in the target area.[105]

The Army, in the face of Air Force opposition, had been arming its helicopters in part to escort its organic transport helicopters into and out of landing zones and to protect them from enemy attack while they off-loaded their troops or cargo. In an effort to demonstrate that the Air Force could perform this mission with its existing planes, fighter-bombers during Indian River evolved tactics and techniques for escorting helicopters and fixed-wing transports as a new facet of close air support. Tactical fighters first cleared the route through enemy territory along which the airmobile force would pass by striking targets or threats to helicopters uncovered by reconnaissance. The fighter escorts then flew a modified racetrack pattern around the helicopters, provided suppressive fire, struck targets of opportunity, or were directed to strikes on targets by a FAC flying in the lead helicopter. Once again the fighters showed that they were flexible enough for effective close air strikes while escorting helicopters and aircraft.[106]

In Indian River III tactical fighters also provided cover for armored columns on the move, a type of close air support performed successfully during World War II. When artillery support was not immediately available to moving columns, tactical fighters worked closely with FACs in each column to strike enemy forces in the event of ambush or attack.[107]

The follow-on joint Gold Fire I exercise went off as planned. For two weeks, between October 29 and November 11, Air Force and Army units maneuvered through a two-million-acre tract of leased land in and around Fort Leonard Wood in south central Missouri, using a scenario that reflected the Air Force's concepts of airmobility. The Air Force set out to prove, under Joint

Close Air Support and Flexible Response

Strike Command supervision and evaluation, that a current Army ROAD Division with its full complement of equipment, which included 97 helicopters when teamed with Air Force units with first-line equipment. The division was fully capable of providing the Army with enough mobility, combat strength, and staying power to overcome the most powerful potential enemy. The Air Force used three tactical fighter squadrons, one tactical reconnaissance squadron, two C–130 troop carrier squadrons, and one CH–3C helicopter squadron. These units, together with their command and support elements totaled 4,900 men. Army forces consisted of a reinforced infantry brigade, almost division size with about 8,700 men. Evaluators from the Strike Command measured the effectiveness of the Air Force's ideas in the areas of organizational and tactical doctrine, command, control, and communication (C3), the use of aviation, logistical concepts, intelligence and reconnaissance, close air support procedures, and control of the airspace.

The scenario called for an allied military support task force (Ozark) to defend an imaginary underdeveloped country, Oroland, against a task force (Sioux) invasion from its aggressive neighbor, Argentia. Task Force Ozark, the force being tested, employed the Air Force's airmobility concept.[108] The conflict was conventional, with a low nuclear threat and was divided into five phases. The first phase, a three-day deployment, consisted of a simulated strategic airlift by 110 C–130s of Task Force Ozark into Oroland, with fighters providing close air support, air, and convoy cover.[109] The planned second phase, a three-day counterinsurgency operation against Argentan guerrillas was a failure as the Ozark forces could not get organized. The Argentan invasion, which began on November 4, was the third phase of the scenario. Task Force Sioux drove 24 miles inside Oroland before the end of the day. During the advance, Sioux fighters made repeated strikes against the Ozark ground troops and demonstrated the value of the latest in smoke screening devices, a CBU that expelled a series of smoke-producing bomblets to screen the advance. On the following day, the fifth, the invaders, still enjoying excellent close air support, advanced another 24 miles before being stopped by Ozark units that had been newly deployed by C–130s. During the ensuing three-day defensive phase, aircraft on both sides flew extensive air superiority, interdiction, and close air support missions. F–100s and F–105s on both sides struck heavily, pouring simulated napalm, CBUs, and 20-mm cannon fire into enemy ground positions. As the fighters inflicted crippling blows on the ground troops, C–130s continued to resupply the Ozark forces. The final, offensive, phase opened in the predawn hours of November 10 when Ozark forces began an all-out counteroffensive, completed by the end of the following day, to drive the invaders from their homeland.[110]

Close air support planes in the exercise were controlled by the task-force commander who established mission priorities. Although this was standard Air Force doctrine for command and control, the fact that the Ozark task-force

Help from Above

commander in Gold Fire I was an Air Force officer elicited an official comment by CONARC observers who were present that the organization of the task force "seemed to be more 'air-minded' than is desirable in a conflict which is essentially a land battle."[111]

A full panoply of air-ground facilities was constructed for the exercise. Tactical air control parties were attached to the Army units from the battalion level on up. Sorties were allocated through a DASC that demonstrated its ability to be transported by air. A CRC handled the direction of airspace. During the fourth, defensive, phase of the operation, F–100s used "Night Owl" techniques to fly support missions at night. In the final offensive phase, F–105s, F–100s, and F–4Cs provided column cover and suppressive fire for helicopters, which carried 400 troops and 23 vehicles into the battle. In the final push to expel the invaders, Ozark forces enjoyed free movement throughout the battlefield thanks to close air support missions that kept the Sioux forces pinned down.[112]

The Air Force was satisfied with Gold Fire I, and was convinced that it had demonstrated its ability to support ground forces. The most dramatic demonstration of this ability came in the use of assault airlift to support the Ozark ground forces, but several experiments in close air support also paid off. The soundness of centralizing all tactical air support under a newly instituted Deputy Air Force Commander for Direct Air Support at the Army component headquarters became evident during the offensive phase when this Air Force officer quickly and effectively advised the Army commander on which ground attack plans could be supported by air. Another addition that was, on the whole, successful was that of using direct air support teams at Army levels below divisions. These teams, which served the same function as DASCs at higher echelons, proved effective in reducing response times. The most successful tactical experiment was the use of eight SAC KC–135 tankers to refuel the fighters, thereby extending their loiter time.[113]

On the down side, both Army and Air Force observers agreed that the Ozark ground area was "saturated" with Air Force personnel, 184 by Army count.[114] The Air Force admitted that it was "trying to run too large an operation at too low a level." Due to the unwieldy size of the direct support organization, many subordinate units were more rigidly controlled from above than they would have been under normal field conditions, and therefore could not be accurately evaluated. The exercise showed that direct air support teams, while effective, were too large, restricting their movement and making them healthy targets from the air. Tactical air control parties at the battalions were also overmanned, leading to the recommendation that they be reduced to one, rather than the existing two FACs. Overall, the Air Force concluded that the exercise had been "invaluable in getting a feel for Army requirements and Air Force capabilities," and represented "another step forward in bringing the Army and Air Force components close together in joint operations."[115]

Close Air Support and Flexible Response

An F–111F refueling from a KC–135E Stratotanker.

The Army was less sanguine. Observers on the scene from CONARC deemed the Air Force concept, which emphasized the joint task force command, as inappropriate for many situations, as tilted too much toward air power, and as having failed to increase the tactical mobility and combat effectiveness of the Ozark force. In addition, the emphasis on control at the higher echelon resulted in too much high-level meddling in the tactical affairs of the brigade. The same observers used the difficulties experienced by Air Force helicopters in the exercise to conclude that Army organic airlift would have been preferred.[116] In their report to the Army staff, they judged the close air support as "fair," pointing out that the brigade received more close air support than would be the case under battle conditions. This was due to the absence of artillery and was made possible by air refueling. It also noted that no close air support was available during bad weather and that, given the high number of aircraft provided the brigade, the "results did not reflect the improvement which could be expected."[117] In addition, the observers, unable to make a reasonable evaluation of the control of airspace, simply noted the continuing clash between the Army concept, in which the Army must be free to use the airspace contiguous to the combat zone vertically to an altitude of 5,000 feet, and the Air Force's view that control of airspace was a corollary of air defense and therefore belonged to the air component commander.

While the Air Force's airmobility concept was undergoing joint evaluation in the Strike Command's test in Missouri, the Army was conducting its

Help from Above

final unilateral test of the Howze Board concept in the maneuver areas of the Carolinas. Phase One of this evaluation had begun over a year and a half earlier, in February 1963, with the Army's activation of a provisional division, the 11th Air Assault Division (**Figure 14**), and the 10th Air Transport Brigade at Fort Benning. The Army was allowed to increase its size temporarily by 15,000 personnel for the tests. Some equipment and personnel were transferred from existing units. In May the Air Force formally agreed to support the tests and to provide liaison officers.[118]

The second phase of Army tests began in July 1963, with various battalion tests lasting into the fall. In a third phase, during the summer of 1964, the Army held tests, called Hawk Star, using brigades of the 11th Air Assault Division. Typical of the Army's use of armed helicopters for close air support was their role in one of the many small operations during Hawk Star. Before a helicopter landing assault against an enemy headquarters, a helicopter gunship reconnoitered the area, found a good landing zone, and radioed back to the transport helicopters to come ahead. After marking the landing zone with rockets, the gunship made pass after pass firing its guns and rockets to keep the enemy pinned down while the friendly troops landed. When the troops were safely on the ground, the gunship hovered protectively over them, swooping down at 90 knots while firing against any targets that threatened the disembarked soldiers. Gunships also covered the troops as they were picked up after the operation.[119] These were functions the Air Force always performed for the Army and continued to view as part of its mission.

For the final exercise in the fall of 1964, the Army committed 500 aircraft and 32,000 soldiers of the 11th Air Assault Division and the 82d Airborne Division from Fort Bragg. This maneuver, called Air Assault II, was the culminating test of 83 major efforts undertaken by the Army's Combat Developments Command to test the airmobility idea. This was by far the most comprehensive series of tests ever conducted by a unit of the American army, and probably on any army in the world.

Unlike Gold Fire I, which was a joint evaluation of the Air Force's concept, Air Assault II was a unilateral Army exercise. Although the Air Force supported the operation with airlift, reconnaissance, close air support, and paradrop missions, it participated only to provide realism, not for comparison with Army concepts. The tests were conducted "as though the Air Force did not exist."[120] The two fighter wings, three airlift wings, and one reconnaissance wing with their associated units and equipment that participated did so only to support the Army's airmobile concept, not the Air Force's. The Army was testing only Army concepts.[121]

Air Assault II took place in the maneuver area between Fort Bragg, North Carolina, and Fort Jackson, South Carolina, from October 14–November 12, 1964. Air Force observers agreed that an airlifted division had the advantages of mobility, flexibility, and response over conventional

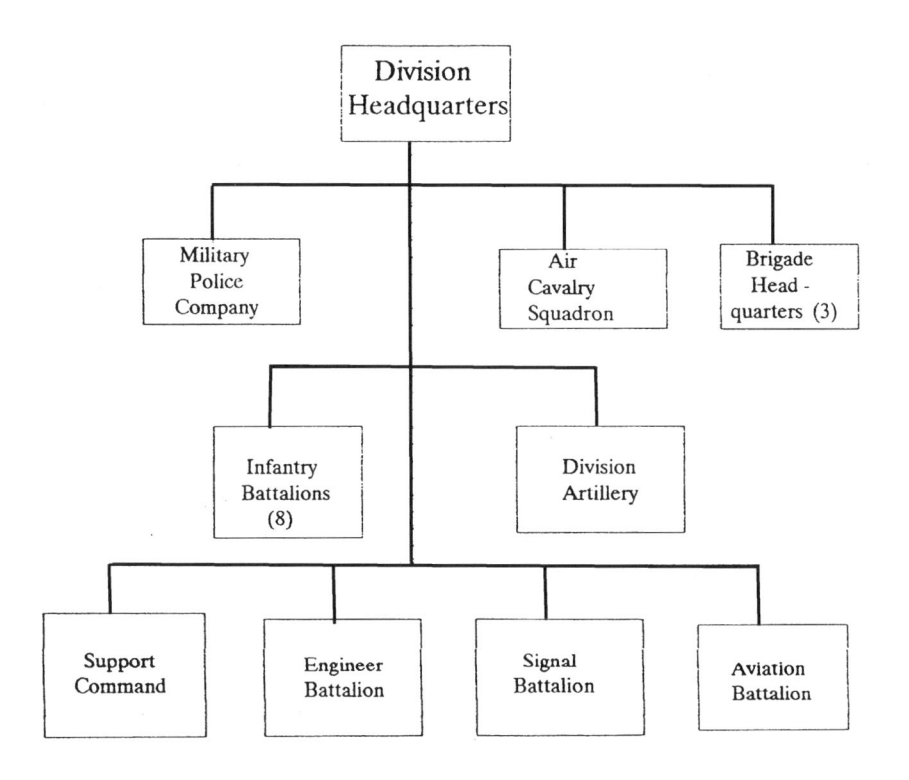

```
                    ┌─────────────────┐
                    │     Division    │
                    │  Headquarters   │
                    └────────┬────────┘
        ┌────────────────────┼────────────────────┐
┌───────┴───────┐    ┌───────┴───────┐    ┌───────┴───────┐
│   Military    │    │      Air      │    │    Brigade    │
│    Police     │    │    Cavalry    │    │    Head -     │
│    Company    │    │   Squadron    │    │  quarters (3) │
└───────────────┘    └───────────────┘    └───────────────┘
                     ┌───────┴───────┐
             ┌───────┴───────┐   ┌───┴───────────┐
             │   Infantry    │   │   Division    │
             │  Battalions   │   │   Artillery   │
             │      (8)      │   │               │
             └───────────────┘   └───────────────┘
     ┌──────────────┬──────────┴─────┬──────────────┐
┌────┴────┐   ┌─────┴─────┐   ┌──────┴────┐   ┌─────┴─────┐
│ Support │   │ Engineer  │   │  Signal   │   │ Aviation  │
│ Command │   │ Battalion │   │ Battalion │   │ Battalion │
└─────────┘   └───────────┘   └───────────┘   └───────────┘
```

Figure 14
Organization of the 11th Air Assault Division, 1963–1964

Help from Above

Army divisions, and that the airmobile concept improved the effectiveness of airlifted, but ground-based, firepower systems, such as some types of artillery. Aerial firepower systems, such as the helicopter rocket force, while proving useful when hidden from ground fire during periods of bad weather and at night, had little chance of survival against a sophisticated defense. Further, they could not deliver sufficient firepower to destroy hard targets, such as tanks and concrete emplacements. The air cavalry, whose job was to locate targets for air assault, usually did a good job, but the few instances when it did not resulted in utter confusion. Since air superiority was assumed and enemy antiaircraft and automatic weapons fire was virtually ignored, the air cavalry flew unopposed behind enemy lines. Army members of the aggressor force stated that if real bullets had been used the air cavalry would have been annihilated early in the exercise.[122]

The Air Force noted, and the Army often agreed, that there were some major problems with the airmobile test and concept. For one thing, by assuming complete air superiority, the test failed to include such important functions as camouflaging of helicopters, equipment, and command posts; accounting for losses of assault aircraft and flying command posts; or the loss of tactical air allocated to the air battle. One item on which both services agreed was that the helicopter showed itself to be highly vulnerable. Despite expectations to the contrary, reconnaissance planes had no difficulty detecting them flying close to the earth, where small arms fire could destroy them. An Army spokesman admitted this vulnerability and asked for better active and passive improvements to reduce it.[123]

There was also agreement that the air assault division concept presented major maintenance problems. The more candid among Army leaders admitted that the helicopter was still too complex a machine. They did maintain the minimum 75 percent in-commission rate for all their aircraft during the exercise, but in the exercise the "war" lasted only five days, followed by a four-day recess, making it relatively simple to maintain such a high rate. In the view of experienced Air Force officials, this would not have been possible in real battle conditions.[124]

Another conclusion of the Ninth Air Force, which provided the aircraft for the Air Assault II exercise, was that Army's organic air was not adequate to support the operation, either in airlift or close air support (fire-support). In the area of close air support, it pictured the gap between powerful jet fighters and an infantryman on foot as too great to be filled by Mohawks and helicopters firing from the air, as the Army tried to do, or by jet fighters themselves. The gap needed filling by an aircraft that could fire immediately in front of the combat infantryman, could perform during periods of bad weather, and could provide constant column cover or instantaneous response in the immediate battle area. It would require an unrealistic number of jet fighters to do this, and to use them exclusively for these missions would be "fighting the problem." What

Close Air Support and Flexible Response

was needed to accompany the all-powerful, heavy-fire "Sunday punch" of tactical air was an Air Force plane tailored to the specific needs of the air assault concept.[125] Air Force voices calling for development of a specific close air support plane were proliferating.

One major problem during Air Assault II was the absence of coordination between the Army's Mohawks and the Air Force's jet fighters in the battle area. This proved to be one of the weakest points of the entire maneuver. Frequently, Mohawk pilots did not seem to be controlled by the fire-support elements that controlled all other firepower, including tactical aircraft. Time and time again, Air Force fighters that had been cleared to their targets by the Army Fire Support Coordinator encountered Mohawks over their objective. Often coordinators could not establish radio contact with the Mohawks to order them off and allow the fighters to attack. In the view of Ninth Air Force, if the Army could not control the Mohawks, they should give that function to someone who could.[126]

In its overall evaluation of the exercise, Ninth Air Force saw that an air assault attack would be practical only in severely circumscribed situations. It might achieve some success where it enjoyed total air supremacy, where the enemy's whereabouts was known exactly, where the helicopters and Army fixed-wing planes could avoid antiaircraft ground fire, where the weather was good, and where there was close coordination between the helicopter-borne air attack and follow-on tactical air and ground support. In a telling conclusion, knowledgeable Army and Air Force personnel at the working level were convinced that the need for tactical air power, including fighters, reconnaissance, and airlift planes, was greater in the air assault concept than in conventional Army warfare. "Instead of taking away any of the USAF missions and roles," Ninth Air Force added, "they have laid more requirements upon us."[127]

Army leaders, while generally supportive of the results of Air Assault II, differed in their opinions. As would be expected, those directly involved with the tests in the field were the most laudatory concerning the results. The commander of the aggressor force, the 82d Airborne Division, saw airmobility as a revolutionary military concept with "dynamic potential." The leader of the 11th Air Assault Division was impressed by those abilities of the air mobility division that the standard Army ROAD division did not possess. The test director, to whom these commanders reported, praised the prototypical air assault division as the most versatile force that could be added to the Army. He urged that the division, which was scheduled to be disbanded in February 1965, not only be spared fragmentation and dispersal, but that it be formally inducted into the Army's force structure.[128]

Some Army officers in the Pentagon were more cautious. The Deputy Commander of the Army staff office responsible for force development, and therefore for incorporating the air mobility division into the force structure

Help from Above

should it be so decided, noted that an air mobility division cost about half again as much as a standard ROAD division, and it was imperative to determine whether, on a cost-effectiveness basis, the Air Assault Division was worth the difference. His judgment on the joint aspects of the air assault test mirrored that of the working-level airmen and soldiers in the tests. The Air Assault Division, he said:

> may need at least as much Air Force support as do our conventional divisions. The unit, since it takes greater risks for greater gains, needs more deep reconnaissance of the type that can best be performed by the Air Force. It can also use at least as much close air support and wholesale logistical support as is required by our conventional units.[129]

This was one of the very few Army critiques that acknowledged the existence of an Air Force tactical air support capability. Virtually all of the others judged the division's performance *in vacuo*, as if there were no Air Force. This narrow focus had been the basis of the Air Force's complaint with the Army position from the beginning. Throughout 1963 and 1964, as the Air Force tested its concept of airmobility jointly with the Army through the Strike Command, the Army declined to perform similar joint testing. Although the Secretary of Defense, as early as December 1962, instructed that both services' test their differing airmobile concepts under the aegis of the Strike Command,[130] McNamara changed his mind in March 1964 and approved a recommendation by the Joint Chiefs that joint comparative testing of the Army concept be deferred, that the Army proceed with its unilateral tests in 1964, and that the Army then recommend to the Joint Chiefs what part, if any, of the airmobile test warranted joint evaluation. In May, Air Force Secretary Eugene M. Zuckert reiterated the desirability of joint comparative testing.[131]

In January 1965, two months before the Gold Fire I and Air Assault II reports were sent on to the Office of the Secretary of Defense (OSD), the Joint Chiefs recommended, and the secretary approved, cancellation of Gold Fire II, the proposed Joint Strike Command test of the Army's concept.[132] This was a major defeat for the Air Force, for it meant, in effect, that a successful test of the Air Force concept depended upon the effectiveness of Army troops and the positive judgment of Army evaluators, while the Army tested its own concept with its own judges.[133] General John P. McConnell, who replaced General LeMay as the Air Force's Chief of Staff the following month, vociferously dissented from the JCS position, arguing that it was only fair for both concepts to be evaluated equally by a third party.

In March 1965 Secretary Zuckert, commenting on the reports from Gold Fire I and Air Assault II, recommended modifying the 1957 roles and mission statement in light of the new airmobility concept.[134] He noted that past efforts

Secretary of the Air Force Eugene M. Zuckert

to delineate the air functions of the two services, first by restricting the weight of Army aircraft and then by defining the areas in which they could operate in terms of distance from the front line, had not been effective because they did not take into account technological changes and changes in combat requirements. To Zuckert, the Gold Fire I and Air Assault II tests provided the basis for a reasonable and workable solution to this venerable problem. Based on the data that emerged from the tests, he proposed that the Air Force own and operate all major combat and combat support fixed-wing and cargo-coded rotary-wing planes that directly support the Army: C–130s, Caribous, and CH–3, CH–47, and CH–54 helicopters for air assault lift; Air Force jets and Mohawks for reconnaissance; and Air Force fighters for close air support. The Army would own and operate light and utility helicopters for airmobile operations, visual reconnaissance and fire adjustment, utility airlift within the division area, and local aeromedical evacuation, and liaison.[135] While these suggestions spoke primarily to the airlift and reconnaissance functions of tactical aircraft, they also were designed to restrict the close air support functions that were being performed by helicopters and Mohawks. This suggestion formed the basis for a key agreement the following year between the chiefs of both services over the employment of helicopters and fixed-wing planes.

Following months of speculation about the possible fate of the 11th Air Assault Division, ranging from having it replace either the 101st Airborne or the 82d Airborne Divisions, to organizing air assault brigades in one or both of these divisions,[136] in March 1965, the Joint Chiefs, minus McConnell, approved the Army's recommendation that the air mobility division replace one of the its infantry divisions and sent the recommendation to OSD.[137] Secretary McNamara approved the recommendation on June 15, and the air mobility division replaced the 2nd Infantry Division, which then exchanged its colors

Help from Above

with the 1st Cavalry Division in Korea to become the 1st Cavalry Division (Airmobile).

There were at least three reasons, all peripheral to what was learned in the tests, for this failure to test the Army concept as fully and objectively as the Air Force concept one and for the decision to keep the air mobility division alive. First, the Army had convinced a large segment of the military establishment that further large-scale tests were unnecessary. This argument was accompanied by a sense of urgency, as the test division was scheduled to be inactivated at the end of June and its units had already begun to disperse throughout the Army. Secondly, even though the Strike Command and even some elements within the Army and OSD were not satisfied with the results of the unilateral airmobile tests, there were no funds for further testing in 1965.

The most important reason for the acceptance of the air mobility division were the escalating events in Vietnam, which made the air mobility division appear attractive to many.[138] On August 2, 1964, as both services were gearing up for the airmobile tests, American destroyers in the Gulf of Tonkin reported being attacked by North Vietnamese torpedo boats. In response, Congress authorized President Lyndon B. Johnson to use all measures, including military force, to defend South Vietnam against the north. Three months later, on November 1, as the Gold Fire and Air Assault maneuvers were entering their final fortnight, Viet Cong squads killed 4 Americans and destroyed 5 bombers and damaged 19 others when they shelled the crowded airfield at Bien Hoa, South Vietnam. On Christmas eve, as the Army and Air Force evaluators at home were preparing their final reports of the exercises, the Viet Cong exploded a powerful charge in the Brink Hotel bachelor officers quarters in Saigon, killing 2 and wounding 71 Americans. Three days later, the conflict escalated from an insurgency to a conventional war when the Viet Cong opened a six-day battle in which they destroyed two South Vietnamese battalions at Binh Gia on the southern Ca Mau peninsula. In February 1965, 8 Americans lost their lives and more than 100 others were wounded and 5 helicopters destroyed at Pleiku in the central highlands when enemy mortars struck the American advisory compound there. Navy planes responded by striking North Vietnamese army barracks in the north, only to have the Viet Cong, in retaliation, blow up an American enlisted men's barracks at Qui Nhon, killing 23 Americans and 7 Vietnamese, and wounding many others. The following month, as the Joint Chiefs were recommending retention of the air mobility division, the American commander in Vietnam, General Westmoreland, requested an American army division for the Pleiku area to hold the line against enemy escalation for a few months while the badly mauled South Vietnamese army brought themselves up to full strength.

These events marked a turning point for the United States in the war. Earlier discussions in Washington about withdrawing advisors were replaced with recommendations for sending additional forces to the area. On March 9,

Close Air Support and Flexible Response

1965, the first brigade of Marines landed at Da Nang in the northern part of South Vietnam, followed in May by the arrival of the first U.S. Army brigade. It was within this context of rapidly deploying American combat forces to Vietnam that Secretary McNamara decided in June to retain the new air mobility division and make it a replacement for the 1st Cavalry Division. It would seem that the sense of urgency engendered by the escalating conflict in Vietnam outweighed the airmobile tests in arriving at the decision to retain an air mobility division.

* * *

Although emphasis on the strategic nuclear arena since the World War II had, by 1965, rendered the Air Force and Army less than totally prepared for the coming ground war in Southeast Asia, sufficiently significant improvements were made between 1960 and 1965 to raise close air support consciousness and capabilities to the point where the two services were able to adapt quickly to the fast-paced developments in Southeast Asia. The catalyst for these improvements was the advent of the Flexible Response strategy with its accompanying accent on military doctrine, strategy, tactics, and force structures to deter wars below the strategic nuclear level. Of equal importance with this new strategy was Secretary McNamara's support of the Army's bid to raise its mobility by employing organic aircraft to supplant some Air Force missions. This challenge stirred the Air Force to sharpen its own concept of airmobility, which was to use existing Air Force resources with standard Army divisions, rather than create new resources and divisions.

This Air Force claim that its own tactical air support resources could do the job for the Army led it to improve its close air support assets in preparation for a test against the Army's airmobile concept. As the Army built up its organic support air units, the Air Force enhanced its close air support aircraft, weapons, armament, tactics, and control system. It tested a whole series of new conventional weapons, improved its ability to perform close air support missions at night, stepped up its training with the Army and tilted its own unit and individual training programs more toward close air support, and placed some Air Force officers on permanent assignment with the Army to coordinate their activities. Even though most of these measures were directed toward a potential conventional conflict in Europe, they represented a turn from strictly nuclear strategic planning, a change that made the close air support mission more adaptable in Southeast Asia than would otherwise have been the case.

The contest between the two visions of airmobility was played out during this period, with the Air Force's traditional close air support role, among other missions, at least partially at stake. The clash of the Howze and Disosway concepts of airmobility in stateside tests resulted in a compromise. Both concepts were validated: the Air Force's by the joint Strike Command, the Army's unilaterally by its own judges. Although the Air Force's claim to control helicopters, part of whose mission was emerging as close air support, was weakened, other facets of close air support were strengthened. Several Army observers of the tests suggested that the Army's new airmobile idea actually increased the need for Air Force close air support. This conclusion was to be repeated in Vietnam.

The ultimate outcome of the competing concepts, however, was postponed, as the testing ground moved from the United States to South Vietnam. Both systems of tactical and close air support were transported there. With the air mobility division's deployment, in the fall of 1965, and the Air Force's subsequent installation of a full-fledged tactical air control system and a wing structure, complete with jet aircraft, the stage was set for the final competition between two close air support systems.

6 | The Vietnam Era: 1965–1973

The U.S. Air Force agrees to relinquish all claims for helicopters and follow-on rotary wing aircraft which are designed and operated for intra-theater movement, fire support, supply and resupply of Army forces.

— USAF/USA Agreement, April 1966

The Air Force (is to) take immediate and positive action to obtain a specialized close air support aircraft specifically designed for the lower spectrum of the close air support mission in low order of conflict.

— USAF Chief of Staff, September 1966

By mid-1968, following three years of intensive ground warfare in South Vietnam, the United States was no longer willing to continue an economically and politically enervating military stalemate. Late in that year Pres. Lyndon B. Johnson began to withdraw American troops and to bolster the South Vietnamese to defend themselves against the North. The four-year extraction of American forces, continued by Johnson's successor, Richard M. Nixon, was complete by early 1973.

The causes of this military stalemate were manifold. Regardless of how much the American ground strategy in South Vietnam contributed to the deadlock, the Air Force's function in South Vietnam was to back up with air support whatever American ground strategy was employed. The issue of how successful the Air Force was in supporting this strategy is separate from the question of how well-considered and successful the strategy proved to be.

Help from Above

The Strike Command's validation of the Air Force's concept of airmobility, namely, to provide tactical air support to standard Army ROAD divisions, encouraged the Air Force to improve the effectiveness of its close air support in Vietnam between 1965 and 1973. Air Force close air support recorded many successes. In the summer of 1965, Air Force operations restrained the tide of enemy attacks on South Vietnamese forces long enough for the U.S. Army to deploy its initial forces and get them ready for battle, and on frequent subsequent occasions, Air Force close air support averted the defeat of American and South Vietnamese troops. Army commanders on the whole were enthusiastic about the close air support they received from the Air Force.

Many of the close air support issues that had divided the Army and Air Force for decades were brought into sharper focus and, in some cases, resolved. While many old practices were improved, several new measures were added to prewar close air support techniques. The Tactical Air Control System adapted smoothly to the alien environment. One long-standing controversy was laid to rest, as jets fitted into the close air support role with a minimum of disruption. Communication equipment and procedures, which had often impaired earlier close air support, were vastly improved when the Air Force assumed responsibility for the air request net. The creation and successful placing of close air support control agencies at the corps level under Air Force direction went part way toward satisfying the Army's demand for more control over Air Force close air support missions. The expanded employment of airborne FACs represented a successful culmination of a practice that began tentatively during World War II. Another novelty, the effective use of B–52s for close air support, was a reversal of the preceding tendency to use tactical aircraft for strategic purposes, while the successful use of ground-controlled bombing equipment added a new dimension to close air support, particularly at night and during periods of poor weather.

At the same time as the Air Force was honing its close air support resources to provide major support for the Army's ground operations in Vietnam, it was also modifying its earlier positions on two major close air support issues: the role of armed helicopters in close air support, and the development of a close air support aircraft. Regarding the first of these issues, the Air Force's earlier hope of extending its doctrine of centralization of air power to helicopters ended when the Army proved unwilling to place its helicopters under the Air Force control system in Vietnam, when the Army introduced its airmobile division into the war, and finally, when the Air Force and Army chiefs agreed that the Air Force would relinquish its claim to helicopters in return for the Army's abandonment of its nascent fixed-wing close air support capability.

This defection of yet another facet of air power from Air Force jurisdiction represented only the latest in a series of such estrangements. The first revision of the Air Force's dream of controlling everything that flies came on its very birthday in 1947 when, in order to obtain the Navy's concurrence with the National Security Act, the Air Force agreed to the Navy's retention of its own aviation, including land-based planes. At the same time, the Marine Corps was permitted to keep its supporting air units. The Army, likewise, was given the green light to develop its own organic aircraft. Despite strenuous Air Force efforts, over succeeding years, to limit the hemorrhaging from centralized air power these decisions encouraged, the dissipation of air resources continued. The Army's *fait accompli* in the early 1960s in creating an airmobile organization, testing it unilaterally, and securing Defense Secretary McNamara's acquiescence in deploying it to Vietnam over the vociferous objections of the Air Force Chief of Staff, created yet another separate packet of air power outside the control of and unaccountable to the Air Force which, in Vietnam at least, was theoretically responsible for the activities of all air units within the theater.

Emboldened by the performance of its armed helicopters in Vietnam, Army leaders set about to develop a stronger, second-generation of helicopters for ground troop support. This led to the second major shift during the Vietnam period in the Air Force's position regarding close air support. For a number of reasons, some directly related to Vietnam, others to the Army's continued criticism at home, and still others to the economic realities of the defense budget, the Air Force reversed its traditional stance on whether or not to develop a plane specifically for close air support. For almost three decades it had resisted Army calls for such a plane, arguing both doctrinally and economically against limiting a plane's potential by restricting it to only one mission. Now the Air Force, in the face of a growing Army helicopter capability for close air support, changed its mind and set out to develop an attack plane designed solely for close air support of the Army.

Air Force Close Air Support Validated in Vietnam

Much has been written about the purported unpreparedness of the American military as it plunged into the Vietnam War in the summer of 1965. Generalizations abound in the attempts to document, in the case of the Air Force, such deficiencies as an absence of guns on fighter planes, a dearth of conventional munitions, a shortage in the Air Force's inventory of light planes for FACs, and, in general, a service that had permitted the close air support capability it had built up in Korea to decay in the face of the subsequent demands of a nuclear deterrent strategy.

Viewed solely from a technological perspective, there is an element of truth in this indictment. At least until 1961, the nuclear role strongly influenced fighter aircraft configurations and pilot training. Pilot competency in conventional close air support tactics, however, never completely disappeared, as pilots were always required to maintain dual proficiency in both

Help from Above

nuclear and nonnuclear techniques. Moreover, the Air Force closed down production lines of conventional iron bombs, relying on the Navy for what it anticipated as a small future demand and, in the face of the growth of Army aviation, the Air Force not only neglected helicopters, but light planes as well. When the need for a multitude of small, conventional, FAC planes arose in Vietnam, the Air Force had to get them from the Army. Likewise, at the outset, the Air Force had to acquire propeller-driven A–1 close air support planes from the Navy.

Yet to place too great an emphasis on the importance of these technological shortcomings, which could be and, in fact, were quickly rectified, can obscure the generally healthy condition of the Air Force's underlying tactical air control system, that was ultimately of greater importance than these temporary technological deficiencies. Close air support is more than just the aircraft that place munitions on targets. It is an entire tactical air control system that must regulate planes so that they can be shifted, reallocated, and concentrated where the enemy action is being felt, sometimes under adverse weather conditions. The air commander relies on this integrated system to carry out air support requirement of the the theater.[1]

The Tactical Air Control System, which provided the structure for Air Force close air support of ground forces, was installed in Vietnam along the lines of the *JAGOS Manual* of 1957. Although still not approved as a joint publication by the Joint Chiefs, the *JAGOS Manual* had received the imprimatur of both services, and its prescriptions for training and operating together had seeped into the consciousness of both soldiers and airmen to form the basis of instruction at the many schools that treated the subject of air-ground operations. Early in 1965, the reaffirmation by the Strike Command following the Gold Fire I exercise of the validity of this system for close air support ensured that the Army and the Air Force were basically well prepared for joint operations in Vietnam. By the time, starting in 1965, the Air Force was called upon to use its Tactical Air Control System to support American ground forces, it had already amassed nearly four years of valuable experience supporting the South Vietnamese.

The Air Force began to build its Tactical Air Control System in Vietnam long before the infusion of large-scale American combat units in 1965. Just after it assumed the mission of advising the small South Vietnamese Air Force (VNAF) in January 1962, the U.S. Air Force installed the initial segments of a tactical air control system to provide a communications link between ground forces and the air resources that existed to support them.[2] This system, designed to plan, direct, and coordinate air operations, was a textbook application of the prescriptions of the *JAGOS Manual*. Since at the time the Air Force had only 16 combat planes in the country, which it used to train Vietnamese airmen, the introduction of such a compendious air control system pointed to a large increase in air activities sometime in the future.

The Vietnam Era

As introduced in 1962, the original Tactical Air Control System consisted of an Air Operations Center (AOC) and a Control and Reporting Center (CRC) at Tan Son Nhut air base in Saigon; two Control and Reporting Posts at Da Nang in the north and at Pleiku in the center of the country; and Air Support Operations Centers (ASOCs) in Saigon, Da Nang and Pleiku. Also, a number of ALOs served with the Vietnamese at their corps headquarters, and a pool of five FACs, were assigned to the AOC in Saigon where they trained Vietnamese controllers, but from there they could be temporarily attached, when the situation warranted, to ground forces that expected to contact the enemy.

Since the *JAGOS Manual*, upon which this system was modeled, was not designed for application to an advisory situation or in jungle terrain like that in Vietnam, some adjustments had to be made during the advisory period (1961–1964). Two parallel structures were set up within the Tactical Air Control System, one for Air Force and VNAF planes that were supporting South Vietnamese ground operations, the other for the much smaller number of Air Force planes (mostly airlift) that were assisting U.S. Army ground advisors. American and Vietnamese officers worked side by side at all levels of the system, from the AOC down. Each directed his own national units and personnel.

The hub of the system during the early advisory years was the Air Operations Center as prescribed by the 1957 *JAGOS Manual*. Located in Saigon, this center served as the command post for both the VNAF commander and the commander of the USAF headquarters, the 2d Advanced Echelon (ADVON). Its director was Vietnamese, its deputy director American. The latter was responsible for all USAF operations, including close air support, reconnaissance, airlift, and special missions requested by the Vietnamese. The Air Operations Center was also the focal point for coordinating U.S. Army and Navy fixed-wing air flights.[3] Since these were few before 1965, the Tactical Air Control System was largely an instrument for the Air Force to advise the Vietnamese.

Next door to the AOC at Tan Son Nhut was a radar site, called a CRC, which displayed, based on information received from its local Control and Reporting Posts at Da Nang and Pleiku, the entire aerial picture in South Vietnam. As with other parts of the system, VNAF personnel were included in the center's manning and received training.

The Tactical Air Control System in Vietnam reflected the Air Force's concept of centralized control and decentralized operation of aircraft. While the AOC in Saigon was the central agency for planning and controlling air missions, these missions were under the immediate direction of the center's tentacles, the ASOCs, located at each of the three (and later four) local Vietnamese corps tactical zone headquarters. The 1957 manual called for these local centers to be highly mobile in order to keep up with the army's moving front line. Since there were no front battle lines in Vietnam, and since

Help from Above

the country was small, these centers became permanent parts of the ground-force headquarters. One ASOC was located with the Vietnamese I Corps headquarters at Da Nang and another with the II Corps headquarters at Pleiku, while the Saigon AOC itself served as the third, for operations in III Corps. After the Vietnamese created a fourth corps tactical zone in the southern Mekong Delta in March 1963, a fourth center was set up in the Vietnamese headquarters at Can Tho. The Saigon AOC allocated sorties for the directors of the local centers to use in close air support or reconnaissance missions requested by the Vietnamese corps commanders. Requests that came into these local centers for interdiction, airlift, or psychological warfare missions, none of which the center could handle, were passed up to the Saigon AOC.[4]

Other ingredients of the Vietnamese environment led to further adjustments of the basic Tactical Air Control System before 1965. The original *JAGOS Manual* had been conceived for a conventional, European-style war between political opponents who subscribed essentially to Western military practices as they had matured over many centuries. Wars between Western sovereign states had historically been characterized by clearly defined but fluid forward battle lines, fairly easily recognizable targets, and relatively open terrain. None of these conditions existed in Vietnam—there were no forward battle lines, the targets were elusive and poorly defined, and the thick jungle foliage presented unanticipated challenges to close air support. The standard control system also had to be modified to allow for local restrictions on air power and for the fact that requests for close air support came separately and uncoordinated from both the civilian and military leaders of the country.

During most of the advisory period the Vietnamese Air Force provided poor close air support to the Vietnamese Army (ARVN). This was attributed mainly to South Vietnamese unfamiliarity with American culture and air practices. However, one part of the Tactical Air Control System, the air-request net, contributed to the problem. According to the *JAGOS Manual*, the Army was responsible for providing the men and equipment and for operating the air-request net that ground forces used to request emergency air strikes. Requests emanating from a company or higher level had to work their way up this Army-owned- and-operated communications ladder. At each level, the request was scrutinized to see if some other form of fire support might not be more appropriate and, if not, it was passed on to the next echelon. Not until it finally arrived at, and was approved by, ground officers at the field army level was the request transmitted to the Air Force's ASOC for response.

In Vietnam during this early period where the U.S. Army was performing only an advisory role, the requirement that the Army operate the request net meant that the ARVN operated the net. This opened the door to an influx of "political, religious, personal or social background and customs of the ARVN and civilian officials,"[5] which jammed up the system. For example, very few requests for immediate assistance reached the Air Force, having been

The Vietnam Era

Maj. Gen. Joseph H. Moore

held up or diverted along the way by such indigenous impediments as language difficulties, religious prohibitions, local political jealousies, and ignorance on the part of many South Vietnamese of the benefits of air support.

In May 1964, Maj. Gen. Joseph H. Moore, 2d Air Division Commander, overhauled the system along the lines suggested earlier by the Close Air Support Board. To the cumbersome ARVN request net he added a VNAF air-request net. Thereafter, TACPs made up of both American and Vietnamese officers and radio operators, radioed requests for immediate air strikes from their battalions directly to the ASOCs. While the center was preparing its planes to respond, the radio request continued up the ARVN request net where it was monitored simultaneously at all echelons, each of which had only five minutes to object. Silence meant approval.[6] By the time the request exited from the ARVN system, the planes were ready for takeoff. By the end of 1964, the four ASOCs were equipped with enough radios and ALOs to make the system work efficiently. Judging from the modest increase in requests it evoked, the reform was only partially successful in convincing South Vietnamese ground commanders of the value of tactical air support. Its greater importance, however, came in the later years of the war when the Air Force applied the new practice to its support of the U.S. Army.

None of these modifications affected the basic organizational structure of the Tactical Air Control System. By the time it came to be used principally in support of the U.S. Army, its organization was sound and well tested. This shift to supporting principally American ground units came about between 1965 and 1966, as American air and ground troops took over the war from the South Vietnamese who barely avoided defeat in the summer of 1965. The Tactical Air Control System was strengthened in the spring of that year when General McConnell and Gen. Harold K. Johnson signed yet another agree-

305

Help from Above

ment, a "Concept for Improved Joint Air-Ground Coordination." By this new directive the Army agreed to continued centralized control of Air Force tactical aircraft under the air component commander, while the Air Force accepted decentralized execution of tactical missions by placing them under the control of the ASOCs, which were soon to be renamed Direct Air Support Centers (DASCs), in each corps.[7]

A further step in linking the Air Force's Tactical Air Control System to the Army's air-ground system occurred in May 1966 when Military Assistance Command, Vietnam established the Joint Air-Ground Operations System (**Figure 15**). This new arrangement united the Air Force's Tactical Air Control System with the Army's air-ground system, and later with the Marine's air control structure in I Corps in the north. This attempt to bring together the various and sometimes competing air systems into one unified process succeeded quite well before 1968 in coordinating Army, Air Force, and Navy fixed-wing missions. In 1968 Marine aircraft grudgingly became part of the system, although not until they were on the eve of departing the country.

This Army air-ground system, which was paired with the Air Force's tactical air control system, set up Army agencies parallel to those of the Air Force's system. Its purpose was to evaluate and process requests for fire support (air or otherwise) and reconnaissance that came in from battalions or higher level units. At the apex of the system, on the same level with the Air Force's Tactical Air Control Center, or TACC, was the Army's Tactical Air Support Element, which allocated available sorties to ground commanders and passed on to the TACC all approved preplanned strike requests for execution. This procedure was used only for preplanned close air support strikes, that is, those that had been agreed upon 24 hours before the missions were flown. Requests for immediate strikes, which went directly from the field unit to the Air Force's DASC, bypassed this Army Tactical Air Support Element.[8]

Just as the Air Force's TACC had its local branches, the DASCs, so the Army's Tactical Air Support Element had corresponding units at each subordinate Army level down to battalion. These units, called Tactical Operations Centers (TOC) at corps and divisions and Fire Support Coordination Centers (SCC) at lower levels, were headed by Army officers who were part of the commander's staff at each level. These G–2/G–3 Air officers advised their commanders on all aspects of tactical air support that affected their operations. In addition to these G–2/G–3 Air officers at Army headquarters, the Tactical Air Support Element attached ground liaison officers at U.S. strike air bases, where they briefed pilots on the ground situation they were about to enter, and debriefed them after their missions.[9]

Important to the effectiveness of the Air Force's close air support of the Army in Vietnam was the speed with which the Tactical Air Control System assisted aircraft responding to requests for air strikes. Despite its apparent complexity, the elements of the request system had been reduced to the barest

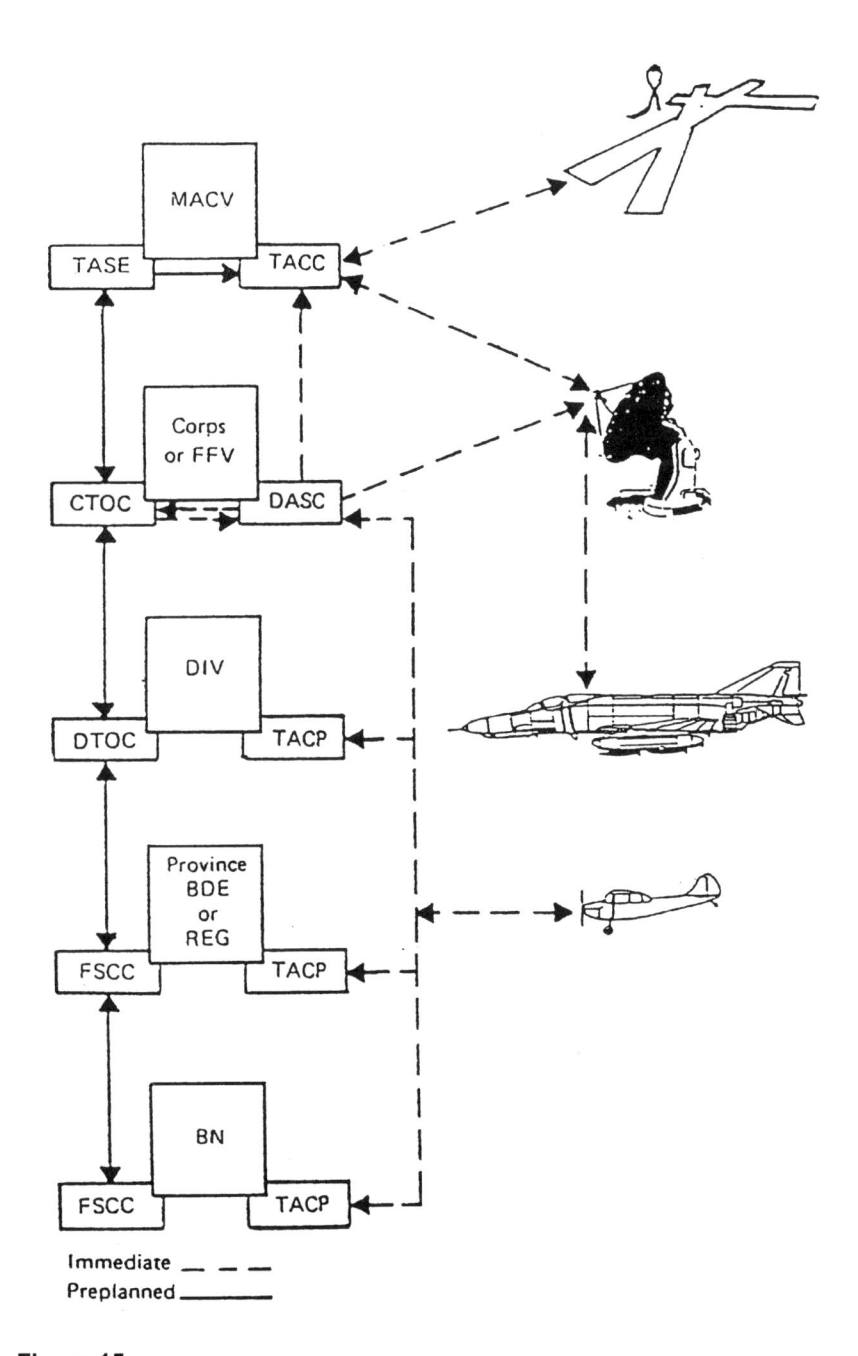

**Figure 15
Joint Air-Ground Operations System**

Help from Above

minimum needed for operations. Requests for immediate, emergency strikes, which possessed greater urgency, moved through the revamped system differently than did the more standard, less time-sensitive requests that were preplanned beforehand. Immediate air requests, which could arrive from any Army level, were dispatched directly by an Air Force TACP or airborne FAC at the battalion directly to the closest Air Force DASC. The DASC began readying aircraft to reply while simultaneously clearing the request with the Army's Corps TOC located alongside. This arrangement, initiated by General Moore in 1964, ensured that the needed aircraft would be ready for takeoff by the time the Army's Corps Tactical Operations Center gave final approval. The DASC could divert FACs and strike planes from lower priority preplanned missions or from airborne alert. Yet scrambling ground-alert planes or diverting planes from another corps area could be done only by the higher level TACC in Saigon.[10]

Preplanned air support missions, on the other hand, since they were not so time-sensitive, were more thoroughly scrubbed before orders were issued for takeoff. Although requests for these sorties could originate at any Army level, planning normally took place at a battalion conference the afternoon before a scheduled ground operation. Unlike immediate requests that went directly from the battalion to the Air Force's DASC, preplanned requests were sent over the Army's net up to the next level, the brigade. If the brigade decided that Army artillery or aircraft could do the job, the request went no farther. If not, the request continued on up the line to the Tactical Air Support Element. Here it was coordinated with the Air Force's Tactical Air Control Center, or TACC, which gave it a priority and issued a strike order, called a frag order.[11]

Once again, the modifications made to the Tactical Air Control System after 1964, to make it an efficient provider of close air support and reconnaissance for the U.S. Army, did not change the system's basic structure. Alterations occurred to accommodate such developments as the introduction of jet aircraft in February 1965, the opening of the air war against North Vietnam the following month, the creation in April of a separate Air Force immediate-request net, the use of B–52s for close air support in South Vietnam starting in June, the expansion of the role and number of FACs, the inauguration of a visual reconnaissance program in August 1965, the initial employment of an airborne command and control plane the following September, the introduction of a ground-controlled radar bombing system in March of 1966, and the merging of the Air Force's Tactical Air Control System with the Army's air-ground system in May of that year. Some long-term, internal changes were also made by the Air Force. For example, when Gen. William W. Momyer took over Seventh Air Force in 1966, he started a movement to take the Air Force's Tactical Air Control System out of the hands of communicators, where the Hawaiian air command had lodged it, and give it to operators. In his view the system was an operational element of command rather

The Vietnam Era

A B–52 bomber.

than simply a technical means of passing orders. In order to be responsive to the operational commander, he wrote, the communications units in the Tactical Air Control System should be organic to the system, not borrowed from communicators.[12] Each of these changes improved an already well-functioning system and represented an important contribution to the Air Force's fixed-wing close air support of the U.S. Army in the conflict.

The Air Force's responsibilities in Southeast Asia quickly overflowed the boundaries of South Vietnam. Since December 1964, fighter-bomber pilots, in addition to training and supporting the VNAF inside South Vietnam, had been attacking men and supplies as they moved down the Ho Chi Minh Trail in neighboring Laos. In March 1965, Air Force and Navy planes began the Rolling Thunder bombing campaign against North Vietnam. As the types of aircraft missions expanded, so did the need to refine the agencies that controlled them. In August 1965, the 2d Air Division in Saigon, the successor to the 2d ADVON, split its existing control organization into two, one to handle operations inside South Vietnam and the other to control missions outside the country. The AOC assumed responsibility for in-country operations and was renamed the Tactical Air Control Center, or TACC, while its local ASOCs were redesignated Direct Air Support Centers, or DASCs. A fifth DASC was added in the center of the country at Nha Trang. Control and coordination of air missions outside South Vietnam was vested in a separate "Blue Chip" organization at Seventh Air Force headquarters.

After 1964 these changes in the control system, together with deployments of first-line tactical aircraft, improved the Air Force's ability to provide close air support to the Army. The 2,392 strike sorties that the Air Force flew in January 1965, when the Air Force was still primarily supporting the South Vietnamese, rose to 13,274 by December, by which time the U.S. Army had become the principal customer for close air support.[13] The inventory of Air

Help from Above

Force strike planes for close air support at the beginning of the year included only 48 single-engine, propeller-driven A–1E attack planes and 20 B–57 turbojet twin-engine bombers at Bien Hoa, still dedicated primarily to training and supporting the South Vietnamese. Although there were 30 F–100 jets temporarily stationed at Da Nang at the time, these could not be used in South Vietnam until the ban on jets was lifted in February. Things changed dramatically after midyear. In October, five permanent F–100 squadrons were stationed at Bien Hoa and Da Nang. During the following month the advanced elements of an F–4C fighter wing landed at Cam Ranh Bay. By the end of the year, 388 of the more than 500 Air Force planes in Vietnam were fighter-bombers that were being flown mainly in support of the rapidly deploying American ground forces. The average monthly strike sortie total continued to climb early in the following year until it reached a peak of about 15,000, where it leveled off. Meanwhile, the number of strike aircraft in the country increased to 633, mostly jets, by the end of the following year, 1967. The transition from propeller planes to jets was complete. During November and December of 1967 the last remaining Air Force A–1 Skyraiders were transferred from South Vietnam to Thailand.[14] The close air support program had become totally a jet show.

This transition from propeller-driven attack planes to jets did not take place without some controversy. Many in the Army still believed that the jets were too fast and consumed too much fuel to serve as effective close air support planes. They opted, in their arguments, for propeller aircraft that flew more slowly and could spend more time over the battlefield, thereby allowing the pilots to see more of the ground action they were supporting. While the Army's increasing use of its organic helicopters in Vietnam muted some of its criticism of jets, there remained, among many Air Force pilots of these older, nonjet strike planes—the T–28s, A–1Es, and B–26s—a vocal residue of sentiment for retaining these vestiges of a disappearing generation. The experiences of these pilots convinced them that the greater visibility afforded the pilot from, and the longer staying power of, the prop aircraft made them a more effective close air support plane than the newer jets in the limited, jungle war environment of Vietnam. They were correct in that the slow cruise speed—of the A–1, for example—allowed it to make strikes underneath ceilings as low as 300 feet and with two miles visibility. Jet fighters, on the other hand, had a difficult time performing strikes below ceilings of 1,200 feet and with four miles of visibility. The main advantage of the jets, however, was that their speed, three times that of the prop planes, gave them the element of surprise, making them less vulnerable to the ground fire that was decimating the slower planes. The principal close air support planes throughout most of the war were the F–100 Super Sabre and the F–4 Phantom II.

Although the first two configurations of the F–100, the A and C models, were designed and equipped primarily as air-superiority fighters and only sec-

The Vietnam Era

ondarily as fighter-bombers, the F–100D, which first came into the inventory in 1956 and which predominated in Vietnam, was built primarily as a sophisticated fighter-bomber with only a secondary mission as a day fighter. It required virtually no modification for the basic close air support role in Vietnam. More than 90 percent of its sorties in Vietnam were of that type. As originally configured, the F–100D carried externally up to 7,000 pounds of bombs and rockets while internally it had four M–39 20-mm cannons, with room for 800 rounds of ammunition.[15] With a 335-gallon fuel tank hanging from each wing, the F–100 had a combat radius of 275 miles with 15 minutes in the target area. The Super Sabre was among the most accurate bomber of all the planes in Vietnam, its average circular error being 130 feet.[16] Although most of the F–100 models were one-seaters, the F model had two seats that allowed it to be used, among other things, as a jet forward air control, or FAC, planes in those regions where the slower O–1s and O–2s could not operate, and as Wild Weasel escort warning planes in strikes against North Vietnam.

Since the original F–100Ds and Fs were designed to carry most, but not all, nonnuclear weapons, a 1962 program to extend their life, undertaken long before their use in Vietnam was anticipated, also increased their ability to deliver all conventional ordnance. Additional minor modifications were made after they were deployed to Southeast Asia. Weapons release and firing systems were improved, and new guns and a more accurate target-marking system were provided. In 1966, all F–100s in Vietnam were equipped with a radar transmitter that allowed them to operate at night and during poor weather using the new Combat Skyspot ground-controlled bombing system.[17] None of these alterations, however, were sufficiently extensive to justify the assertion that the original F–100D and Fs were unprepared for close air support in Vietnam.

McDonnell-Douglas's two-seater F–4 Phantom II, originally a Navy interceptor, proved to be the most versatile fighter in Southeast Asia. Although it was used in many different roles, including some outside South Vietnam, it also performed many close air support functions. Within two years of its arrival in the theater in the spring of 1965, the F–4 was stationed at bases throughout Vietnam and Thailand, participating in interdiction, armed-reconnaissance, air superiority, escort, and close air support operations. The Phantom's ordnance load was phenomenal. Its normal external load weighed between 6,000 and 9,000 pounds of bombs and rockets, but it could be loaded up to 16,000 pounds. A low-altitude speed of 700 knots let the plane enter and leave a high-threat area before the enemy could track it. It also required less runway distance for takeoff than the other jets. These advantages outweighed the plane's weaknesses. Its high speed forced it to bomb from higher altitudes where its accuracy suffered. Not until the E model were the Phantoms equipped with internal cannons. Previously, when strafing was necessary, a 20-mm cannon was attached to the plane's centerline station. Its relatively large

Help from Above

turning and maneuver radius cut down its flexibility, and its short loiter time, 20 minutes at a 200-mile range, kept it from being used on airborne alert.[18]

The Phantom required more modification for its Vietnam role than did the Super Sabre. The early models sent to Southeast Asia, the F–4Cs, lacked internal guns and had to add external gun pods for 20-mm guns. Its ability, however, to carry Sparrow and Bullpup missiles, as well as napalm and all types of conventional bombs, gave it an advantage over the early F–100s. While the Phantoms experienced delays in being retrofitted for Wild Weasel missions, the modifications required for the close air support role were performed expeditiously. When the later models, the F–4Ds, reached Vietnam in 1967 they, like the F–100s, were rapidly equipped with X-band radar transmitters that allowed them to bomb with the radar Combat Skyspot system.[19]

Between the autumns of 1964 and 1969, the Air Force also used the B–57 Canberra bomber for close air support. This plane, adapted from Great Britain's first jet bomber, was the first Air Force jet to drop bombs in Vietnam. It could carry 10,000 pounds of ordnance and could mount either eight 50-caliber cannons or four 20-mm guns externally. The B–57 could fly 200 miles to the scene of an action and remain there for an hour and a half. Its two-man crew made it particularly useful at night when the second pilot performed myriad functions to support the first pilot as he flew the plane. A number of serious drawbacks, however, led to its disappearance from Vietnam by October 1969, by which time the Super Sabres and Phantoms had taken over most of the close air support missions. As an older and foreign plane, replacement aircraft and parts for the Canberra became very difficult to obtain. Moreover, the B–57 could not be refueled in flight, and the pilot's view was hampered by the plane's large wing.[20]

The F–4E Phantom II.

The Vietnam Era

Several F–4D Phantom IIs taxi on a runway with their drogue chutes extended.

Two late arrivals made their debut to the close air support function during the final phases of the war in Vietnam—the A–37 and the A–7. The attachment to these planes of the designation "A" (for "attack"), which had not been used since World War II, foreshadowed a softening of the Air Force's long-standing opposition to fighter planes that could be used for only one of the three tactical missions of air superiority, interdiction, and close air support. The A–37 Dragonfly was a converted trainer that underwent successful testing in Vietnam during the second half of 1967. This twin-engine light fighter was a replacement for the A–1s and F–100s later in the war. It carried about 2,500 pounds of bombs in wing ordnance racks and flew at a top airspeed of 416 knots. Its slim silhouette made it difficult to hit from the ground. The Dragonfly was easily maintained in the field, and its 2,800-foot takeoff distance permitted it to be stationed at every hard-surface field in Vietnam. In some ways, however, it was inferior to the F–100, as it could barely reach targets more than 170 miles from home and its loiter time was less than that of the Super Sabre. Its slower attack speed improved its accuracy but heightened its chance of being hit, and the cockpit visibility of the A–37 was inferior to that of the F–100. On balance, however, the Dragonfly was deemed a suitable replacement to take over the close air support functions of the Super Sabre.[21]

The A–7D did not enter the war until October 1972, long after it could support the U.S. Army, which had almost totally left the country. Yet the Air Force's adaptation of this plane from the Navy's A–7A, its designation of it as an attack aircraft, and the hope the plane raised of becoming an interim close air support vehicle, reflect the imminent change of heart that would result in the abandonment by the Air Force of its traditional animus against single-purpose aircraft. The A–7D carried 16,000 pounds of bombs, rockets, napalm, and Sidewinder missiles, and an internally mounted Gatling gun made this model excellent for ground strafing. With a top speed of 575 knots, a combat radius of 400 miles, and 30 minutes of loiter time it fulfilled many of the requirements for a close air support plane.[22]

There was no way that the conservative defenders of the continued use of propeller-driven planes could have won their argument against the partisans

Help from Above

An A–7K Corsair II flying with an A–7D Corsair II (top)
and an A–37 Dragonfly (bottom).

of jet aircraft. Both the Army and the Air Force viewed the war in Vietnam, at least in part, as a test bed for future equipment, munitions, and personnel practices as much as they saw it as an exercise in defeating an enemy. Since the conflict was interpreted largely as a one-time aberration from the contemporary national strategy of nuclear deterrence and, should deterrence fail, full-scale conventional ground warfare in Europe, both services were reluctant to invest in outmoded equipment that would prove useless beyond the present conflict. Thus, for example, evidence put forward by prop-plane advocates showing that the A–1 was superior to the F–100 or F–4 for spotting and strik-

The Vietnam Era

ing targets and in remaining aloft for longer periods fell largely on deaf ears as Air Force planners and commanders clung to the prevailing concept of the future Air Force as a jet service. As it turned out, they were correct, but not only for the reasons they enunciated. Army helicopters, possessing advantages identical to those claimed for fixed-wing propeller planes, would soon take over many of the operations of these reciprocating-engine aircraft, leaving those missions the helicopters could not perform for jets.

Second only to the exile of propeller planes from South Vietnam as an illustration of the Air Force's reluctance to build up too large an equity in past technology was the case of fixed-wing gunships. The idea of placing a side-firing machine gun in the door of the Air Force's venerable C–47 Skytrain (nicknamed the Gooney Bird) cargo plane that the pilot could fire from up front was the brainchild of two captains in the Air Force's Systems Command. The two junior officers fought a wall of opposition before the idea was given serious attention. The strongest resistance came from the professional military, namely, TAC, the Air Staff, and the Joint Chiefs. The civilian hierarchy consisting of the Secretary of the Air Force and the Secretary of Defense, on the other hand, supported the development of additional and improved fixed-wing gunships. The TAC commander, Gen. Walter C. Sweeney Jr., opposed the development on several grounds. First, he believed that these low, slow, and bulky planes were too vulnerable to avoid ground fire in the Vietnam environment. Second, he did not want to set the precedent of using a transport plane for close air support, since in his view this could encourage the Army to increase its ongoing experiments in arming its Mohawk planes. Primarily, however, the TAC commander was convinced that incorporation of such outmoded planes into the Air Force inventory could prove "disastrous in some future conflict."[23] Plans, budgets, and doctrine for the future of TAC revolved around a jet force capable of conducting a technologically sophisticated war in Europe. The development of slow, propeller planes did not fit into this scenario.

Sweeney was overruled by General McConnell, and a squadron of several gunships entered Vietnam in November 1965. The unit soon increased to 20 planes. Within two years a second squadron of 16 additional gunships joined them. For nearly four years these armed Gooney Birds performed such diverse functions as close air support for troops in contact; defense of besieged U.S. and friendly military outposts; support of hamlets, villages, and towns; armed reconnaissance and interdiction; search and rescue; forward air control; night armed escort; and illumination of night-fighter strikes. Four of these activities were strictly close air support missions. The largest number involved aerial strikes against enemy soldiers who were attacking U.S. or friendly military outposts throughout South Vietnam. Also, the corps Direct Air Support Centers frequently instructed the gunships to scatter enemy troops that were in direct contact with friendly forces. The gunships were particularly useful dur-

Help from Above

ing night battles by dropping flares to light up the battlefield for fighter planes and by raining down hails of bullets on the enemy from its miniguns. Finally, in situations where a FAC was unavailable, the gunships sometimes performed that role as well.

Although, quantitatively, the missions of these venerable planes represented only a small portion of the Air Force's close air support of the Army during the war, their results were impressive. At the end of 1969 the tired AC–47s were replaced in South Vietnam by another veteran of past wars, AC–119s, which soon were turned over to the South Vietnamese Air Force as part of the Vietnamization program.[24]

Of all the Air Force personnel involved in the close air support aspects of the Tactical Air Control System, none had a more critical and gruelling day-to-day job in cooperating with friendly ground forces than did the airborne FAC. The Tactical Air Control System as described in the 1957 *JAGOS Manual* was designed primarily with a war in Europe in mind. Accordingly, although the manual did not rule out using airborne FACs, its emphasis was on Air Force officers who controlled air strikes from ground positions. The Air Force FACs that accompanied some of the first U.S. Army units to Vietnam had been trained at the Air-Ground Operations School at Hurlburt Field, Florida, to direct strikes from the ground. But the heavy double- and triple-canopied jungle terrain in Vietnam, which severely limited sighting distance from the ground, rendered these ground controllers ineffective. The Air Force quickly adapted its practices to the local conditions by placing its controllers in light aircraft, from which they could better grasp the ground situation and control fighter strikes.

This changeover was rapid. In 1964 the Air Force had only one squadron, called a Tactical Air Support Squadron, of FAC pilots and planes in Vietnam. This squadron had 23 former Army Cessna L–19s, which the Air Force renamed O–1 Bird Dogs, and 44 pilots. Earlier, the Air Force had tried with little success to use this squadron to train Vietnamese FACs. An experiment with turning the squadron over to the Vietnamese in 1964 proved so unfortunate that the squadron, and the forward air control mission, was back in Air Force hands by January 1965.[25]

The following March the Army and Air Force agreed that the latter should create its own channel for transmitting immediate requests for close air support from the requesting unit to the Air Force planes. The Air Force took over from the Army the responsibility for providing the vehicles and communications facilities for this new net.[26] Also as a result of this agreement, coupled with the large influx of American forces during the second half of 1965, the need for FACs burgeoned. The 2d Air Division added three new tactical air support squadrons, bringing the number of Bird Dogs to 121 by year's end, and the cadre of FACs operating out of over 50 locations in Southeast Asia to 172.[27] Most of the additional Bird Dogs came from Army resources in Korea.

The Vietnam Era

More than half of the 123 FACs who were in South Vietnam were assigned to U.S. Army units for close air support.

Unlike the FACs who worked with the South Vietnamese or outside Vietnam, and who were assigned to geographical regions, those who assisted the U.S. Army were attached to army units as part of TACPs. They acted as advisors on the ground, and the Army looked on them as part of the ground team. And while all controllers, whether working with the Vietnamese, with the U.S. Army, or out of the country, had the dual roles of controlling strikes and performing visual reconnaissance, those attached to the U.S. Army were concerned almost exclusively with the former function.[28]

FACs directed fighters performing all types of close air support: preparing landing zones, escorting road convoys, hitting enemy troops who were in contact with friendlies, and covering troop helicopter airlift flights. On preplanned missions, the FAC was briefed the night before by the ALO. The controller's first job on a mission was to pinpoint the target himself so he could pass its location on to the oncoming fighters. This normally presented little problem, as he arrived about half an hour before strike time and learned by radio from the ground commander the target's description, the results that the commander hoped to get from the strike, and the location of the nearest friendly troops. The controller then advised the ground commander of what ordnance his fighters were carrying, what the plan of attack was, and how the ground troops should prepare themselves and mark the target with smoke.

After vectoring the fighters into the target area, the controller briefed them by radio on the target's characteristics, the weather, what ground fire to expect, the location of the friendly units, how the fighters should orbit while the controller marked the target with smoke rockets, where the controller would be during the target runs, in which sequence the fighters should drop their ordnance, the best headings for the fighters to use for their strikes, how they should break away after their runs, and the location of the nearest airfields and best bailout areas should a strike pilot experience an emergency.

One 2.75 white-phosphorous marker rocket, or smoke rocket, usually sufficed for the controller to mark the target for the fighters. The fighters ordinarily made three to five passes on the target, first dropping hard bombs followed by cluster bombs and napalm. The controller looked on from a nearby position where he monitored the action and, if necessary, adjusted his smoke markings between passes. He guided in the fighters on each pass, always keeping an eye on the friendly positions to avoid striking them by accident.

The controllers final responsibility during a strike was to evaluate the results. While the strike planes orbited overhead, the FAC flew over and around the target to perform a bomb damage assessment (BDA). He then gave his preliminary damage report to the flight leader of the strike planes and released them to return to their bases.

Help from Above

For immediate strikes the controller process was almost identical to that of preplanned requests, with two exceptions. In the first instance, since it was an emergency, the controller had to identify the target and the location of the friendly units much more rapidly than with preplanned missions. The shortness of time made this a particularly difficult procedure. Second, the FAC had to decide quickly whether to radio back to the division or brigade for additional strikes from the DASC. Other than this urgency, the sequence of events was similar to that performed on preplanned missions.[29]

By late 1966 it became apparent that the O-1 Bird Dog was rapidly becoming obsolete as a forward air control plane. Its lack of armor, speed, a *zoom* capability, and an adequate number of rockets, were making it more and more vulnerable in an increasingly hostile ground environment. Communication and performance problems were multiplying. Forward Air Controllers were limited in their ability to direct strikes because the Bird Dogs could carry only four to eight marking rockets, their slow airspeed increased their reaction time to immediate requests for strikes, and their fuel limitations restricted the time they could spend over the target. These disadvantages were somewhat offset by the minimum amount of maintenance they required, which allowed them to operate efficiently from primitive fields. The overhead wing of the O-1 provided the pilot with excellent visibility.

Nevertheless, the Air Force began a search for a replacement. As early as 1964 the Defense Department had approved the development of a new aircraft, the OV-10 Bronco, which was to be the first plane designed specifically for airborne forward control duty.[30] Since the Bronco would not be available until 1968, however, the Air Force purchased the Cessna 337 Super Skymaster, called the O-2A, *off the shelf* to serve as an interim control aircraft.

This second-generation O-2A controller plane had several advantages over the O-1. It had two engines, one forward of the cockpit that pulled the plane, and one aft that pushed. It also had more sophisticated communications equipment, greater speed, and longer endurance than the Bird Dog, and with its 14 rockets its pilot could direct more strikes. It too, however, had limitations. Despite its two engines, the O-2A flew well on one engine only when that one engine was the rear one. It had visibility problems. Since it carried two pilots seated side by side, it was difficult when being flown with only one pilot aboard for that pilot to see across the front seat to the opposite window. Unlike its predecessor, the O-2A was ill-suited to operate from forward airfields. On unimproved runways its front engine would kick dirt and rocks into the rear engine. Further, its landing gear had not been built for the rough use it would have to endure on unimproved surfaces.[31]

By 1968, the OV-10 Bronco was beginning to replace its two predecessors and quickly demonstrated its superiority to them. Like the O-2 it had two engines, but in tandem, and could fly better on one than could the Super Skymaster. It had better visibility than both, could fire either 28 rockets, four

The Vietnam Era

An OV–10 Bronco.

rockets and eight flares, or a combination of these. The OV–10 cruised at between 150 and 180 knots and could dive at 400 knots. The Bronco also had instruments for night and all-weather flying. One clear advantage was its ability to rendezvous with fighters at 10,000 feet and lead them to the target with little warning to the enemy. Radios allowed the Bronco pilot to talk directly to the DASC as well as to the fighters and ground commanders.[32]

A recurring issue with these light controller planes was their vulnerability to ground fire. As early as 1967 the OH–1s could no longer operate in the demilitarized zone (DMZ) and the Tally Ho region directly to its north. In these highly defended areas the Air Force experimented with using jet planes, initially Misty F–100s and, later, Tiger and Stormy F–4s, to control the armed-reconnaissance and interdiction strikes of the fighter planes.[33] Within South Vietnam, suggestions to arm the controller planes began as early as 1965. Proponents argued that armed forward air control planes would reduce the response time by having these light planes serve as stopgap attack planes until the heavier fighters arrived. They pointed out, further, that many of the calls for close air support were for minor actions against small knots of enemy troops that did not need heavy fighters. Armed small controller planes could hit these small targets, saving the fighters and gunships for larger actions. At first Seventh Air Force, swayed by the argument that armed controllers, who were trained fighter pilots, would forget about directing strikes and be tempted into carrying out the strikes themselves, opposed arming them. This argument had some merit for, despite the ban, some FACs found ways to arm themselves with grenades, machine guns, and rifles.[34]

The advent of the Bronco in Vietnam in 1968 revived the controversy. The OV–10 was an ideal plane to serve as an armed FAC. It was designed to

319

Help from Above

be able to carry four forward-firing M–60 machine guns and 3,600 pounds of ordnance. Tests in III Corps in 1969 showed that armed Broncos responded more quickly to immediate requests than did the strike aircraft. Furthermore, the Broncos handled successfully 80 percent of the requests themselves without the need for fighters. These results led the Seventh Air Force commander, General George S. Brown, to order the arming of all Broncos in Vietnam. By the time the process of arming the Broncos was completed in 1970, however, the policy of Vietnamization was rapidly reducing the U.S. Army's presence in Vietnam.[35]

A more persistent weakness of close air support over the decades had been the Air Force's limited ability to support ground forces at night and in bad weather. In Vietnam, the enemy initially took advantage of this weakness by launching most of his attacks at these times when both FACs and fighters had either to remain on the ground or face obstacles in flight that reduced their effectiveness. One of the more graphic instances of the success of this enemy tactic took place in March 1966, when Viet Cong forces seized a key friendly outpost at A Shau (**Figure 16**). This Vietnamese border camp, which was manned by 210 Vietnamese irregular troops and 10 American advisers, was situated near the Laotian border in I Corps. The post was one of about 50 along the border that served as launching sites for attacks on enemy guerrillas and as stations for keeping an eye on enemy infiltrators from the nearby Ho Chi Minh Trail. For several weeks in February, the Viet Cong and North Vietnamese had been infiltrating soldiers until by the first week in March, 2,000 of them surrounded the camp. On the ninth, under a cloud cover of 500 feet, they attacked, destroying the camp's supply area before retreating. Only one AC–47 gunship was able to penetrate the ceiling later in the morning when the enemy resumed his attack, and it was shot down. The following morning, with a ceiling now down to 200 feet, the enemy flooded into the camp and by noon had taken it. Despite heroic efforts by the individual pilots of a pair of Skyraiders, some C–123s, and a USAF helicopter, the poor weather kept most planes on the ground and was primarily responsible for this serious loss.[36]

One of the most frustrating challenges to those pilots that were able to fly at night and in bad weather was their inability to distinguish friendly troops from enemy targets. Without a visible horizon to use as a reference, air crews were frequently disoriented spatially. Determining closure rates became more difficult and the chances of midair collisions increased.[37]

The Air Force tried a variety of both makeshift and high-tech means to match wits with the enemy. At night and during bad weather, missions were flown under the light of flares dropped from either fixed-wing gunships, fighters, or FAC planes. This was a far from perfect solution to the problem. Flares often blinded the air crews, heightened ground glare, and helped enemy gunners track the fighters. If dropped too high, the flares burned out before being useful. If dropped too low, they did not light up the battlefield. The 2.75-inch smoke

The Vietnam Era

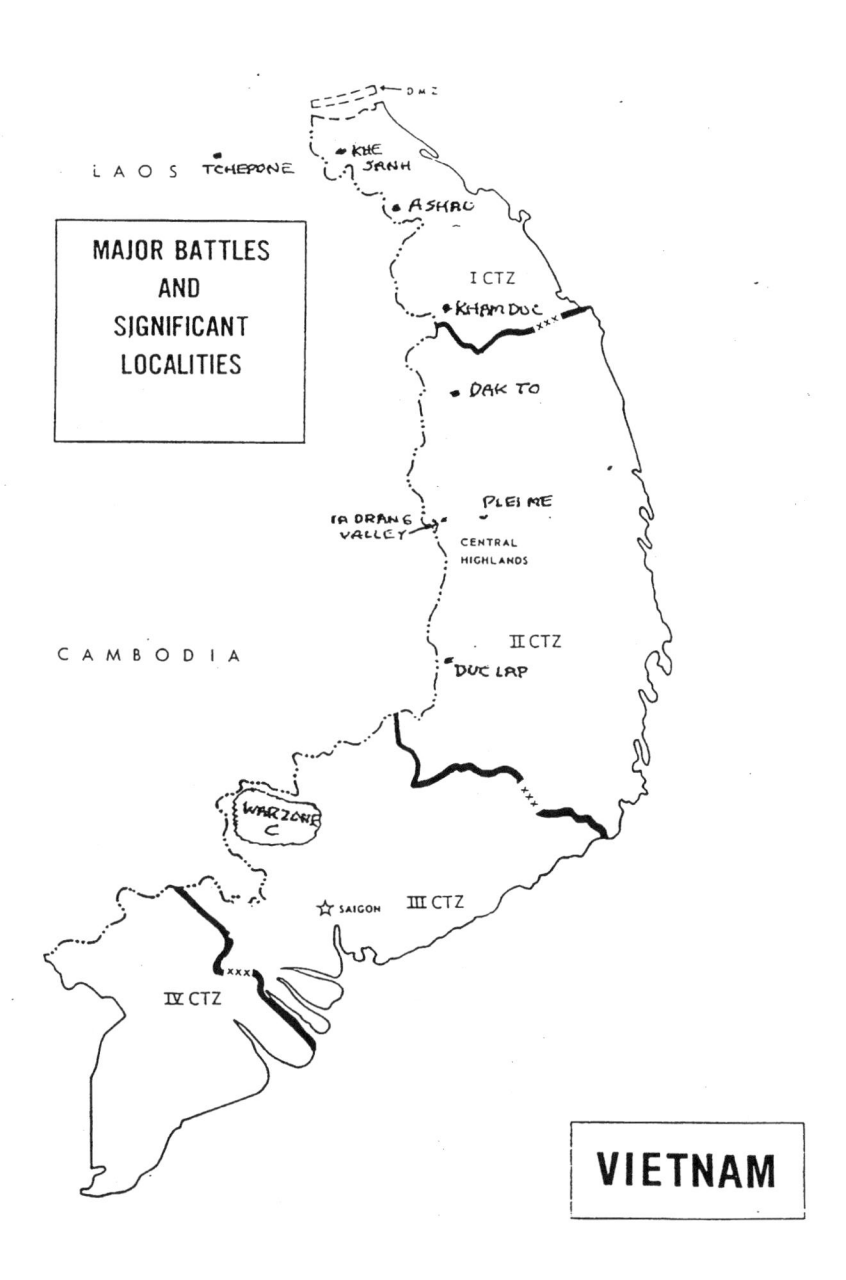

Figure 16
Major Battles and Significant Localities, Vietnam

Help from Above

rocket, which worked well during the day in marking targets with smoke, was useless under the light of the flare because the smoke from the rocket lasted only two or three minutes and often could not be seen at all.

Several experimental attempts to solve the problem met with mixed success. At the urging of one FAC, units of the 1st Cavalry Division began marking their positions with torches fashioned out of 105-mm shell casings. The same units experimented with 50-gallon oil drums cut in half, filled with jellied gasoline, and ignited. Ground marker logs, which were dropped from planes and ignited after hitting the ground, did some good in pinpointing friendly positions, until the resourceful enemy countered by lighting his own fires to confuse the air controller. Some success was achieved by adapting the Army's rifle-mounted starlight scope for use in FAC planes and gunships, and by the middle of 1967, a new starlight scope was installed in the OH–2As and C–123/C–130 flareships.[38]

The most effective attempt to provide close air support around the clock and in bad weather came in the spring of 1966 with the introduction of a ground-controlled radar bombing system called Combat Skyspot or, more frequently, simply Skyspot. For years, the SAC at home had been scoring their simulated bomb runs on a van-mounted computer, the MSQ 35. Weapons ballistic information and target coordinates were entered into the computer and compared with air speed, altitude, and heading information from the plane at the time of the bomb's release to calculate the accuracy of the drop.

A Fairchild C–123 transport.

The Vietnam Era

Experiments using this radar equipment in reverse were successful. Now the plane's air speed, altitude, and heading were entered into the computer to determine the release point of bombs for the target. The Air Force upgraded the radar equipment into an MSQ 77, which had a vastly increased range of 200 miles.

The first Skyspot equipment arrived in Vietnam in March 1966 and was installed at Bien Hoa. Additional Skyspot radars were soon positioned at Pleiku, Dong Ha, and Da Lat, providing coverage of virtually the entire country except the southernmost IV Corps region in the Mekong Delta. During the first year of operation the new system directed more than 1,500 strike sorties, almost all of them by F–100s. Skyspot possessed two advantages over visual, FAC-directed strikes. It proved to be more accurate, allowing pilots to drop bombs closer to friendly units. Second, the pilots could release their ordnance from higher altitudes, well above the range of ground fire.[39] This security from enemy threat increased the pilots' confidence and ability to concentrate on the accuracy of their drops. It also increased the confidence of the supported ground troops.

When bombing under Skyspot control, pilots did not need FACs, who were usually grounded by weather or darkness at any rate. When the bomb run began, the DASC turned the pilot over to a radar controller at the nearest Skyspot site. The radar controller, serving the same function as a FAC, coordinated target information and ordnance types between the pilot and the commander of the requesting ground unit. He then entered flight and target information into his computer. Using the calculations that emerged from this information, the radar controller talked the pilot, who was flying at about 25,000 feet, from the initial point to the bomb release point.[40]

The Skyspot system experienced normal growing pains. Although the radar sets had a range of 200 miles, unreliable UHF radio communications limited their use to about 150 miles. Coverage did not extend to all of the southern corps of Vietnam, and all of IV Corps and part of III Corps depended on the one Skyspot installation at Bien Hoa. At first, only the F–100s at Bien Hoa had the proper beacon transponders to use the system.[41] As additional emergency beacons were rushed to Vietnam, however, this obstacle disappeared. By the end of 1967, B–52s were using Skyspot with pinpoint accuracy to provide close air support to U.S. Army units in South Vietnam.

A dramatic illustration of the success of the new system took place during January, February, and March of the following year. In the process of breaking the enemy's siege of the Marine outpost at Khe Sanh in northwestern I Corps (**Figure 16**), the Air Force flew over 24,000 tactical air sorties, many in close air support, while 2,700 B–52 sorties dropped 110,000 tons of bombs. Because of poor weather, 62 percent of all these strikes were made under the direction of Combat Skyspot.[42]

The presence of B–52 Stratofortresses during the Khe Sanh operation indicates a novel facet of close air support in Vietnam—the use of a strategic

Help from Above

nuclear bomber for close air support and battlefield air interdiction in a nonnuclear, midintensity war. Although the big bombers at Khe Sanh were supporting a Marine outpost rather than a U.S. Army unit, a large majority of its sorties in Southeast Asia were conducted in South Vietnam and most of those were in support of the U.S. Army.

Stratofortresses entered the theater in February 1965 when 30 of them flew from the States to Andersen AFB on the island of Guam, accompanied by an equal number of supporting KC–135 tankers, which landed at both Guam and Okinawa. The planes were sent in anticipation of flying against North Vietnam in retaliation for a murderous Viet Cong raid earlier that month against American soldiers at Pleiku. A State Department objection, that using B–52s against North Vietnam would signal an escalation of the conflict to a level unintended by the American government, kept the planes on the ground on Guam until June, when they were first sent against targets in South Vietnam. It was almost another year, in April 1966, before the B–52s were used over North Vietnam and, after that, only sparingly over that area.

For these nonnuclear, Arc Light missions, as they were called, racks were installed in the bomb bays of the B–52s, which increased their internal load of 500- and 750-pound bombs from 27 to 84. In addition, they carried 24 bombs on wing racks. For the first two years, the bombers flew only from Guam, which involved a round-trip time of 13 hours. With the opening of a second B–52 operation from the U Tapao Royal Thai Air base in Thailand in April 1967, the flight time was reduced to between four and ten hours, and most of the bombers began staging from the new base.

Fifty-four percent of all B–52 sorties flown in Southeast Asia dropped their bombs in South Vietnam. Missions over Laos accounted for another quarter of the sorties, while 13 percent of the sorties were put into Cambodia. A meager six percent joined the bombing campaigns against the north, and 60 percent of these were employed during the 11-day Linebacker II raids in December 1972.[43]

It could be argued that, technically, the majority of the more than 67,000 Arc Light sorties over South Vietnam were close air support flights, since they had to be coordinated with ground operations. Due to the vagaries of the reporting system, however, and the ambiguity surrounding the definitions of some types of missions, it is not possible to posit with any degree of certainty the specific proportion of B–52 missions that were in close air support of ground units vis-à-vis those that were performing battlefield interdiction tasks. Often the two types of missions were indistinguishable. Narrative statements from ground observers suggest that, in some cases, most of these sorties directly assisted ground units in contact with the enemy. Such was the case, for example, during one week of a two-month siege of a Special Forces camp at Ben Het, west of Dak To in western II Corps (**Figure 16**) in June 1969, when most of the 98 flights flown by the B–52s were close air support sorties.[44]

The Vietnam Era

General Westmoreland, and Army commanders whose operations benefitted from the bombers, were generous in their praise of the Arc Light raids. After the war, almost half of 110 Army generals who had commanded units in Vietnam and had voiced their opinion about operations there, rated the B–52s as "very valuable." Another third considered them useful but not vital, while 15 percent said that they were not worth the effort. This divergence is understandable, given the wide variety of operations that were going on simultaneously in different parts of the country. Results of the bombing varied not only from place to place, but from time to time. As one Army general commented:

> In my first tour B–52s were not particularly decisive. They added to our arsenal of weapons significantly but I can't see where they spelled the difference between success and failure in any operation. During my second tour they were decisive and enabled us to stop the advance of the NVA [North Vietnamese Army] toward Hue and to retake Quang Tri in 1972.[45]

Arc Light also contributed indirectly to close air support in Vietnam. Of equal importance with the strikes of the Stratofortresses was the fact that the big bombers could release large numbers of fighters for close air support and battlefield interdiction missions, which was what led to using the strategic bombers in a tactical role in Vietnam in the first place. This was vividly illustrated one day in mid-April, 1965, when the Military Assistance Command, Vietnam (MACV), sent Air Force, Marine, Navy, and Vietnamese tactical fighters on around-the-clock strikes against an enemy base camp in III Corps. For 12 uninterrupted hours the planes mounted over 400 sorties, dropping more than 800 tons of bombs on the small camp. By midafternoon the entire area was engulfed in smoke from bombs and grass fires, making it impossible for later waves of fighters to see targets from the air.[46] Westmoreland was disappointed with this operation. The length of time it took allowed the enemy to flee the area. Too much ordnance was used, and fighters had to be diverted to the area from other air missions, particularly close air support. As a result, B–52s soon took over some of the strikes against base areas, allowing the fighters to concentrate on their more productive close air support missions.

The first Arc Light operation of the war was an interdiction mission flown by 30 B–52s on June 18 against another base camp in III Corps. Later the size of these missions was reduced, usually to six aircraft, as they came to include additional types of operations. The first close air support mission was conducted on November 15 when B–52s were diverted from raids farther south to the Ia Drang Valley. The newly arrived 1st Cavalry Division had chased enemy forces across the valley and into the Chu Pong range near the Cambodian border. While Air Force A–1Es, F–100s, B–57s, and F–4s, and

Help from Above

Marine A–4s helped to hold the enemy at bay, 18 B–52s dropped over 900 bombs on the enemy close to friendly troops.[47] Westmoreland was so satisfied with the big bombers that he ordered daily close air support strikes for the remainder of the operation.[48]

Since the B–52s continued to be responsible for their worldwide nuclear mission of deterrence, SAC retained operational control, through its deputy for operations, of the Arc Light operation in South Vietnam. This represented another instance in Vietnam, along with those of Army helicopters, Marine and Navy aircraft, and Air Force C–130 airlift planes, where an element of air power eluded centralized control by being kept out of Seventh Air Force's tactical air control system. Until January 1967, the SAC exercised its control in Vietnam through a liaison office (SACLO), which after that date, became the Strategic Air Command Advance Echelon (SAC ADVON). This office coordinated all Arc Light and tanker refueling, called Young Tiger, operations with SAC, the 3rd Air Division on Guam, which had the planes, and some offices of Seventh Air Force and MACV.

The SAC ADVON's point of contact with Seventh Air Force was with the Bomber Plans Branch of the latter's TACC. Here advance echelon representatives coordinated with Seventh Air Force officers in order to receive tactical support for the Arc Light strikes and to integrate the Arc Light flights into the dense air traffic over Vietnam.[49] In short, Seventh Air Force, having no role in selecting targets or controlling the big bombers, was limited to coordinating the bomber's flights with other tactical missions being flown in the country and to protecting the Stratofortresses.[50]

The Army thought more highly of the Arc Light program than did many in the Air Force.[51] Strategic Air Command was concerned lest the use of the planes for tactical, conventional missions interfere with their primary mission of nuclear readiness and airborne alert. Several times the command requested that the planes be returned to their home bases in the United States. General Momyer, the Seventh Air Force commander between 1966 and 1969, considered the B–52 missions to be an inefficient use of air power. While SAC relied on the principle of centralization of air power to keep its planes from falling under MACV, Momyer used the same principle to argue that the Arc Light operations should be folded into the Tactical Air Control System in Vietnam. Since the B–52s were being used the same way as were his tactical planes, they should follow the same rules. The commander closest to the battlefield should decide which types of planes, B–52s or fighter-bombers, was better suited for particular targets. Momyer deemed it wasteful to use B–52s as long-range artillery against suspected, and often questionable, enemy supply areas rather than to employ them selectively and in moderation against specific targets.[52]

The Air Force relied on the elements of this tactical air control system to perform a variety of close air support functions for the U.S. Army in Vietnam.

The Vietnam Era

Its fighters, bombers, and gunships, under the direction of FACs or ground radar, helped defend Army Special Forces camps and other defended outposts and villages, provided close air support strikes to back up infantry units on search and destroy missions, prepared landing zones for Army helicopters, and kept them free of enemy soldiers during landings and extractions. The aircraft also escorted Army helicopters, ground convoys, and marching troops, provided fighter cover and resupply for long- and short-range American reconnaissance patrols, and struck enemy units that were outside the reach of American artillery. Besides the thousands of small, often undramatic, close air support missions, two types of operations best illustrate the effectiveness of fixed-wing aircraft in the close air support role: the defense of special forces camps and villages against enemy attacks or their evacuation when defense was impossible, and the support of U.S. Army ground operations against an entrenched or threatening enemy.

Air Force participation in defending or evacuating special forces camps typifies the tactics, techniques, and effectiveness of close air support. Along with the South Vietnamese, the United States built a string of fortified camps in remote areas along South Vietnam's western border astride infiltration routes from Laos and Cambodia. These posts were manned by between 200 and 400 irregular South Vietnam Montagnard troops, who were advised and supported logistically by a small team of highly trained U.S. Army Special Forces troops. The camps kept an eye on communist infiltrators and sent out patrols to intercept and ambush them. Soldiers from the camps also protected the inhabitants of local villages, most of whom were made up of their families and relatives. Isolated as they were, one of the camps' main sources of contact with the outside world was through the FACs.

The first major enemy assault against one of these camps after the arrival of American ground forces occurred in October 1965, with a 10-day siege of a Special Forces outpost and its attached village at Plei Me in the central highlands, south of Pleiku and 20 miles from the Cambodian border (**Figure 16**). The attack was conceived by its North Vietnamese commander as a prelude to a full-scale autumn invasion of South Vietnam, an invasion that was to be followed by a drive to the coast to cut the country in half before the newly arrived American airmobile 1st Cavalry Division could become sufficiently organized to thwart it.

In the evening of October 19, a combined enemy force of two North Vietnamese regiments, a heavy mortar battalion, an antiaircraft battalion, and a Viet Cong battalion, attacked the fort from the north.[53] For five days and nights FACs directed A–1Es, B–57s, F–100s, and F–8s in raining general-purpose and fragmentation bombs, napalm, rockets, cluster bomb units, and 20-mm cannon fire on enemy positions as close as 35 meters from the outpost's walls. At night, AC–47 gunships dropped flares and fired their miniguns against the attackers. The enemy broke contact on the twenty-fourth and for

Help from Above

five more days the planes undertook an around-the-clock interdiction role, blocking enemy withdrawal routes and concentration points. By October 29 the enemy was completely routed and withdrew into the Chu Pong mountains, which form the border with Cambodia.[54]

Of the 696 strike sorties flown in and around Plei Me, 585 were mounted by the Air Force. Within the short span of 10 days the enemy had absorbed 866,000 pounds of general-purpose bombs, over 250,000 pounds of fragmentation bombs, close to 486,000 pounds of napalm, plus rockets, CBUs, and machine gun fire.[55] The successful defense of Plei Me from the air convinced many, including General Westmoreland, that the Tactical Air Control System could be used to place massive amounts of ordnance on pinpoint targets in support of ground forces. The subsequent American pursuit of the fleeing enemy in the Ia Drang Valley campaign was the first instance in the war where the allied forces followed up their defeat of an enemy force.

Before the advent of Skyspot, fighters found it difficult to defend the camps against enemy attack when the weather was bad. Such was the case with the loss of the A Shau camp and valley in March 1966 (**Figure 16**). Three days of poor weather and very low ceilings prevented adequate air strikes and resupply in what General Westmoreland called the most significant setback of the year.[56]

In some cases the American and South Vietnamese forces did not wait for a strike on a camp but hit the gathering enemy before he could attack. In October 1967, four North Vietnamese regiments began moving toward Dak To, a special forces camp and complex in Kontum Province, north of Pleiku and 20 miles inside South Vietnam from the point where the joint Laotian/Cambodian border abuts South Vietnam (**Figure 16**). The allies responded by sending what eventually amounted to three American brigades and six Vietnamese battalions into the area. Before the enemy could launch his attack, the Americans and South Vietnamese had established artillery fire-support bases and attacked the infiltrators.[57]

The American portion of the operation took place in separate hills around the camp. Triple canopy hindered both ground and air forces. The enemy hugged American troops, making the use of heavy ordnance and antipersonnel cluster bombs dangerous to the friendly troops. Nevertheless, nearly 2,100 close air support sorties using largely napalm, 750-pound bombs, and 20-mm cannons, were instrumental in turning back the North Vietnamese. Air strikes accounted for one-third of the estimated 1,600 enemy dead and were a major factor in stopping the four enemy regiments and driving them back across the border.[58]

In one typical close air support operation during the campaign, air strikes extricated a U.S. Army company that was surrounded by the North Vietnamese. On November 6, 1966 when the enemy converged on the besieged company with automatic weapons, the company commander called for air strikes. Within

The Vietnam Era

15 minutes two F–4s arrived with napalm and 750-pound bombs, set up corridors of napalm 75 meters east and west of the besieged company, and then dropped their bombs on the enemy close to the friendly positions. During a subsequent attack by an enemy company, the FAC, ignoring the cardinal rule of always delivering ordnance parallel to friendly forces, ran a set of F–4s directly at the friendly positions, dropping napalm within 20 meters of the troops. After the enemy retreated, the company commander reported that the napalm routed the enemy and "left only fifteen charred bodies as evidence."[59]

In the largest wartime defense of a border camp against infiltrating North Vietnamese, at Khe Sanh (**Figure 16**) early in 1968, air power was used to support U.S. Marines rather than American army units. Yet one of the principal outcomes of this successful defense of this outpost was the introduction of a more effective system for controlling close air support operations—a system that would benefit the U.S. Army in the future in the northern reaches of the country.

Until late in 1967, the northernmost tactical zone in South Vietnam, I Corps, was essentially the province of the U.S. Marines. Since Marine ground troops performed virtually all of the ground operations in the area, they employed their own air doctrine, which restricted the use of their air-

A Marine with an M–16 rifle.

Help from Above

craft to the support of their own troops. Despite much importuning by General Westmoreland and his air deputy, General Momyer, the Marines continued, over the years, to deny MACV the use of their planes for the close air support of units outside the corps' boundaries. Starting late in 1967, however, U.S Army troops began to enter I Corps in large numbers, and by the following April, Army battalions outnumbered Marine battalions 30 to 24.[60] The situation had clearly changed and the control arrangements for close air support had to change with it. The defense of the base at Khe Sanh provided Westmoreland and Momyer the opportunity to bring about that change.

An air campaign, called Operation Niagara, was carried out between January 22 and March 31, 1968, in northwestern I Corps and the neighboring areas of Laos, to frustrate an anticipated major enemy offensive. The Marine outpost at Khe Sanh was at the hub of the expected enemy invasion, lying directly in the path of North Vietnamese units that were bypassing the DMZ to the west when passing from North to South Vietnam. The base was valuable as a jumping off point for allied ground operations against these infiltration routes as well as for attacks on North Vietnamese supply areas across the Laotian border. General Westmoreland decided to hold it.

By January 1968, two enemy divisions were in the immediate vicinity of Khe Sanh, with a third division in reserve a short distance away. Inside the base, which had earlier been an Army Special Forces camp, were three Marine infantry battalions, totaling about 6,000 men, and an artillery battalion of 18 105-mm howitzers, six 155-mm howitzers, and six mortars. The Army built a 1,500-foot airstrip within the perimeter. By the end of March, when the North Vietnamese abandoned attempts to seize the base, Air Force, Navy, and

An XM–198 155-mm howitzer.

The Vietnam Era

Marine tactical planes dropped 40,000 tons of bombs on communist positions, B–52s added another 60,000 tons, while Air Force planes dropped 12,000 tons of supplies into the beleaguered outpost to sustain it during the continuous shellings and probing attacks.[61]

General Momyer, who was responsible for coordinating and directing all air resources in Operation Niagara, made it clear at the outset of the operation that close air support would receive the first priority for aircraft. In his orders concerning the battle for Khe Sanh he noted that:

> we must provide close air support to troops who are in contact. It doesn't matter where this is. These requirements will be met above all others. I construe troops in contact to also include helicopters, AC–47s, or any other air vehicle which is engaging enemy troops.[62]

Despite his responsibility for all air resources in the operation, Momyer was not given operational control of the Marine planes of the 1st Marine Aircraft Wing when the campaign began. Westmoreland, reluctant to resurrect the high-level roles and missions arguments that were sure to follow the appointment of a single air manager, decided to move cautiously. At first, instead of transferring operational control of all aircraft to his Deputy for Air, General Momyer, he agreed to a compromise, linking the Air Force and Marine control mechanisms in an Airborne C–130 Battlefield Command and Control Center (ABCCC). This arrangement allowed the Marines to keep control of all the air strikes in those sectors closest to the Khe Sanh base, while "other air resources took on more distant targets."[63]

This arrangement interfered seriously, however, with the Air Force's responsibility for the air campaign. The Air Force was unable to integrate the Marine planes into the overall air campaign because Marine airmen, disregarding the airborne control center, fought their own private war over and near the base. In addition to the problems encountered by close air support operations, the system failed to provide integrated reconnaissance on the status of enemy forces.

Finally, early in March, Westmoreland convinced the Joint Chiefs and his superiors in Hawaii that the changed situation in I Corps demanded centralization of all air assets in his and General Momyer's hands.[64] Admiral Ulysses S. Grant Sharp, Jr., Commander in Chief, Pacific, approved of the single-manager concept, but with two amendments: that in emergencies the Marines be relieved of the requirement of going through Seventh Air Force in Saigon for their close air support, and that the Marines have the right to appeal any decisions they believed detrimental to the effectiveness of their operations.[65]

It was not until the last week in March, after 85 percent of the Operation Niagara sorties had already been flown, that the new single-manager concept

Help from Above

became fully operational. Therefore, its effect on the campaign was minimal. The idea was further watered down by the Marines' success in having the unified manager concept recognized as applicable only to the Khe Sanh operation and as not necessarily providing a precedent for future campaigns.[66] Conceptually, however, it gave an important boost to the Air Force's traditional contention that close air support and other forms of air power were more effective when directed by a centralized mind that comprehended the big picture than when controlled by a profusion of scattered agencies that lacked the panoramic view.

Within several weeks the new system of control passed its first test at Kham Duc (**Figure 16**), the last remaining outpost in I Corps, south of Khe Sanh. Early on May 12 General Westmoreland, convinced that the special forces camp possessed neither the importance nor the "defensive potential" of Khe Sanh,[67] ordered its 1,700 Americans and Vietnamese to evacuate the camp. Two hundred and seventy-two of these were Vietnamese dependents, the remainder were American Army, Marine, and Air Force personnel, including engineers, advisors, and Vietnamese Montagnard soldiers. Included was a battalion task force of 600 U.S. Army troops from the American division that had been flown into the camp two days earlier.[68]

Two North Vietnamese regiments had battered the camp with heavy mortar and recoilless rifle fire for several days. The camp's inhabitants survived these attacks, however, largely due to the air support they received from AC–47 gunships and tactical fighter sorties. On the twelfth, firepower from tactical fighter planes permitted Army and Marine helicopters and Air Force C–130s to fly over 1,400 people out of the camp. In its first important exercise of the newly approved single-manager concept, an ABCCC C–130 orchestrated the operation by controlling the air-refueling tankers, assigning parking orbits to fighters awaiting their turn to strike, and handing off the fighters to the FACs. All told, during the day, the C–130 integrated about 16 Marine A–6D sorties, at least two Navy fighter flights, six F–5 sorties from the Vietnamese Air Force, and more than 120 USAF sorties into a smooth operation.[69] Although the ABCCC had no control over or contact with Army and Marine helicopters or the ground commander, its success in coordinating Marine and Air Force fighters with a large number of FACs led General Momyer to declare the operation "the real test of the single management system."[70]

Later that year, in August, a special forces complex at Duc Lap (**Figure 16**), near Ban Me Thuot in II Corps, came under attack by 4,000 North Vietnamese regular soldiers of the 1st Division. Most of the 2,500 defenders were paramilitary Montagnards, reinforced by two battalions of South Vietnamese regulars and advised by U.S. Green Berets. The onset of the attack on the 23d triggered an immediate air reaction. Fortunately, the commander of the parent Vietnamese division had established an operations center at his

The Vietnam Era

headquarters consisting of a TACP, U.S. Army G–3 and G–3 Air officers, and artillery and intelligence advisors.

The Air Force's ALO at the division took immediate charge of the close air support of the beleaguered camp. He directed that two airborne FACs be in the area during all daylight hours until relieved by night-flying gunships, and that fighters arrive every 20 to 25 minutes. The FACs directed 392 fighter sorties, 100 gunship sorties, adjusted artillery more than 50 times, and directed fire suppression from six helilifts. After two days, the enemy broke off his attempt to take the camp, persuaded to withdraw by 581,000 pounds of bombs, 485,000 pounds of napalm, 200,000 pounds of cluster bombs, 1,140 rockets, and 36,000 rounds of ammunition.

The senior Army adviser at Duc Lap, in attributing the successful defense of the camp to the excellent coordination of close air support, noted:

> I've never seen closer cooperation between the TAC Air and ground forces than was exhibited at Duc Lap and I think that is one reason it is still in existence today. Had it not been for the job done by TAC Air and by the Spooky [gunship] operations at night, I'm sure this outpost would have gone down.... The coordination was primarily carried on by our ALO.... I've never seen a better performance by any portion of the Armed Forces.[71]

In addition to helping defend its border posts, Air Force close air support contributed in a major way to the Army's search and destroy missions and their

A drawing of a Lockheed C–130.

Help from Above

sweeps against the enemy throughout South Vietnam. During the first major American ground battle, late in 1965, against communist units in the Ia Drang Valley (**Figure 16**) following the breaking of the siege of Plei Me, Air Force tactical fighters added 753 close air support and interdiction sorties and 96 sorties by B–52s to the considerable firepower of the newly deployed 1st Cavalry Division. The battle occupied almost the entire month of November, during which American forces inflicted heavy casualties and drove the tattered remnants of three enemy regiments back across the border into Cambodia. Although Air Force airlift planes provided the most dramatic and critical assistance to the airmobile division, flying over 5,000 sorties to deliver fuel and supplies after Army helicopters and Caribous had to be diverted from these missions to transport troops, close air support strikes proved valuable in keeping the enemy off balance, severely depleting his units, and forcing his retreat across the border. After the battle several battalion commanders commented on the important role of tactical fighter strikes. The use of so much Air Force tactical air led General Westmoreland to wonder, following this first combat test of the airmobility concept, whether the airmobile division had enough inherent firepower to carry out search and destroy missions by itself. As we have seen, the division commander concluded, essentially, that it did not, and that both Air Force and Army close air support resources had to be combined to make the airmobile idea effective.[72]

The Ia Drang battle was dwarfed, in the spring of 1967, by a massive sweep of 35,000 allied soldiers into War Zone C (**Figure 16**), aimed at clearing out this major enclave northwest of Saigon that the enemy had long been using as a jumping off point for attacks throughout III Corps, as a logistic support base, a training center, a rest camp, and a hospital. The campaign, called Junction City, entailing the equivalent of more than two divisions on each side, unfolded in five phases, each featuring critical battles in which tactical fighters, flying immediate and diverted close air support missions, were major factors in turning a potential disaster into an allied victory. All told, between the first week in February and May 14, Air Force fighters flew 5,000 sorties, with B–52s adding 126 more.[73] Over 2,700 enemy soldiers died, and hundreds of base camps, defensive positions, supply depots, and training areas were destroyed. In a later summation of his experience during the campaign as assistant commander of the U.S. 1st Infantry Division, one of the two American divisions involved in Junction City, Gen. Bernard W. Rogers recorded the importance of Air Force close air support to the success of the operation:

> Another outstanding aspect of…Junction City was the close air support provided by the Air Force; it was typical of the support the Air Force always gave the Big Red One, the only outfit for which I can speak authoritatively. The short reaction time; the intense desire of the forward air controller—

and the pilots of the flight he was directing—to put the ordnance exactly on the spot desired by the ground commander; the ability to bring in air strikes at night under artificial illumination where one slight mistake in depth perception meant 'so long,' were all capabilities which left a lasting impression upon us infantrymen. Surely there were occasions when the flight arrived over the target without the kind of ordnance requested, but not often. I could not be more outspoken in my praise for the professionalism displayed by the supporting Air Force personnel.[74]

With the cessation of large-scale sweeps and search and destroy missions, and the shift toward Vietnamization of the war after the Tet upheavals in the spring of 1968, close air support missions decreased and reverted to smaller operations in support of a dwindling U.S. Army presence, and to training the Vietnamese Air Force.

On the whole most Army generals surveyed after the war, 64 percent were satisfied with the quantity of Air Force close air support they had received during the conflict. Surprisingly, a substantial minority, 28 percent, felt that there was too much reliance on air strikes. This opinion would seem to be part of a larger dissatisfaction with the use of firepower in general, including not only aerial firepower but artillery that, in the view of many, was excessive given the nature of the war. But, in general, those who had first hand experience with the Air Force's close air support operations were satisfied that they received the support they requested. General John J. Tolson, a former Director of Army Aviation and a commander of the 1st Cavalry Division in Vietnam, praised the "magnificent support that the Air Force provided, and the trust and confidence that was generated in the minds of every major ground commander." In his experience in Vietnam, "the close integration and timing of Air Force support to the organic Army support could not have been improved."[75]

Armed Helicopters Also Legitimized

While Air Force support operations in Vietnam were justifying the Strike Command's 1963 validation of the Air Force concept of close air support, the U.S. Army was simultaneously increasing the number of its own close air support armed helicopters in Vietnam. The Army referred to this mission of these helicopters as *direct aerial fire support* (DAFS), rather than as *close air support*. The service's adoption of this terminology, far from being merely an exercise in semantics, was doctrinally grounded and based on several assumptions. First, the close air support its armed helicopters provided, whether as

Help from Above

armed gunship escorts for its transport helicopters, as aerial rocket artillery, or as air cavalry, was, in its view, simply another type of Army combat support, comparable to that provided by artillery, which had always been referred to as fire support. Since armed helicopters, in the Army view, served the same purpose as other forms of fire support, the same label was deemed appropriate.

Second, the use of the term *direct aerial fire support* reflected the strong doctrinal conviction on the part of most ground commanders that what the armed helicopters were doing was generically different from what the Air Force *close air support* missions were providing. Army aviators at all levels had been working for years to acquire tactical air resources they could control and, prior to Vietnam, had realized considerable success in the areas of aerial transportation and reconnaissance. They accomplished this by convincing Secretary McNamara that a gap existed[76] between their "reasonable" tactical needs, which the Air Force was required by the DOD Directive to satisfy,[77] and the Air Force's ability (or willingness) to carry out this responsibility. Since it was up to the Army to decide which of its needs were "reasonable," the way was cleared for it to expand its aerial resources by adjusting upward its subjective evaluation of what was "reasonable." In Vietnam, the movement to gain control of aerial assets progressed from the fields of transportation and reconnaissance into that of close air support.

A final reason why the Army found it advantageous to refer to the operations of its armed helicopters as *direct aerial fire support*, rather than as *close air support*, was to avoid running afoul of the numerous roles and missions agreements and directives that, since 1947, clearly assigned the close air support mission to the Air Force and specifically prohibited the Army from duplicating any of the missions of its sister service. Disregard of the close air support stipulations of these directives by Secretary McNamara, and in some instances positive statements to the effect that he did not intend to be limited by them, encouraged the Army to consider them dead letters. This was particularly true of the 1957 DOD Directive 5160.22. Following the secretary's example, for instance, the Army Chief of Force Development admitted in 1965 that the entire Howze Board proceedings and the airmobility concept were in violation of that directive. This did not matter, however, since the Army did not feel bound by what "a piece of paper said twenty years ago."[78] By adopting the term *direct aerial fire support*, and defining it as something different from *close air support*, the Army could avoid the complex doctrinal entanglements that were certain to flow from what would appear to be a contravention of the roles and missions agreements.

The Army moved early in Vietnam to assure control of its helicopters. It was strongly assisted in this by the command and control system it developed virtually single-handedly for the country. The Military Assistance Command, Vietnam, or MACV, which controlled military activity in the theater, was a subunified command subordinate to the unified Pacific Com-

The Vietnam Era

mand in Hawaii. The position of MACV commander was designated to be filled by an Army general who, according to the organizational rules ordained for a unified command, was to act independently of his own service and upon the advice of, and after consultation with, the component commanders of the services engaged in the conflict—in this case the Army, the Navy, and the Air Force. This arrangement was designed to ensure that a unified commander operated as an autonomous and objective arbiter between the often competing requirements, strategies, and ambitions of the participating services.

General Paul D. Harkins, the first MACV commander, as well as his successor General Westmoreland, did not, however, name a separate Army component commander. Instead, they assumed for themselves leadership of the Army's component command, the U.S. Army, Vietnam, which they added to their responsibilities atop the unified command. As a result, the operations of the two commands, unified and Army component, became intermingled. The MACV staff, to a large extent, reflected the personnel doctrine and methods of the Army, while the Air Force and the Navy, including their doctrines and techniques, were afforded token roles in the planning and conduct of military operations.

From the beginning, this organizational arrangement helped the Army counter Air Force efforts to exercise the control over aerial resources legally assigned to it, particularly control of close air support resources and operations. As the Army was starting to introduce helicopters into Vietnam at the end of 1961, measures taken by the Air Force commander there, Brig. Gen. Rollin H. Anthis, to abide by the agreements assigning him responsibility for close air support were countermanded by the MACV. Late in 1962 Anthis issued a document assigning fighter-bombers the responsibility for protecting Army helicopters en route to and from their landing zones, except during the final minute before landing and the one minute before extraction, when the armed helicopters could engage targets.[79] The thrust of the memo was that helicopters were to act only defensively. In the middle of the following year, Anthis complained to MACV that Army helicopters were being used for close air support and that requests from Army units in the field for Air Force support, which should have been passed on to the Air Force through its Air Support Operations Center (ASOC) in Saigon, were often intercepted at higher Army headquarters and filled by Army resources. Military Assistance Command, Vietnam replied to this bid by the Air Force commander to centralize air assets with a reiteration of Army doctrine:

> …all incidents mentioned occurred in the immediate battle areas of the ground units. These are not subjects for ASOC/TOC coordination but rather matters for the ground commander to handle as he deems appropriate. Direct support aviation is controlled by the ground element command-

er and requires no supervision or control by a tactical air control system far removed from the ground battle.[80]

This early reference to helicopters as "direct support aviation" and the separation of helicopter operations out from under the Air Force's Tactical Air Control System assured that the Army would control all helicopter missions throughout the war, whether for airlift, reconnaissance, or close air support.

Efforts by the Air Force Chief of Staff, General McConnell, to limit the spread of Army helicopters in Vietnam were to no avail. In the summer of 1965, shortly after assuming leadership of the Air Force, he strongly dissented from the other chiefs' decision to send the airmobile division to Vietnam. That spring, the South Vietnamese army had suffered a string of defeats that convinced General Westmoreland that the enemy was about to cut the country in two at its narrow waist in II Corps. The Joint Chiefs met to consider his June request for additional troops, including the airmobile division that had been tested unilaterally, then partially disbanded, and was at the time being reassembled. Over the objections of the other chiefs, McConnell opposed sending the division until air power had been given an opportunity to knock out the North Vietnamese.

McConnell's main concern was with how the Air Force could provide close air support to the division in Vietnam. He doubted that, as envisioned, its organic airmobile resources could themselves support the division over lines of communication that would have to run from the coast through hostile territory to the division's proposed inland base. Since the division had not held joint tests with the Air Force, the chief had little idea what kind of close air, airlift, and reconnaissance support the Army would need from the Air Force. McConnell's discomfiture stemmed from the Army's view of airmobility as an internal, unilateral affair, a view that excluded the Air Force from participating in a joint evaluation of its capability. The Army had reiterated this position by declaring, at the time of the cancellation of the proposed joint Gold Fire II airmobility test, that it learned all it needed to know and that joint testing was unnecessary. The Strike Command director, Army Gen. Paul D. Adams, agreed that this appeared to be the Army's interpretation, but he did not agree that joint testing was not needed. After stating that a joint field test was essential for evaluating the suitability of airmobility in joint operations, he noted:

> The Army reflects overriding interest in airmobility as a unilateral rather than a joint matter...I have had the impression, in this connection, that the Army views its concept and that of the Air Force as involving two different things. On the one hand, the Army desires fullest support by the Air Force, and

The Vietnam Era

>acknowledges need for appropriate coordination and control measures.... On the other hand the Army, from our [Strike Command] viewpoint, looks upon development of airmobile units as an internal undertaking largely divorced from joint consideration.
>
>This approach does not, in my estimation, contribute to an Army posture designed to simplify joint operations and facilitate their support...[81]

Despite his agreement with General Adams over the inadvisability of inserting the airmobile division into a joint operation at that time, McConnell drew silent stares from the other service chiefs at a meeting in late June 1965 when he told them that they would be criminally responsible if they recommended sending the division to Vietnam without tethering it to the coast with secure links. At a subsequent session, when asked how the Air Force would support the division if it were sent inland, the Air Force chief replied that it would not have to be supplied for long since it would soon be destroyed by the Viet Cong.[82] McConnell's objections to the airmobile idea and stated preference for using a standard ROAD division supported by Air Force aircraft reflected the long-standing Air Force perception that the Army, in its eagerness to go it alone, had consistently failed, when planning for joint operations, to factor in Air Force tactical air resources and their assigned roles.

Over the objections of the Air Force chief, the 1st Cavalry Division (Airmobile), with its 434 aircraft (**Figure 17**), arrived in Vietnam in September 1965, and by November was engaged in its first action against the Viet Cong in the Ia Drang Valley of II Corps (**Figure 16**). In this month-long series of battles, the division, strongly supported by Air Force fighters, bombers, gunships, and transports, killed almost 2,000 of the enemy, forcing his retreat across the border into Cambodia.[83]

The success of this initial operation in halting the enemy and disabusing him of his belief that American forces were unwilling and unable to fight, and the manner in which this result was achieved, reinforced the conviction among Air Force commanders that major airmobile operations could not be conducted successfully without the support of non-organic, non-Army airlift and fighter planes. The Army's airlift helicopters proved inadequate for the task. After the first several days the supply of helicopter aviation fuel, which was supposed to be airlifted by organic helicopters, was so depleted that the division commander, Maj. Gen. Harry O. Kinnard, called on the Air Force for assistance. The division's logistics officer later admitted that without the resulting steady stream of emergency deliveries to forward bases by Air Force C–123s and C–130s, "we would have had to grind to a halt for lack of fuel."[84] In the close air support area, Air Force fighter-bombers flew 753, and B–52 bombers

Help from Above

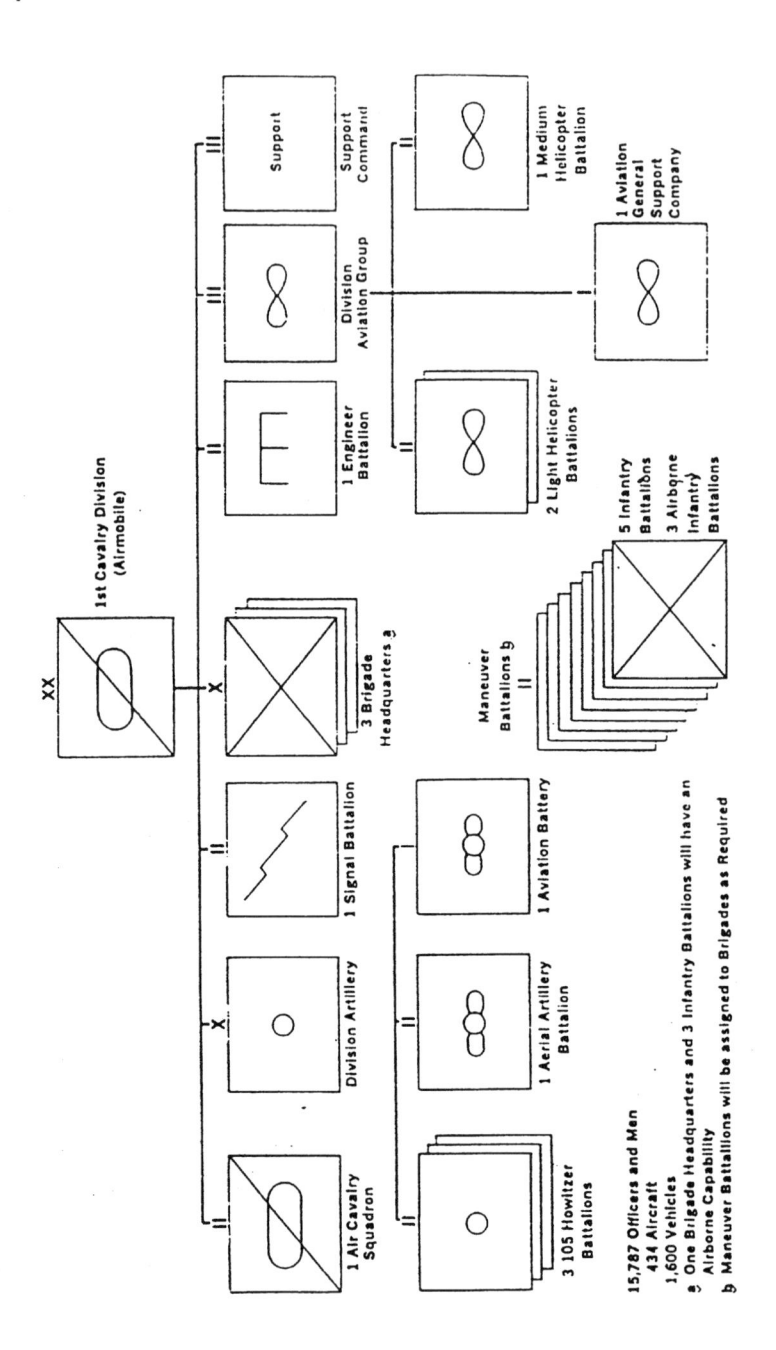

FIGURE 17
1st Cavalry Division (Airmobile) Organization

The Vietnam Era

96, sorties. After the dust settled, General Kinnard in December 1965 concluded that an airmobile division had even greater need of Air Force close air support, airlift, and reconnaissance aircraft than did other Army divisions.[85]

To the Army, Kinnard's conclusion was consistent with its view that Air Force close air and other tactical air support was something generically different from the battlefield support that armed helicopters and airlift and reconnaissance rotary-wing vehicles provided to the division. It was in no way an admission of the inadequacy of these organic planes. Air Force commanders, on the other hand, who recognized no difference between the close air support missions performed by fighter-bombers and the direct aerial fire support provided by helicopters, saw this conclusion as an admission of a defect in the airmobile concept. This impression was heightened when Westmoreland, commenting on the campaign, questioned whether the airmobile division as then constituted had enough firepower and endurance for the Vietnam mission.[86]

One fact was incontrovertible—despite room for improvement in their techniques and equipment, helicopters were there to stay. They were too numerous and too integrated into the Army's force structure to encourage continued efforts to remove them. It was in recognition of this *fait accompli* that General McConnell, the following spring, made a highly controversial agreement with the Army Chief of Staff, Gen. Harold K. Johnson, that revised the aviation roles and missions for their respective services.

Following a series of personal negotiating sessions, the two chiefs on April 6, 1966, unveiled an agreement on a new division of labor between fixed-wing aircraft and helicopters.[87] Henceforth, the Army would have the primary claim on helicopters and the Air Force on fixed-wing planes. The Air Force surrendered all claims to helicopters for close air support, intratheater movement, and resupply of Army forces. The Army, on the other hand, gave up its title for the present and the future to operating fixed-wing planes, such as the Caribou, which were competing with the Air Force's C–123s and C–130s in Vietnam, the Mohawk, and the next generation Buffalo. Both services, stated the accord, would work jointly to develop vertical takeoff and landing (VTOL) planes. To take some of the sting out of this Solomonic division, the chiefs allowed some minor exceptions. The Air Force could continue to employ helicopters on special warfare missions and for search and rescue. The Army could keep some of its small fixed-wing planes for administrative flights. As a small bow to the Army's desire for control, it was agreed that, when the unified theater commander deemed it advisable, Air Force troop-lift planes could be attached to ground commands.[88]

While the Air Force's main objective in this agreement was to curb the Army's growing fixed-wing force, which in Vietnam alone numbered 96 small CV–7 airlift Caribous and the 56 fixed-wing reconnaissance planes, the implications were far broader, particularly for close air support. When the agreement was signed, the United States had close to 1,800 helicopters in Vietnam,

Help from Above

most of them employed by the Army both in the airmobile division and in nondivisional groups and battalions. Attack helicopters were averaging over 27,000 sorties per month, nearly three times the number of fixed-wing attack sorties.[89] McConnell acknowledged the existence of these close air support helicopters as an accomplished fact, one that the Air Force could hardly undo. In his estimation, however, it could contain the spread of the Army's armed fixed-wing planes (including transports), like the Mohawk, that were gradually acquiring close air support capabilities akin to those of Air Force aircraft.

Neither chief found it easy to sign this compromise. Those Army aviators who had fought so hard to create not only a helicopter close air support capability, but a fixed-wing one as well, felt that Johnson was unnecessarily sacrificing the latter. Others doubted the strength of Johnson's commitment to Army aviation. Earlier, as commander of the Command and General Staff College, he was reported to have eliminated Army aviation departments in the school. His exasperation with the inordinate amount of time he had to spend defending the Army's use of armed Mohawk planes against the other chiefs was well known. Most Army officers, however, seemed willing, however grudgingly, to accept the decision, since it also gave the Army control over the close air support functions of their armed helicopters, the Hueys, the Cobras, and later, it was hoped, the planned Cheyenne.[90] A leading advocate of Army organic aviation, for example, came to terms with the agreement by reasoning that it was quite possible that the compromise prevented "an all-out battle on the very right of the Army to own any aircraft."[91]

General McConnell also faced formidable opposition from some of his staff, who continued to feel strongly about preventing further scattering of the nation's military air resources. It still rankled many that there were separate air forces in the Navy and Marines, and that the Army's air force was expanding. McConnell's focus, however, was pragmatic. He concentrated primarily on the Army's increasing airlift capability, aware that if he were unable to reach an accord with the Army, the simmering controversy over roles and missions would likely be decided by the Secretary of Defense, a prospect that, in the context of the time, was uninviting. He also firmly believed, based on wide-ranging input from Vietnam, that the Air Force's control of all fixed-wing airlift would enhance America's conduct of the war.[92]

Given this potential opposition, both chiefs met without fanfare for several months before reaching the accord. They briefed only a handful of people on their respective staffs, and discouraged proposals or amendments from them. When the Air Force chief sent a draft of the final agreement to staff members, he accompanied it with a warning that anyone who attempted to change the meaning of the agreement would be fired.[93]

This accord represented the Magna Carta of Army helicopters as close air support vehicles. By the end of 1969, at its peak, there were over 6,400 helicopters in Vietnam, 3,600 of which were armed attack aircraft. In December of

The Vietnam Era

that year, attack helicopters flew 80,734 sorties, a record number that began to drop the following month as Vietnamization took hold. In 1966, at the time of the accord, attack helicopters flew 2 1/2 times as many sorties as did fixed-wing attack planes. By 1970 the difference had increased to 10 times.[94] Given the dissimilarity in flight durations and in the method of counting sorties between helicopters and fixed-wing planes, these figures do not present a useful picture of the relative weight of effort between fixed-wing aircraft and helicopters. The figures can be used only to illustrate in a general way that helicopters had taken their place alongside fixed-wing planes in the close air support role.

Army helicopters in Vietnam were organized in one of two ways. Either they were integral parts of an airmobile division or they were assigned to aviation brigades for use by nonairmobile divisions and smaller units. All Army divisions in Vietnam had, as an integral part of their force, some aviation resources. Each of the two airmobile divisions there—the 1st Cavalry and, later, the 101st Airborne—had about 434 aircraft as part of its permanent force. Within each division, these aircraft, mostly helicopters, were organized into an assigned aviation group containing three aviation battalions, two or three assigned aviation companies, and an indefinite number of attached (borrowed) companies, such as aerial weapons and assault helicopter companies. Each of the six other nonairmobile, standard ROAD infantry divisions (or their equivalents) in Vietnam had between 85 and 100 helicopters and fixed-wing aircraft, whose companies belonged to an aviation battalion, and an air cavalry troop.[95]

Besides these divisional helicopters, there was an enormous aggregation of helicopters in separate aviation brigades that were used to support Army units that either lacked their own aviation or needed reinforcement for their own helicopters. The largest of these, the 1st Aviation Brigade (**Figure 18**), was activated in May 1966. At its height, it possessed 641 fixed-wing aircraft, 441 Cobra attack helicopters, 311 cargo helicopters, 635 observation helicopters, and 2,200 UH–1 utility helicopters, some of which were used for close air support.[96]

At each of the two U.S. corps areas, called *Field Forces* so as not to confuse them with the four Vietnamese Corps Tactical Zones, nondivisional Army helicopters and fixed-wing planes were formed into an aviation battalion that acted as a pool to respond to requests from units throughout the corps. It was the job of the Field Force operations officer (G–3) to allocate helicopters and fixed-wing planes to ground commanders for a specified period of time.[97] These nondivisional aircraft were centralized in a way, that on paper, differed only marginally from the way the Air Force believed air power should be organized. The only real difference was that they were centralized in Army, rather than Air Force, hands. The same centralization existed with divisional aviation, although there the helicopters were controlled at one level lower (the division) than was the case with nondivisional aviation (the corps).

Nevertheless, in neither case did the Army's control system in Vietnam provide ground commanders below the division level a measurable increase of

Help from Above

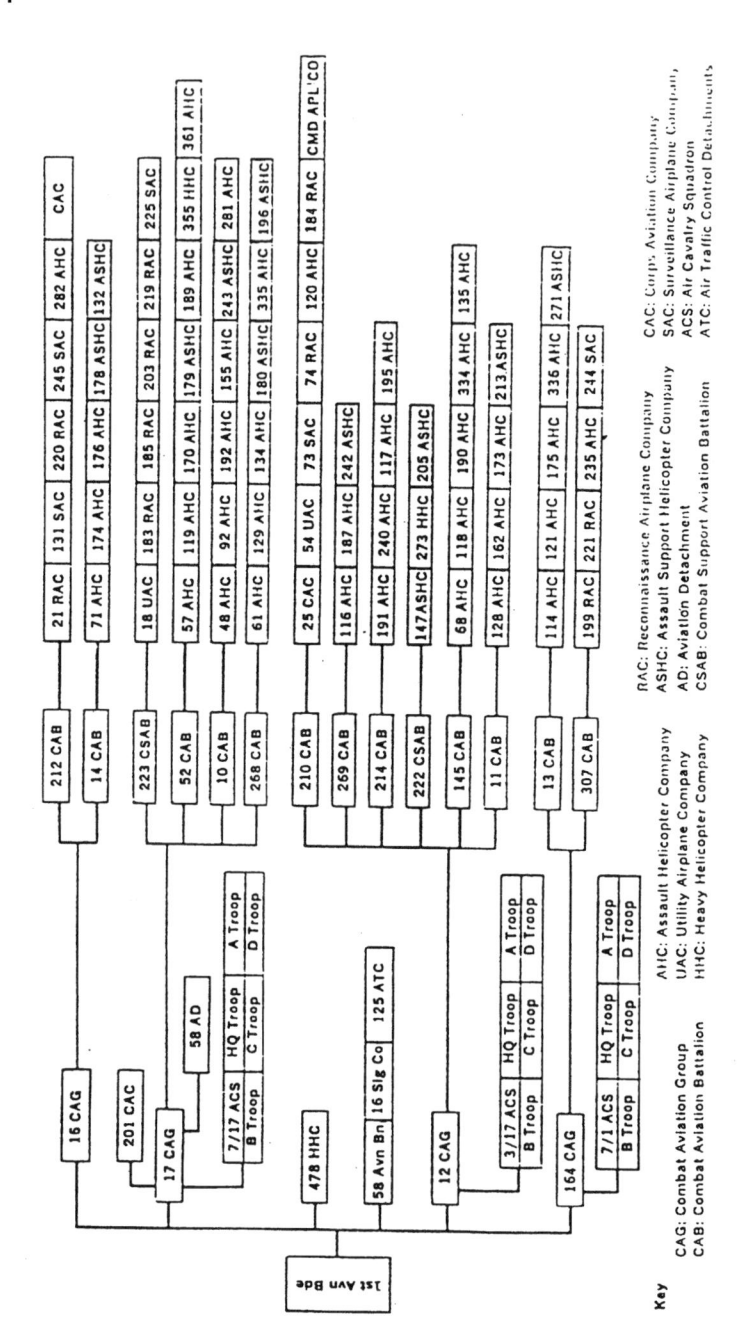

FIGURE 18
1st Aviation Brigade Organization, August 1, 1968

The Vietnam Era

personal control of aircraft than did the Air Force's system. The vast majority of Army aviation in the conflict—80 to 90 percent by one estimate—was assigned to and controlled at levels higher than the division. The commander of a nonairmobile division controlled less than 100 small aircraft for logistics, reconnaissance, and command and control. When he needed additional aircraft, he had to obtain them from resources that were pooled at the corps or higher level. Even the commanders of the two airmobile divisions, each of whom controlled over 400 aircraft, had to supplement these with planes kept at higher organizational levels.[98] This strongly suggests that once having gained a modicum of control over their helicopters, the Army discovered what the Air Force had learned in World War II and had been practicing since, namely, that air assets were most effective when placed under central control but decentralized for operations. In this light, the Army's argument for control of close air support (and airlift and reconnaissance) aircraft by ground commanders appears to have been based less on a desire for lower level control than on a general desire on the part of the Army to control these assets.

This conclusion is further suggested by the seemingly contradictory fact that, in the face of this centralization, Army commanders in Vietnam still considered the armed helicopters to be more responsive to their specific needs than were Air Force tactical fighters. By this they meant they had the helicopters available on a continuing basis and as close to their unit as possible. On paper, the helicopters were not that much more available and responsive than were fighters, but the perception was almost universal among Army commanders that they were.[99]

Not only did gunship and artillery helicopters perform close air support missions similar to those being conducted, frequently against the same target, by Air Force fighter-bombers, but their armament often duplicated much of that which adorned the fixed-wing close air support planes. The earlier Huey helicopter gunships (UH–1B/C) as well as the later Cobras (AH–1G) and aerial rocket helicopters featured 40-mm grenade launchers, door-sited miniguns, wing-mounted high-rate 20-mm machine guns, and pods for launching 2.75-inch folding-fin aerial rockets.[100] Even the ground-alert system for Army helicopters replicated that which Air Force fighters were using. Aerial rocket-artillery helicopters generally remained on call on the ground. One group stayed on two-minute, another on five-minute, alert. When the first section departed on an emergency mission, the second section moved up to two-minute alert and was replaced with new five-minute alert forces. As with the close air support provided by fighters, this system made continuous firepower available.[101]

By the end of 1971, Army helicopters had logged nearly four million attack sorties, 11 percent of the 36 million helicopter sorties flown in the war. Over the years, rotary-wing pilots in South Vietnam had developed a *modus operandi* with Air Force fighter planes and devised techniques that

Help from Above

resulted in fairly smooth cooperation between the two on close air support missions. Air Force planes, with their heavier armament loads, performed many missions for the ground forces that were beyond the capability of helicopters. A major close air support function of the Air Force, for example, was to prepare landing zones for Army assault helicopters. Sometimes these landing zones were carved out of the jungle instantaneously by a 15,000-pound BLU–82 bomb with an extended fuse (called Commando Vault), dropped from a C–130 to clear an area that could handle up to three helicopters. Air Force F–4s and F–100s also made the helicopter assault landings and extractions possible by suppressing enemy ground fire in and around the cleared zone. The highest priority for fighter-bombers in close air support was given to situations in which friendly troops were in contact with the enemy. Also preparing the way for helicopter operations were B–52 Arc Light close air support missions, which dropped tons of munitions on suspected enemy redoubts in and around the area of operations. Other Air Force planes also joined in with helicopters in providing close air support. Fixed-wing gunships proved invaluable on many occasions in forcing an enemy to break contact.

The integration of fighter-bombers with helicopters in battle, however, did not occur without its difficulties. One of the main problems created for the Air Force Component Commander was that of air-space control. The presence in the same area of helicopters lifting troops into landing zones, suppressing enemy resistance with fire support, and resupplying troops; fighter-bombers clearing landing zones, escorting helicopters, and striking ground targets; B–52s dropping bombs unseen from above; and FAC planes and command helicopters, often created highly congested traffic situations over the battlefield. A temporary solution was found in empowering the FAC to clear the target area of other traffic for fighter strikes. But this did not always work, and there were frequent reports of near misses in the air. The frequency of these instances convinced many that, while the situation was tolerable in Vietnam, in a conflict where enemy air traffic would be added to the equation, much more positive control of traffic would be needed.[102]

The perceived success of helicopters in Vietnam convinced many Army commanders of the soundness of their original airmobile conception. Air Force leaders pointed out, however, that the airmobile division as envisioned by the Howze Board and the Air Assault II exercises was designed for a European scenario in NATO rather than for a limited, jungle war of the Vietnamese type. Its relative success in Southeast Asia, in their eyes, was attributable to factors that would most likely be absent in a full-intensity conflict: the lack of enemy air resistance and the general effectiveness of the Air Force in suppressing ground fire. The Air Force continued to maintain that the helicopter's vulnerabilities restricted its employment to situations where it could be protected by fixed-wing close air support planes.

The Vietnam Era

This conclusion was reinforced, in Air Force eyes, early in 1971 by the outcome of a one-month ground operation aimed at attacking the North Vietnamese supply routes in neighboring Laos. The objective of the campaign by South Vietnamese ground forces, called Lam Son 719, was to strike enemy supply areas near the town of Tchepone, 27 miles inside Laos (**Figure 16**) Tchepone was a hub on the enemy's main conduit for infiltration into the south, the Ho Chi Minh Trail. The trail, which ran from the western exits of North Vietnam down through the Laotian panhandle, whence men and materiel were siphoned into South Vietnam, was also used as a sanctuary for shielding enemy troops and storing supplies. Having lost their sea supply route to Cambodia the previous year, the North Vietnamese were seeking, early in 1971, to compensate for the loss by extending the trail southward into Cambodia. One goal of the allied invasion was to frustrate that design.

The incursion was carried out by three South Vietnamese division-equivalents, commanded by General Lam, and supported by U.S. Army helicopters and ground artillery of the 101st Airborne Division (Airmobile) and by Seventh Air Force fighters, gunships, B–52s, and FACs. Since no Americans were allowed on the ground in Laos, the operation was run from Khe Sanh across the nearby border inside South Vietnam. Ground commanders of the U.S. Army XXIV Corps[103] did the initial major planning. Hypnotized by more than four years of successful fighter-bomber-supported helicopter operations in South Vietnam, the ground-oriented planners overestimated the ability of their helicopters to go it alone in creating and clearing landing zones in the face of the enemy's withering automatic weapons and barrage-fire technique, and in countering armored attacks by enemy tanks. The North Vietnamese had built an integrated air-defense network of some 575 antiaircraft artillery (AAA) guns—37-mm, 23-mm, and 57-mm—along the trail in Laos. In addition, against low-flying aircraft they frequently used artillery, tank, and infantry weapons, while SA–2 missiles were fired at B–52s. Against helicop-

A Soviet 7.62-mm AK–47 assault rifle.

Help from Above

ters entering or leaving a landing zone or a besieged area, the North Vietnamese realized great success with barrage fire by infantrymen discharging 7.62-mm small arms and 12.7-mm machine guns simultaneously.

Although the Air Force had become familiar with these enemy defenses in the Laotian panhandle during the seven years it had been flying there, and advised the Army of the seriousness of the threat, the Army did not consider it significant enough to refrain from using its helicopters for resupply, troop movement, and close air support. It was not long into the operation, however, before the vulnerabilities of the inadequately supported helicopters became apparent, leading to increased reliance on the Air Force's close air support planes.

Before the operation began, the Air Force presented Army planners with a proposal for countering the expected formidable enemy ground opposition through a combination of B–52 sorties, Commando Vault drops, and tactical fighter strikes in three-hour-long sustained strikes to prepare landing zones for helicopter assaults. Each landing zone, according to the plan, would initially be hit before 0700 hours by 15 Arc Light sorties, followed by a Commando Vault drop. Six or seven flights of fighters would then strike the potential landing zone with daisy cutters, which burst above the ground, and antipersonnel (CBU) ordnance. Finally, 15 sets of fighters would pound the zone for two hours with 500-pound bombs and napalm to clean out any remaining enemy

A Soviet-made ZU–23 23-mm antiaircraft gun.

The Vietnam Era

weapons. Just before the lift helicopters arrived, two fighters would create a smoke screen to hide their assault.[104]

Vietnamese and U.S. Army generals initially rejected this suggestion. They said it would unnecessarily delay the combat assaults they wanted completed early in the day so that night defensive positions could be established before dark.[105] Instead, they planned to use only individual segments of this massive fixed-wing force to construct and prepare landing zones, supplementing them with Army artillery firing across the border, aerial rocket artillery helicopters, and helicopter gunships.

Disregard for importance of fighter support for helicopters became apparent at the outset as the troops first moved into Laos. The first major objective of the South Vietnamese forces was a major crossroads at A Luoi, half way to Tchepone. Since it was a South Vietnamese operation, tactical decisions were made by the indigenous commander, General Lam, in coordination with South Vietnamese President Nguyen Van Thieu, but too frequently without coordinating the decisions with Seventh Air Force. The action around Landing Zone Lo Lo, just west of A Luoi, illustrated the disastrous consequences that could result from attempting helicopter assault landings without sufficient reliance on fixed-wing aircraft strikes.

South Vietnamese troops crossed over into Laos on February 8, 1971. Within two days their 1st Airborne Division air penetrated into A Luoi, 16 kilometers into Laos. Although at the outset enemy opposition was relatively

A Soviet-made M–1939 37-mm antiaircraft gun.

Help from Above

light, thereby boosting allied confidence in the invulnerability of its rotary planes, enemy resistance stiffened after A Luoi. During the next three weeks the drive bogged down in the face of heavy enemy resistance, during which 31 helicopters were lost and more than 230 damaged. The drive westward was resumed on March 2. On the following day, however, major difficulties at Landing Zone Lo Lo shattered the earlier confidence in the ability of helicopters to provide close air support without the assistance of fixed-wing planes.

Between 8:00 and 9:30 on the morning of March 3, an Air Force FAC, under the direction of a U.S. Army Air Mission Commander, prepared the landing zone at Lo Lo first by guiding six fighters in dropping 500-, 1,000-, and 2,000-pound general-purpose bombs with fuze extenders, then sending in three fighters to expend antipersonnel munitions and strafe the area with their 20-mm guns. This preparation, far short of what the Air Force believed was necessary, proved highly inadequate. The assault helicopters, which began to arrive at 10:00, were greeted with withering fire from automatic weapons and mortars, which shot down four of the first nineteen helicopters and heavily damaged many others. The assault was stopped for six hours while 30 more fighters, along with helicopter gunships and artillery, battered the area. The lift was finally completed at 6:30 that evening, over 10 hours after it began. Forty-two helicopters were hit, 20 shot down and declared unflyable, and seven destroyed in the operation.[106]

This disastrous helicopter assault at Lo Lo changed the Army's attitude. General Creighton W. Abrams, the MACV commander, directed that closer coordination be given landing zone preparation. Not only were more fixed-wing strikes used in future landing zone preparations, but the daily sortie rate for direct support of ground forces more than doubled from the pre-Lo Lo average of 104 to 211 sorties in the latter part of the operation.[107]

The Army helicopter losses for the entire Lam Son 719 operation were officially placed at 105 with over 600 others damaged, 20 percent of which were not expected to fly again. Since no American advisors accompanied the South Vietnamese into Laos, these figures were probably low.

In addition to being unable to withstand determined barrages of enemy ground fire, the Army's gunship helicopters also were not strong enough to destroy the tanks the North Vietnamese introduced into the conflict. Throughout the operation, ground forces relied on Air Force tactical aircraft to destroy tanks. Normally, when gunships of the Army's air cavalry reconnaissance unit sighted enemy tanks, they would request fighter assistance, and then maintain contact with them until the fixed-wing planes arrived. When fighters were not available, helicopter gunships would fire at the tanks until their ordnance was gone. Rarely, however, did they carry enough ordnance to destroy the tanks. Between opening day, February 8, and March 24, 1971 air cavalry units sighted 66 tanks, but could destroy only six. The rest were turned over to the Air

The Vietnam Era

Force. The weapons system of the Army's most advanced gunship, the AH–1G Huey Cobra, had little or no effect against a tank such as the T–54.[108] In its final report, the 101st Airborne Division noted that:

> the Army needs new tank-defeating armed helicopters. Had the Division entered LAMSON 719 with a helicopter armed with an accurate, lethal, relatively long-range anti-tank weapon, it would have destroyed many more NVA tanks and would have rendered more effective close support to RVNAF ground forces.[109]

The reliance of Army airmobility on the close air support assistance of fixed-wing planes, which General Kinnard characterized as crucial in the Ia Drang Valley operation, was reinforced in the operation in Laos. "Lam Son 719 reaffirmed," stated the Army's evaluation of the campaign, "that air cavalry squadrons, to be fully effective, must have immediate access to USAF support." While the air cavalry could locate and record targets, it frequently lacked the firepower to destroy them.[110] In analyzing firepower during the campaign, the Army division commander concluded:

> While all sources of firepower contributed to the success of airmobile operations, the mass of destructive firepower was delivered by the USAF. Multiple B–52 strikes prepared objective areas. Commando Vaults and daisy cutter bombs constructed landing and pickup zones and alternate touchdown points. Bombs, rockets, CBU, napalm, and 20-mm gunfire destroyed or neutralized enemy weapons positions and troop units. Then the USAF aircraft laid a smoke screen to shield troop-lift aircraft from enemy fire and observations as they entered and departed landing or pickup zones.[111]

While Army helicopters proved to be excellent vehicles for lifting troops, artillery, and supplies into and extracting them from virtually inaccessible areas, their vulnerability and short standoff range limited their usefulness in providing close air support firepower. Army helicopters could not survive ground fire from weapons of 23-mm or larger. On numerous occasions helicopters were forced to abort missions because of heavy antiaircraft fire in the landing zone. Whenever Army air cavalry helicopters encountered antiaircraft weapons, for example, they requested fighter-bombers, since "the USAF has the standoff range and the firepower to engage antiaircraft weapons at a more acceptable risk level than does the Cav with organic gunships."[112]

Initial Army estimates of how many helicopter gunships would be required for the operation fell far short of what was actually needed. Planners

Help from Above

began the campaign by assigning two gunships to cover 20 lift helicopters and ended it using two gunships for every five UH–1Hs.[113] This reduced the close air support efficiency of the rotary-wing aircraft.

The helicopter losses in Lam Son 719 intensified the debate over helicopters between the Army, which saw the solution to the problem in developing larger and more potent helicopters such as the Cheyenne, which was fast approaching the size, weight, and characteristics of a fighter-bomber, and the Air Force, which sought to forestall this by acquiring an airplane that would be devoted solely to the close air support mission.

Toward a Specialized Close Air Support Plane

During the Vietnam period the Air Force, in addition to losing a portion of its close air support mission to armed helicopter gunships, abandoned a second long-standing tenet of close air support, namely, that the planes it used for close air support should also be able to perform air combat and interdiction roles. As early as 1965, pressure from many directions, including the Secretary of Defense, the Congress, the Army, and the military budget, was compelling the Air Force to reevaluate this time-honored conviction. As a consequence, in September 1966, General McConnell made the significant decision to proceed with the design, development, and purchase of the Air Force's first specialized close air support aircraft.

McConnell's decision was the culmination of a series of events and studies suggesting that if the Air Force did not move in that direction, the entire close air support mission could be lost to the Army's growing fleet of increasingly sophisticated attack helicopters. Important in this train of events was Secretary McNamara, who periodically prodded the Air Force to improve its close air support aircraft. The secretary's support of the Army's development of helicopters to improve its mobility also affected Air Force thinking. In January 1965, for example, McNamara directed the Air Force to examine the requirements for both an interim and long-term close air support plane.[114] In September, three months after he approved the airmobile division for the Army, and while that division was en route to Vietnam, he sent a memo to the retiring Air Force secretary, Eugene M. Zuckert, endorsing the steps the Army was taking to arm its helicopters to perform certain close air support functions. He found it quite appropriate, he wrote, that aircraft of every service go into battle with armament, not only for self-defense, but also for attacking tanks and performing any other close air support operations that the battlefield situation required.[115]

Concurrent with McNamara's memorandum was a congressional investigation of close air support in Vietnam. This occurred between September 22 and October 14, 1965, even before the U.S. Army and Air Force's first major cooperative battle against the enemy in the Ia Drang Valley. New York

Representative Otis G. Pike, a Marine fighter pilot in World War II, convened a subcommittee of the House Armed Services Committee, to examine the adequacy of air superiority, support facilities for tactical aircraft, and close air support in Vietnam. Citing time limitations, the committee considered only the latter question, and quickly narrowed the close air support issue to an examination of the type of aircraft that should perform the function.[116]

The fact that close air support had yet to be performed to any sizable degree in Vietnam, combined with the chairman's known propensity for Marine aviation, resulted in a final report that relied heavily on *a priori* positions rather than on evidence from the war. While ignoring testimony favorable to past close air support operations,[117] the committee report emphasized the traditional differences between the two services as reported by the Army and Air Force Close Air Support Boards in 1963. It was the view of the nine committee members that a gulf existed between what the Army wanted as a close air support aircraft and what the Air Force "wanted to provide them."[118] Underscoring that contention, the Air Force was roundly criticized for having to obtain O–1 FAC planes for Vietnam from the Army and close air support A–1 strike planes from the Navy, and for failing to design its own attack plane for close air support.

The committee's expressed unalloyed adulation in its final report for the control system and aircraft used by the Marine corps for close air support:

> The Navy-Marine Corps doctrine, organization, and the equipment employed in close tactical air support of ground forces are obviously superior to that of the other armed services. They meet the requirements for limited war operations, such as the current conflict in South Vietnam, and are readily adaptable to an escalating conflict.[119]

Virtually ignoring the Air Force's argument that multipurpose, supersonic aircraft were both more efficient and more effective in a multiplicity of roles, including close air support, the report strongly urged the Army/Air Force team to emulate "the knowledge, the technique, the capability for effective close air support" as practiced by the Marine Corps. This was a clear call for the Air Force to rectify past omissions and develop a close air support aircraft as had the Navy and Marine Corps. Specifically, it touted the effectiveness of the Navy's A–7A. The Air Force was unconvinced by the report's closing disclaimer that it did not want the report "to be construed as a unilateral, or perhaps even a parochial, attack upon one service."[120]

While the defense secretary and Congress were expressing in words their desire that the Air Force develop a close air support plane, the Army was pursuing initiatives that would push the Air Force even farther in that direction. Buoyed by the results of its field tests, by the support it believed it had from Secretary McNamara, and by the Air Force's acquiescence, however reluctant,

Help from Above

in its airmobile concept, the Army pushed ahead to develop a larger and more powerful helicopter that could provide even greater fire support for its ground forces.

The generally laudatory view of the Air Force's close air support operations that Army commanders on the ground in Vietnam expressed was not universally shared by their confreres on the Army staff in Washington. This dichotomy of views between those engaged with an enemy on the battlefield and those in the higher reaches of service planning was not unusual, given the different perspectives and objectives at work at the two levels. The goals of those engaged in battle are more immediate and relatively transitory, namely, to use all available military assets to defeat the enemy. Such goals do not outlive the enemy's demise. In a theater of war, military resources are treasured more for their effective contribution to the immediate military objective than for their effect on the future design of a military service. On the other hand, those off the battlefield, but responsible for the long-range existence and vitality of a military service, are guided at least as strongly by the effects battles and wars have on the future resources and doctrines of the service as by their contribution to the conflict.

Consequently, the satisfaction that many ground commanders in Vietnam expressed with the Air Force response to requests for close air support was not reflected in Washington and largely failed to alter the Army's on-going program to develop a helicopter that could take over a larger share of the close air support mission. With the shift in national strategy to Vietnamization late in 1968, with its concurrent downgrading of counterinsurgency, military planning was returning to an emphasis on scenarios for mid- and high-level conflicts in Europe. Despite the effectiveness of the Huey and Huey Cobra helicopters in Vietnam, these systems had been *ad hoc* additions to the airmobile division and did not fulfill the requirements for a European conflict. Both were essentially helicopters to which ground weapons had been added for suppressive fire missions. What was needed now, in the view of the Army, was a helicopter designed from the outset as a weapons system whose integrated weapons made it more efficient in the amount and types of ammunition it carried, the accuracy of its firing, and its ability to survive in more hostile environments.[121]

Consistent with its conviction that these helicopters were not usurping the Air Force's close air support mission, the Army ceased describing their mission as *close air support*, which was clearly an Air Force mission, in favor of calling it *direct aerial fire support*. In the new lexicon, an armed helicopter became an advanced aerial fire-support system (AAFSS). By 1970 Army manuals were defining direct aerial fire support as:

> fires delivered by aerial vehicles organic to land forces against surface targets and in support of land operations. Such fire support supplements, is integrated with, and is con-

The Vietnam Era

trolled similarly to Army surface weaponry. It is a complement rather than a substitute for ground-based fire or close air support.[122]

The attack helicopter was described as a weapon system for "offensive, defensive and other operations which contribute to the location and destruction of hostile targets to include self-protection, escort, fire suppression, reconnaissance, security, raids, screening, and anti-tank operations."[123]

The Air Force viewed both the idea that this new category of support was something different from close air support, and the Army's program to develop improved attack helicopters, as a circumvention of DOD Directive 5160.22.[124] It also recognized that earlier roles and missions agreements unequivocally gave the close air support mission to the Air Force. Congress also agreed at times. In a 1970 report, for example, the House Appropriations Committee observed that the Army's description of the Cheyenne as an AAFSS, to provide *direct aerial fire support*, as opposed to *close air support*, was "obviously an artificial distinction even by definition."[125] This congressional view was reinforced when the Army readopted the phrase *close air support* after Secretary of Defense Melvin R. Laird rescinded the directive in 1971,[126] making the distinction no longer necessary.

As early as February 1965, however, the Army took initial steps to improve the ability of its attack helicopters to escort troop-carrying helicopters, attack armor, and provide close air support to the ground troops. On the nineteenth the Army let its first definition phase contracts for an AAFSS that would exceed 200 knots. In November the Lockheed Corporation was named as the contractor to develop prototypes of what by then was called the AH–56A Cheyenne.[127]

An AH–56A Cheyenne attack helicopter, Fort Polk, Louisiana.

Help from Above

The Army expected great things from the Cheyenne. In an attempt to close even further the gap between the close air support the Air Force was providing and what it believed the Air Force was not able to provide, the Army was designing the Cheyenne to operate around the clock, day and night, and in bad weather; to destroy tanks and other hard targets with missiles and rockets; and to act as either a rotary-wing or a fixed-wing aircraft. It was hoped that this latter capability would result from combining both a helicopter rotor and a modified fixed wing in the same airframe. When flying forward at high speed the rotor would be disengaged, allowing the wing to carry most of the weight. Ideally, the Cheyenne would blend the maneuverability of a helicopter with the payload and high speed of a fixed-wing aircraft.[128]

In 1966, a bid by Air Force Secretary Harold Brown to persuade the Secretary of Defense that the new Army helicopter was designed primarily to deliver fire power and would compete with rather than complement Air Force fixed-wing attack planes, went nowhere. Throughout the controversy OSD approached the issue from a fundamentally different direction than did the Air Force. While the Air Force stressed the roles and missions underpinning close air support, and in doing so, relied heavily on the numerous agreements and directives that, over the years, had clearly made the Air Force responsible for close air support of the Army, OSD frequently overlooked roles and missions and based their close air support decisions on the *ad hoc* effectiveness of each aircraft system as it arose, regardless of which service was proposing to perform the mission. This case of the new attack helicopter was no different. The OSD supported the Army's contention that an armed helicopter was an effective part of the ground commander's arsenal and saw no conflict between it and the Air Force's strike aircraft.[129] Two years later, in 1968, the Department of Defense approved the procurement of 375 Cheyenne helicopters by the Army. Production of the Cheyenne was halted the following year as the result of production delays by Lockheed and the death of a test pilot in a crash.[130] Research continued, however, and costs soared—$420 million by 1972 and over $5 million per copy, according to one estimate. The Cheyenne was permanently canceled in August 1972 after a study showed the costs to be prohibitive and that there were less expensive alternatives.[131] The failure of the Cheyenne, however, did not end the attack helicopter/A–X controversy. At the same time that it announced the end of the Cheyenne program, the Army initiated a new advanced attack helicopter (AAH) program to find a replacement for the discontinued helicopter.[132]

This renewed attempt to develop a second-generation armed attack helicopter gunship was seen by the Air Force as the next logical phase of the Army's step-by-step quest to acquire some of its own close air support assets. It was apparent to General McConnell and to some congressmen that, in order to avoid further Army cooptation of the close air support mission, the Air Force had to develop an airplane tailored exclusively to that mission.[133] He chose to do this along the lines of McNamara's earlier directive

The Vietnam Era

to develop both an interim close air support plane and one for the long term. Like the Army, the Air Force was looking beyond the low-intensity environment of Vietnam to the requirements for mid- and high-intensity European war scenarios.

In November 1965, McConnell recommended that the Air Force satisfy the need for an interim close air support plane by buying a limited number of A–7Ds, a variation of the Navy's A–7A (VAL) light attack plane, for close air support and interdiction.[134] McConnell's hopes that the A–7D would solve the problem of an interim close air support replacement soon ran into trouble.

The modifications that had to be made to adapt the plane for close air support and interdiction's role rapidly escalated its cost to the level of that of the proven F–4E. It was also discovered that the A–7D required a longer hard-surface runway than the F–4 and had to be based far back from the front lines. With 74 of the 387 proposed planes already on hand by the end of 1970, McConnell could neither persuade the Navy to take them nor find an economical way to stop production. At the urging of the secretary of defense, the Air Force ended up with three wings of the planes, one of which arrived in Thailand in October 1972, a bare four months before the end of American air operations in the theater. Despite the good record of the A–7D during these months—close to 6,000 attack sorties, 540 sorties escorting search and rescue helicopters, and 230 sorties during the Christmas time Linebacker II bombing campaign over North Vietnam[135]—the plane proved too costly and lacked many close air support performance capabilities.

Although it did minimally fulfill the interim requirement, the A–7D was not a specialized close air support plane that could satisfy the need for an aircraft for the long-term future and in conflicts at a higher level of intensity, particularly in Europe. By June of 1966, the escalating use of helicopters by the Army in Vietnam, together with the Army's increased spending for Huey Cobra helicopter gunships and for development of the Cheyenne, moved General McConnell to commission a close air support study to examine what areas of close air support were not being provided to the Army by the Air Force and, if a gap existed, what steps should be taken to get the necessary equipment to fill it.

The study, completed in August, presented several important conclusions. First, all evidence indicated that the Army ground commanders in Vietnam were satisfied with the Air Force's response to their requests for close air support. Second, however, the report pointed out that there were many instances in Vietnam where the ground commanders did not request Air Force assistance so that they could use their own organic helicopters for close air support. This practice notwithstanding, continued the report, Air Force planes had not been effective in two types of close air support: escorting helicopters and suppressing enemy fire, particularly in landing zones. As a result, the Army had effectively filled this gap with its organic armed helicopters which, even though less accurate than Air Force fighters, were suc-

Help from Above

cessful in keeping the enemy at bay while transport helicopters discharged their infantrymen.[136]

In conclusion, the report urged that the Air Force embark on a crash program to obtain a close support plane that was simpler and cheaper than the A–7D and that would be better suited for the long-term close air support needs. This was the background to the chief of staff's directive of September 8, which set in motion the development of the Air Force's first specialized close air support plane, called the A–X during development.

The decision in September 1966 by the Air Force to go ahead with the A–X gave a new life to the debate over whether attack helicopters were usurping the close air support mission and, specifically, whether the attack helicopter and the A–X were complementary or competitive. By 1970, the nature of the debate had been modified in part by the fact that many of the leading decision makers on both sides, who earlier had worked together in Vietnam on this question, brought their battlefield harmony home with them. General Westmoreland was now the Army's Chief of Staff and his air deputy in Vietnam, General Momyer, TAC commander, was to be the principal user of the new aircraft. The agency charged with developing the Cheyenne, the Army's Combat Developments Command, was headed by General Kinnard, a leader in generating the airmobile idea and the first commander of the airmobile division in Vietnam.

The mutual experiences these commanders had in integrating armed helicopters and fixed-wing planes during close air support operations in Vietnam led them, outwardly, to submerge their differences, modify their public statements so as to stress the complementary nature of the two weapons systems, and downplay the competition between them. Pressure to do so also came from the OSD, which continued to look with favor on the Army's position. In response to a request from Deputy Defense Secretary David L. Packard, in January 1970, that the two services reach agreement on the complementary nature of the two systems,[137] the service secretaries replied in a startlingly neutral manner by stating that:

1. The AAFSS and the A–X were competitive because they operated the same mission.

2. The AAFSS and the A–X were complementary because they had different flight characteristics that influenced degree of suitability for specific missions.

3. Agreement had not been reached on the degree to which the two systems were competitive and/or complementary.

4. Research and development should continue for both the A–X and the AAFSS at least through prototype development.[138]

The Vietnam Era

The Cheyenne/A–X controversy resulted in an interesting role reversal by both services. For decades the Army had been pressuring the Air Force to develop a specialized close air support plane that could be assigned to ground commanders. The Air Force resisted this idea, arguing that since close air support planes had to fly other tactical missions in addition to close air support, missions that were of little direct concern to the Army, Army control of the close air support planes would weaken the ability of these planes to perform these other operations. Now that the Army had its own close air support helicopters, it reversed its former position and adopted the earlier Air Force rationale. When some in the Air Force suggested in 1969, for example, that the A–X then under development could be dedicated to Army control by being assigned to particular Direct Air Support Centers (DASCs) for use by specific Army units, the Army rebuttal echoed earlier Air Force arguments:

> There are other factors which militate against (placing close air support strikes under Army control)—prime of which is that fixed-wing close air aircraft are multi-capable.... The joint commander retains control of his fixed-wing close air support assets because they can contribute to other elements of his tactical air mission.... To assign these aircraft to the Army would reduce the responsiveness from the viewpoint of the joint force commander.[139]

Although General Westmoreland said he believed the two systems were complementary, he assigned the A–X to what the Air Force would call an interdiction role. The Cheyenne, in his view, would deliver fire along front lines and in situations requiring a quick response, a high order of accuracy, and a night and bad weather capability. The A–X, on the other hand, would expend heavier munitions against less fleeting targets, presumably away from the front lines. Although he agreed that there would be some overlap, he felt it would be unavoidable, small, and even desirable.[140]

The Air Force, on the other hand, seeking to preserve what was left of its close air support mission by building a specialized close air support plane, also underwent a doctrinal metamorphosis. A major voice in the debate was that of General Momyer, the commander of TAC. His support for the A–X, however, was based less on his view of it as a competitor with Army helicopters than on the economics of the situation. The traditional Air Force preference for multipurpose fighters for air superiority, interdiction, and close air support was based on the understanding that most of the force would be devoted first to gaining air superiority, without which none of the other missions mattered. Once air superiority was achieved, the planes would then turn to interdicting enemy movements and striking his forces. Regardless of the continuing theoretical validity of this concept, noted Momyer, the economic realities of the

Help from Above

late 1960s made it impossible to equip all tactical air wings with first-line F–15 fighters that could be diverted to close air support after achieving air superiority. To shift F–15s to close air support, as had been done with fighters in the past, would be to jeopardize the Air Force's ability to withstand a Soviet air attack. Further, argued Momyer, allied ground forces in Europe would come under attack simultaneously with the air battle, requiring a specific close air support plane to respond from the outset of hostilities.[141]

To him, the issue was less one of the A–X versus the Cheyenne, than it was of whether the roles and missions of the Air Force were to be changed. His 30 years of dealing with this question and his consistent involvement with close air support of the Army left no doubt in his mind that the Air Force would never be able to satisfy the Army on close air support no matter what kind of plane it built to do the job. The Army could never abandon its fundamental view of air power as a form of artillery that must remain in the hands of the commander doing the fighting. What he saw being done by the Army's Combat Developments Command reinforced his conviction that the Army saw the entire tactical air mission as being divided into two parts: the battlefield component, which belonged to the Army and was to be supported by Army airlift, reconnaissance, and close air support planes, and the Air Force component, comprising everything beyond 60 nautical miles of the front line, which was the realm for the Air Force to exercise its reconnaissance, airlift, and close air support. Given this orientation, the A–X/Cheyenne argument was, in Momyer's view, only an outward manifestation of the deeper roles and mission disagreement.[142]

Momyer's more holistic understanding of the controversy as a roles and missions issue rather than a debate over hardware was rejected by the Deputy Secretary of Defense in a 1971 review of close air support. In January, the Packard Committee, named after its chairman, replied to a congressional request that it reevaluate the roles and missions and aircraft options available for close air support. At Packard's direction, the committee ignored the question of roles and missions, which it considered secondary, and analyzed such items as the capabilities of the current close air support systems (the A–X, the Cheyenne, and the Marines' Harrier), how they could be improved, what missions required new systems, and how the tank threat in Europe could best be met. By concentrating on these tactical 'hardware' questions, the group disregarded the roles and missions and doctrinal aspects of close air support, that is, questions of who should furnish close air support, who should control it, and how it was performed. In narrowing the study, as was its wont, to questions of hardware and cost-effectiveness, the secretary bypassed the question of service responsibilities. This order of priorities, which was frequent within the Department of Defense, was seen by some as a means of avoiding prickly interservice issues that could lead to public controversy and unpleasant political consequences for the department. The end result in this case, however, was

The Vietnam Era

to leave the fundamental issues that lay behind the A–X/Cheyenne debate untouched. The committee endorsed continued development of all three close air support systems. Many of those close to the committee believed that until the roles and missions and doctrinal implications were sorted out, there remained little hope of resolving the close air support question.[143]

McConnell's 1966 order to procure a close air support plane moved slowly through the system, due in part to the relaxation of pressure occasioned by the adequacy of the A–7D. At the end of 1970 contracts were let to Fairchild Industries and Northrop for each to develop two turbofan prototypes, and both planes, Northrop's A–9 and Fairchild's A–10 were first flown in May 1972. Pitted against each other in a series of flyoffs between October and December the following year,[144] Fairchild's A–10 won, becoming the first aircraft in four decades developed by the Air Force solely to provide close air support to the U.S. Army.

An A–10 Thunderbolt II during an exercise (top) and an A–10 Thunderbolt II firing a GAU–8/A 30-mm cannon (bottom).

Help from Above

* * *

During the critical years of the Vietnam War, between 1965 and the end of the decade, Air Force close air support had evolved in several different directions. One direction in the Tactical Air Control System in Vietnam, was inspired by the Strike Command's approval of the Air Force's concept of air mobility, which resulted in important improvements. Principal among these improvements were the employment for the first time on a grand scale of airborne FACs, and the incorporation within the tactical air control system of DASCs, which allowed centrally controlled air resources to be operated decentrally. Both of these innovations were extremely successful in validating the Air Force's air-ground doctrine and in averting even more serious assaults on its close air support system. Further advancements were made in communications, ground-controlled bombing, the ability to strike at night and in poor weather, and the employment of B–52s in the ground-support role.

Despite the frequently unsympathetic reception accorded its roles and missions arguments by successive secretaries of defense, however, the Air Force emerged from this period with its doctrine for close air support still largely intact, if somewhat dented. The key tenet of that doctrine, namely, centralized control of close air support assets in the hands of the tactical air-component commander, had, with the exception of helicopters, been preserved in the face of continued Army preference to decentralize all close air support resources. Although helicopters were lost to the Air Force, its claim to preeminence between the two services in the field of fixed-wing aircraft was established.

A second direction in which the Air Force had traveled by 1973 was the virtual abandonment of its aspiration to incorporate armed helicopters in its close air support inventory. Helicopters, whose future integration in large numbers into the Army appeared in jeopardy in 1965, had by 1973 been irrevocably absorbed into the very marrow of Army divisions. Army rotary-wing aircraft were being used to support virtually every function of land combat: command and control, logistics, reconnaissance, maneuver, and firepower.[145] The Army had about 1,200 aircraft, and more fliers (24,000) than the Air Force. About 36 Army generals and 230 Army colonels were drawing flight pay.[146]

The degree to which helicopters had come to be accepted as an integral part of ground combat was reflected in the gradual acceptance by both services of an expanded definition of close air support. In the 1950s and early 1960s, the Joint Chiefs described close air support as air action against hostile targets that were in close proximity to friendly forces and required detailed integration of each air mission with the fire and movement of those forces.[147] This definition stressed the geographical nearness of the air action to the friendly

The Vietnam Era

ground forces and the need for close coordination with the fire and movement of those forces. Historically, both the *fire* and the *movement* were from and on the ground, and the air action was the realm of fixed-wing planes.

By 1970, the Army and Air Force had greatly broadened this definition to incorporate the new reality that helicopters now also constituted instruments of firepower and movement. The new characterization expanded the concept of close air support by adding to its traditional tasks those of preparing landing zones for helicopter assaults, striking the enemy during insertions and extractions, escorting helicopters to protect them from both air and ground attacks, and supporting air cavalry operations and helicopter rescue missions.[148] Such a broad conception would, of course, have been unthinkable 15 years earlier.

The third direction that the Air Force took in close air support during this period was its decision to forgo the long-standing practice of acquiring only multipurpose tactical fighter planes and develop an aircraft to be used solely for close air support. This decision was prompted primarily by a damage-limiting desire to avoid giving the Army a further rationale for developing its advance attack helicopters, and secondarily, by the escalating costs of developing military aircraft in the face of stringent defense budgets. Even as the decision was being made, however, some of the backers of the new close air support plane, the A–10, harbored lingering doubts. General Momyer, his support for the plane notwithstanding, cautioned against committing it totally to close air support. For years he had been able to point to the multiple missions of Air Force tactical planes in successfully countering the claim that the Army should control them. Too much emphasis on the A–10 as only a close air support plane, in his estimation, would strip him of this argument and could possibly open the way to validating the claim that the A–10 should be organic to the Army.[149] Despite these fears, the Air Force, largely as a result of its experiences in Vietnam, embarked on a new chapter in its close air support relations with the Army.

7 | Conclusions

In one respect, during the three decades between World War II and America's departure from Vietnam, both the concept and the system by which the Air Force provided the Army with aerial firepower changed very little, yet in another respect underwent important modification. Two general types of influences were at work to bring about these developments: those that came from outside the military services and over which the Army and Air Force exercised little control, and those that arose from within, generated by traditional service interests and disagreements.

The broadest and most pervasive external influence on close air support was the geostrategic environment spawned by the cold war. America's national security policy of containing the spread of USSR communism, a policy that remained vigorous throughout the period, was expressed, during the first half of this thirty-year interval, in a national strategy of Massive Retaliation. During the remaining years, it was gradually transformed into a strategy of Flexible Response. Each of these strategies in turn had profound effects within the services. Questions of technological development, procurement of equipment and personnel, doctrine, and training, were affected and these, in turn, colored each service's thinking, planning, and performance in the area of close air support.

Emphasis on nuclear deterrence and warfighting during the first half of the period propelled the Air Force into a dominant position in the military hierarchy. More than any other service, the Air Force emerged from World War II with a doctrine, a nucleus of resources, and the experience that best met the contemporary need for worldwide nuclear preparedness and for a quick and effective reaction in the event of a major nuclear war. Consequently, attention and money were funneled primarily to the Air Force to build a nuclear arsenal capable of either discouraging nuclear adventures by the USSR or, should such preventative measures fail, of successfully defeating this enemy in a major nuclear war.

Help from Above

Until the end of the 1950s, despite the evidence of the Korean War, the persistence of the existing belief that the existence of a large nuclear retaliatory force would deter the USSR from embarking on more limited military adventures, resulted in a degradation of the military resources required for smaller conflicts. Among the neglected assets were those the Air Force needed to provide close air support to the Army's ground forces. Perhaps even more important than the slighted resources was the evolution of a mind-set among many in the Air Force that saw the new emphasis on global nuclear military power as not only a justification of what airmen had been proclaiming since the 1930s, but also as a final repudiation of the classic model of warfare as a clash of two armed forces on the ground whose outcome was decided by the defeat of one of the forces. To many airmen (although not to all), such local, tactical, ground encounters, and the military equipment needed to wage them, had become anachronisms.

While propelling the Air Force into the forefront, the new nuclear strategy simultaneously presented the other services, particularly the Army, with major challenges. With its traditional mission of defeating enemy ground forces in jeopardy, the Army, in order to remain a major military actor, had to create a new mission for itself in the nuclear age. This task was rendered doubly difficult by the fact that it alone of the services lacked a force that was considered to be a requirement for membership in the nuclear club—a major aviation branch. In its first attempt to create a nuclear mission during this early period, the Army succeeded in gaining a near monopoly on using ground-to-air missiles for air defense. Yet this remained a minor mission. Unable, due to its lack of an aviation force, to become a major player under the new rules that favored the strategic air mission, the Army set about with considerable success to change the rules. It succeeded in convincing the national decision makers to modify the national strategy of Massive Retaliation, with its airpower emphasis, in the direction of a strategy of Flexible Response, which returned some of the spotlight to traditional ground power, with air power in a supporting role. At the same time, the Army set about building its own aviation force. Thus, the all but dormant controversy over the nature of close air support and who should control it was revived. Close air support remained a flashpoint between the two services throughout the period.

A second external influence on the fortunes of close air support was the startling pace of technological progress in the United States during the three postwar decades. The maturation of nuclear energy, jet propulsion, advanced electronics, and missiles profoundly affected the services. Technological development, however, was not an inert, undirected phenomenon that descended haphazardly with equal force upon the services. It was neutral and its direction was determined by its utility to the military mission. Military technology was limited to those facets that could best serve the contemporary national strategy, first of Massive Retaliation, then of Flexible Response. As a result, the perfec-

Conclusions

tion of nuclear weapons in the first half of the period, along with the advent of jet aircraft, catapulted the Air Force into service primacy. While this was a case of technology creating (or exacerbating) service envy, it also proved to be an example of how technology could be used by one service to revive its declining fortunes. This is most clearly seen in the case of close air support, where the Army took advantage of progress in aviation technology to develop, not only armed helicopters, but a close air support mission for them with which it recaptured a portion of the limelight.

A third major external factor, one that influenced both the geostrategic environment and the pace of technological progress as well as military development, was the unprecedented economic boom the United States enjoyed after World War II. A constantly rising gross national product, relatively low inflation rates, high employment, and an excellent balance of trade with foreign nations propelled the United States far ahead of other nations in its ability to devote resources to military expansion without harming the civilian sector of the economy. Although initially constrained, the military budget constantly expanded and very little was denied to the military. As a result, the American armed forces had the luxury of being able to build redundancy into its weapons systems, a redundancy that few other nations of the world could afford.

This duplication of capabilities was evident across the spectrum of military equipment and personnel. It permitted each service, for example, to procure close air support assets, apart from those possessed by the other services, to fulfill its own conception of what that mission entailed. As close air support resources proliferated, particularly after the acceptance of the Flexible Response policy, military leaders gradually came to alter their view of them from being redundant to being complementary. Each service generated various rationales for its own system, explaining how its close air support requirements differed, however slightly, from those of the other military organizations. Such a development was possible only because money was not in short supply and was tolerated only because of the ever looming military threat posed by the USSR. This installation of expensive, duplicative systems would later present major problems when both the ready availability of funds and the threat from the USSR evaporated, simultaneously.

While these three external factors had fundamental effects on the Army and Air Force, their impact was long term, and was modified by traditional service interests that became the ultimate shapers of the details of the close air support debate. The relative influence on the controversy of such concerns as budget competition, service doctrine and tradition, pride in accomplishing the mission, interservice contention, careerism, territorialism, and, at times, just plain obtuseness, was particularly strong in determining the progress, or lack thereof, of the many elements that combined to constitute the term *close air support*.

Help from Above

In the midst of diversity and change, one factor remained a constant force in virtually every aspect of the close air support debate. This unyielding issue was that of command and control that, in almost every instance, had some influence in either bringing about a change or preventing one from occurring. For the Air Force, the principle of command and control derived from the doctrinal conviction, born before World War II and proven correct (to the Air Force) in that conflict, that air power was most efficient and effective when it was controlled and directed by airmen. Airmen were more familiar than ground officers with both the potentialities of aircraft and with military requirements of modern global warfare that transcended the immediate battlefield. Even in the tactical area of close air support, planes could provide better support when a single force was able to move them rapidly from one trouble spot to another. To tie them down to specific ground units was to deprive them of the ability to perform most effectively.

For the Army officer, on the other hand, backed up by the lessons culled from several millennia of military experience, the clash of infantry forces on the ground, supported by artillery both from the ground and from the air, constituted the heart of warfare. All other military elements, be they artillery, armor, cavalry, or aviation, existed only to serve the infantry, the *Queen of Battles*. Although many other factors, such as budget competition, interservice rivalry, careerism, misplaced loyalty, and sheer recklessness, played roles from time to time, the most immediate influence on the outcome of the close air support debate was exerted by these two diametrically opposed visions of what close air support aircraft were all about and, ultimately, who should direct them.

During the three decades, some close air support issues hardly changed at all, while others were altered substantially. The areas of close air support that underwent relatively minor changes over the years included those of tactical air priorities, joint training and joint doctrine, official statements of roles and missions, and service attitudes. The command and control issue figured prominently in each of these.

The idea of assigning the first priority for tactical aircraft to air superiority missions, the second to interdiction sorties, and the last to close air support, was a logical extension of the ideas of Air Vice Marshal Sir Arthur Coningham in World War II. During the campaign in North Africa, the British Air Commander succeeded in gaining acceptance for his view that tactical planes should be used first to acquire air superiority, rather than, as was then being done, to serve as umbrellas to protect ground forces. Although Coningham emphasized only the primacy of air superiority, and placed no priorities between interdiction and close air support, the tripartite idea of priorities became rigid at the Army Air Forces' School of Applied Tactics in Florida early in 1943 and was formally published in July of that year in F.M. 100–20. This concept of the relative effectiveness of the various types of tactical air power quickly became a bedrock of postwar Air Force doctrine.

Conclusions

Because of its disagreement with these priorities, the Army tried to expunge them. Shortly after the war it appeared, on paper, to succeed. The first postwar manual on air-ground operations in 1946 omitted any mention of priorities, leaving their determination up to the air commander on the scene. By enjoining air commanders to give precedence to missions that provided long-term effectiveness to the entire force over missions that conferred local, temporary assistance to only a portion of that force, however, the manual encouraged retention of the earlier priorities. Both air superiority and interdiction missions provided longer term effectiveness to a larger portion of the force than did close air support missions.

The Army continued to seek a change of priorities. For example, in the summer of 1949, their representatives on the Board of Review for Tactical Operations hoped to accomplish this by proposing a revision of the existing joint manuals for close air support. The issue arose again the following year in Korea. The Far East Command of General Douglas A. MacArthur, staffed essentially by Army personnel, at first insisted on using B–29 bombers almost exclusively for close air support. When the leaders of MacArthur's component air command, the Far East Air Forces, or FEAF, objected and opted for a more balanced employment of the aircraft, to include more interdiction missions, they were faulted for relegating close air support to a third priority. A similar charge was made against them by the ground commander of the X Corps, who sang the praises of Marine aviation because close air support was its sole priority. The Air Force airmen denied that close air support was necessarily a third priority, responding that tactical aircraft missions were determined by the existing battlefield situation and in consultation with ground forces.

This same ambivalence over the relative position of close air support in the hierarchy of tactical missions continued into the 1950s as the Air Force published its first doctrinal manuals. While proclaiming that priorities could not be established arbitrarily, and that they kept changing with the degree of battlefield success, these same manuals speculated that air superiority and interdiction missions were actually more useful to surface actions than were close air support sorties.

The issue was largely muted in Vietnam by two factors. In the first place, since there were enough planes in the country to satisfy the demands of all three priorities, competition for limited resources seldom arose. Second, the planes used inside South Vietnam for close air support were to a large extent separated physically and administratively from those employed for interdiction and air supremacy in Laos and North Vietnam. Since there were enough resources to go around, the issue of priorities seldom caused problems.

Nevertheless, the question of priorities for tactical air power was driven primarily by the larger command and control issue. It was its adherence to the principle that airmen should control airplanes, including the selection of the missions they flew, that perpetuated the Air Force's relegation, whether explic-

Help from Above

it or implicit, of close air support to a position, in time if not necessarily in importance, behind air supremacy and interdiction. In addition to being convinced that close air support was normally less effective than, and distracted from, other tactical missions, it was felt by some in the Air Force that assigning too much importance to close air support would lessen the control that airmen exercised over their aircraft. To support the Army entailed letting ground commanders in on the planning and giving them some say concerning targets, munitions, and other facets of air operations that the airmen viewed as solely their province in air combat and interdiction operations.

Another close air support area with a disappointing history during the three decades, due in large part to command and control controversy, was that of joint air-ground training. There had been little time for such training during World War I, and little progress was made between the world wars. Air-ground exercises at the Air Corps Tactical School were not realistic, and when the airmen's attention turned toward strategic bombing and away from attack aviation after 1935, joint air-ground practice received even less emphasis. As the United States prepared for World War II, the diversion of American aircraft to allies already at war crippled the Air Corps' ability to perform meaningful joint exercises with the Army. Following the war, the newly organized Tactical Air Command, or TAC, at first undertook an ambitious program of cooperation with the Army, providing air indoctrination courses to Army personnel and operating with them in combined exercises. These were demonstrations rather than realistic training exercises, and many Army leaders came to characterize them as *strictly an Air Force show*. The revision of the air-ground operations manual in 1946 went largely unheeded, as American strategy emphasized the defense. The Army felt little need to cross-train their troops in joint operations with the Air Force. The Air Force increasingly concentrated on the global threat from the USSR, with the result that TAC was reduced in size and influence.

Command and control differences surfaced during the infrequent joint exercises that did take place. The Army's experiment in 1949 with a Fire Support Coordination Center in the Tarheel maneuver suggested a diminution of the airmen's control. During two exercises the following year, strong differences of opinion arose as to whether control of the supporting aircraft should be decentralized by being given to assault battalions or whether the planes should retain their flexibility by continuing to be controlled from higher levels.

The results of this unhappy state of joint training in the late 1940s quickly became apparent in the opening phase of the Korean War. The Army found itself without officers trained for detailed coordination with the Air Force. This proved disastrous during the first month of the war, when lack of coordination between the two services resulted in several Air Force personnel being trapped behind enemy lines. The Air Force was hardly better prepared. Its sole Tactical Control Group, which was the main vehicle for coordinating with the Army

Conclusions

and controlling close air support missions, did not arrive in Korea until three months after hostilities began and, even then, was not totally proficient, due to lack of joint training. Pilots who flew close air support missions complained of not having had enough training with ground forces to enable them to shift easily from defensive to offensive operations. Both Army and Air Force high-level reports from the field placed the responsibility for these initial close air support problems on the lack of previous joint training. Predictably, each side often attributed these failures to the other. Although most of these problems were settled as the war progressed, the high price paid at the outset for lack of joint training was evident.

With the advent of Massive Retaliation after Korea, a malaise descended on air-ground cooperation and joint training. The Army filled only about half its quota of officers for the Air Force's Air-Ground Operations School, and command and control disagreements continued to plague air-ground exercises. The problem was exacerbated with the introduction of tactical nuclear weapons into training exercises. The Air Force withdrew from several exercises in the 1950s over the question of who should control nuclear weapons, and a major disagreement in 1955 over control of nuclear weapons almost scuttled the Sage Brush maneuver. The Air Force objected to the Army's insistence on controlling and targeting air-delivered weapons. The joint chiefs resolved the dispute with a temporary compromise that left the basic issue of command and control unresolved.

With the establishment of the unified Strike Command in 1961, joint training between the Army and Air Force enjoyed a revival. Dozens of joint exercises were held in the next two years. Although the overarching command and control questions remained unresolved, some cooperation was realized through numerous small adjustments to the existing Tactical Air Control System, the Air Ground Operating System, and exchange programs. Command and control differences, however, remained a stumbling block to truly effective joint training.

As the Army developed its airmobile concept in 1962, which featured increased reliance on its own close air support armed helicopters and fixed-wing planes, its appetite for joint exercises waned. The Army's decision to conduct the Air Assault II test unilaterally in 1964 and to cancel the planned joint Gold Fire II test early the following year signaled a retreat from cooperation with the Air Force and toward an isolation made possible by the substantial degree of self-sufficiency in close air support capability the Army had attained.

One of the chief barriers to joint training in close air support over the years was the failure of the services to agree on a joint doctrine. Contention over command and control of close air support aircraft was a major disruptive obstacle. In 1946, the Army approved a new manual on air ground operations, but only with reluctance. Its leaders were uncomfortable with the document's

Help from Above

command and control stipulations, such as that calling for a centralized Joint Operations Center, which reflected the Army Air Forces's experience in the war in Europe rather than ground-force doctrine. The document was published as a field manual and never attained joint status. Several other attempts to formulate joint doctrine in the late 1940s also foundered on disagreements over control of planes in amphibious operations.

Doctrinal differences over command and control also intervened to dash hopes of revising the 1946 air-ground operations manual as a joint manual four years later. This time the debate took place primarily within the Air Force. The Army and Air Force tactical commands had hammered out a joint training directive that each published separately as a service manual. The opportunity to have it approved as a joint statement on air-ground operations, however, was lost when higher Air Force headquarters objected to the document's implication that warfare was primarily surface action and that the mission of tactical air forces was solely to support ground battles. Although the procedures it outlined were used in Korea, the joint training directive never acquired the status and force of accepted joint doctrine.

Training exercises throughout the 1950s also suffered from a dearth of clear guidelines for the command and control of operations that a mutually agreed-upon joint doctrine could have provided. The Southern Pine maneuver in 1951 was almost canceled when the Army and Air Force spent valuable time reaching an agreement over who would control the fighter bombers and air-delivered weapons. The absence of a definitive joint doctrine on control of forces resulted in the Army's chief of staff concluding, after the Long Horn exercise the following year, that the control system for close air support was too slow and unmanageable. A definitive joint position on command and control for close air support could have avoided the embarrassing and contentious preliminaries that led up to the Sage Brush exercise in 1955. Although there was no shortage of Defense Department declarations outlining the services' roles and missions, there was a noticeable reticence to put into writing a joint doctrine for close air support. It can only be surmised that this lacuna existed because the close air support issue cut to the very heart of the two services' basic doctrine on command and control, and it was deemed preferable to let the services arrive at mutually acceptable practices through trial and error, without raising larger, controversial, doctrinal matters.

Another area that underwent little change during the period, at least on the surface, was that of official statements on roles and missions. The Air Force, in presenting its case for retaining control of close air support aircraft and operations, relied heavily, and perhaps too heavily, on repeated pronouncements from service and defense secretaries confirming close air support as a primary mission solely of the Air Force. Early roles and missions statements were somewhat vague, but became more specific with the passage of time. The first Executive Order, which accompanied its birth in 1947, gave the new Air Force the gener-

Conclusions

al responsibility for supporting the ground forces. Conferees at Key West the following year made this mission more specific by characterizing the Air Force's responsibility as that of providing close combat air support to the Army. By 1952 it had become even clearer, through a series of agreements between Army and Air Force leaders, that one of the Air Force's primary tasks was to provide close air support to the Army, and that the Army was prohibited from providing its own close air support. A Defense Department directive in 1956 again specifically forbade the Army to use its aircraft for close air support.

The Air Force's tendency to rely on the inviolability of the written word, while understandable, proved to be naive in the face of the Army's determination to establish for itself an airmobile mission. While Air Force leaders continued to interpret the close air support controversy as an *a priori* roles and missions issue and to argue against an Army close air support capability on that basis, the Army, supported by later secretaries of defense, saw it primarily *a posteriori* as a practical question that came down basically to hardware. The Army succeeded in creating an aerial branch whose success in providing close air support eventually overrode the stipulations of written documents. "Here, as with other technological developments," concluded one historian, "the service that developed a weapons system had an excellent chance to get to be the user, whether it had the mission or not."[1]

One other item in the close air support equation that changed little between World War II and Vietnam was the reciprocal attitudes with which members of both the Army and the Air Force viewed the actions and interpreted the motives of the other. At the higher headquarters levels, where cooperation was considered a prerequisite for effectiveness, the Joint Chiefs often displayed, at least on the surface, considerable sensitivity toward the other service's positions. Service chiefs and secretaries frequently made objective and honest attempts to resolve some of the knotty issues of close air support, although these efforts more often than not resulted in temporary accommodations rather than long-term solutions. By the same token, there was a noted tendency, especially at the Defense Secretary and Joint Chiefs levels, to avoid pronouncements on the larger issues of tactical air power that could turn out to be too absolute and permanent, and to rely instead on temporary and changeable accommodations, such as the stipulations concerning aircraft weights or designs. This avoidance of the absolute was due in part to the prevailing attitude of compromise and the unwillingness to arouse interservice antipathies of sufficient intensity to impair future working relations. This proclivity to emphasize the ephemeral was also a result of the recognition that, regardless of how absolute an official statement was intended to be, its shelf life was limited and some change would most likely be forthcoming.

Mutual suspicion of the other service's motives was more pronounced at the next lower echelon. Many Army leaders in the field held the conviction, at times fueled by the Air Force's own actions, that the Air Force was not totally

Help from Above

serious about close air support, was giving the Army only what it had left over from its more important missions, and that therefore the Army could do better and should assume the responsibility for close air support. Air Force leaders were cognizant of this attitude, as it was frequently conveyed to them by Army leaders. To them, this suspicion arose from what they saw as an Army view of the nature of warfare that was too narrow. Airmen looked at close air support not as an end in itself but as one facet of tactical air operations, and often a lesser one at that. That this often resulted in assigning higher priorities to air-to-air combat or to interdiction did not mean close air support and the success of the ground troops were being neglected. Throughout the period, the steps taken by Air Force leaders to change the Army's attitude were consistent, from Lt. Gen. Elwood R. Quesada's programs in the 1940s to demonstrate the Air Force's ability to perform the mission, through the Gold Fire tests over two decades later designed to show that Air Force tactical air support, when added to an Army ROAD division, could be just as effective as the proposed airmobile division.

Air Force suspicions that the Army was attempting a takeover of part of the close air support mission were unallayed. As in other areas of close air support, the question of command and control loomed large. Just as some Air Force actions and statements seemed to confirm the Army's suspicions, so the Army's unremitting crusade to gain control, first of the development and then of the operation of close air support planes, created a defensive attitude on the part of many Air Force officers. It can be rightfully asked why the Air Force insisted on retaining the close air support mission that was causing it so much controversy and discord with so little return. Some Air Force officers, especially the more strategically minded, did not favor keeping the mission. But two reasons pushed the prevailing sentiment in the direction of preserving it. On a more abstract level, Air Force doctrineers and traditionalists believed that air power was indivisible and that its effectiveness would suffer from the detachment of one of its functions from the whole. More pragmatically, the assignment of a mission to a service was accompanied by budgeted funds to accomplish that mission. Loss of the close air support mission would entail a budget reduction for the Air Force, a prospect that any service would seek to avoid.

Fortunately, the attitudes of pilots and soldiers at the subordinate operating levels, once the chaos of the opening phase of wars subsided, most often took the form of light-hearted rivalry and seldom, whether in World War II, in Korea, or in Vietnam, prevented them from cooperating effectively in carrying out close air support missions. Army and Air Force interaction in Vietnam was exceptionally smooth and effective. The question of whether this cooperation, which appears to have greatly improved since the Korean War, reflected true progress toward better close air support policies and procedures between the wars, or whether the Army, having acquired some of its own close air support

Conclusions

capability and eliminated some of its reliance on the Air Force, was less prone to criticize Air Force support, cannot be answered. On the whole these attitudes seem to have changed little over the years and were to form an important factor in post-1973 close air support discussions between the Army and the Air Force.

While the status of priorities, joint training and doctrine, official statements of roles and missions, and service attitudes remained fairly static since World War II, more substantive transformations took place in other close air support areas. Three issues underwent deep-seated changes: the definition and range of close air support, the tactics, techniques and procedures for controlling and executing close air support strikes, and, most radical of all, the question of the most suitable type of close air support aircraft.

The formal definition of close air support, as it was understood by both services, did not change appreciably over these decades. The essential elements of close air support, which remained constant, included aerial activity directed against enemy ground units that were close enough to friendly troops to require that the air strikes be coordinated with the ground troops who were receiving the assistance.

While the formal definition was general enough to avoid substantial alteration, there was considerable activity in interpreting the official pronouncement. From time to time attempts were made to modify the definition in response to political or technological developments. During the 1950s, for example, the Army seemed at times to wish to include reconnaissance and even airlift sorties within the definition of close air support, although the Air Force always looked upon these types of sorties as part of the more comprehensive tactical mission called tactical air support. As one of its many arguments to support the idea of an airmobile unit, the Howze Board in 1963 sought to modify the definition of close air support by separating it into two missions: close air support, which the Air Force could properly provide, and aerial fire support, which required more intimate coordination with infantry, tank, and armored units—coordination that could only be achieved, in Howze's view, if the Army controlled its own close air support assets. Once the airmobile concept was approved and the Army acquired its own organic close air support capability, however, this distinction between close air support and aerial fire support disappeared from the service literature.

One of the major claims proffered by the U.S. Marines in arguing for the superiority of their system of close air support was that Marine aircraft, thanks to the constant training of its pilots with its infantry units, were able to strike enemy forces much closer to friendly troops than could Air Force planes. While this was often true, it was also irrelevant when contrasting the two incompatible systems. Unlike Marine close air support, in which aircraft seldom performed in concert with other types of firepower, Air Force close air support missions were intimately tied in with other concurrent forms of fire-

Help from Above

power, principally artillery. As a result, the effectiveness of Air Force close air support sorties was determined by how closely they meshed with ground artillery and how decisive was the outcome of combined air and ground firepower upon the enemy. Proximity of the strikes to friendly forces was seldom considered important. Quite the contrary. Since the inception of military air power, the Air Force and its predecessors consistently looked down upon such close-in strikes as the least productive way to use aircraft.

Since the Army/Air Force system seldom required aircraft to strike particularly close to friendly forces, especially against targets that were more suitable for artillery, the degree of proximity to friendly troops was not as essential a part of the definition of close air support for these services as it was for the Marines. Over the decades, more attention has been paid by the Army and Air Force to the relationship between aerial firepower and artillery. In fact, the arena for close air support was ordinarily determined around the capabilities of artillery. Before World War II, attack planes were prohibited from striking anywhere within the range of artillery. This area ban was gradually lifted during the war. By the time hostilities ended, fighter-bombers were allowed to strike in areas that were within artillery range, but were limited to striking only those targets that artillery could not effectively hit. Subsequent technological progress extended the area where close air support could be most profitably employed, pushing it out to the edge of the interdiction region where coordination with the ground forces was not required. Later refinements would result in referring to the aerial activity in this hybrid border region as battlefield air interdiction.

While technological changes over the decades were influential in expanding the range of close air support operations, it was the command and control issue, more than technology, that encouraged attempts to modify the concept of close air support. In particular, efforts to create a distinction between two categories of close air support, and even to change the name, were inspired by the Army's conviction that some types of close air support could be performed only by pilots and planes devoted solely to that mission. That meant personnel and equipment commanded and controlled by the Army. Once the Army achieved its own close air support capability in the form of armed helicopters, the crusade to alter the definition and description of close air support ended.

The same ancillary position that technology occupied in relation to command and control decisions in the case of defining close air support can also be seen in the improvements made to the tactics and techniques used by the services in performing the close air support mission. This primarily involved changes to the Tactical Air Control and Air-Ground Operations Systems, which were responsible for close air support. The technological advances in jet propulsion, missile technology, and armaments and communications constituted an important factor in enhancing the effectiveness of air-ground operations.

Conclusions

A UH–1H Iroquois during a training flight.

Yet, unless managed by a control structure that used it to its best advantage, the most sophisticated technology would have remained neutral, a force for neither improvement nor regression. The introduction during this period of major improvements in two elements of the Tactical Air Control System, namely, the ground elements and the airborne elements that control close air support planes in the battle zone, can be more fruitfully viewed as resulting primarily from command and control decisions rather than from technological breakthroughs.

One of these improvements consisted of an incremental refinement of the ground elements of the air-ground system that controlled strike aircraft. This witnessed a gradual change of the locus of control from the highly centralized and relatively unsophisticated Air Support Commands of World War II to the Direct Air Support Centers, or DASCs, that proved their worth in Vietnam. At the same time this represented a decentralization of close air support operations about as far down the line as it could go without contravening the Air Force's doctrine of centralized control.

During World War II, many soldiers expressed dissatisfaction with the air support commands that, in their opinion, coordinated the air and ground action at too high a level, the field army echelon, to allow them to make any meaningful input into decisions concerning close air support missions. They wanted a larger voice in determining the types of missions, targets, and armaments that close air support aircraft provided. After the war, these air commands were replaced by a system featuring a Joint Operations Center, or JOC that, on paper, seemed to place Army and Air Force members on an equal footing in controlling close air support planes. In reality, the JOC, like its predecessor,

Help from Above

was also located at the field army level, and became an organizational part of a numbered Air Force for controlling Air Force planes. Army generals complained about this in Korea, where one of them refused to deal with the center and instead tried to circumvent it by using Marine planes.

In Vietnam, a substantial portion of the authority to control close air support planes was moved down one echelon from the field army and placed in Air Support Operations Centers at the corps level. The absence of battle lines and the fluidity of combat resulted in increased responsibilities for these centers, which in 1965, were renamed DASCs. This added responsibility was in accordance with the Air Force's policy of centralized control and decentralized operation of close air support aircraft. As experience mounted in Vietnam, airmen became increasingly proficient in using these DASCs to control close air support missions by performing such functions as scrambling aircraft from alert, synchronizing forward air controllers with strike aircraft, plotting coordinates, and avoiding border violations and short rounds. Air Force doctrine, published in the late 1960s, enshrined the DASC as the primary element of the Tactical Air Control System for executing close air and other tactical air support functions.

Part of the reason for the acceptance of the lower level DASC was the on-going efforts by the Air Force to decrease the unacceptably long amount of time it had been taking planes to respond to emergency immediate calls for help from ground units engaged with an enemy. The 100-minute response times of World War II were reduced to about 90 minutes in the late 1950s. In the hit-and-run war in Vietnam, however, such lengthy waits for help were particularly unsatisfactory; frequently the enemy had fled to safety before the planes arrived. Several changes to the Tactical Air Control System reduced this time considerably. In 1964 the Air Force established its own air-request net in Vietnam that allowed requests for immediate strikes to go directly from battalions to the Air Support Operations Centers (later DASCs). In the absence of a veto from any of the intervening levels of command, which monitored the requests, the center launched the mission. This represented an extension of an air-request practice established seven years earlier in the Joint Air-Ground Operations Manual.

Several methods adopted for launching close air support missions also helped to reduce response times. Most of the planes that the DASCs sent on immediate strike missions were ones that had been scheduled the day before for preplanned missions and were either still at home base or were already airborne. A large number of immediate strike planes were also called from airfields where they had been standing by on 15-minute alerts. A smaller number were summoned from airborne alert. Response times of these aircraft varied depending upon their status. Although impossible to quantify with any assurance, or to generalize about such a variety of different types of response, the overall result of these measures was a considerable reduction of response time,

Conclusions

to a point where user dissatisfaction became muted and an occasional criticism even began to be heard of strike planes arriving too early over their targets.

In addition to improvements in the ground element of the Tactical Air Control System, advances in the airborne elements were also instrumental in streamlining the close air support system in Vietnam. The most dramatic of these improvements was the increased use of airborne forward air controllers, or FACs. Although on rare occasions during World War II controllers took to the air, the postwar manuals and agreements on air-ground operations spoke almost exclusively of FACs as members of the ground Tactical Air Control Parties, or TACPs. The question of whether or not controllers should fly became an issue between the Air Force and the Army, with many airmen favoring airborne controllers and many soldiers preferring the controllers to remain on the ground. The issues of both command and control and effectiveness figured into the debate. In Korea, the Army commander of X Corps considered ground TACPs to be superior to the airborne Mosquito FACs, in part because he had more control over officers who were on the ground. He hoped to increase this control by relaxing the requirement that the groundborne controllers be fighter pilots, and even proposed using nonrated Army officers in that position. This suggestion, which resurfaced later in the 1960s as a recommendation of the Close Air Support Board, was not acted upon.

Not all Air Force commanders in Korea were sold on the idea of airborne controllers. The loss of combat pilots to serve as Mosquitoes caused hardships to many fighter squadrons. Some commanders agreed with the Army that nonrated officers could perform the functions of FACs as well as their rated confreres.

Vietnam settled the issue. The geography and terrain of the country made the job of ground-based controllers virtually impossible. The dense jungle terrain and undergrowth not only rendered much of their equipment unusable, but also severely impaired their ability to see clearly enough to obtain a contextual vision of the battle. The enormous influx of airborne FACs, their excellent training, and the effectiveness of their performance quelled any move toward relying on ground personnel.

Whether or not the planes flown by these FACs should be armed or not was also an issue of control, and was largely one that took place within the Air Force. The early spotter planes, the OH–1 Bird Dogs and the OH–2s, were civilian planes that had not been built with an eye toward installing guns or cannons. Although the pilots of these planes often expressed the desire to have an armed controller aircraft, this was not feasible with this first-generation of planes. Air Force commanders at first opposed the idea of arming the control planes, fearing that such a move would divert the FACs, who were fighter pilots, away from their primary missions of controlling other fighters and performing visual reconnaissance, and turn their flights into strike missions.

Help from Above

Despite the ban, many FACs in the early days carried rifles, pistols, and even grenades, which they used on their missions.

Two considerations swung the balance in favor of arming the FAC aircraft. First was the argument that the majority of contacts were with small groups of the enemy that could be attacked by small armed planes without having to resort to the overkill that was often the result of calling in heavy, expensive jet fighter-bombers. Therefore, many of the enemy who were currently escaping could be struck. Second, the new FAC plane, the OV–10 Bronco, was configured from the beginning with gun stations. Within a year of its introduction into the war in 1968, Seventh Air Force ordered that they be armed and permitted controllers to fire at enemy troops under certain conditions. Earlier fears proved unfounded, as the pilots displayed remarkable restraint in carrying out their responsibilities as controllers.

Among the more pervasive changes brought about in the area of close air support by Army/Air Force disagreements, primarily over the issue of command and control, were those concerning the type of plane that could best accomplish the close air support mission. This drama unfolded in three sequential acts. The initial controversy arose when the Air Force, despite Army discomfiture, began to substitute jet fighter-bombers for its propeller-driven aircraft for close air support. A second conflagration was touched off when the Army, over rather half-hearted and ineffectual Air Force opposition, integrated organic armed helicopters into its ground forces and began to employ them as close air support vehicles. Finally, the period witnessed an attempt by the Air Force to slow down the Army's powerful momentum toward obtaining larger and more expensive close air support helicopters by developing its own close air support plane, despite its traditional hesitancy to spend money on planes that could perform only one mission.

The first change came with the gradual acceptance, after much debate, of jet aircraft in the close air support role. Although technology made this change possible, and probably even inevitable, the controversy that preceded the endorsement of jets was waged primarily over the question of their effectiveness on the battlefield and ultimately, as with other issues, over the question of who should control them on close air support missions.

As soon as the Air Force approved its first jet fighter-bomber, the F–80, for tactical missions, including close air support, in 1947, the Army began to express doubts about the suitability of any jet to satisfy its close air support requirements. The Army's list of the jets' deficiencies was long. The planes' high rate of fuel consumption kept them from remaining over the battlefield long enough to reassure the ground troops. This in fact often proved to be the case in Korea. In addition, the need for additional fuel and maintenance that jet planes generated placed unnecessary added burdens on logistics personnel and facilities. The jets' extremely wide radius of turn made it difficult for pilots to pinpoint targets. At first, jets were unable to carry all the ordnance, such as

Conclusions

napalm, which the Army requested. Jet engines, in the view of some Army officers, were highly vulnerable to ground fire. Jet planes needed large and fully equipped airfields, which were not always available and took long to construct. The needs of propeller-driven aircraft, on the other hand, were believed by the Army to be fewer and more easily obtainable.

The Air Force's reply, based on the results of both joint maneuvers and unilateral tests, stressed that jets were faster and quieter and therefore more capable of surprising the enemy, that the absence of torque in their engines increased a pilot's accuracy, that they were more rugged and more easily maintained than propeller planes, that they had better guns, and that they could fly during weather conditions that normally would ground nonjet planes.

Technological and budgetary concerns partly account for this difference of opinion. To the Air Force, to whom jet propulsion represented the future of aviation, retention of nonjet aircraft was seen as an unacceptable drain on its finite budget with little to show in higher effectiveness. Since jets were indisputably better for the air superiority and interdiction roles, and since the same planes performed close air support, the solution to overcoming potential shortcomings of the jets in close air support lay in improving jet planes and the tactics and techniques of their pilots, not in reverting to the employment of outmoded aircraft. In the Air Force view, planes designed for the least significant function had no place in an air force made up of multipurpose aircraft.

Behind these technological and budgetary considerations, however, were questions of command and control. Throughout the period one of the Army's unswerving aspirations was to increase its influence over the close air support function, either by adjusting the mechanisms that controlled close air support airplanes or by acquiring its own close air support aircraft. It became evident soon after World War II, as the Air Force entered the jet age, that the Army could not follow suit. It lacked the resources and the incentive to establish a full-fledged research and development, production, training, and maintenance capability for jet planes. Smaller, slower, less expensive propeller-driven planes, on the other hand, provided the Army with an asset that would permit it to compete for a portion of the close air support mission without diverting appreciable funds from other branches of the service. The question of the relative effectiveness of jet and propeller-driven aircraft, although normally in the forefront of studies and reports on the issue, frequently was merely the outer manifestation of a hidden command and control agenda.

Unable to persuade the Air Force to assign it specific air units for close air support, the Army developed its own close air support resources. To achieve this it relied on two basic elements: the opening offered it by the National Security Act and the Executive Order in 1947 to retain its own organic aircraft, and its felt need to offset the superiority in importance that firepower was enjoying by increasing its own mobility. Command and control of close air support planes became the recurring theme throughout all the discussions and

Help from Above

studies between the two services. While the Army maintained that control of the planes by ground commanders was essential, the Air Force over the years sought to allay the Army's fears by demonstrating that it could provide effective close air support. In Korea the Army was unsuccessful, despite sustained efforts on the part of its top commanders, in having the Air Force assign airplanes permanently to specific ground units. Throughout the remainder of the 1950s, Army studies, such as the *Tactical Air Support Feasibility* study, reiterated the theme that close air support airplanes, like artillery and other forms of ground firepower, were tools of the ground commander, who should have the authority to decide on their employment.

The bible of airmobility was the final report of the Howze Board in 1962. As with the other studies, the underlying thesis of this report was that the Army's organic planes, principally helicopters, if integrated into Army divisions and controlled by division commanders, would provide more mobility and be more effective for some tactical air missions, including close air support, than the existing system that relied on Air Force fighter planes. Some close air support functions were to be retained by the Air Force, namely in instances requiring a mass of planes to attack a single target. Yet for the day-to-day needs, it was essential that the ground commander be in control. These day-to-day needs, as outlined in the report, included such existing Air Force close air support missions as accompanying troop carrier helicopters into battle, providing suppressive fire and close air support after the troops landed, and

A crewman mans an M–60 machine gun on an Iroquois helicopter.

Conclusions

protecting marching columns from threats from the air and from the ground. The study envisioned using helicopters for tactical envelopment of the enemy up to 300 miles.

The Air Force's response to the Howze report also stressed the command and control issue. It held that in unified operations, which were the only kind envisioned for the future, the priorities and decisions about how to use air power should be the prerogative of the unified commander, who was responsible for the overall operation, and not be left to any one of his subordinate component commanders. Aircraft were present for use throughout the entire theater, not for employment in only one segment of the theater's operations.

Approval of the airmobile division concept with its organic close air support capability encouraged the Army to build larger and more expensive helicopters that were soon approaching the size and cost of Air Force fighters. The Air Force's response was to develop a specific close air support plane. Two reasons were normally offered for this decision, which reversed earlier tradition. The first reason contributed to the command and control argument. Despite the claims of complementarity by both services, research on this A–X aircraft was a logical step in the ongoing Air Force campaign to convince the Army that it could provide it with the required close air support. The A–X was envisioned within the Air Force as a substitute for, not a complement to, the Army's advanced helicopter. And since the proposed plane would remain within the Air Force, the doctrine of centralized control would be maintained.

The second explanation offered for developing the close air support plane was an economic one. At the time the Air Force was also developing a new fighter plane, the F–15, as its front line fighter. Fighter planes, however, had become so expensive to build and maintain that not enough of them could be purchased to serve the triple role of air superiority, interdiction, and close air support. It was argued that it made more economic sense to build a plane just for close air support, whose simpler requirements would make it less expensive, than to divert expensive front line planes that were in short supply to close air support. Doing the latter ran the risk of losing the front line battle, in which case close air support would be of no avail. As it turned out, initial fears expressed by some that such a plane would end up in Army hands proved unfounded.

In sum, close air support issues developed at an uneven pace between 1946 and 1973. While the basic assumptions within both the Army and the Air Force relating to the command and control of air power remained undented, a series of compromises on peripheral issues produced a veneer of change. The most substantive change occurred with the official approval of the airmobile idea. Despite a later political agreement between the chiefs of staff of the two services to the effect that Army helicopter missions were not to be defined as close air support, these rotary vehicles did displace some Air Force functions in that role. Acceptance of the airmobile concept represented a further step in the dissipation of air power.

Help from Above

The Army's single-mindedness of purpose does not in itself explain the success of armed helicopters in assuming a portion of the close air support mission. Air Force naiveté and complacency played their part. Throughout the period, the Air Force relied heavily—probably too heavily—on the authority of official statements that assigned the close air support function to it as a primary mission while excluding the Army from sharing in the mission: the National Security Act of 1947, the Key West and Newport Agreements of 1948, arrangements between service secretaries and between chiefs of staff, the Wilson Memorandum of 1957, and others. This credulous overreliance on the written word, along with a tendency to endow doctrine with too much importance, blinded many Air Force leaders, causing them to underestimate the effectiveness of the Army's more pragmatic approach. Since these agreements militated against their position, Army decision makers circumvented them by treating them as dead letters. This attitude was neatly reflected in the 1965 assertion from the Army staff that the Army did not feel bound by any 20-year-old piece of paper. In this they were encouraged by the secretaries of defense of the 1960s who, like the Army thinkers, placed more weight on future effectiveness than on past promises.

Air Force complacency was also a factor. Secure in the permanency of America's strategic policy and of its preeminent role in that strategy, the Air Force immediately after World War II invested its immediate future and funds in strategic deterrence and war-fighting capabilities. In so doing, it overlooked the potential of helicopters, over which it had a monopoly at the time and which it deemed to be both aerodynamically and tactically ineffectual, by giving them away to the Army. The Army, on the other hand, searching for a mission in the nuclear age, was quick to take advantage of the potential of rotary wing aircraft and capitalized on the Air Force's distraction. The result was a diminution of the centralization of air assets that the Air Force traditionally placed as a centerpiece of its air doctrine.

On balance, however, the Air Force managed to retain both close air support as a primary mission and most of the resources to perform the mission. As a result, the controversy with the Army had run only half its course by 1973. The familiar positions and arguments of the two services would be repeated in the following decades as the Army adopted the AirLand Battle strategy. On the broader, defense-wide scale, the question of redundancy of close air support assets remained below the surface, shielded by agreement across the board on the complementarily of close air support capabilities.

Notes

Chapter 1

1. What distinguishes a close air support mission from other tactical air missions is its proximity to ground forces sufficient to require intimate coordination with those forces. Since almost all Air Service missions in World War I called for a close working relationship with the ground forces, they were close air support sorties, even though the name is of later vintage.

2. Karl von Clausewitz, *On War*, ed. and trans. Michael Howard and Peter Paret (Princeton, NJ: Princeton University Press, 1976); Raymond Aron, *Clausewitz: Philosopher of War* (London: Routledge and Kegan Paul, 1983); Michael Howard, *Clausewitz* (New York: Oxford University Press, 1983); Michael J. Handel, ed., *Clausewitz and Modern Strategy* (New York: Frank Cass, 1989).

3. Clausewitz's discussions of targets other than the opposition's army are dotted throughout Clausewitz, *On War*. The clearest statements appear on pp 595–96.

4. War Department, *Field Service Regulations, United States Army, 1914*, in Maurer Maurer, *The U.S. Air Service in World War I*, 4 vols., (Washington, DC: Office of Air Force History, 1978–1979), vol. 2, pp 23, 25.

5. House Committee on Military Affairs, *Act to Increase the Efficiency in the Aviation Service: Hearings before the Committee on Military Affairs*, 63d Cong., 1st sess., 1913. In Maurer, *Air Service*, vol. 2, pp 3–7.

6. Capt William Mitchell's testimony in Maurer, *Air Service*, vol. 2, p 10.

7. An interesting analysis of World War I aviation as defensive is presented by Charles D. Bright, "Air Power in World War I: Sideshow or Decisive Factor?," *Aerospace Historian*, Jun 1971, pp 52–62.

8. Alfred Goldberg and Lt Col Donald Smith, *Army-Air Force Relations: The Close Air Support Issue*, (Santa Monica, Calif: The RAND Corporation, #R-906-PR, 1971), p 1.

9. Observation missions were ordered by the Army G–2 for army reconnaissance flights and by the Army G–3 for command reconnaissance sorties. The Army G–3 section also issued orders for artillery adjustment missions, pursuit missions involving patrolling, tactical bombing missions, and balloon surveillance missions. At the Corps level, visual observation flights were ordered by the Corps G–2, while the Corps G–3 issued operational orders for command reconnaissance and balloon surveillance missions. The Army division commander controlled liaison flights, and the division artillery commander ordered artillery liaison sorties. The only types of missions left to the discretion of the Air Service commander were pursuit missions flown to protect observation aircraft. Maurer, *Air Service*, vol. 3, pp 5–6.

10. Memo, Col William Mitchell to Col Hugh Drum, Sep 7, 1918, in Maurer, *Air Service*, vol. 3, pp 102–103.

11. For one among many such complaints see that of Col Frank P. Lahm, Army Air Service Commander, 2d Army, "Lessons Learned," in Maurer, *Air Service*, vol. 4, p 356.

12. "Post-War Review: Lessons Learned," in Maurer, *Air Service*, vol. 4, p 218.

13. Maj F.M. Shumaker, radio officer, I Corps Observation Group, "Lessons Learned," in Maurer, *Air Service*, vol. 4, p 213.

14. Col Walter C. Kilner, chief, Training Section, Air Service, AEF, "Lessons Learned," in Maurer, *Air Service*, vol. 4, pp 324–27.

15. James J. Hudson, *Hostile Skies: A Combat History of the American Air Service in World War I* (Syracuse, NY: Syracuse University Press, 1968), p 58; Ltr, Maj Gen Malin Craig to Col William Mitchell, in Benjamin D. Foulois, "Air Service, American Expeditionary Forces, 1917–1919" in Gen B.D. Foulois collection, (United States Air Force Historical Research Center, Maxwell AFB, Ala); William Mitchell,

Help from Above

Memoirs of World War I (NY: Random House, 1960), p 10.

16. "Final Report of the Chief of the Air Service," in Maurer, *Air Service*, vol. 1, p 47.

17. For example, the basic doctrinal manual for observation aircraft (*Instruction on Liaison for Troops of All Arms*) issued by AEF headquarters in August 1917, was a direct translation of the French Army's manual of the previous December. Likewise, a French revision of the manual in December 1917 was translated and issued as an American manual (*Liaison for All Arms*) six months later. See Edgar Raines's notes on the manuscript, Jun 18, 1993, in the Center of Air Force History.

18. Memo, Maj William Mitchell, Aviation Section, Signal Corps, to Chief of Staff (CofS), American Expeditionary Forces, Jun 1917, in Maurer, *Air Service*, vol. 2, pp 108, 111.

19. Air Service Information Circular, vol. 1, no. 72, Jun 12, 1920, in Maurer, *Air Service*, vol. 2, p 304.

20. Provisional Manual of Operations for Air Service Units, Coblenz, Germany, Dec 23, 1918, in Maurer, *Air Service*, vol. 2, p 290.

21. Lt Col William O. Sherman, "Tentative Manual for the Employment of Air Service," in Maurer, *Air Service*, vol. 2, p 314.

22. Holley, I.B. Jr., *Ideas and Weapons: Exploitation of the Aerial Weapon By the United States During World War I* (Hamden, Conn.: Archon Books, 1951), p 127.

23. Maj George E.A. Reinburg, Commanding Officer (CO), 2d Day Bombardment Group, in Maurer, *Air Service*, vol. 4, pp 84–85.

24. Field Order no. 41, Annex no. 2: Plan for the Air Service, Sep 9, 1918, in Maurer, *Air Service*, vol. 3, p 113; Historical Summaries, 8th and 90th Aero Squadrons in Maurer, *Air Service*, vol. 3, pp 690–92; Lessons Learned, 90th Aero Squadron, in Mauer, *Air Service*, vol. 4, p 126; 2d Lt Adolph O. Devre, Liaison Officer, 50th Aero Squadron, in Mauer, *Air Service*, vol. 4, pp 180–182.

25. Capt Stephen H. Noyes, CO, Corps Observation Group, First Army, "Lessons Learned" in Maurer, *Air Service*. vol. 4, p 115; 90th Aero Squadron, in Maurer, *Air Service*. vol. 4, p 126.

26. Capt Harlowe Hardinge, Radio Division, Office of the Chief Signal Officer, AEF, "Lessons Learned" in Maurer, *Air Service*, vol. 4, pp 252–53, 256.

27. *Ibid*, p 254; William Mitchell, "Leaves From My War Diary," in Frank C. Platt, comp., *Great Battles of World War I: In the Air* (New York: Signet, 1966), pp 175–76.

28. Memo, HQ Air Service, First Army, "Army Dropping Point for Messages Via Airplane," Sep 4, 1918, in Maurer, *Air Service*, vol. 3, pp 82–83.

29. Mitchell, "Leaves," pp 176–77.

30. 90th Aero Squadron, "Lessons Learned," in Maurer, *Air Service*, vol. 4, p 128.

31. HQ, Chief of Air Service, First Army, "Circular No 1," Aug 19, 1918, in Maurer, *Air Service*, vol. 3, pp 32–33.

32. 90th Aero Squadron, "Lessons Learned," in Maurer, *Air Service*, vol. 4, p 127.

33. Field Order no. 41, Annex A 5th Division, Sep 9, 1918, in Maurer, *Air Service*, vol. 3, p 117.

34. *Ibid*.

35. See, for example, Rpt, Lt Col Davenport Johnson, CO, 2d Pursuit Group, in Maurer, *Air Service*, vol. 4, p 40; HQ, Chief of Air Service, First Army, "Circular No. 1," Aug 19, 1918, in Maurer, *Air Service*, vol. 3, p 43.

36. Capt Stephen H. Noyes, CO, Corps Observation Group, First Army, in Maurer, *Air Service*, vol. 4, p 108.

37. Lt Col George W. D'Armond, Chief, Personnel Section, Air Service, AEF, in Maurer, *Air Service*, vol. 4, p 310.

38. Lt Col Philip A. Carroll, Assistant Chief, Training Section, Air Service, AEF, in Maurer, *Air Service*, vol. 4, p 313.

39. Mitchell, "Leaves," pp 148, 155–56.

40. *Ibid*, p 122, 314.

41. Chief of Air Service, AEF, "Final Report," in Maurer, *Air Service*, vol. 1, p 89.

42. Col Thomas DeWitt Milling, Army Air Service Commander, First Army, in Maurer, *Air Service*, vol. 4, p 359.

43. Col Frank P. Lahm, Army Air Service Commander, Second Army, in Maurer, *Air Service*, vol. 4, p 356.

44. Mitchell, "Leaves," p 112.

45. Maj Howard S. Curry, CO, HQ Detchament, Third Aviaton Training Center, in Maurer, *Air Service*, vol. 4, p 337.

46. Chief of Air Service, "Final Report," 1919, in Maurer, *Air Service*, vol. 1, p 89.

47. 1st Lt Pressley B. Shuss, Observer, 90th Aero Squadron, in Maurer, *Air Service*, vol. 4, pp 185, 189.

48. 2d Lt Fred E. D'Amour, Operations Officer, 1st Aero Aquadron, in Maurer. *Air Service*, vol. 4, pp 171–72.

49. *Ibid,* pp 171–72, 188, 190.

50. Maj F.N. Shumaker, OIC, Air Service Section, Radio Division, OCSO, AEF, in Maurer, *Air Service*, vol. 4, pp 263–66, 270.

51. D'Amour, in Maurer, *Air Service*, vol. 4, p 171.

52. *General der Flieger* a. D. Paul Deichmann, *German Air Force Operations in Support of the Army*, USAF Historical Study no. 163 (Maxwell AFB: Research Studies Institute, Jun 1962), p 5; Richard P. Hallion, *Strike From the Sky* (Washington, DC: Smithsonian Institution Press, 1989), pp 19–22.

53. Proceedings, *Attack Aviation,* Air Corps Tactical School (ACTS), Maxwell Field, Ala, 1936–1937, AFHRC 248.2201B, pp 2–4.

54. Course, *Attack Aviation: History and Development*, ACTS, Maxwell Field, Ala, 1935–1936, K248. 2205B, p 3.

55. Deichmann, *German Air Force*, pp 5–7.

56. Attack Aviation, Training Division, *Training Manual No 2: Air Force*, part 3, Air Corps Advanced Flying School, Kelly Field, Texas, 1927, AFHRC 248.222-55B, p 5; Proceedings, *Attack Aviation*.

57. "Tactical History of Pursuit Aviation," in Maurer, *Air Service*, vol. 1, p 326.

58. Course, *Attack Aviation*, pp 2, 5.

59. "Tactical History of Pursuit Aviation," in Maurer, *Air Service*, vol. 1, p 331; Mitchell, "Leaves," p 167; 5th Division, *Field Order No. 41*, Sep 9, 1918, Annex no. 2: Plan for Air Service, in Maurer, *Air Service*, vol. 3, p 112; Brereton Greenhous, "Close Support Aircraft in World War I: The Counter-Tank Role," *Aerospace Historian*, Jun 1974, vol. 21, pp 87–93.

60. 91st Aero Squadron, "Lessons Learned," in Maurer, *Air Service*, vol. 4, p 130.

61. 2d Lt W.J. Rogers, Observer, 50th Aero Squadron, in Maurer, *Air Service*, vol. 4, p 177.

62. 1st Lt Dogan M. Arthur, Pilot, 12th Aero Squadron, in Maurer, *Air Service*, vol. 4, pp 147–48.

63. 2d Lt H.L. Borden, Observer, 90th Aero Squadron, in Maurer, *Air Service*, vol. 4, p 192.

64. Capt John Wentworth, Assistant Operations Officer, 1st Pursuit Wing, in Maurer, *Air Service*, vol. 4, p 50.

65. 2d Lt William Nickel, Aerial Gunner, 99th Aero Squadron, in Maurer, *Air Service*, vol. 4, pp 192, 195.

66. For example, see *Ibid*, p 42.

67. Robert Sherrod, *History of the Marine Corps Aviation in World War II* (Washington, DC: Combat Forces Press, 1952), pp 11–18.

68. War Department Training Regulation 440–15, *Fundamental Principles for the Employment of the Air Service*, Jan 26, 1926, AFHRC 248.211-65a.

69. *Employment of Combined Air Force*, Air Service Tactical School text, Apr 6, 1926.

70. "Provisional Manual of Operations," Dec 23, 1918, in Maurer, *Air Service*, vol. 2, p 267.

71. *Ibid*; "Tentative Manual for the Employment of Air Service," 1919, in Mau-

rer, *Air Service*, vol. 2, pp 290–95; 369–375.

72. Training Regulation 440–l5, "Air Tactics," Air Service Field Officers School, Langley, Va, 1922, AFHRC 248.101-4A, pp 7–8, 11–13.

73. Maurer Maurer, *Aviation in the U.S. Army, 1919–1939* (Washington, DC: Office of Air Force History, 1987), Appendices 2 and 3.

74. Course, *Attack Aviation*; Proceedings, Maurer Maurer, ed., *Air Force Combat Units of World War II* (Washington DC: Office of Air Force History, 1983), p 61; Maurer, *Aviation*, p 473.

75. Ltr, ACTS to Chief of the Air Corps, "Attack Aviation," Jan 7, 1928, AFHRC 248.2201B, Frames 111ff.

76. Memo, ACTS to Chief of the Air Corps, May 27, 1938, AFHRC 248.2206B-1, p 3; ACTS, "The Development of a Special Attack Plane for Support of Ground Troops," May 14, 1937, AFHRC 248.222-54, p 5.

77. Maj Omer O. Niergarth, *The Attack Airplane in Support of Ground Forces*, ACTS, 1937–1938, AFHRC Reel A2796, 248.222-56, Frames 49ff, pp 5, 9; Course, *Attack Aviation*, p 1.

78. See, for example, such papers written at the school as Capt R.C. Blatt, Cavalry Officer, "The Effect of Attack Aviation on Ground Troops," Mar 14, 1928, AFHRC Reel 2796, 248.222-56, Frames 798ff; Maj George Arneman, Field Artillery Officer, "The Artillery-Air Corps Team," May 15, 1928, AFHRC Reel 2771, 248.211-103, Frames 1329ff; Maj O. Morales, Air Corps, "Aerial Machine Gun Fire on Ground Troops," May 15, 1928, AFHRC Reel A2796, 248.222-68E; Capt Stuart Cutter, Infantry Officer, "The Effect of Aviation on Troop Movements," AFHRC 248.222-56, Frames 946-61.

79. Ltr, Office of the Chief of Air Corps to Commandant, ACTS, "Marine Corps Activities in Nicaragua," Apr 20, 1928, with attachment, "Marine Corps Operations in Nicaragua," Commandant, USMC, Feb 21, 1928, AFHRC Reel 2796, 248.222-56, Frames 1027ff.

80. Memo, Assistant Commandant, ACTS, "The Effect of Attack Aviation on Ground Troops," Langley Field, Va, Mar 14, 1928, AFHRC 248.222-68, pp 7–8.

81. Memo, Assistant Commandant, ACTS, Maxwell Field, Ala, "The Future of Attack Aviation," Dec 2, 1936, AFHRC 248.220lB, Frames 1458ff, p 3.

82. Proceedings, *General Requirements of an Attack Airplane*, Apr 8, 1929, AFHRC Reel A2796 248.222-52; TR 440-15, Jan 26, 1926, II, 7, g; Course, *Attack Aviation*, 1938–39, AFHRC 248.2208B-2, pp 5–6.

83. "Present Status of Attack Aviation and Its Trend of Development," ACTS, Maxwell Field, Ala 1931–1932, p 5. AFHRC Reel 2796, 248.222-56, Frames 40ff.

84. Maurer, *Aviation*, p 214.

85. F.M. 1–5, *Employment of Aviation of the Army*, April 15, 1940, officially eliminated the category of attack aviation and established the light bomber as the basic unit for support forces. See Thomas H. Greer, *The Development of Air Doctrine In the Army Air Arm, 1917–1941*, USAF Historical Studies, no. 89 (Maxwell AFB, Ala: Research Studies Institute, 1955), p 122.

86. Maurer, *Aviation*, pp 158–59, 231–34.

87. Gen Vernon E. Megee, USMC (Ret), "The Genesis of Air Support in Guerrilla Operations," *U.S.Naval Institute Proceedings*, vol. 91, Jun 1965, pp 53–54.

88. John Schlight, "Elwood R. Quesada: Tac Air Comes of Age," in John L. Frisbee, ed., *Makers of the United States Air Force* (Washington, DC: Office of Air Force History, 1987), p 181.

89. Maurer, *Aviation*, pp 314–15, 415.

90. ACTS, "Report on Bombing and Machine Gun Firing Conducted by the Air Corps Tactical School, or ACTS, April 13, 17 and 23, 1931, Against Targets Representing a Small Infantry Column," Langley Field, Va, 1930–1931, AFHRC 248.2201B, Frames 84ff, figures 1–2 and 1–3.

Notes

91. Maurer, *Aviation*, pp 239–253.

92. Lt Col Donald Wilson, 1st Ind to Memo, Department of Air Tactics and Strategy ACTS to Assistant Commandant, ACTS, Dec 8, 1936, AFHRC 248.2201B, Frame 1462.

93. Deichman, *German Air Force*, pp 10–11; Williamson Murray. *Strategy for Defeat: The Luftwaffe, 1933–1945* (Maxwell AFB, Ala: Air University Press, 1983), pp 3–21; Kenneth A. Steadman, *A Comparative Look at Air-Ground Support Doctrine and Practice in World War II* (Leavenworth, Kansas: Combat Studies Institute, 1982), pp 2–5; Hallion, *Strike*, pp 111–114.

94. Deichman, *German Air Force*, pp 69–82; Steadman, *Comparative Look*, pp 3–4.

95. War Department, Field Manual (F.M.) 31–35, *Aviation in Support of Ground Forces*, Apr 9, 1942. This document, published under the auspices of HQ AAF, indicates a growing awareness on the part of the AAF of the need to organize close air support.

96. Air Support Commands (ASCs) were approved in July 1941 as part of the overall reorganization of the AAF into numbered air forces, which were further subdivided into functional commands—bomber, interceptor, air support, and air force base. Although ASCs had as their primary mission the support of ground forces, this did not preclude using aircraft from other types of commands for the same purpose. Directive, AG, War Department, to Chief, AAF, Jul 25, 1941, "Air Support Aviation"; Herman S. Wolk, *Planning and Organizing the Post-War Air Force, 1943–1947* (Washington, DC: Office of Air Force History, 1948), pp 21–22.

97. F.M. 31–35, pp 3, 11–12.

98. *Ibid*, p 2, 3.

99. *Ibid*, pp 9–10.

100. F.M. 1–5.

101. *Ibid*, p 11.

102. I.B. Holley, "Evolution of the Liaison-Type Airplane, 1917–1944," *Army Air Forces Historical Studies, no. 44* (Washington DC: AAF Historical Office, 1946), p 19.

103. Mary Self, *Reconnaissance Aircraft and Aerial Photographic Equipment, 1915–1945*, (Wright Field, Ohio: Intelligence Historical Division, 1946), pp 135–146.

104. F.M. 31–35, pp 19–31.

105. Genevieve Brown, *Development of Transport Airplanes and Air Transport Squadrons* (Wright Field, Ohio: Air Technical Service Command, 1946), AFHRC 201.7.

106. F.M. 31–35, pp 32–41.

107. Brown, *Transport Squadrons*, p 131.

108. *Ibid*, pp 132–39.

109. Kent R. Greenfield, *Army Ground Forces and the Air-Ground Battle Team, Including Organic Light Aviation*, Study no. 35 (Washington, DC: Historical Section, Army Ground Forces, 1948), pp 9–22; James A. Huston, "Tactical Use of Air Power in World War II," *Military Review*, vol. 14, 1950, pp 165–200.

110. Lt Gen Elwood Quesada, "Air University Interview," Hobe Sound, Florida, Apr 10, 1988 and May 3, 1989, Document PDOC-89076.

111. Ltr, Brig Gen Laurence Kuter to Gen Henry Arnold, May 12, 1943, quoted in Michael L. Wolfert, *From ACTS to COBRA: Evolution of Close Air Support Doctrine in World War II* (Maxwell AFB, Ala: Air War College, 1988), p 29.

112. Steadman, *Comparative Look*, p 6.

113. Vincent Orange, *Coningham: A Biography of Air Marshall Sir Arthur Coningham* (London: Methuen, 1990, Reprint: Washington DC: Center for Air Force History, 1992), p 79.

114. Wesley Frank Craven and James Lea Cate, eds., The Army Air Forces in World War II, vol. 2, *Europe: Torch to Pointblank, Aug 1942 to Dec 1943* (Chicago: University of Chicago Press, 1949; reprinted, Washington: Office of Air Force History, 1984), p 168.

115. *Ibid*, pp 153–161.

116. *Ibid*, pp 166–206.

117. Daniel R. Mortensen, *A Pattern for Joint Operations: World War II Close Air Support, North Africa* (Washington, DC: Office of Air Force History and the U.S. Army Center of Military History, 1987), p 66.

118. In fact, the Army ground forces official history, produced shortly after the war, maintains that F.M. 31–35 "remained the only authoritative guide to tactical cooperation between air and ground until the publication of "Training Circular no. 17" on Apr 20, 1945. Greenfield, *Army Ground Forces*, p 3, 85; XII ASC, *Report of Tunisian Operations*, Apr 10 to May 13, 1943; Craven and Cate, eds., vol. 2, *Europe: Torch to Pointblank*, p 154, 205.

119. F.M. 100–20, *Field Service Regulations: Command and Employment of Air Power*, Jul 21, 1943.

120. *Ibid*, p 11.

121. *Ibid*, p 12. The strongly felt differences between the ground and air forces over the twin questions of control of tactical air power and the priorities for its employment are most starkly presented in the postwar interpretations of the wartime F.M. 31–35 and F.M. 100–20 as penned by official historians of the U.S. Army ground forces and those of the U.S. Air Force. Kent Roberts Greenfield, in his official history of the Army Ground Forces, published in 1948 (*Army Ground Forces*), depicts F.M. 31–35 as the only authoritative manual for air-ground operations throughout the war (p 3). Field Manual 100–20 was too incomplete to serve as a guide. In his view, technological developments go farther to explain the later success of close air support operations than do the command and control stipulations of this manual. He attempts to show that Montgomery himself did not apply his own principles, which formed the basis for F.M. 100–20, in his campaign from El Alamein to Tunisia, whereas it was the employment of these very principles by the American forces in North Africa prior to the fall of Tunis that produced such disastrous results (p 48). Conversely, Air Force observers and historians, both at the time and since, have emphasized F.M. 100–20 as a "declaration of independence" whose liberation of air power from the stultifying practices of ground forces led to the subsequent successful development of close air support. See Goldberg and Smith, *Close Air Support*, pp 2–4; Robert F. Finney, *The Development of Tactical Air Doctrine in the U.S. Air Force, 1917–1951* (Maxwell AFB, Ala: Air University Press, 1952), pp 27–44; Charles W. Dickens, *A Survey of Air-Ground Operations* (Langley AFB, Va: TAC Study no. 34, 1958), p 7; Robert F. Futrell. *Ideas, Concepts, Doctrine: A History of Basic Thinking in the United States Air Force, 1907–1984*, 2 vols. (Maxwell AFB, Ala: Air University Press, 1989), vol. 1, pp 137–38. The overpowering quantitative superiority of American air resources after late 1943 prevented a true test of these two opposing views and opened the way for predispositions to color conclusions.

122. Sherrod, *Marine Corps Aviation in WWII*, p 291.

123. Craven and Cate, eds., vol. 2, *Europe: Torch to Pointblank*, p 486.

124. Greenfield, *Army Ground Forces*, p 78.

125. *Ibid*, pp 79–80.

126. *Ibid*, p 81.

127. Craven and Cate, eds., vol. 2, *Europe: Torch to Pointblank*, p 493, note.

128. Greenfield, *Army Ground Forces*, pp 82, 92–93.

129. *Ibid*, pp 69–76.

130. HQ AAF, *Condensed Analysis of Ninth Air Force in the European Theater of Operations* (1946; reprint, Washington: Office of Air Force History, 1984).

131. In an AAF reorganization late in 1943, ASCs were replaced by Tactical Air Commands (TACs) that were subordinate to Tactical Air Forces and on an equal level with ground armies. Tactical Air Forces were equivalent to army groups.

132. Air Evaluation Board, "Report on

Notes

Tactical Air Cooperation, Organization, Methods, and Procedures with Special Emphasis on Phase III Operations," Orlando Army Air Base, Jul 31, 1945, AFHRC Reel A1174, Frames 0586ff, pp 100–115.

133. Study, 12th Army Group, "Effects of Air Power on Military Operations, Western Europe," quoted in HQ AAF, *Condensed Analysis, Ninth AF*, p 26–27, 123.

134. *Ibid*, p 29.

135. *Ibid*, pp 37–38.

136. The German commander during the Battle of the Bulge, Field Marshall von Rundstedt, called the fighter-bomber attacks on armored spearheads decisive in stopping the offensive. Rprt, Air Evaluation Board, *Phase III Operations*, p 16.

137. Intvw, Quesada, Apr 10, 1988 and May 3, 1989.

138. Rpt, AAF Evaluation Board, "Tactics and Techniques Developed by the United States Tactical Air Commands in the European Theater of Operations," Mar 1, 1945, AFHRC Reel A1174, Frames 414–496, pp 39–48; Rprt, Air Evaluation Board, *Phase III Operations*, sec. R, "Ground Control of Aircraft."

139. Joe G. Taylor, *Development of Night Air Operations, 1941–1952*. USAF Historical Studies, #92 (Maxwell AFB, Ala: Aerospace Research Institute, 1953), p 3.

140. AAFEB-ETO, *Tactics and Techniques*, pp 21–25; Rpt, Air Evaluation Board, *Phase III Operations*, pp 403–404.

141. Intvw, Quesada, Apr 10, 1988 and May 3, 1989; HQ AAF, *Condensed Analysis, Ninth AF*, p 42.

142. Ltr, Gen Kenney to Gen Arnold, Feb 28, 1943, in Joe G. Taylor, *Close Air Support in the War Against Japan*, USAF Historical Studies: no. 86 (Maxwell AFB, Ala: Research Studies Institute, 1955), p 57.

143. *Ibid*, p 62.

144. *Ibid*, p 2.

145. These latter were at first called Support Aircraft Parties (SAPs) but soon, probably under the influence of F.M. 100–20 which expunged the word *support*, they came to be called Air Liaison Parties (ALPs).

146. Taylor, *War Against Japan*, p 58.

147. *Ibid*, pp 2, 38–39, 55.

148. William A. Jacobs, "Tactical Air Doctrine and AAF Close Air Support in the European Theater, 1944–1945," *Aerospace Historian*, Mar 1980, p 46.

149. Taylor, *War Against Japan*, pp 44–45.

150. *Ibid*, pp 127–31.

151. *Ibid*, pp 132–217.

152. *Ibid*, p 206.

153. Sherrod, *Marine Corps Aviation*, pp 294–97; Taylor, *War Against Japan*, p 240.

154. *Ibid*, p 243.

155. *Ibid*, p 244.

156. HQ AAF, *Condensed Analysis, Ninth AF*, p 94.

Chapter 2

1. "Interim Plan for Permanent Military Establishment of the AUSA," Sep 3, 1945. Record Group 337, Decimal File 370.01/10, National Archives.

2. Richard H. Kohn and Joseph P. Harahan eds., *Air Superiority in World War II and Korea* (Washington, DC: Office of Air Force History, 1983), pp 64–65; Intvw, Elwood R. Quesada, by Lt Col Stephen W. Long, Jr., USAF and Lt Col Ralph W. Stephenson, USAF, May 12–13, 1975, AFHRC K239.0512-838, Reel 34851, Iris no. 1037750, pp 31–33, quoted in Wolk, *Planning and Organizing*, p 130; U.S. Congress. House Committee on Expenditures in the Executive Departments, 78th Cong., 1st sess., 1947, pp 294–300 and 328–336. Other, more practical, considerations also figured into Eisenhower's support for Air Force separation. The Navy's opposition was one factor. Also, Eisenhower was well aware that Army retention of its own tactical air

Help from Above

force would saddle the Army with responsibility not only for airplanes, but for their entire support structure, including research and development, maintenance, aircraft warning units, and air communications. It is little wonder that he concluded that "The Army does not belong in the air—it belongs on the ground." Memo, Gen Dwight David Eisenhower, CofS, U.S. Army to Secretary of Defense, "Tactical Air Support," Nov 3, 1947, in Dickens, *Survey of Air-Ground Doctrine*, Appendix 1; Intvw, Quesada, May 12–13, 1975; Ltr, "from Dwight Eisenhower to all members of the Army," Jul 26, 1947, Record Group 165: Records of the Army CofS, Decimal File, NA, Box 365, Book 1.

3. The origins and development of this bureaucratic insurgency are traced in Frederic A. Bergerson, *The Army Gets an Air Force* (Baltimore, MD: The Johns Hopkins Press, 1980).

4. Gen Henry H. Arnold, Gen George C. Marshall, and Adm Ernest King, *The War Reports* (New York: Lippincott and Company, 1947), pp 453 and 469.

5. Kohn and Harahan, eds., *Air Superiority*, pp 64–65.

6. Intvw, Quesada, May 12–13, 1975, pp 273–276; Wolk, *Planning and Organizing*, p 130.

7. Ltr, HQ AAF to President, AAF Board, "Tactical Air Force Development Program," Jun 13, 1944, in AFHRC K239.0429-3653Q, Frames 1830–32.

8. "Tactical Air Force Development Program, 1944–1947," AFHRC K239.0429-3653Q and the following six entries on Reel K2613.

9. *Ibid*.
10. *Ibid*.
11. *Ibid*.
12. F.M. 31–35, *Air-Ground Operations*, Aug 1946, p 67.
13. *Ibid*, p 64.
14. *Ibid*, pp 55–56.
15. *Ibid*, p 22.
16. *Ibid*, p 64.
17. Ltr, Lt Gen Mark W. Clark to Army CofS, "Tactical Air Support of Ground Forces," Sep 13, 1951, quoted in Futrell, *Ideas*, vol. 1, *1907–1964*, p 156.

18. "Experts Disagree on Economy And Atomic War," *The Washington Post*, Sunday, 5 Oct, 1947; Ltr, Gen Eisenhower to Devers, Oct 6, 1947, in Devers Papers, York County Historical Society, York, Pa.

19. Maj Gen W.R. Wolfinbarger, Cmdr, 9th Air Force to HQ TAC, "Review of Tactical Air in Joint Operations," Sep 1950 in *History of the Tactical Air Command, Jul 1, 1950–Nov 30, 1950*, vol. 3, doc. #631; Dickens, *Survey of Air-Ground Doctrine*, p 21.

20. HQ TAC, "Minutes of Air Ground Conference," Jul 26–27, 1946, AFHRC 417.151-2, Reel 4025, Fr 0948ff, p 13.

21. Ltr, CG AAF to CG TAC, "Interim Mission," Mar 12, 1946, in *History of TAC, Mar–Dec 1946*, vol. 1, AFHRC 417.01, p 56.

22. Elwood R. Quesada, "Tactical Air Power," *Air University Quarterly Review*, vol. 1, no. 4, Spring 1948, pp 37–45; Futrell, *Ideas*, vol. 1, *1907–1964*, pp 177–78.

23. Intvw, Quesada, May 12–13, 1975.
24. HQ TAC, *Air-Ground Conference*, p 34.
25. *Ibid*, p 17, 18.
26. *Ibid*, pp 20–21, 22.

27. Students attended from the Armed Forces Staff College, the Army Command and General Staff College, the Infantry, Armored, and Artillery Schools, the Ground General School, and the Air University. Army and Navy Register, Feb 1, 1947, p 2; Mar 1, 1947, p 5; May 10, 1947, p 7.

28. Ltr, HQ TAC to HQ AAF, "Air Indoctrination Course," May 28, 1947, in "Resume of Individual, Unit and Joint Training Activities Covering Tactical Air Operations for 1946–1950," Appendix to *Board of Review for Tactical Operations, 1949–1951*, vol. 15, AFHRC K168.15-43, Reel K1269, p 2.

29. Ltr, OCAFF to G3-USA, "Training," Aug 15, 1950, RG 337, l1949-51, Box 479, Decimal File 353, Item 38, NA.

30. Until after it gained independence in Sep 1947, the Air Force retained the pursuit

Notes

duty prefix "P" for its fighter aircraft. On Jun 11, 1948 the designation changed to "F" for Fighter.

31. Marcelle Size Knaack, *Encyclopedia of USAF Aircraft and Missile Systems, vol. 1, Post-World War II Fighters, 1945–1973* (Washington, DC: Office of Air Force History, l978), pp 1–6; E.T. Wooldrige, Jr, *The P–80 Shooting Star: Evolution of a Jet Fighter* (Washington, DC: Smithsonian Institution Press, 1979); Enzo Angelucci, *The American Fighter* (New York: Orion Books, 1985), pp 273–277; Memo, to Dpty CG for Education, "Tactical Test of the P–80 Aircraft," Aug 14, 1947, and Tab B: Report of the First Fighter Group. AFHRC K239.0429-4841Q, Reel K2615 Fr1058ff.

32. Memo, to Dpty CG for Education, "Test of P–80."

33. Lt Gen William H. Simpson, "Partners in Battle," *Air Force*, Aug 1945.

34. Project Q–4876, "Development of Doctrine and Techniques for a Tactical Night Striking Unit Employing Light Bombardment Aircraft," May 3, 1946, AFHRC K239.0429-4876Q, Reel K2615; Taylor, *Night Operations*, pp 188–195.

35. "Tactical Air Force Development Program."

36. Taylor, *Night Operations*, p 192.

37. "An Evaluation of the Effectiveness of the United States Air Force in the Korean Campaign," vol. 3, *Operations and Tactics*, AFHRC K168.1504A3, p 78, quoted in Taylor, *Night Operations*, p 188.

38. Senate Committee on Military Affairs, Department of the Armed Forces and Department of Military Security: *Hearings on S 84 and S 1482*, 79th Cong., 1st sess., 1945; Senate Committee on Naval Affairs; *Unification of the Armed Services: Hearings on S 2044*, 79th Cong., 2d sess., 1946; House Committee on Expenditures in the Executive Branch, *National Security Act of 1947: Hearings on HR 2319*, 80th Cong., 1st sess., 1947; Senate Committee on Armed Services, *National Defense Establishment (Unification of the Armed Services): Hearings on S 758*, 80th Cong., 1st sess., 1947.

39. The Navy's arguments are presented most succinctly by David Alan Rosenberg, "American Postwar Air Doctrine and Organization: The Navy Experience," in Alfred F. Hurley and Robert C. Ehrhart, eds., *Air Power and Warfare, Proceedings of the 8th Military History Symposium*, USAF Academy, Oct 18–20, 1978 (Washington, DC: Office of Air Force History, 1979), pp 245–71.

40. Senate Committee on Military Affairs, *Department of Armed Forces, Department of Military Security: Hearings on S 84 and S 1482*, 79th Cong., 1st sess., 1945, pp 504–511; Joseph William Caddell, "Orphan of Unification: The Development of the United States Tactical Air Power Doctrine, 1945–1950" (Ph.D. diss., Duke University, Durham, NC, 1984), pp 193f, pp 194–95; Senate Committee, *Hearings on S84 and S1482*, pp 547–590.

41. House Committee, *National Security Act of 1947*, pp 689–710.

42. Public Law 253, 80th Cong., 1st sess., "*The National Security Act of 1947*," Jul 26, 1947, 61 Stat, Chap 343; Richard I. Wolf, ed., *The United States Air Force Basic Documents on Roles and Missions* (Washington, DC: Office of Air Force History, 1987), pp 61–83; Executive Order 9877, "Functions of the Armed Forces," Jul 26, 1947, in Wolf, *Basic Documents*, pp 85–92.

43. Wolf, *Basic Documents*, p 90.

44. *Ibid*, pp 71, 87.

45. "Functions of the Armed Forces and the Joint Chiefs of Staff," Apr 21, 1948, in Wolf, *Basic Documents*, pp 151–167.

46. *Ibid*, p 165.

47. *Ibid*, p 156.

48. *Ibid*, p 182.

49. Study, Plans and Requirements Division, TAC, "Liaison Aircraft Activities," Mar 19, 1948, AFHRC 417.01, Reel A4023, Supporting Document #179, pp 5, 8; Earl R. McClendon, *Army Aviation, 1947–1953*. Air

University Documentary Study no. 48 (Maxwell AFB, Ala, 1954), p 5.

50. Wolf, *Basic Documents*, p 91.

51. Intvw, Gen Jacob Devers by Col Thomas Griess, Ft McNair and Ft Monroe, Apr 5–7, 1972, Tape 20, page 32, in Devers Papers, York County Historical Society, York, Pa.

52. *Ibid*, pp 33–34, 37.

53. Memo, Maj Gen Curtis E. LeMay to CG, AGF, "Curtailment of Air Force Development Projects of Ground Forces Interest," in John A. Bonin, "Combat Copter Cavalry: A Study in Conceptual Confusion and Inter-Service Misunderstanding in the Exploitation of Armed Helicopters as Cavalry in the US Army, 1950–1965," (Ph.D. diss., Duke University, Durham, NC, 1982) p 64.

54. James M. Gavin, *War and Peace in the Space Age* (New York: Harper & Son, 1958), pp 109–11.

55. Intvw, Devers, Apr 5–7, 1972, p 36.

56. Memo, CofS, USA to Secretary of Defense, "Tactical Air Support," Nov 3, 1947.

57. "An Evaluation of Jet Fighter Aircraft for Tactical Air Operations," Langley Air Force Base, Va, May 1949, pp 21–22. AFHRC Reel A4024, Frame 1028.

58. *History of the Tactical Air Command* (*TAC History*), Jan 1–Nov 30, 1948, p 39. AFHRC 417.01, Reel A4023.

59. *TAC History, 1948*, pp 34–36.

60. Lecture, Maj Donald A. Kersting, "Current Trends in Air-Ground Operations," Air University, nd (1949?), in RG 337, Box 479, Decimal File 353, Item 41, NA.

61. J–3 Final Report, Exercise ASSEMBLY, in HQ, JTF Lucky Final Report, Exercise Assembly, Jun 11, 1948, Annex 3, cited in Ralph D. Bald, *Air Force Participation in Joint Army-Air Force Training Exercises, 1947–1950* (Maxwell AFB, Ala: USAF Historical Division, l953), Air Historical Studies no. 30.

62. Memo, Col William W. Momyer, Director, Plans and Requirements, TAC, Jul 1948, "Comments on the Report Rendered by the Senior Marine Observer on Exercise 'Assembly,'" in *TAC History, 1948*, Fr 0233ff, p 2, 4.

63. *Ibid*, p 3.

64. *Ibid*, p 2.

65. Ninth Air Force, "Operation Combine III: Air Ground Team in Action," nd, p 1.

66. *Ibid*, pp 6–8.

67. *Ibid*, pp 16–18.

68. Study, TAC, "Liaison Activities," in *TAC History, 1948*.

69. *TAC History, 1948*, p 98.

70. Study, TAC, "Liaison Activities," p 17.

71. *Ibid*, p 16.

72. Joint Army and Air Force Adjustment Regulation 5-10-1 (JAAFAR 5-10-1), "Combat, Joint Operations: Employment of Aircraft for Performance of Certain Missions," May 20, 1949, discussed in Goldberg, *Close Air Support*, pp 8–9; McClendon, *Army Aviation*, pp 6–9.

73. Noel F. Parrish, "Hoyt S. Vandenberg: Building the New Air Force," in Frisbee, *Makers*, p 214.

74. Message, CG TAC to CG Ninth AF et al, in *TAC History, 1948*. The corresponding Army and Air Force commands, which had identical geographic limits, were:

ARMY	AIR FORCE
1st	1st
2nd	14th
3rd	9th
4th	12th
5th	10th
6th	4th

75. Col William H. Wise, "Future of the Tactical Air Force," *Air University Quarterly Review*, Spring 1949, p 36.

76. Gen William Momyer, in Kohn and Harahan, eds., *Air Superiority*, p 62.

77. Intvw, Quesada, Apr 10, 1988 and May 3, 1989, pp 33–36.

78. Board of Review 49, Formal Report, Jun 10, 1949–Oct 1949, AFHRC 168.15-43, vol. 6, p 8.

79. Futrell, *Ideas*, vol. 1, *1907–1964*, pp 241–242; Rosenberg, *Navy Experience*, p 258; Board of Review, 49, vol. 6, p 8.

80. Rprt, Plans and Operations, OCAFF, "Naval Air Support of Army Ground Forces," Jun 20, 1949, RG 319, 373, National Archives.

81. Ltr, Gen Jacob Devers to Gen Hoyt Vandenberg, "Tactical Air Support of Ground Forces," nd (Spring 1949), AU Library, no. M-36650, cited in Caddell, "Orphan," p 210.

82. ConAC Reg 26-2, "Organization of the Tactical Air Force (Provisional)," Jul 16, 1949.

83. Gen William Momyer, *Manuscript Seminar*, (Center of Air Force History, Bolling AFB, Washington, DC, Jun 17, 1993).

84. Memo, Muir S. Fairchild, VCSAF, to Gen Quesada, "Board of Review for Tactical Air Operations," Jun 10, 1949, Quesada Papers, Box 6, Manuscript Division, Library of Congress (LOC).

85. Board of Review 49, vol. 6, tab C, First Meeting, Jun 21, 1949, p 1.

86. Board of Review 49, vol. 6, tab C, Third Meeting, Jul 14–15, 1949, pp 1–2.

87. *Ibid*, p 3.

88. *Ibid*, p 2.

89. *Ibid*, p 2.

90. *Ibid*, p 5.

91. *Ibid*, p 3.

92. Board of Review 49, vol. 8, *TAC Briefing*, Jun 21, 1949.

93. *Ibid*, p 7.

94. Board of Review 49, vol. 8, "Allocation of Effort," p 2.

95. Board of Review 49, vol. 8, "Aircraft Requirements," p 3.

96. Board of Review 49, vol. 6, "Formal Report," Tab E: "The Conventional Versus Jet Fighter in the Tactical Air Role," pp 1–4.

97. *Ibid*, Tab J: "Field Exercises," p 3, Ralph D. Bald, *Air Force Participation in Joint Amphibious Training Exercises, 1946–1950*, USAF Historical Studies, no. 94 (Maxwell AFB, Ala: Research Studies Institute, 1954), chap. 5.

98. Board of Review 49, Transcript of Proceedings, Fourth Meeting, Sep 16, 1949, p 22.

99. Board of Review 49, Transcript of Proceedings, Fourth Meeting, "Formal Report," pp 3–5.

100. *Ibid*, p 9.

101. *Ibid*, p 11–12.

102. *Ibid*, p 12, 15, 20.

103. Memo, Gen Quesada to Secretary of the Air Force, Oct 13, 1949, in Devers Papers, York County Historical Society, York, Pa.

104. *Ibid*.

105. Paper, "Basic Issues Underlying Service Differences as Evidenced During H\R Armed Services Committee Investigation of the B–36 and Related Matter," p 8, RG 319, P&O 452.1, Box 704, Entry 704.

106. *Ibid*.

107. Ltr, Gordon Gray, Secretary of the Army, to Honorable Carl Vinson, Chairman, Committee on Armed Services, Jul 11, 1949, p 2. RG 319, P&O 452.1, Box 704, Entry 153.

108. Paper, "Basic Issues," p 10.

109. *Ibid*, p 24.

110. Ltr, Gray to Chairman, Armed Services Committee, Jul 11, 1949, pp 2–3.

111. Paper, "Basic Issues," p 24.

112. *Ibid*, p 25.

113. *Ibid*, p 26.

114. House Committee on Armed Services, *Hearings: The National Defense Program—Unification and Strategy*, 81st Cong., 1st sess., 1949, pp 193–200.

115. "Papers Prepared for Rebuttal to Brig Gen Magee's Testimony Before the Vinson Committee Investigating the B–36, Nov–Dec 1949" AFHRC, 168.7010-45.

116. *Ibid*.

117. OCAFF and HQ TAC, "Joint Training Directive for Air-Ground Operations, Sep 1, 1950," in RG 337, Box 480 Decimal File 353.01, National Archives; Bald, *Joint Amphibious Training*, pp 18–36.

118. AAF Technical Report 5502, in *An Evaluation of Jet Fighter Aircraft*, pp 7–8.

119. *Ibid*, pp 9–11.

120. *Ibid*, pp 11–12.

121. *Ibid*, pp 12–13.

Help from Above

122. *Radius of action* is the maximum distance that an aircraft can fly from and return to its home base under specified conditions. This varies with each individual aircraft, depending upon its useful load, power settings, altitude during flight, the arrangement of bombs and ammunition, rate and time of each climb and descent, and the amount of fuel to be reserved as a safety factor. The amount of fuel required to start, warm up, taxi, take-off and land must also be taken into consideration.

123. *Evaluation of Jet Aircraft*, pp 13–14.
124. *Ibid*, p 16.
125. *Ibid*, pp 16–20.
126. *Ibid*, pp 24–27.
127. Memo, HQ USAF to CG, CONAC, "Tactical Suitability Tests, F–80C With Pylon Bomb Racks," nd, in *TAC History, 1949*, Supporting Document #79. AFHRC, Reel A4024, Fr 0356; "Evaluation of the F–80C, F–84E and F–86A," in *TAC History, 1949*, Fr 0365ff.
128. *Evaluation of Jet Aircraft*, p 2; Memo, HQ USAF to CG TAC, "Penetration Fighter Study," Jul 7, 1949, in *TAC History, 1949*, Supporting Document 260.
129. The world-renowned T–33 trainer was derived from this *stretch* Shooting Star. The T–33 remained in production until 1959 and served in the air forces of no fewer than 30 countries. Angelucci, *American Fighter*, p 274; Memo, CG TAC to CG CONAC, "Current Activities of the Tactical Air Command," nd, p 5. AFHRC, Reel A4024, Fr 1115.
130. Ltr, Gen Mark W. Clark, OCAFF, to Gen Robert M. Lee, Apr 3, 1950. AFHRC Reel A4025, Fr 0016.
131. Bald, *Joint Amphibious Training*, pp 108–110.
132. *Ibid*, p 111.
133. *Ibid*.
134. *Ibid*, pp 112–113.
135. *Ibid*, pp 115–116.
136. *Ibid*, pp 116–118.
137. Intvw, Lt Col McBride, CO, 502d Tactical Control Group, *An Evaluation of the Effectiveness of the United States Air Force in the Korean Campaign,* Oct 21, 1950, vol. 6, *Logistics*, Part IV, Book II, Air-Ground Team.
138. Exercise Swarmer, "Final Report," Fort Meade, Md, Nov 1950, RG 218, Decimal File 354, National Archives; Bald, *Training Exercises*, pp 37–74.
139. Intvw, Lt Col McBride, Oct 21, 1950.
140. Ltr, OCAFF to G–3, GSUSA, "Training," Aug 15, 1950, in RG 337, Box 479, Decimal File 353, Item 38.
141. Exercise Swarmer, "Final Report," p 32.
142. Ltr, HQ USAF to CG, Air University, "Joint Training Directive for Air-Ground Operations," Mar 9, 1951. The National Military Establishment was renamed the Department of Defense in the 1949 amendments to the National Security Act of 1947; Wolf, *Basic Documents*, pp 187–200.
143. Staff Study, Assistant for Evaluation, DCS/Development USAF, "What Can and Should the USAF Do to Increase the Effectiveness of Air-Ground Operations?," Dec. 1950, pp 6–7, in Futrell, *Ideas*, vol. 1, *1907–1964*, p 178.
144. Ltr, 1st Ind, AU to CSUSAF, Apr 16, 1951, to USAF AU, "Joint Training Directive for Air-Ground Operations," Mar 9, 1951.
143. Discussion between Quesada, Lee, Momyer, and Ferguson, in Kohn and Harahan, eds., *Air Superiority*, pp 61–66; McClendon, *Army Aviation*, p 12.

Notes

Chapter 3

1. James F. Schnabel, *Policy and Direction: The First Year*, "United States Army in the Korean War" (Washington, DC: Office of the Chief of Military History, 1972), pp 46–49.

2. Intvw, Gen Otto P. Weyland, USAF Academy, Dec 1968, K239.0512-798, p 35.

3. James A. Winnefeld and Dana J. Johnson. *Command and Control of Joint Air Operations* (Santa Monica, CA: RAND R-4045-RC, 1991), p 33.

4. Intvw, Gen Earle E. Partridge, USAF Academy, Apr 1974, 55.560-61, K239.0512-730.

5. On September 17, 1947 (the birth date of the new USAF) all bombers were reclassified according to range, rather than according to weight, which had been the earlier practice. Bombers with a range of over 2,500 miles, such as the imminent B–36 and B–52, were classified as *heavy*. Those with ranges between 1,000 and 2,500 miles, including the formerly heavy B–29 and B–50, along with the B–47 and B–58, became *medium*. Those with ranges below 1,000 miles, such as the B–45, B–57, and B–66, were designated *light* bombers. See Marcelle Size Knaack, *Post-World War II Bombers, 1945–1973*, in *Encyclopedia of US Air Force Aircraft and Missile Systems*, vol. 2 (Washington, DC: Office of Air Force History,1988), n45, 488, pp 21.

6. Diary, Col Ethelred L. Sykes, Jul 22, 1950, in Col Ethelred L. Sykes, *An Evaluation of the Effectiveness of the United States Air Power in the Korean Conflict*, Appendix 2, Book 1; *Command and Organization*, Jun 25–Jul 23, 1951, K168.041-1.

7. Rpt, Secretary of Defense to President, "Operations in Korea During the Period Jun 25, 1950 to Jul 8, 1951," pt. 2, K 160.04B, pp 14–15.

8. Diary, Sykes, Jul 7, 1950.

9. Intvw, Lt Col Dean E. Hess, AF Advisor to the Korean Government, P'Yongyang, Korea, Nov 3, 1950, p 2, 3.

10. Allan R. Millett, "Korea, 1950–1953," in Benjamin Franklin Cooling, ed., *Close Air Support* (Washington, DC: Office of Air Force History, 1990), p 395.

11. Rprt, SECDEF to President, "Ops in Korea," p 8.

12. Diary, Sykes, Jul 18 and 24, 1950; "Air War in Korea: II," *Air University Quarterly Review*, Spring 1951, p 59.

13. For a few from among many encomia heaped upon FEAF's close support air effort during the retreat, see: Partridge Interview, p 587; Roger F. Kropf, "The US Air Force in Korea: Problems that Hindered the Effectiveness of Air Power," *Air Power Journal*, Spring 1990, pp 31 and 35; "Has the Air Force Done Its Job in Korea?" *Air Force*, March 1951, p 41; Roy E. Appleman, *South to the Naktong, North to the Yalu: June–November 1950* (Washington, DC: Office of the Chief of Military History, 1961), pp 476–77; Msg, Fifth AF to FEAF, 10 Aug 1950, annex 5, in *FEAF Operations History*, vol. 1, pp 263–64; "Summary," in Sykes, *Korean Evaluation*, p 9; Diary, Sykes, Jul 12 and 24, 1950; Dickens, *Survey of Air-Ground Doctrine*, pp 31–39.

14. On July 8, General MacArthur was appointed Commanding General, United Nations forces.

15. Diary, Sykes, Jul 24, 1950.

16. *Ibid*, Jul 14, 1950.

17. Diary, Stratemeyer, Jul 25, 1950, Original Copy, Office of Air Force History.

18. For example, see Diary, Stratemeyer, Jul 19, 1950.

19. Diary, Sykes, Jul 23, 1950.

20. Appleman, *South to Naktong, North to Yalu*, p 490.

21. Maj Gen Earle E. Partridge, Oral History, April 1974, USAFA, AFHRC K239.0512-729, pp 601–602.

22. Diary, Sykes, Jul 24, 1950.

23. Diary, Sykes, Aug 15, 1950; FEAF, *Report on the War in Korea*, vol. 1, K740-04D, pp 41–50; Diary, Sykes, Aug 1950.

Help from Above

24. Kenneth R. Whiting, "The Korean War," in J.H. Scrivner, ed., *Studies in the Employment of Air Power, 1947–1972*, Jun 1973 (Air University, Maxwell AFB, AL), pp 27–28.
25. Memo, GHQ, FEC to Commander, NAVFE and CG, FEAF, "Coordination of Air Effort of Far East Air Forces and United States Naval Forces, Far East, Jul 8, 1950," in FEAF Operations History, vol. 1, annex 1.
26. Appleman, *South to Naktong, North to Yalu*, pp 266–88.
27. Redline Msg, Norstad to Stratemeyer, Aug 14, 1950, in Vandenberg Papers, LOC Box 86.
28. Diary, Stratemeyer, Aug 18 and Sep 9, 1950.
29. Redline Msg, V0193CG, FEAF to HQ USAF, Personal Stratemeyer to Norstad, Aug 16, 1950, in Vandenberg Papers, LOC, Box 86.
30. Diary, Stratemeyer, 23 Aug 1950.
31. FEAF, *Report on the War in Korea*, vol. 2, AFHRC K720-04D, p 89.
32. Redline Msg, Personal Stratemeyer to Norstad, Aug 16, 1950, LOC.
33. Diary, Stratemeyer, Aug 26 and Sep 8, 1950.
34. FEAF, *Report*, vol. 1, pp 39–53.
35. Diary, Stratemeyer, Aug 16, 18, and 19, 1950; Diary, Sykes, Aug 15 and 16, 1950.
36. Diary, Sykes.
37. Annexes E and F to CINCFE Operational Order #1, Aug 30, 1950; Sykes, *Korean Evaluation*, vol. 1, book 1, Command and Organization, pp 22–23.
38. Coordination memo, Jul 8, 1950; in fact, this memo became familiarly known as "the Almond directive of 8 July." Sykes, *Korean Evaluation*, vol. 1, book 1, Command and Organization, p 11.
39. TWX 10261, X Corps to CINCFE, Sep 28, 1950, in Sykes, *Korean Evaluation*, vol. 1 book 1, p 23; TWX KF OPR-372, Fifth Air Force to FEAF, Sept 29, 1950, in Sykes, *Korean Evaluation*, vol. 1, book 1, p 24.
40. TWX 1666B, FEAF to CINCFE, Sep 29, 1950, in Sykes, *Korean Evalua-*

tion, vol. 1, book 1, p 24; Diary, Sykes, Sep 28, 1950.
41. Diary, Sykes, Oct 1, 1950.
42. USAF Statistical Digest, Korean War, Table 21, Airborne Sorties by Type Mission.
43. Annexes E and F to CINCFE Operations Order #2, Oct 2, 1950, in Sykes, *Korean Evaluation*, vol. 1, book 1, p 25.
44. TWX 328, FEAF to CINCFE, Oct 7, 1950, in Sykes, *Korean Evaluation*, vol. 1, book 1, p 26.
45. Diary, Stratemeyer, Oct 25 and Nov 5, 1950; Time, Pacific Edition, Nov 6, 1950, p 7.
46. Coordination memo, Jul 8, 1950; Robert F. Futrell, *The United States Air Force in Korea, 1950–1953*, rev. ed. (Washington, DC: Office of Air Force History, 1983), pp 212–214.
47. Appleman, *South to Naktong, North to Yalu*, p 684.
48. Memo, Stratemeyer to GHQ, "Signal from X Corps to CINCUNC," cite X11894, Nov 2, 1950; Radio signal, Partridge to Stratemeyer, Nov 5, 1950; Diary, Stratemeyer, Nov 2 and 5, 1950.
49. *Ibid*.
50. Ltr, Stratemeyer to Spaatz, Oct 8, 1950, in Diary, Stratemeyer, Oct 8, 1950; Ltr, Stratemeyer to Vandenberg, Oct 16, 1950, in Diary, Stratemeyer, Oct 16, 1950.
51. Diary, Stratemeyer, Nov 16 and 18, 1950.
52. *Ibid*, Oct 7, 1950.
53. Msg, Fifth Air Force to FEAF, Aug 10, 1950, annex 5, FEAF Operations History, vol. 1, pp 263–64; Kropf, *AF in Korea: Problems*, p 31; Cline, Timothy, "Has the Air Force Done Its Job in Korea?" *Air Force*, Mar 1951, p 41; *Air University Quarterly Review*, Spring 1951, p 59; Appleman, *South to Naktong, North to Yalu*, p 476; Diary, Sykes, Jul 12 and 24, 1950.
54. Kropf, *AF in Korea: Problems*, p 35; Appleman, *South to Naktong, North to Yalu*, p 476.
55. Ltr, Maj Gen Hobart Gay to Maj Gen Earle Partridge, Oct 21, 1950; Ltr, HQ

Notes

Eighth Army, APO 301, to Stratemeyer, Nov 7, 1950.

56. Rpt, Dr Stearns to Stratemeyer, on conversations with MacArthur, Dec 20, 1950, in Diary, Stratemeyer, Dec 20, 1950. Dr. Robert Stearns, President of the University of Colorado, was in the Far East as head of an Air Force investigative committee examining the effectiveness of close air support.

57. Ltr, Brig Gen Sladen Bradley, USA, Asst Div Commander 2d Inf Div to Gen Stratemeyer, Dec 25, 1950, in Diary, Stratemeyer, Dec 26, 1950; Futrell, *Korea*, pp 254–55; Ltr, Maj Gen J.B. Keiser CG 2d Inf Div to Gen Partridge, Dec 18, 1950, quoted in Diary, Stratemeyer, Dec 21, 1950.

58. Otto P. Weyland, "The Air Campaign in Korea," *Air University Quarterly Review*, Fall 1953, p 20.

59. *Ibid*.

60. FEAF, *Report*, vol. 2, p 35.

61. USAF Statistical Summary, Korea, Table 21.

62. Msg, Stratemeyer to Partridge, Dec 20, 1950, in Diary, Stratemeyer, Dec 20, 1950.

63. F.M. 31–35, Aug 1946, chap. 4.

64. *Ibid*.

65. *Ibid*.

66. Memo, HQ FEAF to CINCFE, "Air-Ground Operations, Aug 13, 1950," in FEAF, *Operations History*, vol. 1, annex 6.

67. Diary, Sykes, Jul 7, 1950.

68. FEAF, *Report*, vol. 2, p 81.

69. Sykes, *Korean Evaluation*, vol. 2, chap. 1, sec. 3, AGOS, pp 23–26.

70. *Ibid*.

71. Memo, CG Fifth Air Force to CG FEAF, Dec 21, 1950, in Diary, Stratemeyer, Dec 1, 1950.

72. FEAF, *Report*, vol. 2, p 81.

73. Ltr, Partridge to Walker, Aug 4, 1950, in Diary, Stratemeyer, Aug 8, 1950.

74. Diary, Stratemeyer, Aug 13, 1950.

75. Intvw, Lt Col McBride, CO 502d Tactical Control Group, HQ Fifth Air Force Advanced, AFHRC K168.O41-1.

76. Futrell, *Korea*, p 266.

77. The I, IX, and X Corps.

78. Msg, FEAF AG No. 19985, Apr 19, 1951, "Extracts of Reports on Night Bombing," in Diary, Stratemeyer, May 16, 1951.

79. Ltr, Stratemeyer to Idwal Edwards, in Diary, Stratemeyer, May 16, 1951.

80. FEAF, *Report*, vol. 2, pp 84–85.

81. Intvw, Lt G.W. Rutter, 51st Fighter Wing, K-14, AFHRC K168.041-1.

82. Intvw, Capt Smith and Lt Small, 8th Fighter Bomber Group, AFHRC K168.041-1.

83. Intvw, Lt Duerksen, Tactical Air Controller, Air Support Detachment 1, 620th AC&W Unit, AFHRC K168.041-1.

84. Intvw, Lt Walter G. Center, 49th Fighter Group, K-2, Taegu, AFHRC K168.041-1.

85. Conference, "Mosquito Squadron Operations," P'Yongyang, Korea, Nov 4, 1950, AFHRC K168.041-1.

86. FEAF, *Report*, vol. 2, p 90; Intvw, Lt Col John L. Throckmorton, Maj Elmer G. Owens, and Lt George N. Edwards, 5th Regimental Combat Team; Intvw, Capt Smith and Lt Small, 8th Fighter Bomber Group; Intvw, 1st Lt Audrey C. Edenberg, 51st Fighter Interceptor Group, AFHRC K168.041-1.

87. Intvw, Lts Gossen and Lamar, 35th Fighter Group, AFHRC K168.041-1; Futrell, *Korea*, p 708.

88. Futrell, *Korea*, pp 86–87.

89. F.M. 31–35, chap. 5, sec. 6, p 64.

90. Conference, "Mosquito Squadron Ops," p 20.

91. Futrell, *Korea*, pp 462–63.

92. Timothy Cline, "Forward Air Control in the Korean War," *Journal of the American Aviation Society*, 1976, p 258.

93. Futrell, *Korea*, p 463.

94. FEAF, *Report*, vol. 2, p 31.

95. *Ibid*; For a description of this experiment with the "Misawa" tank, see Intvw, Col Stanton T. Smith, Jr, Director of Combat Operations, 5th Air Force, Seoul, Korea, Nov 14, 1950, AFHRC K168.041-1.

96. FEAF, *Report*, vol. 2, p 31.
97. Table 13, Operations Statistics Division, Directorate of Statistical Services, DCS Office of the Comptroller.
98. Sykes, *Korean Evaluation*, vol. 3, pp 26–29.
99. Intvw, Col Smith, Nov 14, 1950, pp 29–30.
100. Sykes, *Korean Evaluation*, pp 30–34; Intvw, Col Smith, Nov 14, 1950, pp 10–11.
101. Sykes, *Korean Evaluation*, vol. 3, pp 35–38.
102. Intvw, Col Smith, Nov 14, 1950, p 19.
103. For example, see Intvw, Maj A.N. Lien, 27th Fighter Escort Group, Dec 22, 1950, AFHRC K168.041-1.
104. The first unit to fly F–84s in Korea in December 1950 was the 27th Fighter Escort Wing in escorting B–29s on bomber missions. When the swept-wing MiG–15 appeared over the battlefield, the F–84s were shifted to close air support and interdiction missions where they excelled. During 1951 and 1952 Thunderjets were acquired by the 49th, 58th, and 474th Fighter Bomber Groups.
105. See Note 97.
106. Intvw, Maj Lien, Dec 22, 1950, p 6.
107. *Ibid*, p 4.
108. Ltr, Brig Gen Gerald J. Higgins, Director, Army Air Support Center, Ft Bragg, N.C., to Chief of Army Field Forces, Ft Monroe, Va, with 1 enclosure, "Air Support in Korean Campaign, Dec 1, 1950," AFHRC K239.04291-1
109. *Ibid*; Dickens, *Survey of Air-Ground Doctrine*, pp 31–35.
110. Staff Study, "Army Tactical Air Support Requirements" (Almond Report), HQ X Corps, Dec 25, 1950, AFHRC K239.04291-1, p 1.

111. *Ibid*, p 6.
112. *Ibid*, p 7.
113. "Coordination Between Headquarters, X Corps, and Headquarters, Fifth Air Force in Korea," in Sykes, *Korean Evaluation*, vol. 1, book 1, *Command and Organization*, pp 83–87.
114. Comments on Staff Study, "Army Tactical Air Support Requirements, Headquarters X Corps," by Gen Otto P. Weyland, HQ FEAF, Jan 18, 1951.
115. Memo, Gen Collins to Gen Vandenberg, "Close Air Support of Ground Operations," Nov 21, 1950, Vandenberg Papers, Box 83, LOC.
116. Vandenberg-Collins Memorandum of Agreement, Aug 1, 1950, in Wolf, ed., *Basic Documents*, pp 219–222.
117. Enclosure to Collins memo, *Close Air Support*.
118. *Ibid*.
119. Sykes, *Korean Evaluation*, vol. 2, "Air-Ground Operations," pp 34–37.
120. *Ibid*, pp 34–35.
121. *Ibid*, p 37.
122. Study, "Tactical Air Support, X Corps, May 10–June 5, 1951," HQ X Corps, Jul 15, 1951, AFHRC K239.04291-1.
123. Minimum response time was 18 minutes, the maximum 145 minutes.
124. Study, "X Corps," p 4.
125. *Ibid*, pp 6–7.
126. *Ibid*, p 10.
127. Memo, HQ Fifth Air Force to OSAF, "Van Fleet Meeting with Everest," Dec 17, 1951, AFHRC K239.04291-1, p 2.
128. Ltr, HQ EUSAK to CINCFEC, "Close Air Support," Dec 20, 1951, AFHRC K239.04291-1.
129. *Ibid*, p 2.
130. *Ibid*.
131. *Ibid*, pp 2–3.

Notes

Chapter 4

1. John C. Donovan, "NSC 68: The Acheson-Nitze Hard Line, 1950," in *The Cold Warriors* (Lexington, Mass: D.C. Heath and Company, 1974), pp 81–103.

2. Donovan, "NSC 68."

3. "A New Look at Tactical Air Power," Study, 1954, quoted in *TAC History*, Jan–Jun 1963, p 445.

4. Too many commentators and analysts underestimate the degree to which TAC retained a nonnuclear, conventional strike capability throughout the 1950s. Some extremists go so far as to assert that "it was in the 1950s…that the Air Force set itself up to lose the war in Vietnam." See Earl H. Tilford, Jr., *Setup*, (Maxwell AFB, Ala: Air University Press, 1991), p 25. What might be forgotten here is that, in the 1950s, the Air Force developed its force structure capability for nuclear and conventional war in a manner consistent with established security policy as found in NSC 162/2, a policy that placed principal emphasis on nuclear deterrence.

5. History of the 9th Air Force, 1954–55, in *TAC History*, Jan–Jun 1963, p 446, 447.

6. History of the 9th Air Force, Jan–Jun 1956, p 168, in *TAC History*, Jan–Jun 1963, p 447.

7. History of the 9th Air Force, Jan–Jun 1956, p 182, in *TAC History*, Jan–Jun 1963, p 448.

8. History of the 9th Air Force, Jul–Dec 1958, p 100, in *TAC History*, Jan–Dec 1963, p 450.

9. Ltr, TAC to USAF, "Conventional Armament Objectives for Tactical Air Forces," May 26, 1958, in *TAC History*, Jan–Jun 1963, p 450.

10. History of TAC, Jan–Jun 1959, in *TAC History*, Jan–Jun 1963, p 451.

11. *TAC History*, Jul–Dec 1953, vol. 4, *Training*, pp 74–79.

12. *Ibid*, p 80.

13. Knaack, *Fighter Encyclopedia*, p 121.

14. *TAC History*, Jul–Dec 1957, AFHRC Reel K4357, Frame 1062.

15. Angelucci, *American Fighter*, pp 308–309.

16. *Ibid*, pp 282–287.

17. Knaack, *Fighter Encyclopedia*, p 205.

18. History of TAC, Jul–Dec 1959, in *TAC History*, Jan–Jun 1963, p 451.

19. Speech, Gen O.P. Weyland to AFA Industrial Associates, in *TAC History*, Jan–Jun 1955, vol. 3, Supporting Document 2, K417.01.

20. Ltr, Gen O.P. Weyland, Commander TAC to Gen Laurence S. Kuter, Commander FEAF, Dec 16, 1955, in *TAC History*, Jan–Jun 1956, vol. 1, Supporting Document 11, K417.01.

21. Senate Committee on Armed Services, Subcommittee on the Air Force, *Hearing on the Study of Airpower*, 84th Cong, 2d sess., May 8, 1956, part 7, p 463.

22. For example, AFM 1–2, *United States Air Force Basic Doctrine*, Mar 1953, pp 7–8, 11; AFM 1–2, *United States Air Force Basic Doctrine*, Apr 1, 1954, pp 1–2, 8, and 11; and AFM 1–3, *Theater Air Operations*, Sep 1, 1953, pp 1–3.

23. Lecture, Col Shannon Christian, "Force Relations in Theater Tasks," Air War College, Feb 25, 1955, AFHRC K239.716255-9, p 20.

24. Memo, CG TAC to CG Air Materiel Command, nd (1953), "Concepts of Operations (F–84F, F–86F, F–86H, and F–100)," in *TAC History*, Jan–Jun 1953.

25. Msg, HQ USAF to CG TAC, Mar 26, 1958, in *TAC History*, Jan–Dec 1958, Supp Doc #41.

26. Gen Maxwell Taylor, Army Commanders Conference, Fort Bliss, Tex, Apr 5, 1956, in *Taylor Papers*, National Defense University.

27. AFM 1–2, *USAF Basic Doctrine*, Apr 1, 1954, pp 1–32 and 1–35.

28. Lecture, Col Christian, "Theater Tasks," Feb 25, 1955, p 20.

29. Memo, Adj Gen, Dept of the Army, to Distribution, "Distribution of Editorial," *Air Facts*, May 18, 1955.

30. *Ibid*, pp 8–11.

31. *Ibid*, p 10.

32. *Ibid*, p 12.

33. *Ibid*, p 13.

34. Memo, Maj Gen Paul D. Adams, ACS, G–3, Army Aviation Division, to CofS and SA, "Army Position in Forthcoming Conversations with Air Force Staff Representatives on Army's Need for Aviation," Jun 30, 1955, in U.S. Army Chief of Military History, File: Army Aviation.

35. Col T.H. Dupuy, "Does Army Thinking on Tactical Air Violate Unity of Command?" *Air Force*, Nov 1955, pp 46–49.

36. *Ibid*, p 47.

37. *Ibid*.

38. Memo, HQ CONARC, to Gen M.D. Taylor, Dec 12, 1955, cited in Bonin, *Combat Copter Cavalry*, pp 96, 98–99.

39. Gen Maxwell D. Taylor, *The Uncertain Trumpet,* (New York: Harper and Brothers, 1959), pp 168–69.

40. *Ibid*.

41. Wolf, *Documents*, p 90, 163.

42. *Ibid*, p 237; Goldberg and Smith, *Close Air Support*, pp 8–9.

43. Wolf, *Documents*, p 239, 243; Goldberg and Smith, *Close Air Support*, pp 10–12.

44. Memo, SecDef, "Clarification of Roles and Missions to Improve the Effectiveness of Operation of the Department of Defense," Nov 26, 1956, in Wolf, *Documents*, pp 297, 299.

45. DoD Directive 5160.22, "Clarification of Roles and Missions of the Departments of the Army and the Air Force Regarding Use of Aircraft," Mar 18, 1957, in Wolf, *Documents*, pp 317–324.

46. *Ibid*, p 320.

47. Memo, OCS/DA to DCSOPS, "Outline Plan for Assumption of Certain Tactical Air Support Functions," Oct 28, 1959, with Incl. 2 *Tactical Air Support Feasibility Study*, and Annex: *Close Air Support*, in U.S. Army Center of Military History, File: Army Aviation.

48. "Outline Plan for the Assumption by the Army of Certain Tactical Air Support Functions," Office of Deputy CofS for Military Operations, Dec 2, 1959, Summary, 2, a.

49. Army, "Tactical Air Support Feasibility Study," Aviation Section, DCSOPS, Nov 20, 1959, p 4, and Annex C "Close Support of Ground Operations," p 12.

50. *Ibid*, p 6.

51. *Ibid*, pp 4–5.

52. *Ibid*, p 7.

53. *Ibid*, p 21.

54. *Ibid*, p 25.

55. *Ibid*, p 2.

56. Brig Gen Clifton F. von Kann, USA, "The Real Goal of Army Aviation," *U.S. Army Aviation Digest*, Mar 1960, p 36.

57. Quoted in Lt Gen John J. Tolson, *Airmobility* (Washington, DC: Department of the Army, 1973), p 14.

58. In the summer of 1956 FEAF headquarters were transferred to Hawaii, where it joined with the Pacific air headquarters to form PAC/FEAF. A year later FEAF was fully incorporated in the Pacific Air Forces (PACAF).

59. The U.S. Air Forces, Europe (USAFE) was the component air command of the unified European Command (EUCOM) as well as the U.S. air component of the NATO command.

60. Joint Army-Air Force Exercises: Southern Pines and Long Horn, 1951–1952, in *TAC History*, Jul–Dec 1954, vol. 5, AFHRC Reel K4347, K417.01, pp 1–13.

61. The Joint Tactical Air Support Board was one of six joint boards set up by the Joint Chiefs of Staff in 1951 to implement the roles and missions and doctrinal measures it fashioned in its Joint Action Armed Forces manual that year. The Air Force was responsible for this Tactical Air Support Board along with a Joint Air Defense Board and a Joint Air Transportation Board. The Army was responsible for a Joint Airborne Troop Board, the Marines for a Joint Landing Force

Notes

Board, and the Navy for a Joint Amphibious Board. See Futrell, *Ideas*, vol. 1, *1907–1964*, pp 379, 401–403. These boards proved sterile and the JCS dissolved them early in Dec 1954. See Sunderland, *Evolution*, p 31.

62. *Ibid*, pp 15–31; Dickens, *Survey*, p 45.

63. *Ibid*.

64. Memo, Lt Gen McAuliffe, DCS Operations and Administration to CofS USAF, "U.S. Air Force Responsibilities in Support of Army Operations," Mar 24, 1953, in *TAC History*, Jan–Jun 1953, Supporting Document 93, K417.01.

65. "Tactical Air Command Role in the Development of Joint Doctrine since the Publication of the Joint Training Directive," in *TAC History*, Jan–Jun 1954, vol. 4, K417.01, pp 6–9.

66. Ltr, TAC to Dir Ops USAF, "Joint Training Directive for Air-Ground Operations," Feb 3, 1951.

67. Ltr, HQ USAF to CG Air University, "Joint Training Directive for Air-Ground Operations," Mar 9, 1951.

68. "TAC's Role in Joint Doctrine," pp 12–13.

69. Ltr, CG TAC to CofS USAF, "Joint Tactical Air Support Board," in "TAC's Role in Joint Doctrine," Document 20.

70. Ltr, TAC to Director JTASB, "JTASB Project No 2-53," June 22, 1954, in "TAC's Role in Joint Doctrine," Document 22; Caroline Frieda Zemke, "In the Shadow of the Giant: USAF Tactical Air Command in the Era of Strategic Bombing: 1945–1955," unpublished dissertation, Ohio State University, Columbus, 1989, pp 278–82.

71. "TAC's Role in Joint Doctrine," Supporting Document 18; Memo, HQ TAC to Director of Requirements USAF, "Report of Temporary Duty Subpanel, Working Party 42," Sep 15, 1953.

72. "TAC's Role in Joint Doctrine," Supporting Document 19: "ABC Manual for Tactical Air Operations," pp 14–15.

73. AFM 1–3, "Air Doctrine: Theater Air Operations," Apr 1, 1954, p 8.

74. AFM 1–7, "Air Doctrine: Theater Air Forces in Counter Air, Interdiction, and Close Air Support Operations," Mar 1, 1954, p 1.

75. AFM 1–3, p 9.

76. *Ibid*, pp 3–4.

77. *Ibid*, p 19.

78. AFM 1–3, pp 9, 18.

79. AFM 1–7, p 3, 16, 18–19.

80. Ltr, Gen Weyland to Gen Dahlquist, Oct 7, 1954, in *TAC History*, Jul–Dec 1955, vol. 8, Supporting Document 34, K417.01.

81. Ltrs, Gen Weyland to Gen Dahlquist, Dec 22, 1954 and Mar 1, 1955 in *TAC History*, Jul–Dec 1955, vol. 8, Supporting Documents 35 and 37.

82. *TAC History*, Jul–Dec 55, vol. 8, *Exercise Sage Brush*, K417.01, p 59, 60.

83. Ltr, DCS/Ops, HQ USAF to Gen Weyland, maneuver director Sage Brush, "Control of Atomic Weapons Play in Exercise Sage Brush," Jun 30, 1955, in *TAC History*, Jul–Dec 1955, vol. 8, *Exercise Sage Brush*, pp 62–64 and Supporting Documents 42 and 43; Ltr, Actg DCS/Ops, HQ USAF to Gen Weyland, maneuver director, Sage Brush, "Control of Atomic Weapons Play in Exercise Sage Brush," Jul 12, 1955.

84. Msg, SecAF to Gen Weyland, Nov 15, 1955, in *Ibid*, pp 69–70.

85. HQ XVIII Airborne Corps, "Final Report of the Aggressor Army: Exercise Sage Brush," Ft Bragg, N.C., Mar 20, 1956, p 2.

86. "Report of Army Tests, Exercise Sage Brush," Jan 20, 1956, Appendix 22, Annex H, in Bonin, *Combat Copter Cavalry*.

87. Maj Gen Hamilton H. Howze, "The Last Three Years of Army Aviation," *Army Aviation Digest*, Mar 1958, p 15.

88. Col Gordon A. Moon II, "Needed: Joint Doctrine on Close Air Support," *Military Review*, Jul 1956, p 8.

89. *Final Report, Exercise Sagebrush*, Section 1 (Langley AFB, Va, Feb 15, 1956), p iii.

90. Memo, Director of Doctrine, HQ TAC, "Joint Air-Ground Operations Manual," Jul 11, 1956, in Dickens, *Survey of Air-Ground Doctrine*, p 49; Lt Col Lytle R. Perkins, "Army-Air Force Relations Rela-

Help from Above

tive to Tactical Air Support," Air University, War College Thesis, Apr 1962, AFHRC K239.042-2416. Perkins was a TAC representative at these meetings and has recorded the proceedings in this paper.

91. Dickens, *Survey of Air-Ground Doctrine*, p 57.

92. Dickens, *Survey of Air-Ground Doctrine*, p 52; "Doctrinal Problems, TAC-ARMY," *TAC History*, Jan–Jun 1957, AFHRC K417.01.

93. *Ibid*.

94. *Ibid*.

95. Memo, for Armed Forces Policy Council, "Clarification of Roles and Missions to Improve the Effectiveness of Operation of the Department of Defense," Nov 26, 1956, in Wolf, *Documents*, p 298.

96. HQ CONARC and HQ TAC, CONARC TT 110-100-1/TACM 55-3, "Tactical Air Control and Operations System," chap. 5 in *Joint Air-Ground Operations (JAGOS)*, Sep 1, 1957, AFHRC K417.549-3, p 43; Dickens, *Survey of Air-Ground Doctrine*, p. 58.

97. The manual bore the dual designation of CONARC TT (Training Text) 110-100-1 and TACM 55-3, stamping it as a less-than-official statement of joint doctrine.

98. HQ CONARC and HQ TAC, *JAGOS*, p ii.

99. HQ CONARC and HQ TAC, *JAGOS*, pp 15–16.

100. Moon, "Joint Doctrine," p 10; Maj Robert C. Brotherton, "Close Air Support in the Nuclear Age," *Military Review*, Apr 1959, pp 32–33.

101. Brotherton, "Close Air Support Nuclear Age," p 34.

102. HQ CONARC and HQ TAC, *JAGOS*, Sep 1, 1957, pp 59–60 and 67.

103. *Ibid*, p 35, 36.

104. *Ibid*, p 73.

105. *Ibid*, chap. 5.

106. *Ibid*, "Air Control Team," p 70.

107. Ltr, Gen Everest, CG USAFE to Gen O.P. Weyland, CG TAC, Mar 10, 1958, in *USAFE History*, Jan–Dec 1958, vol. 4, Suppl Doc 4 to chap. 3, K570.01

108. *USAFE History*, Jul–Dec 1955, vol. 1, chap. 4, AFHRC K570.10, pp 97–99.

109. *Ibid*, p 1.

110. *Ibid*, p 2.

111. *Ibid*.

112. *Ibid*.

113. Ltr, F.F. Everest, CG USAFE to O.P. Weyland, CG TAC, May 19, 1958, in *TAC History*, Jan–Jun 1958, Supporting Document 51.

114. Ltr, Everest to Weyland, Mar 10, 1958.

115. Von Kann, "Army Aviation," p 35; Col Jay D. Vanderpool, "Aerial Vehicles in the Ground Role," *Military Review*, Oct, 1958, pp 59–60.

116. Vanderpool, "Aerial Vehicles," pp 60–61.

117. JAAFAR 5-10-1; Goldberg and Smith, *Close Air Support*, pp 8–9; AR 700-50/AFR 65-7, *Supplies and Equipment: Army Aircraft and Allied Equipment*, Mar 23, 1950; McClendon, *Army Aviation*, pp 6–9.

118. Wolf, *Documents*, pp 239–240; Goldberg and Smith, *Close Air Support*, pp 10–12.

119. Wolf, *Documents*, pp 243–45; Goldberg and Smith, *Close Air Support*, pp 11–12.

120. Memo, Matthew B. Ridgway, CofS USA to Distribution (all commanders), "Air Transportability," Jun 28, 1955, Army Center of Military History, File: Army Aviation.

121. Claude Witze, "Army Aviation Buying Fight Looms," *Aviation Week*, Jan 10, 1955.

122. Col Melvin Zais, "New Tactics for the New Gear," *U.S. Army Combat Forces Journal*, Jun 1953, p 23, in Bonin, *Combat Copter Cavalry*, p 79.

123. James M. Gavin, "Cavalry, and I Don't Mean Horses!" *Harpers*, Apr 1954.

124. "Army Creates Aviation Division," *Aviation Week*, Mar 21, 1955.

125. Maj Gen Ernest F. Easterbrook, USA, "Army Aviation Looks Ahead," *U.S. Army Aviation Digest*, Dec 1959, pp 3–4.

Notes

126. "Army Aviation Operations," chap. 5, sec. I: "General Objectives," in *Combat Developments Objectives Guide*, reprinted, in *U.S. Army Aviation Digest*, Jul 1962, pp 2–3.

127. Thomas Garrett, "Close Air Support: Which Way Do We Go?" *Parameters*, Dec 1990, p 40; Richard P. Hallion. *Battlefield Air Support: A Time For Retrospective Assessment* (Andrews AFB. Md: HQ AFSC, Feb 17, 1989), p 37.

128. Brig Gen Carl I. Hutton, "The Commandant's Column," *Army Aviation Digest*, vol. 1, May 1955, pp 3–4.

129. Hutton, "Commandant's Column," Jul 1955, p 3.

130. Howze, "Last Three Years," p 58.

131. CONARC Training Memorandum 13, Jun 4, 1956.

132. Lt Col Charles O. Griminger, "The Armed Helicopter Story: Part I: The Origins," *U.S. Army Aviation Digest*, Jul 1971, p 17.

133. *Ibid*, p 18.

134. Howze, "Last Three Years," p 59.

135. Griminger, "Armed Helicopter Story," p 18.

136. Howze, "Last Three Years," p 60.

137. Tolson, *Airmobility,* p 6.

138. *U.S. Army Aviation Digest*, June 1961, p 6; Thomas R. Hill, "ARST: The 'Saber in the Sky' Grows Longer and Sharper, Promises to be a Major Force of Modern Army," *U.S. Army Aviation Digest*, May 1960, p 2.

139. Tolson, *Airmobility*, p 13, 22.

140. "Policy-Bound Army Hunts for Air Tools," *Aviation Week*, Feb 25, 1957, p 88.

141. Gen William Momyer, *Seminar Discussion*, Jun 17, 1993.

142. Tolson, *Airmobility*, p 13.

143. "Gavin Says Wilson Directive Crippling," *Aviation Week*, May 6, 1957, p 30.

144. Paper, "Air Force-Army Aviation," nd, in Twining papers, USAFA, pp 2, 3–4.

Chapter 5

1. Arthur M. Schlesinger, Jr, *A Thousand Days: John F. Kennedy in the White House* (Cambridge, Mass: Houghton Mifflin Co., 1965), p 310, 311; Gen Maxwell D. Taylor, *The Uncertain Trumpet* (New York: Harper and Brothers, 1959, 1960).

2. Schlesinger, Jr, *A Thousand Days*, p 315.

3. Gen Walter C. Sweeney, CG TAC, *Current Status Presentation*, Jul 9, 1962, in *TAC History*, Jan–Jun 1963, p 440. Although in theory the terms *non-nuclear* and *close air support* are not synonymous, in reality, at least since the Sage Brush exercise in 1955, where it was determined that for all practical purposes nuclear close air support was impractical, the term *non-nuclear* is shorthand for the traditional tactical air missions including close air support.

4. *TAC History*, Jan–Jun 1963, (Langley AFB, VA), pp 458–463.

5. *Ibid*, pp 463–467.

6. The U.S. Strike Command (STRICOM), which was formed by integrating the Strategic Army Corps and TAC, became operational on December 28, 1961. The mission of this unified command was to provide combat-ready reinforcements to other unified commands. It also was tasked with developing joint Army/Air Force tactical doctrine and conducting joint training for these forces. It was deeply involved in the burning question of doctrine and techniques for close air support of ground troops.

7. Air Force Manuals 51–100; USAF Aircrew Training Manual F–100D/F and 51–105; USAF Aircrew Training Manual F–105D/F, Ap 1963; Air Force Regulations 55–25 and 55–89.

8. Close Air Support Board, Final Report, Aug 1963, vol. 5, Tab A to Appendix 4 to Annex H, p 4.

9. Annex J to USCONARC Training Directive, "Air-Ground Operations Training," Sep 30, 1961, in Close Air Support Board, Final Rpt, pp 11–17.

10. Ltr, TAC No 1–2, "Informal Liaison Between Army and Air Force Units," Nov 23, 1962; Msg, HQ USCONARC, ATUTR-TNG, Oct 20, 1962.

11. Army, Navy, Air Force Register and Journal, Sep 21, 1963, p 12.

12. Close Air Support, Final Rpt, pp 5–10.

13. Memo, SECDEF to Mr. Stahr, Apr 19, 1962, p. 2; Memo, SECDEF to SECARMY, "Army Aviation," Apr 19, 1962, K177.1511, p. 2.

14. Memo, SECDEF to Mr. Stahr, Apr 19, 1962 p 2.

15. Bergerson, *Army Gets an Air Force*, pp 110–111; a similar suggestion of the lower-level genesis of these memos is made by Sheridan Stuart, "Air Concepts on a Collision Course," *Air Force/Space Digest*, Aug 1964, p 36.

16. Bergerson, *Army Gets an Air Force*, pp 146–147.

17. Tolson, *Airmobility*, p 19.

18. *Ibid*.

19. Memo, HQ Off of the Adj Gen US Army to CG USCONARC, "Army Aviation Requirements," Apr 29, 1962, Appendix "Guidelines: U.S. Army Tactical Mobility Requirements Board," AFHRC K177.1511.

20. *Ibid*, p 111.

21. Ltr, Gen W.C. Sweeney Jr to Gen C.E. LeMay, AFCS, Jun 25, 1962, in *TAC History*, Jul–Dec 1962, pp 5–6.

22. Army Tactical Mobility Requirements Board (Howze Board), "Final Report," AFHRC K177-1511, Appendix 11, Technological Forecasts to Annex I, "Long Range Concepts and Requirements," Annex P, "Industry Inputs," p 2.

23. *Ibid*, Annex B, "Report of Southeast Asia Visit," Annex J, "Special Warfare Concepts and Requirements," Annex M, "War Games."

24. Tolson, *Airmobility*, p 22.

25. Howze Board, "Final Rpt," Annex O, "Field Tests."

26. Bergerson, *Army Gets an Air Force*, p 112.

27. Ltr, Brig Gen T.H. Watkins, AF Liaison Officer to Howze Board, to Gen W.G. Sweeney, Jr CG TAC, Jul 30, 1962, in *TAC History*, Jul–Dec 1962, p 7.

28. Ltr, Deputy for Plans TAC to Gen Sweeney, "U.S. Army Long Range Concepts and Requirements for the 1969–1975 Time Frame Study by Army Tactical Mobility Requirements Board," Aug 1, 1962, in *TAC History*, Jul–Dec 1962, pp 7–8.

29. Howze Board, "Final Rpt," IV, "Response to the Requirement," pp 18–19.

30. *Ibid*, "Tactical Concepts," p 23.

31. *Ibid*, p 28.

32. *Ibid*, p 37, 39.

33. *Ibid*, pp 39–41.

34. *Ibid*, p 64.

35. Howze Board, "Final Rpt," Annex I, "Long Range Concepts and Requirements," pp 6–8.

36. *Ibid*, p 5.

37. *Ibid*, p 2.

38. *Ibid*, p 14, 19.

39. Howze Board, "Final Rpt," vol. 8, *Joint Considerations*, pp 70–72. The persistence of this issue is amazing, although too often the argument for colocation degenerates from the lofty and logical tone of the Howze Board to green-eyed personal grousing about living conditions. Instead of stressing the tactical advantages to be gained by having Army soldiers and Air Force tactical pilots live under the same roof, Army complaints too often sound like whining about the better living conditions and the Air Force officers' alleged aversion to getting their hands dirty.

40. *Ibid*, Annex B, "Southeast Asia Trip Report," Jul 31, 1962, pp.7, 8.

41. *Ibid*, p 5 and incl 2, "Specific Topics for Discussion Proposed by Committee," p 7.

42. *Ibid*, incl 2, "Specific Topics for Discussion Proposed by Committee," p 7.

Notes

43. *TAC History*, Jul–Dec, 1962, p 6; *TAC History*, Jan–Jun, 1963, p 96; *TAC History*, Jul–Dec, 1963, p 91.

44. Ltr, CofS, USAF, "Tactical Air Support Requirements (Disosway Board)," Jul 23, 1962.

45. USAF Tactical Air Support Requirements Board (Disosway Board), p iii; List of Members, AFHRC K177.1512-2.

46. Memo, to Gen Curtis E LeMay, CofS USAF, "Comments on Report of Army Tactical Mobility Requirements (Disosway) Board," Aug 14, 1962, p 12.

47. Comments on the Brief by the President of the Army Board. One: Equipment in Disosway Board, "Final Rpt," pp 3, 4.

48. Memo, "Disosway Board," pp 4–5.

49. *Commander-in-Chief Dispatch, North African Campaign, 1942–43*, p 38, in *Ibid*, p 5.

50. Memo, "Disosway Board," p 3.

51. *Ibid*, p 5.

52. Disosway Board, "Final Rpt," pp 13, 14–15, and Appendix 1 to Annex O; "Evaluation of Field Tests Conducted in Support of the U.S. Army Tactical Mobility Requirements Board."

53. *Ibid*, p 12.

54. Memo, "Disosway Board," p 6.

55. U.S. House, *Department of Defense Appropriations for 1964*, 88th Cong, lst sess., p 415, quoted in Futrell, *Ideas*, vol. 2, *1961–1984*, pp 180–81.

56. Memo, SECDEF to Secretaries of the Army and Air Force, "Close Air Support," Feb 16, 1963.

57. *Ibid*.

58. Futrell, *Ideas*, vol. 2, *1961–1984*, p 182.

59. Memo, *Central Army Position*, Incl 3, ODC&A to General Hamlett, "Army/Air Force Differences," Apr 24, 1963, pp 1–6.

60. See Appendix I.

61. Ltr, Gen McKee to Gen Hamlett, May 20, 1963.

62. *Forward Edge of the Battle Line (FEBA)*: The furthermost limit of an area where ground combat units, except covering or screening forces, are deployed. The FEBA is used to coordinate fire support, position forces, and maneuver units. *Forward Bomb Lines*: Land lines determined by a troop commander beyond which he considers that bombing need not be coordinated with his own forces. *Tactical Bomb Lines*: Land lines prescribed by a troop commander beyond which he considers that properly coordinated bombing would not endanger his own forces (JCS Pub. 1, *Dictionary of United States Military Terms for Joint Usage*, Feb 1, 1964, pp 60, 140).

63. Close Air Support Board, Final Rpt, vol. 1, *Summary*, p 5.

64. These requirements were set down in DoD Directive Number 5160.22, "Clarification of Roles and Missions of the Departments of the Army and the Air Force Regarding Use of Aircraft," Mar 18, 1957.

65. Close Air Support Board, Final Rpt, vol. 5, Appendix 1-1 to Annex H, pp 1–14, and Incl 1 to Appendix 1.

66. *Ibid*, Appendix 1-2 to Annex H, pp 1–7.

67. Memo, Rand, RM-3295-PR, "An Operations Model for Estimating the Effectiveness and Attrition of Tactical Aircraft When Penetrating Defenses at Low Altitude (U)," Dec 1962.

68. Close Air Support Board, Final Rpt, vol. 5, Tab A-1 to Appendix 2-1 to Annex H, pp 5–7.

69. Close Air Support Board, Final Rpt, vol. 5, Appendix 2-1 to Annex H, pp 4–5; Futrell. *Ideas*, pp 379–380.

70. The attrition rate is the number of aircraft lost per sortie. Losses refer to aircraft destroyed as a result of combat actions on the ground as well as in the air.

71. Close Air Support Board, Final Rpt, vol. 5, Tab A to Appendix 2-2 to Annex H, pp 2–3.

72. Study, "A Critical Analysis of Army Positions in Aviation in 1961–1963 as Compared With Historical Experience" (Aerospace Studies Institute, Maxwell AFB, Oct 1963), pp 31–43.

73. *Ibid*, pp 11–12.

Help from Above

74. Memo, SecNav-LA to SecNav, CNO, Cdt, Marine Corps, "Congressional Committee Hearings, Report," Feb 24, 1964, p 1.

75. Close Air Support Board, Final Rpt, vol. 5, Tab B to Appendix 22 to Annex H, pp 5–11.

76. See Chapter 4 of this book.

77. Draft Manual, Headquarters STRICOM, *Joint Task Force Operations*, Apr 1, 1963. Actually this draft proposal, like its 1957 predecessor, was the product of work by TAC, CONARC and the Army's Combat Developments Command, which were the component commands of the unified Strike Command.

78. Close Air Support Board, Final Rpt, vol. 5, Tab C to Appendix 3 to Annex H, pp 4–6.

79. *Ibid*, Incl 1 to Tab C to Appendix 3 to Annex H, pp 1–3.

80. *Ibid*, pp 7–13.

81. JCS Publications 1: JCS Publication 2, "Unified Action Armed Forces (UNAAF), Nov 1962.

82. Close Air Support Board, Final Rpt, vol. 5, Tab D to Appendix 3 to Annex H, pp 3–5, 11.

83. *Ibid*, p 8.

84. *Ibid*, Appendix 4; "Training and Indoctrination," to Annex H, pp 1–12, Tab A; "Training," to Appendix 4, pp 1–18, Tab B, "Schools," to Appendix 4, pp 1–7.

85. *Ibid*, Tab A; "Base Facilities," to Appendix 5, "Resources," to Annex H, pp 2–3, 8, 15.

86. *Ibid*, Tab B: Communications, to Appendix 5, Resources, to Annex H, p 22, Tabs B and C to Appendix 3, "Procedures, Tactics and Techniques," to Annex H, p 13.

87. *Ibid*, Appendix 5, "Resources," pp 7–8.

88. *Ibid*, p 18.

89. CINCSTRIKE Test and Evaluation Plan, HQ Strike, Apr 19, 1963.

90. *Ibid*, p 536.

91. *Ibid*, p 535.

92. *Ibid*, p 536.

93. *Ibid*, p 537–538.

94. *Ibid*, p 543.

95. Inter-office Communication, DPLPO to TAC Staff, "Report of TAC Briefing for CSAF," Nov 21, 1963, in *TAC History*, Jul–Dec 1963, p 95.

96. Close Air Support Board, Final Rpt, vol. 5, Appendix 4, "Training and Indoctrination," p 3.

97. Ltr, Gen Sweeney to Gen G.P. Disosway, CINCUSAFE, Nov 14, 1963; Ltr, Gen Sweeney to Gen Jacob E. Smart, CINCPACAF, Nov 18, 1963, discussed in *TAC History*, Jul–Dec 1963, pp 110–111.

98. Final Report, "Indian River Field Exercises," vol. 1, Jan 1965, p 1.1, in *History of the Tactical Air Warfare Center, Jul–Dec 1964* (Eglin AFB, FL), K417.0732.

99. *Ibid*, p 1–7.

100. TACM 1-1, Tactical Air Control System, June 1964.

101. Rpt, "Indian River," p 2.8. For a description of all the potential facilities that made up the Tactical Air Control System in 1964, see Appendix 2.

102. *Ibid*, pp 3.10–3.21.

103. *Ibid*, pp 3.27–3.29.

104. Memo, HQ TAWC to HQ TAC, "TAWC Accomplishments Since Activation," Sep 26, 1964, Tab C; "USAF Tactical Air Concepts for Test and Evaluation," p 2, in *TAWC History*, Jul–Dec 1964, K417.0732.

105. Rpt, "Indian River," pp 3.34–3.36.

106. Memo, HQ TAWC to HQ TAC, "TAWC Accomplishments," Sep 26, 1964, p 1; Rpt, "Indian River," p 3.38.

107. Rpt, "Indian River," p 3.39.

108. History of the Ninth Air Force, *Jul–Dec 1964*, vol. 1, p 175; Brig Gen Andrew S. Low, Jr., "Air Mobility in the Field Test Laboratory," *Air University Review*, Jul–Aug 1965, p 17; Maj Robert G. Sparkman, "Exercise Gold Fire I," *Air University Review*, Mar–Apr 1965, p 23ff; Memo, Assistant CofS for Force Development, US Army (ACSFOR), "Comments on Joint Test and Evaluation Exercise Gold Fire 1," Dec 8, 1964.

Notes

109. Ninth AF Hist, *Jul–Dec 1964*, p 178.

110. Sparkman, "Gold Fire 1"; Memo, ACofSFOR, "Gold Fire."

111. Memo, ACofSFOR, "Gold Fire," p 3.

112. Sparkman, "Gold Fire I."

113. Final Report, AFFOR OZARK, Nov 19, 1964, in Ninth AF Hist, *Jul–Dec 1964*, p 180; Memo, ACoSFOR, "Gold Fire," p 5.

114. Memo, ACofSFOR, "Gold Fire," p 4.

115. Ninth AF Hist, *Jul–Dec 1964*, pp 186–187.

116. Memo, ACoSFOR, "Gold Fire," pp 4–5.

117. Memo, DCS/MILOPS to ACSFOR, "USCONARC Observer Team Report of Observations, JTEX Gold Fire 1," nd, Spreadsheet, Close Air Support.

118. Statement of Agreement of CofS Army and CofS Air Force, May 23, 1963.

119. William H. Smith. "Hawk Star," *U.S. Army Aviation Digest*, Sept 1964, pp 27–32.

120. Ninth AF Hist, *Jul–Dec 1964*, p 190.

121. Memo, HQ 354th Tactical Fighter Wing, "TACOP Final Report-Air Assault II," Nov 25, 1964, p 1, in Ninth AF Hist, *Jul–Dec 1964*, vol. 2, Supporting Document #200.

122. Memo, HQ 354th Tactical Fighter Wing, "TACOP Final Report," Nov 25, 1964, pp 26–27.

123. *Ibid*, p 28; Lt Gen Edward Rowny, "An Army View on Air Mobility," *Supplement to Air Force Policy Letter to Commanders*, #1, 1965, p 13.

124. Memo, HQ 354th Tactical Fighter Wing, "TACOP Final Report," Nov 25, 1964, p 29; Rowny, "Army View," p 13.

125. Memo, HQ 354th Tactical Fighter Wing, "TACOP Final Report," Nov 25, 1964, pp 30–31.

126. *Ibid*, p 31.

127. Ninth AF Hist, *Jul–Dec 1964*, vol. 1, p 197.

128. Tolson, *Airmobility*, pp 55–57.

129. Rowny, "Army View," p 14.

130. Memo, SecDef to CJCofS, "Approval of JCSM-936-62 (Joint Testing)," Dec 5, 1962.

131. Tolson, *Airmobility*, p 57; Memo, SecAF to SecDef, "Progress in Improving Air Force Capability to Support the Army," May 22, 1964.

132. JCSM-51-65, Jan 21, 1965; Memo, SecDef to CJCofS, Jan 21, 1965.

133. Bergerson, *Army Gets an Air Force*, p 114.

134. DoD Directive 5160.22, "Clarification of Roles and Missions of the Departments of the Army and Air Force Regarding the Use of Aircraft," Mar 18, 1957.

135. Memo, SecAF to SecDef, "A Proposed Method for Clarifying Air Force and Army Aviation Functions and Use of Aerial Vehicles," Mar 18, 1965.

136. Journal of the Armed Forces, vol. 102, no. 10, Nov 7, 1964 and no. 22, Jan 30, 1965, p 5.

137. JCSM-205-65, Mar 20, 1965.

138. Tolson, *Airmobility*, pp 60–61.

Chapter 6

1. Lecture, Gen W.W. Momyer, Commander, TAC, U.S. Marine Corps Command and Staff College, Quantico, Va., Oct 20, 1972, pp 37–38.
2. Gen B.A. Schriever, "Close Air Support (1965)," in *The Journal of the Armed Forces*, vol. 103, Feb 19, 1966, pp 15, 25.
3. Rpt, TAC, *Close Air Support*, pp 51–54
4. *Ibid*, p 53.
5. Msg, MACV to CINCPAC, Nov 29, 1962, in Schriever, "Close Air Support," p 58.
6. Melvin J. Porter, "Air Response to Immediate Air Requests in SVN," Project Checo, HQ PACAF, Jul 15, 1969, p 2; Warren A. Trest, "Control of Air Strikes in SEA, 1961–1966," Project Checo, HQ PACAF, Mar 1, 1967, p 17; Schriever, "Close Air Support," p 58.
7. Futrell, *Ideas*, vol. 2, *1961–1984*, p 518.
8. Rprt, TAC, *Close Air Support*, pp 62–66.
9. *Ibid*.
10. Ralph A. Rowley, *Tactics and Techniques of Close Air Support Operations, 1961–1973*, in "The Air Force in Southeast Asia" series (Washington, D.C.: Office of Air Force History, 1976), pp 59–62; Louis M. McDermott, "III DASC Operations," Project Checo, HQ PACAF, Aug 1, 1969, pp 6–8; Thomas D. Wade. "Seventh Air Force Tactical Air Control Center," Project Checo, HQ PACAF, 1968, pp 32–34.
11. Rowley, *Close Air Support*, p 62; Porter, "Air Response," pp 5–11.
12. Ltr, Gen Momyer to Gen Nazzaro, SAC, Oct 1, 1970.
13. Trest, "Control," p 29; Porter, "Air Response," p 5.
14. History, Seventh Air Force, *Jul–Dec 1967*, p xxii.
15. Marcelle Size Knaack, *Post-World War II Fighters, 1945–1973*, in "Encyclopedia of U.S. Air Force Aircraft and Missile Systems" series, vol. 1 (Washington, D.C.: Office of Air Force History, 1978), pp 113–133.
16. Rowley, *Close Air Support*, p 66.
17. Knaack, *Fighters*, pp 126–127.
18. Rowley, *Close Air Support*, pp 68–69.
19. Knaack, *Fighters*, pp 267, 274.
20. Rowley, *Close Air Support*, pp 67–68.
21. *Ibid*, pp 69–70.
22. *Ibid*, pp 139–140.
23. Kenneth Sams, "First Test and Combat Use of the AC–47," Project Checo, HQ PACAF, 1965, p 2; Jack Ballard, *Development and Employment of Fixed-Wing Gunships, 1962–1972* (Washington, D.C.: Office of Air Force History, 1982), pp 13–15, 142; John Schlight, *The War in South Vietnam: The Years of the Offensive, 1965–1968*, The United States Air Force in Southeast Asia Serves (Washington, D.C.: Office of Air Force History, 1988), pp 90–91.
24. Ballard, *Gunships*, pp 28–75.
25. Schlight, *Offensive*, p 6.
26. Trest, "Control," p 36.
27. James B. Overton. "FAC Operations in Close Air Support Role," Project Checo, HQ PACAF, Jan 31, 1969, p 4.
28. *Ibid*, p 6.
29. *Ibid*, pp 16–23.
30. Rowley, *Close Air Support*, p 65.
31. Overton, "FAC Operations," pp 34–6.
32. *Ibid*, pp 36–40.
33. John Schlight, "Jet Forward Air Controllers in SE Asia," Project Checo, HQ PACAF, 1969.
34. Rowley, *Close Air Support*, pp 129–130.
35. Msg, 7AF to 504 TASG, "Arming OV–10 FAC Aircraft," Jun 5, 1969; Joseph V. Potter, "OV–10 Operations in SE Asia," Project Checo, HQ PACAF, Sep 15, 1959, p 15, 133.
36. Kenneth Sams, "The Fall of A Shau," Project Checo, HQ PACAF, Apr 18, 1966, p 1; Kenneth Sams and Bert Aton, "USAF Support of Special Forces," Project Checo, HQ PACAF, Mar 10, 1969, p 8; Weekly Air

Notes

Intelligence Summary, Apr 16, 1966, p 24; PACAF Summary of Air Operations in SEA, vol. 19, pp 4–7 and 4–8; Schlight, *Offensive*, pp. 198–201.

37. Rowley, *Close Air Support*, p 104.
38. *Ibid*, pp 105–107.
39. *Ibid*, pp 91–92.
40. *Ibid*, pp 92–93.
41. Trest, "Control," pp 38–41.
42. Carl Berger, ed., *The United States Air Force in Southeast Asia*, (Washington, D.C.: Office of Air Force History, 1977) pp 52, 56.
43. The Arc Light sortie figures for 1965–1973 are as follows:

South Vietnam	67,477
Laos	33,350
Cambodia	16,527
North Vietnam	7,303
TOTAL	124,657

Statistics compiled by AF/XOOCOAB from OPREP-5s, the SEADAB, JCS Stratops, and SAC COACT.

44. For example, Berger, ed., *AF in Southeast Asia*, p 160.
45. Douglas Kinnard, *The War Managers* (Wayne, N.J.: Avery Publishing Co., 1985), p 49.
46. Msg, MACV to CINCPAC, "USMACV Military Report," Apr 19, 1965; Msg, PACAF to CINCPAC, "Summary of Air Activities," Apr 22, 65; Schlight, *Offensive*, pp 29–30.
47. History, SAC, *Jul–Dec 1965*, vol. 2, p 280.
48. Schlight, *Offensive*, p 105.
49. Rpt, TAC, *Close Air Support*, pp 67–68.
50. Schlight, *Offensive*, pp 148–149.
51. For example, General Westmoreland's laudatory statements about Arc Light in Gen W.C. Westmoreland, *Report on the War in Vietnam (as of Jun 30, 1968)*, Section II: Report on Operations in South Vietnam, Jan 1964–Jun 1968 (Washington, D.C.: Government Printing Office, nd), p 103.

52. Gen Momyer, W.W., *Airpower in Three Wars* (Washington, D.C.: 1978), pp 99–102; Wesley R.C. Melyan, "Arc Light, 1965–1966," Project Checo, HQ PACAF, 1967, p. 249; Schlight, *Offensive*, pp 148–154.
53. Westmoreland, *Report*, p 110.
54. Rpt, TAC, *Close Air Support*, p 83–84; Warren A. Trest, "History of the 2d Air Division, Jul–Dec 1965," vol. 2, pp 35–37; Essay, Richard R. Sexton, "The Battle of Plei Me, Republic of Vietnam," Jun 2, 1967.
55. Rpt, TAC, *Close Air Support*, p 83.
56. Westmoreland, *Report*, p 124.
57. William Thorndale, "Battle for Dak To," Project Checo, HQ PACAF, Jun 21, 1968; John A. Cash et al., *Seven Firefights in Vietnam* (Washington, D.C.: Office of the Chief of Military History, 1970), pp 85–108; Westmoreland, *Report*, pp 138–139; Rpt, TAC, *Close Air Support*, pp 88–89.
58. Westmoreland, *Report*, p 139; Rpt, TAC, *Close Air Support*, p 89; Thorndale, "Dak To," p 5.
59. Thorndale, "Dak To," pp 9–10; Rpt, TAC, *Close Air Support*, p 89.
60. Bernard C. Nalty, *Air Power and the Fight for Khe Sanh* (Washington, D.C.: Office of Air Force History, 1973), p 77.
61. *Ibid*, pp 103–105; Alan L. Gropman, "Airpower and the Airlift Evacuation of Kham Duc," USAF Southeast Asia Monograph Series, vol. 5, Monograph 7 (Maxwell AFB, Ala: Airpower Research Institute, 1979), p 1.
62. Rpt, TAC, *Close Air Support*, p 90; Warren A. Trest, "Khe Sanh (Operation Niagara), Jan 22–Mar 31, 1968," Project Checo, HQ PACAF, 1968, p 23.
63. Maj Gen N.J. Anderson, commander of the 1st Marine Aircraft Wing, cited in Nalty, *Khe Sanh*, p 73.
64. Memo, Gen W.C. Westmoreland, COMUSMACV to CJCS, "Single Management of Fighter/Bomber, Recon Assets," Feb 24, 1968, cited in Robert Burch, "Single Manager for Air in SVN," Project Checo, HQ PACAF, 1969, p 6.

411

Help from Above

65. Nalty, *Khe Sanh*, p 77.
66. *Ibid*, pp 81–82.
67. Gropman, "Kham Duc," pp 10–11.
68. *Ibid*, p 4; Kenneth Sams and A.W. Thompson, "Kham Duc," Project Checo, HQ PACAF, Jul 8, 1968, pp 5–6.
69. *Ibid*, p 25.
70. Nalty, *Khe Sanh*, p 80.
71. AAR, 23d Div (ARVN) USAF TACP, "The Battle of Duc Lap, Aug 23–Sep 8, 1968"; AAR, 21st Mil Hist Det, 5th Special Forces Gp, 1st Spl Forces, Nov 27, 1968, cited in Rpt, TAC, *Close Air Support*, pp 91–92.
72. Schlight, *Offensive*, Appendix 6, "USAF Support of Major U.S. Ground Operations," 1965–1967; Westmoreland, *Report*, p 110; Msg, CINCPACAF to CSAF, Dec 1, 1965, in Schlight, *Offensive*, pp 6, 106.
73. Schlight, *Offensive*, Appendix 6.
74. Lt Gen B.W. Rogers, *Cedar Falls–Junction City: A Turning Point*, (Washington, D.C.: Department of the Army, 1974), p 155.
75. Kinnard, *Managers*, p 47; Tolson, *Airmobility*, p 256.
76. Rprt, HQ USAF, DCS/Plans and Operations, "A Study of Aviation Responsibilities: Air Force-Army," Jun 1962, pp 22–28.
77. DoD Directive 5160.22, "Clarification of the Roles and Missions of the Department of the Army and the Department of the Air Force Regarding the Use of Aircraft," Mar 1957.
78. Senate, FY 1966 Appropriations, p 305, in Futrell, *Ideas*, vol. 2, *1961–1984*, p 517.
79. Tolson, *Airmobility*, p 31.
80. *Ibid*, p 32.
81. USSTRICOM, *Summarization of Air Mobility Test and Evaluation Activities*, Jun 30, 1965, pp 17–18, and JCS 1478/115-2, Aug 13, 1965, pp 3–14, both in Goldberg and Smith, *Close Air Support*, pp 22–23.
82. CofS's Notebook, Item 186, Jun 25, 1965; CofS's Notebook, Item 190, Jul 2, 1965.
83. Schlight, *Offensive*, pp 103–108.
84. Intvw, Col Kampe, USA, 1st Cav Div G–4, Corona Harvest Interview #101.
85. Ltr, Maj Gen H.W.O. Kinnard, USA, Cmdr, 1st Cav Div to Lt Gen Joseph H. Moore, 2d Air Division, Nov 21, 1965.
86. Msg, CINCPACAF to CSAF, Dec 1, 1965.
87. "Air Force, Army Agree on Roles, Missions," *Aviation Week and Space Technology*, Apr 27, 1966, pp 26–27; Tolson. *Airmobility*, pp 104–108; Bergerson, *Army Gets an Air Force*, pp 117–120; Goldberg and Smith, *Close Air Support*, pp 29–30; Schlight, *Offensive*, pp 122–125.
88. Agreement Between CofS USA and CofS USAF, Apr 6, 1966; See Appendix 5.
89. Sortie rates of helicopters versus fixed-wing aircraft must be treated gingerly. The term *sortie* meant different things for the two types of aircraft. In Vietnam, a sortie for a fixed-wing plane constituted one takeoff and one landing. However, by specific exception, MACV permitted armed helicopters that escorted troop-carrying helicopters to log one sortie into the landing zone and one out of it, whether they landed or not. Therefore, helicopter sorties were often multiple-counted over fixed-wing aircraft. For example, if an F–100 took off, escorted a train, performed a close air support strike, then returned home without an intermediate landing, it was credited with one sortie. A UH–1B helicopter, performing the same task would be credited with two sorties. In addition, helicopter flights often consumed less than half an hour, compared to several hours for fighters. Thus, a helicopter could amass multiple sorties during the same time frame that a fixed-wing plane was performing the same task and being credited with one sortie. Schlight, *Offensive*, Appendix 2: "Sorties vs Tasks," pp 319–320.
90. Bergerson, *Army Gets an Air Force*, p 118.
91. Tolson, *Airmobility*, p 107.
92. Schlight, *Offensive*, pp 122–124.

Notes

93. Ltr, Gen McConnell to Ray Bowers, Oct 3, 1972.
94. Table 6: Statistics on Southeast Asia, Comptroller, Office of the Secretary of Defense, Mar 25, 1971.
95. Ernest Montagliani, "Army Aviation in RVN–A Case Study," Project Checo, HQ PACAF, Jul 11, 1970, p xi; Shelby L. Stanton, *Vietnam Order of Battle* (New York: Galahad Books, 1986).
96. Stanton, *Order of Battle*, p 109.
97. *Ibid*, p xiv.
98. Goldberg and Smith, *Close Air Support*, pp 47–48.
99. Montagliani, "Army Aviation," p 48.
100. Stanton, *Order of Battle*, p 293.
101. Tolson, *Airmobility*, p 122.
102. Rprt, "History of USAF Close Air Support Command and Control, Directorate, Studies and Analysis, Tactical Air Command," May 1, 1973, p 73.
103. The U.S. XXIV Corps was a third Field Force introduced into Vietnam in 1968 after the Tet Offensive to control Army units in the northernmost I Corps.
104. Col J.F. Loye, Jr. et al., *Lam Son 719, Jan 30–Mar 24, 1971: The South Vietnamese Incursion into Laos*, HQ PACAF, Project Checo, Mar 24, 1971, p 93.
105. *Ibid*, p 108.
106. *Ibid*, p 97.
107. *Ibid*, p 7.
108. Rpt, "Airmobile Operations in Support of Lam Son 719," Feb 8–Apr 6, 1971, 101st Airborne Division (Airmobile), Camp Eagle, Vietnam, May 1, 1971, vol. 2, pp 1V–12, IV–32.
109. *Ibid*, vol. 1, p I–52.
110. *Ibid*, vol. 2, p IV–14.
111. *Ibid*, vol. 1, p I–32.
112. *Ibid*, vol. 2, p IV–11, IV–40.
113. *Ibid*, p IV–29.
114. Memo, SECDEF to SECAF, "Close Support and SAW Aircraft," Jan 7, 1965. This memo can be found as Document #6 in Edward C. Mishler, "The A–X Specialized Close Air Support Aircraft: Origins and Concept Phase, 1961–1970" (Andrews AFB, Washington, D.C.: Office of History, AFSC, nd).
115. Memo, R.S. McNamara to SECAF, "Operation and Management of Army and Air Force Aviation," Sept 11, 1965; Mishler, "The A–X," p 15; Goldberg and Smith, *Close Air Support*, pp 28–29.
116. House Committee on Armed Services, *Close Air Support: Report of Special Subcommittee on Tactical Air Support* (Pike Hearings), 89th Cong., 2nd sess. Feb 1, 1966.
117. The Air Force presented its views on close air support in Vietnam to the committee in the form of a detailed analysis called "Close Air Support (1965)." There is no indication in the committee's final report that this document was used. It was printed in full in *The Journal of the Armed Forces*, vol. 103, Feb 19, 1966, pp 15, 25.
118. House Committee, *Close Air Support,* Pike Hearings.
119. *Ibid*, p 4872.
120. *Ibid*, p 4873.
121. Intvw, Gen Harry O. Kinnard, in *Armed Forces Journal*, Dec 14, 1968, p 30.
122. Army F.M. 100–2, The Air-Ground Operations System, Jan 1970, Glossary 4, p 2–2, in Goldberg and Smith, *Close Air Support*, p 32.
123. *Ibid*.
124. See Appendix 6.
125. Rpt, House Appropriations Committee, Oct 6, 1970, cited in *Armed Forces Journal*, Oct 19, 1970, p 41.
126. Goldberg and Smith, *Close Air Support*, p 32.
127. Mishler, "The A–X," pp 9–10; Joseph Volz, "A–X vs. AH–56: Competitive or Complementary?," *Armed Forces Journal*, Apr 25, 1970, p 25; Walter Andrews, "Rugged Tests and a Rugged Machine," *Armed Forces Journal*, Dec 14, 1968, p 17.
128. Walter Andrews, "A Weapons Ship For All Environments," *Armed Force Journal*, Dec 14, 1968, p 12; Andrews, Walter, "There Are No Red Flags Flying," *Armed Forces Journal*, Dec. 14, 1968, p 20.

413

129. Memo, Cyrus Vance to Secretary of the Air Force, "Evaluation of Helicopter Fire Support System," Aug 27, 1966, in Goldberg and Smith, *Close Air Support*, p 34.

130. Bergerson, *Army Gets an Air Force*, p 122.

131. Brooke Nihart, "Cheyenne Dead After Lingering Illness," *Armed Forces Journal*, Sep 1972, pp 61–62; Futrell, *Ideas*, vol. 2, *1961–1984*, p 527.

132. Brooke Nihart, "Army Gets Go-Ahead for Scrubbed Down AAH," *Armed Forces Journal*, Dec 1972, p 14; Futrell, *Ideas*, vol. 2, *1961–1984*, p 527.

133. Bergerson, *Army Gets an Air Force*, p 131.

134. Mishler, "The A–X," p 13; Golberg and Smith, *Close Air Support*, pp 30–31; Futrell, *Ideas*, vol. 2, *1961–1984*, p. 472.

135. Futrell, *Ideas*, vol. 2, *1961–1984*, p 483.

136. *Analysis of Close Air Support Operations*, HQ USAF (AFXDO), Aug 14, 1966; Mishler, "The A–X," pp 15–16; Goldberg and Smith, *Close Air Support*, pp 32–33.

137. Memo, David Packard to Secretary of Army and Secretary of the Air Force, "Systems for Air Delivered Fire Support of Ground Forces," Jan 22, 1970, in Goldberg and Smith, *Close Air Support*.

138. Memo, Stanley R. Resor, Secretary of Army and Robert C. Seamans, Jr., Secretary of the Air Force to Deputy Secretary of Defense, "Systems for Air Delivered Fire Support of Ground Forces," Mar 26, 1970, in Goldberg and Smith, *Close Air Support*, p 35.

139. Futrell, *Ideas*, vol. 2, *1961–1984*, p 520.

140. Volz, "Competitive," p 25.

141. Lecture, Gen W.W. Momyer, Army Command and General Staff College, Fort Leavenworth, Kan., Oct 27, 1972, pp 33–37.

142. Ltr, Gen W.W. Momyer to Gen John Ryan, CofS USAF, Mar 2, 1970.

143. *Armed Forces Journal*, Jun 21, 1971, p 18; Goldberg and Smith, *Close Air Support*, p 38.

144. Edgar Ulsamer, "The A–10 Approach to Close Air Support," *Air Force Magazine*, May 1973, p 43; Mishler, "The A–X," p 1; Futrell, *Ideas*, vol. 2, *1961–1984*, p 528.

145. Bergerson, *Army Gets an Air Force*.

146. Maureen Mylander, *The Generals* (New York: Dial Press, 1974), p 188 in Bergerson, *Army Gets an Air Force*, pp 121–122.

147. JCS Pub 1, *Dictionary of United States Military Terms for Joint Usage*, Feb 1, 1964, p 27.

148. House, 1971 DoD Appropriations, pt. 6:678, in Futrell, *Ideas*, vol. 2, *1961–1984*, p 522.

149. Ltr, Momyer to Ryan, Mar 2, 1970.

Chapter 7

1. Goldberg and Smith, *Close Air Support,* p 40.

Glossary

AAF	Army Air Forces
AAFSS	advanced aerial fire-support system
AAH	advanced attack helicopter
ABCCC	Airborne Battlefield Command and Control Center
ABM	antiballistic missile
ACR	aerial combat reconnaissance
ACTS	Air Corps Tactical School
ADC	Air Defense Command
ADVON	2d Advanced Echelon (commander of USAF HQ)
AEF	American Expeditionary Force
AGF	Army Ground Forces
AGOS	Air-Ground Operations School
ALO	air liaison officer
ALPs	air liaison parties
AOC	Air Operations Center
ARVN	Vietnamese Army
ASC	Air Support Command
ASOC	Air Support Operations Center
BDA	bomb damage assessment
CASF	Composite Air Strike Force
CBU	cluster bomb unit
CINCAFFE	Commander of Army Forces, Far East
CINCFE	Commander in Chief, Far East Command
CINCUNC	Commander in Chief, United Nations Command
CO	commanding officer
CofS	Chief of Staff
CONAC	Continental Air Command
CONARC	Continental Army Command
CRC	Control and Reporting Center
CSA	commander of support aircraft
DAFS	direct aerial fire support
DASC	Direct Air Support Center
DAST	Direct Air Support Team
DCSOPS	Deputy Chief of Staff for Operations
DMZ	demilitarized zone
EUCOM	U.S. European Command

Help from Above

FAC	forward air controller
FDL	fast development logistics
FEAF	Far East Air Forces
FEBAs	forward edges of the battle area
FEC	Far East Command
FM	frequency-modulation
F.M.	Field Manual
FSCCs	Fire Support Coordination Centers
GCA	ground-controlled approach
GHQ	General Headquarters
GLO	ground liaison officer
HF	high frequency
JAAF	Joint Action Armed Forces
JAAFAR	Joint Army and Air Force Adjustment Regulations
JAGIT	Joint Air-Ground Instruction Team
JAGOS	*Joint Air-Ground Operations Manual*
JATO	jet assisted takeoff
JCS	Joint Chiefs of Staff
JOC	Joint Operations Center
JTD	Joint Training Directive
LOC	Library of Congress
MACV	Military Assistance Command, Vietnam
NATAF	Northwest African Tactical Air Force
NATO	North Atlantic Treaty Organization
NAVFE	Naval Forces, Far East
NCOs	noncommissioned officers
NKPA	North Korean Peoples Army
NLT	not later than
NSC	National Security Council
OCAFF	Office of the Chief of Army Field Forces
OSD	Office of the Secretary of Defense
PACAF	Pacific Air Forces
POL	petroleum, oil, and lubricants
PSP	pierced-steel plank
RAF	Royal Air Force
ROAD	Reorganization Objective Army Division
ROKA	Republic of Korea Army

Glossary

ROTC	Reserve Officer's Training Corps
SAC	Strategic Air Command
SACADVON	Strategic Air Command Advance Echelon
SACEUR	Supreme Allied Commander, Europe
SACLO	Strategic Air Command liaison office
SAM	surface-to-air missile
SATS	Short Airfield of Tactical Support
SCAP	Supreme Commander Allied Powers
SHAPE	Supreme Headquarters Allied Powers Europe
SHORAN	Short-range Radar and Navigation
STRICOM	United States Strike Command
STOL	short-takeoff-and-landing
TAC	Tactical Air Command
TACAN	tactical air navigation
TACC	Tactical Air Control Center
TACPs	Tactical Air Control Parties
TADCs	Tactical Air Direction Centers
TADP	Tactical Air Direction Post
TAWC	Tactical Air Warfare Center
TOC	Tactical Operations Center
TSC	Tactical Support Center
UHF	ultrahigh frequency
UN	United Nations
USA	United States Army
USAF	United States Air Force
USAFE	United States Air Force Europe
USAFFE	United States Army Forces, Far East
USARPAC	Army of the Pacific
USSR	Union of Soviet Socialist Republics
VAL	visual light attack
VHF	very high frequency
VNAF	South Vietnamese Air Force
VTOL	vertical-takeoff-and-landing

Bibliography

1 | The Birth of Close Air Support

ARTICLES

Bright, Charles D. "Air Power in World War I: Sideshow or Decisive Factor?" *Aerospace Historian* (June 1971): 52–62.

Cameron, Rebecca H. "The Air Corps Tactical School, 1920–1940." Speech, American Military Institute, Fall 1988.

Cooper, Malcolm. "The Development of Air Policy and Doctrine on the Western Front, 1914–1918," *Aerospace Historian* (March 1981): 38–51.

Dater, Henry M. "Tactical Use of Air Power in World War II: The Navy Experience," *Military Affairs*, 14 (1950): 192–200.

Eaker, Ira C. "Toward the Sound of Guns," *Aerospace Historian* (summer 1967): 69–76.

Elmhirst, Sir T. W. Air Marshal, RAF. "Some Aspects and Lessons of Air Warfare, 1939–1945," *Royal Air Force Quarterly Journal,* 19, no. 3: 143–49.

Finney, Robert T. "Early Air Corps Trainings and Tactics," *Military Affairs* (fall 1956): 154–161.

Hezlet, Arthur. "Development of U.S. Naval Aviation and the British Fleet Arm Between the Wars," *Aerospace Historian* (1971).

Hitchhold, Maj. Gen. Hubertus. "German Close-Support Aviation," *Military Review* (March 1951): 95–100.

Huston, James A. "Tactical Use of Air Power in World War II," *Military Affairs*, 14 (1950): 165–185.

Jacobs, William A. "Tactical Air Doctrine and AAF Close Air Support in the European Theater, 1944–1945," *Aerospace Historian* (March 27, 1980).

Loose, Gerhard. "The German High Command and the Invasion of France," *Military Affairs*, 11, no. 3: 159–164.

Mayock, Thomas J. "Notes on the Development of AAF Tactical Air Doctrine," *Military Affairs*, 14 (1950): 186–191.

Megee, Gen. Vernon E. "The Genesis of Air Support in Guerrilla Operations," *U.S. Naval Institute Proceedings*, 91 (June 1965): 48–59.

Milling, Thomas DeW. "Early Flying Experiences," *Air Power Historian* (January 1956): 99–101.

Shiner, John. "Birth of the GHQ Air Force," *Military Affairs* (Oct. 1978): 113–120.

Help from Above

Trest, Warren. "Scores of Pilots, Clouds of Planes," *Airpower Journal* (summer 1987): 42–54.

BOOKS

Arnold, Henry H. *Global Mission*. New York: Harper and Brothers, Publishing, 1949.

Blumenson, Martin. *Breakout and Pursuit* (U.S. Army in World War II: European Theater of Operations). Washington, D.C.: Office of the Chief of Army History, 1961.

Bradley, Omar N. *A Soldier's Story*. New York: Henry Holt and Co., 1951.

Brereton, Lewis H. *The Brereton Diaries: The War in the Air in the Pacific, Middle East and Europe, 3 Oct 1941–8 May 1945*. New York: William Morrow and Company, 1946.

Butcher, Henry C. *My Three Years With Eisenhower*. New York: Simon & Shuster, 1946.

Canham, Doris A. *Development and Production of Fighter Aircraft for the USAF*. (Air Materiel Command Monographs). Wright Field, Ohio, 1946.

Chandler, Charles DeForest. *How Our Army Grew Wings: Airmen and Aircraft Before 1914*. New York: Ronald Press Co., 1943.

Copp, DeWitt S. *Forged in Fire*. Garden City, N.Y.: Doubleday and Co., 1982.

———. *A Few Great Captains*. Garden City, N.Y.: Doubleday Co., 1980.

Craven, Frank, and James Lea Cate, eds. *The Army Air Forces in World War II*. 7 vols. Chicago: University of Chicago Press, 1948–1958. Reprint. Office of Air Force History, 1983.

Cuneo, John. *The Air Weapon, 1914–1916*. Harrisburg, Pa.: The Telegraph Press, 1947.

Eisenhower, Dwight D. *Crusade in Europe*. Garden City, N.Y.: Doubleday and Co., 1948.

———. *The Papers of Dwight David Eisenhower*. Edited by Alfred D. Chandler, Jr. 5 vols. Baltimore: Johns Hopkins Press, 1970.

Ellis, L. F. *Victory in the West*. Vol 1, *Battle for Normandy*. London: Her Majesty's Stationery Office, 1962.

Emme, Eugene M. *The Impact of Air Power: National Security and World Politics*. New York: Van Nostrand Company, 1959.

Ethell, Jeffrey. *Mustang: A Documentary History of the P–51*. London: Jane's, 1981.

Foulois, Benjamin D., and C. V. Glines. *From the Wright Brothers to the Astronauts: The Memoirs of Benjamin D. Foulois*. New York: McGraw-Hill, 1968.

Frisbee, John L., ed. *Makers of the United States Air Force*. Washington, D.C.: Office of Air Force History, 1987.

Bibliography

Futrell, Robert F. *Ideas, Concepts, Doctrine: A History of Basic Thinking in the United States Air Force, 1907–1984.* 2 vols. Maxwell AFB, Ala.: Air University Press, 1989.

Garland, Albert W., Howard McGaw Smyth, and Martin Blumenson. *Sicily and the Surrender of Italy*. U.S. Army in World War II: European Theater of Operations. Washington, D.C.: Chief of Military History, 1965.

Goldberg, Al, ed. *A History of the Unites States Air Force, 1907–1957.* Princeton N.J.: Van Nostrand, 1957.

Gray, P., and O. Thetford. *German Aircraft of the First World War*, 2d ed. London: Putnam, 1970.

Greenfield, Kent Robert. *American Strategy in World War II: A Reconsideration*. Westport, Conn.: Greenwood Press, 1963.

———. *Army Ground Forces and the Air-Ground Battle Team Including Organic Light Aviation*. Study no. 35. Historical Section, Army Ground Forces, 1948.

———. *Command Decisions*. United States Army in World War II series. Washington, D.C.: Office of the Chief of Army History, 1971.

Hallion, Richard P. *Strike From the Sky: The History of Battlefield Air Attack. 1911–1945*. Washington, D.C.: Smithsonian Institution Press, 1989.

———. *Rise of the Fighter Aircraft, 1914–1918*. Annapolis, Md.: Nautical & Aviation Publication Co. of America, 1984.

Hastings, Max. *OVERLORD: D-Day and the Battle for Normandy*. New York: Simon & Shuster, Inc., 1984.

Holley, I. B., Jr. *Ideas and Weapons: Exploitation of the Aerial Weapon By the United States During World War I*. Hamden, Conn.: Archon Books, 1951.

Howe, George F. *Northwest Africa: Seizing the Initiative in the West* U.S. Army in World War II series. Washington, D.C.: Office of the Chief of Military History, 1957.

Hudson, James J. *Hostile Skies: A Combat History of the American Air Service in World War I*. Syracuse, N.Y.: Syracuse University Press, 1968.

Hurley, Alred F. *Billy Mitchell: Crusader for Air Power*. Bloomington, Ind: University of Indiana Press, 1964.

Keegan, John. *Six Armies in Normandy*. New York: Viking Press, 1982.

Kenney, George C. *General Kenney Reports*. New York: Duell, Sloan, and Pearce, 1949; Washington D.C.: Office of Air Force History, 1987.

Jones, H. A., and Walter Raleigh. *The War in the Air: Being the Story of the Part Played in the Great War by the Royal Air Force*. 6 vols. Oxford: The Clarendon Press, 1922–1937.

Lamberton, W. M., and E. F. Cheesman, eds. *Reconnaissance and Bomber Aircraft of the 1914–1916 War*. Letchworth, Herts., England, Harley Ford Publications, 1962.

Help from Above

Liddel Hart, B. H. *The German Generals Talk*. New York: William Morrow and Company, 1948.

Mansfield, Harold. *Vision: A Saga of the Sky*. New York, Duell, Sloan, & Pierce, 1956.

Maurer, Maurer. *The U.S. Air Service in World War I*. 4 vols. Washington, D.C.: Government Printing Office, 1979.

———. *Aviation in the U.S. Army, 1919–1939*. Washington, D.C.: Office of Air Force History, 1987.

Mitchell, Brig. Gen. William. "Leaves From My War Diary," in *Great Battles of World War I: In the Air*. Edited by Frank C. Platt. New York: Signet, 1966.

Murray, Williamson. *The Luftwaffe*. Baltimore: Nautical and Aviation Publishing Company of America, 1985.

Patrick, Mason M. *The United States in the Air*. Garden City, N.Y.: Doubleday, Dovant & Co, 1928.

Patton, George S. *The Patton Papers*. Edited by Martin Blumenson. 2 vols. Boston: Houghton Mifflin, 1972–1974.

Penrose, Harald. *British Aviation, The Great War and Armistice, 1915–1919*. London: Putnam, 1969.

———. *British Aviation, The Ominous Skies, 1935–1939*. London: Her Majesty's Stationery Office, 1980.

Pershing, John J. *My Experiences in the World War*. 2 vols. New York: Fredrick A. Stokes Co., 1931.

Pogue, Forrest C. *The Supreme Command*. U.S. Army in World War II: The European Theater of Operations. Washington, D.C.: Office of the Chief of Army History, 1954.

Richards, Denis, and Hilary St.George Saunders. *The Royal Air Force, 1939–45*. 2 vols. London: Her Majesty's Stationery Office, 1953–1954.

Saunders, Hilary St.George. *Per Ardua: The Rise of British Air Power, 1911–1939*. London: Oxford University Press, 1945.

Sherrod, Robert. *History of Marine Corps Aviation in World War II*. Washington, D.C.: Combat Forces Press, 1952.

Shiner, John. *Foulois and the U.S. Army Air Corps, 1931–1935*. Washington, D.C.: Office of Air Force History, 1983.

Shores, Christopher. *Ground Attack Aircraft of World War II*. London: McDonald & Jane's, 1977.

Slessor, J. C. *Air Power and Armies*. London: Oxford University Press, 1936.

Tantum, W. H., and E. J. Hoffschmidt. *The Rise and Fall of the German Air Force, 1933–45*. Old Greenwich, Conn.: WE, Inc., 1969.

Tedder, Arthur William. *With Prejudice: The War Memoirs of Marshall of the Royal Air Force, Lord Tedder*. Boston: Little, Brown, 1966.

Terraine, John. *A Time For Courage: The Royal Air Force in the European War, 1939–1945*. New York: Macmillan, 1985.

Bibliography

Thompson, Wayne, ed. *Air Leadership*. Washington, D.C.: Office of Air Force History, 1986.

Turnbull, Archibald D., and Clifford L. Lord. *History of the United States Naval Aviation*. New Haven: Yale University Press, 1949.

Weigley, Russell F. *Eisenhower's Lieutenants*. Bloomington, Ind.: Indiana University Press, 1981.

DOCUMENTS

Air Corps Newsletters

Air Corps Tactical School

Course. "Air Force Immediate Support of Ground Forces," 1936.

Course. "Attack of Mechanized and Motorized Columns on the Road by Attack Aviation," 1938–1939.

Course. "Practical Flying-Attack," 1933–1934.

Courses. "Attack Aviation," Dept. of AT&S, 1929–1940.

FM 1–10. Air Corps Field Manual: Tactics and Techniques of Air Attack, 1940.

FM 1–15. Army Air Force Field Manual: Tactics and Techniques of Air Fighting, Apr. 10, 1942.

FM 10–15. Field Service Regulations: Larger Units, June 29, 1942.

FM 31–35. Basic Field Manual: Aviation in Support of Ground Forces, 1942.

FM 100–20. Command and Employment of Air Power, July 21, 1943.

Hopkins, 1Lt Joseph G. "The Development of a Special Attack Plane for Support of Ground Forces," May 14, 1937.

Manual. "Aerial Machine Gun Fire on Ground Troops," May 15, 1928.

Memo. "Effect of Attack Aviation on Ground Troops," March 14, 1928.

Memo. Maj. Lotha Smith to Asst Commandant, ACTS, "The Future of Attack Aviation," December 2, 1936.

Proceedings. Board of Officers to Determine the General Requirements of an Attack Airplane. War Department, April 1929.

Report. "Air Force Support for a Field Army, 1936–1937."

Report. "Report of Cooperation Between the Air Service and the Artillery at Fort Sill, Okla., During Maneuvers, May 22–26, 1924,"

Report, Committee. "Characteristics of an Air Force of the Army to Provide Immediate Support for Ground Forces," May 1936.

Report, Committee. "Support of Tanks By Other Arms." n.d.

Schedule. Regular Course, 1933–1934.

Help from Above

Stearley, Ralph. "The Conquest of Ethiopia and the Use of Aircraft in the Operation," February 1939.
Study. "The Artillery-Air Corps Team," May 1928.
Study. "The Attack Airplane in Support of Ground Forces," Maj. Omar O. Niergrath, 1937.
Training Regulations No. 440-15, Air Service Tactical School, 1922.

INTERVIEWS

Barnes, Earl W. By Hugh Amman. July 1974. Intvw. 828, USAF Oral History Program.
Eaker, Ira. By Richard Tobin. March 1974. Intvw. 918, USAF Oral History Program.
Foulois, Benjamin D. By Alfred Goldberg. December 1965. Intvw. 766, USAF Oral History Program.
Hansell, Maj. Gen. Haywood S. By Dr. Daniel Mortensen. 18 November 1981.
Johnson, Leon W. By James Hasdorff. August 1975. Intvw. 865, USAF Oral History Program.
Kenny, Gen. George C. By Dr. James C. Hasdorff. Bay Harbor Islands, Fla., 10–21 August 1974. Intvw. 806, USAF Oral History Program.
Kuter, Lawrence S. By Tom Sturm and Hugh Amman. October 1974. Intvw. 810, USAF Oral History Program.
Partridge, Earle. By Lt. Col. Collins (919) and Arthur K. Marmor (610). August 1966 and April 1968. Intvws. 610 and 919, USAF Oral History Program.

REPORTS

Claussen, Martin P. *Material Research and Development in the Army Air Arm, 1914–1945.* USAF Historical Study 50. Maxwell AFB, Ala., 1946.
Coles, Harry L. *Ninth Air Force in the Western Desert Campaign to 23 Jan 1943.* Army Air Forces Historical Studies no. 30. February 1945.
———. *Participation of the Ninth and Twelfth Air Forces in the Sicilian Campaign.* Army Air Forces Historical Study no. 37. 1945.
Deichman, Paul. *German Air Force Operations in Support of the Army.* Maxwell AFB, Ala., Research Studies Institute, 1962.
Finney, Robert T. *History of the Air Corps Tactical School, 1920–1940.* USAF Historical Study no. 100. Maxwell AFB, Ala., 1955.
———. "The Development of Tactical Air Doctrine in the U.S. Air Force, 1917–1951," n.p, n.d.
Futrell, Robert F. *Command of Observation Aviation: A Study in Control of Tactical Air Power.* USAF Historical Study 24. Maxwell AFB, Ala., 1956.

Bibliography

George, Robert H. *Ninth Air Force: Apr to Nov 1944*. Army Air Forces Historical Studies no. 36. October 1945.

Greer, Thomas H. *The Development of Air Doctrine in the Army Air Arm, 1917–1941*. USAF Historical Study no. 89. Manhattan, Kan: MA/AH Publishing, September 1955.

———. *History of the XIX Tactical Air Command: 1 Jul 1944–28 Feb 1945*. 7 parts, n.d.

———. *IX Tactical Air Command (European Theater of Operations: IX TAC in Review, Nov 1943 to May 1945*, n.p., n.d.

Kohn, Richard H., and Joseph P. Harahan. *Condensed Analysis of the Ninth Air Force in the European Theater of Operations*. Washington, D.C.: Office of Air Force History, 1984.

Kuter Report. "Organization of American Air Forces in Northwest African Tactical Air Forces," to Commanding General, AAF. 12 May 1943.

Mortensen, Daniel R. *A Pattern for Joint Operations: World War II Close Air Support, North Africa*. Washington, D.C.: Office of Air Force History and the U.S. Army Center of Military History, 1987.

Ramsey, John F. *Ninth Air Force in the ETO, 16 Oct 1943 to 16 Apr 1944*. Army Air Forces Historical Studies #32. May 1945.

"Report on the Activities of the Ninth Air Force from 6 Jun to 20 Aug 1944." From IX TAC to Maj. Gen. L. S. Kuter. 27 September 1944.

"Report on Air-Ground Collaboration in Italy." HQ First U.S. Army Group. 18 January 1944.

Schulz, General Karl Heinrich. "The Collaboration Between the Army and the Luftwaffe Support of the Army by the Luftwaffe on the Battlefield." Translation of POW report of General Schulz. 12 December 1947. Translated by Charles E. Weber, MS #B791. Fort Leavenworth, Kan.

"Statistical Summary: Ninth Air Force Operations, Oct 16, 1943–May 8, 1945." HQ Ninth Air Force, 26th Statistical Control Unit.

Steadman, Kenneth A. *A Comparative Look at Air-Ground Support Doctrine and Practice in World War II*. Leavenworth, Kan: Combat Studies Institute, 1982.

Tate, James. *The Army and Its Air Corps: A Study of the Evolution of Army Policy Toward Aviation, 1919–1941*. Ph.D. Dissertation, Indiana, 1976.

Wolfert, Michael L. *From ACTS to COBRA: Evolution of Close Air Support Doctrine in World War Two*. Maxwell AFB, Ala.: Air Command and Staff College, 1988.

2 | Close Air Support Enfeebled: 1945–1950

ARTICLES

"AAF Tactical Demonstration," *Army and Navy Register* (10 May 1947): 3.
"AAF to Hold Maneuver," *Army and Navy Register* (16 August 1947): 1.
"AGF-AAF Indoctrination Course," *Army and Navy Register* (1 February 1947): 2.
"Army-Air Force Agreements," *Army and Navy Register* (20 September 1947): 1.
Futrell, Robert F. "Preplanning the USAF: Dogmatic or Pragmatic?" *Air University Review*, 22 (January–February 1971).
Goldberg, Alfred. "General Carl A. Spaatz," in *The War Lords: Military Commanders of the Twentieth Century*. Edited by Sir Michael Carver. Boston: Little, Brown, 1976.
Hansell, Haywood S. "General Lawrence S. Kuter, 1905–1979," *Aerospace Historian* (summer 1980).
Holley, I. B., Jr. "An Air Force General: Lawrence Sherman Kuter," *Aerospace Historian* (summer 1980).
Quesada, Elwood P. "Tactical Air Power," *Air University Quarterly Review*, 11 (spring 1959).
———. "The Tactical Air Command Today," *Military Review* (September 1947): 3–8.
"Tactical Air Exercises," *Army and Navy Register* (1 March 1947): 5.

BOOKS

Bald, Ralph D., Jr. *Air Force Participation in Joint Army-Air Force Training Exercises, 1941–1950*. Maxwell AFB, Ala.: AU Press, 1953.
Chennault, Claire L. *Way of a Fighter: The Memoirs of Claire Lee Chennault*. New York: G. P. Putnam's Sons, 1969.
Cole, Alice C., Alfred Goldberg, Samuel A. Tucker, and Rudolph A. Winnaker, eds. *Documents on Establishment and Organization 1944–1978*. Washington, D.C.: Historical Office, Office of the Secretary of Defense, 1978.
Davis, Vincent. *Post War Defense Policy and the U.S. Navy, 1943–1946*. Chapel Hill, N.C.: University of North Carolina Press, 1966.
Goldberg, Alfred, ed. *A History of the United States Air Force, 1907–1957*. Princeton, N.J.: D. Van Nostrand Co., Inc., 1957.

Huzar, Elias. *The Purse and the Sword: Control of the Army by Congress Through Military Appropriations, 1933–1950*. Ithaca, N.Y.: Cornell University Press, 1950.

Knaack, Marcelle S. *Encyclopedia of U.S. Air Force Aircraft and Missile Systems*. Vol 1, *Post World War II Fighters*. Washington, D.C.: Office of Air Force History, 1978.

Mets, David R. *A Master of Airpower: General Carl A. Spaatz*. Novato, Calif.: Presidio Press, 1988.

Smith, Perry McCoy. *The Air Force Plans for Peace, 1943–1945*. Baltimore, Md.: Johns Hopkins Press, 1970.

Williams, Susan Mercer, and Frank J. Mirande. *"When the Chips Are Down...,"* A Historical Sketch of Close Air Support. Marietta, Ga: Lockheed Aeronautical Systems Co., 1988.

Wolk, Herman S. *Planning and Organizing the Postwar Air Force, 1943–1947*. Washington, D.C.: Office of Air Force History, 1982.

DISSERTATIONS

Caddell, Joseph William. "Orphan of Unification: The Development of United States Air Force Tactical Air Power Doctrine, 1945–1950," Duke University, Durham, N.C., 1984.

Martin, Jerome Vernon. "Reforging the Sword: United States Tactical Air Forces, Air Power Doctrine, and National Security Policy, 1945–1956." Ohio State University, Columbus, Ohio, 1988.

Mrozek, Donald John. "Peace Through Strength: Strategic Air Power and the Mobilization of the United States for the Pursuit of Foreign Policy, 1945–1955," Rutgers University, New Brunswick, N.J., 1972.

Zemke, Caroline. "Tactical Air Doctrine, 1945–1950" (draft). Ohio State University, Columbus, Ohio, n.d.

DOCUMENTS

Dickens, Charles. "A Survey of Air-Ground Doctrine." Tactical Air Command Historical Study no. 34. April 1958.

FM 31–35. Air-Ground Operations, August 1946.

Histories. Tactical Air Command.

Histories. Continental Army Command.

Histories. Continental Air Command.

Memo. Army Chief of Staff to Secretary of Defense. "Tactical Air Support," March 9, 1950.

Memo. Army Chief of Staff (Eisenhower) to Secretary of Defense. "Tactical Air Support, November 3, 1947.

Help from Above

Plan. *Development Planning Objective for Tactical Air*, n.d.
Speech. Nathan Twining. "Development of the U.S. Air Force Philosophy of Air Warfare Prior to Our Entry into World War II," n.d.

INTERVIEWS

Quesada, Elwood P. By Lt. Col. Steve Long and Lt. Col. Ralph Stephenson, Intvw 838, May 1975.
———. By John Schlight, November 1981.

3 | Korea

ARTICLES

Cline, Timothy. "Forward Air Control in the Korean War," *Journal of the American Aviation Society* (1976).
"Has the Air Force Done Its Job in Korea?" *Air Force* (March 1951).
Kropf, Roger F. "The US Air Force in Korea: Problems that Hindered the Effectiveness of Air Power," *Air Power Journal* (spring 1990).
Weyland, Otto P. "The Air Campaign in Korea," *Air University Quarterly Review* (fall 1953).
Wykeham-Barnes, Wing Commander P.G. "Air Power Difficulties in the Korean Conflict," *Military Review* (April 1953): 73–81.

BOOKS

Appleman, Roy E. *South to the Naktong, North to the Yalu (June–Nov 1950)*. Washington, D.C.: Office of the Chief of Military History, 1961.
Futrell, Robert F. *The United States Air Force in Korea, 1950–1953*. Reprint, Washington, D.C.: Office of Air Force History, 1983.
Millett, Allan R. "Korea, 1950–1953," in *Close Air Support*. Washington, D.C.: Office of Air Force History, 1990: 345–410.
Schnabel, James F. *Policy and Direction: The First Year*. United States Army in the Korean War series. Washington, D.C.: Office of the Chief of Military History, 1972.
Whiting, Kenneth R. "The Korean War," in J. H. Scrivner, ed. *Studies in the Employment of Air Power, 1947–1972*. Maxwell AFB, Ala.: Air University, June 1973.

Bibliography

Wolf, Richard I., ed. *The United States Air Force Basic Documents on Roles and Missions*. Washington, D.C.: Office of Air Force History, 1987.

Y'Blood, William T., ed. *The Three Wars of Lt. Gen. George E. Stratemeyer: His Korean War Diary*. Washington, D.C.: Air Force History and Museums Program, 1999.

DIARIES

Sykes, Colonel Ethelred L. In "An Evaluation of the Effectiveness of the United States Air Power in the Korean Conflict." Appendix 2, Book I: *Command and Organization*. K168.041-1.

DOCUMENTS

Conference. "Mosquito Squadron Operations," P'Yongyang, Korea, November 4, 1950. K168.041-1.

Intelligence Roundup. FEAF. "Fifth Air Force Interdiction and Close Support Operations, Beginning Feb 1951."

Intelligence Summaries, Fifth Air Force. July 1–15, 1952; August 1–15, 1952.

Letter. Maj. Gen. Hobart Gay to Maj.Gen. Earle Partridge, October 21, 1950.

Letter. Commanding General, Fifth Air Force to Commanding General, FEAF, "Suitability of the F–86 in Interdiction and Close Air Support Missions," July 13, 1953.

Letter. Stratemeyer to Spaatz, October 8, 1950.

Letter. HQ, Eighth Army to Stratemeyer, November 7, 1950.

Letter. Brig. Gen. Sladen Bradley, Asst. Div. Commander, 2d Inf. Div. to Gen. Stratemeyer, Dec. 25, 1950.

Letter. Maj. Gen. J. B. Keiser, Commanding Gen., 2d Inf. Div., to Partridge, Dec. 18, 1950.

Letter. Partridge to Walker, August 4, 1950.

Letter. Stratemeyer to Idwal Edwards, May 16, 1951.

Letter. HQ, EUSAK to CINCFE, "Close Air Support," Dec. 20, 1951. K239.04291-1.

Log. Fifth Air Force, "Close Air Support." June 17, 1952–March 4, 1953.

Manual. Air War College. *Close Air Support Operations, 1951–1953*.

Momyer Collection on close air support in Korea, reports and memoranda on doctrine of close air support, 1951–1954.

Memo. Collins to Vandenberg. "Close Air Support of Ground Operations," November 21, 1950. Vandenberg Papers, Library of Congress, Box 83.

Help from Above

Memo. FEAF, Operations Analysis Office. "Combat Test of the F–86A as a Ground Support Airplane," February 10, 1951.
Memo. GHQ, FEC to Commander, NAVFE and Commanding Gen., FEAF. "Coordination of Air Effort of Far East Air Forces and United States Naval Forces, Far East," July 8, 1950.
Memo. Stratemeyer to GHQ. "Signal from X Corps to CINCUNC," November 2, 1950.
Memo. HQ, FEAF to CINCFE. "Air-Ground Operations," August 13, 1950.
Memo for the Record. Commanding Gen., Fifth Air Force to Commanding Gen., FEAF, Dec. 21, 1950.
Memo for the Record. HQ, Fifth Air Force to OSAF. "Van Fleet Meeting with Everest," December 17, 1951. K239.04291-1.
Memorandum of Agreement. Vandenberg-Collins, August 1, 1950.
Message. FEAF to CINCFE. "Extracts of Reports on Night Bombing," May 16, 1951.
Message, Redline. "Norstad to Stratemeyer," Aug. 14, 1950. Vandenberg Papers, Library of Congress, Box 86.
Message, Redline. Personal, "Stratemeyer to Norstad," August 16, 1950, Vandenberg Papers, LOC, Box 86.
Papers, Partridge. "Differences of Opinion Concerning Quality and Quantity of Close Air Support Given by the Fifth Air Force in Support of the Eighth Army." 4 vols. 1950–1951.
Special Projects. "Marine System of Close Support Was Superior to the USAF System."
Staff Study. "*Army Tactical Air Support Requirements*," HQ, X Corps, December 25, 1950. With comments by General Weyland. K239.04291-1.
Statistical Digest. USAF. "Korean War."
Study. DAF. "An Evaluation of the Effectiveness of the USAF in the Korean Campaign," June 25–December 31, 1950.
Study. "Tactical Air Support, X Corps, 10 May–5 Jun 1951," HQ, X Corps, July 15, 1951. K239.04291-1.

HISTORIES

FEAF Histories. June 1950–December 1953.
FEAF Operations Histories. 2 vols.
Histories. Fifth Air Force. June 1950–December 1953.
History. Commander Naval Forces, Far East. March–April 1953.
History. 136th Fighter Bomber Wing. "Tactical Doctrine for Conduct of Close Support Missions." March 1952.
"History of USAF Close Air Support Command and Control." Directorate, Studies and Analysis, DCS Plans, Tactical Air Command, May 1, 1973. XPS R-73-13.

Bibliography

INTERVIEWS

Center, Lt. Walter G., 49th Fighter Group, K-2, Taegu. K168.041-1.
Duerksen, Lt., Tactical Air Controller, Air Support Detachment 1, 620th AC&W Unit. K168.041-1.
Edenberg, 1st Lt. Audrey C., 51st Fighter Interceptor Group. K168.041-1.
Gossen, Lt. and Lt. Lamar, 35th Fighter Group. K168.041-1.
Hess, Lt. Col. Dean E., AF Advisor to the Korean Government, 3 November 1950.
Lien, Maj. A. N., 27th Fighter Escort Group. K168.041-1.
McBride, Lt. Col., Commanding Officer, 502d Tactical Control Group. K168.041-1.
Partridge, Gen. Earle E., USAF Academy. April 1974. K239.0512-730.
Rutter, Lt. G. W., 51st Fighter Wing, K-14. K168.041-1.
Smith, Capt. and Lt. Small, 8th Fighter Bomber Group. K168-041-1.
Smith, Maj. Gen., Commanding Gen., 1st Marine Division. On the quality of close air support as used by the Marine Corps.
Smith, Jr., Col. Stanton, Director of Combat Operations, Fifth Air Force, Seoul, Korea. November 14, 1950. K168.041-1.
Throckmorton, Lt. Col. John L., Maj. Elmer G. Owens, and Lt. George N. Edwards, 5th Regimental Combat Team. K168.041-1.
Weyland, Gen. Otto P. USAF Academy. December 1968. K239.0512-798.

LECTURES

Barcus, Maj. Gen. Glenn O. "Appraisal of Korean Operations." Air War College, 9 October 1951.
Timberlake, Maj. Gen. Edward J. "Early Stages of the Korean Operation." Air War College, 8 October 1951.

ORAL HISTORIES

Partridge, Maj. Gen. Earle E. April 1974. USAFA. K239.0512-729.

REPORTS

Report. ACS, Studies and Analysis. "Quantitative Comparison Between Land-based and Carrier-based Air During the Early Days of the Korean War," June 1972.

Help from Above

Report. Air War College. "Requirements for Tactical Air Control Parties." 31 July 1952.
Report. Brig. Gen. Gerald J. Higgins, U.S. Army. *Air Support in the Korean Campaign*. 1 December 1950. K239.04291-1.
Report. FEAF. "A General Review of United States Tactical Air Support in Korea, June 28–Sept. 8, 1950."
Report. *FEAF Report on the War in Korea*. 2 vols. K740-04D.
Report. Fifth Air Force. "Report of Mis-use and Criticism of Close Air Support." 25 November 1951.
Report. Fifth Air Force. "Communications Principles Applicable to Joint Operations Involving Combat Air Support of Land Campaigns." 15 June 1953.
Report. Gen. O. P. Weyland, Commanding General, FEAF. "FEAF Report on the Korean War, June 25, 1950–July 27, 1953."
Report. Secretary of Defense to President. "Operations in Korea During the Period June 25, 1950 to July 8, 1951." K160.04B.
Reports. FEAF. "Collection on Air-Ground Support in the Korean Campaign, 1950–1952."
Reports. FEC. "Collection of Reports on Close Air Support in the Korean Campaign, 1952."

4 | Close Air Support Under the New Look

ARTICLES

"Army Aviation," *Air Facts* (April 1, 1955): 7–14.
"Aviation Combat Developments Agency," *U.S. Army Aviation Digest* (April 1963): 9–11.
Cairns, Brig. Gen. Bogardus. "Army Aviation = Battlefield Mobility," *Army Information Digest*, 13 (August 1958).
"Combat Developments and Research and Development Systems of the Army," *U.S. Army Aviation Digest* (March 1960): 1–7.
Easterbrook, Brig. Gen. Ernest F. "The Increasing Requirement for Army Aviation Staff Officers," *U.S. Army Aviation Digest* (May 1958): 3–5.
———. "Army Aviation Looks Ahead," *U.S. Army Aviation Digest* (December 1959): 1–4.
Forrest, Col. Frank G. "Effect of Clarification of Roles and Missions on Army Aviation," *U.S. Army Aviation Digest* (April 1957): 22–26.

Bibliography

"Fort Rucker's Combat Command," *U.S. Army Aviation Digest* (August 1957): 20–21.

Gavin, Lt. Gen. James M. "Cavalry, And I Don't Mean Horses," *Harpers* (April 1954).

Gonseth, Col. Jules E. "Tactical Air Support for Army Forces," *Military Review* (July 1955): 3–16.

Greene, Lt. Col. T. N. "Support by Fire: Part Three Close Air Support: Quo Vadis?" *Marine Corps Gazette* (September 1959): 38–42.

Griffin, Capt. William P. "Column Support by Armed Helicopter," *U.S. Army Aviation Digest* (October 1963): 6–11.

Hewin, Larry M. "Helicopter Future," *U.S. Army Aviation Digest* (April 1956): 5–12.

Hill, Thomas R. "ARST: The 'Saber in the Sky' Grows Longer and Sharper, Promises to be a Major Force of Modern Army," *U.S. Army Aviation Digest* (May 1960): 1–6.

Howze, Maj. Gen. Hamilton H. "Future Direction of Army Aviation," *Army*, 7 (December 1956).

———. "Future of Army Aviation," *U.S. Army Aviation Digest* (June 1957): 5–6.

———. "Army Aviation Looks Ahead," *Army Information Digest*, 12 (July 1957).

———. "The Use of the Helicopter as a Reconnaissance Vehicle," *U.S. Army Aviation Digest* (July 1957): 2–4.

———. "Notes from the Pentagon," *Army Aviation Digest* (September 1957): 2–4.

———. "Meditations on Helicopter Vulnerability," *Army Aviation Digest* (October 1957): 2–4.

———. "The Last Three Years of Army Aviation," *U.S. Army Aviation Digest* (March 1958).

Hutton, Brig. Gen. Carl I. "Interdiction and Close Support," *U.S. Army Aviation Digest* (May 1955): 3–4.

———. "An Air Fighting Army?" *U.S. Army Aviation Digest* (July 1955): 2–3.

———. "Imbalance Between Firepower and Mobility," *U.S. Army Aviation Digest* (August 1955): 3–4.

———. "The Age of the Offensive," *U.S. Army Aviation Digest* (February 1956): 3–4.

———. "Universal Highway," *U.S. Army Aviation Digest* (May 1956): 3–4.

———. "Joint Strategy," *U.S. Army Aviation Digest* (July 1956): 3–4.

———. "Helicopter-Borne Operations," *U.S. Army Aviation Digest* (October 1958): 5–8.

"Impressive Buildup Continues at Rucker," *U.S. Army Aviation Digest* (January 1964): 24–25.

Help from Above

Kay, Capt. William K. "The Army Aviation Story," *U.S. Army Aviation Digest* (June 1961): 1–7.

Lang, M/Sgt. Thomas M. "The Army Aviation Story," Part 3: "Fixed Wing Aircraft," *U.S. Army Aviation Digest* (August 1962): 9–19.

McKenney, S. L. "Sky Cav Operations During Exercise Sage Brush," *Military Review*, 35 (June 1956).

MacMichael, Capt. D. C. "Bottleneck in Close Air Support," *Marine Corps Gazette* (May 1959).

Matheny, Col. Charles W. "Aerial Vehicle Transport for Combat Units," *Army Aviation Digest* (June 1956): 5–12.

"Mohawk AO-1-AF," *U.S. Army Aviation Digest* (September 1960): 1–5.

Moon, Col. Gordon A. "Needed: Joint Doctrine on Close Air Support," *Military Review* (July 1956): 8–13.

Neumann, Lt. Col. James D. "Self-propelled Airtillery," *U.S. Army Aviation Digest* (May 1960): 7–8.

Oswalt, Lt. Col. John W. "Shooting Copters. Why and How the Army Arms for Battle," *Army*, 8 (May 1958).

———. "Report on the Rogers' Board," *U.S. Army Aviation Digest* (February 1961): 15–17.

Pickett, Brig. Gen. George B. "The Army's Tactical Mobility Concept," *U.S. Army Aviation Digest* (November 1964): 1–5.

Rawlings, Lt. Col. Morris G. "The Objectives of Army Aviation," *U.S. Army Aviation Digest* (July 1962): 1–4.

"Report from Camp Wolters," *Army Aviation Digest* (April 1957): 20–21.

Rich, Maj. Gen. Charles W. G. "Industry and Air Assault," *U.S. Army Aviation Digest* (February 1964): 2–6.

Rougeron, Camille. "Tactical Aviation," *Military Review* (October 1957): 96–105.

Swink, Capt. Paul C. "How Modern is Our Concept?" *U.S. Army Aviation Digest* (June 1961): 8–9.

Shamburek, Maj. Roland H., and Col. Spurgeon H. Neel. "The Army Aviation Story," Part 8: "Army Aviation Medicine," *U.S. Army Aviation Digest* (January 1963): 34–39.

Smith, William H. "Hawk Star," *U.S. Army Aviation Digest* (September 1964): 27–32.

"The U.S. Army Aviation Board," *U.S. Army Aviation Digest* (October 1957): 14–18.

Tierney, Richard K. "The Army Aviation Story," Part 1. *U.S. Army Aviation Digest* (June 1962): 2–25.

———. "The Army Aviation Story," Part 2: "Academics and Training." *U.S. Army Aviation Digest* (July 1962): 10–31.

———. "The Army Aviation Story," Part 6: "North Africa, Sicily, Italy." *U.S. Army Aviation Digest* (November 1962): 34–47.

———. "The Army Aviation Story," Part 7: "Europe, Pacific, Korea." *U.S. Army Aviation Digest* (December 1962): 26–38.
Vance, William E. "History of Army Aviation," *U.S. Army Aviation Digest* (June 1957): 7–20.
Vanderpool, Col. Jay D. "Aerial Vehicles in the Ground Role," *Military Review*, 38 (October 1958): 59–65.
———. "We Armed the Helicopters," *U.S. Army Aviation Digest*, 17 (June 1971).
van Kann, Brig. Gen. Clifton F. "The Real Goal of Army Aviation," *U.S. Army Aviation Digest* (March 1960): 35–37.
Weyland, Gen. O. P. "Tactical Air Power," *Ordnance* (March–April 1958): 798–801.
Wheeler, Gen. Earle G. "Airmobility," *U.S. Army Aviation Digest* (October 1963): 2–5.
———. "A Perspective on Firepower and Mobility," *U.S. Army Aviation Digest* (March 1964): 2–6.

BOOKS

Bergerson, Frederick A. *The Army Gets an Air Force*. Baltimore: The Johns Hopkins Press, 1980.
Eisenhower, Dwight D. *Mandate for Change, 1953–56*. Garden City, N.Y.: Doubleday and Co., 1963.
Ridgway, Matthew B. *Soldier: The Memoirs of Matthew B. Ridgway*. New York: Harper and Brothers, 1956.
Weinert, Richard P. *History of Army Aviation, 1950–1962. Phase II: 1955–1962*. Fort Monroe, Va.: Historical Office, TRADOC, 1976.
Weston, Leonard C., and Clifford W. Stephens. *The Development, Adaptation, and Production of Armament for Army Helicopters, 1957–1963*. Rock Island, Ill.: HQ, U.S. Army Armament Command, n.d.

DOCUMENTS

"A Critical Analysis of Army Positions on Aviation in 1961–1963 as Compared with Historical Experience," USAF Historical Division, Aerospace Studies Institute, Maxwell AFB, Ala. October 1963. K239.046-34,1961–63 (HC).
AFM 3–1. "Tactical Fighter Weapons Employment." November 1, 1965; January 25, 1967; March 20, 1970. K168.13-1 (HC).

Help from Above

"Air/Ground Attack Operations in Night and Adverse Weather Conditions: A Survey of Past Combat Experience." By C. B. East and E. H. Sharkey, RAND Note: N-1228-AF. August 1979. K146.003-379 (HC).

History. Directorate, Studies and Analysis, DCS Plans, Tactical Air Command. "USAF Close Air Support Command and Control." May 1, 1973. K417.04-7 (HC).

Hutton, Brig. Gen. Carl I. "Without Trumpets and Drums: Recollections of Thirty-Six Months with the Army Aviation School, June 1954–June 1957." Bound unpublished document. U.S. Army Aviation Center Library, Fort Rucker, Alabama.

———. "Airmobility: Collected Papers, 1952–1956." Bound unpublished document. U.S. Army Aviation Center Library, Fort Rucker, Alabama.

———. Statement of Plan. "A History of the Development of Army Aviation from 1940 to 1957." June 1959. To support Guggenheim application.

Memo. Army Chief of Staff to All Commands. "Air Transportability," June 28, 1955.

Memo. G-3, Army Aviation Division to Army Chief of Staff. "Army Position in Forthcoming Conversations with Air Force Staff Representatives on Army's Needs for Aviation." June 30, 1955.

Outline Plan. "Assumption by the Army of Certain Tactical Air Support Functions, Office, Deputy Chief of Staff for Military Operations, Department of the Army, Dec. 2, 1959."

Policy Decision. Secretary of Defense, Nov. 26, 1956. "Clarification of roles and missions to improve the effectiveness of operation of the Department of Defense," *U.S. Army Aviation Digest* (December 1956): 5–12.

Study. Joint Staff Task Force, Phase 2. "Close Air Support Study." 1972. K178.05-2 (HC).

TACM/PACAFM/USAFM 3-1. Part 2, Chapter 8: *Close Air Support*. September 30, 1971. K168.13 (HC).

5 | Flexible Response: 1960–1965

ARTICLES

"AF Documents Views on Close Air Support," *The Journal of the Armed Forces*, 103 (February 19, 1966): 15, 25.

Air Mobility Symposium. *Army*, 14 (December 1963): 64–71.

"Army and AF Mobility Concepts in Crucial Tests," *The Journal of the Armed Forces*, 102 (November 7, 1964): 16.

"Army Asks for More Airborne Firepower," *Business Week* (December 5, 1961): 31.

"Army Chief Gives Views on Howze Board Report," *Army, Navy, Air Force Journal and Register*, 100 (April 27, 1963): 33.

"Army Demands Aviation Control," *Army, Navy, Air Force Journal and Register*, 100 (September 15, 1962): 3.

"Army to Ignore 1948 (Key West) Agreements in Air Buildup," *Air Force Times*, 23 (May 1, 1963): 2.

Asprey, Robert B. "Close Air Support: How Do We Get It?" *Army*, 11 (November 1961): 33–37.

Donovan, S. J. "Tactical Air Command," *Army Information Digest* (October 1961): 15–21.

Dupuy, R. Ernest. "New Tactical Command: Big Step in the Right Direction," *The Army, Navy, Air Force Register* (October 21, 1961): 19.

Eliot, Maj. George Fielding. "STRICOM's Big Job," *Ordnance* (January–February 1963): 422–424.

Erbe, Maj. Robert L. "Army Tactical Mobility," *Military Review*, 42 (December 1962): 75–79.

Fowler, Lt. Col. Delbert M. "Close Air Support," *Military Engineer*, 52 (November–December 1960): 461–462.

Gavin, Lt. Gen. James M. "The Mobility Differential," *Army*, 13 (June 1963): 34–36.

Guntharp, Lt. Col. Walter A. "Where's TAC Air?" *Army*, 11 (February 1961): 55–57.

Harvey, Thomas H. "Air Cavalry in Battle: A New Concept in Action," *Armor* (May–June 1968): 5–10.

"Irwin School's Summer Term: How the Howze Board Did Its Work," *Army*, 12 (September 13, 1962): 74ff.

Kann, Clifton F. von. "Vulnerability of Army Aircraft," *Military Review* (November 1961): 2–8.

Help from Above

"Keep on Top of Close Air Support," *The Journal of the Armed Forces*, 103 (February 12, 1966): 11, 28.

"LeMay to Propose End of 'Army Air,'" *Army Times* (December 30, 1964): 1, 14.

Low, Brig. Gen. Andrew S. "Air Mobility in the Field Test Laboratory," *Air University Review* (July–August 1965): 14–27.

MacIntyre, Col. N. R. "Close Air Support," *Ordnance*, 47 (November–December 1962): 305–308.

McNamara, Robert S. and Gen. Earle G. Wheeler. "The Prospects for Army Air Mobility," *Army*, 13 (March 1963): 20–21.

Meyer, Maj. Gen. R. D. "Army's Air Plans Don't Conflict with Air Force's," *Army, Navy, Air Force Register*, 82 (March 25, 1961): 24–25.

Mitchell, Col. Douhet. "Aircraft for the Ground Battle," *Army*, 13 (February 1963): 24–28.

Poe, Perry. "How's Air Mobility?" *Army*, 13 (June 1963): 25–28.

Pickett, Brig. Gen. George B. "The Army's Tactical Mobility Concept," *U.S. Army Aviation Digest* (November 1964): 1–5.

Pouget, J. "The Armed Helicopter," *Military Review*, 44 (March 1964): 81–96.

Rathbun, Frank F. "Tasks of the Airmobile Test Team," *Army*, 13 (June 1963): 37–42.

"Report on Close Air Support Criticizes AF, DoD Failures," *The Journal of the Armed Forces* (February 12, 1966): 1–2, 14–15, 25, 29.

Rowny, Maj. Gen. E. L. "Air Mobility Problems," *Air Force Policy Letter for Commanders*, 23 (December 1964): 2–3.

Smith, William H. "Hawk Star," *U.S. Army Aviation Digest* (September 1964): 27–32.

Sparkman, Robert G. "Exercise Gold Fire I," *Air University Review* (March–April 1965): 22–44.

Steinkraus, Robert F. "Air/Ground Coordination," *Marine Corps Gazette*, 50 (May 1966): 29–31.

Stuart, Sheridan. "Air Concepts on a Collision Course," *Air Force/Space Digest* (August 1964): 34–39.

Sweeney, W. C., Jr. "Tactical Air Command Today," *The Army, Navy, Air Force Journal and Register*, 99 (June 9, 1962): 24–25.

"TAC Tells Help It Gives Army," *The Army, Navy, Air Force Journal and Register*, 101 (September 21, 1963): 12.

"Tactical Air Plays Top Role in 3 Exercises," *The Journal of the Armed Forces*, 102 (October 17, 1964): 11.

"Tactical Air Power," *Ordnance* (March–April 1968): 463–466.

"Tactical Aviation Conflict Sharpens," *The Journal of the Armed Forces*, 101 (July 18, 1964): 1, 25.

Weller, Jack "Gunships: Key to a New Kind of War," *The National Guardsman* (October 1968): 2–8.

Bibliography

BOOKS

Tolson, John. *Airmobility.* Washington, D.C.: Center of Military History, 1978.

DOCUMENTS

AFM 1–1. United States Air Force Basic Doctrine, August14, 1964. Paper. *AFM 1–1: An Audit Trail, 1943–1975.* Origin Unknown.
Appendix. "Notes on Agreements and Doctrine, U.S. Army-Air Force Aircraft," n.d.
Briefing. U.S. Strike Command to USAF Representatives Conference. Maxwell AFB, Ala., February 12, 1964.
Chronology. *Army Air Mobility Concept,* n.d. (last entry July 1965).
Draft Position Papers on Howze Board Findings, June 20, 1963.
Letter. Secretary of Defense to Secretary of Army, "Army Tactical Mobility," April 19, 1962.
Letter. Daley to Army Chief of Staff. "Improved Army Mobility," September 7, 1962.
Letter. Vice Chief of Staff to Daley. "Air Assault Division," February 11, 1963.
Letter. Hammett to McKee. "Army/Air Force Areas of Divergency," n.d. (April 1963?).
Letter. McKee to Hamlett. "The Central Air Force Position on Close Air Support," May 20, 1963.
Letter. ACS/FD to USACDC. "Army Air Mobility Program Projects," September 10, 1964.
Letter. Corcoran to Johnson. "General LeMay's Concern About Evaluation of Air Mobility Tests," October 2, 1964.
Letter. Rich to USAF Reps. "USAF Support, Air Assault II," October 26, 1964.
Letter. Beach to Abrams. "Gold Fire I," December 18, 1964.
Memo. DCS\MO to Army Chief of Staff. "USCONARC Observer Team Report of Observations, JTEX Goldfire I," n.d.
Memo. Secretary of Defense to Secretary of Army. "Army Aviation," April 10, 1962.
Memo. Secretary of Army to Army Chief of Staff. August 1, 1962.
Memo. Decker to CG/USACDC. "Improved Army Mobility." August 24, 1962.
Memo. Army Chief of Staff to DCSs. "Department of the Air Force Analysis of Final Report," Army Tactical Mobility Board. September 21, 1962.
Memo. Army Vice Chief of Staff to Air Force Vice Chief of Staff "Identification of Basic Issues." April 1963.

Help from Above

Memo, SGS to Army Vice Chief of Staff. "Army/Air Force Differences." April 25, 1963.

Memo. Dept of Navy, OLL to Secretary of Navy. "Report of Congressional Committee Hearings." February 24, 1964.

Memo. DCS\MO to Army Chief of Staff. "Senate Preparedness Investigating Subcommittee Hearings on Vietnam." June 1964.

Memo. ACSFD for Vice Chief of Staff. "Gold Fire I." October 22, 1964.

Memo, Abrams to Johnson. "Visit by General LeMay to Air Assault II." Oct. 30, 1964.

Memo. Army Chief of Staff to DCSs. "JTEX Gold Fire I and Army Air Assault II." November 18, 1964.

Memo. 354th Tactical Fighter Wing. "TACOP Final Report–Air Assault II." November 25, 1964.

Memo. Zuckert to Secretary of Defense. "Department of the Air Force Proposal for Clarification of Air Force/Army Aviation Functions and Use of Aerial Vehicles." March 18, 1965.

Memo. Secretary of Defense to Army Chief of Staff. "Organization of an Airmobile Division." n.d. (April 1965?).

Memo. ACSFOR to Army Chief of Staff. "'New Focus' Committee Visit to Vietnam." November 16, 1965.

Memo SGS, Army to Army Chief of Staff. "Army-Air Force Interface." April 7, 1966.

MFR. "Meeting Between Dr. Harold Brown and Brig. Gen. R. R. Williams." December 1, 1964.

MFR. ACS/FD. "Army Tactical Mobility: Issues and Opportunities–Stockfish Report." December 5, 1964.

MFR. Army Chief of Staff. "Comments on Joint Test and Evaluation Exercise Gold Fire I." December 8, 1964.

MFR. "Chronology of Airmobile Division." August 6, 1965.

Report. Army Tactical Mobility Requirements Board (Howze Board). *Final Report, U.S. Army Tactical Mobility Requirements Board*. Fort Bragg, NC, August, 1962. Lt. Gen. H. H. Howze, USA, President.

Report. (Disosway Board). *USAF Tactical Air Support Requirements Board Comments on U.S. Army Tactical Mobility Requirements Board Report.* August 14, 1962.

Report. *Army Position Concerning Organic Army Aircraft*. May 2, 1963.

Report. *Army Position Concerning Organic Army Aircraft*. 1964.

Report. DCS/MO. *Army Aviation Guidelines, FY1961–FY1970*. n.d.

Speech. Brig. Gen. John J. Tolson. "Army Aviation and Air Mobility," September 22, 1964.

Speech. Maj. Gen. E. L.Rowny to Association of U.S. Army. "An Army View of Air Mobility," November 17, 1964. In *Supplement to Air Force Policy Letters for Commanders*, #1, 1965, pp. 9–14.

Talking Paper. Gen. McKee. *Army/Air Force Divergencies*. April 11, 1963.
Talking Paper. *Army-AF Differences*. May 22, 1963.
Talking Paper. *Army and Air Force Responsibilities Regarding the Use of Aerial Vehicles*. 1963?

HISTORIES

Tactical Air Command, 1963–1965. K417.01
Tactical Air Warfare Center, 1963–1964. K417.0732
Ninth Air Force, 1963–1965. K533.01
The United States Strike Command, 1964. K177.01

6 | The Vietnam Era

ARTICLES

"Air Force, Army Agree on Roles, Mission," *Aviation Week and Space Technology* (April 27, 1966): 26–27.
Andrews, Walter. "Rugged Tests and a Rugged Machine," *Armed Forces Journal* (December 14, 1968).
———. "A Weapons Ship For All Environments," *Armed Forces Journal* (December 14, 1968).
———. "There Are No Red Flags Flying," *Armed Forces Journal* (December 14, 1968).
"Close Air Support (1965)," Air Force report. *The Journal of the Armed Forces*, 103 (February 19, 1966).
Nihart, Brooks. "Cheyenne Dead After Lingering Illness," *Armed Forces Journal* (September 1972).
———. "Army Gets Go-Ahead for Scrubbed Down AAH," *Armed Forces Journal* (December 1972).
Ulsamer, Edgar. "The A–10 Approach to Close Air Support," *Air Force Magazine* (May 1973).
Volz, Joseph. "A–X vs. AH–56: Competitive or Complementary?" *Armed Forces Journal* (April 1970).

Help from Above

BOOKS

Ballard, Jack S. *Development and Employment of Fixed-Wing Gunships, 1962–1972*. The United States Air Force in Southeast Asia series. Washington, D.C.: Office of Air Force History, 1982.

Berger, Carl, ed. *The United States Air Force in Southeast Asia*. Washington, D.C.: Office of Air Force History, 1977.

Cash, John et al. *Seven Firefights in Vietnam*. Washington, D.C.: Office of the Chief of Military History, 1970.

Eckhardt, George S. *Command and Control, 1950–1969*. U.S. Army Vietnam Studies. Washington, D.C.: Department of the Army, 1974.

Futrell, Robert F. *The Advisory Years*. The United States Air Force in Southeast Asia series. Washington, D.C.: Office of Air Force History. 1981.

Gropman, Alan L. *Airpower and the Airlift Evacuation of Kham Duc*. Maxwell AFB, Ala: Airpower Research Institute, 1979.

Hay, Lt. Gen. John H, Jr. *Tactical and Materiel Innovations*. U.S. Army Vietnam Studies. Washington, D.C.: Department of the Army, 1974.

Kinnard, Douglas. *The War Managers*. Wayne, NJ: Avery Publishing Co., 1985.

Knaack, Marcelle Size. *Post-World War II Fighter, 1945–1973*. Encyclopedia of U.S. Air Force Aircraft and Missile systems series, vol. 1. Washington, D.C.: Office of Air Force History, 1978.

Momyer, William W. *Airpower in Three Wars*. Washington, D.C.: Government Printing Office, 1978.

Nalty, Bernard C. *Air Power and the Fight for Khe Sanh*. Washington, D.C.: Office of Air Force History, 1973.

Pearson, Willard. *The War in the Northern Provinces*. U.S. Army Vietnam Studies. Washington, D.C.: Department of the Army, 1975.

Rogers, Lt. Gen. Bernard W. *Cedar Falls-Junction City: A Turning Point*. U.S. Army Vietnam Studies. Washington, D.C.: Department of the Army, 1974.

Schlight, John. *The War in South Vietnam: The Years of the Offensive, 1965–1968*. The United States Air Force in Southeast Asia series. Washington, D.C.: Office of Air Force History, 1988.

Stanton, Shelby. *Vietnam Order of Battle*. New York: Galahad Books, 1986.

Tilford, Earl H. Jr. *Setup: What the Air Force Did in Vietnam and Why*. Maxwell AFB, AL: Air University Press, 1991.

Tolson, John J. *Airmobility, 1961–1971*. U.S. Army Vietnam Studies. Washington, D.C.: Department of the Army, 1973.

Bibliography

DOCUMENTS

Agreement. Between Army Chief of Staff and Air Force Chief of Staff, April 6, 1966.
Letter. Maj. Gen. H.W.O. Kinnard, CG 1st Cav Div to Lt. Gen. Joseph H. Moore, 2d Air Division, Nov. 21, 1965.
Memo. SECDEF to SECAF. "Close Support and SAW Aircraft," January 7, 1965.
Memo. Robert S. McNamara to Secretary of the Air Force. "Operation and Management of Army and Air Force Aviation," September 11, 1965.
Memo. Cyrus Vance to Secretary of the Air Force. "Evaluation of Helicopter Fire Support System," August 27, 1966.
Memo. David Packard to Secretaries of the Army and Air Force. "Systems for Air Delivered Fire Support of Ground Forces," January 22, 1970.
Memo. DEPSECDEF to Secretaries of the Army and Air Force. "Systems for Air Delivered Fire Support of Ground Forces, March 26, 1970.
Notebooks. USAF Chief of Staff.
Summary. PACAF. Air Operations in SEA.

HISTORIES

2d Air Division, July–December 1965.
Strategic Air Command, July–December 1965.

INTERVIEWS

Kampe, Col., USA, 1st Cavalry Division G-4, Corona Harvest # 101.
Kinnard, Gen. Harry O. In *Armed Force Journal* (December 14, 1968).

REPORTS

"101st Airborne Division (Airmobile). Final Report, "Air Mobile Operations in Support of Lam Son 719 Feb 8–Apr. 6, 1971," vol. 1, May 1, 1972. Momyer Collection. 168.7041-152
101st Airborne Division (Airmobile), Camp Eagle, Vietnam. "Airmobile Operations in Support of Lam Son 719, Feb 8–Apr. 6, 1971," Final Report. May 1, 1971.
Abbey, Tom G. "The Role of USAF in Support of Special Activities in SEA," Project Checo, HQ PACAF. July 1, 1976.
"A Chronology of Significant Airpower Events in Southeast Asia, 1950–1968," Project Corona Harvest. May 1969.

Help from Above

"Activities Input for Corona Harvest: In-Country and Out-Country Strike Operations in Southeast Asia, Jan 1, 1965–Mar. 31, 1968," Project Corona Harvest. March 1968.

Anthony, Victor B. "The Air Force in Southeast Asia: Tactics and Techniques of Night Operations,1961–1970," Office of Air Force History, 1973.

"A Study of Aviation Responsibilities: Air Force-Army," HQ USAF, DCS Plans and Operations. June 1962.

Bates, William and Kenneth Sams. "Operation Masher/White Wing," Project Checo, HQ PACAF. September 9, 1966.

Burch, Robert. "Single Management of Air in SVN," Project Checo, HQ PACAF. March 18, 1969.

"Evaluation of Command and Control of Southeast Asia Operations, Jan 1, 1965–Mar 31, 1968," Project Corona Harvest, n.d.

Goldberg, Alfred and Donald Smith, "Army-Air Force Relations: The Close Air Support Issue." Santa Monica, CA: the RAND Corporation, 1971. R-906-PR

Hickey, Lawrence J. "Operation Junction City," Project Checo, HQ PACAF, 17 November 1967

——— and James G. Bruce. "Operation Attleboro." Project Checo, HQ PACAF, 14 April 1967.

"History of USAF Close Air Support Command and Control." Directorate, Studies and Analysis, DCS Plans, Tactical Air Command. 1 May 1973. XPS R 73-13

"In-Country Air Strike Operations, Southeast Asia, Jan 1, 1965–Mar 31, 1968." Project Corona Harvest, May 1971

"The Joint Chiefs of Staff and the War in Vietnam, 1960–1968." JCS History Office.

Lane, John J., Jr. "Command and Control and Communications Structures in Southeast Asia." Maxwell AFB, AL: Air University Press, 1981.

Loye, Col. J.F. Jr. et al. "Lam Son 719, 30 January–24 March 1971: The South Vietnamese Incursion Into Laos." Project Checo, HQ PACAF, 14 March 1971. K717.0413-98

McDermott, Louis M. "III DASC Operations." Project Checo, HQ PACAF, 1 August 1969.

Melyan, Wesley. "The War in Vietnam, 1965." Project Checo, HQ PACAF, 25 January 1967.

———. "Arc Light, 1965–1966." Project Checo, HQ PACAF, 1967.

Mishler, Edward C. "The A-X Specialized Close Air Support Aircraft: Origins and Concept Phase, 1961–1970." Andrews AFB: Air Force Systems Command.

Montagliani, Ernest. "Army Aviation in RVN-A Case Study," Project Checo, HQ PACAF. 11 July 1970.

Bibliography

Overton, James B. "FAC Operations in Close Air Support Role." Project Checo, HQ PACAF. 31 January 1969.

Porter, Melvin F. "Silver Bayonet," Project Checo, HQ PACAF. 28 February 1966.

———. "Air Response to Immediate Air Request in SVN." Project Checo, HQ PACAF. 15 July 1969.

Potter, Joseph V. "OV–10 Operations in SEAsia." Project Checo, HQ PACAF. 15 September 1969.

Rowley, Ralph A. "USAF FAC Operations in SEA, 1961–1965." Office of Air Force History, 1972.

———. "The Air Force in Southeast Asia: FAC Operations, 1965–1970." Office of Air Force History, 1975.

———. "The Air Force in Southeast Asia: Tactics and Techniques of Close Air Support Operations, 1961–1973." Office of Air Force History, 1976.

Sams, Kenneth. "The Fall of A Shau," Project Checo, HQ PACAF. 18 April 1966

———. "First Test and Combat Use of the AC–47." Project Checo, HQ PACAF. 1965.

——— and Bert Aton. "USAF Support of Special Forces." Project Checo, HQ PACAF. 10 March 1969.

——— and A.W. Thompson. "Kham Duc," Project Checo, HQ PACAF. 8 July 1968.

Schlight, John. "Jet Forward Air Controllers in SEAsia," Project Checo, HQ PACAF. 15 October 1969.

Sexton, Richard R. "The Battle of Plei Me, Republic of Vietnam." (Essay) 2 June 1967.

"Summarization of Air Mobility Test and Evaluation Activities." 30 June 1965.

Thorndale, William. "Battle for Dak To," Project Checo, HQ PACAF. 21 June 1968.

Trest, Warren A. "Control of Air Strikes in SEA, 1961–1966." Project Checo, HQ PACAF. 1 March 1967.

———. "Khe Sanh (Operation Niagara)." Project Checo, HQ PACAF. 1968.

U.S. House (Pike) Committee on Armed Services. *Report of Special Subcommittee on Tactical Air Support*. 89th Cong., 2d sess., February 1, 1966.

"United States-Vietnam Relations, 1945–1967." Pentagon Papers, 12 vols. Washington, D.C.: Government Printing Office, 1971.

Wade, Thomas D. "Seventh Air Force Tactical Air Control Center." Project Checo, HQ PACAF, 1968.

Westmoreland, William C. and U.S.G. Sharp. "Report on the War in Vietnam (as of 30 June 1968)." Washington, D.C.: Government Printing Office, 1968.

Help from Above

Winnefeld, James A. and Dana J. Johnson. "Command and Control of Joint Operations: Some Lessons Learned from Four Case Studies of an Enduring Issue." Santa Monica, CA; The RAND Corporation, 1991. R-4045-RC

SPEECHES

Momyer, Gen. William W., Cdr, TAC. U.S. Marine Corps Command and Staff College, Quantico, Va. October 20, 1972.
———. Army Command and General Staff College, Fort Leavenworth, Kansas. October 27, 1972.
Schriever, Gen. Bernard A. "Close Air Support (1965)." Printed in *Journal of the Armed Forces*, 103 (February 19, 1966).

Index

2d Advanced Echelon (ADVON): 303, 309, 326
ABC Manual for Tactical Operations: 205
Abrams, Creighton W.: 350
Adams, Paul D.: 179, 210, 257, 338, 339
advanced aerial fire-support system (AAFSS): 354, 355, 358
advanced attack helicopter (AAH): 356
aerial combat reconnaissance (ACR): 227, 228
Air Assault II: 290, 292, 293, 294, 295, 346, 371
Airborne Battlefield Command and Control Center (ABCCC): 331, 332
Air Corps Tactical School (ACTS): 1, 2, 20, 22, 28, 43, 124, 370
Air Defense Command (ADC): 56, 63, 83
Air Service Liaison Officer: 9
Air Support Operations Center (ASOC): 211, 217, 218, 220, 241, 277, 280, 303, 304, 305, 306, 309, 337
Air Transport Command: 36
Aircraft: 57, 62, 67–69, 73, 74, 114, 186, 220, 222, 231, 301, 352–362
    A–1: 302, 310, 313, 314, 353, 340, 342, 368
    A–1E: 310, 325, 327
    A–3: 24, 26
    A–4: 324
    A4D: 270
    A4D-5: 265
    A4E: 265
    A–6D: 332
    A6A: 265, 270
    A–7: 313
    A–7A: 313, 353, 357
    A–7D: 313, 314, 353, 357, 358, 361
    A–7K: 314
    A–9: 361
    A–10: 271, 361, 363
    A–17: 24, 26
    A–18: 26
    A–20: 27
    A–26: 63, 64, 69
    A–37: 313, 314
    AC–47: 316, 320, 327, 331, 332
    AC–119: 316
    AD–2: 92
    AD–4: 199
    AD–6: 199
    AF–2: 199
    AH–1G: 345, 351
    AM–1: 92
    B–17: 22, 38, 187
    B–24: 36
    B–25: 41, 49
    B–26: 41, 117, 118, 120, 148, 149, 152, 168, 183, 310
    B–29: 117, 118, 120, 122, 123, 124, 125, 126, 127, 131, 132, 149, 235, 369
    B–36: 88, 95, 187
    B–52: 236, 300, 308, 309, 323, 324, 325, 326, 331, 334, 339, 346, 347, 348, 351, 362
    B–57: 183, 241, 253, 310, 312, 325, 327
    B–57A: 183
    B–66: 184, 253
    B–66A: 185
    B–70: 199, 236
    Brequet: 7, 14
    Bristol: 14
    C–5A: 236
    C–7: 246
    C–46: 38, 39, 62
    C–47: 38, 39, 62, 315
    C–54: 38, 39
    C–82: 38, 62, 77
    C–123: 320, 322, 339, 341
    C–130: 246, 283, 287, 295, 322, 326, 331, 332, 333, 339, 341, 346
    Caproni: 7, 8
    Caribou: 246, 250, 265, 295, 334, 341
    Corsair: 126, 129
    Curtiss A–3: 24, 26
    Curtiss A–8: 24
    Curtiss A–12 Shrike: 24
    Curtiss O–1: 24
    Curtiss XA–8: 26

447

Help from Above

Curtiss Y1A–18: 27
CV–7: 341
DC–3: 38
DeHavilland: 18
DH–4: 7, 8, 10, 24
Douglas A–20: 27
Douglas O–2: 24
F–4: 236, 255, 262, 270, 310, 311, 314, 325, 329, 346
F–4C: 265, 270, 271, 278, 283, 285, 288, 310, 312
F–4D: 312, 313
F–4E: 312, 357
F–5: 36, 37, 332
F–5A: 265, 270
F–6: 36, 37, 77
F–7: 36
F–7A: 36
F–8: 327
F–9: 36
F–15: 360, 383
F–47: 77, 92, 99
F–51: 77, 92, 99, 120, 121, 122, 128, 130, 139, 153, 154–155, 168
F–80: 68, 75, 92, 99, 101, 104, 117, 120, 122, 128, 130, 139, 154–155, 157, 168, 380
F–80C: 100
F–82: 92, 117, 159
F–84: 92, 99, 139, 157, 159, 168, 183, 253
F–84B: 99
F–84E: 100, 102, 104, 106, 108, 157
F–86: 92, 139, 158, 183, 184, 241
F–86A: 100, 104
F–86F: 199
F–89: 68
F–94: 68
F–100: 183, 185, 187, 199, 200, 237, 238, 240, 241, 253, 265, 283, 287, 288, 310, 311, 312, 313, 314, 319, 323, 325, 327, 346
F–100D: 184, 187, 188, 270, 311
F–101: 187, 270
F–101A: 188, 189
F–104: 185, 187, 188
F–105: 187, 188, 199, 236, 238, 253, 255, 265, 270, 283, 285, 287, 288
F–111: 234, 265, 271
F–111A: 270, 271
F–111F: 289
Fi–156: 267, 268
G–91: 199, 265
Halberstadt CL: 14
Handley Page: 7
Hannoveraner: 14
Henschel Hs 126: 267
JN–4: 7
Ju–87: 267, 268
Junkers-Fokker CL–1: 14
KC–135: 288, 324
KC–135E: 289
L–5: 44, 151, 152
L–16: 83
L–17: 83
L–19: 153, 193, 316
MIG–15: 139, 157
Morane: 14
Mosquito: 122, 132, 139, 144, 150, 163, 167
Mureaux-115: 267
Nieuport: 7, 14
O–1: 311, 316, 318, 353
O–2: 311
O–2A: 318
OH–1: 319, 379
OH–2: 379
OH–2A: 322
OV–1: 228, 229
OV–10: 318, 318, 380
P–38: 35, 36, 41, 49
P–39: 35, 42, 49
P–40: 35, 41, 49, 157
P–47: 36, 46, 49, 90, 102, 157
P–51: 36, 63
P–61: 47, 68, 69
P–80: 63, 65, 67
P–80A: 67
RF–80: 99
Salmson: 7
Sopwith Camel: 14
Spad: 7, 8, 14

Index

Stork: 267
T–6: 122, 151, 152, 153, 167, 168
T–28: 310
Westland Lysander: 267, 269
XBIA: 24
XF–86: 158
XL–19B: 193
Air Forces (numbered):
   Eighth: 40
   Fifth: 48, 49, 50, 51
   Ninth: 45, 47
Air-Ground Operations School (AGOS): 186
air liaison officer (ALO): 186, 241, 242, 273, 277, 280, 303, 305, 317, 333
air liaison parties (ALPs): 50
Air Operations Center (AOC): 211, 218, 303, 309
Air Support Command (ASC): 38, 48
AK–47 assault rifle: 347
Almond, Edward M.: 113, 123, 124–125, 131, 132, 133, 135–138, 144, 150, 151, 161, 162, 163, 164, 165, 166, 167, 168, 169, 170, 175, 203
American Expeditionary Force (AEF): 3, 5, 11, 12, 20
Amiens: 14
AN/CPS–5: 106
Anthis, Rollin H.: 337
AN\TRC–7: 107
antiballistic missle (ABM): 236
Arc Light: 324, 325, 326, 346, 348
ARC–27 UHF radio: 150, 280
ARC–3 VHF radio: 150, 155
ARC–7 radio: 150
Ardennes: 3, 47
Argonne: 10, 14, 15, 18, 20
Armistice: 3, 7
Armies (numbered):
   Eighth: 40, 115, 118, 126, 127, 129, 131, 132, 133, 135, 136, 137, 138, 139, 140, 142, 143, 144, 146, 148, 149, 150, 151, 152, 159, 164, 167, 168, 169, 171, 172, 174, 175
   Fifth: 38
Army Air Forces (AAF): 32, 35, 38, 40, 42, 44, 46, 47, 48, 49, 51, 53, 54, 55, 56, 58, 61, 62, 65, 67, 70, 71, 91, 97, 110
Army Air Forces Board (AAF Board): 57, 62, 67
Army Ground Forces (AGF): 38, 42, 45, 61, 62, 63, 65, 70, 72, 74, 75, 110
Army of the Pacific (USARPAC): 242
Arnold, Henry H.: 32, 33, 38, 42, 48, 55, 83
Artillery Brigade: 9
Barcus, Glenn O.: 99, 100, 166, 167
Barcus Report: 113
Barksdale Field: 22, 23
Barksdale Hamlett: 257
Bastogne: 47
Battle of the Somme: 13
Bizerte: 41
BLU–82: 346
Board of Review for Tactical Operations: 88
bomb damage assessment (BDA): 317
Bradley, Omar N.: 46, 52, 70, 87, 197
Brown, George S.: 320
Brown, Harold: 356
Bullpup: 271
Calais: 18
Cannon, John K.: 182, 203
Casablanca: 40
CAV–58: 71
CBU–2A: 237
Chambley: 15
Chateau-Thierry: 5
Churchill, Winston: 40
Circular #17: 58
Circular #30: 58
Clark, Mark W.: 61, 104, 129, 137, 171
cluster bomb unit (CBU): 238, 287, 328, 348, 351
Collins, Joseph L.: 70, 88, 90, 96, 97, 130, 137, 164, 165, 166, 171, 172, 175
Combine III: 81, 82, 83
Commands (numbered):
   IX Air Support: 46, 47
   IX Tactical Air: 46, 47, 62

449

Help from Above

XII Air Support: 41, 43, 44
XIX Tactical Air: 46, 47
Commander in Chief, Far East Command (CINCFE): 115, 116, 117
Commander in Chief, United Nations Command (CINCUNC): 115, 116
Commander of Army Forces, Far East (CINCAFFE): 115, 116
commander of support aircraft (CSA): 50
Composite Air Strike Force (CASF): 183
CONARC TT 110-100-1: 213
Coningham, Arthur: 1, 40, 41, 42, 368
Continental Air Command (CONAC): 83, 84, 86, 87, 88, 99
Continental Army Command (CONARC): 195, 200, 206, 208, 211, 212, 213, 219, 227, 228, 240, 241, 244, 260, 271, 275, 288, 289
Control and Reporting Center (CRC): 284, 288, 303
Corps (numbered):
   I: 132, 149, 173, 306, 320, 323, 329, 330, 331, 332
   II: 324, 332, 338, 339
   III: 241, 304, 320, 323, 325, 334
   IV: 323
   V: 89, 203
   IX: 147
   X: 117, 133, 135, 136, 137, 138, 144, 146, 149, 150, 151, 161, 163, 164, 166, 167, 168, 169, 369, 379
   XVIII Airborne: 241, 244
   XXIV: 347
Corps of Engineers: 5
Dahlquist, John E.: 195, 208, 227
Deputy Chief of Staff for Operations (DCSOPS): 198
Dean, William F.: 121, 122, 138, 144
Decker, George H.: 200, 201
demilitarized zone (DMZ): 241, 319, 330
Denfeld, Louis E.: 96
Devers, Jacob L.: 61, 62, 66, 67, 70, 72, 74, 75, 84, 87, 88, 104
direct aerial fire support (DAFS): 335
Direct Air Support Center (DASC): 241, 273, 277, 278, 280, 281, 284, 288, 306, 308, 309, 315, 318, 319, 323, 359, 362, 377, 378
Direct Air Support Team (DAST): 284
Disosway, Gabriel P.: 252, 253, 256, 257, 297
Divisions (numbered):
   III Marine: 49
DoD Directive 5160.22: 336, 355
Douglas Aircraft Company: 38
Douhet, Giulio: 40
Drum, Hugh: 4, 5
Dulles, John F.: 182, 234
Eaker, Ira C.: 76
Eisenhower, Dwight D.: 52, 55, 56, 61, 68, 70, 75, 110, 130, 165, 181, 191, 196, 254
European Theater of Operations (ETO): 254
Everest, Frank F.: 169, 171, 175, 219, 220
Far East Air Forces (FEAF): 115, 117, 118, 120, 121, 122, 123, 124, 125, 126, 127, 129, 130, 131, 132, 133, 134, 135, 136, 137, 138, 139, 140, 141, 144, 148, 149, 154, 164, 168, 172, 174, 182, 201, 369
Far East Command (FEC): 115, 116, 120, 123, 124, 131, 136, 143, 144, 161, 169
fast development logistics (FDL): 236
Ferguson, James: 146, 147
Field Manual (F.M.): 33
   F.M. 100-20: 42, 43, 45, 58, 79, 90, 205, 368
   F.M. 31-35: 33, 36, 38, 40, 42, 45, 48, 58, 60, 61, 62, 66, 75, 78, 79, 89, 109, 110, 137, 141, 142, 144, 146, 148, 159, 167, 204, 205, 211
Field Service Regulations: 3
Finletter, Thomas K.: 197
Fire Support Coordination Centers (FSCCs): 78, 99, 100
Flanders coast: 14
Forrestal, James: 72
Fort Crockett: 22
Fort Knox: 28
Fort Sam Houston: 13

Index

forward air controller (FAC): 60, 77, 99, 107, 122, 149, 150, 151, 152, 163, 166, 172, 174, 176, 218, 241, 242, 254, 273, 274, 276, 277, 278, 282, 283, 284, 286, 288, 300, 301, 302, 308, 311, 316, 317, 318, 319, 320, 322, 323, 327, 329, 332, 333, 334, 346, 347, 350, 353, 362, 379, 380
forward edge of the battle area (FEBA): 249, 260
Foulois, Benjamin D.: 12, 13, 18, 20
Frederick the Great: 2
frequency-modulation: 82
G–2 Air Section: 46
G–3 Air Section: 44, 46
GAU–8/A cannon: 361
Gavin, James M.: 74, 223, 225, 226, 230
Gay, Hobart R.: 138
General Headquarters (GHQ) Air Force: 19, 24, 26, 35
Gold Fire I: 283, 285, 286, 288, 290, 294, 295, 296, 302, 374
Gold Fire II: 283, 294, 296, 338, 371, 374
Gray, Gordon: 96, 97
Great War: 1, 22
ground controlled approach (GCA): 278
Groups (numbered):
    First Surveillance: 22
ground liaison officer (GLO): 186, 241, 275
Harkins, Paul D.: 337
Hawk Star: 290
Helicopters: 180, 181, 192, 209, 217, 218, 221, 222, 223–230, 231, 245, 246, 247, 248, 249, 286, 345, 380
    AH–56A: 355
    CH–3: 295
    CH–3C: 283, 287
    CH–21: 227
    CH–47: 295
    CH–54: 295
    Cobra: 342, 343, 345, 351, 354, 357
    H–25: 227
    OH–13: 227
    UH–1: 343

UH–1B: 345
UH–1C: 345
UH–1H: 352, 377
UH–19: 227
Hess, Dean E.: 121
Hickey, Doyle D.: 124
Higgins, Gerald J.: 159, 161, 166
high frequency (hf): 82, 144
Howze, Hamilton H.: 194, 225, 244, 252, 253, 255, 256, 375
HU-1: 249
Hutton, Carl I.: 194, 224, 226, 227
Indian River I: 283, 285
Indian River II: 283, 284, 285
Indian River III: 283, 284, 285, 286
Iwo Jima: 50
jet assisted takeoff (JATO): 103
Johnson, Harold K.: 305, 341, 342
Johnson, Louis: 95
Johnson, Lyndon B.: 296, 299
Joint Action Armed Forces (JAAF): 208
Joint Air-Ground Instruction Team (JAGIT): 186
Joint Air-Ground Operations Manual (JAGOS): 213, 217, 218, 219, 220, 240, 271, 272, 302, 303, 304, 316, 378
Joint Army and Air Force Adjustment Regulations (JAAFAR) 5-10-1: 222
Joint Chiefs of Staff (JCS): 257, 275
Joint Operations Center (JOC): 58, 60, 66, 77, 78, 80, 81, 99, 107, 121, 122, 127, 132, 136, 137, 142, 143, 144, 145–149, 151, 152, 159, 163, 168, 169, 171, 172, 173, 174, 176, 186, 202, 207, 209, 210, 211, 217, 249, 250, 372, 377
Joint Training Directive (JTD): 186, 202, 203, 204, 205, 208, 210, 211, 213
Joint Training Directive for Air-Ground Operations: 109
Joy, C. Turner: 115
Junction City: 334
Kasserine Pass: 41, 42
Kean, William B.: 121, 122, 138
Keiser, J.B.: 139

451

Help from Above

Kelly Field: 22, 23
Kennedy, John F.: 196, 231, 234, 236, 237
Kenney, George C.: 48, 55
Kinnard, Harry O.: 339, 341, 351, 358
klaxon horn: 10
Kuter, Laurence S.: 200
Laird, Melvin R.: 355
Lam: 347, 349
Lam Son: 347, 350, 351, 352
LAU–10: 237
Lee, Robert M.: 85, 86, 87, 88, 89, 90, 91, 92, 104
LeMay, Curtis E.: 74, 234, 235, 245, 251, 252, 256, 270, 294
Lemnitzer, Lyman L.: 198
Linebacker II: 324, 357
Long Horn: 203, 372
Luftwaffe: 29, 32, 38, 40, 41, 45, 47
M–2 machine gun: 155
M–3 machine gun: 155
M–16 rifle: 236, 329
M–39 jeep: 150
M–60: 320
M–1939: 349
MacArthur, Douglas: 48, 115, 117, 120, 122, 123, 124, 126, 131, 132, 135, 136, 141, 143, 169, 369
Macon, Robert C.: 88
March Field: 22
Marianas-Bonin Command: 115
Mars-la-Tour: 15
Marshall, George C.: 32, 33, 42, 52
McAuliffe, Anthony C.: 203
McConnell, John P.: 294, 295, 305, 315, 338, 339, 341, 342, 352, 356, 357, 361
McKee, William F.: 259
McNair, Lesley J.: 38, 55
McNamara, Robert S.: 188, 234, 235, 236, 242, 243, 244, 256, 257, 258, 260, 265, 271, 279, 294, 295, 297, 301, 336, 352, 353, 356
M-day: 29
Megee, Vernon E.: 97, 98
Mesquite: 75

Meuse-Argonne: 15, 18, 20
Meyers, Gilbert L.: 146, 281, 282
Military Assistance Command, Vietnam (MACV): 306, 325, 326, 330, 336, 337
Mitchell, William "Billy": 4, 5, 6, 9, 12, 19, 20, 180, 221
MK–24: 237
MK–6: 237
Momyer, William W.: 79, 80, 308, 326, 330, 331, 332, 358, 359, 360, 363
Montdidier: 15
Montgomery, Bernard L.: 40, 86, 164
Moore, Joseph H.: 305, 308
Mosquitoes: 130, 137, 151–153, 168, 172, 174
Motor Transport Corps: 5
MPQ–2: 81
MPQ–2 radar: 149
MSQ 35: 322
MSQ 77: 323
MSQ–1 radar: 149
Napoleon: 2
National Security Act: 71, 72, 73
National Security Council (NSC): 181
Naval Forces, Far East (NAVFE): 115, 116
Nguyen Van Thieu: 349
Niagara: 330, 331
Nicaragua: 23, 28
Nixon, Richard M.: 299
noncommissioned officer (NCO): 12, 32, 273
Norstad, Lauris: 87, 107, 108
North Atlantic Treaty Organization (NATO):
North Korean Peoples Army (NKPA): 118, 127, 133
Northwest African Tactical Air Force (NATAF): 41
not later than (NLT): 285
NSC 68: 181
NSC 162/2: 181
Nugent, Richard E.: 88, 89
O'Donnell, Emmett: 120, 131
Office of the Chief of Army Field Forces (OCAFF): 206

Index

Office of the Secretary of Defense (OSD): 294, 295, 296
Ordnance Department: 5
Ozark: 287–289
Pace, Frank, Jr.: 197
Pacific Air Forces (PACAF): 238, 240, 241, 242
Packard, David L.: 358, 360
Partridge, Earl E.: 124, 125, 126, 131, 133, 135, 136, 137, 138, 144, 146, 163, 164
Patton, George S.: 46, 124, 254
peace dividend: 53
penny packets: 54, 86
Pershing, John J.: 3, 4, 5, 11
petroleum, oil, and lubricants (POL): 99
Phase I: 57
Phase II: 57
Phase III: 57
Picardy: 14
pierced-steel plank (PSP): 103
Pike, Otis G.: 353
Quarles, Donald A.: 209
Quesada, Elwood R.: 46, 47, 56, 58, 62, 64, 65, 70, 72, 76, 81, 84, 85, 87, 88, 93, 94, 147, 186, 374
Question Mark airplane: 28
Radford, Arthur W.: 96
RAND: 263
Reorganization Objective Army Division (ROAD): 245, 247, 248, 255, 279, 287, 293, 294, 300, 339, 343, 374
Republic of Korea Army (ROKA): 117, 129, 136, 169
Reserve Officer's Training Corps (ROTC): 63
Ridgway, Matthew B.: 138, 169, 171, 180, 191, 196, 210, 223, 224
Rogers, Bernard W.: 334
Rommel: 40, 41
Royal Air Force (RAF): 14, 15, 18, 40
Ryukus Command: 115
SA–2 missile: 266, 347
SA–3 missile: 266
Sage Brush: 184, 206, 208, 209, 210, 226, 371, 372

SCR–130: 28
SCR–193: 169
SCR–399: 144, 169
SCR–522 radio: 155
SCR–584: 47
Sharp, Ulysses S. Grant: 331
Sherman, William T.: 3
Short Airfield of Tactical Support (SATS): 278
Short-range Radar and Navigation (SHORAN): 69, 70, 81
short-takeoff-and-landing (STOL): 264, 266, 267
Shrike: 266, 288
Signal Corps: 3, 5, 28
Signal Officer: 9
Sioux: 287
Skyspot: 311, 312, 322, 323, 328
Smith, Oliver P.: 162
Snakeye: 279
Southern Pine: 202, 203, 372
South Vietnamese Air Force (VNAF): 302, 303, 305, 309, 316
Spaatz, Carl A.: 56, 74, 83, 84, 85
Spanish Civil War: 26
Sparrow: 270, 271
Squadrons (numbered):
 1st Aero: 12
 1st Photographic: 35
 12th Aero: 15
 90th Aero: 12
St. Benôit: 15
St. Lo: 46
St. Mihiel: 3, 5, 9, 10, 15, 16, 20
Stahr, Elvis J.: 242
Stearns, Robert: 166
Strategic Air Command (SAC): 56, 81, 83, 95, 97, 182, 183, 187, 188, 190, 199, 202, 235, 281, 322, 326
Strategic Air Command Advance Echelon (SAC ADVON): 326
Strategic Air Command liaison office (SACLO): 326
Stratemeyer, George E.: 85, 115, 121, 122, 123, 124, 127, 129, 130, 131, 132, 135, 136, 137, 143, 146, 149

Help from Above

Sunday Punch: 293
Supreme Allied Commander, Europe (SACEUR): 219, 220
Supreme Commander Allied Powers (SCAP): 115
Supreme Headquarters Allied Powers Europe (SHAPE): 219
surface-to-air missile (SAM): 265, 266
Sweeney, Walter C.: 235, 236, 241, 245, 251, 252, 282, 283, 315
Swift Strike III: 237, 279, 280, 281
Symington, Stuart: 94, 97
T–34 tank: 118
T–54 tank: 351
Tactical Air Command (TAC): 56, 57, 58, 62, 63, 64, 65, 66, 67, 68, 75, 76, 79, 80, 82, 83–95, 99, 102, 103, 106, 107, 108, 109, 110, 146, 176, 179, 182, 184, 185, 186, 187, 188, 189, 199, 200, 201, 202, 203, 204, 205, 206, 208, 211, 213, 218, 219, 229, 235, 237, 238, 240, 241, 245, 246, 251, 252, 257, 262, 271, 275, 278, 281, 282, 284, 315, 333, 358, 359, 368, 370
TACM 55-3: 213
Tactical Air Control Center (TACC): 60, 64, 77, 79, 80, 81, 99, 106, 107, 144, 145, 147, 148, 167, 241, 284, 306, 308, 309, 326
Tactical Air Control Group: 60, 66, 106
Tactical Air Control Parties (TACPs): 60, 66, 77, 79, 99, 122, 127, 130, 131, 132, 137, 139, 143, 144, 145, 146, 147, 149–151, 152, 162, 164, 166, 167, 169, 172, 174, 175, 176, 181, 183, 218, 241, 273, 277, 278, 280, 281, 305, 308, 317, 333, 379
Tactical Air Control System: 58, 60, 65, 66, 76, 77, 102, 104, 106, 107, 110, 137, 140, 142, 145, 176
Tactical Air Direction Center (TADC): 60, 66, 77, 81, 99, 106, 107, 145, 147, 148, 167, 168
Tactical Air Direction Post (TADP): 149
Tactical Air Force: 57, 67, 80, 87, 89, 93, 164

tactical air navigation (TACAN): 278
Tactical Air Support Board: 202, 204
Tactical Air Warfare Center (TAWC): 252, 281, 282
Tactical Operations Center (TOC): 306, 308, 337
Tactical Support Center (TSC): 211, 217, 218, 219
Tarheel: 99
Taylor, Maxwell D.: 179, 180, 190, 191, 196, 198, 234, 246
Tolson, John J.: 223, 335
Toul: 12
TRC–1 radio: 150
Troop Carrier Command: 36
Truman, Harry S.: 53, 71, 72, 86, 181, 197
Tunis: 41, 42
ultrahigh-frequency (UHF): 278, 280, 281
Union of Soviet Socialist Republics (USSR): 179, 180, 181, 182, 235, 236, 365, 366, 367, 370
United States Army Forces, Far East (USAFFE): 115
UPS–1: 284
U.S. Army of the Pacific (USARPAC): 242
USAF Tactical Review Board: 53
United Nations (UN): 115, 123, 126, 129, 132, 136, 138, 140, 160
United States Air Force (USAF): 86, 87, 105, 108, 164
United States Air Force Europe (USAFE): 201, 219, 220
United States European Command (EUCOM): 219
Vandenberg, Hoyt S.: 83, 84, 85, 87, 96, 97, 110, 123, 164, 165, 171, 197, 198, 203
Van Fleet, James A.: 169, 171–175
vertical-takeoff-and-landing (VTOL): 249, 341
very high frequency (VHF): 43, 44–46
Very pistol: 9, 10
Vietnamese Army (ARVN): 304, 305

Index

Vignuelles: 15
visual light attack (VAL): 265, 270
von Clausewitz, Karl: 2
von Kann, Clifton F.: 198, 201
Walker, Walton H.: 121, 122, 127, 129, 130, 131, 133, 135, 136, 138, 141, 146, 151, 169
Walleye: 279
Watkins, Tarleton H.: 246
Wedemeyer, Albert C.: 88
Westmoreland, William C.: 281, 296, 325, 326, 328, 330, 331, 332, 334, 337, 338, 341, 358, 359
Weyland, Otto P.: 46, 88, 124–125, 136, 139, 164, 182, 185, 188, 189, 196, 202, 206, 208, 209, 210, 211, 213
White, Thomas D.: 185, 201, 228, 229
Whitehead, Ennis C.: 88
Willoughby, Charles A.: 124
Wilson, Charles E.: 197, 213, 230
Wilson Memorandum: 384
Wyman, Willard G.: 211, 213, 227
ZU–23: 348
Zuckert, Eugene M.: 294, 295, 352

ISBN 0-16-051552-1